Documents Set

Volume II

OUT OF MANY

A History
of the
American People

Fourth Edition

JOHN MACK FARAGHER

Yale University

Mari Jo Buhle

Brown University

Daniel Czitrom

Mount Holyoke College

Susan H. Armitage

Washington State University

Revised and Updated by
Kathryn A. Abbott

Western Kentucky University

Prentice Hall, Upper Saddle River, New Jersey 07458

©2003 by Pearson Education
Upper Saddle River, New Jersey 07458

Printed in the United States of America

ISBN 0-13-098929-0

Prentice Hall International (UK) Limited, *London*
Prentice Hall of Australia Pty. Limited, *Sydney*
Prentice Hall Canada Inc., *Toronto*
Prentice Hall Hispoamericana, S.A., *Mexico*
Prentice Hall of India Private Limited, *New Delhi*
Prentice Hall of Japan, Inc., *Tokyo*
Simon & Schuster Asia Pte. Ltd., *Singapore*
Editora Prentice-Hall do Brasil, *Rio de Janeiro*

Documents Set

OUT OF MANY: A History of the American People, Fourth Edition

Volume II

by Faragher / Buhle / Czitrom / Armitage

Chapter 27. America at Midcentury, 1952–1963   390

Chapter 28. The Civil Rights Movement, 1945–1966   406

Chapter 29. War Abroad, War at Home, 1965–1974   432

Chapter 30. The Conservative Ascendancy, 1974–1987   458

Chapter 31. Toward a Transitional America, since 1988   475

chapter 17

Reconstruction, 1863–1877

17-1 Charlotte Forten, Life on the Sea Islands, 1864

In 1862, after Union troops captured Port Royal off the coast of South Carolina, the surrounding Sea Islands became the site of the first major attempts to aid freed people. Charlotte Forten was part of a wealthy free black family in Philadelphia. She was one of many Northern teachers who volunteered to help educate ex-slaves and demonstrate that African Americans were capable of self-improvement. The following selection, published in 1864, was compiled from letters she wrote to her friend, the poet John Greenleaf Whittier.

SOURCE: Atlantic Monthly (1864).

The Sunday after our arrival we attended service at the Baptist Church. The people came in slowly; for they have no way of knowing the hour, except by the sun. By eleven they had all assembled, and the church was well filled. They were neatly dressed in their Sunday attire, the women mostly wearing clean, dark frocks, with white aprons and bright-colored head-hand-kerchiefs. Some had attained to the dignity of straw hats with gay feathers, but these were not nearly as becoming nor as picturesque as the handkerchiefs. The day was warm, and the windows were thrown open as if it were summer, although it was the second day of November. It was very pleasant to listen to the beautiful hymns, and look from the crowd of dark, earnest faces within, upon the grove of noble oaks without. The people sang, "Roll, Jordan, roll," the grandest of all their hymns. There is a great, rolling wave of sound through it all....

Harry, the foreman on the plantation, a man of a good deal of natural intelligence, was most desirous of learning to read. He came in at night to be taught, and learned very rapidly. I never saw any one more determined to learn. We enjoyed hearing him talk about the "gun-shoot,"—so the people call the capture of Bay Point and Hilton Head. They never weary of telling you "how Massa run when he hear de fust gun."

"Why did n't you go with him, Harry?" I asked. "Oh, Miss, 't was n't 'cause Massa did n't try to 'suade me. He tell we dat de Yankees would shoot we, or would sell we to Cuba, an' do all de wust tings to we, when dey come, 'Berry well, Sar,' says I. 'If I go wid you, I be good as dead. If I stay here, I can't be no wust; so if I got to dead, I might 's well dead here as anywhere. So I'll stay here an' wait for de "dam Yankees." 'Lor', Miss, I knowed he was n't tellin' de truth all de time."

"But why did n't you believe him, Harry?"

"Dunno, Miss; somehow we hear de Yankees was our friends, an' dat we'd be free when dey come, an' 'pears like we believe *dat.*"

I found this to be true of nearly all the people I talked with, and thought it strange they should have had so much faith in the Northerners. Truly, for years past, they had but little cause to think them very friendly. Cupid told us that his master was so daring as to come back, after he had fled from the island, at the risk of being taken prisoner by our soldiers; and that he ordered the people to get all the furniture together and take it to a plantation on the opposite side of the creek, and to stay on that side themselves. "So," said Cupid, "dey could jus' sweep us all up in a heap, an' put us in de boat. An' he telled me to take Patience—dat's my wife—an' de chil'en down to a certain pint, an' den I could come back, if I choose. Jus' as if I was gwine to be sich a goat!" added he, with a look and gesture of ineffable contempt. He and the rest of the people, instead of obeying their master, left the place and hid themselves in the woods; and when he came to look for them, not one of all his "faithful servants" was to be found. A few, principally house-servants, had previously been carried away.

In the evenings, the children frequently came in to sing and shout for us. These "shouts" are very strange,—in truth, almost indescribable. It is necessary to hear and see in order to have any clear idea of them. The children form a ring, and move around in a kind of shuffling dance, singing all the time. Four or five stand apart, and sing very energetically clapping their hands, stamping their feet, and rocking their bodies to and fro. These are the musicians, to whose performance the shouters keep perfect time. The grown people on this plantation did not shout, but they do on some of the other plantations. It is very comical to see little children, not more than three or four years old, entering into the performance with all their might. But the shouting of the grown people is rather solemn and impressive otherwise. We cannot determine whether it has a religious character or not. Some of the people tell us that it has, others that it has not. But as the shouts of the grown people are always in connection with their religious meetings, it is probable that they are the barbarous expression of religion, handed down to them from their African ancestors, and destined to pass away under the influence of Christian teachings. The people on this island have no songs. They sing only hymns, and most of these are sad. Prince, a large black boy from a neighboring plantation, was the principal shouter among the children. It seemed impossible for him to keep still for a moment. His performances were most amusing specimens of Ethiopian gymnastics. Amaretta the younger, a cunning, kittenish little creature of only six years old, had a remarkably sweet voice. Her favorite hymn, which we used to hear her singing to herself as she walked through the yard, is one of the oddest we have heard:—

> "What makes ole Satan follow me so?
> Satan got nuttin' 't all fur to do wid me.
> CHORUS
> "Tiddy Rosa, hold your light!
> Bradder Tony, hold your light!
> All de member, hold bright light
>   On Canaan's shore!"

This is one of the most spirited shouting-tunes. "Tiddy" is their word for sister.

A very queer-looking old man came into the store one day. He was dressed in a complete suit of brilliant Brussels carpeting. Probably it had been taken from his master's house after the "gun-shoot"; but he looked so very dignified that we did not like to question him about

it. The people called him Doctor Crofts,—which was, I believe, his master's name, his own being Scipio. He was very jubilant over the new state of things, and said to Mr. H.,—"Don't hab me feelins hurt now. Used to hab me feelins hurt all de time. But don't hab 'em hurt now no more." Poor old soul! We rejoiced with him that he and his brethren no longer have their "feelins" hurt, as in the old time.

* * * * * *

1. *How would you describe Forten's attitudes toward the freed people of the Sea Islands? What differences seem apparent between their world and the one she comes from?*

2. *How does Forten compare the Sea Island religious practices to those that she is used to? Why were they so different?*

3. *What feelings do the Sea Islanders express toward education and freedom?*

17–2   Lincoln's Second Inaugural Address, 1865

In the summer of 1864 Abraham Lincoln's reelection chances looked bleak. Public opinion on the war and emancipation remained deeply divided, and many Radical Republicans lacked confidence in the President. But General Sherman's capture of Atlanta in September lifted Northern morale and contributed to Lincoln's victory over Democratic candidate General George B. McClellan. Lincoln's Second Inaugural was one of the briefest yet most memorable ever delivered.

SOURCE: Richardson, ed., *Messages and Papers*, Vol. VI, p. 276 ff.

Lincoln's Second Inaugural Address

FELLOW–COUNTRYMEN:—At this second appearing to take the oath of the presidential office there is less occasion for an extended address than there was at the first. Then a statement somewhat in detail of a course to be pursued seemed fitting and proper. Now, at the expiration of four years, during which public declarations have been constantly called forth on every point and phase of the great contest which still absorbs the attention and engrosses the energies of the nation, little that is new could be presented. The progress of our arms, upon which all else chiefly depends, is as well known to the public as

to myself, and it is, I trust, reasonably satisfactory and encouraging to all. With high hope for the future, no prediction in regard to it is ventured.

On the occasion corresponding to this four years ago all thoughts were anxiously directed to an impending civil war. All dreaded it, all sought to avert it. While the inaugural address was being delivered from this place, devoted altogether to *saving* the Union without war, insurgent agents were in the city seeking to *destroy* it without war—seeking to dissolve the Union and divide effects by negotiation. Both parties deprecated war, but one of them would *make* war rather than let the nation survive, and the other would *accept* war rather than let it perish, and the war came.

One eighth of the whole population was colored slaves, not distributed generally over the Union, but localized in the southern part of it. These slaves constituted a peculiar and powerful interest. All knew that this interest was somehow the cause of the war. To strengthen, perpetuate, and extend this interest was the object for which the insurgents would rend the Union even by war, while the Government claimed no right to do more than to restrict the territorial enlargement of it. Neither party expected for the war the magnitude or the duration which it has already attained. Neither anticipated that the *cause* of the conflict might cease with or even before the conflict itself should cease. Each looked for an easier triumph, and a result less fundamental and astounding. Both read the same Bible and pray to the same God, and each invokes

His aid against the other. It may seem strange that any men should dare to ask a just God's assistance in wringing their bread from the sweat of other men's faces, but let us judge not, that we be not judged. The prayers of both could not be answered. That of neither has been answered fully. The Almighty has His own purposes. "Woe unto the world because of offenses; for it must needs be that offenses come, but woe to that man by whom the offense cometh." If we shall suppose that American slavery is one of those offenses which, in the providence of God, must needs come, but which, having continued through His appointed time, He now wills to remove, and that He gives to both North and South this terrible war as the woe due to those by whom the offense came, shall we discern therein any departure from those divine attributes which the believers in a living God always ascribe to Him? Fondly do we hope, fervently do we pray, that this mighty scourge of war may speedily pass away. Yet, if God wills that it continue until all the wealth piled by the bondsman's two hundred and fifty years of unrequited toil shall be sunk, and until every drop of blood drawn with the lash shall be paid by another drawn with the sword, as was said three thousand years ago, so still it must be said, "The judgments of the Lord are true and righteous altogether."

With malice toward none, with charity for all, with firmness in the right as God gives us to see the right, let us strive on to finish the work we are in, to bind up the nation's wounds, to care for him who shall have borne the battle and for his widow and his orphan, to do all which may achieve and cherish a just and lasting peace among ourselves and with all nations.

* * * * * *

1.   *To what extent does the address outline Lincoln's plan for Reconstruction?*

2.   *How would you compare the Second Inaugural to the First Inaugural in tone and style? How do both treat the issue of slavery?*

17–3   *The Freedmen's Bureau Bill, 1865*

Congress established the Bureau of Refugees, Freedmen, and Abandoned Lands to provide aid for freed people and to oversee free labor arrangements in the South. President Andrew Johnson's policy of liberally pardoning ex-confederates and returning their land frustrated Bureau commissioner General O. O. Howard's efforts to resettle freed people on confiscated lands. Congress extended the life of the Bureau in 1866 over Johnson's veto. Always underfunded, the Bureau nonetheless succeeded in helping establish schools, overseeing free labor contracts, and providing legal support for freed people.

SOURCE: Henry Steele Commager, *Documents of American History* (1973); *U.S. Statutes at Large*, Vol. XIII, p. 507ff.

AN ACT TO ESTABLISH A BUREAU FOR THE RELIEF OF FREEDMEN AND REFUGEES

Be it enacted, That there is hereby established in the War Department, to continue during the present war of rebellion, and for one year thereafter, a bureau of refugees, freedmen, and abandoned lands, to which shall be committed, as hereinafter provided, the supervision and management of all abandoned lands, and the control of all subjects relating to refugees and freedmen from rebel states, or from any district of country within the territory embraced in the operations of the army, under such rules and regulations as may be prescribed by the head of the bureau and approved by the President. The said bureau shall be under the management and control of a commissioner to be appointed by the President, by and with the advice and consent of the Senate....

SEC. 2. That the Secretary of War may direct such issues of provisions, clothing, and fuel, as he may deem needful for the immediate and temporary shelter and supply of destitute and suffering refugees and freedmen and their wives and children, under such rules and regulations as he may direct.

SEC. 3. That the President may, by and with the advice and consent of the Senate, appoint an assistant commissioner for each of the states declared to be in insurrection, not exceeding ten in number, who shall, under the direction of the commissioner, aid in the execution of the provisions of this act;...And any military officer may be detailed and assigned to duty under this act without increase of pay or allowances....

SEC. 4. That the commissioner, under the direction of the President, shall have authority to set apart, for the use of loyal refugees and freedmen, such tracts of land within the insurrectionary states as shall have been abandoned, or to which the United States shall have acquired title by confiscation or sale, or otherwise, and to every male citizen, whether refugee or freedman, as aforesaid, there shall be assigned not more than forty acres of such land, and the person to whom it was so assigned shall be protected in the use and enjoyment of the land for the term of three years at an annual rent not exceeding six per centum upon the value of such land, as it was appraised by the state authorities in the year eighteen hundred and sixty, for the purpose of taxation, and in case no such appraisal can be found, then the rental shall be based upon the estimated value of the land in said year, to be ascertained in such manner as the commissioner may by regulation prescribe. At the end of said term, or at any time during said term, the occupants of any parcels so assigned may purchase the land and receive such title thereto as the United States can convey, upon paying therefor the value of the land, as ascertained and fixed for the purpose of determining the annual rent aforesaid....

* * * * * *

1.   *How does the Bill treat the issue of abandoned lands in the South? What hope did it offer freed people?*

17–4   *Black Code of Mississippi, 1865*

In the aftermath of Emancipation, Southern states passed a variety of laws known as "Black Codes." Although these codes varied from state to state, they were all aimed at tightly controlling the lives and labor of newly freed people. The codes angered Congress and the Northern public, who viewed them as Southern attempts to roll back Emancipation and subvert Reconstruction. The Civil Rights Act of 1866, the Fourteenth Amendment, and the Military Reconstruction Act of 1867 were all designed in part to counter the Black Codes.

SOURCE: Henry Steele Commager, *Documents in American History* (1973): *Laws of Mississippi, 1865*, p. 82ff.

BLACK CODE OF MISSISSIPPI, 1865

1. CIVIL RIGHTS OF FREEDMEN IN MISSISSIPPI

Sec. 1. *Be it enacted,...*That all freedmen, free negroes, and mulattoes may sue and be sued, implead and be impleaded, in all the courts of law and equity of this State, and may acquire personal property, and choses in action, by descent or purchase, and may dispose of the same in the same manner and to the same extent that white persons may: *Provided,* That the provisions of this section shall not be so construed as to allow any freedman, free negro, or mulatto to rent or lease any lands or tenements except in incorporated cities or towns, in which places the corporate authorities shall control the same....

Sec. 3....All freedmen, free negroes, or mulattoes who do now and have herebefore lived and cohabited together as husband and wife shall be taken and held in law as legally married, and the issue shall be taken and held as legitimate for all purposes; that it shall not be lawful for any freedman, free negro, or mulatto to intermarry with any white person; nor for any white person to intermarry with any freedman, free negro, or mulatto; and any person who shall so intermarry, shall be deemed guilty of felony, and on conviction thereof shall be confined in the State penitentiary for life; and those shall be deemed freedmen, free negroes, and mulattoes who are of pure negro blood, and those descended from a negro to the third generation, inclusive, though one ancestor in each generation may have been a white person....

Sec. 6....All contracts for labor made with freedmen, free negroes, and mulattoes for a longer period than one month shall be in writing, and in duplicate, attested and read to said freedman, free negro, or mulatto by a beat, city or county officer, or two disinterested white persons of the county in which the labor is to be performed, of which each party shall have one; and said contracts shall be taken and held as entire contracts, and if the laborer shall quit the service of the employer before the expiration of his term of service, without good cause, he shall forfeit his wages for that year up to the time of quitting.

Sec. 7....Every civil officer shall, and every person may, arrest and carry back to his or her legal employer any freedman, free negro, or mulatto who shall have quit the service of his or her employer before the expiration of his or her term of service without good cause; and said officer and person shall he entitled to receive for arresting and carrying back every deserting employe aforesaid the sum of five dollars, and ten cents per mile from the place of arrest to the place of delivery; and the same shall be paid by the employer, and held as a set-off for so much against the wages of said deserting employe: *Provided,* that said arrested party, after being so returned, may appeal to the justice of the peace or member of the board of police of the county, who, on notice to the alleged employer, shall try summarily whether said appellant is legally employed by the alleged employer, and has good cause to quit said employer; either party shall have the right to appeal to the county court, pending which the alleged deserter shall be remanded to the alleged employer or otherwise disposed of, as shall be right and just; and the decision of the county court shall be final....

Sec. 9....If any person shall persuade or attempt to persuade, entice, or cause any freedman, free negro, or mulatto to desert from the legal employment of any person before the expiration of his or her term of service, or shall knowingly employ any such deserting freedman, free negro, or mulatto, or shall knowingly give or sell to any such deserting freedman, free negro, or mulatto, any food, raiment, or other thing, he or she shall be guilty of a misdemeanor, and, upon conviction, shall be fined not less than twenty-five dollars and not more than two hundred dollars and the costs; and if said fine and costs shall not be immediately paid, the court shall sentence said convict to not exceeding two months' imprisonment in the county jail and he or she shall moreover be liable to the party injured in damages: *Provided,* if any person shall, or shall attempt to, persuade, entice, or cause any freedman, free negro, or mulatto to desert from any legal employment of any person, with the view to employ said freedman, free negro, or mulatto without the limits of this State, such person, on conviction, shall be fined not less than fifty dollars, and not more than five hundred dollars and costs; and if said fine and costs shall not be immediately paid, the court shall sentence said convict to not exceeding six months imprisonment in the county jail....

2. MISSISSIPPI APPRENTICE LAW

(LAWS OF MISSISSIPPI, 1865, p. 86.)

Sec. 1....It shall be the duty of all sheriffs, justices of the peace, and other civil officers of the several counties in this State, to report to the probate courts of their respective counties semi-annually, at the January and July terms of said courts, all freedmen, free negroes, and mulattoes, under the age of eighteen, in their respective counties, beats or districts, who are orphans, or whose parent or parents have not the means or who refuse to provide for and support said minors; and thereupon it shall be the duty of said probate court to order the clerk of said court to apprentice said minors to some competent and suitable person, on such terms as the court may direct, having a particular care to the interest of said minor: *Provided,* that the former owner of said minors shall have the preference when, in the opinion of the court, he or she shall be a suitable person for that purpose....

Sec. 3....In the management and control of said apprentice, said master or mistress shall have the power to inflict such moderate corporal chastisement as a father or guardian is allowed to inflict on his or her child or ward at common law. *Provided,* that in no case shall cruel or inhuman punishment inflicted.

Sec. 4....If any apprentice shall leave the employment of his or her master or mistress, without his or her consent, said master or mistress may pursue and recapture said apprentice, and bring him or her before any justice of the peace of the county, whose duty it shall be to remand said apprentice to the service of his or her master or mistress; and in the event of a refusal on the part of said apprentice so to return, then said justice shall commit said apprentice to the jail of said county, on failure to give

bond, to the next term of the county court; and it shall be the duty of said court at the first term thereafter to investigate said case, and if the court shall be of opinion that said apprentice left the employment of his or her master or mistress without good cause, to order him or her to be punished, as provided for the punishment of hired freedmen, as may be from time to time provided for by law for desertion, until he or she shall agree return to the service of his or her master or mistress:...if the court shall believe that said apprentice had good cause to quit his said master or mistress, the court shall discharge said apprentice from said indenture, and also enter a judgment against the master or mistress for not more than one hundred dollars, for the use and benefit of said apprentice....

3. MISSISSIPPI VAGRANT LAW

(LAWS OF MISSISSIPPI, 1865, p. 90)

Sec. 1. *Be it enacted,* etc.,...That all rogues and vagabonds, idle and dissipated persons, beggars, jugglers, or persons practicing unlawful games or plays, runaways, common drunkards, common night-walkers, pilferers, lewd, wanton, or lascivious persons, in speech or behavior, common railers and brawlers, persons who neglect their calling or employment, misspend what they earn, or do not provide for the support of themselves or their families, or dependents, and all other idle and disorderly persons, including all who neglect all lawful business, habitually misspend their time by frequenting houses of ill-fame, gaming-houses, or tippling shops, shall be deemed and considered vagrants, under the provisions of this act, and upon conviction thereof shall be fined not exceeding one hundred dollars, with all accruing costs, and be imprisoned at the discretion of the court, not exceeding ten days.

Sec. 2....All freedmen, free negroes and mulattoes in this State, over the age of eighteen years, found on the second Monday in January, 1866, or thereafter, with no lawful employment or business, or found unlawfully assembling themselves together, either in the day or night time, and all white persons so assembling themselves with freedmen, free negroes or mulattoes, or usually associating with freedmen, free negroes or mulattoes, on terms of equality, or living in adultery or fornication with a freed woman, free negro or mulatto, shall be deemed vagrants, and on conviction thereof shall be fined in a sum not exceeding, in the case of a freedman, free negro or mulatto, fifty dollars, and a white man two hundred dollars, and imprisoned at the discretion of the court, the free negro not exceeding ten days, and the white man not exceeding six months....

4. PENAL LAWS OF MISSISSIPPI
(*LAWS OF MISSISSIPPI,* 1865, p. 165.)

Sec. 1. *Be it enacted,…*That no freedman, free negro, or mulatto, not in the military service of the United States government, and not licensed so to do by the board of police of his or her county, shall keep or carry fire-arms of any kind, or any ammunition, dirk or bowie knife, and on conviction thereof in the county court shall be punished by fine, not exceeding ten dollars, and pay the costs of such proceedings, and all such arms or ammunition shall be forfeited to the informer; and it shall be the duty of every civil and military officer to arrest any freedman, free negro, or mulatto found with any such arms or ammunition, and cause him or her to be committed to trial in default of bail.

2.…Any freedman, free negro, or mulatto committing riots, routs, affrays, trespasses, malicious mischief, cruel treatment to animals, seditious speeches, insulting gestures, language, or acts, or assaults on any person, disturbance of the peace, exercising the function of a minister of the Gospel without a license from some regularly organized church, vending spirituous or intoxicating liquors, or committing any other misdemeanor, the punishment of which is not specifically provided for by law, shall, upon conviction thereof in the county court, be freed not less than ten dollars, and not more than one hundred dollars, and may be imprisoned at the discretion of the court, not exceeding thirty days.

Sec. 3.…If any white person shall sell, lend, or give to any freedman, free negro, or mulatto any firearms, dirk or bowie knife, or ammunition, or any spirituous or intoxicating liquors, such person or persons so offending, upon conviction thereof in the county court of his or her county, shall be fined not exceeding fifty dollars, and may be imprisoned, at the discretion of the court, not exceeding thirty days.…

Sec. 5.…If any freedman, free negro, or mulatto, convicted of any of the misdemeanors provided against in this act, shall fail or refuse for the space of five days, after conviction, to pay the fine and costs imposed, such person shall be hired out by the sheriff or other officer, at public outcry, to any white person who will pay said fine and all costs, and take said convict for the shortest time.

* * * * * *

1. *How did these laws limit the freedom of movement of ex-slaves? Why was this so important to the Mississippi legislature?*

2. *Apprenticeship laws provoked especially bitter complaints from African Americans. How would you explain this?*

3. *Why did the Black Codes pay so much attention to limiting the social lives of freed people, for example, sexuality, drinking, recreation?*

17–5 Frederick Douglass, Speech to the American Anti-Slavery Society, 1865

Congress approved the Thirteenth Amendment abolishing slavery in February 1865, and the Union's final military victory over the Confederacy that spring assured the destruction of the slave system. The American Anti-Slavery Society, long in the forefront of the abolitionist movement, met in May 1865, to discuss its future. Black leader Frederick Douglass addressed the Society, urging it not to disband but to continue the fight against racial discrimination.

SOURCE: Philip S. Foner, ed., *The Life and Writings of Frederick Douglass,* Vol. IV (1955).

…I do not wish to appear here in any fault-finding spirit, or as an impugner of the motives of those who believe that the time has come for this Society to disband. I am conscious of no suspicion of the purity and excellence of the motives that animate the President of this Society

[William Lloyd Garrison], and other gentlemen who are in favor of its disbandment. I take this ground; whether this Constitutional Amendment [the thirteenth] is law or not, whether it has been ratified by a sufficient number of States to make it law or not, I hold that the work of Abolitionists is not done. Even if every State in the Union had ratified that Amendment, while the black man is confronted in the legislation of the South by the word "white," our work as Abolitionists, as I conceive it, is not done. I took the ground, last night, that the South, by unfriendly legislation, could make our liberty, under that provision, a delusion, a mockery, and a snare, and I hold that ground now. What advantage is a provision like this Amendment to the black man, if the Legislature of any State can to-morrow declare that no black man's testimony shall be received in a court of law? Where are we then? Any wretch may enter the house of a black man, and commit any violence he pleases; if he happens to do it only in the presence of black persons, he goes unwhipt of justice ["Hear, hear."] And don't tell me that those people down there have become so just and honest all at once that they will not pass laws denying to black men the right to testify against white men in the courts of law. Why, our

Northern States have done it. Illinois, Indiana and Ohio have done it. Here, in the midst of institutions that have gone forth from old Plymouth Rock, the black man has been excluded from testifying in the courts of law; and if the Legislature of every Southern State to-morrow pass a law, declaring that no Negro shall testify in any courts of law, they will not violate that provision of the Constitution. Such laws exist now at the South, and they might exist under this provision of the Constitution, that there shall he neither slavery not involuntary servitude in any State of the Union....

Slavery is not abolished until the black man has the ballot. While the Legislatures of the South retain the right to pass laws making any discrimination between black and white, slavery still lives there. [Applause.] As Edmund Quincy once said, "While the word 'white' is on the statute-book of Massachusetts, Massachusetts is a slave State. While a black man can he turned out of a car in Massachusetts, Massachusetts is a slave State. While a slave can be taken from old Massachusetts, Massachusetts is a slave State." That is what I heard Edmund Quincy say twenty-three or twenty-four years ago. I never forget such a thing. Now, while the black man can be denied a vote, while the Legislatures of the South can take from him the right to keep and bear runs, as they can—would not allow a Negro to walk with a cane where I came from, they would not allow five of them to assemble together—the work of the Abolitionists is not finished. Notwithstanding the provision in the Constitution of the United States, that the right to keep and bear arms shall not be abridged, the black man has never had the right either to keep or bear arms; and the Legislatures of the States will still have the power to forbid it, under this Amendment. They can carry on a system of unfriendly legislation, and will they not do it? Have they not got prejudice there to do it with? Think you, that because they are for the moment in the talons and beak of our glorious eagle, instead of the slave being there, as formerly, that they are converted? I hear of the loyalty at Wilmington, the loyalty at South Carolina—what is it worth?

["Not a straw."]

Not a straw. I thank my friend for admitting it. They are loyal while they see 200,000 sable soldiers, with glistening bayonets, walking in their midst. [Applause.] But let the civil power of the South be restored, and the old prejudices and hostility to the Negro will revive. Aye, the very fact that the Negro has been used to defeat this rebellion and strike down the standards of the Confederacy will be a stimulus to all their hatred, to all their malice, and lead them to legislate with greater stringency toward-

sthis class than ever before. [Applause.] The America. people are bound—bound by their sense of honor (I hope by their sense of honor, at least, by a just sense of honor), to extend the franchise to the Negro; and I was going to say, that the Abolitionists of the American Anti-Slavery Society were bound to "stand still, and see the salvation of God," until that work is done. [Applause.] Where shall the black man look for support, my friends, if the American Anti-Slavery Society fails him? ["Hear, hear."] From whence shall we expect a certain sound from the trumpet of freedom, when the old pioneer, when this Society that has survived mobs, and martyrdom, and the combined efforts of priest-craft and state-craft to suppress it, shall all at once subside, on the mere intimation that the Constitution has been amended, so that neither slavery not involuntary servitude shall hereafter be allowed in this land? What did the slaveholders of Richmond say to those who objected to arming the Negro, on the ground that it would make him a freeman? Why, they said, "The argument is absurd. We may make these Negroes fight for us; but while we retain the political power of the South, we can keep them in their subordinate positions." That was the argument; and they were right. They might have employed the Negro to fight for them, and while they retained in their hands power to exclude him from political rights, they could have reduced him to a condition similar to slavery. They would not call it slavery, but some other name. Slavery has been fruitful in giving itself names. It has been called "the peculiar institution," "the social system," and the "impediment," as it was called by the General conference of the Methodist Episcopal Church. It has been called by a great many names, and it will call itself by yet another name; and you and I and all of us had better wait and see what new form this old monster will assume, in what new skin this old snake will come forth. [Loud applause.]

* * * * * *

1. *What rights does Douglass see as crucial to establishing full citizenship for African Americans?*

2. *How does Douglass compare black civil rights in the Northern and Southern states?*

3. *What course does Douglass advise for dealing with the defeated Confederacy?*

17–6   *The Civil Rights Act of 1866*

Passed over President Johnson's veto in April 1866, the Civil Rights Act provided the first statutory definition of American citizenship. By conferring citizenship rights upon freed people, it negated the Supreme Court's Dred Scott decision of 1857, which had held that a black person could not be a citizen of the United States. The Civil Rights Act proposed that the federal government guarantee the principle of equality before the law, regardless of race.

SOURCE: Henry Steele Commager, *Documents of American History* (1973), pp. 14-15: *U.S. Statutes at Large*, Vol. XIV, p. 27ff.

An Act to protect all Persons in the United States in their Civil Rights, and furnish the Means of their Vindication.

Be it enacted, That all persons born in the United States and not subject to any foreign power, excluding Indians not taxed, are hereby declared to be citizens of the United States; and such citizens, of every race and color, without regard to any previous condition of slavery or involuntary servitude, except as a punishment for crime whereof the party shall have been duly convicted, shall have the same right, in every State and Territory in the United States, to make and enforce contracts, to sue, be parties, and give evidence, to inherit, purchase, lease, sell, hold, and convey real and personal property, and to full and equal benefit of all laws and proceedings for the security of person and property, as is enjoyed by white citizens, and shall be subject to like punishment, pains, and penalties, and to none other, any law, statute, ordinance, regulation, or custom, to the contrary notwithstanding.

SEC. 2. *And be further enacted,* That any person who, under color of any law, statute, ordinance, regulation, or custom, shall subject, or cause to be subjected, any inhabitant of any State or Territory to the deprivation of any right secured or protected by this act, or to different punishment, pains or penalties on account of such person having at any time been held in a condition of slavery or involuntary servitude, except as a punishment for crime whereof the party shall have been duly convicted, or by reason of his color or race, than is prescribed for the punishment of white persons, shall be deemed guilty of a misdemeanor, and, on conviction, shall be punished by fine not exceeding one thousand dollars, or imprisonment not exceeding one year, or both, in the discretion of the court.

SEC. 3. *And be it further enacted,* That the district courts the United States,…shall have, exclusively of the courts of the several States, cognizance of all crimes and offences committed against the provisions of this act, and also, concurrently with the circuit courts of the United States, of all causes, civil and criminal, affecting persons who are denied or cannot enforce in the courts or judicial tribunals of the State or locality where they may be any of the rights secured to them by the first section of this act.…

SEC. 4. *And be it further enacted,* That the district attorneys, marshals, and deputy marshals of the United States, the commissioners appointed by the circuit and territorial courts of the United States, with powers of arresting, imprisoning, or bailing offenders against the laws of the United States, the officers and agents of the Freedmen's Bureau, and every other officer who may be specially empowered by the President of the United States, shall be, and they are hereby, specially authorized and required, at the expense of the United States, to institute proceedings against all and every person who shall violate the provisions of this act, and cause him or them to be arrested and imprisoned, or bailed, as the case may be, for trial before such court of the United States or territorial court as by this act has cognizance of the offence.…

SEC. 8. *And be it further enacted,* That whenever the President of the United States shall have reason to believe that offences have been or are likely to be committed against the provisions of this act within any judicial district, it shall be lawful for him, in his discretion, to direct the judge, marshal, and district attorney of such district to attend at such place within the district, and for such time as he may designate, for the purpose of the more speedy arrest and trial of persons charged with a violation of this act; and it shall be the duty of every judge or other officer, when any such requisition shall be received by him, to attend at the place and for the time therein designated.

SEC. 9. *And be it further enacted,* That it shall be lawful for the President of the United States, or such person as he may empower for that purpose, to employ such part of the land or naval forces of the United States, or of the militia, as shall be necessary to prevent the violation and enforce the due execution of this act.

SEC. 10. *And be it further enacted,* That upon all questions of law arising in any cause under the provisions of this act a final appeal may be taken to the Supreme Court of the United States.

* * * * * *

1.   *How does the act specifically define civil rights and those who may enjoy them?*

2.   *What provisions does the act make for enforcement of these rights?*

17–7   President Johnson's Veto of the Civil Rights Act, 1866

The Civil Rights Act was the first major piece of legislation to become law over a president's veto. Johnson's veto message helped make the estrangement between Congress and the president irreparable. Johnson's constitutional arguments induced Congress to enact the Fourteenth Amendment, which forbade individual states to deprive citizens of the "equal protection of the laws."

SOURCE: Richardson, ed., *Messages and Papers*, Vol. VI, p. 405ff.

WASHINGTON, D.C., *March 27, 1866. To the Senate of the United States:*

I regret that the bill, which has passed both Houses of Congress, entitled "An act to protect all persons in the United States in their civil rights and furnish the means of their vindication," contains provisions which I can not approve consistently with my sense of duty to the whole people and my obligations to the Constitution of the United States. I am therefore constrained to return it to the Senate, the House in which it originated, with my objections to its becoming a law.

By the first section of the bill all persons born in the United States and not subject to any foreign power, excluding Indians not taxed, are declared to be citizens of the United States.... It does not purport to give these classes of persons any status as citizens of States, except that which may result from their status as citizens of the United States. The power to confer the right of State citizenship is just as exclusively with the several States as the power to confer the right of Federal citizenship is with Congress.

The right of Federal citizenship thus to be conferred on the several excepted races before mentioned is now for the first time proposed to be given by law. If, as is claimed by many, all persons who are native born already are, by virtue of the Constitution, citizens of the United States, the passage of the pending bill can not be necessary to make them such. If, on the other hand, such persons are not citizens, as may be assumed from the proposed legislation to make them such, the grave question presents itself whether, when eleven of the thirty-six States are unrepresented in Congress at the present time, it is sound policy to make our entire colored population and all other excepted classes citizens of the United States. Four millions of them have just emerged from slavery into freedom....It may also be asked whether it is necessary that they should be declared citizens in order that they may be secured in the enjoyment of the civil rights proposed to be conferred by the bill. Those rights are, by Federal as well as State laws, secured to all domiciled aliens and foreigners, even before the completion of the process of naturalization; and it may safely be assumed that the same enactments are sufficient to give like protection and benefits to those for whom this bill provides special legislation. Besides, the policy of the Government from its origin to the present time seems to have been that persons who are strangers to and unfamiliar with our institutions and our laws should pass through a certain probation, at the end of which, before attaining the coveted prize, they must give evidence of their fitness to receive and to exercise the rights of citizens as contemplated by the Constitution of the United States. The bill in effect proposes a discrimination against large numbers of intelligent, worthy, and patriotic foreigners, and in favor of the negro, to whom, after long years of bondage, the avenues to freedom and intelligence have just now been suddenly opened....

The first section of the bill also contains an enumeration of the rights to be enjoyed by these classes so made citizens "in every State and Territory in the United States." These rights are "to make and enforce contracts; to sue, be parties, and give evidence; to inherit, purchase, lease, sell, hold, and convey real and personal property," and to have "full and equal benefit of all laws and proceedings for the security of person and property as is enjoyed by white citizens." So, too, they are made subject to the same punishment, pains, and penalties in common with white citizens, and to none other. Thus a perfect equality of the white and colored races is attempted to be fixed by Federal law in every State of the Union over the vast field of State jurisdiction covered by these enumerated rights. In no one of these can any State ever exercise any power of discrimination between the different races....

Hitherto every subject embraced in the enumeration of rights contained in this bill has been considered as exclusively belonging to the States. They all relate to the internal police and economy of the respective States. They are matters which in each State concern the domestic condition of its people, varying in each according to its own peculiar circumstances and the safety and well-being of its own citizens. I do not mean to say that upon all these subjects there are not Federal restraints—as, for instance, in the State power of legislation over contracts there is a Federal limitation that no State shall pass a law impairing the obligations of contracts; and, as to crimes, that no State shall pass an *ex post facto* law; and, as to money, that no State shall make anything but gold and silver a legal tender; but where can we find a Federal prohibition against the power of any State to discriminate, as do most of them, between aliens and citizens, between artificial persons, called corporations, and natural persons, in the right to hold real estate? If it be granted that Congress can repeal all State laws discriminating between whites and blacks in the subjects covered by this bill, why, it may be asked, may not Congress repeal in the same way all State laws discriminating between the two races on the subjects of suffrage and office? If Congress can declare by law who shall hold lands, who shall testify, who shall have capacity to make a contract in a State, then Congress can by law also declare who, without regard to color or race, shall have the right to sit as a juror or as a judge, to hold any office, and, finally, to vote "in every State and Territory of the United States." As respects the Territories, they come within the power of Congress, for as to them the lawmaking power is the Federal power; but as to the States no similar provision exists vesting in Congress the power "to make rules and regulations" for them.

The object of the second section of the bill is to afford discriminating protection to colored persons in the full enjoyment of all the rights secured to them by the preceding section....

This provision of the bill seems to be unnecessary, as adequate judicial remedies could be adopted to secure the desired end without invading the immunities of legislators, always important to be preserved in the interest of public liberty; without assailing the independence of the judiciary, always essential to the preservation of individual rights; and without impairing the efficiency of ministerial officers, always necessary for the maintenance of public peace and order. The remedy proposed by this section seems to be in this respect not only anomalous, but unconstitutional; for the Constitution guarantees nothing with certainty if it does not insure to the several States the right of making and executing laws in regard to all matters arising within their jurisdiction, subject only to the restriction that in cases of conflict with the Constitution and constitutional laws of the United States the latter should be held to be the supreme law of the land....

The fourth section of the bill provides that officers and agents of the Freedmen's Bureau shall be empowered to make arrests, and also that other officers may be specially commissioned for that purpose by the President of the United States. It also authorizes circuit courts of the United States and the superior courts of the Territories to appoint, without limitation, commissioners, who are to be charged with the performance of *quasi* judicial duties. The fifth section empowers the commissioners so to be selected by the courts to appoint in writing, under their hands, one or more suitable persons from time to time to execute warrants and other processes described by the bill. These numerous official agents are made to constitute a sort of police, in addition to the military, and are authorized to summon a *posse comitatus,* and even to call to their aid such portion of the land and naval forces of the United States, or of the militia, "as may be necessary to the performance of the duty with which they are charged." This extraordinary power is to be conferred upon agents irresponsible to the Government and to the people, to whose number the discretion of the commissioners is the only limit, and in whose hands such authority might be made a terrible engine of wrong, oppression, and fraud....

The ninth section authorizes the President, or such person as he may empower for that purpose, "to employ such part of the land or naval forces of the United States, or of the militia, as shall be necessary to prevent the violation and enforce the due execution of this act." This language seems to imply a permanent military force, that to is to be always at hand, and whose only business is to be the enforcement of this measure over the vast region on where it is intended to operate....

In all our history, in all our experience as people living under Federal and State law, no such system as that contemplated by the details of this bill has ever before been proposed or adopted. They establish for the security of the colored race safeguards which go infinitely beyond any that the General Government has ever provided for the white race. In fact, the distinction of race and color is by the bill made to operate in favor of the colored and against the white race. They interfere with the municipal legislation of the States, with the relations existing exclusively between a State and its citizens, or between inhabitants of the same State—an absorption and assumption of power by the General Government which, if acquiesced in, must sap and destroy our federative system of limited powers and break down the barriers which preserve the rights of the States. It is another step, or rather stride, toward centralization and the concentration of all legislative powers in the National Government. The tendency of the bill must be to resuscitate the spirit of rebellion and to arrest the progress of those influences which are more closely drawing around the States the bonds of union and peace....

ANDREW JOHNSON.

* * * * * *

1.   *What is Johnson's "state's rights" argument against the notion of federal citizenship?*

2.   *How do Johnson's racial views mesh with his constitutional interpretation?*

3.   *How and why does Johnson extend his argument to a critique of the Freedmen's Bureau?*

17–8 *The First Reconstruction Act, 1867*

Radical Republicans made President Johnson's intransigence the central issue in the election campaign of 1866. Northern voters overwhelmingly rejected Johnson's policies and strengthened the Radicals' control of Congress. At the same time, all the Southern states (except Tennessee) rejected the Fourteenth Amendment. In response, Congress passed the following act in March 1867, outlining the main principles of Congressional Reconstruction.

SOURCE: Henry Steele Commager, *Documents in American History* (1973): *U.S. Statutes at Large*, Vol. XIV, p. 428ff.

An Act to provide for the more efficient Government of the Rebel States

WHEREAS no legal State governments or adequate protection for life or property now exists in the rebel States of Virginia, North Carolina, South Carolina, Georgia, Mississippi, Alabama, Louisiana, Florida, Texas, and Arkansas; and whereas it is necessary that peace and good order should be enforced in said States until loyal and republican State governments can be legally established: Therefore,

Be it enacted, That said rebel States shall be divided into military districts and made subject to the military authority of the United States as hereinafter prescribed, and for that purpose Virginia shall constitute the first district; North Carolina and South Carolina the second district; Georgia, Alabama, and Florida the third district; Mississippi and Arkansas the fourth district; and Louisiana and Texas the fifth district.

SEC. 2. That it shall be the duty of the President to assign to the command of each of said districts an officer of the army, not below the rank of brigadier-general, and to detail a sufficient military force to enable such officer to perform his duties and enforce his authority within the district to which he is assigned.

SEC. 3. That it shall be the duty of each officer assigned as aforesaid, to protect all persons in their rights of persons and property, to suppress insurrection, disorder, and violence, and to punish, or cause to be punished, all disturbers of the public peace and criminals; and to this end he may allow local civil tribunals to take jurisdiction of and to try offenders, or, when in his judgment it may be necessary for the trial of offenders, he shall have power to organize military commissions or tribunals for that purpose, and all interference under color of State authority with the exercise of military authority, under this act, shall be null and void.

SEC. 4. That all persons put under military arrest by virtue of this act shall be tried without unnecessary delay, and no cruel or unusual punishment shall be inflicted, and no sentence of any military commission or tribunal hereby authorized, affecting the life or liberty of any person, shall be executed until it is approved by the officer in command of the district, and the laws and regulations for the government of the army shall not be affected by this act, except in so far as they conflict with its provisions: *Provided,* That no sentence of death under the provisions of this act shall be carried into effect without the approval of the President.

SEC. 5. That when the people of any one of said rebel States shall have formed a constitution of government in conformity with the Constitution of the United States in all respects, framed by a convention of delegates elected by the male citizens of said State twenty-one years old and upward, of whatever race, color, or previous condition, who have been resident in said State for one year previous to the day of such election, except such as may be disfranchised for participation in the rebellion or for felony at common law, and when such constitution shall provide that the elective franchise shall be enjoyed by all such persons as have the qualifications herein stated for electors of delegates, and when such constitution shall he ratified by a majority of the persons voting on the question of ratification who are qualified as electors for delegates, and when such constitution shall have been submitted to Congress for examination and approval, and Congress shall have approved the same, and when said State, by a vote of its legislature elected under said constitution, shall have adopted the amendment to the Constitution of the United States, proposed by the Thirty-ninth Congress, and known as article fourteen, and when said article shall have become a part of the Constitution of the United States said State shall be declared entitled to representation in Congress, and senators and representatives shall he admitted therefrom on their taking the oath prescribed by law, and then and thereafter the preceding sections of this act shall he inoperative in said State: *Provided,* That no person excluded from the privilege of holding office by said proposed amendment to the Constitution of the United States, shall be eligible to election as a member of the convention to frame a constitution for any of said rebel States, nor shall any such person vote for members of such convention.

SEC. 6. That, until the people of said rebel States shall be by law admitted to representation in the Congress of the United States, any civil governments which may exist therein shall he deemed provisional only, and in all respects subject to the paramount authority of the United States at any time to abolish, modify, control, or supersede the same; and in all elections to any office under such provisional governments all persons shall be entitled to vote, and none others, who are entitled to vote, under the provisions of the fifth section of this act; and no persons shall be eligible to any office under any such provisional governments who would be disqualified from holding office under the provisions of the third *article* of said constitutional amendment.

* * * * * *

1. *Why did Congress define its Reconstruction policy in military terms?*

2. *What provisions did it make for the readmission of Southern states to the Union? How did these differ from the policy followed by President Johnson?*

17–9   *Organization and Principles of the Ku Klux Klan, 1868*

Founded in Pulaski, Tennessee, in 1866, the Ku Klux Klan spread quickly throughout the South under the leadership of former Confederate General Nathan Bedford Forrest, its first Grand Wizard. The Klan became a potent instrument of terror against freed people, their white allies, and Republican state governments. The Klan was strongest in rural areas and operated locally, with little central control. Most Klan leaders came from local landholding and professional elites.

SOURCE: Walter L. Fleming, ed., *The Ku Klux Klan* (1905), p. 154ff.

ORGANIZATION AND PRINCIPLES OF THE KU KLUX KLAN
APPELLATION

This Organization shall be styled and denominated, the Order of the * * *

CREED

We, the Order of the * * *, reverentially acknowledge the majesty and supremacy of the Divine Being, and recognize the goodness and providence of the same. And we recognize our relation to the United States Government, the supremacy of the Constitution, the Constitutional Laws thereof, and the Union of States thereunder.

CHARACTER AND OBJECTS OF THE ORDER

This is an institution of Chivalry, Humanity, Mercy, and Patriotism; embodying in its genius and its principles all that is chivalric in conduct, noble in sentiment, generous in manhood, and patriotic in purpose; its peculiar objects being

First: To protect the weak, the innocent, and the defenseless, from the indignities, wrongs, and outrages of the lawless, the violent, and the brutal; to relieve the injured and oppressed; to succor the suffering and unfortunate, and especially the widows and orphans of Confederate soldiers.

Second: To protect and defend the Constitution of the United States, and all laws passed in conformity thereto, and to protect the States and the people thereof from all invasion from any source whatever.

Third: To aid and assist in the execution of all constitutional laws, and to protect the people from unlawful seizure, and from trial except by their peers in conformity to the laws of the land.

TITLES

Sec. I. The officers of this Order shall consist of a Grand Wizard of the Empire, and his ten Genii; a Grand Dragon of the Realm, and his eight Hydras; a Grand Titan of the Dominion, and his six Furies; a Grand Giant of the Province, and his four Goblins; a Grand Cyclops of the Den, and his two Night Hawks; a Grand Magi, a Grand Monk, a Grand Scribe, a Grand Exchequer, a Grand Turk, and a Grand Sentinel.

Sec. 2. The body politic of this Order shall be known and designated as "Ghouls."

TERRITORY AND ITS DIVISIONS

Sec. 1. The territory embraced within the jurisdiction of this Order shall be coterminous with the States of Maryland, Virginia, North Carolina, South Carolina, Georgia, Florida, Alabama, Mississippi, Louisiana, Texas, Arkansas, Missouri, Kentucky, and Tennessee; all combined constituting the Empire.

Sec. 2. The Empire shall be divided into four departments, the first to be styled the Realm, and coterminous with the boundaries the several States; the second to be styled the Dominion and to be coterminous with such counties as the Grand Dragons of the several Realms may assign to the charge of the Grand Titan. The third to be styled the Province, and to be coterminous with the several counties; *provided* the Grand Titan may, when he deems it necessary, assign two Grand Giants to one Province, prescribing at the same time, the jurisdiction of each. The fourth department to be styled the Den, and shall embrace such part of a Province as the Grand Giant shall assign to the charge of a Grand Cyclops....

INTERROGATIONS TO BE ASKED

1st. Have you ever been rejected, upon application for membership in the * * *, or have you ever been expelled from the same?

2d. Are you now, or have you ever been, a member of the Radical Republican party, or either of the organizations known as the "Loyal League" and the "Grand Army of the Republic"?

3d. Are you opposed to the principles and policy of the Radical party, and to the Loyal League, and the Grand Army of the Republic, so far as you are informed of the character and purposes of those organizations?

4th. Did you belong to the Federal army during the late war, and fight against the South during the existence of the same?

5th. Are you opposed to negro equality, both social and political?

6th. Are you in favor of a white man's government in this country?

7th. Are you in favor of Constitutional liberty, and a Government of equitable laws instead of a Government of violence and oppression?

8th. Are you in favor of maintaining the Constitutional rights of the South?

9th. Are you in favor of the reenfranchisement and emancipation of the white men of the South, and the restitution of the Southern people to all their rights, alike proprietary, civil, and political?

10th. Do you believe in the inalienable right of self-preservation of the people against the exercise of arbitrary and unlicensed power?...

...9. The most profound and rigid secrecy concerning any and everything that relates to the Order, shall at all times be maintained.

10. Any member who shall reveal or betray the secrets of this Order, shall suffer the extreme penalty of the law.

* * * * * *

1. *How do the Klan "Interrogations" for prospective members reflect the lingering ideals of the Confederacy?*

2. *Why did the Klan place so much emphasis upon ritual secrecy and grand titles?*

17–10   Blanche K. Bruce, Speech in the Senate, 1876

Born a slave in Virginia, Blanche K. Bruce grew up in Missouri, where he established the state's first school for African Americans during the Civil War. After the war he moved to Mississippi, where he became a Republican political organizer and a large landowner in the Delta region. Bruce won election to the U.S. Senate in 1874, where he was the first African American to serve a full term. Bruce here protests violent election frauds in his home state.

SOURCE: *Congressional Record, 44th Congress, 1st Session* (1876).

The conduct of the late election in Mississippi affected not merely the fortunes of partisans—as the same were necessarily involved in the defeat or success of the respective parties to the contest—but put in question and jeopardy the sacred rights of the citizen; and the investigation contemplated in the pending resolution has for its object not the determination of the question whether the offices shall be held and the public affairs of that State be administered by democrats or republicans, but the higher and more important end, the protection in all their purity and significance of the political rights of the people and the free institutions of the country....

The evidence in hand and accessible will show beyond peradventure that in many parts of the State corrupt and violent influences were brought to bear upon the registrars of voters, thus materially affecting the character of the voting or poll lists; upon the inspectors of election, prejudicially and unfairly thereby changing the number of votes cast; and, finally, threats and violence were practiced directly upon the masses of voters in such measures and strength as to produce grave apprehensions for their personal safety and as to deter them from the exercise of their political franchises....

It will not accord with the laws of nature or history to brand colored people a race of cowards. On more than one historic field, beginning in 1776 and coming down to this centennial year of the Republic, they have attested in blood their courage as well as a love of liberty. I ask Senators to believe that no consideration of fear or personal danger has kept us quiet and forbearing under the provocations and wrongs that have so sorely tried our souls. But feeling kindly toward our white fellow-citizens, appreciating the good purposes and offices of the better classes, and, above all, abhoring a war of races, we determined to wait until such time as an appeal to the good sense and justice of the American people could be made....

The sober American judgment must obtain in the South as elsewhere in the Republic, that the only distinctions upon which parties can be safely organized and in harmony with our institutions are differences of opinion relative to principles and policy of government, and that differences of religion, nationality, or race can neither with safety nor propriety be permitted for a moment to enter into the party contests of the day. The unanimity with which the colored voters act with a party is not referable to any race prejudice on their pan. On the contrary, they invite the political co-operation of their white brethren, and vote as a unit because proscribed as such. They deprecate the establishment of the color line by the opposition, not only because the act is unwise and wrong in principle, but because it isolates them from the white men of the South, and forces them, in sheer self-protection and against their inclination, to act seemingly upon the basis of a race prejudice that they neither respect nor entertain. As a class they are free from prejudices, and have no uncharitable suspicions against their white fellow-citizens, whether native born or settlers from the Northern States. They not only recognize the equality of citizenship and the right of every man to hold, without proscription any position of honor and trust to which the confidence of the people may elevate him; but owing nothing to race, birth, or surroundings, they, above all other classes in the community, are interested to see prejudices drop out of both politics and the business of the country, and success in life proceed only upon the integrity and merit of the man who seeks it.... But withal, as they progress in intelligence and appreciation of the dignity of their prerogatives as citizens, they, as an evidence

of growth begin to realize the significance of the proverb, "When thou doest well for thyself, men shall praise thee;" and are disposed to exact the same protection and concession of rights that are conferred upon other citizens by the Constitution, and that, too, without the humiliation involved in the enforced abandonment of their political convictions....

I have confidence, not only in my country and her institutions, but in the endurance, capacity, and destiny of my people. We will, as opportunity offers and ability serves, seek our places, sometimes in the field of letters, arts, sciences, and the professions. More frequently mechanical pursuits will attract and elicit our efforts; more still of my people will find employment and livelihood as the cultivators of the soil. The bulk of this people—by surroundings, habits, adaptation, and choice—will continue to find their homes in the South, and constitute the masses of its yeomanry. We will there probably, of our own volition and more abundantly than in the past, produce the great staples that will contribute to the basis of foreign exchange, aid in giving the nation a balance of trade, and minister to the wants and comfort and build up the prosperity of the whole land. Whatever our ultimate position in the composite civilization of the Republic and whatever varying fortunes attend our career, we will not forget our instincts for freedom nor our love of country.

* * * * * *

1. *Bruce cultivated a reputation as a racial moderate in Reconstruction politics. How does his speech reflect this?*

2. *What political and economic strategies does he recommend for freed people?*

17–11 A Sharecrop Contract, 1882

During the Reconstruction era, sharecropping emerged as the most common method of organizing and financing Southern agriculture. Large plantations, no longer worked by gangs of slaves, were broken up into small plots worked by individual families. The following contract typifies the sort of formal arrangements that many thousands of poor black and white farmers made with local landowners.

SOURCE: Grimes Family Papers, Southern Historical Collection, University of North Carolina, Chapel Hill, in Robert D. Marcus and David Burner, eds., *America Firsthand* (1992), pp. 306—308.

To every one applying to rent land upon shares, the following conditions must be read, and *agreed to.*

To every 30 or 35 acres, I agree to furnish the team, plow, and farming implements, except cotton planters, and I *do not* agree to furnish a cart to every cropper. The croppers are to have half of the cotton, corn and fodder (and peas and pumpkins and potatoes if any are planted) if the following conditions are compiled with, but—if not—they are to have only two-fifths (2/5). Croppers are to have no part or interest in the cotton seed raised from the crop planted and worked by them. No vine crops of any description, that is, no watermelons, muskmelons,...squashes or anything of that kind, except peas and pumpkins, and potatoes, are to be planted in the cotton or corn. All must work under my direction. All plantation work to be done by the croppers. My part of the crop to be *housed* by them, and the fodder and oats to be hauled and put in the house. All the cotton must be topped about 1st August. If any cropper fails from any cause to save all the fodder from his crop, I am to have enough fodder to make it equal to one half of the whole if the whole amount of fodder had been saved.

For every mule or horse furnished by me there must be 1000 good sized rails...hauled, and the fence repaired as far as they will go, the fence to be torn down and put up from the bottom if I so direct. All croppers to haul rails and work on fence whenever I may order. Rails to be split when I may say. Each cropper to clean out every ditch in his crop, and where a ditch runs between two croppers, the cleaning out of that ditch is to be divided equally between them. Every ditch bank in the crop must be shrubbed down and cleaned off before the crop is planted and must be cut down every time the land is worked with his hoe and when the crop is "laid by," the ditch banks must be left clean of bushes, weeds, and seeds. The cleaning out of all ditches must be done by the first of October. The rails must be split and the fence repaired before corn is planted.

Each cropper must keep in good repair all bridges in his crop or over ditches that he has to clean out and when a bridge needs repairing that is outside of all their crops, then any one that I call on must repair it.

Fence jams to be done as ditch banks. If any cotton is planted on the land outside of the plantation fence, I am to have *three-fourths* of all the cotton made in those patches, that is to say, no cotton must be planted by croppers in their home patches.

All croppers must clean out stables and fill them with straw, and haul straw in front of stables whenever I direct. All the cotton must be manured, and enough fertilizer must be brought to manure each crop highly, the croppers to pay for one half of all manure bought, the quantity to be purchased for each crop must be left to me.

No cropper to work off the plantation when there is any work to be done on the land he has rented, or when his work is needed by me or other croppers. Trees to be cut down on Orchard, House field & Evanson fences, leaving such as I may designate.

Road field to be planted from the *very edge of the ditch to the fence,* and all the land to be planted close up to the ditches and fences. *No stock of any kind* belonging to croppers to run in the plantation after crops are gathered.

If the fence should be blown down, or if trees should fall on the fence outside of the land planted by any of the croppers, any one or all that I may call upon must put it up and repair it. Every cropper must feed, or have fed, the team he works, Saturday nights, Sundays, and every morning before going to work, beginning to feed his team (morning, noon, and night *every day* in the week) on the day he rents and feeding it to and including the 31st day of December. If any cropper shall from any cause fail to repair his fence as far as 1000 rails will go, or shall fail to clean out any part of his ditches, or shall fail to leave his ditch banks, any part of them, well shrubbed and clean when his crop is laid by, or shall fail to clean out stables, fill them up and haul straw in front of them whenever he is told, he shall have only two-fifths (2/5) of the cotton, corn, fodder, peas and pumpkins made on the land he cultivates.

If any cropper shall fail to feed his team Saturday nights, all day Sunday and all the rest of the week, morning/noon, and night, for every time he so fails he must pay me five cents.

No corn nor cotton stalks must be burned, but must be cut down, cut up and plowed in. Nothing must be burned off the land except when it is *impossible* to plow it in.

Every cropper must be responsible for all gear and farming implements placed in his hands, and if not returned must be paid for unless it is worn out by use.

Croppers must sow & plow in oats and haul them to the crib, but *must have no part of them.* Nothing to be sold from their crops, nor fodder nor corn to be carried out of the fields until my rent is all paid, and all amounts they owe me and for which I am responsible are paid in full.

I am to gin & pack all the cotton and charge every cropper an eighteenth of his part, the cropper to furnish his part of the bagging, ties, & twine.

The sale of every cropper's part of the cotton to be made by me when and where I choose to sell, and after deducting all they owe me and all sums that I may be responsible for on their accounts, to pay them their half of the net proceeds. Work of every description, particularly the work on fences and ditches, to be done to my satisfaction, and must be done over until I am satisfied that it is done as it should be.

No wood to burn, nor light wood, nor poles, nor timber for boards, nor wood for any purpose whatever must be gotten above the house occupied by Henry Beasley—nor must any trees be cut down nor any wood used for any purpose, except for firewood, without my permission.

* * * * * *

1. *What responsibilities does the landowner agree to take on in the contract? How do these differ from the cropper?*

2. *What distinctions are made between the growing and selling of cotton and other crops?*

chapter 18

Conquest and Survival: Communities in the Trans-Mississippi West, 1860–1900

18-1   The Oklahoma Land Rush, 1889

Beginning in 1884, white settlers began entering the "Oklahoma District," a fertile area of rich land in the center of Indian Territory owned by no one tribe. Public pressure on Congress mounted to open the region to settlers under the terms of the Homestead Act. President Harrison announced that the district would be open to homesteaders on April 22, 1889, and thousands of would-be settlers, held back by Army troops, lined up to stake their claims. The following eyewitness account captures the bedlam of the "Sooner" land rush.

SOURCE: "The Rush to Oklahoma," *Harper's Weekly* 33 (May 18, 1889), p. 391.

The preparations for the settlement of Oklahoma had been complete, even to the slightest detail, for weeks before the opening day. The Santa Fe Railway, which runs through Oklahoma north and south, was prepared to take any number of people from its handsome station at Arkansas City, Kansas, and to deposit them in almost any part of Oklahoma as soon as the law allowed; thousands of covered wagons were gathered in camps on all sides of the new Territory waiting for the embargo to be lifted. In its picturesque aspects the rush across the border at noon on the opening day must go down in history as one of the most noteworthy events of Western civilization. At the time fixed, thousands of hungry home-seekers, who had gathered from all parts of the country, and particularly from Kansas and Missouri, were arranged in line along the border, ready to lash their horses into furious speed in the race for fertile spots in the beautiful land before them. The day was one of perfect peace. Overhead the sun shone down from a sky as fair and blue as the cloudless heights of Colorado. The whole expanse of space from zenith to horizon was spotless in its blue purity. The clear spring air, through which the rolling green billows of the promised land could be seen with unusual distinctness for many miles, was as sweet and fresh as the balmy atmosphere of June among New Hampshire's hills.

As the expectant home-seekers waited with restless patience, the clear, sweet notes of a cavalry bugle rose and hung a moment upon the startled air. It was noon. The last barrier of savagery in the United States was broken down. Moved by the same impulse, each driver lashed his horses furiously; each rider dug his spurs into his willing steed, and each man on foot caught his breath hard and darted forward. A cloud of dust rose where the home-seekers had stood in line, and when it had drifted away before the gentle breeze, the horses and wagons and men were tearing across the open country like fiends. The horsemen had the best of it from the start. It was a fine race for a few minutes, but soon the riders began to spread out like a fan, and by the time they had reached the horizon they were scattered about as far as eye could see. Even the fleetest of the horsemen found upon reaching their chosen localities that men in wagons and men on foot were there before them. As it was clearly impossible for a man on foot to outrun a horseman, the inference is plain that Oklahoma had been entered hours before the appointed time. Notwithstanding the assertions of the soldiers that every boomer had been driven out of Oklahoma, the fact remains that the woods along the various streams within Oklahoma were literally full of people Sunday night. Nine-tenths of these people made settlement upon the land illegally. The other tenth would have done so had there been any desirable land left to settle upon. This action on the part of the first claim-holders will cause a great deal of land litigation in the future, as it is not to be expected that the man who ran his horse at its utmost speed for ten miles only to find a settler with an ox team in quiet possession of his chosen farm will tamely submit to this plain infringement of the law.

Some of the men who started from the line on foot were quite as successful in securing desirable claims as many who rode fleet horses. They had the advantage of knowing just where their land was located. One man left the line with the others, carrying on his back a tent, a blanket, some camp dishes, an axe, and provisions for two days. He ran down the railway track for six miles, and reached his claim in just sixty minutes. Upon arriving on his land he fell down under a tree, unable to speak or see. I am glad to be able to say that his claim is one of the best in Oklahoma. The rush from the line was so impetuous that by the time the first railway train arrived from the north at twenty-five minutes past twelve o'clock, only a few of the hundreds of boomers were anywhere to be seen. The journey of this first train was well-nigh as interesting as the rush of the men in wagons. The train left Arkansas City at 8:45 o'clock in the forenoon. It consisted of an empty baggage car, which was set apart for the use of the newspaper correspondents, eight passenger coaches, and the caboose of a freight train. The coaches were so densely packed with men that not another human being could get on board. So uncomfortably crowded were they that some of the younger boomers climbed to the roofs of the cars and clung perilously to the ventilators. An adventurous person secured at great risk a seat on the forward truck of the baggage car.

In this way the train was loaded to its utmost capacity. That no one was killed or injured was due as much to the careful management of the train as to the ability of the passengers to take care of themselves. Like their friends in the wagons, the boomers on the cars were exultant with joy at the thought of at last entering into possession of the promised land. At first appearances the land through which the train ran seemed to justify all the virtues that had been claimed for it. The rolling, grassy uplands, and the wooded river-bottoms, the trees, which were just bursting into the most beautiful foliage of early spring, seemed to give a close reality to the distant charm of green and purple forest growths, which rose from the trough of some long swell and went heaving away to meet the brighter hues in the far-off sky. Throughout all the landscape were clumps of trees suggesting apple orchards set in fertile meadows, and here and there were dim patches of gray and white sand that might in a less barbarous region be mistaken for farm-houses surrounded by hedges and green fields. Truly the Indians have well-named Oklahoma the "beautiful land." The landless and home-hungry people on the train might be pardoned their mental exhilaration, when the effect of this wonderfully beautiful country upon the most prosaic mind is fully considered. It was an eager and an exuberantly joyful crowd that rode slowly into Guthrie at twenty minutes past one o'clock on that perfect April afternoon. Men who had expected to lay out the town site were grievously disappointed at the first glimpse of their proposed scene of operations. The slope east of the railway at Guthrie station was dotted white with tents and sprinkled thick with men running about in all directions.

"We're done for," said a town-site speculator, in dismay. "Some one has gone in ahead of us and laid out the town."

"Never mind that," shouted another town-site speculator, "but make a rush and get what you can."

Hardly had the train slackened its speed when the impatient boomers began to leap from the cars and run up the slope. Men jumped from the roofs of the moving cars at the risk of their lives. Some were so stunned by the fall that they could not get up for some minutes. The coaches were so crowded that many men were compelled to squeeze through the windows in order to get a fair start at the head of the crowd. Almost before the train had come to a standstill the cars were emptied. In their haste and eagerness, men fell over each other in heaps, others stumbled and fell headlong, while many ran forward so blindly and impetuously that it was not until they had passed the best of the town lots that they came to a realization of their actions.

I ran with the first of the crowd to get a good point of view from which to see the rush. When I had time to look about me I found that I was standing beside a tent, near which a man was leisurely chopping holes in the sod with a new axe.

"Where did you come from, that you have already pitched your tent?" I asked.

"Oh, I was here," said he.

"How was that?"

"Why, I was a deputy United States marshal."

"Did you resign?"

"No; I'm a deputy still."

"But it is not legal for a deputy United States marshal, or any one in the employ of the government, to take up a town lot in this manner."

"That may all be, stranger; but I've got two lots here, just the same; and about fifty other deputies have got lots in the same way. In fact, the deputy-marshals laid out the town."

At intervals of fifteen minutes, other trains came from the north loaded down with home-seekers and town-site speculators. As each succeeding crowd rushed up the slope and found that government officers had taken possession of the best part of the town, indignation became hot and outspoken; yet the marshals held to their lots and refused to move. Bloodshed was prevented only by the belief of the home-seekers that the government would set the matter right.

This course of the deputy United States marshals was one of the most outrageous pieces of imposition upon honest home-seekers ever practised in the settlement of a new country. That fifty men could, through influence, get themselves appointed as deputy United States marshals for the sole purpose of taking advantage of their positions in this way is creditable neither to them nor to the man who made their appointment possible. This illegal seizure thus became the first matter of public discussion in the city of Guthrie....

It is estimated that between six and seven thousand persons reached Guthrie by train from the north the first afternoon, and that fully three thousand came in by wagon from the north and east, and by train from Purcell on the south, thus making a total population for the first day of about ten thousand. By taking thought in the matter, three-fourths of these people had provided themselves with tents and blankets, so that even on the first night they had ample shelter from the weather. The rest of them slept the first night as best they could, with only the red earth for a pillow and the starry arch of heaven for a blanket. At dawn of Tuesday the unrefreshed home-seekers and town-site speculators arose, and began anew the location of disputed claims. The tents multiplied like mushrooms in a rain that day, and by night the building of frame houses had been begun in earnest in the new streets. The buildings were by no means elaborate, yet they were as good as the average frontier structure, and they served their purpose, which was all that was required.

On that day the trains going north were filled with returning boomers, disgusted beyond expression with the dismal outlook of the new country. Their places were taken by others who came in to see the fun, and perhaps pick up a bargain in the way of town lots or commercial speculation.

* * * * * *

1. *What attention, if any, does the author give to Indian peoples in the settlement area?*

2. *What does the reported role of deputy federal marshals suggest about law and order on the frontier?*

18–2 *The Homestead Act, 1862*

The Homestead Act created the first program for making public lands available to small farmers. Before the Civil War, southern congressmen had opposed homesteading plans' because they feared that rapid western settlement would increase the number and influence of free states. Northern Republicans made homestead legislation a high priority, and after secession they were finally able to get the law through Congress. By the end of the Civil War, some 15,000 homestead claims had been made. Although the Homestead Act did offer new opportunities for some eastern and midwestern farmers, it could not help poor city dwellers and others who lacked the resources to begin farming. Much of the land granted under the Act eventually fell into the hands of speculators, railroads, and mining companies.

SOURCE: *U.S. Statutes at Large*, Vol. XII.

AN ACT to secure homesteads to actual settlers on the public domain.

Be it enacted, That any person who is the head of a family, or who has arrived at the age of twenty-one years, and is a citizen of the United States, or who shall have filed his declaration of intention to become such, as required by the naturalization laws of the United States, and who has never borne arms against the United States Government or given aid and comfort to its enemies, shall, from and after the first of January, eighteen hundred and sixty-three, be entitled to enter one quarter-section or a less quantity of unappropriated public lands, upon which said person may have filed a pre-emption claim, or which may, at the time the application is made, be subject to pre-emption at one dollar and twenty-five cents, or less, per acre; or eighty acres or less of such unappropriated lands, at two dollars and fifty cents per acre, to be located in a body, in conformity to the legal subdivisions of the public lands, and after the same shall have been surveyed: *Provided,* That any person owning or residing

on land may, under the provisions of this act, enter other land lying contiguous to his or her said land, which shall not, with the land so already owned and occupied, exceed in the aggregate one hundred and sixty acres.

Sec. 2. That the person applying for the benefit of this act shall, upon application to the register of the land office in which he or she is about to make such entry, make affidavit before the said register or receiver that he or she is the head of a family, or is twenty-one or more years of age, or shall have performed service in the Army or Navy of the United States, and that he has never borne arms against the Government of the United States or given aid and comfort to its enemies, and that such application is made for his or her exclusive use and benefit, and that said entry is made for the purpose of actual settlement and cultivation, and not, either directly or indirectly, for the use or benefit of any other person or persons whomsoever; and upon filing the said affidavit with the register or receiver, and on payment of ten dollars, he or she shall thereupon be permitted to enter the quantity of land specified: *Provided, however,* That no certificate shall be given or patent issued therefore until the expiration of five years from the date of such entry; and if, at the expiration of such time, or at any time within two years thereafter, the person making such entry—or if he be dead, his widow; or in case of her death, his heirs or devisee; or in case of a widow making such entry, her heirs or devisee, in case of her death—shall prove by two credible witnesses that he, she, or they have resided upon or cultivated the same for the term of five years immediately succeeding the time of filing the affidavit aforesaid, and shall make affidavit that no part of said land has been alienated, and that he has borne true allegiance to the Government of the United States; then, in such case, he, she, or they, if at that time a citizen of the United States, shall be entitled to a patent, as in other cases provided for by law: *And provided, further,* That in case of the death of both father and mother, leaving an infant child or children under twenty-one years of age, the right and fee shall inure to the benefit of said infant child or children; and the executor, administrator, or guardian may, at any time within two years after the death of the surviving parent, and in accordance with the laws of the State in which such children for the time being have their domicile, sell said land for the benefit of said infants, but for no other purpose; and the purchaser shall acquire the absolute title by the purchase, and be entitled to a patent from the United States, on payment of the office fees and sum of money herein specified....

* * * * * *

1.   *How did the terms and language of the Homestead Act reflect the values of the Republican Party in this era?*

2.   *Why were homestead claims limited to small farms*

18–3   Helen Hunt Jackson, The Thrill of Western Railroading, 1878

Perhaps no event in the nation's transportation history captured the public imagination like the transcontinental railroad, completed in 1869. Ordinary Americans could now make the journey from New York to San Francisco in a week, traveling in comfort and style. The burgeoning railroad system encouraged the growth of the vacation industry, bringing attractive vacation spots within the geographical and financial grasp of more people. The following account communicates some of the excitement experienced by first-time travelers through the Far West.

SOURCE: Helen Hunt Jackson, *Bits of Travel at Home* (Boston: Roberts Brothers, 1878), pp. 6–9.

We cross the Missouri at Council Bluffs; begin grumbling at the railroad corporations for forcing us to take a transfer train across the river; but find ourselves plunged into the confusion of Omaha before we have finished railing at the confusion of her neighbor. Now we see for the first time the distinctive expression of American overland travel. Here all luggage is weighed and rechecked for points further west. An enormous shed is filled with it. Four and five deep stand the anxious owners, at a high wooden wall, behind which nobody may go. Everybody holds up checks, and gesticulates and beckons. There seems to be no system; but undoubtedly there is. Side by side with the rich and flurried New-Yorker stands the poor and flurried emigrant. Equality rules. Big bundles of feather-beds, tied up in blue check, red chests, corded with rope, get ahead of Saratoga trunks. Many languages are spoken. German, Irish, French, Spanish, a little English, and all varieties of American, I heard during thirty minutes in that luggage-shed. Inside the wall was a pathetic sight,—a poor German woman on her knees before a chest, which had burst open on the journey. It seemed as if its whole contents could not be worth five dollars,—so old, so faded, so coarse were the clothes and
so battered were the utensils. But it was evidently all she

owned; it was the home she had brought with her from the Fatherland, and would be the home she would set up in the prairie. The railroad-men were good to her, and were helping her with ropes and nails. This comforted me somewhat; but it seemed almost a sin to be journeying luxuriously on the same day and train with that poor soul.

"Lunches put up for people going West." This sign was out on all corners. Piles of apparently owner-less bundles were stacked all along the platforms; but everybody was too busy to steal. Some were eating hastily, with looks of distress, as if they knew it would be long before they ate again. Others, wiser, were buying whole chickens, loaves of bread, and filling bottles with tea. Provident Germans bought sausage by the yard. German babies got bits of it to keep them quiet. Murderous-looking rifles and guns, with strapped rolls of worn and muddy blankets, stood here and there; murderous, but jolly-looking miners, four-fifths boots and the rest beard, strode about, keeping one eye on their weapons and bedding. Well-dressed women and men with polished shoes, whose goods were already comfortably bestowed in palace-cars, lounged up and down, curious, observant, amused. Gay placards, advertising all possible routes; cheerful placards, setting forth the advantages of travellers' insurance policies; insulting placards, assuming that all travellers have rheumatism, and should take "Unk Weed;" in short, just such placards as one sees everywhere,—papered the walls. But here they seemed somehow to be true and merit attention, especially the "Unk Weed." There is such a professional croak in that first syllable; it sounds as if the weed had a diploma.

"All aboard!" rung out like the last warning on Jersey City wharves when steamers push off for Europe; and in the twinkling of an eye we were out again in the still, soft, broad prairie, which is certainly more like sea than like any other land.

Again flowers and meadows, and here and there low hills, more trees, too, and a look of greater richness. Soon the Platte River, which seems to be composed of equal parts of sand and water, but which has too solemn a history to be spoken lightly of. It has been the silent guide for so many brave men who are dead! The old emigrant road, over which they went, is yet plainly to be seen; at many points it lies near the railroad. Its still, grass-grown track is strangely pathetic. Soon it will be smooth prairie again, and the wooden headboards at the graves of those who died by the way will have fallen and crumbled.

Dinner at Fremont. The air was sharp and clear. The disagreeable guide-book said we were only 1,176 feet above the sea; but we believed we were higher. The keeper of the dining-saloon apologized for not having rhubarb-pie, saying that he had just sent fifty pounds of rhubarb on ahead to his other saloon. "You'll take tea there to-morrow night."

"But how far apart are your two houses?" said we.

"Only eight hundred miles. It's considerable trouble to go back an' forth, an' keep things straight; but I do the best I can."

Two barefooted little German children, a boy and girl, came into the cars here, with milk and coffee to sell. The boy carried the milk, and was sorely puzzled when I held out my small tumbler to be filled. It would hold only half as much as his tin measure, of which the price was five cents.

"Donno's that's quite fair," he said, when I gave him

five cents. But he pocketed it, all the same, and ran on, swinging his tin can and pint cup, and calling out, "Nice fresh milk. Last you'll get! No milk any further west." Little rascal! We found it all the way; plenty of it too, such as it was. It must be owned, however, that sage-brush and prickly pear (and if the cows do not eat these, what do they eat?) give a singularly unpleasant taste to milk; and the addition of alkali water does not improve it.

* * * * * *

1.   *What does the author see as peculiarly American about her railroad experience? About the landscape?*

2.   *What evidence does the piece offer about social and cultural life on the 1870s frontier?*

18–4   Bill Haywood, Miners and Cowboys, 1887

William D. "Big Bill" Haywood was born in 1869 in Salt Lake City and began working in the metal mines of Nevada at age fifteen. He also worked as a farmhand and a cowboy and tried his hand at homesteading. In later years, Haywood became an influential leader in two radical labor organizations, the Western Federation of Miners and the Industrial Workers of the World. The harsh working and living conditions he describes here were typical of mining and agricultural communities in the late-nineteenth-century West.

SOURCE: William D. Haywood, *The Autobiography of Big Bill Haywood* (NY: International Publishers, 1929), pp. 32–35. Reprinted by permission.

Some time later I returned to Utah and went to work in the Brooklyn mine. My first job there was firing the boilers and running the top car, taking away the waste and ore that were sent to the surface. The Brooklyn was an inclined shaft fourteen hundred feet deep, in which there was a skip that was hauled up by the engine for which I was firing the boilers. For a while I worked in what was called the Mormon stope; it had been given this name because several of the men employed there were from the San Pete valley, a strictly Mormon section. I worked in several different places in this mine, which was producing lead. There were men going to and coming from the hospital all the time, suffering from lead poisoning. This is one of the serious vocational diseases with which the workers have to contend, but there was no provision made

for them. In that part of the country the miners were sent to hospitals in Salt Lake City which they themselves maintained. Every miner had one dollar a month taken out of his wages by the company for hospital services. Their transportation to and from the hospital the workers had to pay themselves. A crowd of lead miners presents a ghastly appearance, as their faces are ashen pale.

There are many dangers to which a miner is exposed besides rheumatism, consumption, lead poisoning, and other diseases. One of these is the constant danger of falling rock when a mine is not kept closely timbered. I was working but a short distance from Louis Fontaine when he was killed by a slab of rock from the roof that crushed his head on the drill that he was holding. We got the body out of the stope on a timber truck, ran it to the station, and put all that was left of Louis in the skip. We rang three bells for the surface. Some of us laid off to go to the funeral.

The men rode on the skip coming up to dinner at quitting time. Four could sit in the skip on either side, two on the crossbar, and one on the angle to which the steel cable was fastened. One day I got on the cable behind the man on the angle and rode all the way to the top. It was one of the most hair-raising experiences of my life. The cable was whipping the timbers at the top and the rollers on which the skip ran up the steep incline. I was afraid every second that my hands would be caught as I held on to the cable behind my head, and I gripped the man in front of me with both legs to keep from turning on the rope.

While at the Brooklyn mine, I sent to Nevada for my sweetheart, Nevada Jane Minor. We were married and went to live in Salt Lake City, where our first child was born, a boy who died at birth. Shortly afterward we returned to Nevada, where I spent some time doing assessment work for Thad Hoppin, and prospecting. I later went to work on the Hoppin ranch.

A cowboy's life is not the joyous, adventurous existence shown in the moving pictures, read about in cheap novels, or to be seen in World's Exhibitions. The cowboy's work begins at daybreak. If he is on the ranch he rolls out of bed, slips on his pants, boots and hat and goes to the barn to feed his saddle horses. It is his greatest pride that he does not work on foot. Coming back, he washes his face and hands at the pump, and takes his place at the long table; the Chinese cook brings in piles of beefsteaks, potatoes, hot cakes, and "long butter," as the flour-gravy is called, because on a big cattle ranch where there are thousands of cows, ofttimes there will be not one milk cow, and no butter but what is hauled many miles from town to the ranch.

There are various kinds of work for the cowboy to do during the different seasons on a cow ranch. The cattle are not pastured or herded, but run wild on the mountains and sage-brush flats. They are rounded up in the Spring and Fall, the round-up being called the "rodeo." This and other words commonly used in the southwest come down to us from the days when this part of the country was a Spanish colony, and Spanish was the usual language. The foreman, who was called major-domo, of the biggest ranch in the neighborhood issued the call for the rodeo. Cowboys from all the ranches in a radius of a hundred miles or more came with their saddle horses, each bringing three or four. The bedding consisted of a couple of blankets and a bed-canvas. When traveling with the rodeo, the men rolled up their bedding and put it in the chuck wagon which also carried the cooking utensils and the grub. Starting from the home ranch the outfit would camp on the banks of a stream or near a spring or sometimes would be compelled to make a dry camp, in which case they hauled along barrels of water for the emergency. After supper we stretched our beds on the ground, gambled and otherwise amused ourselves, telling stories of past experience and singing lilting and rollicking songs. A horse-wrangler or two guarded the paratha, the herd of saddle horses. We all went to sleep as soon as night fell. At the first break of day, the cook was up getting breakfast. The wranglers brought the horses. The cowboys went to the corral. Each roped his horse out of the band, saddled and bridled it and then went to the chuck wagon for breakfast.

After eating we rolled cigarettes, mounted our horses and started for the mountains, some going up one canyon, some up another. We rode to the highest summits. Turning, we drove before us all the cattle on that part of the range. The round-up took place in the valley below, where the cattle were brought together. The cowboys

formed a circle around them, fifty or a hundred cowboys spaced out around several hundred head of cattle. Two or four cowboys from the biggest ranch rode among the herd and drove out the cows and young calves; they were able to recognize their own by the brands and earmarks on the cows. The task was then for the cowboys from each ranch to brand and earmark the calves that belonged to the ranch they were working for. The parting out continued until all the cows and young calves were separated from the herd. The other cattle were started back to the mountains. Two or three small fires were lit in the corral and the first bunch of cows was driven in; the other bunches were held to await their turn. We roped the calves by the hind legs and dragged them near the fire by taking a turn with the rope around the horns of our saddles. We cut the ears of the calves with our own peculiar marks, crop, underbit, swallow-fork or other designs. The brand of the ranch was burnt into hip or shoulder. This proceeded until all the calves were branded and earmarked, the males gelded, leaving one out of every twenty-five or fifty for breeding purposes, selecting those which in the opinion of the cowboys would make big, strong animals. Outside of the bawling and bellowing of the calves and cows, there was silence; we had little to say while at work, as we were nearly choked with dust.

Meanwhile the chuck wagon had moved on to the next camping ground. If the horses had not had a hard day's work we would start for our supper at a long, swinging lope, singing ribald songs at the top of our voices. Unsaddling the horses where we were going to make our beds for the night, we washed up and were ready with ravenous appetites for grub. The day's work was done. The round-up took several weeks; we went up one side of the valley and down the other side.

Another round-up took place every fall, when beef steers were gathered for the market. It was carried on in much the same way though we used to take more care not to drive the animals fast because of the weight that would be lost from marketable steers.

When beef was needed for the camp, a young heifer or steer was killed. The cowboys as a rule used to barbecue the head and other parts of the animal. This was done by heating rocks which were put into a hole that had been prepared, the head and pieces of meal being wrapped in pieces of wet canvas, put on top of the hot rocks and covered with dirt. In the morning we would dig it out, remove the canvas and the hide, and with a little pepper and salt the main part of our breakfast was ready.

Wild horses are more fleet-footed than cattle and more difficult to handle. After the round-up of horses, those that were wanted for harness and saddle were kept in field or corral until the slack season of fall and winter, when they were broken to work or ride. This was the most exhilarating part of a cowboy's life. There was much excitement in riding wild horses as well as in handling them, not only for the rider but for the onlookers. Some horses were extremely vicious, biting, striking and kicking fiercely, to say nothing of their bucking propensities.

* * * * * *

1.   *What connections can you make between the*

life Haywood depicts and his later turn to radical unionism?

2.   *How does Haywood's portrait of western life in the 1800s compare with popular contemporary images of that world?*

18–5   Red Cloud, Speech at Cooper Union, New York, 1870

An influential Oglala Sioux chief, Red Cloud fought the U.S. Army for nearly a decade during the 1860s in a losing effort to hold onto Sioux lands in the Yellowstone and Powder River valleys. But military expeditions and rapid settlement forced Red Cloud to sign the Fort Laramie treaty of 1868, and he later agreed to live on a reservation. In 1870, while on a trip east to visit President Grant, Red Cloud was persuaded to speak at the Cooper Union Hall in New York City. Red Cloud was given a standing ovation by the New York audience.

SOURCE: *The New York Times*, July 17, 1870.

My brethren and my friends who are here before me this day, God Almighty has made us all, and He is here to bless what I have to say to you today. The Good Spirit made us both. He gave you lands and He gave us lands; He gave us these lands; you came in here, and we respected you as brothers. God Almighty made you but made you all white and clothed you; when He made us He made us with red skins and poor; now you have come.

When you first came we were very many, and you were few; now you are many, and we are getting very few, and we are poor. You do not know who appears before you today to speak. I am a representative of the original American race, the first people of this continent. We are good and not bad. The reports that you hear concerning us are all on one side. We are always well disposed to them. You are here told that we are traders and thieves, and it is not so. We have given you nearly all our lands, and if we had any more land to give we would be very glad to give it. We have nothing more. We are driven into a very little land, and we want you now, as our dear friends, to help us with the government of the United States.

The Great Father made us poor and ignorant—made you rich and wise and more skillful in these things that we know nothing about. The Great Father, the Good Father in heaven, made you all to eat tame food—made us to eat

wild food—gives us the wild food. You ask anybody who has gone through our country to California; ask those who have settled there and in Utah, and you will find that we have treated them always well. You have children; we have children. You want to raise your children and make them happy and prosperous; we want to raise [ours] and make them happy and prosperous. We ask you to help us to do it.

At the mouth of the Horse Creek, in 1852, the Great Father made a treaty with us by which we agreed to let all that country open for fifty-five years for the transit of those who were going through. We kept this treaty; we never treated any man wrong; we never committed any murder or depredation until afterward the troops were sent into that country, and the troops killed our people and ill-treated them, and thus war and trouble arose; but before the troops were sent there we were quiet and peaceable, and there was no disturbance. Since that time there have been various goods sent from time to time to us, the only ones that ever reached us, and then after they reached us (very soon after) the government took them away. You, as good men, ought to help us to these goods.

Colonel Fitzpatrick of the government said we must all go to farm, and some of the people went to Fort Laramie and were badly treated. I only want to do that which is peaceful, and the Great Fathers know it, and also the Great Father who made us both. I came to Washington to see the Great Father in order to have peace and in order to have peace continue. That is all we want, and that is the reason why we are here now.

In 1868 men came out and brought papers. We are ignorant and do not read papers and they did not tell us right what was in these papers. We wanted them to take away their forts, leave our country, would not make war, and give our traders something. They said we had bound ourselves to trade on the Missouri, and we said, no, we did not want that. The interpreters deceived us. When I went to Washington I saw the Great Father. The Great Father showed me what the treaties were; he showed me all these points and showed me that the interpreters had deceived me and did not let me know what the right side of the treaty was. All I want is right and justice....I represent the Sioux Nation; they will be governed by what I say and what I represent....

Look at me. I am poor and naked, but I am the chief of the Nation. We do not want riches, we do not ask for riches, but we want our children properly trained and brought up. We look to you for your sympathy. Our riches will…do us no good; we cannot take away into the other world anything we have—we want to have love and peace.…We would like to know why commissioners are sent out there to do nothing but rob [us] and get the riches of this world away from us?

I was brought up among the traders and those who came out there in those early times. I had a good time for they treated us nicely and well. They taught me how to wear clothes and use tobacco, and to use firearms and ammunition, and all went on very well until the Great Father sent out another kind of men—men who drank whisky. He sent out whiskymen, men who drank and quarreled, men who were so bad that he could not keep them at home, and so he sent them out there.

I have sent a great many words to the Great Father, but I don't know that they ever reach the Great Father. They were drowned on the way, therefore I was a little offended with it. The words I told the Great Father lately would never come to him, so I thought I would come and tell you myself.

And I am going to leave you today, and I am going back to my home. I want to tell the people that we cannot trust his agents and superintendents. I don't want strange people that we know nothing about. I am very glad that you belong to us. I am very glad that we have come here and found you and that we can understand one another. I don't want any more such men sent out there, who are so poor that when they come out there their first thoughts are how they can fill their own pockets.

We want preserves in our reserves. We want honest men, and we want you to help to keep us in the lands that belong to us so that we may not be a prey to those who are viciously disposed. I am going back home. I am very glad that you have listened to me, and I wish you good-bye and give you an affectionate farewell.

* * * * * *

1.   *What are the specific grievances Red Cloud has with the government in Washington?*

2.   *How does Red Cloud suggest common interests between his people and the Americans? What policies does he recommend for the future?*

18–6   Helen Hunt Jackson, A Century of Dishonor, 1881

Born and raised in Massachusetts, Helen Hunt Jackson wrote articles and poems for popular magazines after the Civil War. In 1875, she relocated to Colorado Springs with her husband. She became interested in the plight of Indian peoples and conducted extensive research into the history of their mistreatment by the federal government. In 1881 she published A Century of Dishonor *and sent a copy to every member of Congress. The book inspired a reform movement aimed at helping Indians become full members of American society, ultimately leading to passage of the Dawes Act in 1887.*

SOURCE: Helen Hunt Jackson, *A Century of Dishonor* (Boston: Roberts Brothers, 1881).

There is not among these three hundred bands of Indians [in the United States] one which has not suffered cruelly at the hands either of the Government or of white settlers. The poorer, the more insignificant, the more helpless the band, the more certain the cruelty and outrage to which they have been subjected. This is especially true of the bands on the Pacific slopes. These Indians found themselves of a sudden surrounded by and caught up in the great influx of gold-seeking settlers, as helpless creatures on a shore are caught up in a tidal wave. There was not time for the Government to make treaties; not even time for communities to make laws. The tale of the wrongs, the oppressions, the murders of the Pacific-slope Indians in the last thirty years would be a volume by itself, and is too monstrous to be believed.

It makes little difference, however, where one opens the record of the history of the Indians; every page and every year has its dark stain. The story of one tribe is the story of all, varied only by differences of time and place; but neither time nor place makes any difference in the main facts. Colorado is as greedy and unjust in 1880 as was Georgia in 1830, and Ohio in 1795; and the United States Government breaks promises now as deftly as then, and with added ingenuity from long practice.

One of its strongest supports in so doing is the widespread sentiment among the people of dislike to the Indian, of impatience with his presence as a "barrier to civilization," and distrust of it as a possible danger. The old tales of the frontier life, with its horrors of Indian warfare, have gradually, by two or three generations' telling, produced in the average mind something like an hereditary instinct of unquestioning and unreasoning aversion which it is almost impossible to dislodge or soften.

There are hundreds of pages of unimpeachable testimony on the side of the Indian; but it goes for nothing, is set down as sentimentalism or partisanship, tossed aside and forgotten.

President after president has appointed commission after commission to inquire into and report upon Indian affairs, and to make suggestions as to the best methods of managing them. The reports are filled with eloquent statements of wrongs done to the Indians, of perfidies on the part of the Government; they counsel, as earnestly as words can, a trial of the simple and unperplexing expedients of telling truth, keeping promises, making fair bargains, dealing justly in all ways and all things. These reports are bound up with the Government's Annual Reports, and that is the end of them. It would probably be no exaggeration to say that not one American citizen out of ten thousand ever sees them or knows that they exist, and yet any one of them, circulated throughout the country, read by the right-thinking, right-feeling men and women of this land, would be of itself a "campaign document" that would initiate a revolution which would not subside until the Indians' wrongs were, so far as is now left possible, righted.

In 1869 President Grant appointed a commission of nine men, representing the influence and philanthropy of six leading States, to visit the different Indian reservations, and to "examine all matters appertaining to Indian affairs."

In the report of this commission are such paragraphs as the following: "To assert that 'the Indian will not work' is as true as it would be to say that the white man will not work.

"Why should the Indian be expected to plant corn, fence lands, build houses, or do anything but get food from day to day, when experience has taught him that the product of his labor will be seized by the white man tomorrow? The most industrious white man would become a drone under similar circumstances. Nevertheless, many of the Indians" (the commissioners might more forcibly have said 130,000 of the Indians) "are already at work, and furnish ample refutation of the assertion that 'the Indian will not work.' There is no escape from the inexorable logic of facts.

"The history of the Government connections with the Indians is a shameful record of broken treaties and unfulfilled promises. The history of the border, white man's connection with the Indians is a sickening record of murder, outrage, robbery, and wrongs committed by the former, as the rule, and occasional savage outbreaks and unspeakably barbarous deeds of retaliation by the latter, as the exception.

"Taught by the Government that they had rights entitled to respect, when those rights have been assailed by the rapacity of the white man, the arm which should have been raised to protect them has ever been ready to sustain the aggressor...."

To assume that it would be easy, or by any one sudden stroke of legislative policy possible, to undo the mischief and hurt of the long past, set the Indian policy of the country right for the future, and make the Indians at once safe and happy, is the blunder of a hasty and uninformed judgment. The notion which seems to be growing more prevalent, that simply to make all Indians at once citizens of the United States would be a sovereign and instantaneous panacea for all their ills and all the Government's perplexities, is a very inconsiderate one. To administer complete citizenship of a sudden, all round, to all Indians, barbarous and civilized alike, would be as grotesque a blunder as to dose them all round with any one medicine, irrespective of the symptoms and needs of their diseases. It would kill more than it would cure. Nevertheless, it is true, as was well stated by one of the superintendents of Indian Affairs in 1857, that, "so long as they are not citizens of the United States, their rights of property must remain insecure against invasion. The doors of the federal tribunals being barred against them while wards and dependents, they can only partially exercise the rights of free government, or give to those who make, execute, and construe the few laws they are allowed to enact, dignity sufficient to make them respectable. While they continue individually to gather the crumbs that fall from the table of the United States, idleness, improvidence, and indebtedness will be the rule, and industry, thrift, and freedom from debt the exception. The utter absence of individual title to particular lands deprives every one among them of the chief incentive to labor and exertion—the very mainspring on which the prosperity of a people depends."

All judicious plans and measures for their safety and salvation must embody provisions for their becoming citizens as fast as they are fit, and must protect them till then in every right and particular in which our laws protect other "persons" who are not citizens.

There is a disposition in a certain class of minds to be impatient with any protestation against wrong which is unaccompanied or unprepared with a quick and exact scheme of remedy. This is illogical. When pioneers in a new country find a tract of poisonous and swampy wilderness to be reclaimed, they do not withhold their hands from fire and axe till they see clearly which way roads should run, where good water will spring, and what crops will best grow on the redeemed land. They first clear the swamp. So with this poisonous and baffling part of the domain of our national affairs—let us first "clear the swamp."

However great perplexity and difficulty there may be in the details of any and every plan possible for doing at this late day anything like justice to the Indian. however hard it may be for good statesmen and good men to agree upon the things that ought to be done, there certainly is, or ought to be, no perplexity whatever, no difficulty whatever, in agreeing upon certain things that ought not to be done, and which must cease to be done before the first steps can be taken toward righting the wrongs, curing the ills, and wiping out the disgrace to us of the present condition of our Indians.

Cheating, robbing, breaking promises—these three are clearly things which must cease to be done. One more thing, also, and that is the refusal of the protection of the law to the Indian's rights of property, "of life, liberty, and the pursuit of happiness."

When these four things have ceased to be done, time, statesmanship, philanthropy, and Christianity can slowly and surely do the rest. Till these four things have ceased to be done, statesmanship and philanthropy alike must work in vain, and even Christianity can reap but small harvest.

* * * * * *

1.   What evidence does Jackson use to make her case?

Why has that evidence not succeeded in convincing the general public?

2.   Does Jackson believe that Indian peoples should be granted U.S. citizenship? What other rights does she see as crucial to improving their lot?

3.   What specific measures, if any, does she recommend for national Indian policy?

18–7   The Dawes General Allotment (Severalty) Act, 1887

The Dawes Act was passed in response to reformers who argued that reservation life and nomadism made it impossible for Indian people to be fully assimilated into American society. In exchange for renouncing their tribal holdings, Indians could become American citizens and gain individual land ownership after the expiration of a twenty-five-year federal trust period. Any remaining lands could be declared surplus and opened for sale to non-Indians. Between 1887 and 1906, the total land in Indian hands fell from 138 million acres to 78 million acres. Although the Dawes Act severely weakened Indian culture, it failed to promote acceptance of Indians by the larger society.

SOURCE: *U.S. Statutes at Large*, Vol. XXIV.

An act to provide for the allotment of lands in severalty to Indians on the various reservations, and to extend the protection of the laws of the United States and the Territories over the Indians, and for other purposes.

Be it enacted, That in all cases where any tribe or band of Indians has been, or shall hereafter be, located upon any reservation created for their use, either by treaty stipulation or by virtue of an act of Congress or executive order setting apart the same for their use, the President of the United States be, and he hereby is, authorized, whenever in his opinion any reservation or any part thereof of such Indians is advantageous for agriculture and grazing purposes to cause said reservation, or any part thereof, to be surveyed, or resurveyed if necessary, and to allot the lands in said reservation in severalty to any Indian located thereon in quantities as follows:

To each head of a family, one-quarter of a section;

To each single person over eighteen years of age, one eighth of a section;

To each orphan child under eighteen years of age, one-eight of a section; and,

To each other single person under eighteen years now living, or who may be born prior to the date of the order of the President directing an allotment of the lands embraced in any reservation, one-sixteenth of a section:…

SEC. 5. That upon the approval of the allotments provided for in this act by the Secretary of the Interior, he shall…declare that the United States does and will hold the land thus allotted, for the period of twenty-five years, in trust for the sole use and benefit of the Indian to whom such allotment shall have been made…and that at the expiration of said period the United States will convey the same by patent to said Indian, or his heirs as aforesaid, in fee, discharged of such trust and free of all charge or incumbrance whatsoever:…

SEC. 6. That upon the completion of said allotments and the parenting of the lands to said allottees, each and every member of the respective bands or tribes of Indians to whom allotments have been made shall have the benefit of and be subject to the laws, both civil and criminal, of the State or Territory in which they may reside;…And every Indian born within the territorial limits of the United States to whom allotments shall have been made under the provisions of this act, under any law or treaty, and every Indian born within the territorial limits of the United States who has voluntarily taken up, within said limits, his residence separate and apart from any tribe of Indians therein, and adopted the habits of civilized life, is hereby declared to be a citizen of the United States, and is entitled to all rights, privileges, and immunities of such citizen whether said Indian has been or not, by birth or otherwise, a member of any tribe of Indians within the territorial limits of the United States without in any manner impairing or otherwise affecting the right of any such Indian to tribal or other property.…

* * * * * *

1.   What specific provisions does the act make for Indian citizenship?

2.   How do the land provisions of the Dawes Act compare with those in the Homestead Act?

18–8   *D. W. C. Duncan, How Allotment Impoverishes the Indian, 1906*

D. W. C. Duncan, a Cherokee leader, testified in 1906 before a Senate committee investigating conditions in the Indian Territory. That year, Congress passed the Burke Act, which waived the twenty-five-year trustee period set forth in the Dawes Act for all Indian peoples judged competent to manage their own affairs.

SOURCE: Senate Report *5013,* 59th Congress (1906), 2nd Session, Part I.

Senators, just let me present to you a picture; I know this is a little digression, but let me present it. Suppose the Federal Government should send a survey company into the midst of some of your central counties of Kansas or Colorado or Connecticut and run off the surface of the earth into sections and quarter sections and quarter quarter sections and set apart to each one of the inhabitants of that county 60 acres, rescinding and annulling all title to every inch of the earth's surface which was not included in that 60 acres, would the State of Connecticut submit to it? Would Colorado submit to it? Would Kansas brook such an outrage? No! It would be ruin, immeasurable ruin—devastation. There is not an American citizen in any one of those States would submit to it, if it cost him every drop of his heart's blood. That, my Senators, permit me—I am honest, candid, and fraternal in my feelings—but let me ask a question: Who is that hastened on this terrible destruction upon these Cherokee people? Pardon me, it was the Federal Government. It is a fact; and, old as I am, I am not capable of indulging in euphuisms.

Before this allotment scheme was put in effect in the Cherokee Nation we were a prosperous people. We had farms. Every Indian in this nation that needed one and felt that he needed one had it. Orchards and gardens—everything that promoted the comforts of private life was ours, even as you—probably not so extensively—so far as we went, even as you in the States. The result has been—which I now want to illustrate, as I set out, by my own personal experience.

Under our old Cherokee régime I spent the early days of my life on the farm up here of 300 acres, and arranged to be comfortable in my old age; but the allotment scheme came along and struck me during the crop season, while my corn was ripening in full ear. I was looking forward to the crop of corn hopefully for some comforts to be derived from it during the months of the winter. When I was assigned to that 60 acres, and I could take no more under the inexorable law of allotment enforced

upon us Cherokees, I had to relinquish every inch of my premises outside of that little 60 acres. What is the result? There is a great scramble of persons to find land—the office was located here in our town—to file upon. Some of the friends in here, especially a white intermarried citizen, goes up and files upon a part of my farm—on a part of my growing crop, upon the crop upon which I had spent my labor and my money, and upon which I had based my hopes. I remonstrated with him. I said to him, "Sir, you don't want to treat me that way. We are neighbors and friends. You can't afford to take my property that way. Of course the Dawes Commission and the Curtis law will give you the land, although I have subdued it, and I have fenced it, and cultivated it. But for God's sake, my friend, don't take my crop." "Well," says he, "I had to surrender my crop to a fellow down here. He allotted on me, and I don't know why I should be any more lenient on you than others are on me. If you don't let that corn alone, I will go to the court and get an order." That was new to me, but when I came to examine the Curtis law, and investigated the orders and rules established by the Dawes Commission, I just folded my hands and said, "I give it up." Away went my crop, and if the same rule had been established in your counties in your State you would have lost your dwelling house; you would have lost your improvements. Now, that is what has been done to these Cherokees....

What a condition! I have 60 acres of land left me; the balance is all gone. I am an old man, not able to follow the plow as I used to when a boy. What am I going to do with it? For the last few years, since I have had my allotment, I have gone out there on that farm day after day. I have used the ax, the hoe, the spade, the plow, hour for hour, until fatigue would throw me exhausted upon the ground. Next day I repeated the operation, and let me tell you, Senators, I have exerted all my ability, all industry, all my intelligence, if I have any, my will, my ambition, the love of my wife—all these agencies I have employed to make my living out of that 60 acres, and, God be my judge, I have not been able to do it. I am not able to do it. I can't do it. I have not been able to clear expenses. It will take every ear of the bounteous crop on that 60 acres—for this year is a pretty good crop year—it will take every bushel of it to satisfy the debts that I have incurred to eke out a living during the meager years just passed. And I am here to-day, a poor man upon the verge of starvation—my muscular energy gone, hope gone. I have nothing to charge my calamity to but the unwise legislation of Congress in reference to my Cherokee people....

I am in that fix, Senators; you will not forget now that when I use the word "I" I mean the whole Cherokee people. I am in that fix. What am I to do? I have a piece of property that doesn't support me, and is not worth a cent to me, under the same inexorable, cruel provisions of the Curtis law that swept away our treaties, our system of nationality, our every existence, and wrested out of our possession our vast territory. The same provisions of that Curtis law that ought to have been satisfied with these achievements didn't stop there. The law goes on, and that 60 acres of land, it says, shall not be worth one cent to me; although the Curtis law has given me 60 acres as the only inheritance I have in God's world, even that shall not be worth anything. Let me explain.

If you had a horse that you couldn't use, and some competent power ordained that that horse should have no value in any market on the face of the earth, and at the same time you should be compelled to keep that horse as long as he should live, or at least twenty-five years, at your expense; now, in the name of common sense, what would you do with that horse? He is not worth anything; his services are not worth anything to me; I can't ride him; I can't use him. There is no man in the world that will give me a cent for him; the law won't allow me to sell him. I would get rid of that horse somehow sure.

The point I am making here is applicable to every species of property, whether real or personal. Prevent the property from being purchasable in open market and you destroy it. Upon the same principle, my allotment up here is absolutely destroyed. What am I going to do with it? What can any Indian do with his allotment under similar circumstances?

Let me allude to myself again. It is not egotism. I will tell you what I am going to do with my allotment. I sat down one day and wrote out my application for the removal of my restrictions. I went to work and pushed it through all the Federal machinery up to the Secretary of the Interior and back again, and a few days ago I was notified my restrictions were raised. Now for the next step. What am I going to do with that worthless piece of property? I am going to hold it—how long I don't know—but I am going to wait until the white population becomes a little more multitudinous, when the price of real estate will rise. When I can get anything like an adequate value for my farm I am going to sell it. It is worthless to me.

The Government of the United States knows that these allotments of the Indians are not sufficient. Congress recognizes the fact forcibly, by implication, that these allotments are not sufficient. Why, one American citizen goes out on the western plain in North Dakota to make a home. What is the amount of land allotted to him? Isn't it 160 acres? Why, it is the general consensus all over the country that nothing less would be sufficient to support any family; and there are many years when you think, too, that 160 acres is not sufficient. Since this country has been split up, the Cherokee government abolished, and the allotments attained, immigration has come in from the surrounding States, consisting of persons of different kinds. I have tested them, and know what I am talking about, personally. Persons in pursuit of a sufficient quantity of land upon which to rear their families and take care of themselves. I have interrogated them time and again. I have said to them. "Look here, my friend, where are you going?" "To Indian Territory." "What for?" "To get a piece of land." "Did you have any land in Missouri or Kansas?" "Yes, sir; I had some up there, but it was too small and wasn't sufficient." "How much was it?" "Eighty or one hundred acres," as the case may be; "I have leased out my land up there to parties, and thought I would come down here and get a larger piece of ground." Well, now, that is the state of the case. I think, gentlemen, when you investigate the case fully you will find that these people have been put off with a piece of land that is absolutely inadequate for their needs.

* * * * * *

1.   *What specific analogies with white farmers and American politics does Duncan make to demonstrate his plight?*

2.   *How does he also use differences between Indian and white culture to make his case?*

18–9 *Charles and Nellie Wooster, Letters from the Frontier, 1872*

Charles and Nellie Wooster left their home in Michigan to make a new life on the western prairie. Charles left first, eventually settling in Nebraska, where his wife joined him nine months later. Their correspondence depicts the everyday life and problems faced by western settlers in the post–Civil War era. Nellie Wooster died five years after

joining her husband; Charles, who eventually became a newspaper editor and local politician in Nebraska, lived until 1923.

SOURCE: William F. Schmidt, ed., "The Letters of Charles and Helen Wooster: The Problems of Settlement," *Nebraska History* 46 (1965), 121–137. Reprinted by permission of the Nebraska State Historical Society.

Silver Creek, Nebraska
[March] 14 6 p.m.

This is a station city or village consisting of the depot, a grocery hotel, and one dwelling house....

It [the country] is as much different from anything that you ever saw in Michigan as can possibly be imagined. What I shall do here I can not possibly say. I do not intend to be in a hurry. I shall probably remain here...some time and then perhaps [go] to Grand Island...You must make up your mind not to get homesick when you come, find what you may. If we find any peace or happiness on this earth, I suppose at least 99 per cent of it will be within our own home....

Silver Glen, Merrick Co., Nebr.
March 27, 1872

My Little Wife

...Although there are Indians to be seen here, almost every day, they are very peaceable and are much more afraid of the whites than the whites are of them. In fact the white people do not fear them at all and I have yet to learn of a woman or child who stands in the slightest dread of them....

When they wish to enter a house they will come and look in at the windows until someone notices them and then if the door is opened they will step right in without further invitation. They most always ask for something to eat, but if one doesn't wish to be troubled with them it is only necessary to refuse and send them on their way.

There is no danger here of raids from wild Indians for the country is settled many miles beyond and the wild Indians are far away...So don't give yourself any concern about Indians. You will stand in no more danger of them than in Michigan and when you have been here a little while you will not be a bit afraid of them....

Charley

Silver Glen, Merrick Co., Nebr.
March 31, 1872

Little Wife

...This suspense is rather trying, but still I think things will come out all right in the end. I don't refer to my claim in this for there I apprehend no trouble, still there is always a *chance* for trouble if one does not go upon his land and stay there. I am well pleased with my land and believe there is no better in the country. If I have average luck I know that I shall make a nicer home of it than any other one in the country. Most people you know don't have much of an idea of beautifying their homes. They only look out for the "almighty dollar." I believe that while I am making the dollars I can just as well make a great many other things to add to our enjoyment that are usually lost sight of and that too without any additional

expense, in fact I believe that in the end there would be the most money in this very course....

Bye bye
Charlie

Silver Glen, Neb.
July 21, 1872

My dear little Wife,

This morning I arose quite early, put my house in order, breakfasted upon a couple of cold pancakes....

I hope you will follow your own advice to me and not allow yourself to feel discouraged....We cannot tell what may be in store for us. Let us do the best we can and not attempt to war against fate. I have some of the best land there is in Nebraska and it is admitted to [by] all who know it. *I will keep it,* and sooner or later we shall surely embrace each other in our "little home.".…

I do not want to put you in a sod house. It would be too bad for such a nice little wife.

I do not fear the Indians, and if it were not for you I would not care how quick they came.

Bye bye love
Charley

Silver Glen, Neb.
July 28, 1872

My dear little Wife

I do not know what to say to you. You inform me that you are coming this fall. I certainly hope you will do so for it is very unpleasant for me to live alone and do my own house work, no less so perhaps than for you to be without any fixed place in Michigan. But these are only a part of the reasons why we wish to be together. It seems to me however that it would not be very wise for us to undertake to go to keeping house when we have no money even to pay your fare here saying nothing about freight, the cost of enough furniture to enable us to live at all which would be 50$ at least, the incidental expense of living and things which it would be necessary to have to supply our table which the farm will not afford. Fuel would necessarily cost something. How could we live without a cow? A good one would cost 50$—a second rate one might be had for 40$. In the spring if I did not have a team and some farming utensils a little money would be almost a necessity. How should we get the seeds that I had intended to, for hedge plants, fruits and forest trees? True my corn crop ought to be worth 200$, but whether I could realize anything on it would be a very doubtful question...You can estimate our resources and the necessary expenses of settling up here as well as I can.

If I said I could live cheap here alone, it has been proved that I was correct for since the 26 day of April, living, fuel, cooking utensils and all probably has not cost me 10$. I have had no butter for two months and I do not use more than a pound of pork in a week. Of course it would be expected that I should supply you in Michigan as well as myself here. Both together would be more than keeping house here…As I said, I have some good land and I intend to keep it. The more I see of some other places the more I think of my own. I can prove up on it next spring and then I could raise money on it if I wish to, though I do not wish to if possible to avoid it. As heretofore I shall *try* to get along as well as possible but, if in so doing my feet should slip from under me and I should slide into hell, I should endeavor to endure the fry with all fortitude.…

Bye bye
Charley

Adams, Mich.
Sept. 29, 1872

My dear Charley,

I rec'd yours of the 22 and sent a short note to you in reply, so as to have it be sure and reach you before it was too late to have the bedroom come in front instead of the buttery. And I wouldn't have you fail to do this for a large sum of money; the flowers etc., will be in the front yard no doubt, and I want my bedroom to be in the pleasantest place possible, and for a thousand reasons, figuratively speaking. I want the bedroom in front, and you will no doubt have it built there; and then another thing *please* don't fail to have a back-door and if it is going to cost so much that you will not have money for a door I will stay in Mich. enough longer to earn money for a door; oh! I do want a back door so much!…You will never be sorry to have a back door and to have the bedroom in front. I shouldn't want to let hired men go into any buttery to wash in the sink (you may though, bless you!) and I don't want the washdish to be in the frontyard, and I expect to have a little standard or something of the kind fixed on purpose for the washdish to stand on while one is washing and then it can be hung on the side of it.…

[Nellie]

Silver Glen, Nebr.
October 2, 1872

My dear Nellie

I am very sorry that I cannot follow your suggestions in regard to the house, but I cannot possibly. Don't "fly off the handle" now but reserve judgement until you come. Things will look very different from what you expect, and I am fully persuaded that you will like my arrangement better than your own. We will have things nicer than anyone else. Now you see. Your flowers will be in front of your bedroom and it will not look out on back yards. If you were on the ground today you could not for your life tell which was the *front*. There are two sides either of which might be considered as such. I cannot possibly give you anything like a true idea of these things.

I intend to plaster if cold weather does not overtake me and it shall not if hard work will prevent it. I shall leave the pantry till you come, and then you can have it finished to suit yourself.

Bye bye
Charley

Silver Glen, Neb.
Oct. 23, '72

Little wife:

I will write a few words today noon so that Mr. Alpaugh can mail the letter tonight. He is at work down at the house now. We shall about get the frame up today. Weather continues fine and I am in hopes he will be able to stay till the house is enclosed. I am getting very much "demoralized" and shall probably go to the devil if you don't come pretty soon. My clothes are all in pieces and many of them are so dirty that I should be ashamed to take them away to be washed.

It will probably not be best for you to start until the things come, but be ready so that you can start any day. I think I will write a letter telling you to come and leave it with the Agent to be mailed immediately on the arrival of the things. If you get such a letter you will *know what it means.*

It may be of interest to you to know that the people here have seen fit to elect me Justice of Peace. I qualified last night.

Bye bye Little Baby
Charley

Silver Glen, Neb.
Nov. 4, 1872

Little Wife

We did not do a thing on the house last week but commenced again today. I hope to get it enclosed this week and then we *can* live in it. I would do most anything to have you here.

I could not have a stove in my sod house, because it is covered with hay. I can make my self tolerably comfortable nights and daytimes. I hope to work hard enough to keep warm.…

Bye bye
Charley

Hillsdale, Mich.
Dec. 9, 1872

My dear Boy

I'm now soon coming to you and am not going to be fooled out of it much longer, for although I have had a pretty hard time to find money, I have succeeded *at last* just as I gave up all hope and had gone to bed with a nervous sick headache. You must be pleased and not frown at me for taking the money in the way I have for it is all the way I can get any at present.

[My father] signed a note with me to get the money from Lawt Thompson. I should not have known that Lawt had any but Cousin Mart unbeknown to me asked him if he had some and would let you have it with pa for a signer and he said he would. So this morning pa came up to Lawts with me, and Lawt drew the note and I signed Chas. Wooster to it and pa signed H. P. Hitchcock…He had only 70$ to let so I took that for six months at 10 per ct. and now you will be pleased than other wise won't you? and don't for Gods sake send it back.…

I am going to start a week from tomorrow (Tuesday) so prepare for my coming and don't you write and say that the floor is not quite laid yet, for if it isn't I can soon hammer it down.…

Write to me as soon as you get this for I want one more letter from you before I go so I can carry it in the cars for company.…

Bye bye, for now I'm surely coming even if you write me the house is burned to ashes. Bye.

Nellie

Silver Glen, Nebraska
Dec. 13, 1872

My Little Wife,

Yours of the 9th was rec'd today.

I am very glad that you are coming at last, and am not at all displeased with your manner of raising the money. Your father was very kind.…

It will probably take Mr. Alpaugh most of next week to finish the house; I shall probably go to Columbus Monday and get things as to make ready for you. Things will not be in very good condition to receive you, but we will try and make ourselves comfortable.

On the road, whatever information you may need you can get of the conductors. Ask them any questions. At Chicago go get your ticket for Omaha. You perhaps might get one to Columbus, but do not do so, as your baggage would stop there and occasion some trouble. At Omaha there is an old grayheaded man who acts as policeman about the station. It would be best for you to let him have your check and he would claim your baggage for you. There is usually a great crowd of men and you could not well attend to it. Have him show you the car and take a seat as soon as convenient as they are often crowded. If you let him take your check, take the number of it with your pencil before doing so. It is his business to attend to the wants of passengers. I spoke to him about you and he said that if you would speak to him he would see that every thing was all right. I will of course meet you at Silver Creek.

…Charley's little love is coming to stay with him and then all her troubles will be at an end.

Charley

* * * * * *

1.   *What difficulties seem most pressing for the Woosters? How were they able to overcome them?*

2.   *In what ways do you think frontier life was different from life in settled areas?*

18–10   *John Wesley Powell, Report on the Arid Lands of the West, 1879*

In 1869, the geologist and explorer John W. Powell received a federal grant to lead a scientific expedition along 900 miles of the Green and Colorado Rivers. He was the first white man to make this trek. Throughout the 1870s, Powell continued his western explorations, and in 1880 he became director of the U.S. Geological Survey. His 1879 report noted that the nation's old land policies, established for the region east of the 100th meridian, would prove inadequate for the arid lands of the West. There, access to water would be the determining factor in settlement and development.

SOURCE: Commager, *Documents of American History,* pp. 102–104; J. W. Powell, *Report on the Lands of the Arid Region of the United States,* 1879, pp. 37ff.

…If the whole of the Arid Region was yet unsettled, it might be wise for the Government to undertake the parceling of the lands and employ skilled engineers to do the work, whose duties could be performed in advance of settlement.…Many of the lands surveyed along the minor streams have been entered, and the titles to these lands are in the hands of actual settlers. Many pasturage farms, or ranches, as they are called locally, have been established throughout the country. These remarks are true of every state and territory in the Arid Region. In the main these ranches or pasturage farms are on Government land, and the settlers are squatters, and some are not expecting to make permanent homes.…It is now too late for the Government to parcel the pasturage lands in advance of the wants of settlers in the most available way, so as to closely group residences and give water privileges to the several farms. Many of the farmers are actually on the ground, and are clamoring for some means by which they can obtain titles to pasturage farms of an extent adequate to their wants, and the tens of thousands of individual interests would make the problem a difficult one for the officers of the Government to solve. A system less arbitrary than that of the rectangular surveys now in vogue, and requiting unbiased judgement, overlooking the interests of single individuals and considering only the interests of the greatest number, would meet with local opposition....

Under these circumstances it is believed that it is best to permit the people to divide their lands for themselves—not in a way by which each man may take what he pleases for himself, but by providing methods by which these settlers may organize and mutually protect each other from the rapacity of individuals. The lands, as lands, are of but slight value, as they cannot be used for ordinary agricultural purposes, i.e., the cultivation of crops; but their value consists in the scant grasses which they spontaneously produce, and these values can be made available only by the use of the waters necessary for the subsistence of stock, and that necessary for the small amount of irrigable land which should be attached to the several pasturage farms. Thus, practically, all values inhere in the water, and an equitable division of the waters can be made only by a wise system of parcelling the lands; and the people in organized bodies can well be trusted with this right, while individuals could not thus be trusted. These considerations have led to the plan suggested in the bill submitted for the organization of pasturage districts....

The lands along the streams are not valuable for agricultural purposes in continuous bodies or squares, but only in irrigable tracts governed by the levels of the meandering canals which carry the water for irrigation, and it would be greatly to the advantage of every such district if the lands could be divided into parcels, governed solely by the conditions under which the water could be distributed over them; and such parcelling cannot be done prior to the occupancy of the lands, but can in only be made *pari passu* with the adoption of a system of canals; and the people settling on these lands should be allowed the privilege of dividing the lands into such tracts as may be most available for such purposes, and they should not be hampered with the present arbitrary system of dividing tracts into rectangular tracts....

...The general subject of water rights is one of great importance. In many places in the Arid Region irrigation companies are organized who obtain vested rights in the waters they control, and consequently the rights to such waters do not inhere in any particular tracts of land.

When the area to which it is possible to take the water of any given stream is much greater than the stream is competent to serve, if the land titles and water rights are severed, the owner of any tract of land is at the mercy of the owner of the water right. In general the lands greatly exceed the capacities of the streams. Thus the lands have no value without water. If the water rights fall into the hands of irrigating companies and the lands into the hands of individual farmers, the farmers then will be dependent upon the stock companies, and eventually the monopoly of water rights will be an intolerable burden to the people.

The magnitude of the interests involved must not be overlooked. All the present and future agriculture of more than four-tenths of the area of the United States is dependent upon irrigation, and practically all values for agricultural industries inhere, not in the lands, but in the water. Monopoly of land need not be feared. The question for legislators to solve is to devise some practical means by which water rights may be distributed among individual farmers and water monopolies prevented....

The pioneer is fully engaged in the present with its hopes of immediate remuneration for labor. The present development of the country fully occupies him. For this reason every effort put forth to increase the area of the agricultural land by irrigation is welcomed. Every man who turns his attention to this department of industry is considered a public benefactor. But if in the eagerness for present development a land and water system shall grow up in which the practical control of agriculture shall fall into the hands of water companies, evils will result therefrom that generations may not be able to correct, and the very men who are now lauded as benefactors to the country will, in the ungovernable reaction which is sure to come, be denounced as oppressors of the people.

The right to use water should inhere in the land to be irrigated, and water rights should go with land titles.

Those unacquainted with the industrial institutions of the far west, involving the use of lands and waters, may without careful thought suppose that the long recognized principles of the common law are sufficient to prevent the severance of land and water rights; but other practices are obtaining which have, or eventually will have, all the force of common law because the necessities of the country require the change, and these practices are obtaining the color of right from state and territorial legislation, and to some extent by national legislation. In all that country the natural channels of the streams cannot be made to govern water rights without great injury to its agricultural and mining industries. For the great purposes of irrigation and hydraulic mining the water has no value in its natural channel. In general the water cannot be used for irrigation on the lands immediately contiguous to the streams—i.e., the flood plains or bottom valleys....The waters must be taken to a greater or less extent on the bench lands to be used in irrigation. All the waters of all the arid lands will eventually be taken from their natural channels, and they can be utilized only to the extent to which they are thus removed, and water rights must of necessity be severed from the natural channels. There is another important factor to be considered. The water when used in irrigation is absorbed by the soil and re-evaporated to the heavens. It cannot be taken from its natural channel, used, and returned. Again, the water cannot in general be properly utilized in irrigation by requiring it to be taken from its natural channel within the limits ordinarily included in a single ownership. In order to conduct the water on the higher bench lands where it is to be used in irrigation, it is necessary to go up the stream until a level is reached from which the waters will flow to the lands to be redeemed. The exceptions to this are so small that the statement scarcely needs qualification. Thus, to use the water it must be diverted from its natural course often miles or scores of miles from where it is to be used.

The ancient principles of common law applying to the use of natural streams, so wise and equitable in a humid region, would, if applied to the Arid Region, practically prohibit the growth of its most important industries. Thus it is that a custom is springing up in the Arid Region which may or may not have color of authority in statutory or common law; on this I do not wish to express an opinion; but certain it is that water rights are practically being severed from the natural channels of the streams; and this must be done. In the change, it is to be feared that water rights will in many cases be separated from all land rights as the system is now forming. If this fear is not groundless, to the extent that such a separation is secured, water will become a property independent of the land, and this property will be gradually absorbed by a few. Monopolies of water will be secured, and the whole agriculture of the country will be tributary thereto—a condition of affairs which an American citizen having in view the interests of the largest number of the people cannot contemplate with favor.

Practically, in that country the right to water is acquired by priority of utilization, and this is as it should be from the necessities of the country. But two important qualifications are needed. The *user right* should attach to the *land* where used, not to the individual or company constructing the canals by which it is used; the priority of usage should secure the right. But this needs some slight modification. A farmer settling on a small tract, to be redeemed by irrigation, should be given a reasonable length of time in which to secure his water right by utilization, that he may secure it by his own labor, either directly by constructing the waterways himself, or indirectly by co-operating with his neighbours in constructing systems of waterways. Without this provision there is little inducement for poor men to commence farming operations, and men of ready capital only will engage in such enterprises....

If there be any doubt of the ultimate legality of the practices of the people in the arid country relating to water and land rights, all such doubts should be speedily quieted through the enactment of appropriate laws by the national legislature. Perhaps an amplification by the courts of what has been designated as the *natural right* to the use of water may be made to cover the practices now obtaining; but it hardly seems wise to imperil interests so great by intrusting them to the possibility of some future court made law.

* * * * * *

1.   *According to Powell, how does agricultural practice in the arid region fundamentally differ from that in the East?*

2.   *What political and legal problems does he foresee as a consequence? What remedies does he suggest?*

3.   *What does Powell's report imply about the long-range relationship between the federal government and agriculture in the arid region?*

chapter 19

The Incorporation of America, 1860–1900

19-1 Paul Bourget, *The Traffic in Meat, 1894*

A well-known French novelist and journalist, Paul Bourget visited the United States in 1894, traveling extensively all over the nation. He described American society, culture, business, and labor in Outre-Mer Impressions of America. *The following excerpt records his impressions of Chicago's "Packingtown."*

SOURCE: Paul Bourget, *Outre-Mer Impressions of America* (N.Y.: Charles Scribner's Sons, 1895), excerpted in Bessie Louise Pierce, ed., *As Others See Chicago: Impressions of Visitors, 1673–1933* (1938), 386–391.

One of the enormous branches of traffic of this city is in meat. The Chicago folk are a little ashamed of it.... They are now tired of hearing their detractors call them the inhabitants of Porkopolis....

...These abattoirs furnish material most precious to the foreigner who desires to understand the spirit in which the Americans undertake their great enterprises. A slaughter-house capable of shipping in twelve months, to the four parts of this immense continent, three million, five hundred thousand dressed cattle is worth the trouble of investigating. Everywhere else the technical details are very difficult to grasp. They are less so here, the directors of these colossal manufactories of roast beef and hams having discovered that the best possible advertisement is to admit the public to witness their processes of working. They have made a visit to their establishments, if not attractive,—physical repulsion is too strong for that,—at least convenient and thorough. On condition of having your nerves wrung once for all, these are among the places where you shall best see how American ingenuity solves the problems of a prodigiously complicated organization.

I therefore did like other unprejudiced tourists, and visited the "stock yards" and the most celebrated among the "packing-houses," as they are called,—cutting-up houses, rather,—which is here in operation; the one, indeed, the statistics of whose operations I have but now quoted. This walk through that house of blood will always remain to me one of the most singular memories of my journey....

To reach the "Union Stock Yards" the carriage crosses an immense section of the city, even more incoherent than those which border on the elegant Michigan Ave....It skirts large plots of ground, where market-gardeners are cultivating cabbages amongst heaps of refuse, and others which bear nothing but advertisements....

The advertising fields give place to more houses, more railways, under a sky black with clouds, or smoke,—one hardly knows which,—and on both sides of the road begin to appear fenced enclosures, where cattle are penned by the hundred. There are narrow lanes between the fence, with men on horseback riding up and down. These are the buyers, discussing prices with the "cowboys" of the West.

You have read stories of the "ranches." This adventurous prairie life has taken hold upon your imagination. Here you behold its heroes, in threadbare overcoats, slouch hats, and the inevitable collar and cuffs of the American. But for their boots, and their dexterity in guiding their horses by the knees you would take them for clerks. They are a proof, among many others, of the instinctive disdain of this realistic people for the picturesque in costume. That impression which I had in the park in New York, almost the first day, as of an immense store of ready-made clothes hurrying hither and thither, has never left me. And yet, nothing can be less "common," in the bad sense of the word, than Americans in general, and these Western cowboys in particular. Their bodies are too nervous, too lithe, under their cheap clothes; their countenances, especially, are too intent and too sharply outlined, too decided and too stern.

The carriage stops before a building which, in its massiveness and want of character, is like all other manufactories. My companions and I enter a court, a sort of alley, crowded with packing-boxes, carts and people. A miniature railway passes along it, carrying packing-boxes to a waiting train, entirely composed of refrigerator cars, such as I saw so many of as I came to Chicago. Laborers were unloading these packing-boxes; others were coming and going, evidently intent upon their respective duties. There was no sign of administrative order, as we conceive it, in this establishment, which was yet so well ordered. But already one of the engineers had led us up a staircase, and we enter an immense hall, reeking with heavy moisture saturated with a strong acrid odor, which seems to seize you by the throat. We are in the department where the hogs are cut up. There are hundreds of men hard at work, whom we have not time so much as to look at. Our guide warns us to stand aside, and before us glides a file of porkers, disemboweled and hung by their hind feet from a rod, along which they slip toward a vaulted opening, where innumerable other such files await them. The rosy flesh, still ruddy with the life that but now animated them, gleams under the electric light that illuminates those depths. We go on, avoiding these strange encounters as best we may, and reach at last, with feet smeared in a sort of bloody mud, a platform whence we can see the initial act of all this labor, which now seems so confused, but which we shall shortly find so simple and easy to understand....

If there was nothing but killing to be seen in this manufacture of food, it would hardly be worthwhile to go through so many bloody scenes for the sake of verifying, in one of its lower extremplifications, what the philosopher Huxley somewhere magnificently calls "the gladiatorial theory of existence," the severe law that murder is necessary to life. But this is only a first impression, to experience before passing to a second, that of the rapidity and ingenuity of the cutting-up and packing of this prodigious quantity of perishable meat. I don't know who it was who sportively said that a pig that went to the abattoir at Chicago came out fifteen minutes later in the form of ham, sausages, large and small, hair oil, and binding for a Bible. It is a witty exaggeration, yet hardly overdone, of the rapid and minute labor which we had just seen bestowed upon the beasts killed before our eyes; and the subdividing of this work, its precision, simplicity, quick succession, succeeding in making us forget the necessary but intolerable brutality of the scenes we had been witnessing.

An immense hall is furnished with a succession of counters placed without much order, where each member of the animal is cut apart and utilized without the loss of a bone or a tendon. Here, with quick, automatic blow, which never misses, a man cuts off first the hams, then the feet, as fast as he can throw them into caldrons, which boil and smoke them before your eyes. Farther along, a hatchet, moved by machinery, is at work making sausage-meat, which tubes of all sizes will pour forth in rolls ready for the skins, that are all washed and prepared....

Elsewhere the head and jowl are cleaned, trimmed, and dressed, to figure in their natural form in the show windows of some American or European market. Elsewhere, again, enormous receptacles are being filled with suet which boils and bubbles, and having been cunningly mixed with a certain proportion of cream will be transformed into margarine, refined in an automatic beating machine of which we admired the artful simplicity.

"A workingman invented that," said our guide. "For that matter," he added, "almost all the machines that are used here were either made or improved by the workmen."

These words shed light for us upon all this vast workshop. We understood what these men require of a machine that for them prolongs, multiplies, perfects the acts of men. Once again we felt how much they have become refined in their processes of work, how they excel in combining with their personal effort the complication of machinery, and also how the least among them has a power of initiative, of direct vision and adjustment.

Seated again in our carriage, and rolling away over the irregular wooden pavement made of round sections of trees embedded at pleasure in the mud, we reflected upon what we had just seen. We tried to discern its intellectual significance, if we may use this word in reference to such an enterprise. And why not? We are all agreed that the first characteristic of this enterprise is the amplitude, or rather the stupendousness, of its conception. For an establishment like this to have, in a few years, brought up the budget of its employees to five million five hundred thousand dollars, that is, to more than twenty-seven millions of francs, its founders must have clearly perceived the possibilities of an enormous extension of business, and have no less clearly perceived, defined, and determined its practical features.

A colossal effort of imagination on the one hand, and, on the other, at the service of the imagination, a clear and carefully estimated understanding of the encompassing reality,—these are the two features everywhere stamped upon the unparalleled establishment which we have just visited. One of us pointed out another fact,—that the principal practical feature is the railway, reminding us that the locomotive has always been an implement of general utility in American hands. By it they revolutionized military art and created a full-panoplied modern warfare, such as the Germans were later to practice at our expense....

Our guide, who listens to our philosophizing without seeming much to disapprove, tells us that this very year, in order to elude a coalition of speculators in grain, which he explains to us, the head of the house which we have just visited was forced to erect in nineteen days, for the housing of his own wheat, a building three hundred feet square by a hundred high!

"Yes, in nineteen days, working night and day," he said, smiling; "but we Americans like 'hard work.'"

With this almost untranslatable word,—to one who has not heard it uttered here,—our visit ends. It sums it up and completes it with a terseness worthy of this people of much action and few phrases!

* * * * * *

1. *How does Bourget situate the Union Stock Yards within the larger Chicago community? To what extent had Packingtown become a tourist attraction for visitors to the city by the 1890s?*

2. *What evidence, if any, of class differences and tensions can you find in Bourget's description?*

19-2   Andrew Carnegie, Wealth, 1889

Born in Scotland in 1835, Andrew Carnegie emigrated to America with his family at age twelve. He began working as a telegrapher for the Pennsylvania Railroad and moved rapidly up its corporate ladder. In the 1870s, Carnegie turned his business talents to the steel industry. He paid close attention to new technologies, invested heavily in capital improvements, and kept wages and salaries low. By keeping costs and prices down, he soon became the dominant figure in American steel and one of the world's richest men. Carnegie became one of the nation's leading philanthropists, arguing that the rich had a moral responsibility to plow back their wealth into the larger society.

SOURCE: Andrew Carnegie, "Wealth," *North American Review* (1889).

The problem of our age is the proper administration of wealth, that the ties of brotherhood may still bind together the rich and poor in harmonious relationship. The conditions of human life have not only been changed, but revolutionized, within the past few hundred years. In former days there was little difference between the dwelling, dress, food, and environment of the chief and those of his retainers. The Indians are today where civilized man then was. When visiting the Sioux, I was led to the wigwam of the chief. It was like the others in external appearance, and even within the difference was trifling between it and those of the poorest of his braves. The contrast between the palace of the millionaire and the cottage of the laborer with us to-day measures the change which has come with civilization. This change, however, is not to be deplored, but welcomed as highly beneficial. It is well, nay, essential, for the progress of the race that the houses of some should be homes for all that is highest and best in literature and the arts, and for all the refinements of civilization, rather than that none should be so. Much better this great irregularity than universal squalor. Without wealth there can be no Maecenas. The "good old times" were not good old times. Neither master nor servant was as well situated then as to-day. A relapse to old conditions would be disastrous to both—not the least so to him who serves—and would sweep away civilization with it. But whether the change be for good or ill, it is upon us, beyond our power to alter, and, therefore, to be accepted and made the best of. It is a waste of time to criticize the inevitable.

It is easy to see how the change has come. One illustration will serve for almost every phase of the cause.

In the manufacture of products we have the whole story. It applies to all combinations of human industry, as stimulated and enlarged by the inventions of this scientific age. Formerly, articles were manufactured at the domestic hearth, or in small shops which formed part of the household. The master and his apprentices worked side by side, the latter living with the master, and therefore subject to the same conditions. When these apprentices rose to be masters, there was little or no change in their mode of life, and they, in turn, educated succeeding apprentices in the same routine. There was, substantially, social equality, and even political equality, for those engaged in industrial pursuits had then little or no voice in the State.

The inevitable result of such a mode of manufacture was crude articles at high prices. To-day the world obtains commodities of excellent quality at prices which even the preceding generation would have deemed incredible. In the commercial world similar causes have produced similar results, and the race is benefited thereby. The poor enjoy what the rich could not before afford. What were the luxuries have become the necessaries of life. The laborer has now more comforts than the farmer had a few generations ago. The farmer has more luxuries than the landlord had, and is more richly clad and better housed. The landlord has books and pictures rarer and appointments more artistic than the king could then obtain.

The price we pay for this salutary change is, no doubt, great. We assemble thousands of operatives in the factory, and in the mine, of whom the employer can know little or nothing, and to whom he is little better than a myth. All intercourse between them is at an end. Rigid castes are formed, and, as usual, mutual ignorance breeds mutual distrust. Each caste is without sympathy with the other, and ready to credit anything disparaging in regard to it. Under the law of competition, the employer of thousands is forced into the strictest economies, among which the rates paid to labor figure prominently, and often there is friction between the employer and the employed, between capital and labor, between rich and poor. Human society loses homogeneity....

There remains, then, only one mode of using great fortunes; but in this we have the true antidote for the temporary unequal distribution of wealth, the reconciliation of the rich and the poor—a reign of harmony, another ideal, differing, indeed, from that of the Communist in requiring only the further evolution of existing conditions, not the total overthrow of our civilization. It is founded upon the present most intense Individualism, and the race is prepared to put it in practice by degrees whenever it pleases. Under its sway we shall have an ideal State, in which the surplus wealth of the few will become, in the best sense, the property of the many, because administered for the common good; and this wealth, passing through the hands of the few, can be made a much more potent force for the elevation of our race than if distributed in small sums to the people themselves. Even the poorest can be made to see this, and to agree that great sums gathered by some of their fellow-citizens and spent for public purposes, from which the masses reap the principal benefit, are more valuable to them than if scattered among themselves in trifling amounts through the course of many years.…

This, then, is held to be the duty of the man of wealth: To set an example of modest, unostentatious living, shunning display or extravagance; to provide moderately for the legitimate wants of those dependent upon him; and, after doing so, to consider all surplus revenues which come to him simply as trust funds, which he is called upon to administer, and strictly bound as a matter of duty to administer in the manner which, in his judgment, is best calculated to produce the most beneficial results for the community—the man of wealth thus becoming the mere trustee and agent for his poorer brethren, bringing to their service his superior wisdom, experience, and ability to administer, doing for them better than they would or could do for themselves.…

The best uses to which surplus wealth can be put have already been indicated. Those who would administer wisely must, indeed, be wise; for one of the serious obstacles to the improvement of our race is indiscriminate charity. It were better for mankind that the millions of the rich were thrown into the sea than so spent as to encourage the slothful, the drunken, the unworthy. Of every thousand dollars spent in so-called charity to-day, it is probable that nine hundred and fifty dollars is unwisely spent—so spent, indeed, as to produce the very evils which it hopes to mitigate or cure. A well-known writer of philosophic books admitted the other day that he had given a quarter of a dollar to a man who approached him as he was coming to visit the house of his friend. He knew nothing of the habits of this beggar, knew not the use that would be made of this money, although he had every reason to suspect that it would be spent improperly. This man professed to be a disciple of Herbert Spencer; yet the quarter-dollar given that night will probably work more

injury than all the money will do good which its thoughtless donor will ever be able to give in true charity. He only gratified his own feelings, saved himself from annoyance—and this was probably one of the most selfish and very worst actions of his life, for in all respects he is most worthy.

In bestowing charity, the main consideration should be to help those who will help themselves; to provide part of the means by which those who desire to improve may do so; to give those who desire to rise the aids by which they may rise; to assist, but rarely or never to do all. Neither the individual nor the race is improved by almsgiving. Those worthy of assistance, except in rare cases, seldom require assistance. The really valuable men of the race never do, except in case of accident or sudden change. Every one has, of course, cases of individuals brought to his own knowledge where temporary assistance can do genuine good, and these he will not overlook. But the amount which can be wisely given by the individual for individuals is necessarily limited by his lack of knowledge of the circumstances connected with each. He is the only true reformer who is as careful and as anxious not to aid the unworthy as he is to aid the worthy, and, perhaps, even more so, for in almsgiving more injury is probably done by rewarding vice than by relieving virtue.

* * * * * *

1.   *What does Carnegie see as the most important benefits of capitalism and mass production? How does he justify the amassing of great fortunes?*

2.   *What specific responsibilities does Carnegie claim for men of wealth? What options does he outline for the disposition of property?*

3.   *Who does Andrew Carnegie believe should be responsible for making social welfare policy? Why?*

19–3 John Morrison, Testimony of a Machinist, 1883

John Morrison was a young machinist who worked in New York City. He was one of hundreds of Americans who testified before a Senate committee investigating the causes of recent industrial strikes. Morrison focused on the changes he had seen in the workplace

over the previous nine years. Like many American workers of the era, he believed that mechanization had led to a decline in both the status and demand for skilled labor.

SOURCE: *Report of the Committee of the Senate upon the Relations between Labor and Capital*, 48th Congress (1885), pp. 755–759.

…Q. Is there any difference between the conditions under which machinery is made now and those which existed ten years ago?—A. A great deal of difference.

Q. State the differences as well as you can.—A. Well, the trade has been subdivided and those subdivisions have been again subdivided, so that a man never learns the machinist's trade now. Ten years ago he learned, not the whole of the trade, but a fair portion of it. Also, there is more machinery used in the business, which again makes machinery. In the case of making the sewing-machine, for instance, you find that the trade is so subdivided that a man is not considered a machinist at all. Hence it is merely laborers' work and it is laborers that work at that branch of our trade. The different branches of the trade are divided and subdivided so that one man may make just a particular part of a machine and may not know anything whatever about another part of the same machine. In that way machinery is produced a great deal cheaper than it used to be formerly, and in fact, through this system of work, 100 men are able to do now what it took 300 or 400 men to do fifteen years ago. By the use of machinery and the subdivision of the trade they so simplify the work that it is made a great deal easier and put together a great deal faster. There is no system of apprenticeship, I may say, in the business. You simply go in and learn whatever branch you are put at, and you stay at that unless you are changed to another.

Q. Does a man learn his branch very rapidly?—A. Yes, sir; he can learn his portion of the business very rapidly. Of course he becomes very expert at it, doing that all the time and nothing else, and therefore he is able to do a great deal more work in that particular branch than if he were a general hand and expected to do everything in the business as it came along....

Q. Do you know from reading the papers or from your general knowledge of the business whether there are other places in other cities or other parts of the country that those men could have gone and got work?—A. I know from general reports of the condition of our trade that the same condition existed throughout the country generally.

Q. Then those men could not have bettered themselves by going to any other place, you think?—A. Not in a body.

Q. I am requested to ask you this question: Dividing the public, as is commonly done, into the upper, middle, and lower classes, to which class would you assign the average workingman of your trade at the time when you entered it, and to which class you would assign him now?—A. I now assign them to the lower class. At the time I entered the trade I should assign them as merely hanging on to the middle class; ready to drop out at any time.

Q. What is the character of the social intercourse of those workingmen? Answer first with reference to their intercourse with other people outside of their own trade— merchants, employers, and others.—A. Are you asking what sort of social intercourse exists between the machin-

ists and the merchants? If you are, there is none whatever, or very little if any.

Q. What sort of social intercourse exists among the machinists themselves and their families, as to visiting, entertaining one another, and having little parties and other forms of sociability, those little things that go to make up the social pleasures of life?—A. In fact with the married folks that has died out—such things as birthday parties, picnics, and so on. The machinists to-day are on such small pay, and the cost of living is so high, that they have very little, if anything, to spend for recreation, and the machinist has to content himself with enjoying himself at home, either fighting with his wife or licking his children.

Q. I hope that is not a common amusement in the trade. Was it so ten years ago?—A. It was not; from the fact that they then sought enjoyment in other places, and had a little more money to spend. But since they have had no organization worth speaking of, of course their pay has gone down. At that time they had a form of organization in some way or other which seemed to keep up the wages, and there was more life left in the machinist then; he had more ambition, he felt more like seeking enjoyment outside, and in reading and such things, but now it is changed to the opposite; the machinist has no such desires.

Q. What is the social air about the ordinary machinist's house? Are there evidences of happiness, and joy, and hilarity, or is the general atmosphere solemn, and somber, and gloomy?—A. To explain that fully, I would state first of all, that machinists have got to work ten hours a day in New York, and that they are compelled to work very hard. In fact the machinists of America are compelled to do about one-third more work than the machinists do in England in a day. Therefore, when they come home they are naturally played out from shoving the file, or using the hammer or the chisel, or whatever it may be, such long hours. They are pretty well played out when they come home, and the first thing they think of is having something to eat and sitting down, and resting, and then of striking a bed. Of course when a man is dragged out in that way he is naturally cranky, and he makes all around him cranky; so, instead of a pleasant house it is every day expecting to lose his job by competition from his fellow-workman, there being so many out of employment, and no places for them, and his wages being pulled down through their competition, looking at all times to be thrown out of work in that way, and staring starvation in the face makes him feel sad, and the head of the house being sad, of course the whole family is the same, so the house looks like a dull prison instead of a home.

Q. Do you mean to say that that is the general condition of the machinists in New York and in this vicinity?—A. That is their general condition, with, of course, a good many exceptions. That is the general condition to the best of my knowledge.

Q. Where do you work?—A. I would rather not have it in print. Perhaps I would have to go Monday morning if I did. We are so situated in the machinist's trade that we daren't let them know much about us. If they know that we open our mouths on the labor question, and try to form organizations, we are quietly told that "business is slack," and we have got to go.

Q. Do you know of anybody being discharged for making speeches on the labor question?—A. Yes; I do know of several. A little less than a year ago several members of the organization that I belong to were discharged because it was discovered that they were members of the organization.

Q. Do you say those men were members of the same organization that you belong to?—A. Yes, sir; but not working in the same place where I work. And in fact many of my trade have been on the "black list," and have had to leave town to find work.

Q. Are the machinists here generally contented, or are they in a state of discontent and unrest?—A. There is mostly a general feeling of discontent, and you will find among the machinists the most radical workingmen, with the most revolutionary ideas. You will find that they don't so much give their thoughts simply to trades unions and other efforts of that kind, but they go far beyond that; they

only look for relief through the ballot or through a revolution, a forcible revolution....

Q. You say they look for relief through a forcible revolution. In the alternative of a forcible revolution have they considered what form of government they would establish?—A. Yes; some of them have and some of them have not.

Q. What kind of government would they establish?—A. Yes. They want to form a government such as this was intended to be, a government "of the people, for the people, and by the people"—different entirely from the present form of government.

* * * * * *

1.   *What specific changes in the workplace has Morrison seen over the last decade?*

2.   *What impact have these changes had on the economic and social lives of machinists? On their home lives?*

3.   *What political remedies, if any, does Morrison propose?*

19–4   *Terence V. Powderly, The Knights of Labor, 1889*

Terence Powderly was born in Pennsylvania in 1849, where he worked for many years as a machinist for the railroads. In 1874, he joined the Knights of Labor, a secret fraternal order of workers. He became leader of the Knights ("Grand Master Workman") in 1879 and moved the organization away from secret rituals and toward militant reform. Under Powderly, the Knights advocated an eight-hour day, the abolition of child labor, a graduated income tax, and equal pay for equal work. Unlike other labor organizations of the day, the Knights organized their locals by industry rather than trade, accepting all skill levels and women as well. Powderly opposed strikes, emphasizing instead boycotts, arbitration, and political activism as the best way to improve the worker's lot.

SOURCE: Terence V. Powderly, *Thirty Years of Labor* (1889).

first committee on constitution of the order of the
\s of Labor, appointed by Mr. Stephens, consisted
\ssentatives Robert Schilling, Chairman; Ralph
\t, Thomas King, T. V. Powderly, and George S.

Boyle. Two members of this committee, Messrs. Schilling and Powderly, were members of the Industrial Brotherhood; and though neither one knew that the other would be present, both brought with them a sufficient supply of constitutions of the I. B. to supply the body. The adoption of the preamble was left to these two, and a glance at it will show what changes were made in the declaration of principles whose history has been traced down from year to year since it was first adopted by the National Labor Union of 1866.

The committee on constitution adopted the constitution of the Industrial Brotherhood so far as practicable. The constitution, when printed, bore the same legend on the title page as was adopted at the Rochester meeting in 1874. The following is the preamble adopted at Reading, January 3, 1878:

> "When bad men combine, the good must associate,
>   else they will fall, one by one, an unpitied sacrifice in
>   a contemptible struggle."

PREAMBLE

The recent alarming development and aggression of aggregated wealth, which, unless checked, will invariably lead to the pauperization and hopeless degradation of the toiling masses, render it imperative, if we desire to enjoy the blessings of life, that a check should be placed upon its power and upon unjust accumulation, and a system adopted which will secure to the laborer the fruits of his toil; and as this much-desired object can only be accomplished by the thorough unification of labor, and the united efforts of those who obey the divine injunction that "In the sweat of thy brow shalt thou eat bread," we have formed the * * * * * with a view of securing the organization and direction, by cooperative effort, of the power of the industrial classes; and we submit to the world the objects sought to be accomplished by our organization, calling upon all who believe in securing "the greatest good to the greatest number" to aid and assist us:—

I. To bring within the folds of organization every department of productive industry, making knowledge a stand-point for action, and industrial and moral worth, not wealth, the true standard of individual and national greatness.

II. To secure to the toilers a proper share of the wealth that they create: more of the leisure that rightfully belongs to them; more societary advantages; more of the benefits, privileges, and emoluments of the world: in a word, all those rights and privileges necessary to make them capable of enjoying, appreciating, defending and perpetuating the blessings of good government.

III. To arrive at the true condition of the producing masses in their educational, moral, and financial condition, by demanding from the various governments the establishment of bureaus of Labor statistics.

IV. The establishment of co-operative institutions, productive and distributive.

V. The reserving of the public lands—the heritage of the people—or the actual settler;—not another acre for railroads or speculators.

VI. The abrogation of all laws that do not bear equally upon capital and labor, the removal of unjust technicalities, delays, and discriminations in the administration of justice, and the adopting of measures providing for the health and safety of those engaged in mining, manufacturing, or building pursuits.

VII. The enactment of laws to compel chartered corporations to pay their employes weekly, in full, for labor performed during the preceding week, in the lawful money of the country.

VIII. The enactment of laws giving mechanics and laborers a first lien on their work for their full wages.

IX. The abolishment of the contract system on national, State, and municipal work.

X. The substitution of arbitration for strikes, whenever and wherever employers and employees are willing to meet on equitable grounds.

XI. The prohibition of the employment of children in workshops, mines and factories before attaining their fourteenth year.

XII. To abolish the system of letting out by contract the labor of convicts in our prisons and reformatory institutions.

XIII. To secure for both sexes equal pay for equal work.

XIV. The reduction of the hours of labor to eight per day, so that the laborers may have more time for social enjoyment and intellectual improvement, and be enabled to reap the advantages conferred by the labor-saving machinery which their brains have created.

XV. To prevail upon governments to establish a purely national circulating medium, based upon the faith and resources of the nation, and issued directly to the people, without the intervention of any system of banking corporations, which money shall be a legal tender in payment of all debts, public or private....

In accepting the preamble of the Industrial Brotherhood, the convention fully realized that for the most part the reforms which were asked for in that preamble must one day come through political agitation and action. The chief aim of those who presented the document to the convention was to place something on the front page of the constitution which, it was hoped, every workingman would in time read and ponder over. It was their hope that by keeping those measures, so fraught with interest to the people, constantly before the eye of the worker, he would become educated in the science of politics to that extent that he would know that those things that were wrong in our political system were wrong simply because he did not attend to his political duties in a proper manner; that the righting of such things as were wrong would not be done by those who had the management of political affairs up to that time, but by himself....

...The belief was prevalent until a short time ago among working men, that only the man who was engaged in manual toil could be called a workingman. The man who labored at the bench or anvil; the man who held the throttle of the engine, or delved in the everlasting gloom of the coal mine, did not believe that the man who made the drawings from which he forged, turned, or dug could be classed as a worker. The draughtsman, the time-keeper, the clerk, the school teacher, the civil engineer, the editor, the reporter, or the worst paid, most abused and illy appreciated of all toilers—woman—could not be called a worker. It was essential that the mechanics of America should know who were workers. A more wide-spread knowledge of the true definition of the word labor must be arrived at, and the true relations existing between all men who labor must be more clearly defined. Narrow prejudice, born of the injustice and oppressions of the past, must be overcome, and all who interest themselves in producing for the world's good must be made to understand that their interests are identical. All the way down the centuries of time in which the man who worked was held in bondage or servitude, either wholly or partially, he was brought directly in contact with the overseer, the superintendent, or the boss. From these he seldom received a word of kindness; indeed it was the recognized rule to treat all men who toiled as if they were of inferior clay.

* * * * * *

It was necessary to teach the laborer that it was not essential for him to grovel in the dust at the feet of a master in order to win his title deed to everlasting bliss in the hereafter; and it can not be wondered at that many who strove to better the condition of the toiler lost all respect for religion when they saw that those who affected to be the most devout worshipers at the foot of the heavenly throne, were the most tyrannical of task masters when dealing with the poor and lowly, whose unfortunate lot was cast within the shadow of their heartless supervision....

...Knowledge for the workingman meant that he should he able to detect the difference between the real and the sham. Whenever a learned man said that which did not appear to be just to labor, he was to be questioned, publicly questioned, as to his base of actual facts. All through the centuries toilers have erected the brass and granite monuments of the world's greatness and have thrown up on hillside and plain the material for other homes than their own. The weary feet of toil have trodden the earth, and strong hands have formed the pillars of the bondage of old. All along the blood-stained march of the years that have flown, the struggling ones have given to earth more of richness in the sweat which fell to earth from their throbbing foreheads; the grain which lifted its head for long ages of time under the care of the toiler, has been enriched by the sweat, the blood, and the flesh of the poor, plodding men of toil. While the sun kissed to warmth and life the wheat and corn which their hands nurtured and cared for, they received the husks and stalks as their recompense for labor done. Their masters took the grain for themselves, but lifted no hand in its production....

* * * * * *

1.   What are the key ideals expressed in the Knights' constitution? How does it propose to empower working people?

2.   How does Powderly define a "workingman"?

3.   What specific political strategies does Powderly suggest for organized labor?

19–5   Samuel Gompers, Testimony on Labor Unions, 1883

Samuel Gompers was born into a working-class Jewish family in London in 1850. The family emigrated to New York City in 1863, where Gompers learned the cigar trade from his father. He became active in New York's labor movement circles during the 1870s and rose to head the Cigar Makers International Union. Gompers was suspicious of political activity, and he came to believe that only strong, centralized trade unions could significantly improve wages and working conditions. In 1886, Gompers helped found the American Federation of Labor, which he led until his death in 1924. As President of the AFL, Gompers focused on organizing skilled craft workers, largely ignoring the less skilled, even as they were becoming a more important part of the labor force.

SOURCE: *Report of the Committee of the Senate upon the Relations between Labor and Capital,* 48th Congress (1885).

The Witness: What I wish to show is the condition of the cigar-makers at that period when there was no organization. When our organization commenced to emerge and reorganize throughout the country, the first year there were seventeen strikes in our trade, of which twelve or thirteen were successful. The rest were either lost or compromised. In the year following we had forty-six strikes, of which thirty-seven, I think, were successful, three lost, and six compromised. In these last two years, since which we have held no convention (we will hold one next year and we will hear the result), I am so convinced that we have had over one hundred and sixty or one hundred and seventy strikes, and the strikes have been successful except in, perhaps, twenty instances where they may have been lost or compromised. The truck system of which I spoke exists no longer in our trade. We have adopted a course of action which our experience has taught us, and that is, in certain periods of the year, when it is generally dull, not to strike for an advance of wages. Formerly, before the organization, men would probably strike for an advance of wages in the dull season, and be content that they were not reduced in the busy season. Our experience has taught us to adopt a different mode of action.

Sen. George: You strike now when business is active?—A. Yes, sir; and then, when we obtain an increase of wages when times are fair, our object is to endeavor to obtain fair wages during the dull season also, and, while we have made provision not to strike for an increase of wages during those periods, we are always in a position to strike against a reduction of wages or the introduction of the truck system, or other obnoxious rules. We have found that, for the purpose of accomplishing this object, it is entirely valueless to organize a union during a strike, and that it is little better than valueless to organize just immediately before a strike. We have found that if we are desirous of gaining anything in a strike, we must prepare in peace for the turbulent time which may come. And the Cigar-makers' International Union, of which I now speak especially, is an organization that has in its treasury between $130,000 and $150,000 ready to be concentrated within five days at any time at any given point. I hold in my hand a copy of the constitution of that organization. Of course I am not desirous of making a propaganda for it, but to illustrate what I have been saying I will read from it this provision: "Any union being directed by the executive board to forward money to another local union, and failing to comply within five days from date of said notice shall be suspended." That is, in the event of a strike at a given point, the international president of the organization is directed to direct or request the nearest union to immediately send on its whole treasury if that is necessary, and the unions throughout the entire country and Canada to forward their entire treasury if necessary, to be placed at the disposal of the organization that is in trouble....

There is nothing in the labor movement that employers who have had unorganized laborers dread so much as organization; but organization alone will not do much unless the organization provides itself with a good fund, so that the operatives may be in a position, in the event of a struggle with their employers, to hold out....

Modern industry evolves these organizations out of the existing conditions where there are two classes in society, one incessantly striving to obtain the labor of the other class for as little as possible, and to obtain the largest amount or number of hours of labor; and the members of the other class, being as individuals utterly helpless in a contest with their employers, naturally resort to combinations to improve their condition, and, in fact, they are forced by the conditions which surround them to organize for self-protection. Hence trades unions. Trades unions are not barbarous, nor are they the outgrowth of barbarism. On the contrary they are only possible where civilization exists. Trades unions cannot exist in China; they cannot exist in Russia; and in all those semi-barbarous countries they can hardly exist, if indeed they can exist at all. But they have been formed successfully in this country, in Germany, in England, and they are gradually gaining strength in France. In Great Britain they are very strong; they have been forming there for fifty years, and they are still forming, and I think there is a great future for them yet in America. Wherever trades unions have organized and are most firmly organized, there are the right

[sic] of the people most respected. A people may be educated, but to me it appears that the greatest amount of intelligence exists in that country or that state where the people are best able to defend their rights, and their liberties as against those who are desirous of undermining them. Trades unions are organizations that instill into men a higher motive-power and give them a higher goal to look to. The hope that is too frequently deadened in their breasts when unorganized is awakened by the trades unions as it can be by nothing else. A man is sometimes reached by influences such as the church may hold out to him, but the conditions that will make him a better citizen and a more independent one are those that are evolved out of the trades union movement. That makes him a better citizen and a better man in every particular. There are only a few who can be reached by the church so as to affect their daily walk in life compared with the numbers reached by these organizations.

Sen. Blair: The outside public, I think, very largely confounds the conditions out of which the trades union grows or is formed, with the, to the general public mind, somewhat revolutionary ideas that are embraced under the names of socialism and communism. Before you get through, won't you let us understand to what extent the trades union is an outgrowth or an evolution of those ideas, and to what extent it stands apart from them and is based on different principles?—A. The trades unions are by no means an outgrowth of socialistic or communistic ideas or principles, but the socialistic and communistic notions are evolved from some of the trades unions' movements. As to the question of the principles of communism or socialism prevailing in trades unions, there are a number of men who connect themselves as workingmen with the trades unions who may have socialistic convictions, yet who never gave them currency; who say, "Whatever ideas we may have as to the future state of society, regardless of what the end of the labor movement as a movement between classes may be, they must remain in the background, and we must subordinate our convictions, and our views and our acts to the general good that the trades-union movement brings to the laborer." A large number of them think and act in that way. On the other hand, there are men—not so numerous now as they have been in the past—who are endeavoring to conquer the trades-union movement and subordinate it to those doctrines, and in a measure, in a few such organizations that condition of things exists, but by no means does it exist in the largest, most powerful, and best organized trades unions. There the view of which I spoke just now, the desire to improve the condition of the workingmen by and through the efforts of the trades unions, is fully lived up to. I do not know whether I have covered, the entire ground of the question.

Sen. George: You state, then, that the trades unions generally are not propagandists of socialistic views?—A. They are not. On the contrary, the endeavors of which I have spoken, made by certain persons to conquer the trades unions in certain cases, are resisted by the trades unionists; in the first place for the trades unions' sake, and even persons who have these convictions perhaps equally as strong as the others will yet subordinate them entirely to the good to be received directly through the trades unions. These last help those who have not such convictions to resist those who seek to use the trades unions to propagate their socialistic ideas.

Q. Do you think the trades unions have impeded or advanced the spread of socialistic views?—A. I believe that the existence of the trades-union movement, more especially where the unionists are better organized, has evoked a spirit and a demand for reform, but has held in check the more radical elements in society....

* * * * * *

1. *How does Gompers justify the use of strikes as a weapon for labor?*

2. *Compare the strategy and philosophy of Gompers with that of Powderly.*

19–6   Lee Chew, Experiences of a Chinese Immigrant, 1903

A native of Canton province, Lee Chew emigrated to San Francisco in 1880, when he was sixteen. In California, he encountered virulent anti-Chinese prejudice, which excluded Chinese from labor unions and sparked frequent outbreaks of violence aimed at Chinese communities. Such sentiment led to passage of the Chinese Exclusion Act in 1882, prohibiting the immigration of Chinese laborers. Lee Chew nevertheless managed to make his way operating laundries for railroad construction gangs and in several cities. He eventually settled in New York City, where he opened a successful import business.

SOURCE: *Independent* 55 (February 19, 1903), 417–423.

My father gave me $100, and I went to Hong Kong with five other boys from our place and we got steerage passage on a steamer, paying $50 each. Everything was new to me. All my life I had been used to sleeping on a board bed with a wooden pillow, and I found the steamer's bunk very uncomfortable, because it was so soft. The food was different from that which I had been used to, and I did not like it at all. I was afraid of the stews, for the thought of what they might be made of by the wicked wizards of the ship made me ill. Of the great power of these people I saw many signs. The engines that moved the ship were wonderful monsters, strong enough to lift mountains. When I got to San Francisco, which was before the passage of the Exclusion act [1882], I was half starved, because I was afraid to eat the provisions of the barbarians, but a few days' living in the Chinese quarter made me happy again. A man got me work as a house servant in an American family, and my start was the same as that of almost all the Chinese in this country.

The Chinese laundryman does not learn his trade in China; there are no laundries in China. The women there do the washing in tubs and have no washboards or flat irons. All the Chinese laundrymen here were taught in the first place by American women just as I was taught.

When I went to work for that American family I could not speak a word of English, and I did not know anything about housework. The family consisted of husband, wife and two children. They were very good to me and paid me $3.50 a week, of which I could save $3.

I did not know how to do anything, and I did not understand what the lady said to me, but she showed me how to cook, wash, iron, sweep, dust, make beds, wash dishes, clean windows, paint and [polish] brass, polish the knives and forks, etc., by doing the things herself and then overseeing my efforts to imitate her. She would take my hands and show them how to do things. She and her husband and children laughed at me a great deal, but it was all good natured....

In six months I had learned how to do the work of our house quite well, and I was getting $5 a week and board, and putting away about $4.25 a week. I had also learned some English, and by going to a Sunday school I learned more English and something about Jesus, who was a great Sage, and whose precepts are like those of Kong-foo-tsze.

It was twenty years ago when I came to this country, and I worked for two years as a servant, getting at the last $35 a month. I sent money home to comfort my parents, but though I dressed well and lived well and had pleasure, going quite often to the Chinese theater and to dinner parties in Chinatown, I saved $50 in the first six months, $90 in the second, $120 in the third and $150 in the fourth. So I had $410 at the end of two years, and I was now ready to start in business.

When I first opened a laundry it was in company with a partner, who had been in the business for some years. We went to a town about 500 miles inland, where a railroad was building. We got a board shanty and worked for the men employed by the railroads. Our rent cost us $10 a month and food nearly $5 a week each, for all food was dear and we wanted the best of everything—we lived principally on rice, chickens, ducks and pork, and did our own cooking. The Chinese take naturally to cooking. It cost us about $50 for our furniture and apparatus, and we made close upon $60 a week, which we divided between us. We had to put up with many insults and some frauds, as men would come in and claim parcels that did not belong to them, saying they had lost their tickets, and would fight if they did not get what they asked for. Sometimes we were taken before Magistrates and fined for losing shirts that we had never seen. On the other hand, we were making money, and even after sending home $3 a week I was able to save about $15. When the railroad construction gang moved on we went with them. The men were rough and prejudiced against us, but not more so than in the big Eastern cities. It is only lately in New York that the Chinese have been able to discontinue putting wire screens in front of their windows, and at the present time the street boys are still breaking the windows of Chinese laundries all over the city, while the police seem to think it a joke.

We were three years with the railroad, and then went to the mines, where we made plenty of money in gold dust, but had a hard time, for many of the miners were wild men who carried revolvers and after drinking would come into our place to shoot and steal shirts, for which we had to pay. One of these men hit his head hard against a flat iron and all the miners came and broke up our laundry, chasing us out of town. They were going to hang us. We lost all our property and $365 in money, which members of the mob must have found....

I have found out, during my residence in this country, that much of the Chinese prejudice against Americans is unfounded, and I no longer put faith in the wild tales that were told about them in our village, tho some of the Chinese, who have been here twenty years and who are learned men, still believe that there is no marriage in this country, that the land is infested with demons and that all the people are given over to general wickedness.

I know better. Americans are not all bad, nor are they wicked wizards. Still, they have their faults, and their treatment of us is outrageous.

The reason why so many Chinese go into the laundry business in this country is because it requires little capital and is one of the few opportunities that are open. Men of other nationalities who are jealous of the Chinese, because he is a more faithful worker than one of their people, have raised such a great outcry about Chinese cheap labor that they have shut him out of working on farms or in factories or building railroads or making streets or digging sewers. He cannot practice any trade, and his opportunities to do business are limited to his own countrymen. So he opens a laundry when he quits domestic service.

The treatment of the Chinese in this country is all wrong and mean. It is persisted in merely because China is not a fighting nation. The Americans would not dare to treat Germans, English, Italians or even Japanese as they treat the Chinese, because if they did there would be a war.

There is no reason for the prejudice against the Chinese. The cheap labor cry was always a falsehood. Their labor was never cheap, and is not cheap now. It has always commanded the highest market price. But the trouble is that the Chinese are such excellent and faithful workers that bosses will have no others when they can get them. If you look at men working on the street you will find an overseer for every four or five of them. That watching is not necessary for Chinese. They work as well when left to themselves as they do when some one is looking at them.

* * * * * *

1.   How would you evaluate Lee Chew's attitude toward business? To what extent do you think he was typical of other American small businessmen of his day?

2.   How does Lee Chew compare American and Chinese prejudices?

19–7 John Hill, Testimony on Southern Textile Industry, 1883

In the 1880s, the center of the nation's textile industry began to shift from New England to the southern Piedmont region. Lower wage rates and close access to raw materials attracted increasing numbers of textile manufacturers. Conditions in southern textile mills were extremely harsh, and most mill towns were thoroughly dominated by company agents and plant superintendents.

Southern mills employed large numbers of women and children from the surrounding towns and countryside. A transplanted northerner, John Hill was a mechanical engineer for the Eagle and Phoenix Manufacturing Company in Columbus, Georgia.

SOURCE: *Report of the Committee of the Senate upon the Relations between Labor and Capital*, 48th Congress, 4 (1885).

Now as to the efficiency of labor in the two sections. The Southern operative is native born, while the average Northern operative is not. They have got more Canadian operatives in Manchester, N.H., than they have natives. Now, as it is a well-known fact to all who have studied the subject, the elements of mind, the general mental make-up and intelligence of the native American exceeds by far the average of like qualities in the lower classes of for-eigners, the classes who immigrate into this country to work in mills. So in the same proportion are you likely to find the comparative intelligence of the Northern and the Southern operatives, the Southern being native and the Northern being a foreigner. There is more endurance in the constitution in a cold climate than in a warm one, and our advantage becomes a disadvantage in this respect, where it is a question of hard, heavy labor. Natural laws would therefore indicate that for heavy labor the Northern operative would be superior to the Southern, but while this is true, it is also true that a warm climate develops the human system earlier, and makes the action of both mind and body quicker than in a cold climate. The natives of warm climates are more impulsive, quicker to learn, and quicker in action, though not so enduring. This climate advances the period of manhood or womanhood fully a year and a half over the average climate of New England, so far as development is concerned. A man or a woman here in Columbus is as far advanced in physical develop-ment at fifteen years of age as a like person would be in Lowell at sixteen and a half years of age.

Now, for cotton manufacturing, capacity to endure hard labor is not a material point, because the labor is not hard. The motions required are quick rather than labori-ous, except in certain departments. In weaving there is probably about as much of one kind as the other, and, of course, weaving is a very important department.

It may be stated as a general fact, therefore, that in this regard the advantages in the South are at least equal to those in the North.

In the matter of education the native American of the North averages superior to the native of the South, owing to the fact that for many years, covering the lives of all the operatives now in the mills of the North, the free-school system has been universal there, and the necessity of education has been generally and fully appre-ciated. In the South, while a free-school system does exist in this State, yet it is not so far advanced as the free-school system in New England; not so liberal; not so easy to be availed of. It furnishes less school accommodation in proportion to population, and there is less disposition on the part of the people to patronize it, and, generally speaking, owing to the very limited time it has been in existence, the advantages of our free-school system here have not been reaped by our people to an extent that will at all compare with the benefits that the New England sys-tem has conferred upon the people there.

But again, as compared with foreign help, the prob-abilities are that even in the matter of education our

Southern operatives have the advantage. In Alabama, South Carolina, and other States, where no attention has been paid to the free-school system, the operatives have not had the advantages that they have in Georgia.

The hours of labor in cotton manufacture in the Eagle and Phoenix mills average eleven per day, but in many mills they average twelve per day. In New England, in some of the States, the law prescribes ten hours as a day's work. That is so in Massachusetts, but not in New Hampshire....

I might state that all mill operatives having to do with the process of cotton manufacturing involving quick perception and manipulation are white. In portions of the work, where it is only a question of muscle, and where intelligence is not a necessity, the laborers employed are either black or white, the preference, where it comes to a matter of mere muscle, being given to the colored labor-er. I refer now to rolling a bale of cotton in, tearing it open, tumbling around boxes and bales, and such heavy work. It has been found, and is a fact patent to all who have studied the question, that the employment of colored labor in the finer processes of manufacturing is a question which is mooted only by those who know nothing about it....It may be regarded as a fact about which those who understand the question can have no dispute, that it will be many years before the present condition of things can be changed. There are places to which each of these labor elements is specially adapted. The supply of both races is about equal to the demand, and there is an opportunity for support and for fair and reasonable prosperity open to one race as well as to the other.

There is a good feeling existing between the employers and the employed, both white and black, at the South, which is not equaled in any other section of this country, or in Europe either. There are no strikes here, no rebellions of the laborers, no disposition on the part of labor to combine against capital, and no disposition on the part of capital to oppress labor. Everything is in harmony, and a state of harmony and of prosperity in this respect exists which is to be found in no other place in the civi-lized world to the same extent as in the cotton States of the South. That is caused by the fact that there is a liber-ality upon the part of the employers which dispenses jus-tice to the employed willingly and cheerfully, and without compulsion. This fact is recognized by the employes, and where there is justice between capital and labor, and no oppression, there is, of course, no necessity for collisions, strikes, or animosities....

Now, I will make another statement which will probably be interesting to people who do not live here. The cotton States of the South are the only portion of the United States where whites and blacks work together upon the same work at the same pay and under the same regulations, the only part of this country where the two races will work side by side, justice being rendered to each, and the laborers of both races working in harmony and in unison, without rebellion and with mutual good-will. I employed on mill No. 3 from fifty to seventy-five brick masons, and probably from fifteen to twenty rock masons. The men of both races were mixed, working side by side, black and white. They were paid equal wages, and there was perfect harmony between them and equal proficiency except in cases where special acquirements were necessary on special work, and, in one instance, for considerable length of time, a state of facts existed that could not exist in any other country in the world, viz, that the entire lot of laborers were [sic] superintended by a colored man. You can't see anything like that in New England, can you? But what I say of the harmonious relations between the laborers of the two races has particular reference to Georgia, and other States where the races have not been antagonized by violent and political agitations in the past....

I have been simply calling attention to the fact that we can do here what you cannot do there; that is, we can work the two races together on the same work in harmony, and I say again that you could not do that in the mines of Pennsylvania, in the rolling mills of Pittsburgh, in the manufacturing establishments of New York, or upon the buildings of New York, Boston, or Chicago. You could not find or get up in any of those places the same harmonious feeling which exists here between the races to-day.

The CHAIRMAN. Then it is not really the race question at all. It is simply this that such a large part of your working population is colored that if you should undertake to exclude them from your labor market there would be nobody to do the work, and therefore, there being sufficient employment for both races, they work quietly alongside of each other, neither feeling that it is necessary to compete with the other for employment.

The WITNESS. Well, always, both before the war and since the war, there has been a better feeling between the two races here than at the North. The question of race, the question of the color of a man's face, does not arise at all in reference to this kind of labor, but in the North it does come in, and the consequence is that you find it impossible there to work the two races together harmoniously as we do here. I simply state this as a fact not generally known by parties at the North who have not investigated it....

It is only in the proper place that the two races can come together harmoniously. They don't come together in the dining-room, they don't come together in society, but there is a place where they can come together harmoniously, and that is right down on this basis where it is a question of labor, and where the common sentiment of the people is that the two races are equal. So far as regards this question of such labor as can earn 60 or 70 cents a day, there is perfect equality between white and black labor here in the South. But that does not mean at all social equality. It has nothing to do with politics or with social equality or anything of the kind. It means just 75 cents a day for a day's work, whether the laborer is white or black, or $2.50 a day for a black mason, and $2.50 for a white mason. We have two blacksmiths at work at the Eagle and Phoenix mill, one of them being white and the other black, and they are on an equality in wages and in work. One of them is a very intelligent white man and the other is a very intelligent colored man. The question of equality does not come up with reference to those two men at all. They are both just blacksmiths working at $2.50 a day each, and drawing that amount of wages at the end of the week, and that is all there is to it. We do not mix the races in the machine shop. It is done only where there seems to be a certain suitableness in it. We do it on our rock walls and our brick walls, and among our carpenters, and we pay each one at the same rate for equal work.

Q. And give neither race the preference in selecting the men to be employed?—A. If I want a man to do certain things I want a colored man every time, while, on the other hand, if I want a man to do certain other things, I want a white man. I don't know that it hinges on the question of the whiteness or blackness of the man's skin; it hinges rather on the adaptability of the man to do the particular work that is required.

* * * * * *

1. *According to Hill, how and why is the southern textile workforce superior to that in the north?*

2. *How does he compare black labor with immigrant labor? How does he differentiate southern race relations inside and outside of the mill?*

19–8   Thorstein Veblen, Conspicuous Consumption, 1899

An iconoclastic economist and social theorist, Thorstein Veblen developed an influential critique of both mainstream economic theory and capitalist society as a whole. The Theory of the Leisure Class, his first book, reached a large audience outside of academia and quickly became a classic indictment of upper-class behavior and values. Using concepts drawn from Darwin's theory of evolution, Veblen attacked America's turn-of-the-century "new rich" as parasites who "retard the adaptation of human nature to the exigencies of modern industrial life." He effectively satirized America's "pecuniary culture," where status was based largely upon wealth, and he noted the tendency of lower- and middle-class people to emulate the rich.

SOURCE: Thorstein Veblen, *The Theory of the Leisure Class* (NY: Macmillan, 1899), pp. 64–70.

Conspicuous consumption of valuable goods is a means of reputability to the gentleman of leisure. As wealth accumulates on his hands, his own unaided effort will not avail to sufficiently put his opulence in evidence by this method. The aid of friends and competitors is therefore brought in by resorting to the giving of valuable presents and expensive feasts and entertainments. Presents and feasts had probably another origin than that of naïve ostentation, but they acquired their utility for this purpose very early, and they have retained that character to the present; so that their utility in this respect has now long been the substantial ground on which these usages rest. Costly entertainments, such as the potlatch or the ball, are peculiarly adapted to serve this end. The competitor with whom the entertainer wishes to institute a comparison is, by this method, made to serve as a means to the end. He consumes vicariously for his host at the same time that he is a witness to the consumption of that excess of good things which his host is unable to dispose of singlehanded, and he is also made to witness his host's facility in etiquette.

In the giving of costly entertainments other motives, of a more genial kind, are of course also present. The custom of festive gatherings probably originated in motives of conviviality and religion; these motives are also present in the later development, but they do not continue to be the sole motives. The latter-day leisure-class festivities and entertainments may continue in some slight degree to serve the religious need and in a higher degree the needs of recreation and conviviality, but they also serve an invidious purpose; and they serve it none the less effectually for having a colorable non-invidious ground in these more avowable motives. But the economic effect of these social amenities is not therefore lessened, either in the vicarious consumption of goods or in the exhibition of difficult and costly achievements in etiquette.

As wealth accumulates, the leisure class develops further in function and structure, and there arises a differentiation within the class. There is a more or less elaborate system of rank and grades. This differentiation is furthered by the inheritance of wealth and the consequent inheritance of gentility. With the inheritance of gentility goes the inheritance of obligatory leisure; and gentility of a sufficient potency to entail a life of leisure may be inherited without the complement of wealth required to maintain a dignified leisure. Gentle blood may be transmitted without goods enough to afford a reputably free consumption at one's ease. Hence results a class of impecunious gentlemen of leisure, incidentally referred to already. These half-caste gentlemen of leisure fall into a system of hierarchical gradations. Those who stand near the higher and the highest grades of the wealthy leisure class, in point of birth, or in point of wealth, or both, outrank the remoter-born and the pecuniarily weaker. These lower grades, especially the impecunious, or marginal, gentlemen of leisure, affiliate themselves by a system of dependence or fealty to the great ones; by so doing they gain an increment of repute, or of the means with which to lead a life of leisure, from their patron. They become his courtiers or retainers, servants; and being fed and countenanced by their patron they are indices of his rank and vicarious consumers of his superfluous wealth. Many of these affiliated gentlemen of leisure are at the same time lesser men of substance in their own right; so that some of them are scarcely at all, others only partially, to be rated as vicarious consumers. So many of them, however, as make up the retainers and hangers-on of the patron may be classed as vicarious consumers without qualification. Many of these again, and also many of the other aristocracy of less degree, have in turn attached to their persons a more or less comprehensive group of vicarious consumers in the persons of their wives and children, their servants, retainers, etc....

In the later development of peaceable industry, the usage of employing an idle corps of uniformed men-at-arms gradually lapses. Vicarious consumption by dependents bearing the insignia of their patron or master narrows down to a corps of liveried menials. In a heightened degree, therefore, the livery comes to be a badge of servitude, or rather of servility. Something of a honorific character always attached to the livery of the armed retainer, but this honorific character disappears when the livery becomes the exclusive badge of the menial. The livery becomes obnoxious to nearly all who are required to wear it. We are yet so little removed from a state of effective slavery as still to be fully sensitive to the sting of any imputation of servility. This antipathy asserts itself even in the case of the liveries or uniforms which some corporations prescribe as the distinctive dress of their employees. In this country the aversion even goes the length of discrediting—in a mild and uncertain way—those government employments, military and civil, which require the wearing of a livery or uniform.

With the disappearance of servitude, the number of vicarious consumers attached to any one gentleman tends, on the whole, to decrease. The like is of course true, and perhaps in a still higher degree, of the number of dependents who perform vicarious leisure for him. In a general way, though not wholly nor consistently, these two groups coincide. The dependent who was first delegated for these duties was the wife, or the chief wife; and, as would be expected, in the later development of the institution, when the number of persons by whom these duties are customarily performed gradually narrows, the wife remains the last. In the higher grades of society a large volume of both these kinds of service is required; and here the wife is of course still assisted in the work by a more or less numerous corps of menials. But as we descend the social scale, the point is presently reached where the duties of vicarious leisure and consumption devolve upon the wife alone. In the communities of the Western culture, this point is at present found among the lower middle class.

And here occurs a curious inversion. It is a fact of common observance that in this lower middle class there is no pretense of leisure on the part of the head of the household. Through force of circumstances it has fallen into disuse. But the middle-class wife still carries on the business of vicarious leisure, for the good name of the household and its master. In descending the social scale in any modern industrial community, the primary fact—the conspicuous leisure of the master of the household—disappears at a relatively high point. The head of the middle-class household has been reduced by economic circumstances to turn his hand to gaining a livelihood by occupations which often partake largely of the character of industry, as in the case of the ordinary business man of today. But the derivative fact—the vicarious leisure and consumption rendered by the wife, and the auxiliary vicarious performance of leisure by menials—remains in a vogue as a conventionality which the demands of reputability will not suffer to be slighted. It is by no means a an uncommon spectacle to find a man applying himself to work with the utmost assiduity, in order that his wife may in due form render for him that degree of vicarious leisure which the common sense of the time demands.

The leisure rendered by the wife in such cases is, of course, not a simple manifestation of idleness or indolence. It almost invariably occurs disguised under some is form of work or household duties or social amenities, which prove on analysis to serve little or no ulterior end beyond showing that she does not occupy herself with anything that is gainful or that is of substantial use. As has already been noticed under the head of manners, the greater part of the customary round of domestic cares to which the middle-class housewife gives her time and effort is of this character. Not that the results of her attention to household matters, of a decorative and mundificatory character, are not pleasing to the sense of men trained in middle-class proprieties; but the taste to which these effects of household adornment and tidiness appeal is a taste which has been formed under the selective guidance of a canon of propriety that demands just these evidences of wasted effort. The effects are pleasing to us chiefly because we have been taught to find them pleasing. There goes into these domestic duties much solicitude for a proper combination of form and color, and for other ends that are to be classed as aesthetic in the proper sense of the term; and it is not denied that effects having some substantial aesthetic value are sometimes attained. Pretty much all that is here insisted on is that, as regards these amenities of life, the housewife's efforts are under the guidance of traditions that have been shaped by the law of conspicuously wasteful expenditure of time and substance. If beauty or comfort is achieved—and it is a more or less fortuitous circumstance if they are—they must be achieved by means and methods that commend themselves to the great economic law of wasted effort. The more reputable, "presentable" portion of middle-class household paraphernalia are, on the one hand, items of conspicuous consumption, and on the other hand, apparatus for putting in evidence the vicarious leisure rendered by the housewife.

The requirement of vicarious consumption at the hands of the wife continues in force even at a lower point in the pecuniary scale than the requirement of vicarious leisure. At a point below which little if any pretense of wasted effort, in ceremonial cleanness and the like, is observable, and where there is assuredly no conscious attempt at ostensible leisure, decency still requires the wife to consume some goods conspicuously for the reputability of the household and its head. So that, as the latter-day outcome of this evolution of an archaic institution, the wife, who was at the outset the drudge and chattel of the man, both in fact and in theory—the producer of goods for him to consume—has become the ceremonial consumer of goods which he produces. But she still quite unmistakably remains his chattel in theory; for the habitual rendering of vicarious leisure and consumption is the abiding mark of the unfree servant.

This vicarious consumption practiced by the household of the middle and lower classes can not be counted as a direct expression of the leisure-class scheme of life, since the household of this pecuniary grade does not belong within the leisure class. It is rather that the leisure-class scheme of life here comes to an expression at the second remove. The leisure class stands at the head of the social structure in point of reputability; and its manner of life and its standards of worth therefore afford the norm of reputability for the community. The observance of these standards, in some degree of approximation, becomes incumbent upon all classes lower in the scale. In modern civilized communities the lines of demarcation between social classes have grown vague and transient, and wherever this happens the norm of reputability imposed by the upper class extends its coercive influence with but slight hindrance down through the social structure to the lowest strata. The result is that the members of each stratum accept as their ideal of decency the scheme of life in vogue in the next higher stratum, and bend their energies to live up to that ideal. On pain of forfeiting their good name and their self-respect in case of failure, they must conform to the accepted code, at least in appearance.

The basis on which good repute in any highly organized industrial community ultimately rests is pecuniary strength; and the means of showing pecuniary strength, and so of gaining or retaining a good name, are leisure and a conspicuous consumption of goods. Accordingly, both of these methods are in vogue as far down the scale as it remains possible; and in the lower strata in which the two methods are employed, both offices are in great part delegated to the wife and children of the household. Lower still, where any degree of leisure, even ostensible, has become impracticable for the wife, the conspicuous consumption of goods remains and is carried on by the wife and children. The man of the household also can do something in this direction, and indeed, he commonly does; but with a still lower descent into the levels of indigence—along the margin of the slums—the man, and presently also the children, virtually cease to consume valuable goods for appearances, and the woman remains virtually the sole exponent of the household's pecuniary decency. No class of society, not even the most abjectly poor, forgoes all customary conspicuous consumption. The last items of this category of consumption are not given up except under stress of the direst necessity. Very much of squalor and discomfort will be endured before the last trinket or the last pretense of pecuniary decency is put away. There is no class and no country that has yielded so abjectly before the pressure of physical want as to deny themselves all gratification of this higher or spiritual need.

* * * * * *

1. *What does Veblen mean by "conspicuous consumption"? What is its impact on society?*

2. *According to Veblen, how and why are the spending habits of the leisure class imitated by other classes? What effect does this have on the economy and social life?*

3. *How would you apply Veblen's analysis to contemporary American life? Is conspicuous consumption a more or less pronounced feature in our culture today?*

19–9   M. Carey Thomas, Higher Education for Women, 1901

Born in 1857, M. Carey Thomas hailed from a prominent Quaker family in Baltimore. She attended Cornell University and Johns Hopkins and later earned a doctorate in literature from the University of Zurich. In 1883, she was appointed dean of Bryn Mawr, a new college for women in Pennsylvania; eleven years later, she became its president. Among the most prominent women educators of her day, Thomas insisted that the standards and curricula for women's colleges be the equal of those of the best men's colleges.

SOURCE: M. Carey Thomas, "Should the Higher Education of Women Differ from that of Men?", *Educational Review 21* (1901).

Once granted that women are to compete with men for self-support as physicians or lawyers,...what is the best attainable training for the physician or the lawyer, man or woman? There is no reason to believe that typhoid or scarlet fever or phthisis can be successfully treated by a woman physician in one way and by a man physician in another way. There is indeed every reason to believe that unless treated in the best way the patient may die, the sex of the doctor affecting the result less even than the sex of the patient. The question needs only to be put for us to feel irrevocably sure that there is no special woman's way of dealing with disease. And so in law, in architecture, in electricity, in bridge-building, in all mechanic arts and technical sciences, our effort must be for the most scientific instruction, the broadest basis of training that will enable men and women students to attain the highest possible proficiency in their chosen profession. Given two bridge-builders, a man and a woman, given a certain bridge to be built, and given as always the unchangeable laws of mechanics in accordance with which this special bridge and all other bridges must be built, it is simply inconceivable that the preliminary instruction given to the two bridge-builders should differ in quantity, quality, or method of presentation because while the bridge is building one will wear knickerbockers and the other a rainy-day skirt. You may say you do not think that God intended a woman to be a bridge-builder. You have, of course, a right to this prejudice; but as you live in America, and not in the interior of Asia or Africa, you will probably not be able to impose it on women who wish to build bridges. You may say that women's minds are such that they cannot build good bridges. If you are right in this opinion you need concern yourselves no further—bridges built by women, will on the whole, tend to fall down, and the competition of men who can build good bridges will force

women out of the profession. Both of these opinions of yours are side issues, and, however they may be decided hereafter, do not in the remotest degree affect the main question of a common curriculum for men and women in technical and professional schools. But you may say that men and women should study bridge-building and medicine and law in separate schools, and not together. You may be foolish enough, and wasteful enough, to think that all the expensive equipment of our technical and professional schools should be duplicated for women, when experience and practice have failed to bring forward a single valid objection to professional coeducation, and when the present trend of public opinion is overwhelmingly against you, and for the sake of argument let us grant that beside every such school for men is to be founded a similar school for women. But this duplication of professional schools for women leaves us just where we were in regard to the curriculum of professional study to be taught in such women's schools. So long as men and women are to compete together, and associate together, in their professional life, women's preparation for the same profession cannot safely differ from men's. If men's preparation is better, women, who are less well prepared, will be left behind in the race; if women's is better, men will suffer in competition with women....

The above argument applies with equal force to the training given by the university graduate school of arts and sciences. Statistics indicate that an overwhelmingly large majority of men and women graduate students are fitting themselves for the profession of higher teaching, that over one-third of all graduate students in the United States are women, and that the annual increase of women graduate students is greater than that of men. In the lower grades of teaching men have almost ceased to compete with women; in the higher grade, that is, in college teaching, women are just beginning to compete with men, and this competition is beset with the bitterest professional jealousy that women have ever had to meet, except perhaps in medicine. There are in the United States only eleven independent colleges for women of at all the same grade as the three hundred and thirty-six coeducational colleges where women and men are taught together, yet only in these separate colleges for women have women an opportunity of competing with men for professors' chairs. It is very rare indeed for coeducational colleges to employ any women instructors, and even then only so many women are as a rule employed as are needed to look after the discipline or home life of the women students. Where women are teaching in coeducational colleges side by side with men their success is regarded by men teachers with profound dislike, and on account of this sex jealousy college presidents and boards of trustees (all of whom are, as a rule, men) cannot, even if they would, materially add to the number of women teachers or advance them. The working of the elective system, however, permits us to see that men students show no such jealousy, but recognize the able teaching of women by overcrowding their classes. Women have succeeded so brilliantly, on the whole so much better than men, as primary and secondary teachers, that they will undoubtedly repeat this success in their college teaching so soon as artificial restrictions are removed. No one could seriously maintain that handicapped as women now are by prejudice in the highest branches of a profession peculiarly their own, they should be further hampered by the professional training different from men's....

But this line of reasoning will be incomplete unless we ask ourselves whether there are not some subjects peculiar to women in which we must maintain special women's technical schools. There are certainly three schools. So long as men and women are to compete professional schools where women students already largely outnumber men: normal schools, including normal departments of universities, schools of nursing, and schools for library study. If cooking and domestic service ever become lucrative professions, and more especially if men of wealth ever come to choose their wives for culinary and sanitary lore instead as at present for social and intellectual charm, such schools will tend to spring up and, like normal schools, will undoubtedly be attended almost exclusively by women. They will beyond question be taught exactly in the same way as if they were to be attended exclusively by men. The method of teaching cooking is one and the same and does not depend on the sex of the cooks....

The burden of proof is with those who believe that the college education of men and women should differ. For thirty years it has been as nearly as possible the same, with brilliantly satisfactory results, so far as concerns women. College women have married as generally as their non-college-bred sisters, and have as a rule married better than their sisters, because they have chosen a larger proportion of professional men; they have not died in childbirth, as was predicted; they have borne their proper proportion of children, and have brought up more than the usual proportion of those born; they have made efficient housekeepers and wives as well as mothers; their success as teachers has been so astonishingly great that already they are driving non-college-bred women teachers out of the field. There is, in short, not a word to be said against the success and efficiency and healthfulness of these women educated by men's curriculum....

Undoubtedly the life of most women after leaving college will differ from that of men. About one-half will marry in a rather deliberate fashion, choosing carefully, and on the whole living very happily a life of comparative leisure, not of self-support; about one-third will become professional teachers, probably for life; and the greater part of the remainder will lead useful and helpful lives as unmarried women of leisure. And just because after leaving college only one-third, and that in the peculiarly limited profession of teaching, are to get the wider training of affairs that educates men engaged in business and in the professions all their lives thru, women while in college ought to have the broadest possible education. This college education should be the same as men's, not only because there is, I believe, but one best education, but because men and women are to live and work together as comrades and dear friends and married friends and lovers, and because their effectiveness and happiness and the welfare of the generation to come after them will be vastly increased if their college education has given them the same intellectual training and the same scholarly and moral ideals.

* * * * * *

1. *Why does Thomas draw so many examples from the fields of science and engineering? How does she use the ideal of competition to make her case?*

2. *How does Thomas evaluate the results of the first thirty years of college education for women? What arguments does she use to answer its critics?*

19–10 B. F. Keith, *The Vogue of Vaudeville, 1898*

Born and raised on a New Hampshire farm, B. F. Keith began his show business career in the 1870s working in circuses. In 1883, he opened a dime museum in Boston and soon began presenting live variety acts in its 300-seat theater. With his partner Edward F. Albee, Keith leased several regular theaters in the northeast, presenting low-priced, completely respectable "vaudeville" shows that ran continuously from morning to night. In the early twentieth century the Keith/Albee Circuit came to dominate big-time vaudeville. In 1898, with his empire still growing, Keith tried to explain the broad appeal of vaudeville theater, as well as his own business success.

SOURCE: B. F. Keith, "The Vogue of Vaudeville," *National Magazine 9* (November 1898), 146–153.

I do not think that the old saw, "Necessity is the mother of invention," ever had a clearer application than in the case of my origination of the continuous performance idea of entertainment. Replying to the query of a friend, not long since, "What first induced you to establish the continuous performance?" I truthfully replied: "Because I had to do something."

A mental retrospection of the years prior to this particular period of "having to do something" discloses the fact that shadowy gleamings of the success that would follow the institution of the new form of amusement were constantly flitting across my mental vision, with the result that I pondered over the problem betwixt waking and sleeping many a restless night.

All at once the full formed idea was made plain, and I never hesitated in putting it into execution. It was clear that the majority of people would stay through an entertainment so long as they could, even sitting out acts that had to be repeated. The old form necessitated a final curtain at a specified time, and the emptying of the house. As a result the succeeding audience gathered slowly, the theatre was necessarily dreary as they came into it, and there was nothing going on. Did you ever notice the hesitancy on the part of early comers to a playhouse to assume their seats in the auditorium, how they hang back until reassured by numbers? Well, that is one of the things the continuous performance does away with. It matters not at what hour of the day or evening you visit, the theatre is always occupied by more or less people, the show is in full swing, everything is bright, cheerful and inviting. In this connection, I remember that in the days of my first shows (prior to the opening of the Bijou), I was always maneuvering to keep patrons moving up and down stairs in view of passersby on the sidewalk for the specific purpose of impressing them with the idea that business was immense.

Beyond making the start in the continuous, I gave little thought to the growth of the business. I was convinced that would come in due course, as amusement seekers became familiar with the new order of things, but I never dreamed of its expanding to its present proportions, nor that it would become such a popular form of entertainment that imitators would spring up all over the country, as they have today.

For the benefit of those who have never enjoyed a vaudeville show of the continuous order, I might explain that it is designed to run twelve hours, during which period performers appear two or three times, as it would be manifestly impossible to secure enough different acts to fill out the dozen hours. The best class of artists appear twice, just as at a matinee and evening performance in a dramatic theatre, and the balance do three "turns." It was this revolution of "turns" that I found most difficult to explain to my employees at the outset. One, who has since risen to a position of trust and prominence in my business, was then lecturing on "The Arctic Moon," a relic of the Greeley expedition which was presented to me by Lieutenant Brainerd. When it came to his turn to go on again, he came to me and said: "Why, Mr. Keith, I can't go out there and make that talk over again; the same people I talked to before are still in the house. If you say so, however, I'll do it." I did say so, as that was my plan, and he went on and began his lecture, and people all over the house got up and left, but their places were soon taken by others, and the continuous performance had its beginning. The gentleman who lectured soon saw the point.

I have to smile now whenever I think of the manner in which my project was received at the outset. I shall never forget the look of sincere pity which o'erspread the countenance of my chief assistant, to whom I unfolded my plans. He did not say a word, simply gave me a look that said as plainly as words could have done that he regarded my scheme as visionary beyond discussion. But then, that was the opinion of people generally, especially managers of other amusement enterprises, not a few of whom predicted my failure within a short period.

Two things I determined at the outset should prevail in the new scheme. One was that my fixed policy of cleanliness and order should be continued, and the other that the stage show must be free from vulgarisms and coarseness of any kind, so that the house and entertainment would directly appeal to the support of ladies and children—in fact that my playhouse must be as "home-like" an amusement resort as it was possible to make it. While a certain proportion of the male sex may favor stage performances of a risqué order, none of them would care to bring the female members of their families, to witness an entertainment of that description, and I think that a majority of men who do visit playhouses where that sort of entertainment is provided have a feeling of shame when they get outside and the glamor is removed. In the early days of my business career, many worthy but mistaken people ridiculed the idea of a clean and respectable house and entertainment being conducted at the then price of admission (only ten cents), but I successfully demonstrated that such a thing was possible. Indeed, I believed then, as now, that one can be just as respectable and clean—always provided they have the desire so to be—in a resort where ten cents defrays the admission, as in one where ten dollars is the charge.

Nowadays, the public has grown very discriminating, and not only do they demand a better quality of acts, but they expect to see the smallest sketch presented with proper stage settings and surroundings, something that was unheard of in the earlier days of vaudeville. Formerly, while any meritorious act was sure of recognition, a decided preference was exhibited for short farces and afterpieces. It was for this reason that for several years after I inaugurated continuous performance, I kept a small stock company, who presented short plays each week, which were always cordially received. One of the most pronounced successes was achieved with a condensed version of "Muldoon's Picnic." It was staged nicely, had a good cast and ran for nearly two months. Another unexpected hit was made with a small panorama illustrating John Brown's famous raid at Harpers Ferry, together with other exciting incidents in the life of the great abolitionist. In connection with this attraction, a half hour descriptive lecture was given, and originally produced on a Monday morning to fill an unlooked-for vacancy. It made such a distinct hit that it was continued for several weeks.

There has been a marked improvement in vaudeville acts in the past few years, as is evidenced by the fact that many of the older performers, who were at the head of the programs in those days, and who persist in following the methods by which they then attained popularity, have been relegated to second and third places, and even then fail to make any marked impression on the amusement-seeking public.

The advent of dramatic players into my theatres has been distinctly beneficial, in that it has added the element of novelty, which is the essence of vaudeville, and has attracted the attention of a desirable class of patrons whose previous knowledge of a variety entertainment had been very vague and largely governed by tradition. As to the sort of entertainment which seems to please most, light, frothy acts, with no particular plot, but abounding in songs, dances, bright dialogue and clean repartee, seem to appeal most to the vaudeville audiences of the present time. But, it is quite evident that a thoroughly good program, in its entirety, is what draws the public, rather than individual acts, the rule being proven, however, by occasional exceptions, notably the Living Picture production, the song-sheet novelty and the Biograph, the most improved of the motion-picture inventions, and a very few of the leading performers who have novelties to offer. The most marked improvement is the tendency of artists to keep their acts clean and free from coarseness, and to do away with the ridiculous costumes which were formerly a glaring defect of nearly all vaudeville entertainments. Added to this is the closer attention paid to stage setting and scenic embellishment generally.

The character of the vaudeville audience has notably improved in recent years, and the entertainment of today is freely patronized and enjoyed by the most intelligent and cultivated people, who flatter me by the assurance which their presence in my theatres brings that they have confidence in my pledge that therein nothing

shall be given which could not with perfect safety be introduced to their homes.

There is (or was) a mistaken impression on the part of some eminent critics, and others, that my scheme of vaudeville simply served the turn of people who desired quantity at the expense of quality, and I remember reading a story, while abroad, in which the Astor tramp yarn was made to do duty as illustrative of this point. For the benefit of those who may never have seen it—or seeing, have forgotten—I will rehearse it as memory serves. The tramp, who, after being arrested for sleeping in the millionaire's bed burglariously, was asked by a reporter what sort of a dinner he would order if he possessed all the wealth of John Jacob Astor. The hobo reflected long and earnestly, and finally replied: "I think," said he, thoughtfully, "if I had all that 'ere Mr. Astor's millions, and I had the choice of a real good dinner, I would order corn beef and cabbage. It's so werry fillin'."

Now, as a matter of fact, there are no audiences anywhere who demand so much that is good in an entertainment as the patrons of the continuous form of amusement. Personally, I care as much for grand opera as I do for a variety show, and I have no doubt but that a large percentage of the patrons of my houses do also. This was demonstrated during a six years' continuous run of opera in my theatres. If quantity and not quality were desired on the part of vaudeville audiences, many thousands of dollars could be saved in a year by the non-employment of high-priced artists from the dramatic stage, the operatic stage and the lyceum platform.

The indications are that vaudeville will be the popular form of entertainment for years to come, and, through the acquisition of new and better material there will be evolved a higher vaudeville, constantly improving in quality, and adapted to the changing conditions of the times.

* * * * * *

1. Why does Keith place so much emphasis on "cleanliness" and "decency" in his shows? How did this help his business?

2. How would you compare the business of vaudeville to other industrial enterprises of the day?

3. What elements made vaudeville so popular? What connections can you make between vaudeville and later twentieth-century entertainment forms?

chapter 20

Commonwealth and Empire, 1870s–1900s

20-1 Edward Bellamy, *Looking Backward, 1888*

Edward Bellamy was born in 1850 in Chicopee Falls, Massachusetts, a typical New England factory town. Bellamy worked as a journalist and wrote short stories before publishing his landmark utopian socialist novel, Looking Backward, *in 1888. The story centers on Julian West, who awakens after a century of sleep and finds that a nonviolent revolution has thoroughly transformed society. The means of production have been nationalized, poverty has been abolished, and all citizens share equally in the nation's wealth. The novel sold over a million copies within a few years, and Bellamy became the leader of what he called the Nationalist Movement, dedicated to peacefully eradicating capitalism. In the following excerpt, Doctor Leete informs Julian West of the momentous political and social changes that have taken place since 1888.*

SOURCE: Edward Bellamy, *Looking Backward* (1888).

"You told me when we were upon the housetop that though a century only had elapsed since I fell asleep, it had been marked by greater changes in the conditions of humanity than many a previous millennium. With the city before me I could well believe that, but I am very curious to know what some of the changes have been. To make a beginning somewhere, for the subject is doubtless a large one, what solution, if any, have you found for the labor question? It was the Sphinx's riddle of the nineteenth century, and when I dropped out the Sphinx was threatening to devour society, because the answer was not forthcoming. It is well worth sleeping a hundred years to learn what the right answer was, if, indeed, you have found it yet."

"As no such thing as the labor question is known nowadays," replied Doctor Leete, "and there is no way in which it could arise, I suppose we may claim to have solved it. Society would indeed have fully deserved being devoured if it had failed to answer a riddle so entirely simple. In fact, to speak by the book, it was not necessary for society to solve the riddle at all. It may he said to have solved itself. The solution came as the result of a process of industrial evolution which could not have terminated otherwise. All that society had to do was to recognize and cooperate with that evolution, when its tendency had become unmistakable."

"I can only say," I answered, "that at the time I fell asleep no such evolution had been recognized."

"It was in 1887 that you fell into this sleep, I think you said."

"Yes, May 30, 1887."

My companion regarded me musingly for some moments. Then he observed, "And you tell me that even then there was no general recognition of the nature of the crisis which society was nearing? Of course, I fully credit your statement. The singular blindness of your contemporaries to the signs of the times is a phenomenon commented on by many of our historians, but few facts of history are more difficult for us to realize, so obvious and unmistakable as we look back seem the indications, which must also have come under your eyes, of the transformation about to come to pass. I should be interested, Mr. West, if you would give me a little more definite idea of the view which you and men of your grade of intellect took of the state and prospects of society in 1887. You must, at least, have realized that the widespread industrial and social troubles, and the underlying dissatisfaction of all classes with the inequalities of society, and the general misery of mankind, were portents of great changes of some sort."

"We did, indeed, fully realize that," I replied. "We felt that society was dragging anchor and in danger of going adrift. Whither it would drift nobody could say, but all feared the rocks."

"Nevertheless," said Doctor Leete, "the set of the current was perfectly perceptible if you had but taken pains to observe it, and it was not toward the rocks, but toward a deeper channel."

"We had a popular proverb," I replied, "that 'hindsight is better than foresight,' the force of which I shall now, no doubt, appreciate more fully than ever. All I can say is, that the prospect was such when I went into that long sleep that I should not have been surprised had I looked down from your housetop today on a heap of charred and moss-grown ruins instead of this glorious city."

Doctor Leete had listened to me with close attention and nodded thoughtfully as I finished speaking. "What you have said," he observed, "will be regarded as a most valuable vindication of Storiot, whose account of your era has been generally thought exaggerated in its picture of the gloom and confusion of men's minds. That a period of transition like that should be full of excitement and agitation was indeed to be looked for; but seeing how plain was the tendency of the forces in operation, it was natural to believe that hope rather than fear would have been the prevailing temper of the popular mind."

"You have not yet told me what was the answer to the riddle which you found," I said. "I am impatient to know by what contradiction of natural sequence the peace and prosperity which you now seem to enjoy could have been the outcome of an era like my own."

"Excuse me," replied my host, "but do you smoke?" It was not till our cigars were lighted and drawing well that he resumed. "Since you are in the humor to talk rather than to sleep, as I certainly am, perhaps I cannot do better than to try to give you enough idea of our modern industrial system to dissipate at least the impression that there is any mystery about the process of its evolution. The Bostonians of your day had the reputation of being great askers of questions, and I am going to show my descent by asking you one to begin with. What should you name as the most prominent feature of the labor troubles of your day?"

"Why, the strikes, of course," I replied.

"Exactly. But what made the strikes so formidable?"

"The great labor organizations."

"And what was the motive of these great organizations?"

"The workmen claimed they had to organize to get their rights from the big corporations," I replied.

"That is just it," said Doctor Leete. "The organization of labor and the strikes were an effect, merely, of the concentration of capital in greater masses than had ever been known before. Before this concentration began, while as yet commerce and industry were conducted by innumerable petty concerns with small capital, instead of a small number of great concerns with vast capital, the individual workman was relatively important and independent in his relations to the employer. Moreover, when a little capital or a new idea was enough to start a man in business for himself, workingmen were constantly becoming employers and there was no hard and fast line between the two classes. Labor unions were needless then, and general strikes out of the question. But when the era of small concerns with small capital was succeeded by that of the great aggregations of capital, all this was changed. The individual laborer, who had been relatively important to the small employer, was reduced to insignificance and powerlessness against the great corporation, while at the same time the way upward to the grade of employer was closed to him. Self-defense drove him to union with his fellows.

"The records of the period show that the outcry against the concentration of capital was furious. Men believed that it threatened society with a form of tyranny more abhorrent than it had ever endured. They believed that the great corporations were preparing for them the yoke of a baser servitude than had ever been imposed on the race, servitude not to men but to soulless machines incapable of any motive but insatiable greed. Looking back, we cannot wonder at their desperation, for certainly humanity was never confronted with a fate more sordid and hideous than would have been the era of corporate tyranny which they anticipated.

"Meanwhile, without being in the smallest degree checked by the clamor against it, the absorption of business by ever-larger monopolies continued. In the United States there was not, after the beginning of the last quarter of the century, any opportunity whatever for individual enterprise in any important field of industry, unless backed by a great capital. During the last decade of the century, such small businesses as still remained were fast-failing survivals of a past epoch, or mere parasites on the great corporations, or else existed in fields too small to attract the great capitalists. Small businesses, as far as they still remained, were reduced to the condition of rats and mice, living in holes and corners, and counting on evading notice for the enjoyment of existence. The railroads had gone on combining till a few great syndicates controlled every rail in the land. In manufactories, every important staple was controlled by a syndicate. These syndicates, pools, trusts, or whatever their name, fixed prices and crushed all competition except when combinations as vast as themselves arose. Then a struggle, resulting in a still greater consolidation, ensued. The great city bazaar crushed its country rivals with branch stores, and in the city itself absorbed its smaller rivals till the business of a whole quarter was concentrated under one roof, with a hundred former proprietors of shops serving as clerks. Having no business of his own to put his money in, the small capitalist, at the same time that he took service under the corporation, found no other investment for his money but its stocks and bonds, thus becoming doubly dependent upon it.

"The fact that the desperate popular opposition to the consolidation of business in a few powerful hands had no effect to check it proves that there must have been a strong economical reason for it. The small capitalists, with their innumerable petty concerns, had in fact yielded the field to the great aggregations of capital, because they belonged to a day of small things and were totally incompetent to the demands of an age of steam and telegraphs and the gigantic scale of its enterprises. To restore the former order of things, even if possible, would have involved returning to the day of stagecoaches. Oppressive and intolerable as was the regime of the great consolidations of capital, even its victims, while they cursed it, were forced to admit the prodigious increase of efficiency which had been imparted to the national industries, the vast economies effected by concentration of management and unity of organization, and to confess that since the new system had taken the place of the old the wealth of the world had increased at a rate before undreamed of. To be sure this vast increase had gone chiefly to make the rich richer, increasing the gap between them and the poor; but the fact remained that, as a means merely of producing wealth, capital had been proved efficient in proportion to its consolidation. The restoration of the old system with the subdivision of capital, if it were possible, might indeed bring back a greater equality of conditions, with more individual dignity and freedom, but it would be at the price of general poverty and the arrest of material progress.

"Was there, then, no way of commanding the services of the mighty wealth-producing principle of consolidated capital without bowing down to a plutocracy like that of Carthage? As soon as men began to ask themselves these questions, they found the answer ready for them. The movement toward the conduct of business by larger and larger aggregations of capital, the tendency toward monopolies, which had been so desperately and vainly resisted, was recognized at last, in its true significance, as a process which only needed to complete its logical evolution to open a golden future to humanity.

"Early in the last century the evolution was completed by the final consolidation of the entire capital of the nation. The industry and commerce of the country, ceasing to be conducted by a set of irresponsible corporations and syndicates of private persons at their caprice and for their profit, were entrusted to a single syndicate representing the people, to be conducted in the common interest for the common profit. The nation, that is to say, organized as the one great business corporation in which all other corporations were absorbed; it became the one capitalist in the place of all other capitalists, the sole employer, the final monopoly in which all previous and lesser monopolies were swallowed up, a monopoly in the profits and economies of which all citizens shared. The epoch of trusts had ended in The Great Trust. In a word, the people of the United States concluded to assume the conduct of their own business, just as one hundred-odd years before they had assumed the conduct of their own government, organizing now for industrial purposes on precisely the same grounds that they had then organized for political purposes. At last, strangely late in the world's history, the obvious fact was perceived that no business is so essentially the public business as the industry and commerce on which the people's livelihood depends, and that to entrust it to private persons to be managed for private profit is a folly similar in kind, though vastly greater in magnitude, to that of surrendering the functions of political government to kings and nobles to be conducted for their personal glorification."

"Such a stupendous change as you describe," said I, "did not, of course, take place without great bloodshed and terrible convulsions."

"On the contrary," replied Doctor Leete, "there was absolutely no violence. The change had been long foreseen. Public opinion had become fully ripe for it, and the whole mass of the people was behind it. There was no more possibility of opposing it by force than by argument. On the other hand the popular sentiment toward the great corporations and those identified with them had ceased to be one of bitterness, as they came to realize their necessity as a link, a transition phase, in the evolution of the true industrial system. The most violent foes of the great private monopolies were now forced to recognize how invaluable and indispensable had been their office in educating the people up to the point of assuming control of their own business. Fifty years before, the consolidation of the industries of the country under national control would have seemed a very daring experiment to the most sanguine. But by a series of object lessons, seen and studied by all men, the great corporations had taught the people an entirely new set of ideas on this subject. They had seen for many years syndicates handling revenues greater than those of states, and directing the labors of hundreds of thousands of men with an efficiency and economy unattainable in smaller operations. It had come to be recognized as an axiom that the larger the business the simpler the principles that can be applied to it; that, as the machine is truer than the hand, so the system, which in a great concern does the work of the master's eye in a small business, turns out more accurate results. Thus it came about that, thanks to the corporations themselves, when it was proposed that the nation should assume their functions, the suggestion implied nothing which seemed impracticable even to the timid. To be sure, it was a step beyond any yet taken, a broader generalization, but the very fact that the nation would be the sole corporation in the field would, it was seen, relieve the undertaking of many difficulties with which the partial monopolies had contended."

* * * * * *

1.   *What did Bellamy regard as the most pressing social issue of his time? Why?*

2.   *How does Doctor Leete explain the transition to the new social system? How do you think this explanation might have contributed to the popularity of Bellamy's novel?*

20–2   E. L. Godkin, A Great National Disgrace, 1877

The great railroad strike of 1877 began in Martinsburg, West Virginia, when, in response to wage cuts made by the Baltimore & Ohio Railroad, workers refused to let any trains move. The strike quickly spread to Baltimore, Pittsburgh, St. Louis, and Chicago. In these and other cities, large crowds of railroad workers and their supporters poured into the streets, venting their rage against railroad barons and other large employers. Pitched battles resulted in deaths, injuries, and the destruction of railroad property. Order was finally restored only with the dispatching of federal troops to several cities. The summer's events showed the widening breach between labor and capital, and conservatives such as E. L. Godkin, editor of The Nation, *saw the strike as a threat to the foundation of American society.*

SOURCE: The Nation 25 (August 2, 1877), 68–69.

It is impossible to deny that the events of the last fortnight constitute a great national disgrace, and have created a profound sensation throughout the civilized world. They are likely to impress the foreign imagination far more than the outbreak of the Civil War, because the probability that the slavery controversy would end in civil war or the disruption of the Union had been long present to people's minds both at home and abroad.... There has for fifty years been throughout Christendom a growing faith that outside the area of slave-soil the United States had— of course with the help of great natural resources—solved the problem of enabling labor and capital to live together in political harmony, and that this was the one country in which there was no proletariat and no dangerous class, and in which the manners as well as legislation effectually prevented the formation of one. That the occurrences of the last fortnight will do and have done, much to shake or destroy this faith, and that whatever weakens it weakens also the fondly cherished hopes of many millions about the future of the race, there is unhappily little question. We have had what appears a widespread rising, not against political oppression or unpopular government, but against society itself. What is most curious about it is that it has probably taken people here nearly as much by surprise as people in Europe. The optimism in which most Americans are carefully trained, and which the experience of life justifies to the industrious, energetic, and provident, combined with the long-settled political habit of considering riotous poor as the products of a monarchy and aristocracy, and impossible in the absence of "down-trodden masses," has concealed from most of the well-to-do and intelligent classes of the population the profound changes which have during the last thirty years been wrought in the composition and character of the population, especially in the great cities. Vast additions have been made to it within that period, to whom American political and social ideals appeal but faintly, if at all, and who carry in their very blood traditions which give universal suffrage an air of menace to many of the things which civilized men hold dear. So complete has the illusion been that up to the day of the outbreak at Martinsburg thousands, even of the most reflective class, were gradually ridding themselves of the belief that force would be much longer necessary, or, indeed, was now necessary in the work of government....

The kindest thing which can be done for the great multitudes of untaught men who have been received on these shores, and are daily arriving, and who are torn perhaps even more here than in Europe by wild desires and wilder dreams, is to show them promptly that society as here organized, on individual freedom of thought and action, is impregnable, and can be no more shaken than the order of nature. The most cruel thing is to let them suppose, even for one week, that if they had only chosen their time better, or had been better led or better armed, they would have succeeded in forcing it to capitulate. In what way better provision, in the shape of public force, should be made for its defense we have no space left to discuss, but that it will not do to be caught again as the rising at Martinsburg caught us; that it would be fatal to private and public credit and security to allow a state of things to subsist in which 8,000 or 9,000 day laborers of the lowest class can suspend, even for a whole day, the traffic and industry of a great nation, merely as a means of extorting ten or twenty cents a day more wages from their employers, we presume everybody now sees. Means of prompt and effectual prevention—so plainly effectual that it will never need to be resorted to—must be provided, either by an increase of the standing army or some change in the organization of the militia which will improve its discipline and increase its mobility. There are, of course, other means of protection against labor risings than physical ones, which ought not to be neglected, though we doubt if they can be made to produce much effect on the present generation. The exercise of greater watchfulness over their tongues by philanthropists, in devising schemes of social improvement, and in affecting to treat all things as open to discussion, and every question as having two sides, for purposes of legislation as well as for purposes of speculation, is one of them. Some of the talk about the laborer and his rights that we have listened to on the platform and in literature during the last fifteen years, and of the capacity even of the most grossly ignorant, such as the South Carolina fieldhand, to reason upon and even manage the interests of a great community, has been enough, considering the sort of ears on which it now falls, to reduce our great manufacturing districts to the condition of the Pennsylvania mining regions, and put our very civilization in peril. Persons of humane tendencies ought to remember that we live in a world of stern realities, and that the blessings we enjoy have not been showered upon us like the rain from heaven. Our superiority to the Ashantees or the Kurds is not due to right thinking or right feeling only, but to the determined fight which the more enlightened part of the community has waged from generation to generation against the ignorance and brutality, now of one class and now of another. In trying to carry on the race to better things nobody is wholly right or wise. In all controversies there are wrongs on both sides, but most certainly the presumptions in the labor controversy have always been in favor of the sober, orderly, industrious, and prudent, who work and accumulate and bequeath. It is they who brought mankind out of the woods and caves, and keep them out, and all discussion which places them in a position of either moral or mental inferiority to those who contrive not only to own nothing, but to separate themselves from property holders in feeling or interest, is mischievous as well as foolish, for it strikes a blow at the features of human character which raise man above the beasts.

* * * * * *

1. *According to Godkin, why was the strike such a shock to both Americans and Europeans? How did it undermine the widespread belief in America's uniqueness?*

2. *What solutions does Godkin propose for preventing another such uprising? To whom does he address his ideas?*

20–3 Roscoe Conkling, Offense of the Spoils System, 1877

A longtime U.S. Senator from New York, Roscoe Conkling was a power in Republican Party circles in the years following the Civil War. He was an ardent defender of the politics of patronage, whereby the party in power was free to appoint its loyalists to positions in the government bureaucracy. Conkling, like most professional politicians of his day, believed that the bureaucracy could not be separated from partisan politics. Civil service reform of the federal government would greatly diminish the enormous personal power of men like Conkling. At a convention of the New York State Republican Party, Conkling attacked fellow Republican and civil service reformer George W. Curtis. This speech gives a good sense of the acrimonious rhetoric that characterized late nineteenth century politics.

SOURCE: A. R. Conkling, *The Life and Letters of Roscoe Conkling* (NY: 1889), pp. 538–541, 546–547.

…We are Republicans. We represent a great party. That party has a battle to fight just now in every county, district and town, and our duty is to Republicans and to their candidates in every locality and school district in the State. Administrations do not make parties. Parties make Administrations. Parties go before Administrations, and live after them. The people make parties. The people made the Republican party, and the people have upheld it in a career of usefulness and achievement such as no other party in history can boast.…

This is a State Convention. Its business is to nominate candidates for State officers, and to declare the principles on which these candidates shall stand and act if they are chosen. Its business is not to hinder, but to help, by the wisdom and harmony of its action, every candidate, not only in the State at large, but upon all tickets which are to run in all counties, towns and localities throughout the State.…I will not assume that any man has been entrusted to introduce matters foreign to our duties and calculated to foment discord among those of the same household of faith. I repel the idea that the national Administration suggests or sanctions any such proceeding. He who volunteers for such a purpose may be found wanting in the discretion of friendship, if not in its sincerity also.…

…To speak plainly, there are special reasons, just now, inviting the Convention to adhere calmly and firmly to its own sense of propriety and wisdom. The Republicans of this State have been summoned for weeks, with somewhat of menace and truculent dictation, to declare this and declare that, and broad hints have been given of retribution if they dare even to remain silent.…Americans, it seems, are now to be chastised for holding their peace. NOT YET. Exotic despotism, revised and improved, will not grow in American soil. It will perish. It would be trodden out, if it did not die out. Who are these oracular censors so busy of late in brandishing the rod over me and every other Republican in this State? Some man has said, "I am of age in the Republican party." So am I. For the last twenty-two years I have labored for it and stood by its flag; and never in twenty-two years have I been false to its principles, its cause, or its candidates. Who are these men who, in newspapers and elsewhere, are cracking their whips over Republicans and playing school-master to the Republican party and its conscience and convictions? They are of various sorts and conditions. Some of them are the non-milliners, the dilettanti and carpet knights of politics men whose efforts have been expended in denouncing and ridiculing and accusing honest men who, in storm and in sun, in war and peace, have clung to the Republican flag and defended it against those who have tried to trail and trample it in the dust. Some of them are men who, when they could work themselves into conventions, have attempted to belittle and befoul Republican administrations and to parade their own thin veneering of superior purity. Some of them are men who, by insisting that it is corrupt and bad for men in office to take part in politics, are striving now to prove that the Republican party has been unclean and vicious all its life, and that the last campaign was venal and wrong and fraudulent, not in some of the States, but in all the States, North and South. For it is no secret that in all States office-holders, in committees, in organizations and everywhere, did all that men could fairly do to uphold the candidates of our party, and that they were encouraged and urged to do so. Some of these worthies masquerade as reformers. Their vocation and ministry is to lament the sins of other people. Their stock in trade is rancid, canting self-righteousness. They are wolves in sheep's clothing. Their real object is office and plunder. When Dr. Johnson defined patriotism as the last refuge of a scoundrel, he was unconscious of the then undeveloped capabilities and uses of the word "Reform."...

...Some of those now laying down new and strange tenets for Republicans, sat but yesterday in Democratic Conventions, some have sought nominations at the hands of Democrats in recent years, and some, with the zeal of neophytes and bitterness of apostates, have done more than self-respecting Democrats would do to vilify and slander their Government and their countrymen. Grant, and all who stood by that upright, fearless magistrate, have been objects of the bitter, truthless aspersions of these men. And now, opposed or laggard in the battles of the past, they leap forward to the feast. They forget that parties are not built up by deportment, or by ladies' magazines, or gush. It used to be said of certain Democrats in Massachusetts that they wanted, by their obnoxious officiousness, to keep the party in that State as small as they could in order to make the stockholders as few and the dividends as large as possible. I hope these new-fledged dictators are not aiming at the same thing in New York. The grasshoppers in the corner of a fence, even without a newspaper to be heard in, sometimes make more noise than the flocks and herds that graze upon a thousand hills....

...Let us agree to put contentions aside and complete our task. Let us declare the purposes and methods which should guide the government of our great State. On this platform let us place upright, capable men, and then let us appeal to the people to decide whether such men shall conduct their affairs on such principles, or whether they would rather trust spurious reformers under the lead and dominion of our political opponents....

* * * * * *

1.   What principles, if any, does Conkling ascribe to Republicans?

2.   What metaphors and images does he use to ridicule reformers?

20–4   *Populist Party Platform, 1892*

The People's (Populist) Party was formally organized in 1892, holding its first national convention in Omaha. It expressed the political grievances of the nation's small producers, especially farmers, in the face of agricultural depression and the growing power of banks, railroads, and other large corporate interests. A direct outgrowth of the Farmers' Alliance of the 1880s, the Populist Party tried to unite farmers and workers in a new third party aimed at radically restructuring American society and politics. Its first presidential candidate, Gen. James B. Weaver, drew over a million votes in 1892, and Populists also won election to Congress and to state legislatures, especially in the west. The party declined rapidly by the late 1890s, but its platform contained many ideas that influenced twentieth century government policy and reform movements.

SOURCE: Commager, *Documents of American History*, pp. 143–146; *Proceedings of the Supreme Council of the National Farmers' Alliance and Industrial Union*, 1890, pp. 32–3.

Assembled upon the 116th anniversary of the Declaration of Independence, the People's Party of America, in their first national convention, invoking upon their action the blessing of Almighty God, put forth in the name and on behalf of the people of this country, the following preamble and declaration of principles:

PREAMBLE

The conditions which surround us best justify our co-operation; we meet in the midst of a nation brought to the verge of moral, political, and material ruin. Corruption dominates the ballot-box, the Legislatures, the Congress, and touches even the ermine of the bench. The people are demoralized; most of the States have been compelled to isolate the voters at the polling places to prevent universal intimidation and bribery. The newspapers are largely subsidized or muzzled, public opinion silenced, business prostrated, homes covered with mortgages, labor impoverished, and the land concentrating in the hands of capitalists. The urban workmen are denied the right to organize for self-protection, imported pauperized labor beats down their wages, a hireling standing army, unrecognized by our laws, is established to shoot them down, and they are rapidly degenerating into European conditions. The fruits of the toil of millions are boldly stolen to build up colossal fortunes for a few, unprecedented in the history of mankind; and the possessors of these, in turn, despise the Republic and endanger liberty. From the same prolific womb of governmental injustice we breed the two great classes—tramps and millionaires.

The national power to create money is appropriated to enrich bond-holders; a vast public debt payable in legal-tender currency has been funded into gold-bearing bonds, thereby adding millions to the burdens of the people.

Silver, which has been accepted as coin since the dawn of history, has been demonetized to add to the purchasing power of gold by decreasing the value of all forms of property as well as human labor, and the supply of currency is purposely abridged to fatten usurers, bankrupt enterprise, and enslave industry. A vast conspiracy against mankind has been organized on two continents, and it is rapidly taking possession of the world. If not met and overthrown at once it forebodes terrible social convulsions, the destruction of civilization, or the establishment of an absolute despotism.

We have witnessed for more than a quarter of a century the struggles of the two great political parties for power and plunder, while grievous wrongs have been inflicted upon the suffering people. We charge that the controlling influences dominating both these parties have permitted the existing dreadful conditions to develop without serious effort to prevent or restrain them. Neither do they now promise us any substantial reform. They have agreed together to ignore, in the coming campaign, every issue but one. They propose to drown the outcries of a plundered people in the uproar of a sham battle over the tariff, so that capitalists, corporations, national banks, rings, trusts, watered stock, the demonetization of silver and the oppressions of the usurers may all be lost sight of. They suppose to sacrifice our homes, lives, and children on the altar of mammon; to destroy of multitude in order to secure corruption funds from the millionaires.

Assembled on the anniversary of the birthday of the nation, and filled with the spirit of the grand general and chief who established our independence, we seek to restore government of the Republic to the hands of the "plain people," with which class it originated. We assert our purposes to be identical with the purposes of the National Constitution; to form a more perfect union and establish justice, insure domestic tranquillity, provide for the common defence, promote the general welfare, and secure the blessings of liberty for ourselves and our posterity.

We declare that this Republic can only endure as a free government while built upon love of the people for each other and the nation; that it cannot be pinned together by bayonets; that the Civil War is over and that every passion and resentment which grew out of it must die with it, and we must be in fact, as we are in name, united brotherhood of free men.

Our country finds itself confronted by conditions for which there is no precedent in the history of the world; our annual agricultural productions amount to billions of dollars in value, which must, within a few weeks or months, be exchanged for billions dollars' worth of commodities consumed in their production; the existing currency supply is wholly inadequate to make this change; the results are falling prices, the formation of combines and rings, the impoverishment of the producing class. We pledge ourselves, if given power, we will labor to correct these evils by wise and reasonable legislation, in accordance with the terms of our platform.

We believe that the power of government—in other words, of the people—should be expanded (as in the case of the postal service) as rapidly and as far as the good sense of an intelligent people and the teachings of experience shall justify, to the end that oppression, injustice, and poverty shall eventually cease in the land.

While our sympathies as a party of reform are naturally upon the side of every proposition which will tend to make men intelligent, virtuous, and temperate, we nevertheless regard these questions, important as they are, as secondary to the great issues now pressing for solution, and upon which not only our individual prosperity but the very existence of free institutions depend; and we ask all men to first help us to determine whether we are to have a republic to administer before we differ as to the conditions upon which it is to be administered, believing that the forces of reform this day organized will never cease to move forward until every wrong is righted and equal rights and equal privileges securely established for all the men and women of this country.

PLATFORM

We declare, therefore—

First.—That the union of the labor forces of the United States this day consummated shall be permanent and perpetual; may its spirit enter into all hearts for the salvation of the Republic and the uplifting of mankind.

Second.—Wealth belongs to him who creates it, and every dollar taken from industry without an equivalent is robbery. "If any will not work, neither shall he eat." The interests of rural and civil labor are the same; their enemies are identical.

Third.—We believe that the time has come when the railroad corporations will either own the people or the people must own the railroads; and should the government enter upon the work of owning and managing all railroads, we should favor an amendment to the constitution by which all persons engaged in the government service shall be placed under a civil-service regulation of the most rigid character, so as to prevent the increase of the power of the national administration by the use of such additional government employees.

FINANCE.—We demand a national currency, safe, sound, and flexible issued by the general government only, a full legal tender for all debts, public and private, and that without the use of banking corporations; a just, equitable, and efficient means of distribution direct to the people, at a tax not to exceed 2 per cent, per annum, to be provided as set forth in the sub-treasury plan of the Farmers' Alliance, or a better system; also by payments in discharge of its obligations for public improvements.

1. We demand free and unlimited coinage of silver and gold at the present legal ratio of 16 to 1.
2. We demand that the amount of circulating medium be speedily increased to not less than $50 per capita.
3. We demand a graduated income tax.
4. We believe that the money of the country should be kept as much as possible in the hands of the people, and hence we demand that all State and national revenues shall be limited to the necessary expenses of the government, economically and honestly administered.
5. We demand that postal savings banks be established by the government for the safe deposit of the earnings of the people and to facilitate exchange.

TRANSPORTATION.—Transportation being a means of exchange and a public necessity, the government should own and operate the railroads in the interest of the people. The telegraph and telephone, like the post-office system, being a necessity for the transmission of news, should be owned and operated by the government in the interest of the people.

LAND.—The land, including all the natural sources of wealth, is the heritage of the people, and should not be monopolized for speculative purposes, and alien ownership of land should be prohibited. All land now held by railroads and other corporations in excess of their actual needs, and all lands now owned by aliens should be reclaimed by the government and held for actual settlers only.

EXPRESSION OF SENTIMENTS

Your Committee on Platform and Resolutions beg leave unanimously to report the following:

Whereas, Other questions have been presented for our consideration, we hereby submit the following, not as a part of the Platform of the People's Party, but as resolutions expressive of the sentiment of this Convention.

1. RESOLVED, That we demand a free ballot and a fair count in all elections, and pledge ourselves to secure it to every legal voter without Federal intervention, through the adoption by the States of the unperverted Australian or secret ballot system.
2. RESOLVED, That the revenue derived from a graduated income tax should be applied to the reduction of the burden of taxation now levied upon the domestic industries of this country.
3. RESOLVED, That we pledge our support to fair and liberal pensions to ex-Union soldiers and sailors.
4. RESOLVED, That we condemn the fallacy of protecting American labor under the present system, which opens our ports to the pauper and criminal classes of the world and crowds out our wage-earners; and we denounce the present ineffective laws against contract labor, and demand the further restriction of undesirable emigration.
5. RESOLVED, That we cordially sympathize with the efforts of organized workingmen to shorten the hours of labor, and demand a rigid enforcement of the existing eight-hour law on Government work, and ask that a penalty clause be added to the said law.
6. RESOLVED, That we regard the maintenance of a large standing army of mercenaries, known as the Pinkerton system, as a menace to our liberties, and we demand its abolition; and we condemn the recent invasion of the Territory of Wyoming by the hired assassins of plutocracy, assisted by Federal officers.
7. RESOLVED, That we commend to the favorable

consideration of the people and the reform press the legislative system known as the initiative and referendum.

8.. RESOLVED, That we favor a constitutional provision limiting the office of President and Vice-President to one term, and providing for the election of Senators of the United States by a direct vote of the people.

9. RESOLVED, That we oppose any subsidy or national aid to any private corporation for any purpose.

10. RESOLVED, That this convention sympathizes with the Knights of Labor and their righteous contest with the tyrannical combine of clothing manufacturers of Rochester, and declares it to be a duty of all who hate tyranny and oppres-

sion to refuse to purchase the goods made by the said manufacturers, or to patronize any merchants who sell such goods.

* * * * * *

1. *How does the language of the Preamble work to make the Populist case?*

2. *What do the Populists see as the fundamental cause of the nation's ills?*

3. *What specific remedies do the Populists propose for the nation's problems?*

20–5   Elizabeth Cady Stanton, The Solitude of Self, 1890

Elizabeth Cady Stanton was among the most influential and determined voices for women's rights in the nation's history. She helped organize the world's first women's rights convention in 1848, the Seneca Falls convention, and she campaigned actively for the abolition of slavery. After the Civil War, Stanton tried unsuccessfully to link the enfranchisement of African-Americans to that of women. She also advocated liberalized divorce laws, reproductive rights, and greater sexual freedom for women. In 1890 she testified before a Senate Committee on women's suffrage, making an appeal for women's emancipation that went far beyond the right to vote.

SOURCE: U.S. Senate Committee on Woman Suffrage, February 20, 1892; in Mari Jo and Paul Buhle, *The Concise History of Woman Suffrage* (University of Illinois Press, 1978), pp. 325–327.

The point I wish plainly to bring before you on this occasion is the individuality of each human soul—our Protestant idea, the right of individual conscience and judgment—our republican idea, individual citizenship. In discussing the rights of woman, we are to consider, first, what belongs to her as an individual, in a world of her own, the arbiter of her own destiny, an imaginary Robinson Crusoe with her woman Friday on a solitary island. Her rights under such circumstances are to use all her faculties for her own safety and happiness.

Secondly, if we consider her as a citizen, as a member of a great nation, she must have the same rights as all other members, according to the fundamental principles of our Government.

Thirdly, viewed as a woman, an equal factor in civilization, her rights and duties are still the same—

individual happiness and development.

Fourthly, it is only the incidental relations of life, such as mother, wife, sister, daughter, which may involve some special duties and training. In the usual discussion in regard to woman's sphere, such men as Herbert Spencer, Frederick Harrison and Grant Allen uniformly subordinate her rights and duties as an individual, as a citizen, as a woman, to the necessities of these incidental relations, some of which a large class of women never assume. In discussing the sphere of man we do not decide his rights as an individual, as a citizen, as a man, by his duties as a father, a husband, a brother or a son, some of which he may never undertake. Moreover he would be better fitted for these very relations, and whatever special work he might choose to do to earn his bread, by the complete development of all his faculties as an individual. Just so with woman. The education which will fit her to discharge the duties in the largest sphere of human usefulness, will best fit her for whatever special work she may be compelled to do.

The isolation of every human soul and the necessity of self-dependence must give each individual, the right to choose his own surroundings. The strongest reason for giving woman all the opportunities for higher education, for the full development of her faculties, her forces of mind and body; for giving her the most enlarged freedom of thought and action; a complete emancipation from all forms of bondage, of custom, dependence, superstition; from all the crippling influences of fear—is the solitude and personal responsibility of her own individual life. The strongest reason why we ask for woman a voice in the government under which she lives; in the religion she is asked to believe; equality in social life, where she is the chief factor; a place in the trades and professions, where she may earn her bread, is because of her birthright to self-sovereignty; because, as an individual, she must rely on herself....

To throw obstacles in the way of a complete education is like putting out the eyes; to deny the rights of property is like cutting off the hands. To refuse political equality is to rob the ostracized of all self-respect, of credit in the market place, of recompense in the world of work, of a voice in choosing those who make and administer the law, a choice in the jury before whom they are tried, and in the judge who decides their punishment. Shakespeare's play of Titus and Andronicus contains a terrible satire on woman's position in the nineteenth century—"Rude men seized the king's daughter, cut out her tongue, cut off her hands, and then bade her go call for water and wash her hands." What a picture of woman's position! Robbed of her natural rights, handicapped by law and custom at every turn, yet compelled to fight her own battles, and in the emergencies of life to fall back on herself for protection.…

How the little courtesies of life on the surface of society, deemed so important from man towards woman, fade into utter insignificance in view of the deeper tragedies in which she must play her part alone, where no human aid is possible!

Nothing strengthens the judgment and quickens the conscience like individual responsibility. Nothing adds such dignity to character as the recognition of one's self-sovereignty; the right to an equal place, everywhere conceded—a place earned by personal merit, not an artificial attainment by inheritance, wealth, family and position. Conceding then that the responsibilities of life rest equally on man and woman, that their destiny is the same, they need the same preparation for time and eternity. The talk of sheltering woman from the fierce storms of life is the sheerest mockery, for they beat on her from every point of the compass, just as they do on man, and with more fatal results, for he has been trained to protect himself, to resist, to conquer.…

In music women speak again the language of Mendelssohn, Beethoven, Chopin, Schumann, and are worthy interpreters of their great thoughts. The poetry and novels of the century are theirs, and they have touched the keynote of reform in religion, politics and social life. They fill the editor's and professor's chair, plead at the bar of justice, walk the wards of the hospital, speak from the pulpit and the platform. Such is the type of womanhood that an enlightened public sentiment welcomes to-day, and such the triumph of the facts of life over the false theories of the past.

Is it, then, consistent to hold the developed woman of this day within the same narrow political limits as the dame with the spinning wheel and knitting needle occupied in the past? No, no! Machinery has taken the labors of woman as well as man on its tireless shoulders; the loom and the spinning wheel are but dreams of the past; the pen, the brush, the easel, the chisel, have taken their places, while the hopes and ambition of women are essentially changed.

We see reason sufficient in the outer conditions of human beings for individual liberty and development, but when we consider the self-dependence of every human soul, we see the need of courage, judgment and the exercise of every faculty of mind and body, strengthened and developed by use, in woman as well as man.…

* * * * * *

1.   How does Stanton use the ideology of individualism to make her argument? Why do you think she invokes the heritage of Protestantism?

2.   What are the implications here for women's rights beyond the right to vote?

20–6   *Pullman Strikers' Statement, 1894*

George Pullman, inventor of the railroad sleeping car, built the company town of Pullman, Illinois, as a site for manufacturing his cars. In response to the economic depression that began in 1893, Pullman fired one-third of his workers and reduced the wages of those who remained by up to 50 percent. But he would not cut the rents or the price of food in the company town. Pullman employees went on strike in June 1894, and they were soon joined by 20,000 members of the American Railway Union, led by Eugene V. Debs. The strikers refused to handle any railroad trains that used Pullman cars, and they succeeded in tying up the nation's railroad system. President Grover Cleveland used court injunctions to arrest union leaders and army troops to break the strike, demonstrating the power of the federal government to suppress organized labor.

SOURCE: U.S. Congress, House, U.S. Strike Commission, *Report on the Chicago Strike of June-July, 1894* (U.S. Government Printing Office, 1895).

Mr. President and Brothers of the American Railway Union: We struck at Pullman because we were without hope. We joined the American Railway Union because it gave us a glimmer of hope. Twenty thousand souls, men, women, and little ones, have their eyes turned toward this convention today, straining eagerly through dark despondency for a glimmer of the heaven-sent message you alone can give us on this earth.

In stating to this body our grievances it is hard to tell where to begin. You all must know that the proximate cause of our strike was the discharge of two members of our grievance committee the day after George M. Pullman, himself, and Thomas H. Wickes, his second vice-president, had guaranteed them absolute immunity. The more remote causes are still imminent. Five reductions in wages, in work, and in conditions of employment swept through the shops at Pullman between May and December, 1893. The last was the most severe, amounting to nearly thirty per cent, and our rents had not fallen. We owed Pullman $70,000 when we struck May 11. We owe him twice as much today. He does not evict us for two reasons: One, the force of popular sentiment and public opinion; the other because he hopes to starve us out, to break through in the back of the American Railway Union, and to deduct from our miserable wages when we are forced to return to him the last dollar we owe him for the occupancy of his houses.

Rents all over the city in every quarter of its vast extent have fallen, in some cases to one-half. Residences, compared with which ours are hovels, can be had a few miles away at the price we have been contributing to make a millionaire a billionaire. What we pay $15 for in Pullman is leased for $8 in Roseland; and remember that just as no man or woman of our 4,000 toilers has ever felt the friendly pressure of George M. Pullman's hand, so no man or woman of us all has ever owned or can ever hope to own one inch of George M. Pullman's land. Why, even the very streets are his. His ground has never been platted of record, and today he may debar any man who has acquiring rights as his tenant from walking in his high-ways. And those streets; do you know what he has named them? He says after the four great inventors in methods of transportation. And do you know what their names are? Why, Fulton, Stephenson, Watt, and Pullman.

Water which Pullman buys from the city at 8 cents a thousand gallons he retails to us at 500 per cent advance and claims he is losing $400 a month on it. Gas which sells at 75 cents per thousand feet in Hyde Park, just north of us, he sells for $2.25. When we went to tell him our grievances he said we were all his "children."

Pullman, both the man and the town, is an ulcer on the body politic. He owns the houses, the schoolhouses, and churches of God in the town he gave his once humble name. The revenue he derives from these, the wages he pays out with one hand—the Pullman Palace Car Company, he takes back with the other—the Pullman Land Association. He is able by this to bid under any contract car shop in this country. His competitors in business, to meet this, must reduce the wages of their men. This gives him the excuse to reduce ours to conform to the market. His business rivals must in turn scale down; so must he. And thus the merry war—the dance of skeletons bathed in human tears—goes on, and it will go on, brothers, forever, unless you, the American Railway Union, stop it; end it; crush it out.

* * * * * *

1. *How did the company town exert control over its employees?*

2. *What were the specific grievances of the strikers?*

20–7   Alfred T. Mahan, *The Influence of Sea Power, 1890*

The historian and naval strategist Alfred T. Mahan believed that the ability to control the sea was the key factor in shaping history. His 1890 book, The Influence of Sea Power Upon History, *was perhaps the single most influential work on the foreign policy and military strategy of his time. Mahan's friends included such powerful political figures as William McKinley and Theodore Roosevelt. His works helped justify and shape the key foreign policy decisions of the era: expansion of the nation's navy, with a new emphasis on battleships; taking possession of Caribbean and Pacific islands; and building the Panama Canal.*

SOURCE: William A. Williams, ed., *The Shaping of American Dipomacy*, Vol. I (1956).

…The conditions which now constitute the political situation of the United States, relatively to the world at large, are fundamentally different from those that obtained at the beginning of the century. It is not a mere question of greater growth, of bigger size. It is not only that we are larger, stronger, have, as it were, reached our majority, and are able to go out into the world. That alone would be a difference of degree, not of kind. The great difference between the past and the present is that we then, as regards close contact with the power of the chief nations of the world, were really in a state of political isolation which no longer exists.…

It is important to recognize this, for it will help clear away the error from a somewhat misleading statement frequently made,—that the United States needs a navy for defence only, adding often, explanatorily, for the defence of our own coasts. Now in a certain sense we all want a navy for defence only. It is to be hoped that the United States will never seek war except for the defence of her rights, her obligations, or her necessary interests. In that sense our policy may always be defensive only, although it may compel us at times to steps justified rather by expediency—the choice of the lesser evil—than by incontrovertible right. But if we have interests beyond sea which a navy may have to protect, it plainly follows that the navy has more to do, even in war, than to defend the coast; and it must be added as a received military axiom that war, however defensive in moral character, must be waged aggressively if it is to hope for success....

Like each man and woman, no state lives to itself alone, in a political seclusion resembling the physical isolation which so long was the ideal of China and Japan. All, whether they will or no, are members of a community, larger or smaller; and more and more those of the European family to which we racially belong are touching each other throughout the world, with consequent friction of varying degree. That the greater rapidity of communication afforded by steam has wrought, in the influence of sea power over the face of the globe, an extension that is multiplying the points of contact and emphasizing the importance of navies, is a fact, the intelligent appreciation of which is daily more and more manifest in the periodical literature of Europe, and is further shown by the growing stress laid upon that arm of military strength by foreign governments; while the mutual preparation of the armies on the European continent, and the fairly settled territorial conditions, make each state yearly more wary of initiating a contest, and thus entail a political quiescence there, except in the internal affairs of each country. The field of external action for the great European states is now the world, and it is hardly doubtful that their struggles, unaccompanied as yet by actual clash of arms, are even under that condition drawing nearer to ourselves. Coincidently with our own extension to the Pacific Ocean, which for so long had a good international claim to its name, that sea has become more and more the scene of political development, of commercial activities and rivalries, in which all the great powers, ourselves included, have a share. Through these causes Central and Caribbean America, now intrinsically unimportant, are brought in turn into great prominence, as constituting the gateway between the Atlantic and Pacific when the Isthmian canal shall have been made, and as guarding the approaches to it. The appearance of Japan as a strong ambitious state, resting on solid political and military foundations, but which scarcely has reached yet a condition of equilibrium in international standing, has fairly startled the world; and it is a striking illustration of the somewhat sudden nearness and unforeseen relations into which modern states are brought,

that the Hawaiian Islands, so interesting from the international point of view to the countries of European civilization, are occupied largely by Japanese and Chinese.

In all these questions we have a stake, reluctantly it may be, but necessarily, for our evident interests are involved, in some instances directly, in others by very probable implication. Under existing conditions, the opinion that we can keep clear indefinitely of embarrassing problems is hardly tenable; while war between two foreign states, which in the uncertainties of the international situation throughout the world may break out at any time, will increase greatly the occasions of possible collision with the belligerent countries, and the consequent perplexities of our statesmen seeking to avoid entanglement and to maintain neutrality....

It is because so much of the world still remains in the possession of the savage, or of states whose imperfect development, political or economical, does not enable them to realize for the general use nearly the result of which the territory is capable, while at the same time the redundant energies of civilized states, both government and peoples, are finding lack of openings and scantiness of livelihood at home, that there now obtains a condition of aggressive restlessness with which all have to reckon.

That the United States does not now share this tendency is entirely evident. Neither her government nor her people are affected by it to any great extent. But the force of circumstances has imposed upon her the necessity, recognized with practical unanimity by her people, of insuring to the weaker states of America, although of racial and political antecedents different from her own, freedom to develop politically along their own lines and according to their own capacities, without interference in that respect from governments foreign to these continents. The duty is self-assumed; and resting, as it does, not upon political philanthropy, but simply upon our own proximate interests as affected by such foreign interference, has towards others rather the nature of a right than a duty. But, from either point of view, the facility with which the claim has been allowed heretofore by the great powers has been due partly to the lack of pressing importance in the questions that have arisen, and partly to the great latent strength of our nation.

...But while our claim thus far has received a tacit acquiescence, it remains to be seen whether it will continue to command the same if the states whose political freedom of action we assert make no more decided advance towards political stability than several of them have done yet, and if our own organized naval force remains as slender, comparatively, as it once was, and even yet is. It is probably safe to say that an undertaking like that of Great Britain in Egypt, if attempted in this hemisphere by a non-American state, would not be tolerated by us if able to prevent it; but it is conceivable that the moral force of our contention might be weakened, in the view of an opponent, by attendant circumstances, in which case our physical power to support it should be open to no doubt.

That we shall seek to secure the peaceable solution of each difficulty as it arises is attested by our whole history, and by the disposition of our people; but to do so whatever the steps taken in any particular case, will bring us into new political relations and may entail serious disputes with other states....A navy, therefore, whose primary sphere of action is war, is, in the last analysis and from the least misleading point of view, a political factor of the utmost importance in international affairs, one more often deterrent than irritant. It is in that light, according to the conditions of the age and of the nation, that it asks and deserves the appreciation of the state, and that it should be developed in proportion to the reasonable possibilities of the political future.

* * * * * *

1.   *According to Mahan, what world changes have occurred that require the United States to re-think its traditional naval strategy?*

2.   *How does Mahan justify the right of the United States to intervene in the affairs of the "weaker states of America"?*

3.   *How does Mahan invoke racial differences to support his arguments?*

20–8   *Frederick Jackson Turner, The Significance of the Frontier in American History, 1893*

Frederick Jackson Turner first presented this essay to a group of historians meeting at the Chicago World Colombian Exposition in 1893. Turner's claim that the frontier held the key to understanding the nation's past revolutionized the scholarly study of American history. His ideas also made a deep impact upon the political debates of the 1890s, particularly those involving foreign policy. Turner's interpretation of the American past was rooted in his own middle-west experiences, and a kind of intellectual declaration of independence from east coast and European influence.

SOURCE: Frederick Jackson Turner, "The Significance of the Frontier in American History," 1893.

IN A RECENT bulletin of the superintendent of the census for 1890 appear these significant words: "Up to and including 1880 the country had a frontier of settlement, but at present the unsettled area has been so broken into by isolated bodies of settlement that there can hardly be said to be a frontier line. In the discussion of its extent, its westward movement, etc., it cannot, therefore, any longer have a place in the census reports." This brief official statement marks the closing of a great historic movement. Up to our own day American history has been in a large degree the history of the colonization of the Great West. The existence of an area of free land, its continuous recession, and the advance of American settlement westward explain American development.

Behind institutions, behind constitutional forms and modifications, lie the vital forces that call these organs into life and shape them to meet changing conditions. The peculiarity of American institutions is the fact that they have been compelled to adapt themselves to the changes of an expanding people—to the changes involved in crossing a continent, in winning a wilderness, and in developing at each area of this progress out of the primitive economic and political conditions of the frontier the complexity of city life. Said Calhoun in 1817, "We are great and rapidly—I was about to say fearfully—growing!" So saying, he touched the distinguishing feature of American life. All peoples show development: the germ theory of politics has been sufficiently emphasized. In the case of most nations, however, the development has occurred in a limited area; and if the nation has expanded, it has met other growing people whom it has conquered. But in the case of the United States we have different phenomenon. Limiting our attention to the Atlantic coast, we have the familiar phenomenon of the evolution of institutions in a limited area, such as the rise of representative government; the differentiation of simple colonial governments into complex organs; the progress from primitive industrial society, without division of labor, up to manufacturing civilization. But we have in addition to this *a recurrence of the process of evolution in each Western area reached in the process of expansion.* Thus American development has exhibited not merely advance along a single line but a return to primitive conditions on a continually advancing frontier line, and a new development for that area. American social development has been continually beginning over again on the frontier. This perennial rebirth, this fluidity of American life, this expansion westward with its new opportunities, its continuous touch with the simplicity of primitive society, furnish the forces dominating American character. The true point of view in the history of this nation is not the Atlantic coast, it is the Great West. Even the slavery struggle, which is made exclusive an object of attention by writers like Professor von Holst occupies its important place in American history because of its relation to westward expansion.

In this advance the frontier is the outer edge of the wave—the meeting point between savagery and civilization. Much has been written about the frontier from the point of view of border warfare and the chase, but as a field for the serious study of the economist and the historian it has been neglected.

What is the [American] frontier? It is not the European frontier—a fortified boundary line running through dense populations. The most significant thing about it is that it lies at the hither edge of free land. In the census reports it is treated as the margin of that settlement which has a density of two or more to the square mile. The term is an elastic one, and for our purpose does not need sharp definition. We shall consider the whole frontier belt, including the Indian country and the outer margin of the "settled area" of the census reports. This paper will make no attempt to treat the subject exhaustively; its aim is simply to call attention to the frontier as a fertile field for investigation, and to suggest some of the problems which arise in connection with it.

In the settlement of America we have to observe how European life entered the continent, and how America modified and developed that life, and reacted on Europe. Our early history is the study of European germs' developing in an American environment. Too exclusive attention has been paid by institutional students to the Germanic origins, too little to the American factors. The frontier is the line of most rapid and effective Americanization. The wilderness masters the colonist. It finds him a European in dress, industries, tools, modes of travel, and thought. It takes him from the railroad car and puts him in the birch canoe. It strips off the garments of civilization, and arrays him in the hunting shirt and the moccasin. It puts him in the log cabin of the Cherokee and the Iroquois, and runs an Indian palisade around him. Before long he has gone to planting Indian corn and plowing with a sharp stick; he shouts the war cry and takes the scalp in orthodox Indian fashion. In short, at the frontier the environment is at first too strong for the man. He must accept the conditions which it furnishes, or perish, and so he fits himself into the Indian clearings and follows the Indian trails.

Little by little he transforms the wilderness, but the outcome is not the old Europe, not simply the development of Germanic germs, any more than the first phenomenon was a case of reversion to the Germanic mark. The fact is that here is a new product that is American. At first the frontier was the Atlantic coast. It was the frontier of Europe in a very real sense. Moving westward, the frontier became more and more American. *As successive terminal moraines result from successive glaciations, so each frontier leaves its traces behind it, and when it becomes a settled area the region still partakes of the frontier characteristics.* Thus the advance of the frontier has meant a steady movement away from the influence of Europe, a steady growth of independence on American lines. And to study this advance, the men who grew up under these conditions, and the political, economic, and social results of it, is to study the really American part of our history.…

GROWTH OF DEMOCRACY

But the most important effect of the frontier has been in the promotion of democracy here and in Europe. As has been pointed out, the frontier is productive of individualism. Complex society is precipitated by the wilderness into a kind of primitive organization based on the family. The tendency is anti-social. It produces antipathy to control, and particularly to any direct control. The tax-gatherer is viewed as a representative of oppression. Professor Osgood, in an able article, has pointed out that the frontier conditions prevalent in the colonies are important factors in the explanation of the American Revolution, where individual liberty was sometimes confused with absence of all effective government. The same conditions aid in explaining the difficulty of instituting a strong government in the period of the confederacy. The frontier individualism has from the beginning promoted democracy.

The frontier states that came into the Union in the first quarter of a century of its existence came in with democratic suffrage provisions, and had reactive effects of the highest importance upon the older states whose peoples were being attracted there. It was *western* New York that forced an extension of suffrage in the constitutional convention of that state in 1821; and it was *western* Virginia that compelled the tidewater region to put a more liberal suffrage provision in the constitution framed in 1830, and to give to the frontier region a more nearly proportionate representation with the tidewater aristocracy. The rise of democracy as an effective force in the nation came in with Western preponderance under Jackson and William Henry Harrison, and it meant the triumph of the frontier—with all of its good and with all of its evil elements.

An interesting illustration of the tone of frontier democracy in 1830 comes from the debates in the Virginia convention already referred to. A representative from western Virginia declared: "But, sir, it is not the increase of population in the West which this gentlemen ought to fear. It is the energy which the mountain breeze and western habits impart to those emigrants. They are regenerated, politically I mean, sir. They soon become *working politicians;* and the difference, sir, between a *talking* and a *working* politician is immense. The Old Dominion has long been celebrated for producing great orators; the ablest metaphysicians in policy; men that can split hairs in all abstruse questions of political economy. But at home, or when they return from congress, they have negroes to fan them asleep. But a Pennsylvania, a New York, an Ohio, or a western Virginia statesman, though far inferior in logic, metaphysics and rhetoric to an old Virginia statesman, has this advantage, that when he returns home he takes off his coat and takes hold of the plough. This gives him bone and muscle, sir, and preserves his republican principles pure and uncontaminated."

So long as free land exists, the opportunity for a competency exists, and economic power secures political power. But the democracy born of free land, strong in selfishness and individualism, intolerant of administrative experience and education, and pressing individual liberty beyond its proper bounds, has its dangers as well as its benefits. Individualism in America has allowed a laxity in regard to governmental affairs which has rendered possible the spoils system and all the manifest evils that follow from the lack of a highly developed civic spirit. In this connection may be noted also the influence of frontier conditions in permitting business honor, inflated paper currency, and wildcat banking. The colonial and Revolutionary frontier was the region whence emanated many of the worst forms of an evil currency. The West in the War of 1812 repeated the phenomenon on the frontier of that day, while the speculation and wildcat banking of

the period of the crisis of 1837 occurred on the new frontier belt of the next tier of states. Thus each one of the periods of lax financial integrity coincides with periods when a new set of frontier communities had arisen, and coincides in area with the successive frontiers, for the most part. The recent Populist agitation is a case in point. Many a state that now declines any connection with the tenets of the Populists itself adhered to such ideas in an earlier stage of the development of the state. A primitive society can hardly be expected to show the intelligent appreciation of the complexity of business interests in a developed society. The continual recurrence of these areas of paper-money agitation is another evidence that the frontier can be isolated and studied as a factor in American history of the highest importance.

* * * * * *

1. *How does Turner define the American frontier? According to Turner, does it still exist?*

2. *How might Turner's arguments be used in the political debates of the 1890s?*

3. *What has been the frontier's most important effect? What is its relation to "democracy" and "individualism"?*

20–9   *Theodore Roosevelt, The Strenuous Life, 1899*

Theodore Roosevelt first won national attention when he led a troop of volunteers, known as the Rough Riders, into battle in Cuba during the Spanish–American War. More than a politician, Roosevelt also became well known as an historian, essayist, naturalist, and moralist. This speech, delivered in Chicago just after he took office as governor of New York, was widely reprinted. It was one of the most forceful and popular expressions of America's imperial role in the world.

SOURCE: *The Works of Theodore Roosevelt* (National Edition), Vol. XIII (1926).

In speaking to you, men of the greatest city of the West, men of the state which gave to the country Lincoln and Grant, men who preeminently and distinctly embody all that is most American in the American character, I wish to preach not the doctrine of ignoble ease but the doctrine of the strenuous life; the life of toil and effort; of labor and strife; to preach that highest form of success which comes

not to the man who desires mere easy peace but to the man who does not shrink from danger, from hardship, or from bitter toil, and who out of these wins the splendid ultimate triumph....

As it is with the individual so it is with the nation. It is a base untruth to say that happy is the nation that has no history. Thrice happy is the nation that has a glorious history. Far better it is to dare mighty things, to win glorious triumphs, even though checkered by failure, than to take rank with those poor spirits who neither enjoy much nor suffer much because they live in the gray twilight that knows neither victory nor defeat. If in 1861 the men who loved the Union had believed that peace was the end of all things and war and strife a worst of all things, and had acted up to their belief, we would have saved hundreds of thousands of lives, we would have saved hundreds of millions of dollars. Moreover, besides saving all the blood and treasure we then lavished, we would have prevented the heartbreak of many women, the dissolution of many homes; and we would have spared the country those months of gloom and shame when it seemed as if our armies marched only to defeat. We would have avoided all this suffering simply by shrinking from strife. And if we had thus avoided it we would have shown that we were weaklings and that we were unfit to stand among the great nations of the earth. Thank God for the iron in the blood of our fathers, the men who upheld the wisdom of Lincoln and bore sword or rifle in the armies of Grant! Let us, the children of the men who proved themselves equal to the mighty days—let us, the children of the men who carried the great Civil War to a triumphant conclusion, praise the God of our fathers that the ignoble counsels of peace were rejected, that the suffering and loss, the blackness of sorrow and despair, were unflinchingly faced and the years of strife endured; for in the end the slave was freed, the Union restored, and the mighty American Republic placed once more as a helmeted queen among nations.

We of this generation do not have to face a task such as that our fathers faced, but we have our tasks, and woe to us if we fail to perform them! We cannot, if we would, play the part of China, and be content to rot by inches in ignoble ease within our borders, taking no interest in what goes on beyond them; sunk in a scrambling commercialism; heedless of the higher life, the life of aspiration, of toil and risk; busying ourselves only with the wants of our bodies for the day; until suddenly we should find beyond a shadow of question, what China has already found, that in this world the nation that has trained itself to a career of unwarlike and isolated ease is bound in the end to go down before other nations which have not lost the manly and adventurous qualities. If we are to be a really great people, we must strive in good faith to play a great part in the world. We cannot avoid meeting great issues. All that we can determine for ourselves is whether we shall meet them well or ill. Last year we could not help being brought face to face with the problem of war with Spain. All we could decide was whether we should shrink like cowards from the contest or enter into it as beseemed a brave and high-spirited people; and, once in, whether failure or success should crown our banners. So it is now. We cannot avoid the responsibilities that confront us in Hawaii, Cuba, Puerto Rico, and the Philippines. All we can decide is whether we shall meet them in a way that will redound to the national credit, or whether we shall make of our dealings with these new problems a dark and shameful page in our history. To refuse to deal with them at all merely amounts to dealing with them badly. We have a given problem to solve. If we undertake the solution there is, of course, always danger that we may not solve it aright, but to refuse to undertake the solution simply renders it certain that we cannot possibly solve it aright.

The timid man, the lazy man, the man who distrusts his country, the overcivilized man, who has lost the great fighting, masterful virtues, the ignorant man and the man of dull mind, whose soul is incapable of feeling the mighty lift that thrills "stern men with empires in their brains"—all these, of course, shrink from seeing the nation undertake its new duties; shrink from seeing us build a navy and army adequate to our needs; shrink from seeing us do our share of the world's work by bringing order out of chaos in the great, fair tropic islands from which the valor of our soldiers and sailors has driven the Spanish flag. These are the men who fear the strenuous life, who fear the only national life which is really worth leading....

I preach to you, then, my countrymen, that our country calls not for the life of ease, but for the life of strenuous endeavor. The twentieth century looms before us big with the fate of many nations. If we stand idly by, if we seek merely swollen, slothful ease, and ignoble peace, if we shrink from the hard contests where men must win at hazard of their lives and at the risk of all they hold dear, then the bolder and stronger peoples will pass us by and will win for themselves the domination of the world. Let us therefore boldly face the life of strife, resolute to do our duty well and manfully; resolute to uphold righteousness by deed and by word; resolute to be both honest and brave, to serve high ideals, yet to use practical methods. Above all, let us shrink from no strife, moral or physical, within or without the nation, provided we are certain that the strife is justified; for it is only through strife, through hard and dangerous endeavor, that we shall ultimately win the goal of true national greatness.

* * * * * *

1.   *How does Roosevelt combine his personal views on the importance of physical exertion with his vision of America's place in the world?*

2.   *How does Roosevelt invoke American history to support his doctrine of "the strenuous life"?*

3.   *What distinction does he make between civilized and "overcivilized"?*

20–10   George F. Hoar, Against Imperialism, 1902

As part of the peace treaty ending the Spanish–American War, Spain ceded to the United States the Philippines, Puerto Rico, and Guam. A national debate ensued between imperialists, who favored the acquisition of these overseas territories, and anti-imperialists, who opposed it. The issue of the Philippines proved the most contentious. In 1899, Emilio Aguinaldo called upon Filipinos to declare their independence, and he led an armed insurrection against U.S. annexation. Over 70,000 U.S. troops were sent to put down the revolt, and fighting continued until 1902. Senator George F. Hoar, Republican of Massachusetts, was one of the staunchest opponents of imperialism. He gave the following speech on the Senate floor in 1902.

SOURCE: Congressional Record, 57th Congress, 1st Session, (1902).

Gentlemen talk about sentimentalities, about idealism. They like practical statesmanship better. But, Mr. President, this whole debate for the last four years has been a debate between two kinds of sentimentality. There has been practical statesmanship in plenty on both sides. Your side have carried their sentimentalities and ideals out in your practical statesmanship. The other side have tried and begged to be allowed to carry theirs out in practical statesmanship also. On one side have been sentimentalities. They were the ideals of the fathers of the revolutionary time, and from their day down till the day of Abraham Lincoln and Charles Sumner was over. The sentimentalities were that all men in political right were created equal; that governments derive their just powers from the consent of the governed, and are instituted to secure that equality; that every people—not every scattering neighborhood or settlement without organic life, not every portion of a people who may be temporarily discontented, but the political being that we call a people— has the right to institute a government for itself and to lay its foundation on such principles and organize its powers in such form as to it and not to any other people shall seem most likely to effect its safety and happiness. Now, a good deal of practical statesmanship has followed from these ideals and sentimentalities. They have built forty-five states on firm foundations. They have covered South America with republics. They have kept despotism out of the Western Hemisphere. They have made the United States the freest, strongest, richest of the nations of the world. They have made the word "republic" a name to conjure by the round world over. By their virtue the American flag—beautiful as a flower to those who love

it; terrible as a meteor to those who hate it—floats everywhere over peaceful seas, and is welcomed everywhere in friendly ports as the emblem of peaceful supremacy and sovereignty in the commerce of the world....

You also, my imperialistic friends, have had your ideals and your sentimentalities. One is that the flag shall never be hauled down where it has once floated. Another is that you will not talk or reason with a people with arms in their hands. Another is that sovereignty over an unwilling people may be bought with gold. And another is that sovereignty may be got by force of arms, as the booty of battle or the spoils of victory.

What has been the practical statesmanship which comes from your ideals and your sentimentalities? You have wasted six hundred millions of treasure. You have sacrificed nearly ten thousand American lives—the flower of our youth. You have devastated provinces. You have slain uncounted thousands of the people you desire to benefit. You have established reconcentration camps. Your generals are coming home from their harvest, bringing their sheaves with them, in the shape of other thousands of sick and wounded and insane to drag out their miserable lives, wrecked in body and mind. You make the American flag in the eyes of a numerous people the emblem of sacrilege in Christian churches, and of the burning of human dwellings, and of the horror of the water torture....

Your practical statesmanship has succeeded in converting a people who three years ago were ready to kiss the hem of the garment of the American and to welcome him as a liberator, who thronged after your men when they landed on those islands with benediction and gratitude, into sullen and irreconcilable enemies, possessed of a hatred which centuries cannot eradicate....

I have sometimes fancied that we might erect here in the capital of the country a column to American Liberty which alone might rival in height the beautiful and simple shaft which we have erected to the fame of the Father of the Country. I can fancy each generation bringing its inscription, which should recite its own contribution to the great structure of which the column should be but the symbol.

The generation of the Puritan and the Pilgrim and the Huguenot claims the place of honor at the base. "I brought the torch of Freedom across the sea. I cleared the forest. I subdued the savage and the wild beast. I laid in Christian liberty and law the foundations of empire."

The next generation says: "What my fathers founded I builded. I left the seashore to penetrate the wilderness. I planted schools and colleges and courts and churches."

Then comes the generation of the great colonial day: "I stood by the side of England on many a hard-fought field. I helped humble the power of France. I saw the lilies go clown before the lion at Louisburg and Quebec. I carried the cross of St. George in triumph in Martinique and the Havana. I knew the stormy pathways of the ocean. I followed the whale from the Arctic to the Antarctic seas, among tumbling mountains of ice and under equinoctial heat, as the great English orator said, 'No sea not vexed by my fisheries; no climate not witness to my toils.'"

Then comes the generation of the revolutionary time: "I encountered the power of England. I declared and won the independence of my country. I placed that declaration on the eternal principles of justice and righteousness which all mankind have read, and on which all mankind will one day stand. I affirmed the dignity of human nature and the right of the people to govern themselves. I devised the securities against popular haste and delusion which made that right secure. I created the supreme court and the Senate. For the first time in history I made the fight of the people to govern themselves safe, and established institutions for that end which will endure forever."

The next generation says: "I encountered England again. I vindicated the fight of an American ship to sail the seas the wide world over without molestation. I made the American sailor as safe at the ends of the earth as my fathers had made the American farmer safe in his home. I proclaimed the Monroe Doctrine in the face of the Holy Alliance, under which sixteen republics have joined the family of nations. I filled the Western Hemisphere with republics from the Lakes to Cape Horn, each controlling its own destiny in safety and in honor."

Then comes the next generation: "I did the mighty deeds which in your younger years you saw and which your fathers told. I saved the Union. I put down the rebellion. I freed the slave. I made of every slave a freeman, and of every freeman a citizen, and of every citizen a voter."

Then comes another who did the great work in peace, in which so many of you had an honorable share: "I kept the faith. I paid the debt. I brought in conciliation and peace instead of war. I secured in the practice of nations the great doctrine of expatriation. I devised the homestead system. I covered the prairie and the plain with happy homes and with mighty states. I crossed the continent and joined together the seas with my great railroads. I declared the manufacturing independence of America,

as my fathers affirmed its political independence. I built up our vast domestic commerce. I made my country the richest, freest, strongest, happiest people on the face of the earth."

And now what have we to say? What have we to say? Are we to have a place in that honorable company? Must we engrave on that column: "We repealed the Declaration of Independence. We changed the Monroe Doctrine from a doctrine of eternal righteousness and justice, resting on the consent of the governed, to a doctrine of brutal selfishness, looking only to our own advantage. We crushed the only republic in Asia. We made war on the only Christian people in the East. We converted a war of glory to a war of shame. We vulgarized the American flag. We introduced perfidy into the practice of war. We inflicted torture on unarmed men to extort confession. We put children to death. We devastated provinces. We baffled the aspirations of a people for liberty."

No, Mr. President. Never! Never! Other and better counsels will yet prevail. The hours are long in the life of a great people. The irrevocable step is not yet taken.

Let us at least have this to say: "We, too, have kept the faith of the fathers. We took Cuba by the hand. We delivered her from her age-long bondage. We welcomed her to the family of nations. We set mankind an example never beheld before of moderation in victory. We led hesitating and halting Europe to the deliverance of their beleaguered ambassadors in China. We marched through a hostile country—a country cruel and barbarous—without anger or revenge. We returned benefit for injury, and pity for cruelty. We made the name of America beloved in the East as in the West. We kept faith with the Philippine people. We kept faith with our own history. We kept our national honor unsullied. The flag which we received without a rent we handed down without a stain."

* * * * * *

1.   *How does Hoar interpret American political history to support his case against imperialism? What aspects of the American past does he ignore?*

2.   *In Hoar's view, what are the most serious political and moral faults following from the imperialist policy?*

chapter 21

Urban America and the Progressive Era, 1900–1920

21-1 Jane Addams, The Subjective Necessity of Social Settlements, 1892

Born in 1860, Jane Addams was part of the first generation of college-educated women in America. She was frustrated by the lack of opportunities available to women seeking professional careers. In 1889, inspired by reformers she had met in England, Addams and her college friend Ellen Starr moved into an old mansion in a Chicago slum and founded the Hull House settlement. Addams dedicated her life to improving the lives of the poor through education, social science research, and political action. Addams strongly believed that settlement workers gained as much, if not more, from immigrants and the poor as they gave. The following essay, first given as an address to a conference of social workers in 1892, became a classic statement of reform commitment in the Progressive era.

SOURCE: Jane Addams, *Twenty Years at Hull House* (Macmillan, 1910), pp. 94–100.

We have in America a fast-growing number of cultivated young people who have no recognized outlet for their active faculties. They hear constantly of the great social maladjustment, but no way is provided for them to change it, and their uselessness hangs about them heavily. Huxley declares that the sense of uselessness is the severest shock which the human system can sustain, and that if persistently sustained, it results in atrophy of function. These young people have had advantages of college, of European travel, and of economic study, but they are sustaining this shock of inaction. They have pet phrases, and they tell you that the things that make us all alike are stronger than the things that make us different. They say that all men are united by needs and sympathies far more permanent and radical than anything that temporarily divides them and sets them in opposition to each other. If they affect art, they say that the decay in artistic expression is due to the decay in ethics, that art when shut away from the human interests and from the great mass of humanity is self-destructive. The tell their elders with all

the bitterness of youth that if they expect success from them in business or politics or in whatever lines their ambition for them has run, they must let them consult all of humanity; that they must let them find out what the people want and how they want it. It is only the stronger young people, however, who formulate this. Many of them dissipate their energies in so-called enjoyment. Others not content with that, go on studying and go back to college for their second degrees; not that they are especially fond of study, but because they want something definite to do, and their powers have been trained in the direction of mental accumulation. Many are buried beneath this mental accumulation which lowered vitality and discontent. Walter Besant says they have had the vision that Peter had when he saw the great sheet let down from heaven, wherein was neither clean nor unclean. He calls it the sense of humanity. It is not philanthropy nor benevolence, but a thing fuller and wider than either of these.

This young life, so sincere in its emotion and good phrase and yet so undirected, seems to me as pitiful as the other great mass of destitute lives. One is supplementary to the other, and some method of communication can surely be devised. Mr. Barnett, who urged the first Settlement—Toynbee Hall, in East London—recognized this need of outlet for the young men of Oxford and Cambridge, and hoped that the Settlement would supply the communication. It is easy to see why the Settlement movement originated in England, where the years of education are more constrained and definite than they are here, where class distinctions are more rigid. The necessity of it was greater there, but we are fast feeling the pressure of the need and meeting the necessity for Settlements in America. Our young people feel nervously the need of putting theory into action, and respond quickly to the Settlement form of activity.

Other motives which I believe make toward the Settlement are the result of a certain renaissance going forward in Christianity. The impulse to share the lives of the poor, the desire to make social service, irrespective of propaganda, express the spirit of Christ, is as old as Christianity itself. We have no proof from the records themselves that the early Roman Christians, who strained their simple art to the point of grotesqueness in their eagerness to record a "good news" on the walls of the catacombs, considered this good news a religion. Jesus had no set of truths labeled Religious. On the contrary, his doctrine was that all truth is one, that the appropriation of it is freedom. His teaching had no dogma to mark it off from truth and action in general. He himself called it a revelation—a life. These early Roman Christians received the Gospel message, a command to love all men, with a certain joyous simplicity. The image of the Good Shepherd is blithe and gay beyond the gentlest shepherd of Greek mythology; the hart no longer pants, but rushes to the water brooks. The Christians looked for the continuous revelation, but believed what Jesus said, that this revelation, to be retained and made manifest, must be put into terms of action; that action is the only medium man has for receiving and appropriating truth; that the doctrine must be known through the will....

In a thousand voices singing the Hallelujah Chorus in Handel's "Messiah," it is possible to distinguish the leading voices, but the differences of training and cultivation between them and the voices of the chorus, are lost in the unity of purpose and in the fact that they are all human voices lifted by a high motive. This is a weak illustration of what a Settlement attempts to do. It aims, in a measure, to develop whatever of social life its neighborhood may afford, to focus and give form to that life, to bring to bear upon it the results of cultivation and training; but it receives in exchange for the music of isolated voices the volume and strength of the chorus. It is quite impossible for me to say in what proportion or degree the subjective necessity which led to the opening of Hull-House combined the three trends: first, the desire to interpret democracy in social terms: secondly, the impulse beating at the very source of our lives, urging us to aid in the race progress; and, thirdly, the Christian movement toward humanitarianism. It is difficult to analyze a living thing; the analysis is at best imperfect. Many more motives may blend with the three trends; possibly the desire for a new form of social success due to the nicety of imagination, which refuses worldly pleasures unmixed with the joys of self-sacrifice; possibly a love of approbation, so vast that it is not content with the treble clapping of delicate hands, but wishes also to hear the brass notes from toughened palms, may mingle with these.

The Settlement, then, is an experimental effort to aid in the solution of the social and industrial problems which are engendered by the modern conditions of life in a great city. It insists that these problems are not confined to any one portion of a city. It is an attempt to relieve, at the same time, the overaccumulation at one end of society and the destitution at the other; but it assumes that this overaccumulation and destitution is most sorely felt in the things that pertain to social and educational privileges. From its very nature it can stand for no political or social propaganda. It must, in a sense, give the warm welcome of an inn to all such propaganda, if perchance one of them be found an angel. The one thing to be dreaded in the Settlement is that it lose its flexibility, its power of quick adaptation, its readiness to change its methods as its environment may demand. It must be open to conviction and

must have a deep and abiding sense of tolerance. It must be hospitable and ready for experiment. It should demand from its residents a scientific patience in the accumulation of facts and the steady holding of their sympathies as one of the best instruments for that accumulation. It must be grounded in a philosophy whose foundation is on the solidarity of the human race, a philosophy which will not waver when the race happens to be represented by a drunken woman or an idiot boy. Its residents must be emptied of all conceit of opinion and all self-assertion, and ready to arouse and interpret the public opinion of their neighborhood. They must be content to live quietly side by side with their neighbors, until they grow into a sense of relationship and mutual interests. Their neighbors are held apart by differences of race and language which the residents can more easily overcome. They are bound to see the needs of their neighborhood as a whole, to furnish data for legislation, and to use their influence to secure it. In short, residents are pledged to devote themselves to the duties of good citizenship and to the arousing of the social energies which too largely lie dormant in every neighborhood given over to industrialism. They are bound to regard the entire life of their city as organic, to make an effort to unify it, and to protest against its overdifferentiation.

It is always easy to make all philosophy point one particular moral and all history adorn one particular tale; but I may be forgiven the reminder that the best speculative philosophy sets forth the solidarity of the human race; that the highest moralists have taught that without the advance and improvement of the whole, no man can hope for any lasting improvement in his own moral or material individual condition; and that the subjective necessity for Social Settlements is therefore identical with that necessity, which urges us on toward social and individual salvation.

* * * * * *

1. *What draws young people to settlement work? According to Addams, why are young women especially suited for and drawn to this work?*

2. *What do settlement workers get from their work in the city slums? What do they give back?*

3. *To what extent is the movement based on Christian ethics? On scientific principles?*

21–2   George Washington Plunkitt, Honest Graft, 1905

George Washington Plunkitt was a longtime state senator from New York City and district leader for Tammany Hall, the Democratic Party machine. In 1905, journalist William Riordon recorded and published a series of informal talks that Plunkitt gave on the art of politics. The resulting book offered a classic statement of the philosophy and workings of the urban political machine. Plunkitt offered a humorous, yet penetrating, analysis of how to succeed in big-city political life.

SOURCE: William Riordon, *Plunkitt of Tammany Hall* (E.P. Dutton, 1905), pp. 3–6.

Everybody is talkin' these days about Tammany men growin' rich on graft, but nobody thinks of drawin' the distinction between honest graft and dishonest graft. There's all the difference in the world between the two. Yes, many of our men have grown rich in politics. I have myself. I've made a big fortune out of the game, and I'm gettin' richer every day, but I've not gone in for dishonest graft—blackmailin' gamblers, saloonkeepers, disorderly people, etc.—and neither has any of the men who have made big fortunes in politics.

There's an honest graft, and I'm an example of how it works. I might sum up the whole thing by sayin': "I seen my opportunities and I took 'em."

Just let me explain by examples. My party's in power in the city, and it's goin' to undertake a lot of public improvements. Well, I'm tipped off, say, that they're going to lay out a new park at a certain place.

I see my opportunity and I take it. I go to that place and I buy up all the land I can in the neighborhood. Then the board of this or that makes its plan public, and there is a rush to get my land, which nobody cared particular for before.

Ain't it perfectly honest to charge a good price and make a profit on my investment and foresight? Of course, it is. Well, that's honest graft.

Or supposin' it's a new bridge they're goin' to build. I get tipped off and I buy as much property as I can that has to be taken for approaches. I sell at my own price later on and drop some more money in the bank.

Wouldn't you? It's just like lookin' ahead in Wall Street or in the coffee or cotton market. It's honest graft, and I'm lookin' for it every day in the year. I will tell you frankly that I've got a good lot of it, too.

I'll tell you of one case. They were goin' to fix up a big park, no matter where. I got on to it, and went lookin' about for land in that neighborhood.

I could get nothin' at a bargain but a big piece of swamp, but I took it fast enough and held on to it. What turned out was just what I counted on. They couldn't make the park complete without Plunkitt's swamp, and they had to pay a good price for it. Anything dishonest in that?

Up in the watershed I made some money, too. I bought up several bits of land there some years ago and made a pretty good guess that they would be bought up for water purposes later by the city.

Somehow, I always guessed about right, and shouldn't I enjoy the profit of my foresight? It was rather amusin' when the condemnation commissioners came along and found piece after piece of the land in the name of George Plunkitt of the Fifteenth Assembly District, New York City. They wondered how I knew just what to buy. The answer is—I seen my opportunity and I took it. I haven't confined myself to land; anything that pays is in my line.

For instance, the city is repavin' a street and has several hundred thousand old granite blocks to sell. I am on hand to buy, and I know just what they are worth.

How? Never mind that. I had a sort of monopoly of this business for a while, but once a newspaper tried to do me. It got some outside men to come over from Brooklyn and New Jersey to bid against me.

Was I done? Not much. I went to each of the men and said: "How many of these 250,000 stones do you want?" One said 20,000, and another wanted 15,000, and other wanted 10,000. I said: "All right, let me bid for the lot, and I'll give each of you all you want for nothin'."

They agreed, of course. Then the auctioneer yelled: "How much am I bid for these 250,000 fine pavin' stones?"

"Two dollars and fifty cents," says I.

"Two dollars and fifty cents!" screamed the auctioneer. "Oh, that's a joke! Give me a real bid."

He found the bid was real enough. My rivals stood silent. I got the lot for $2.50 and gave them their share. That's how the attempt to do Plunkitt ended, and that's how all such attempts end.

I've told you how I got rich by honest graft. Now, let me tell you that most politicians who are accused of robbin' the city get rich the same way.

They didn't steal a dollar from the city treasury. They just seen their opportunities and took them. That is why, when a reform administration comes in and spends a half million dollars in tryin' to find the public robberies they talked about in the campaign, they don't find them.

The books are always all right. The money in the city treasury is all right. Everything is all right. All they can show is that the Tammany heads of departments looked after their friends, within the law, and gave them what opportunities they could to make honest graft. Now, let me tell you that's never goin' to hurt Tammany with the people. Every good man looks after his friends, and any man who doesn't isn't likely to be popular. If I have a good thing to hand out in private life, I give it to a friend. Why shouldn't I do the same in public life?

Another kind of honest graft. Tammany has raised a good many salaries. There was an awful howl by the reformers, but don't you know that Tammany gains ten votes for every one it lost by salary raisin'?

The Wall Street banker thinks it shameful to raise a department clerk's salary from $1500 to $1800 a year, but every man who draws a salary himself says: "That's all right. I wish it was me." And he feels very much like votin' the Tammany ticket on election day, just out of sympathy.

Tammany was beat in 1901 because the people were deceived into believin' that it worked dishonest graft. They didn't draw a distinction between dishonest and honest graft, but they saw that some Tammany men grew rich, and supposed they had been robbin' the city treasury or levyin' blackmail on disorderly houses, or workin' in with the gamblers and lawbreakers.

As a matter of policy, if nothing else, why should the Tammany leaders go into such dirty business, when there is so much honest graft lyin' around when they are in power? Did you ever consider that?

Now, in conclusion, I want to say that I don't own a dishonest dollar. If my worst enemy was given the job of writin' my epitaph when I'm gone, he couldn't do more than write:

"George W. Plunkitt. He Seen His Opportunities, and He Took 'Em."...

This is a record of a day's work by Plunkitt:

2 A.M.: Aroused from sleep by the ringing of his doorbell; went to the door and found a bartender, who asked him to go to the police station and bail out a saloonkeeper who had been arrested for violating the excise law. Furnished bail and returned to bed at three o'clock.

6 A.M.: Awakened by fire engines passing his house. Hastened to the scene of the fire, according to the custom of the Tammany district leaders, to give assistance to the fire sufferers, if needed. Met several of his election district captains who are always under orders to look out for fires, which are considered great vote-getters. Found several tenants who had been burned out, took them to a hotel, supplied them with clothes, fed them, and arranged temporary quarters for them until they could rent and furnish new apartments.

8:30 A.M.: Went to the police court to look after his constituents. Found six "drunks." Secured the discharge of four by a timely word with the judge, and paid the fines of two.

9 A.M.: Appeared in the Municipal District Court. Directed one of his district captains to act as counsel for a widow against whom dispossess proceedings had been instituted and obtained an extension of time. Paid the rent of a poor family about to be dispossessed and gave them a dollar for food.

11 A.M.: At home again. Found four men waiting for him. One had been discharged by the Metropolitan Railway Company for neglect of duty, and wanted the district leader to fix things. Another wanted a job on the road. The third sought a place on the Subway and the fourth, a plumber, was looking for work with the Consolidated Gas Company. The district leader spent nearly three hours fixing things for the four men, and succeeded in each case.

3 P.M.: Attended the funeral of an Italian as far as the ferry. Hurried back to make his appearance at the funeral of a Hebrew constituent. Went conspicuously to the front both in the Catholic church and the synagogue, and later attended the Hebrew confirmation ceremonies in the synagogue.

7 P.M.: Went to district headquarters and presided over a meeting of election district captains. Each captain submitted a list of all the voters in his district, reported on their attitude toward Tammany, suggested who might be won over and how they could be won, told who were in need, and who were in trouble of any kind and the best way to reach them. District leader took notes and gave orders.

8 P.M.: Went to a church fair. Took chances on everything, bought ice cream for the young girls and the children. Kissed the little ones, flattered their mothers and took their fathers out for something down at the corner.

9 P.M.: At the clubhouse again. Spent $10 on tickets for a church excursion and promised a subscription for a new church bell. Bought tickets for a baseball game to be played by two nines from his district. Listened to the complaints of a dozen pushcart peddlers who said they were persecuted by the police and assured them he would go to Police Headquarters in the morning and see about it.

10:30 P.M.: Attended a Hebrew wedding reception and dance. Had previously sent a handsome wedding present to the bride.

12 P.M.: In bed.

* * * * * *

1. *How does Plunkitt distinguish between honest and dishonest graft? Why is politics like a business for him?*

2. *Reformers never tired of exposing the "corruption" of Plunkitt and men like him. Why were they so popular with voters?*

21–3 Louis Brandeis, The Living Law, 1916

Louis Brandeis was the preeminent legal theorist of the Progressive era. As attorney for the National Consumers League in the landmark Muller v. Oregon *Supreme Court case, Brandeis had submitted a unique brief that included detailed sociological, economic, and physiological data in successful defense of a state law setting maximum hours for women workers. The following speech, given just before Woodrow Wilson appointed Brandeis to the Supreme Court in 1916, outlined Brandeis's view that courts had a responsibility to respond to contemporary economic and social conditions.*

SOURCE: Melvin I. Urofsky, *Documents of American Constitutional and Legal History*, V. 2 (Temple University Press, 1989), pp. 72–74.

Since the adoption of the Federal Constitution, and notably within the last fifty years, we have passed through an economic and social revolution which affected the life of the people more fundamentally than any political revolution known to history. Widespread substitution of machinery for hand labor (thus multiplying hundred-fold man's productivity), and the annihilation of space through steam and electricity, have wrought changes in the conditions of life which are in many respects greater than those which had occurred in civilized countries during thousands of years preceding. The end was put to legalized human slavery—an institution which had existed since the dawn of history. But of vastly greater influence upon the lives of the great majority of all civilized peoples was the possibility which invention and discovery created of emancipating women and of liberating men called free from the excessive toil theretofore required to securing food, clothing, and shelter. Yet while invention and discovery created the possibility of releasing men and women from the thraldom of drudgery, there actually came with the introduction of the factory system and the development of the business corporation, new dangers to liberty. Large publicly owned corporations replaced small privately owned concerns. Ownership of the instruments of production passed from the workman to the employer. Individual personal relations between the proprietor and his help ceased. The individual contract of service lost its character, because of the inequality in position between employer and employee. The group relation of employee to employer, with collective bargaining, became common; for it was essential to the workers' protection.

Political as well as economic and social science noted these revolutionary changes. But legal science—the unwritten or judge-made laws as distinguished from legislation—was largely deaf and blind to them. Courts continued to ignore newly arisen social needs. They applied complacently eighteenth-century conceptions of the liberty of the individual and of the sacredness of private property. Early nineteenth-century scientific half-truths like "The survival of the fittest," which, translated into practice, meant "The devil take the hindmost," were erected by judicial sanction into a moral law. Where statutes giving expression to the new social spirit were clearly constitutional, judges, imbued with the relentless spirit of individualism, often construed them away. Where any doubt as to the constitutionality of such statutes could find lodgment, courts all too frequently declared the acts void. Also in other countries the strain upon the law has been great during the last generation; because there also the period has been one of rapid transformation; and the law has everywhere a tendency to lag behind the facts of life. But in America the strain became dangerous; because constitutional limitations were invoked to stop the natural vent of legislation. In the course of relatively few years hundreds of statutes which embodied attempts (often very crude) to adjust legal rights to the demands of social justice were nullified by the courts, on the grounds that the statutes violated the constitutional guaranties of liberty or property. Small wonder that there arose a clamor for the recall of judges and of judicial decisions and that demand was made for amendment of the constitutions and even for their complete abolition....

The challenge of existing law does not, however, come only from the working classes. Criticism of the law is widespread among business men. The tone of their criticism is more courteous than that of the working classes; and the specific objections raised by business men are different. Business men do not demand recall of judges or of judicial decisions. Business men do not ordinarily seek constitutional amendments. They are more apt to desire repeal of statutes than enactment. But both business men and working-men insist that courts lack understanding of contemporary industrial conditions. Both insist that the law is not "up to date." Both insist that the lack of familiarity with the facts of business life results in erroneous decisions....Both business men and working-men have given further evidence of their distrust of the courts and of lawyers by their efforts to establish non-legal tribunals or commissions to exercise functions which are judicial (even where not legal) in their nature, and by their insistence that the commissions shall be manned with business and working-men instead of lawyers. And business men have been active in devising other means of escape from the domain of the courts, as is evidenced by the widespread tendency to arbitrate controversies through committees of business organizations.

The remedy so sought is not adequate, and may prove a mischievous one. What we need is not to displace the courts, but to make them efficient instruments of justice; not to displace the lawyer, but to fit him for his official or judicial task. And, indeed, the task of fitting the lawyer and the judge to perform adequately the functions of harmonizing law with life is a task far easier of accomplishment than that of endowing men, who lack legal training, with the necessary qualifications.

The training of the practicing lawyer is that best adapted to develop men not only for the exercise of strictly judicial functions, but also for the exercise of administrative functions, quasi-judicial in character. It breeds a certain virile, compelling quality, which tends to make the possessor proof against the influence of either fear or favor. It is this quality to which the prevailing high standard of honesty among our judges is due. And it is certainly a noteworthy fact that in spite of the abundant criticism of our judicial system, the suggestion of dishonesty is rare; and instances of established dishonesty are extremely few....

The last fifty years have wrought a great change in professional life. Industrial development and the consequent growth of cities have led to a high degree of specialization—specialization not only in the nature and class of questions dealt with, but also specialization in the character of clientage. The term "corporation lawyer" is significant in this connection. The growing intensity of professional life tended also to discourage participation in public affairs, and thus the broadening of view which comes from political life was lost. The deepening of knowledge in certain subjects was purchased at the cost of vast areas of ignorance and grave danger of resultant distortion of judgment....

Charles R. Crane told me once the story of two men whose lives he should have cared most to have lived. One

was Bogigish, a native of the ancient city of Ragusa off the coast of Dalmatia—a deep student of law, who after gaining some distinction at the University of Vienna, and in France, became professor at the University of Odessa. When Montenegro was admitted to the family of nations, its prince concluded that, like other civilized countries, it must have a code of law. Bogigish's fame had reached Montenegro—for Ragusa is but a few miles distant. So the prince begged the Tsar of Russia to have the learned jurist prepare a code for Montenegro. The Tsar granted the request; and Bogigish undertook the task. But instead of utilizing his great knowledge of laws to draft a code, he proceeded to Montenegro, and for two years literally made his home with the people—studying everywhere their customs, their practices, their needs, their beliefs, their points of view. Then he embodied in law the life which the Montenegrins lived. They respected that law, because it expressed the will of the people.

* * * * * *

1.   What examples of recent American history does Brandeis use to make his argument? Why does he pay special attention to the factory system?

2.   How have changes in the legal profession itself, for better and worse, reflected larger changes in the society? What remedies does Brandeis propose to better the legal system?

21–4   Margaret Sanger, The Case for Birth Control, 1917

Margaret Sanger first became interested in the issue of reproductive rights while working as a nurse among the immigrant poor in New York's Lower East Side. Active in socialist and feminist politics, Sanger began to lecture and write about birth control in 1912. The threat of legal prosecution by the U.S. Post Office forced her to flee to Europe. She returned to the United States in 1915, and the next year she and her sister established the nation's first birth control clinic in Brooklyn. They were arrested, tried, and acquitted in court amidst great publicity. Sanger later founded the American Birth Control League, which ultimately became Planned Parenthood.

SOURCE: Margaret Sanger, *The Case for Birth Control* (New York, 1917).

How often have I stood at the bedside of a woman in childbirth and seen the tears flowing in gladness and

heard the sigh of "Thank God" when told that her child was born dead! What can man know of the fear and dread of unwanted pregnancy? What can man know of the agony of carrying beneath one's heart a little life which tells the mother every instant that it cannot survive? Even were it born alive the chances are that it would perish within a year.

Do you know that three hundred thousand babies under one year of age die in the United States every year from poverty and neglect, while six hundred thousand parents remain in ignorance of how to prevent three hundred thousand more babies from coming into the world the next year to die of poverty and neglect?

I found from records concerning women of the underworld that eighty-five per cent of them come from parents averaging nine living children. And that fifty per cent of these are mentally defective.

We know, too, that among mentally defective parents the birth rate is four times as great as that of the normal parent. Is this not cause for alarm? Is it not time for our physicians, social workers and scientists to face this array of facts and stop quibbling about woman's morality? I say this because it is these same people who raise objection to birth control on the ground that it *may* cause women to be immoral.

Solicitude for woman's morals has ever been the cloak Authority has worn in its age-long conspiracy to keep woman in bondage....

Is woman's health not to be considered? Is she to remain a producing machine? Is she to have time to think, to study, to care for herself? Man cannot travel to his goal alone. And until woman has knowledge to control birth she cannot get the time to think and develop. Until she has the time to think, neither the suffrage question nor the social question nor the labor question will interest her, and she will remain the drudge that she is and her husband the slave that he is just as long as they continue to supply the market with cheap labor.

Let me ask you: Has the State any more right to ravish a woman against her will by keeping her in ignorance than a man has through brute force? Has the State a better right to decide when she shall bear offspring?

Picture a woman with five or six little ones living on the average working man's wage of ten dollars a week. The mother is broken in health and spirit, a worn out shadow of the woman she once was. Where is the man or woman who would reproach me for trying to put into this woman's hands knowledge that will save her from giving birth to any more babies doomed to certain poverty and misery and perhaps to disease and death?

Am I to be classed as immoral because I advocate small families for the working class while Mr. Roosevelt can go up and down the length of the land shouting and urging these women to have large families and is neither arrested nor molested but considered by all society as highly moral?

But I ask you which is the more moral—to urge this class of women to have only those children she desires and can care for, or to delude her into breeding thoughtlessly. Which is America's definition of morality?

You will agree with me that a woman should be free.

Yet no adult woman who is ignorant of the means to prevent conception can call herself free.

No woman can call herself free who cannot choose the time to be a mother or not as she sees fit. This should be woman's first demand.

Our present laws force women into one of two ways: Celibacy, with its nervous results, or abortion. All modern physicians testify that both these conditions are harmful; that celibacy is the cause of many nervous complaints, while abortion is a disgrace to a civilized community. Physicians claim that early marriage with knowledge to control birth would do away with both. For this would enable two young people to live and work together until such time as they could care for a family. I found that young people desire early marriage, and would marry early were it not for the dread of a large family to support. Why will not society countenance and advance this idea? Because it is still afraid of the untried and the unknown.

I saw that fortunes were being spent in establishing baby nurseries, where new babies are brought and cared for while the mothers toil in sweatshops during the day. I saw that society with its well-intentioned palliatives was in this respect like the quack, who cures a cancer by burning off the top while the deadly disease continues to spread underneath. I never felt this more strongly than I did three years ago, after the death of the patient in my last nursing case.

This patient was the wife of a struggling working man—the mother of three children—who was suffering from the results of a self-attempted abortion. I found her in a very serious condition, and for three weeks both the attending physician and myself labored night and day to bring her out of the Valley of the Shadow of Death. We finally succeeded in restoring her to her family.

I remember well the day I was leaving. The physician, too, was making his last call. As the doctor put out his hand to say "Good-bye," I saw the patient had something to say to him, but was shy and timid about saying it. I started to leave the room, but she called me back and said:

"Please don't go. How can both of you leave me without telling me what I can do to avoid another illness such as I have just passed through?"

I was interested to hear what the answer of the physician would be, and I went back and sat down beside her in expectation of hearing a sympathetic reply. To my amazement, he answered her with a joking sneer. We came away.

Three months later, I was aroused from my sleep one midnight. A telephone call from the husband of the same woman requested me to come immediately as she was dangerously ill. I arrived to find her beyond relief. Another conception had forced her into the hands of a cheap abortionist, and she died at four o'clock the same morning, leaving behind her three small children and frantic husband.

I returned home as the sun was coming over the roofs of the Human Bee-Hive, and I realized how futile my efforts and my work had been. I, too, like the philanthropists and social workers, had been dealing with the symptoms rather than the disease. I threw my nursing bag into the corner and announced to my family that I would never take another case until I had made it possible for working women in America to have knowledge of birth control.

I found, to my utter surprise, that there was very little scientific information on the question available in America. Although nearly every country in Europe had this knowledge, we were the only civilized people in the world whose postal laws forbade it.

The tyranny of the censorship of the post office is the greatest menace to liberty in the United States to-day.

The post office was never intended to be a moral or ethical institution. It was intended to be mechanically efficient; certainly not to pass upon the opinions in the matter it conveys. If we concede this power to this institution, which is only a public service, we might just as well give to the street car companies and railroads the right to refuse to carry passengers whose ideas they do not like.

I will not take up the story of the publication of "The Woman Rebel." You know how I began to publish it, how it was confiscated and suppressed by the post office authorities, how I was indicted and arrested for bringing it out, and how the case was postponed time and time again and finally dismissed by Judge Clayton in the Federal Court.

These, and many more obstacles and difficulties were put in the path of this philosophy and this work to suppress it if possible and discredit it in any case.

My work has been to arouse interest in the subject of birth control in America, and in this, I feel that I have been successful. The work now before us is to crystallize and to organize this interest into action, not only for the repeal of the laws but for the establishment of free clinics in every large center of population in the country where scientific, individual information may be given every adult person who comes to ask it.…

The free clinic is the solution for our problem. It will enable women to help themselves, and will have much to do with disposing of this soul-crushing charity which is at best a mere temporary relief.

Woman must be protected from incessant childbearing before she can actively participate in the social life. She must triumph over Nature's and Man's laws which have kept her in bondage. Just as man has triumphed over Nature by the use of electricity, shipbuilding, bridges, etc., so must woman triumph over the laws which have made her a childbearing machine.

* * * * * *

1. *How does Sanger use her practical experiences as a nurse to make her case?*

2. *To what extent does Sanger make a feminist argument—for example, birth control as an issue of women's emancipation? To what extent does she make an argument based on class and economic issues?*

3. *How does Sanger criticize the role of the state in dealing with birth control?*

21–5   Booker T. Washington, The Atlanta Exposition Address, 1895

Born a slave, Booker T. Washington worked his way through the Hampton Institute in Virginia and, in 1881, founded the Tuskeegee Institute in Alabama. There he emphasized practical and vocational training for black students, as opposed to a liberal arts education. By the turn of the century, Washington emerged as the most influential national spokesman for African Americans. By deemphasizing political and social rights for Africa - Americans, he also gained enormous influence among the nation's white political and business elites. His autobiography, Up From Slavery *(1901), won a large readership around the nation and the world.*

SOURCE: Booker T. Washington, *Up From Slavery* (1901).

One-third of the population of the South is of the Negro race. No enterprise seeking the material, civil, or moral welfare of this section can disregard this element of our population and reach the highest success. I but convey to you, Mr. President and Directors, the sentiment of the masses of my race when I say that in no way have the

value and manhood of the American Negro been more fittingly and generously recognized than by the managers of this magnificent Exposition at every stage of its progress. It is a recognition that will do more to cement the friendship of the two races than any occurrence since the dawn of our freedom.

Not only this, but the opportunity here afforded will awaken among us a new era of industrial progress. Ignorant and inexperienced, it is not strange that in the first years of our new life we began at the top instead of at the bottom; that a seat in Congress or the state legislature was more sought than real estate or industrial skill; that the political convention or stump speaking had more attractions than starting a dairy farm or truck garden.

A ship lost at sea for many days suddenly sighted a friendly vessel. From the mast of the unfortunate vessel was seen a signal, "Water, water; we die of thirst!" The answer from the friendly vessel at once came back, "Cast down your bucket where you are." A second time the signal, "Water, water; send us water!" ran up from the distressed vessel, and was answered, "Cast down your bucket where you are." And a third and fourth signal for water was answered, "Cast down your bucket where you are." The captain of the distressed vessel, at last heeding the injunction, cast down his bucket, and it came up full of fresh, sparkling water from the mouth of the Amazon River. To those of my race who depend on bettering their condition in a foreign land or who underestimate the importance of cultivating friendly relations with the Southern white man, who is their next-door neighbour, I would say: "Cast down your bucket where you are"—cast it down in making friends, in every manly way, of the people of all races by whom we are surrounded.

Cast it down in agriculture, mechanics, in commerce, in domestic service, and in the professions. And in this connection it is well to bear in mind that whatever other sins the South may be called to bear, when it comes to business, pure and simple, it is in the South that the Negro is given a man's chance in the commercial world, and in nothing is this Exposition more eloquent than in emphasizing this chance. Our greatest danger is that in the great leap from slavery to freedom we may overlook the fact that the masses of us are to live by the productions of our hands, and fail to keep in mind that we shall prosper in proportion as we learn to dignify and glorify common labour and put brains and skill into the common occupations of life; shall prosper in proportion as we learn to draw the line between the superficial and the substantial, the ornamental gewgaws of life and the useful. No race can prosper till it learns that there is as much dignity in tilling a field as in writing a poem. It is at the bottom of life we must begin, and not at the top. Nor should we permit our grievances to overshadow our opportunities.

To those of the white race who look to the incoming of those of foreign birth and strange tongue and habits for the prosperity of the South, were I permitted I would repeat what I say to my own race, "Cast down your bucket where you are." Cast it down among the eight millions of Negroes whose habits you know, whose fidelity and love you have tested in days when to have proved treacherous meant the ruin of your firesides. Cast down your bucket among these people who have, without strikes and labour wars, tilled your fields, cleared your forests, builded your railroads and cities, and brought forth treasures from the bowels of the earth, and helped make possible this magnificent representation of the progress of the South. Casting down your bucket among my people, helping and encouraging them as you are doing on these grounds, and to education of head, hand, and heart, you will find that they will buy your surplus land, make blossom the waste places in your fields, and run your factories. While doing this, you can be sure in the future, as in the past, that you and your families will be surrounded by the most patient, faithful, law abiding, and unresentful people that the world has seen. As we have proved our loyalty to you in the past, in nursing your children, watching by the sick-bed of your mothers and fathers, and often following them with tear-dimmed eyes to their graves, so in the future, in our humble way, we shall stand by you with a devotion that no foreigner can approach, ready to lay down our lives, if need be, in defence of yours, interlacing our industrial, commercial, civil, and religious

life with yours in a way that shall make the interests of both races one. In all things that are purely social we can be as separate as the fingers, yet one as the hand in all things essential to mutual progress.

There is no defence or security for any of us except in the highest intelligence and development of all. If anywhere there are efforts tending to curtail the fullest growth of the Negro, let these efforts be turned into stimulating, encouraging, and making him the most useful and intelligent citizen. Effort or means so invested will pay a thousand per cent interest. These efforts will be twice blessed—"blessing him that gives and him that takes."

There is no escape through law of man or God from the inevitable:—

> The laws of changeless justice bind
>   Oppressor with oppressed;
> And close as sin and suffering joined
>   We march to fate abreast.

Nearly sixteen millions of hands will aid you in pulling the load upward, or they will pull against you the load downward. We shall constitute one-third and more of the ignorance and crime of the South, or one-third its intelligence and progress; we shall contribute one-third to the business and industrial prosperity of the South, or we shall prove a veritable body of death, stagnating, depressing, retarding every effort to advance the body politic.

Gentlemen of the Exposition, as we present to you our humble effort at an exhibition of our progress, you must not expect overmuch. Starting thirty years ago with ownership here and there in a few quilts and pumpkins and chickens (gathered from miscellaneous sources), remember the path that has led from these to the inventions and production of agricultural implements, buggies, steam-engines, newspapers, books, statuary, carving, paintings, the management of drug-stores and banks, has not been trodden without contact with thorns and thistles. While we take pride in what we exhibit as a result of our independent efforts, we do not for a moment forget that our part in this exhibition would fall far short of your expectations but for the constant help that has come to our educational life, not only from the Southern states, but especially from Northern philanthropists, who have made their gifts a constant stream of blessing and encouragement.

The wisest among my race understand that the agitation of questions of social equality is the extremest folly, and that progress in the enjoyment of all the privileges that will come to us must be the result of severe and constant struggle rather than of artificial forcing. No race that has anything to contribute to the markets of the world is long in any degree ostracized. It is important and right that all privileges of the law be ours, but it is vastly more important that we be prepared for the exercises of these privileges. The opportunity to earn a dollar in a factory just now is worth infinitely more than the opportunity to spend a dollar in an opera-house.

In conclusion, may I repeat that nothing in thirty years has given us more hope and encouragement, and drawn us so near to you of the white race, as this opportunity offered by the Exposition; and here bending, as it were, over the altar that represents the results of the struggles of your race and mine, both starting practically empty-handed three decades ago, I pledge that in your effort to work out the great and intricate problem which God has laid at the doors of the South, you shall have at all times the patient, sympathetic help of my race; only let this be constantly in mind, that, while from representations in these buildings of the product of field, of forest, of mine, of factory, letters, and art, much good will come, yet far above and beyond material benefits will be that

higher good, that, let us pray God, will come, in a blotting out of sectional differences and racial animosities and suspicions, in a determination to administer absolute justice, in a willing obedience among all classes to the mandates of law. This, this, coupled with our material prosperity, will bring into our beloved South a new heaven and a new earth.

* * * * * *

1.   *What does Washington mean by the phrase, "Cast down your bucket where you are"?*

2.   *How does he define the progress made by African Americans since the end of slavery? What strategies for future progress does he outline?*

21–6   Ida B. Wells, A Red Record, 1895

The daughter of slaves, Ida B. Wells began her career as a teacher and journalist in Memphis. During the 1890s, she began speaking out and writing about the taboo subject of lynching. Wells was convinced that lynching formed a critical part of the system of racial oppression in the South, often as tool against successful black businesses. She challenged the myth of black men raping white women, and argued that this myth masked the deeper historical reality of the systematic rape of black women by white men. Wells's carefully researched anti-lynching crusade drew international attention to the issue. She was also active in the black club women's movement, women's suffrage, and was a founding member of the NAACP in 1909.

SOURCE: Ida B. Wells, *A Red Record* (1895).

Not all or nearly all of the murders done by white men, during the past thirty years in the South, have come to light, but the statistics as gathered and preserved by white men, and which have not been questioned, show that during these years more than ten thousand Negroes have been killed in cold blood, without the formality of judicial trial and legal execution. And yet, as evidence of the absolute impunity with which the white man dares to kill a Negro, the same record shows that during all these years, and for all these murders only three white men have been tried, convicted, and executed. As no white man has been lynched for the murder of colored people, these three executions are the only instances of the death penalty being visited upon white men for murdering Negroes.

Naturally enough the commission of these crimes began to tell upon the public conscience, and the Southern white man, as a tribute to the nineteenth century civilization, was in a manner compelled to give excuses for his barbarism. His excuses have adapted themselves to the emergency, and are aptly outlined by that greatest of all Negroes, Frederick Douglass, in an article of recent date, in which he shows that there have been three distinct eras of Southern barbarism, to account for which three distinct excuses have been made.

The first excuse given to the civilized world for the murder of unoffending Negroes was the necessity of the white man to repress and stamp out alleged "race riots." For years immediately succeeding the war there was an appalling slaughter of colored people, and the wires usually conveyed to northern people and the world the intelligence, first, that an insurrection was being planned by Negroes, which, a few hours later, would prove to have been vigorously resisted by white men, and controlled with a resulting loss of several killed and wounded. It was always a remarkable feature in these insurrections and riots that only Negroes were killed during the rioting, and that all the white men escaped unharmed.

From 1865 to 1872, hundreds of colored men and women were mercilessly murdered and the almost invariable reason assigned was that they met their death by being alleged participants in an insurrection or riot. But this story at last wore itself out. No insurrection ever materialized; no Negro rioter was ever apprehended and proven guilty, and no dynamite ever recorded the black man's protest against oppression and wrong....

Then came the second excuse, which had its birth during the turbulent times of reconstruction. By an amendment to the Constitution the Negro was given the right of franchise, and, theoretically at least, his ballot became his invaluable emblem of citizenship....The southern white man would not consider that the Negro had any right which a white man was bound to respect, and the idea of a republican form of government in the southern states grew into general contempt. It was maintained that "This is a white man's government," and regardless of numbers white men should rule. "No Negro domination" became the new legend on the sanguinary banner of the sunny South, and under it rode the Ku Klux Klan, the Regulators, and the lawless mobs, which for any cause chose to murder one man or a dozen as suited their purpose best. It was a long, gory campaign....

The government which had made the Negro a citizen found itself unable to protect him. It gave him the right to vote, but denied him the protection which should have maintained that right. Scourged from his home; hunted through the swamps; hung by midnight raiders, and openly murdered in the light of day, the Negro clung to his right of franchise with a heroism which would have wrung admiration from the hearts of savages. He believed that in the small white ballot there was a subtle something which stood for manhood as well as citizenship, and thousands of brave black men went to their graves, exemplifying the one by dying for the other.

The white man's victory soon became complete by fraud, violence, intimidation and murder. The franchise vouchsafed to the Negro grew to be a "barren ideality," and regardless of numbers, the colored people found themselves voiceless in the councils of those whose duty it was to rule....With the Southern governments all subverted and the Negro actually eliminated from all participation in state and national elections, there could be no longer an excuse for killing Negroes to prevent "Negro Domination."

Brutality still continued, Negroes were whipped, scourged, exiled, shot and hung whenever and wherever it pleased the white man so to treat them, and as the civilized world with increasing persistency held the white people of the South to account for its outlawry, the murderers invented the third excuse—that Negroes had to he killed to avenge their assaults upon women....

Humanity abhors the assailant of womanhood, and this charge upon the Negro at once placed him beyond the pale of human sympathy....

If the Southern people in defense of their lawlessness, would tell the truth and admit that colored men and women are lynched for almost any offense, from murder to a misdemeanor, there would not now be the necessity for this defense. But when they intentionally, maliciously and constantly belie the record and bolster up these falsehoods by the words of legislators, preachers, governors and bishops, then the Negro must give to the world his side of the awful story.

A word as to the charge itself. In considering the third reason assigned by the Southern white people for the butchery of blacks, the question must be asked, what the white man means when he charges the black man with rape. Does he mean the crime which the statutes of the states describe as such? Not by any means. With the Southern white man, any misalliance existing between a white woman and a colored man is a sufficient foundation for the charge of rape. The Southern white man says that it is impossible for a voluntary alliance to exist between a white woman and a colored man, and therefore, the fact of an alliance is a proof of force. In numerous instances where colored men have been lynched on the charge of rape, it was positively known at the time of lynching, and indisputably proven after the victim's death, that the relationship sustained between the man and the woman was voluntary and clandestine, and that in no court of law could even the charge of assault have been successfully maintained.

It was for the assertion of this fact, in the defense of her own race, that the writer hereof became an exile; her property destroyed and her return to her home forbidden under penalty of death, for writing the following editorial which was printed in her paper, the *Free Speech,* in Memphis, Tenn., May 21, 1892:

"Eight Negroes lynched since last issue of the *Free Speech* one at Little Rock, Ark., last Saturday morning where the citizens broke (?) into the penitentiary and got their man; three near Anniston, Ala., one near New Orleans; and three at Clarksville, Ga., the last three for killing a white man, and five on the same old racket—the new alarm about raping white women. The same programme of hanging, then shooting bullets into the lifeless bodies was carried out to the letter. Nobody in this section of the country believes the old threadbare lie that Negro men rape white women. If Southern white men are not careful, they will over-reach themselves and public sentiment will have a reaction; a conclusion will then he reached which will be very damaging to the moral reputation of their women."

But threats cannot suppress the truth, and while the Negro suffers the soul deformity, resultant from two and a half centuries of slavery, he is no more guilty of this vilest of all vile charges than the white man who would blacken his name.

During all the years of slavery, no such charge was ever made, not even during the dark days of the rebellion.... While the master was away fighting to forge the fetters upon the slave, he left his wife and children with no protectors save the Negroes themselves....

Likewise during the period of alleged "insurrection," and alarming "race riots," it never occurred to the white man, that his wife and children were in danger of assault. Nor in the Reconstruction era, when the hue and cry was against "Negro Domination," was there ever a thought that the domination would ever contaminate a fireside or strike to death the virtue of womanhood....

It is not the purpose of this defense to say one word against the white women of the South. Such need not be said, but it is their misfortune that the…white men of that section…to justify their own barbarism…assume a chivalry which they do not possess. True chivalry respects all womanhood, and no one who reads the record, as it is written in the faces of the million mulattoes in the South, will for a minute conceive that the southern white man had a very chivalrous regard for the honor due the women of his race or respect for the womanhood which circumstances placed in his power…. Virtue knows no color line, and the chivalry which depends upon complexion of skin and texture of hair can command no honest respect.

When emancipation came to the Negroes…from every nook and corner of the North, brave young white women…left their cultured homes, their happy associations and their lives of ease, and with heroic determination went to the South to carry light and truth to the benighted blacks….They became social outlaws in the South. The peculiar sensitiveness of the southern white men for women, never shed its protecting influence about them. No friendly word from their own race cheered them in their work; no hospitable doors gave them the companionship like that from which they had come. No chivalrous white man doffed his hat in honor or respect. They were "Nigger teachers"—unpardonable offenders in the social ethics of the South, and were insulted, persecuted and ostracised, not by Negroes, but by the white manhood which boasts of its chivalry toward women.

And yet these northern women worked on, year after year….Threading their way through dense forests, working in schoolhouse, in the cabin and in the church, thrown at all times and in all places among the unfortunate and lowly Negroes, whom they had come to find and to serve, these northern women, thousands and thousands of them, have spent more than a quarter of a century in giving to the colored people their splendid lessons for home and heart and soul. Without protection, save that which innocence gives to every good woman, they went about their work, fearing no assault and suffering none. Their chivalrous protectors were hundreds of miles away in their northern homes, and yet they never feared any "great dark faced mobs."…They never complained of assaults, and no mob was ever called into existence to avenge crimes against them. Before the world adjudges the Negro a moral monster, a vicious assailant of womanhood and a menace to the sacred precincts of home, the colored people ask the consideration of the silent record of gratitude, respect, protection and devotion of the millions of the race in the South, to the thousands of northern white women who have served as teachers and missionaries since the war.…

* * * * * *

1. *Why does Wells devote so much space to southern race relations of the past? How does she interpret the Reconstruction era and use it for her argument?*

2. *Compare the tone and substance of Wells's piece with that of Washington's, written in the same year. How do you think he might have responded to her work?*

21–7 The Niagara Movement, Declaration of Principles, 1905

Despite Booker T. Washington's acknowledged preeminence, other African-American voices made themselves heard in the Progressive era. Led by W. E. B. DuBois, author of The Souls of Black Folk *(1903), a group of African-American leaders convened at Niagara Falls in the summer of 1905 to develop a more militant racial strategy as an alternative to Washington's. In 1909, their declaration of principles found concrete institutional expression when a group of African-Americans and white Progressives founded the National Association for the Advancement of Colored People.*

SOURCE: The Niagara Movement Declaration of Principles (1905).

Progress: The members of the conference, known as the Niagara Movement, assembled in annual meeting at Buffalo, July 11th, 12th and 13th, 1905, congratulate the Negro-Americans on certain undoubted evidences of progress in the last decade, particularly the increase of intelligence, the buying of property, the checking of crime, the uplift in home life, the advance in literature and art, and the demonstration of constructive and executive ability in the conduct of great religious, economic and educational institutions.

Suffrage: At the same time, we believe that this class of American citizens should protest emphatically and continually against the curtailment of their political rights. We believe in manhood suffrage; we believe that no man is so good, intelligent or wealthy as to be entrusted wholly with the welfare of his neighbor.

Civil Liberty: We believe also in protest against the curtailment of our civil rights. All American citizens have the right to equal treatment in places of public entertainment according to their behavior and deserts.

Economic Opportunity: We especially complain against the denial of equal opportunities to us in economic life; in the rural districts of the South this amounts to peonage and virtual slavery; all over the South it tends to crush labor and small business enterprises; and everywhere American prejudice, helped often by iniquitous laws, is making it more difficult for Negro-Americans to earn a decent living.

Education: Common school education should be free to all American children and compulsory. High school training should be adequately provided for all, and college training should be the monopoly of no class or race in any section of our common country. We believe that, in defense of our own institutions, the United States should aid common school education, particularly in the South, and we especially recommend concerted agitation to this end. We urge an increase in public high school facilities in the South, where the Negro-Americans are almost wholly without such provisions. We favor well-equipped trade and technical schools for the training of artisans, and the need of adequate and liberal endowment for a few institutions of higher education must be patient to sincere well-wishers of the race.

Courts: We demand upright judges in courts, juries selected without discrimination on account of color and the same measure of punishment and the same efforts at reformation for black as for white offenders. We need orphanages and farm schools for dependent children, juvenile reformatories for delinquents, and the abolition of the dehumanizing convict-lease system.

Public Opinion: We note with alarm the evident retrogression in this land of sound public opinion on the subject of manhood rights, republican government and human brotherhood, and we pray God that this nation will not degenerate into a mob of boasters and oppressors, but rather will return to the faith of the fathers, that all men were created free and equal, with certain unalienable rights.

Health: We plead for health—for an opportunity to live in decent houses and localities, for a chance to rear our children in physical and moral cleanliness.

Employers and Labor Unions: We hold up for Public execration the conduct of two opposite classes of men: The practice among employers of importing ignorant Negro-American laborers in emergencies, and then affording them neither protection nor permanent employment; and the practice of labor unions in proscribing and boycotting and oppressing thousands of their fellow-toilers, simply because they are black. These methods have accentuated and will accentuate the war of labor and capital, and they are disgraceful to both sides.

Protest: We refuse to allow the impression to remain that the Negro-American assents to inferiority, is submissive under oppression and apologetic before insults. Through helplessness we may submit, but the voice of protest of ten million Americans must never cease to assail the ears of their fellows, so long as America is unjust.

Color-Line: Any discrimination based simply on race or color is barbarous, we care not how hallowed it be by custom, expediency or prejudice. Differences made on account of ignorance, immorality, or disease are legitimate methods of fighting evil, and against them we have

no word of protest; but discriminations based simply and solely on physical peculiarities, place of birth, color of skin, are relics of that unreasoning human savagery of which the world is and ought to be thoroughly ashamed.

"Jim Crow" Cars: We protest against the "Jim Crow" car, since its effect is and must be to make us pay first-class fare for third-class accommodations, render us open to insults and discomfort and to crucify wantonly our manhood, womanhood and self-respect.

Soldiers: We regret that this nation has never seen fit adequately to reward the black soldiers who, in its five wars, have defended their country with their blood, and yet have been systematically denied the promotions which their abilities deserve. And we regard as unjust, the exclusion of black boys from the military and naval training schools.

War Amendments: We urge upon Congress the enactment of appropriate legislation for securing the proper enforcement of those articles of freedom, the thirteenth, fourteenth and fifteenth amendments of the Constitution of the United States.

Oppression: We repudiate the monstrous doctrine that the oppressor should be the sole authority as to the rights of the oppressed. The Negro race in America stolen, ravished and degraded, struggling up through difficulties and oppression, needs sympathy and receives criticism; needs help and is given hindrance, needs protection and is given mob-violence, needs justice and is given charity, needs leadership and is given cowardice and apology, needs bread and is given a stone. This nation will never stand justified before God until these things are changed.

The Church: Especially are we surprised and astonished at the recent attitude of the church of Christ—of an increase of a desire to bow to racial prejudice, to narrow the bounds of human brotherhood, and to segregate black men to some outer sanctuary. This is wrong, unchristian and disgraceful to the twentieth century civilization.

Agitation: Of the above grievances we do not hesitate to complain, and to complain loudly and insistently. To ignore, overlook, or apologize for these wrongs is to prove ourselves unworthy of freedom. Persistent manly agitation is the way to liberty, and toward this goal the Niagara Movement has started and asks the cooperation of all men of all races.

Help: At the same time we want to acknowledge with deep thankfulness the help of our fellowmen from the Abolitionist down to those who today still stand for equal opportunity and who have given and still give of their wealth and of their poverty for our advancement.

Duties: And while we are demanding and ought to demand, and will continue to demand the rights enumerated above, God forbid that we should ever forget to urge corresponding duties upon our people:

The duty to vote.

The duty to respect the rights of others.

The duty to work.

The duty to obey the laws.

The duty to be clean and orderly.

The duty to send our children to school.

The duty to respect ourselves, even as we respect others.

This statement, complaint and prayer we submit to the American people, and Almighty God.

* * * * * *

1. *Compare and contrast this document with both Washington and Wells.*

2. *What do the Niagara principles urge with regard to government action? What do they emphasize in the way of self-help within the African-American community?*

21-8 Declaration of the Conservation Conference, 1908

Theodore Roosevelt's most lasting legacy was arguably his effort to draw attention to and conserve the nation's natural resources. In 1908, Roosevelt convened a conference of governors, congressmen, judges, and other prominent officials to consider the broad issue of conservation. The conference recommended creation of a National Conservation Commission, of which Gifford Pinchot was named chairman. In 1909, the Commission submitted to President Roosevelt a systematic study of the nation's mineral, water, forest, and soil resources, the first such overview in American history.

SOURCE: *Proceedings of a Conference of Governors*, May 13–15, 1908, p. 192 ff.

We the Governors of the States and Territories of the United States of America, in Conference assembled, do hereby declare the conviction that the great prosperity of our country rests upon the abundant resources of the land chosen by our forefathers for their homes and where they laid the foundation of this great Nation.

We look upon these resources as a heritage to be made use of in establishing and promoting the comfort, prosperity, and happiness of the American People, but not to be wasted, deteriorated, or needlessly destroyed.

We agree that our country's future is involved in this; that the great natural resources supply the material basis on which our civilization must continue to depend, and on which the perpetuity of the Nation itself rests.

We agree, in the light of facts brought to our knowledge and from information received from sources which we can not doubt, that this material basis is threatened with exhaustion. Even as each succeeding generation from the birth of the Nation has performed its part in promoting the progress and development of the Republic, so do we in this generation recognize it as a high duty to perform our part; and this duty in large degree lies in the adoption of measures for the conservation of the natural wealth of the country.

We declare our firm conviction that this conservation of our natural resources is a subject of transcendent importance, which should engage unremittingly the attention of the Nation, the States, and the People in earnest cooperation. These natural resources include the land on which we live and which yields our food; the living waters which fertilize the soil, supply power, and form great avenues of commerce; the forests which yield the materials for our homes, prevent erosion of the soil, and conserve the navigation and other uses of our streams; and the minerals which form the basis of our industrial life, and supply us with heat, light, and power.

We agree that the land should be so used that erosion and soil-wash shall cease; that there should be reclamation of arid and semi-arid regions by means of irrigation, and of swamp and overflowed regions by means of drainage; that the waters should be so conserved and used as to promote navigation, to enable the arid regions to be reclaimed by irrigation, and to develop power in the interests of the People; that the forests which regulate our rivers, support our industries, and promote the fertility and productiveness of the soil should be preserved and perpetuated; that the minerals found so abundantly beneath the surface should be so used as to prolong their utility; that the beauty, healthfulness, and habitability of our country should be preserved and increased; that the sources of national wealth exist for the benefit of the People, and that monopoly thereof should not be tolerated.

We commend the wise forethought of the President in sounding the note of warning as to the waste and exhaustion of the natural resources of the country, and signify our high appreciation of his action in calling this Conference to consider the same and to seek remedies therefor through cooperation of the Nation and the States.

We agree that this cooperation should find expression in suitable action by the Congress within the limits of and coextensive with the national jurisdiction of the subject, and, complementary thereto, by the legislatures of the several States within the limits of and coextensive with their jurisdiction.

We declare the conviction that in the use of the natural resources our independent States are interdependent and bound together by ties of mutual benefits, responsibilities and duties.

We agree in the wisdom of future conferences between the President, Members of Congress, and the Governors of States on the conservation of our natural resources with a view of continued cooperation and action on the lines suggested; and to this end we advise that from time to time, as in his judgment may seem wise, the President call the Governors of the States and Members of Congress and others into conference.

We agree that further action is advisable to ascertain the present condition of our natural resources and to promote the conservation of the same; and to that end we recommend the appointment by each State of a Commission on the Conservation of Natural Resources, to cooperate with each other and with any similar commission of the Federal Government.

We urge the continuation and extension of forest policies adapted to secure the husbanding and renewal of our diminishing timber supply, the prevention of soil erosion, the protection of headwaters, and the maintenance of the purity and navigability of our streams. We recognize that the private ownership of forest lands entails responsibilities in the interests of all the People, and we favor the enactment of laws looking to the protection and replacement of privately owned forests.

We recognize in our waters a most valuable asset of the People of the United States, and we recommend the enactment of laws looking to the conservation of water resources for irrigation, water supply, power, and navigation, to the end that navigable and source streams may he brought under complete control and fully utilized for every purpose. We especially urge on the Federal Congress the immediate adoption of a wise, active, and thorough waterway policy, providing for the prompt improvement of our streams and the conservation of their watersheds required for the uses of commerce and the protection of the interests of our People.

We recommend the enactment of laws looking to the prevention of waste in the mining and extraction of coal, oil, gas, and other minerals with a view to their wise conservation for the use of the People, and to the protection of human life in the mines.

Let us conserve the foundations of our prosperity.

* * * * * *

1.   *How does the declaration define natural resources? Why are they of such "transcendent importance"?*

2.   *What role does the declaration recommend for the government in conservation? Would you describe this approach as "progressive"?*

21-9   Woodrow Wilson, The New Freedom, 1913

Woodrow Wilson centered his successful 1912 presidential campaign around the concept of "the new freedom." In speeches and writings, he argued that government must play a larger role in the national life in order to preserve the economic and political freedoms that Americans had historically enjoyed. After the election, Wilson published a compilation of speeches in a book titled The New Freedom; *it won a wide audience and was considered the central philosophical expression of Wilson's version of progressivism.*

SOURCE: Woodrow Wilson, *The New Freedom* (1913).

There is one great basic fact which underlies all the questions that are discussed on the political platform at the present moment. That singular fact is that nothing is done in this country as it was done twenty years ago.

We are in the presence of a new organization of society. Our life has broken away from the past. The life of America is not the life that it was twenty years ago; it is not the life that it was ten years ago. We have changed our economic conditions, absolutely, from top to bottom; and, with our economic society, the organization of our life. The old political formulas do not fit the present problems; they read now like documents taken out of a forgotten age. The older cries sound as if they belonged to a past age which men have almost forgotten. Things which used to be put into the party platforms of ten years ago would sound antiquated if put into a platform now. We are facing the necessity of fitting a new social organization, as we did once fit the old organization, to the happiness and prosperity of the great body of citizens; for we are conscious that the new order of society has not been made to fit and provide the convenience or prosperity of the average man. The life of the nation has grown infinitely varied. It does not centre now upon questions of governmental structure or of the distribution of governmental powers. It centres upon questions of the very structure and operation of society itself, of which government is only the instrument. Our development has run so fast and so far along the lines sketched in the earlier day of constitutional definition, has so crossed and interlaced those lines, has piled upon them such novel structures of trust and combination, has elaborated within them a life so manifold, so full of forces which transcend the boundaries of the country itself and fill the eyes of the world, that a new nation seems to have been created which the old formulas do not fit or afford a vital interpretation of.

We have come upon a very different age from any that preceded us. We have come upon an age when we do not do business in the way in which we used to do business,—when we do not carry on any of the operations of manufacture, sale, transportation, or communication as men used to carry them on. There is a sense in which in our day the individual has been submerged. In most parts of our country men work, not for themselves, not as partners in the old way in which they used to work, but generally as employees, in a higher or lower grade,—of great corporations. There was a time when corporations played a very minor part in our business affairs, but now they play the chief part, and most men are the servants of corporations.

You know what happens when you are the servant of a corporation. You have in no instance access to the men who are really determining the policy of the corporation. If the corporation is doing the things that it ought not to do, you really have no voice in the matter and must obey the orders, and you have oftentimes with deep mortification to co-operate in the doing of things which you know are against the public interest. Your individuality is swallowed up in the individuality and purpose of a great organization.

It is true that, while most men are thus submerged in the corporation, a few, a very few, are exalted to a power which as individuals they could never have wielded. Through the great organizations of which they are the heads, a few are enabled to play a part unprecedented by anything in history in the control of the business operations of the country and in the determination of the happiness of great numbers of people.

Yesterday, and ever since history began, men were related to one another as individuals. To be sure there were the family, the Church, and the State, institutions which associated men in certain wide circles of relationship. But in the ordinary concerns of life, in the ordinary work, in the daily round, men dealt freely and directly with one another. Today, the everyday relationships of men are largely with great impersonal concerns, with organizations, not with other individual men.

Now this is nothing short of a new social age, a new era of human relationships, a new stage-setting for the drama of life.

In this new age we find, for instance, that our laws with regard to the relations of employer and employee are in many respects wholly antiquated and impossible. They were framed for another age, which nobody now living remembers, which is, indeed, so remote from our life that it would be difficult for many of us to understand it if it were described to us. The employer is now generally a corporation or a huge company of some kind; the employee is one of hundreds or of thousands brought together, not by individual masters whom they know and with whom they have personal relations, but by agents of one son or another. Workingmen are marshaled in great numbers for the performance of a multitude of particular tasks under a common discipline. They generally use dangerous and powerful machinery, over whose repair and renewal they have no control. New rules must be devised with regard to their obligations and their rights, their obligations to their employers and their responsibilities to one another. Rules must be devised for their protection, for their compensation when injured, for their support when disabled.

There is something very new and very big and very complex about these new relations of capital and labor. A new economic society has sprung up, and we must effect a new set of adjustments. We must not pit power against weakness. The employer is generally, in our day, as I have said, not an individual, but a powerful group; and yet the workingman when dealing with his employer is still, under our existing law, an individual.

Why is it that we have a labor question at all? It is for the simple and very sufficient reason that the laboring man and the employer are not intimate associates now as they used to be in time past. Most of our laws were formed in the age when employer and employees knew each other, knew each other's characters, were associates with each other, dealt with each other as man with man. That is no longer the case. You not only do not come into personal contact with the men who have the supreme command in those corporations, but it would be out of the question for you to do it. Our modern corporations employ thousands, and in some instances hundreds of thousands, of men. The only persons whom you see or deal with are local superintendents or local representatives of a vast organization, which is not like anything that the workingmen of the time in which our laws were framed knew anything about. A little group of workingmen, seeing their employer every day, dealing with him in a personal way, is one thing, and the modern body of labor engaged as employees of the huge enterprises that spread all over the country, dealing with men of whom they can form no personal conception, is another thing. A very different thing. You never saw a corporation, any more than you ever saw a government. Many a workingman to-day never saw the body of men who are conducting the industry in which he is employed. And they never saw him. What they know about him is written in ledgers and books and letters, in the correspondence of the office, in the reports of the superintendents. He is a long way off from them.

So what we have to discuss is, not wrongs which individuals intentionally do,—I do not believe there are a great many of those,—but the wrongs of a system. I want to record my protest against any discussion of this matter which would seem to indicate that there are bodies of our fellow-citizens who are trying to grind us down and do us injustice. There are some men of that sort. I don't know how they sleep o' nights, but there are men of that kind. Thank God, they are not numerous. The truth is, we are all caught in a great economic system which is heartless. The modern corporation is not engaged in business as an individual. When we deal with it, we deal with an impersonal element, an immaterial piece of society. A modern corporation is a means of cooperation in the conduct of an enterprise which is so big that no one man can conduct it, and which the resources of no one man are sufficient to finance. A company is formed; that company puts out a prospectus; the promoters expect to raise a certain fund as capital stock. Well, how are they going to raise it? They are going to raise it from the public in general, some of whom will buy their stock. The moment that begins, there is formed—what? A joint stock corporation. Men begin to pool their earnings, little piles, big piles. A certain number of men are elected by the stockholders to be directors, and these directors elect a president. This president is the head of the undertaking, and the directors are its managers.

Now, do the workingmen employed by that stock corporation deal with that president and those directors? Not at all. Does the public deal with that president and that board of directors? It does not. Can anybody bring them to account? It is next to impossible to do so. If you undertake it you will find it a game of hide and seek, with the objects of your search taking refuge now behind the tree of their individual personality, now behind that of their corporate irresponsibility.

And do our laws take note of this curious state of things? Do they even attempt to distinguish between a man's act as a corporation director and as an individual? They do not. Our laws still deal with us on the basis of the old system. The law is still living in the dead past which we have left behind. This is evident, for instance, with regard to the matter of employers' liability for workingmen's injuries. Suppose that a superintendent wants a workman to use a certain piece of machinery which it is not safe for him to use, and that the workman is injured by that piece of machinery. Some of our courts have held that the superintendent is a fellow-servant, or, as the law states it, a fellow-employee, and that, therefore, the man cannot recover damages for his injury. The superintendent who probably engaged the man is not his employer. Who is his employer? And whose negligence could conceivably come in there? The board of directors did not tell the employee to use that piece of machinery; and the president of the corporation did not tell him to use that piece of machinery. And so forth. Don't you see by that theory that a man never can get redress for negligence on the part of the employer? When I hear judges reason upon the analogy of the relationships that used to exist between workmen and their employers a generation ago, I wonder if they have not opened their eyes to the modern world. You know, we have a right to expect that judges will have their eyes open, even though the law which they administer hasn't awakened.

Yet that is but a single small detail illustrative of the difficulties we are in because we have not adjusted the law to the facts of the new order.

* * * * * *

1. *What key changes does Wilson see in American life over the preceding generation? How does his view compare with that of Brandeis (Document 21–4)?*

2. *What political solutions does Wilson propose for dealing with contemporary problems?*

3. *How does Wilson hope to resolve the growing tensions between individuals and the growing sense that people "have no control over the course of affairs"?*

chapter 22

World War I, 1914–1918

22–1 The President's Commission at Bisbee, 1917

Reacting to pressure from organized labor, President Wilson launched a federal investigation into the wartime deportation of striking copper miners from Bisbee, Arizona. The incident had received widespread coverage in the national press, and it embodied the growing tensions among mobilization for war, freedom of speech, and union activism. This editorial appeared in the New Republic, *a liberal magazine that supported the war effort.*

SOURCE: *New Republic,* December 8, 1917.

Bisbee, Arizona, is at the heart of one of the largest copper producing areas in the world. As the administrative headquarters of the Copper Queen branch of the Phelps Dodge corporation it is the virtual capital of the copper industry of the Southwest. In times of peace the Copper Queen is an important barometer of the nation's industrial prosperity; in times of war the administrative efficiency of the Phelps Dodge corporation in Bisbee is measurable in terms of life and death among our soldiers and the soldiers of our Allies at the front.

On June 27, 1917, the employees of the Copper Queen and of the neighboring properties, the Calumet and Arizona and the Shattuck, Arizona, went out on strike. On July 12, 1917, an armed mob under the nominal leadership of the county sheriff overwhelmed eleven hundred and eighty-six strikers and their alleged sympathizers, herded them aboard a train of cattle and box cars especially provided by the El Paso and Southwestern, a subsidiary of the copper companies, and under the muzzles of rifles, revolvers and machine guns deported them into the New Mexican desert. One man was killed while defending his home against illegal invasion. Others had their scalps and bones broken. Hundreds of homes were broken up. The ranking officer of the Phelps Dodge corporation in Bisbee had given out an interview in which he denounced the strikes in Bisbee and the other copper camps of Arizona as of pro-German origin and advocated deportations as the patriotic remedy.

After an interval of more than two months, President Wilson at the instance of Mr. Samuel Gompers appointed a commission headed by Secretary Wilson of the Federal Department of Labor to adjust the industrial disputes which continued seriously to restrict the output of the copper mines, and, incidentally, to make an investigation and report upon the Bisbee deportations and their effect upon our military preparations. The conclusions of the commission with respect to the industrial policy pursued by the managers of the great copper properties in Bisbee throw a flood of light upon the causes of the widespread industrial unrest that has held back our shipping, aeroplane and munitions program to the verge of a national scandal.

"The deportations of the 12th of July last from the Warren district of Arizona," begins the report, "as well as the practices that followed such deportations have deeply affected the opinions of laboring men as well as the general public throughout the country. They have been made the basis of an attempt to affect adversely public opinion among some of the people of the Allies...."

The commission found that while the miners had grievances, which they sincerely felt called for rectification by the companies, these grievances were not of a nature to justify a strike, provided some rational machinery had existed for the peaceful adjustment of disputes. But the companies created no such machinery, neither did the government attempt to supply it until months after the most pressing need for it had passed. The strikers formulated their grievances and invited the managers to a conference for their adjustment. The managers in Bisbee explain their refusal to confer on the ground that the strike had been called by the I. W. W. In their opinion, which was without foundation in the statutes of Arizona or the United States, the I. W. W. in and of itself and irrespective of proscribed conduct by individual members was an outlaw organization. But in the course of their investigations the commission found that representatives of the Phelps Dodge corporation had taken the same "no conference no compromise" attitude toward the miners' union affiliated with the A. F. of L. on strike in other copper camps owned by the corporation. Rather than deal with their employees through trade union officials they preferred to see their mines crippled until they could settle on their own terms.

The overt reason for the Bisbee deportations, the President's commission found, was "the belief in the minds of those who engineered them that violence was contemplated by the strikers, that life and property would be unsafe unless the deportations were undertaken," but the commission could discover no justification for this belief....

It was because the deportations were without justification, either in fact or in law that, as the commission reports, "those who planned and directed them," including "managers and other officials of the Phelps Dodge corporation Copper Queen division and of the Calumet and Arizona Mining Company, purposely abstained from consulting about their plans either with the United States attorney in Arizona or the law officers of the state....

This brutal resort to the spirit of mob violence has sent a blaze of industrial unrest and suspicion throughout our industrial army. Wage-workers suspected of harboring disloyal sentiments have been apprehended and thrown into jail. Managers who instigated and helped to execute plans "wholly illegal and without authority in law either state or federal" have been given commissions in the American army and invited into the innermost councils of the government. What is the result? We are months behind in the production of munitions...months behind in the production of aeroplanes. Agents of the government report that, since the Bisbee deportations, the strength of the I. W. W. in the timber camps of the Northwest has increased two and three hundred per cent. The spruce industry is completely paralyzed, and without spruce the construction of aeroplanes stops. "Talk to the lumber jacks," these agents say, "and they will answer you in terms of Bisbee."

...The Commission urges upon the President "the wisdom of recommending to the Congress that...deportations such as we have set forth...be made criminal under the federal law." These recommendations are excellent, as recommendations for the future, but they do not restore deportees to their homes, neither do they vindicate the constitutional rights of citizens which have been ignored by processes not provided by law. The wage-workers are not doctors of law. Their sole guide is common sense and it baffles their layman's reason to understand how it is pos-

sible to jail them on suspicion of holding illegal opinions, while both federal and state authorities are helpless to redress wrongs "wholly illegal" committed against them.

The report of the President's commission gives to the administration at Washington an opportunity to restore the confidence of the wage-workers in the majesty of the law and the determination of the government to render even-handed justice....The facts reported by the commission are records of actual interference with the law that have glistened on the surface for months. They have been known to the United States attorney in Arizona. They should have been known in the office of the attorney general at Washington. If we urge that they be given not only appropriate but also prompt attention, it is because there is abundant evidence to show that prompt attention is essential to the restoration of that confidence among tens of thousands of wage-workers without which appeals to patriotism may fall upon doubting and distrustful ears.

* * * * * *

1. *How does the writer try to balance sympathy for the striking copper miners with support for war mobilization? What criticisms does he make of both Phelps Dodge and the I. W. W.?*

2. *What danger does the writer see if the federal government fails to intervene more decisively to protect the rights of organized labor?*

22–2   *Theodore Roosevelt, Corollary to the Monroe Doctrine, 1904*

When the Dominican Republic went bankrupt in 1904, German and other European investors protested loudly, and the threat of armed intervention loomed. Only two years earlier, Germany and Italy had bombarded Venezuela during a similar crisis. To prevent European intervention in the Caribbean and restore financial stability, President Roosevelt issued his corollary to the Monroe Doctrine in a message to Congress. The United States took over customs collections and debt management in the Dominican Republic and thus established an important precedent for active intervention in the internal affairs of Caribbean nations. Roosevelt and later presidents invoked the corollary to justify intervention in Cuba, Nicaragua, Mexico, and Haiti.

SOURCE: President Theodore Roosevelt, Annual Messages to the United States Congress, December 6, 1904, and December 5, 1905.

Annual Message from President Roosevelt to the United States Congress, December 6, 1904.

It is not true that the United States feels any land hunger or entertains any projects as regards the other nations of the Western Hemisphere save such as are for their welfare. All that this country desires is to see the neighboring countries stable, orderly, and prosperous. Any country whose people conduct themselves well can count upon our hearty friendship. If a nation shows that it knows how to act with reasonable efficiency and decency in social and political matters, if it keeps order and pays its obligations, it need fear no interference from the United States. Chronic wrongdoing, or an impotence which results in a general loosening of the ties of civilized society, may in America, as elsewhere, ultimately require intervention by some civilized nation, and in the Western Hemisphere the adherence of the United States to the Monroe Doctrine may force the United States, however reluctantly, in flagrant cases of such wrongdoing or impotence, to the exercise of an international police power. If every country washed by the Caribbean Sea would show the progress in stable and just civilization which with the aid of the Platt amendment Cuba has shown since our troops left the island, and which so many of the republics in both Americas are constantly and brilliantly showing, all question of interference by this Nation with their affairs would be at an end. Our interests and those of our southern neighbors are in reality identical. They have great natural riches, and if within their borders the reign of law and justice obtains, prosperity is sure to come to them. While they thus obey the primary laws of civilized society they may rest assured that they will be treated by us in a spirit of cordial and helpful sympathy. We would interfere with them only in the last resort, and then only if it became evident that their inability or unwillingness to do justice at home and abroad had violated the rights of the United States or had invited foreign aggression to the detriment of the entire body of American nations. It is a mere truism to say that every nation, whether in America or anywhere else, which desires to maintain its freedom, its independence, must ultimately realize that the right of such independence can not be separated from the responsibility of making good use of it.

In asserting the Monroe Doctrine, in taking such steps as we have taken in regard to Cuba, Venezuela, and Panama, and in endeavoring to circumscribe the theater of war in the Far East, and to secure the open door in China, we have acted in our own interest as well as in the interest of humanity at large.

Annual Message from President Theodore Roosevelt to the United States Congress, December 5, 1905.

...There are certain essential points which must never be forgotten as regards the Monroe Doctrine. In the first place we must as a nation make it evident that we do not intend to treat it in any shape or way as an excuse for aggrandizement on our part at the expense of the republics to the south. We must recognize the fact that in some South American countries there has been much suspicion lest we should interpret the Monroe Doctrine as in some way inimical to their interests, and we must try to convince all the other nations of this continent once and for all that no just and orderly government has anything to fear from us. There are certain republics to the south of us which have already reached such a point of stability, order, and prosperity that they themselves, though as yet hardly consciously, are among the guarantors of this Doctrine. These republics we now meet not only on a basis of entire equality, but in a spirit of frank and respectful friendship, which we hope is mutual. If all of the republics to the south of us will only grow as those to which I allude have already grown, all need for us to be the especial champions of the Doctrine will disappear, for no stable and growing American Republic wishes to see some great non-American military power acquire territory in its neighborhood. All that this country desires is that the other republics on this Continent shall be happy and prosperous; and they can not be happy and prosperous unless they maintain order within their boundaries and behave with a just regard for their obligations toward outsiders....

Moreover, we must make it evident that we do not intend to permit the Monroe Doctrine to be used by any nation on this Continent as a shield to protect it from the consequences of its own misdeeds against foreign nations. If a republic to the south of us commits a tort against a foreign nation, such as an outrage against a citizen of that nation, then the Monroe Doctrine does not force us to interfere to prevent punishment of the tort, save to see that the punishment does not assume the form of territorial occupation in any shape. The case is more difficult when it refers to a contractual obligation. Our own Government has always refused to enforce such contractual obligations on behalf of its citizens by an appeal to arms. It is much to be wished that all foreign governments would take the same view. But they do not; and in consequence we are liable at any time to be brought face to face with disagreeable alternatives. On the one hand, this country would certainly decline to go to war to prevent a foreign government from collecting a just debt; on the other hand, it is very inadvisable to permit any foreign power to take possession, even temporarily, of the customhouses of an American Republic in order to enforce the payment of its obligations; for such temporary occupation might turn into a permanent occupation. The only escape from these alternatives may at any time be that we must ourselves undertake to bring about some arrangement by which so much as possible of a just obligation shall be paid. It is far better that this country should put through such an arrangement, rather than allow any foreign country to undertake it. To do so insures the defaulting republic from having to pay debts of an improper character under duress, while it also insures honest creditors of the republic from being passed by in the interest of dishonest or grasping creditors. Moreover, for the United States to take such a position offers the only possible way of insuring us against a clash with some foreign power. The position is, therefore, in the interest of peace as well as in the interest of justice. It is of benefit to our people; it is of benefit to foreign peoples; and most of all it is really of benefit to the people of the country concerned....

* * * * * *

1. *How does Roosevelt link the economic interests of Caribbean nations and those of the United States? What does he mean by "the primary laws of civilized society"?*

2. *What are the military implications of the policy?*

3. *How does the new policy reflect a new U.S. attitude toward U.S. relations with the entire Caribbean region?*

22–3 *Woodrow Wilson, War Message to Congress, 1917*

Wilson's re-election in 1916 owed a great deal to the campaign slogan, "He kept us out of war." But the resumption of unrestricted submarine warfare by Germany in 1917 significantly changed the international situation. Several U.S. merchant ships were sunk in March by German U-boats. That April, Wilson called Congress into extraordinary session to ask for a declaration of war against Germany. Within four days, both the Senate and the House voted overwhelmingly to support the President.

SOURCE: Address delivered at Joint Session of the Two Houses of Congress, April 2, 1917; U.S. 65th Congress, 1st Session, Senate Document 5.

On the third of February last I officially laid before you the extraordinary announcement of the Imperial German Government that on and after the first day of February it was its purpose to put aside all restraints of law or of humanity and use its submarines to sink every vessel that sought to approach either the ports of Great Britain and Ireland or the western coasts of Europe or any of the ports controlled by the enemies of Germany within the Mediterranean. That had seemed to be the object of the German submarine warfare earlier in the war, but since April of last year the Imperial Government had somewhat restrained the commanders of its undersea craft in conformity with its promise then given to us that passenger boats should not be sunk and that due warning would be given to all other vessels which its submarines might seek to destroy, when no resistance was offered or escape attempted, and care taken that their crews were given at least a fair chance to save their lives in their open boats. The precautions taken were meager and haphazard enough, as was proved in distressing instance after instance in the progress of the cruel and unmanly business, but a certain degree of restraint was observed. The new policy has swept every restriction aside. Vessels of every kind, whatever their flag, their character, their cargo, their destination, their errand, have been ruthlessly sent to the bottom without warning and without thought of help or mercy for those on board, the vessels of friendly neutrals along with those of belligerents. Even hospital ships and ships carrying relief to the sorely bereaved and stricken people of Belgium, though the latter were pro-

vided with safe conduct through the proscribed areas by the German Government itself and were distinguished by unmistakable marks of identity, have been sunk with the same reckless lack of compassion or of principle.

I was for a little while unable to believe that such things would in fact be done by any government that had hitherto subscribed to the humane practices of civilized nations. International law had its origin in the attempt to set up some law which would be respected and observed upon the seas, where no nation had right of dominion and where lay the free highways of the world....This minimum of right the German Government has swept aside under the plea of retaliation and necessity and because it had no weapons which it could use at sea except these which it is impossible to employ as it is employing them without throwing to the winds all scruples of humanity or of respect for the understandings that were supposed to underlie the intercourse of the world. I am not now thinking of the loss of property involved, immense and serious as that is, but only of the wanton and wholesale destruction of the lives of non-combatants, men, women, and children, engaged in pursuits which have always, even in the darkest periods of modern history, been deemed innocent and legitimate. Property can be paid for, the lives of peaceful and innocent people cannot be. The present German submarine warfare against commerce is a warfare against mankind.

It is a war against all nations. American ships have been sunk, American lives taken, in ways which it has stirred us very deeply to learn of, but the ships and people of other neutral and friendly nations have been sunk and overwhelmed in the waters in the same way. There has been no discrimination. The challenge is to all mankind. Each nation must decide for itself how it will meet it. The choice we make for ourselves must be made with a moderation of counsel and a temperateness of judgment befitting our character and our motives as a nation. We must put excited feeling away. Our motive will not be revenge or the victorious assertion of the physical might of the nation, but only the vindication of right, of human right, of which we are only a single champion.

With a profound sense of the solemn and even tragical character of the step I am taking and of the grave responsibilities which it involves, but in unhesitating obedience to what I deem my constitutional duty, I advise that the Congress declare the recent course of the Imperial German Government to be in fact nothing less war against the government and people of the United States; that it formally accept the status of belligerent which has thus been thrust upon it; and that it take immediate steps not only to put the country in a more thorough state of defense but also to exert all its power and employ all its resources to bring the Government of the German Empire to terms and end the war.

While we do these things, these deeply momentous things, let us be very clear, and make very clear to all the world what our motives and our objects are. My own thought has not been driven from its habitual and normal course by the unhappy events of the last two months, and I do not believe that the thought of the Nation has been altered or clouded by them. I have exactly the same things in mind now that I had in mind when I addressed the Senate on the twenty-second of January last; the same that I had in mind when I addressed the Congress on the third of February and on the twenty-sixth of February. Our object now, as then, is to vindicate the principles of peace and justice in the life of the world as against selfish and autocratic power and to set up amongst the really free and self-governed peoples of the world such a concert of purpose and of action as will henceforth insure the observance of those principles. Neutrality is no longer feasible or desirable where the peace of the world is involved and the freedom of its peoples, and the menace to that peace and freedom lies in the existence of autocratic governments backed by organized force which is controlled wholly by their will, not by the will of their people. We have seen the last of neutrality in such circumstances. We are at the beginning of an age in which it will be insisted that the same standards of conduct and of responsibility for wrong done shall be observed among nations and their governments that are observed among the individual citizens of civilized states.

We have no quarrel with the German people. We have no feeling towards them but one of sympathy and friendship. It was not upon their impulse that their government acted in entering this war. It was not with their previous knowledge or approval. It was a war determined upon as wars used to be determined upon in the old, unhappy days when peoples were nowhere consulted by their rulers and wars were provoked and waged in the interest of dynasties or of little groups of ambitious men who were accustomed to use their fellow men as pawns and tools....

We are accepting this challenge of hostile purpose because we know that in such a Government, following such methods, we can never have a friend; and that in the presence of its organized power, always lying in wait to accomplish we know not what purpose, there can be no

assured security for the democratic Governments of the world. We are now about to accept gauge of battle with this natural foe to liberty and shall, if necessary, spend the whole force of the nation to check and nullify its pretensions and its power. We are glad, now that we see the facts with no veil of false pretense about them, to fight thus for the ultimate peace of the world and for the liberation of its peoples, the German peoples included: for the rights of nations great and small and the privilege of men everywhere to choose their way of life and of obedience. The world must be made safe for democracy. Its peace must be planted upon the tested foundations of political liberty. We have no selfish ends to serve. We desire no conquest, no dominion. We seek no indemnities for ourselves, no material compensation for the sacrifices we shall freely make. We are but one of the champions of the rights of mankind. We shall be satisfied when those rights have been made as secure as the faith and the freedom of nations can make them.

It is a distressing and oppressive duty, Gentlemen of the Congress, which I have performed in thus addressing you. There are, it may be, many months of fiery trial and sacrifice ahead of us. It is a fearful thing to lead this great peaceful people into war, into the most terrible and disastrous of all wars, civilization itself seeming to be in the balance. But the right is more precious than peace, and we shall fight for the things which we have always carried nearest our hearts,—for democracy, for the right of those who submit to authority to have a voice in their own Governments, for the fights and liberties of small nations, for a universal dominion of right by such a concert of free peoples as shall bring peace and safety to all nations and make the world itself at last free. To such a task we can dedicate our lives and our fortunes, everything that we are and everything that we have, with the pride of those who know that the day has come when America is privileged to spend her blood and her might for the principles that gave her birth and happiness and the peace which she has treasured. God helping her, she can do no other.

* * * * * *

1. *How does Wilson justify the declaration of war on both legal and moral grounds?*

2. *How does he seek to differentiate American war aims from those of belligerents?*

3. *Why does he make careful distinction between the German government and the German people?*

22–4   George Norris, Against Entry into War, 1917

An agrarian Progressive Republican from Nebraska, George Norris was one of only six senators to oppose Wilson's declaration of war. His views reflected the doubts of many Americans, especially in the isolationist Midwest. Norris would also oppose the Versailles Peace Treaty as well, although he later supported the American entry into World War II. He delivered the following speech two days after Wilson's war message.

SOURCE: George Norris, Speech before the Senate, April 4, 1917; U.S. 65th Congress, 1st Session.

There are a great many American citizens who feel that we owe it as a duty to humanity to take part in this war. Many instances of cruelty and inhumanity can be found on both sides. Men are often biased in their judgment on account of their sympathy and their interests. To my mind, what we ought to have maintained from the beginning was the strictest neutrality. If we had done this I do not believe we would have been on the verge of war at the present time. We had a right as a nation, if we desired, to cease at any time to be neutral. We had a technical right to respect the English war zone and to disregard the German war zone, but we could not do that and be neutral. I have no quarrel to find with the man who does not desire our country to remain neutral. While many such people are moved by selfish motives and hopes of gain, I have no doubt but that in a great many instances, through what I believe to be a misunderstanding of the real condition, there are many honest, patriotic citizens who think we ought to engage in this war and who are behind the President in his demand that we should declare war against Germany. I think such people err in judgment and to a great extent have been misled as to the real history and the true facts by the almost unanimous demand of the great combination of wealth that has a direct financial interest in our participation in the war. We have loaned many hundreds of millions of dollars to the allies in this controversy. While such action was legal and countenanced by international law, there is no doubt in my mind but the enormous amount of money loaned to the allies in this country has been instrumental in bringing about a public sentiment in favor of our country taking a course that would make every bond worth a hundred cents on the dollar and making the payment of every debt certain and sure. Through this instrumentality and also through the instrumentality of others who have not only made millions out of the war in the manufacture of munitions, etc., and who would expect to make millions more if our coun-

try can be drawn into the catastrophe, a large number of the great newspapers and news agencies of the country have been controlled and enlisted in the greatest propaganda that the world has ever known, to manufacture sentiment in favor of war. It is now demanded that the American citizens shall be used as insurance policies to guarantee the safe delivery of munitions of war to belligerent nations. The enormous profits of munition manufacturers, stockbrokers, and bond dealers must be still further increased by our entrance into the war. This has brought us to the present moment, when Congress, urged by the President and backed by the artificial sentiment, is about to declare war and engulf our country in the greatest holocaust that the world has ever known....

To whom does the war bring prosperity? Not to the soldier who for the munificent compensation of $16 per month shoulders his musket and goes into the trench, there to shed his blood and to die if necessary; not to the broken-hearted widow who waits for the return of the mangled body of her husband; not to the mother who weeps at the death of her brave boy; not to the little children who shiver with cold; not to the babe who suffers from hunger; nor to the millions of mothers and daughters who carry broken hearts to their graves. War brings no prosperity to the great mass of common and patriotic citizens. It increases the cost of living of those who toil and those who already must strain every effort to keep soul and body together. War brings prosperity to the stock gambler on Wall street—to those who are already in possession of more wealth than can be realized or enjoyed. [A Wall Street broker] says if we can not get war, "it is nevertheless good opinion that the preparedness program will compensate in good measure for the loss of the stimulus of actual war." That is, if we can not get war, let us go as far in that direction as possible. If we can not get war, let us cry for additional ships, additional guns, additional munitions, and everything else that will have a tendency to bring us as near as possible to the verge of war. And if war comes do such men as these shoulder the musket and go into the trenches?

Their object in having war and in preparing for war is to make money. Human suffering and the sacrifice of human life are necessary, but Wall Street considers only the dollars and the cents. The men who do the fighting, the people who make the sacrifices, are the ones who will not be counted in the measure of this great prosperity he depicts. The stock brokers would not, of course, go to war, because the very object they have in bringing on the war is profit, and therefore they must remain in their Wall Street offices in order to share in that great prosperity which they say war will bring. The volunteer officer, even the drafting officer, will not find them. They will be concealed in their palatial offices on Wall Street, sitting behind mahogany desks, covered up with clipped coupons—coupons soiled with the sweat of honest toil, coupons stained with mothers' tears, coupons dyed in the lifeblood of their fellow men.

We are taking a step today that is fraught with untold danger. We are going into war upon the command of gold. We are going to run the risk of sacrificing millions of our countrymen's lives in order that other countrymen may coin their lifeblood into money. And even if we do not cross the Atlantic and go into the trenches, we are going to pile up a debt that the toiling masses that shall come many generations after us will have to pay. Unborn millions will bend their backs in toil in order to pay for the terrible step we are now about to take. We are about to do the bidding of wealth's terrible mandate. By our act we will make millions of our countrymen suffer,

and the consequences of it may well be that millions of our brethren must shed their lifeblood, millions of broken-hearted women must weep, millions of children must suffer with cold, and millions of babes must die from hunger, and all because we want to preserve the commercial right of American citizens to deliver munitions of war to belligerent nations.

* * * * * *

1.   *How does Norris's understanding of the motives for war differ from Wilson's?*

2.   *How does Norris invoke the imagery and results of war in his speech?*

22–5   George Creel,
How We Advertised America, 1920

In 1917, President Wilson appointed George Creel, a progressive midwestern journalist, to head the Committee on Public Information. His task was to mold American public opinion in support of the war effort. Creel presided over a highly centralized and effective government propaganda effort that was unique in American history to that point. After the Armistice, Creel wrote a widely read book that detailed and justified the work of the CPI.

SOURCE: George Creel, *How We Advertised America* (Macmillan, 1920), pp. 3–9.

How We Advertised America
I

THE "SECOND LINES"

Back of the firing-line, back of armies and navies, back of the great supply-depots, another struggle waged with the same intensity and with almost equal significance attaching to its victories and defeats. It was the fight for the *minds* of men, for the "conquest of their convictions," and the battle-line ran through every home in every country.

It was in this recognition of Public Opinion as a major force that the Great War differed most essentially from all previous conflicts. The trial of strength was not only between massed bodies of armed men, but between opposed ideals, and moral verdicts took on all the value of military decisions. Other wars went no deeper than the physical aspects, but German *Kultur* raised issues that had to be fought out in the hearts and minds of people as well as on the actual firing-line. The approval of the world

meant the steady flow of inspiration into the trenches; it meant the strengthened resolve and the renewed determination of the civilian population that is a nation's second line. The condemnation of the world meant the destruction of morale and the surrender of that conviction of justice which is the very heart of courage.

The Committee on Public Information was called into existence to make this fight for the "verdict of mankind," the voice created to plead the justice of America's cause before the jury of Public Opinion. The fantastic legend that associated gags and muzzles with its work may be likened only to those trees which are evolved out of the air by Hindu magicians and which rise, grow, and flourish in gay disregard of such usual necessities as roots, sap, and sustenance. *In no degree was the Committee an agency of censorship, a machinery of concealment or repression. Its emphasis throughout was on the open and the positive. At no point did it seek or exercise authorities under those war laws that limited the freedom of speech and press.* In all things, from fast to last, without halt or change, it was a plain publicity proposition, a vast enterprise in salesmanship, the world's greatest adventure in advertising.

Under the pressure of tremendous necessities an organization grew that not only reached deep into every American community, but that carried to every corner of the civilized globe the full message of America's idealism, unselfishness, and indomitable purpose. We fought prejudice, indifference, and disaffection at home and we fought ignorance and falsehood abroad. We strove for the maintenance of our own morale and the Allied morale by every process of stimulation; every possible expedient was employed to break through the barrage of lies that kept the people of the Central Powers in darkness and delusion; we sought the friendship and support of the neutral nations by continuous presentation of facts. We did not call it propaganda, for that word, in German hands, had come to be associated with deceit and corruption. Our effort was educational and informative throughout, for we had such confidence in our case as to feel that no other argument was needed than the simple, straightforward presentation of facts.

There was no part of the great war machinery that we did not touch, no medium of appeal that we did not employ. The printed word, the spoken word, the motion picture, the telegraph, the cable, the wireless, the poster, the sign-board—all these were used in our campaign to make our own people and all other peoples understand the causes that compelled America to take arms. All that was fine and ardent in the civilian population came at our call until more than one hundred and fifty thousand men and women were devoting highly specialized abilities to the work of the Committee, as faithful and devoted in their service as though they wore the khaki.

While America's summons was answered without question by the citizenship as a whole, it is to be remembered that during the three and a half years of our neutrality the land had been torn by a thousand divisive prejudices, stunned by the voices of anger and confusion, and muddled by the pull and haul of opposed interests. These were conditions that could not be permitted to endure. What we had to have was no mere surface unity, but a passionate belief in the justice of America's cause that should weld the people of the United States into one white-hot mass instinct with fraternity, devotion, courage, and deathless determination. The *war-will,* the will-to-win, of a democracy depends upon the degree to which each one of all the people of that democracy can concentrate and consecrate body and soul and spirit in the supreme effort of service and sacrifice. What had to be driven home was that all business was the nation's business, and every task a common task for a single purpose.

Starting with the initial conviction that the war was not the war of an administration, but the war of one hundred million people, and believing that public support was a matter of public understanding, we opened up the activities of government to the inspection of the citizenship. A voluntary censorship agreement safeguarded information of obvious value to the enemy, but in all else the rights of the press were recognized and furthered. Trained men, at the center of effort in every one of the war-making branches of government, reported on progress and achievement, and in no other belligerent nation was there such absolute frankness with respect to every detail of the national war endeavor.

As swiftly as might be, there were put into pamphlet form America's reasons for entering the war, the meaning of America, the nature of our free institutions, our war aims, likewise analyses of the Prussian system, the purposes of the imperial German government, and full

exposure of the enemy's misrepresentations, aggression, and barbarities. Written by the country's foremost publicists, scholars, and historians, and distinguished for their conciseness, accuracy, and simplicity, these pamphlets blew as a great wind against the clouds of confusion and misrepresentation. Money could not have purchased the volunteer aid that was given freely, the various universities lending their best men and the National Board of Historical Service placing its three thousand members at the complete disposal of the Committee. Some thirty-odd booklets, covering every phase of America's ideals, purposes, and aims, were printed in many languages other than English. Seventy-five millions reached the people of America, and other millions went to every corner of the world, Carrying our defense and our attack.

The importance of the spoken word was not underestimated. A speaking division toured great groups like the Blue Devils, Pershing's Veterans, and the Belgians, arranged mass-meetings in the communities, conducted forty-five war conferences from coast to coast, coordinated the entire speaking activities of the nation, and assured consideration to the crossroads hamlet as well as to the city.

The Four Minute Men, an organization that will live in history by reason of its originality and effectiveness, commanded the volunteer services of 75,000 speakers, operating in 5,200 communities, and making a total of 755,190 speeches, every one having the carry of shrapnel.

With the aid of a volunteer staff of several hundred translators, the Committee kept in direct touch with the foreign-language press, supplying selected articles designed to combat ignorance and disaffection. It organized and directed twenty-three societies and leagues designed to appeal to certain classes and particular foreign-language groups, each body carrying a specific message of unity and enthusiasm to its section of America's adopted peoples.

It planned war exhibits for the state fairs of the United States, also a great series of interallied war expositions that brought home to our millions the exact nature of the struggle that was being waged in France. In Chicago alone two million people attended in two weeks, and in nineteen cities the receipts aggregated $1,432,261.36.

The Committee mobilized the advertising forces of the country—press, periodical, car, and outdoor—for the patriotic campaign that gave millions of dollars' worth of space to the national service.

It assembled the artists of America on a volunteer basis for the production of posters, window-cards, and similar material of pictorial publicity for the use of various government departments and patriotic societies. A total of 1,438 drawings was used.

It issued an official daily newspaper, serving every department of government, with a circulation of one hundred thousand copies a day. For official use only, its value was such that private citizens ignored the supposedly prohibitive subscription price, subscribing to the amount of $77,622.58.

It organized a bureau of information for all persons who sought direction in volunteer war-work, in acquiring knowledge of any administrative activities, or in approaching business dealings with the government. In the ten months of its existence it gave answers to eight-six thousand requests for specific information.

It gathered together the leading novelists, essayists, and publicists of the land, and these men and women, without payment, worked faithfully in the production of brilliant comprehensive articles that went to the press as syndicate features.

One division paid particular attention to the rural press and the plate-matter service. Others looked after the specialized needs of the labor press, the religious press, and the periodical press. The Division of Women's War Work prepared and issued the information of peculiar interest to the women of the United States, also aiding in the task of organizing and directing.

Through the medium of the motion picture, America's war progress, as well as the meanings and purposes of democracy, were carried to every community in the United States and to every corner of the world. "Pershing's Crusaders," "America's Answer," and "Under Four Flags" were types of feature films by which we drove home America's resources and determinations, while other pictures, showing our social and industrial life, made our free institutions vivid to foreign peoples. From the domestic showings alone, under a fair plan of distribution, the sum of $878,215 was gained, which went to support the cost of the campaigns in foreign countries where the exhibitions were necessarily free.

Another division prepared and distributed still photographs and stereopticon slides to the press and public. Over two hundred thousand of the latter were issued at cost. This division also conceived the idea of the "permit system," that opened up our military and naval activities to civilian camera men, and operated it successfully. It handled, also, the voluntary censorship of slide and motion pictures in order that there might be no disclosure of information valuable to the enemy. The number of pictures reviewed averaged seven hundred a day.

* * * * * *

1.   *According to Creel, how did this war differ from all previous conflicts?*

2.   *Why and how does Creel distinguish the work of the CPI from "propaganda"?*

3.   *Why were new mass media so crucial to the Committee on Public Information?*

22–6   *Diary of an Unknown Aviator, 1918*

World War I introduced new technologies of death into armed combat: the machine gun, the tank, and the airplane. Conditions on the battlefield, particularly in the trenches of France, bore little resemblance to the descriptions of war that many soldiers had gleaned from romantic fiction or heard firsthand from Civil war veterans in their communities. The following diary excerpt from an American pilot gives a good sense of the battlefield experience.

SOURCE: *War Birds: Diary of an Unknown Aviator* (Doran, 1926), p. 71.

We've lost a lot of good men. It's only a question of time until we all get it. I'm all shot to pieces. I only hope I can stick it. I don't want to quit. My nerves are all gone and I can't stop. I've lived beyond my time already.

It's not the fear of death that's done it. I'm still not afraid to die. It's this eternal flinching from it that's doing it and has made a coward out of me. Few men live to know what real fear is. It's something that grows on you, day by day, that eats into your constitution and undermines your sanity. I have never been serious about anything in my life and now I know that I'll never be otherwise again. But my seriousness will be a burlesque for no one will recognize it. Here I am, twenty-four years old, I look forty and I feel ninety. I've lost all interest in life beyond the next patrol. No one Hun will ever get me and I'll never fall into a trap, but sooner or later I'll be forced to fight against odds that are too long or perhaps a stray shot from the ground will be lucky and I will have gone in vain. Or my motor will cut out when we are trench straffing or a wing will pull off in a dive. Oh, for a parachute! The Huns are using them now. I haven't a chance, I know, and it's this eternal waiting around that's killing me. I've even lost my taste for licker. It doesn't seem to do me any good now. I guess I'm stale. Last week I actually got frightened in the air and lost my head. Then I found ten Huns and took them all on and I got one of them down out of control. I got my nerve back by that time and came back home and slept like a baby for the first time in two months. What a blessing sleep is! I know now why men go out and take such long chances and pull off such wild stunts. No discipline in the world could make them do what they do of their own accord. I know now what a brave man is. I know now how men laugh at death and welcome it. I know now why Ball went over and sat above a Hun airdrome and dared them to come up and fight with him. It takes a brave man to even experience real fear. A coward couldn't last long enough at the job to get to that stage. What price salvation now?

War is a horrible thing, a grotesque comedy. And it is so useless. This war won't prove anything. All we'll do when we win is to substitute one sort of Dictator for another. In the meantime we have destroyed our best resources. Human life, the most precious thing in the world, has become the cheapest. After we've won this war by drowning the Hun in our own blood, in five years' time the sentimental fools at home will be taking up a collection for these same Huns that are killing us now and our fool politicians will be cooking up another good war. Why shouldn't they? They have to keep the public stirred up to keep their jobs and they don't have to fight and they can get soft berths for their sons and their friends' sons. To me the most contemptible cur in the world is the man who lets political influence be used to keep him away from the front. For he lets another man die in his place.

The worst thing about this war is that it takes the best. If it lasts long enough the world will be populated by cowards and weaklings and their children. And the whole thing is so useless, so unnecessary, so terrible!...

The devastation of the country is too horrible to describe. It looks from the air as if the gods had made a gigantic steam roller, forty miles wide and run it from the coast to Switzerland, leaving its spike holes behind as it went....

I've lost over a hundred friends, so they tell me— I've seen only seven or eight killed—but to me they aren't dead yet. They are just around the corner, I think, and I'm still expecting to run into them any time. I dream about them at night when I do sleep a little and sometimes I dream that some one is killed who really isn't. Then I don't know who is and who isn't. I saw a man in Boulogne the other day that I had dreamed I saw killed and I thought I was seeing a ghost. I can't realize that any of them are gone. Surely human life is not a candle to be snuffed out....

* * * * * *

1. *What is the worst aspect of combat for this soldier? How has the war changed him?*

2. *What problems can you imagine this soldier encountering if he survives the war to return home?*

22–7 *Anna Howard Shaw, Woman's Committee of the Council of National Defense, 1917*

World War I proved a boon for the woman suffrage movement. With the American entry into the fighting, the National American Woman Suffrage Association (NAWSA) urged its members to find ways to aid mobilization, and by 1919 NAWSA's membership had doubled to over two million. Only reluctantly, under pressure from NAWSA and the more radical National Woman's Party, did President Woodrow Wilson come to support woman suffrage. At the 1917 NAWSA convention, its former President Anna Howard Shaw outlined the importance of war work for women.

SOURCE: Anna Howard Shaw, NAWSA Convention, 1917, in Mari Jo and Paul Buhle eds., *The Concise History of Woman Suffrage* (University of Illinois Press, 1978), pp. 438–440.

In a stirring address Dr. Shaw showed what the country expected of women at this critical time, saying:

We talk of the army in the field as one and the army at home as another. We are not two armies; we are one— absolutely one army—and we must work together. Unless the army at home does its duty faithfully, the army in the field will be unable to carry to a victorious end this war which you and I believe is the great war that shall bring to the world the thing that is nearest our hearts—democracy, that "those who submit to authority shall have a voice in the government" and that when they have that voice peace shall reign among the nations of men.

The United States Government, learning from the weaknesses and the mistakes of the governments across the sea, immediately after declaring war on Germany knew that it was wise to mobilize not only the man power of the nation but the woman power. It took Great Britain a long time to learn that—more than a year—and it was not until 50,000 women paraded the streets of London with banners saying, "Put us to work," that it dawned upon the British government that women could be mobilized and made serviceable in the war. And what is the result? It has been discovered that men and women alike have within them great reserve power, great forces which are called out by emergencies and the demands of a time like this.

Dr. Shaw described the forming of the Woman's Committee of the Council of National Defense by the Government and her selection as its chairman. She said she had no idea what the committee was expected to do, so she went to the Secretary of the Navy to find out, and continued: "I learned that the Woman's Committee was to be the channel through which the orders of the various departments of the Government concerning women's war work were to reach the womanhood of the country; that it was to conserve and coordinate all the women's societies in the United States which were doing war work in order to prevent duplication and useless effort. This was very necessary, not because our women are not patriotic but because they are so patriotic that every blessed woman in the country was writing Washington, or her organization was writing for her, asking the Government what she could do for the war and of course the Government did not know; it has not yet the least idea of what women can do."

An amusing picture was given of men supervising a department of the Red Cross where women were knitting, making comfort bags, etc. She showed how for the past forty years women in their clubs and societies had been going through the necessary evolution, "until today," she said, "they are a mobilized army ready to serve the country in whatever capacity they are needed. So when the Council of National Defense laid upon the Woman's Committee the responsibility of calling them together to mobilize women's war work, we knew exactly how to do it....It is not a question of whether we will act or not, the Government has said we *must* act; it is an order as much as it is an order that men shall go and fight in the trenches. It is an order of the Government that the women's war work of the country shall be coordinated, that women shall keep their organizations intact, that they shall get together under directed heads. I said to the gentlemen here in Washington, when at first they feared our women might not be willing to cooperate: 'If you put before them an incentive big enough, if you appeal to them as a part of the Government's life, not as a by-product of creation or a kindergarten but as a great human, living energy, ready to serve the country, they will respond as readily as the men.'"

We must remember that more and more sacrifices are going to be demanded but I want to say to you women, do not meekly sit down and make all the sacrifices and demand nothing in return. It is not that you want pay but we all want an equally balanced sacrifice. The Government is asking us to conserve food while it is allowing carload after carload to rot on the side tracks of railroad stations and great elevators of grain to be consumed by fire for lack of proper protection. If we must eat Indian meal in order to save wheat, then the men must protect the grain elevators and see that the wheat is saved. We must demand that there shall be conservation all along the line. I had a letter the other day giving me a fearful scorching because of a speech I made in which I said that we women have Mr. Hoover looking into our refrigerators, examining our bread to see

what kind of materials we are using, telling us what extravagant creatures we are, that we waste millions of money every year, waste food and all that sort of thing, and yet while we are asked to have meatless days and wheatless days, I have never yet seen a demand for a smokeless day! They are asking through the newspapers that we women shall dance, play bridge, have charades, sing and do everything under the sun to raise money to buy tobacco for the men in the trenches, while the men who want us to do this have a cigar in their mouth at the time they are asking it! I said that if men want the soldiers to have tobacco, let them have smokeless days and furnish it! If they would conserve one single cigar a day and send it to the men in the trenches the soldiers would have all they would need and the men at home would be a great deal better off. If we have to eat rye flour to send wheat across the sea they must stop smoking to send smokes across the sea.

There is no end to the things that women are asked to do. I know this is true because I have read the newspapers for the last six months to get my duty before me. The first thing we are asked to do is to provide the enthusiasm, inspiration and patriotism to make men want to fight, and we are to send them away with a smile! That is not much to ask of a mother! We are to maintain a perfect calm after we have furnished all this inspiration and enthusiasm, "keep the home fires burning," keep the home sweet and peaceful and happy, keep society on a level, look after business, buy enough but not too much and wear some of our old clothes but not all of them or what would happen to the merchants?...

We are going to rise as women always have risen to the supreme height of patriotic service....

The Woman's Committee of the Council of National Defense now asks for your cooperation, that we may be what the Government would have us be, soldiers at home, defending the interests of the home, while the men are fighting with the gallant Allies who are laying down their lives that this world may be a safe place and that men and women may know the meaning of democracy, which is that we are one great family of God. That, and that only, is the ideal of democracy for which our flag stands.

* * * * * *

1. *What does it mean for women to be "soldiers at home"?*

2. *What sense does Shaw give of being dissatisfied with the position of American women?*

3. *Why doesn't Shaw specifically link women's war service with the right to vote?*

22–8 Eugene V. Debs, Statement to the Court, 1918

Eugene V. Debs was a longtime labor leader and perennial presidential candidate of the Socialist Party who opposed American involvement in the First World War. After making an anti-war speech in Canton, Ohio, Debs was arrested in June 1918 and charged with violating the Espionage Act. Convicted and sentenced to ten years in federal prison, the incarcerated Debs ran once again for president in 1920, receiving over 90,000 votes. He served thirty-two months in prison before being pardoned by President Harding on Christmas Day, 1921. Debs made the following statement before going to the federal penitentiary in Atlanta.

SOURCE: Eugene V. Debs, *Writings and Speeches* (1948).

Your honor, years ago I recognized my kinship with all living beings, and I made up my mind that I was not one bit better than the meanest on earth. I said then, and I say now, that while there is a lower class, I am in it, while there is a criminal element, I am of it, and while there is a soul in prison, I am not free.

I listened to all that was said in this court in support and justification of this prosecution, but my mind remains unchanged. I look upon the Espionage Law as a despotic enactment in flagrant conflict with democratic principles and with the spirit of free institutions....

Your Honor, I have stated in this court that I am opposed to the social system in which we live; that I believe in a fundamental change—but if possible by peaceable and orderly means....

Standing here this morning, I recall my boyhood. At fourteen I went to work in a railroad shop; at sixteen I was firing a freight engine on a railroad. I remember all the hardships and privations of that earlier day, and from that time until now my heart has been with the working class. I could have been in Congress long ago. I have preferred to go to prison....

I am thinking this morning of the men in the mills and factories; of the men in the mines and on the railroads. I am thinking of the women who for a paltry wage are compelled to work out their barren lives; of the little children who in this system are robbed of their childhood and in their tender years are seized in the remorseless grasp of Mammon and forced into the industrial dungeons, there to feed the monster machines while they themselves are being starved and stunted, body and soul. I see them dwarfed and diseased and their little lives broken and blasted because in this high noon of our twentieth-century Christian civilization money is still so much

more important than the flesh and blood of childhood. In very truth gold is God today and rules with pitiless sway in the affairs of men.

In this country, the most favored beneath the bending skies—we have vast areas of the richest and most fertile soil, material resources in inexhaustible abundance, the most marvelous productive machinery on earth, and millions of eager workers ready to apply their labor to that machinery to produce an abundance for every man, woman, and child—and if there are still vast numbers of our people who are the victims of poverty and whose lives are an unceasing struggle all the way from youth to old age, until at last death comes to their rescue and stills their aching hearts and lulls these hapless victims to dreamless sleep, it is not the fault of the Almighty: it cannot be charged to nature, but it is due entirely to the outgrown social system in which we live, that ought to be abolished not only in the interest of the toiling masses but in the higher interest of all humanity....

I believe, Your Honor, in common with all Socialists, that this nation ought to own and control its own industries. I believe, as all Socialists do, that all things that are jointly needed and used ought to be jointly owned—that industry, the basis of our social life, instead of being the private property of the few and operated for their enrichment, ought to be the common property of all, democratically administered in the interest of all....

I am opposing a social order in which it is possible for one man who does absolutely nothing that is useful to amass a fortune of hundreds of millions of dollars, while millions of men and women who work all the days of their lives secure barely enough for a wretched existence.

This order of things cannot always endure. I have registered my protest against it. I recognize the feebleness of my effort, but fortunately I am not alone. There are multiplied thousands of others who, like myself have come to realize that before we may truly enjoy the blessings of civilized life, we must reorganize society upon a mutual and co-operative basis; and to this end we have organized a great economic and political movement that spreads over the face of all the earth.

There are today upwards of sixty millions of Socialists, loyal, devoted adherents to this cause, regardless of nationality, race, creed, color, or sex. They are all making common cause. They are spreading with tireless energy the propaganda of the new social order. They are waiting, watching, and working hopefully through all the hours of the day and the night. They are still in a minority. But they have learned how to be patient and to bide their time. They feel—they know, indeed—that the time is coming, in spite of all opposition, all persecution, when this emancipating gospel will spread among all the peoples, and when this minority will become the triumphant majority and, sweeping into power, inaugurate the greatest social and economic change in history.

In that day we shall have the universal commonwealth—the harmonious co-operation of every nation with every other nation on earth....

* * * * * *

1. *How does Debs's anti-war position compare with that of George Norris (Document 22–4)?*

2. *How does Debs turn his legal conviction under the Espionage Act into a celebration of his beliefs?*

22–9 Letters on the Great Migration, 1916–1917

The wartime economic boom spurred what came to be known as the "great migration" of southern African Americans to northern cities. Opportunities in northern factories, mills, meatpacking plants, and other industries attracted hundreds of thousands of rural African Americans looking to earn higher wages and escape repressive racial conditions. The following letters were written mostly to the Chicago Defender, *a black newspaper, and reflect the immediate concerns of would-be migrants.*

SOURCE: Emmett J. Scott, "Letters of Negro Migrants of 1916–1918," *The Journal of Negro History 4* (1919).

Sherman, Ga., Nov. 28, 1916

Dear Sir: This letter comes to ask for all infirmations concerning employment in your connection in the warmest climate. Now I am in a family of (11) eleven more or less boys and girls (men and women) mixed sizes who want to go north as soon as arrangements can be made and employment given places for shelter and so on (etc) now this are farming people they were raised on the farm and are good farm hands I of course have some experience and qualefication as a coman school teacher and hotel waiter and along few other lines.

I wish you would write me at your first chance and tell me if you can give us employment at what time and about what wages will you pay and what kind of arrangement can be made for our shelter. Tell me when can you best use us now or later.

Will you send us tickets if so on what terms and at what price what is the cost per head and by what route should we come. We are Negroes and try to show ourselves worthy of all we may get from any friendly source we endeavor to be true to all good causes, if you can we thank you to help us to come north as soon as you can.

Sanford, Fla., April 27, 1917.

Dear sir. I have seen through the Chicago Defender that you and the people of Chicago are helping newcomers. I am asking you for some information about conditions in

some small town near Chicago.

There are some families here thinking of moving up, and are desirous of knowing what to expect before leaving. Please state about treatment, work, rent and schools. Please answer at some spare time.

Anniston, Ala., April 23, 1917.

Dear sir: Please gave me some infamation about coming north i can do any kind of work from a truck gardin to farming i would like to leave here and i cant make no money to leave I must make enough to live one please let me here from you at once i want to get where i can put my children in schol.

Cedar Grove, La., April 23, 1917.

Dear sir: to day I was advise by the defendent offices in your city to communicate with you in regards to the labor for the colored of the south as I was lead to beleave that you was in position of firms of your city & your near by surrounding towns of Chicago. Please state me how is the times in & around Chicago place to locate having a family dependent on me for support. I am informed by the Chicago Defender a very valuable paper which has for its purpose the Uplifting of my race, and of which I am a constant reader and real lover, that you were in position to show some light to one in my condition.

Seeking a Northern Home. If this is true Kindly inform me by next mail the next best thing to do Being a poor man with a family to care for, I am not coming to live on flowry Beds of ease for I am a man who works and wish to make the best I can out of life I do not wish to come there hoodwinked not knowing where to go or what to do so I Solicite your help in this matter and thanking you in advance for what advice you may be pleased to Give I am yours for success.

P.S. I am presently imployed in the I C RR. Mail Department at Union Station this city.

Brookhaven, Miss., April 24, 1917.

Gents: The cane growers of Louisiana have stopped the exodus from New Orleans, claiming shortage of labor which will result in a sugar famine.

Now these laborers thus employed receive only 85 cents a day and the high cost of living makes it a serious question to live.

There is a great many race people around here who desires to come north but have waited rather late to avoid car fare, which they have not got, isnt there some way to get the concerns who wants labor, to send passes here or elsewhere so they can come even if they have to pay out of the first months wages? Please done publish this letter but do what you can towards helping them to get away. If the R. R. Co. would run a low rate excursion they could leave that way. Please ans.

Savannah, Ga., April 24, 1917.
Sir: I saw an advertisement in the Chicago Ledger where you would send tickets to any one desireing to come up there. I am a married man with a wife only, and I am 38 years of age, and both of us have so far splendid health, and would like very much to come out there provided we could get good employment regarding the advertisement.

Fullerton, La., April 28, 1917.
Dear sir: I was reading about you was neading labor ninety miles of Chicago what is the name of the place and what R R extends ther i wants to come north and i wants a stedy employment ther what doe you pay per day i dont no anything about molding works but have been working around machinery for 10 years. Let me no what doe you pay for such work and can you give me a job of that kind or a job at common labor and let me no your prices and how many hours for a day.

De Ridder, La., April 29, 1917.
Dear sir: there is lots of us southern mens wants transportation and we want to leave ratway as soon as you let us here from you some of us is married mens who need work we would like to bring our wife with us there is 20 head of good mens want transportation and if you need us let us no by return mail we all are redy only wants here from you there may be more all of our peoples wont to leave here and i want you to send as much as 20 tickets any way I will get you up plenty hands to do most any kind of work all you have to do is to send for them. looking to here from you. This is among us-collerd.

Atlanta, Ga., April 30, 1917
Dear Sir: In reading the Chicago Defender I find that there are many jobs open for workmen, I wish that you would or can secure me a position in some of the northern cities; as

a workman and not as a loafer. One who is willing to do any kind of hard in side or public work, have had broad experience in machinery and other work of the kind. A some what alround man can also cook, well trained devuloped man; have travel extensively through the western and southern states; A good strong *morial religious* man no habits. I will accept transportation on advance and deducted from my wages later. It does not matter where, that is; as to city, country, town or state since you secure the positions. I am quite sure you will be delighted in securing a position for a man of this description. I'll assure you will not regret of so doing. Hoping to hear from you soon.

Houston, Tx. April 30, 1917
Dear Sir: wanted to leave the South and Go any Place where a man will be any thing Except a Ker I thought would write you for Advise as where would be a Good Place for a Comporedly young man That want to Better his Standing who has a very Promising young Family.

I am 30 years old and have Good Experience in Freight Handler and Can fill Position from Truck to Agt.

would like Chicago or Philadelphia But I dont Care where so long as I Go where a man is a man.

Beaumont, Texas, May 7, 1917.
Dear Sir: I see in one of your recent issue of collored men woanted in the North I wish you would help me to get a position in the North I have no trade 1 have been working for one company eight years and there is no advancement here for me and I would like to come where I can better my condition I woant work and not affraid to work all I wish is a chance to make good. I believe I would like machinist helper or Molder helper. If you can help me in any way it will be highly appreciate hoping to hear from you soon.

* * * * * *

1.   *What sorts of practical issues most concern the letter writers? How would you compare these concerns with those of immigrants of Europe?*

2.   *What evidence do the letters offer about racial oppression in the South? What do they suggest about the role of families in the "great migration"?*

22–10   Woodrow Wilson, The Fourteen Points, 1918

By late 1917 the Russian Revolution and a flurry of diplomatic overtures had created international pressure for a statement of war aims and an outline for a possible settlement. In response, President Wilson addressed Congress in January 1918, offering a program that soon became known as the Fourteen Points. Wilson called them "the only possible program for peace" from the American standpoint. The Fourteen Points were later taken as the basis for the peace negotiations in Paris.

SOURCE: Woodrow Wilson, Address to Congress, January 8, 1918.

It will be our wish and purpose that the processes of peace, when they are begun, shall be absolutely open and that they shall involve and permit henceforth no secret understandings of any kind. The day of conquest and aggrandizement is gone by; so is also the day of secret covenants entered into in the interest of particular governments and likely at some unlooked-for moment to upset the peace of the world. It is this happy fact, now clear to the view of every public man whose thoughts do not still linger in an age that is dead and gone, which makes it possible for every nation whose purposes are consistent with justice and the peace of the world to avow now or at any other time the objects it has in view.

We entered this war because violations of right had occurred which touched us to the quick and made the life of our own people impossible unless they were corrected and the world secured once for all against their recurrence. What we demand in this war, therefore, is nothing peculiar to ourselves. It is that the world be made fit and safe to live in; and particularly that it be made safe for every peace-loving nation which, like our own, wishes to live its own life, determine its own institutions, be assured of justice and fair dealing by the other peoples of the world as against force and selfish aggression. All the peoples of the world are in effect partners in this interest, and for our own part we see very clearly that unless justice be done to others it will not be done to us. The program of the world's peace, therefore, is our program; and that program, the only possible program, as we see it, is this:

I. Open covenants of peace, openly arrived at, after which there shall be no private international understandings of any kind but diplomacy shall proceed always frankly and the public view.

II. Absolute freedom of navigation upon the seas, outside territorial waters, alike in peace and in war, except as the seas may be closed in whole or in part by international action for the enforcement of international covenants.

III. The removal, so far as possible, of all economic barriers and the establishment of an equality of trade conditions among all the nations consenting to the peace and associate themselves for its maintenance.

IV. Adequate guarantees given and taken that national armaments will be reduced to lowest point consistent with domestic safety.

V. A free, open-minded, and absolutely impartial adjustment of all colonial claims, based upon a strict observance of the principle that in determining all such questions of sovereignty the interests of the populations concerned must have equal weight with the equitable claims of the government whose title is to be determined.

VI. The evacuation of all Russian territory and such a settlement of all questions affecting Russia as will secure the best and freest cooperation of the other nations of the world in obtaining for her an unhampered and unembarrassed opportunity for the independent determination of her own political development and national policy and assure her of a sincere welcome into the society of free nations under institutions of her own choosing; and, more than a welcome, assistance also of every kind that she may need and may herself desire. The treatment accorded Russia by her sister nations in the months to come will be the acid test of their good will, of their comprehension of her needs as distinguished from their own interests, and of their intelligent and unselfish sympathy.

VII. Belgium, the whole world will agree, must be evacuated and restored, without any attempt to limit the sovereignty which she enjoys in common with all other free nations. No other single act will serve as this will serve to restore confidence among the nations in the laws which they have themselves set and determined for the government of their relations with one another. Without this healing act the whole structure and validity of international law is forever impaired.

VIII. All French territory should be freed and the invaded portions restored, and the wrong done to France by Prussia in 1871 in the matter of Alsace-Lorraine, which has unsettled the peace of the world for nearly fifty years, should be righted, in order that peace may once more be made secure in the interest of all.

IX. A readjustment of the frontiers of Italy should be effected along clearly recognizable lines of nationality.

X. The peoples of Austria-Hungary, whose place among the nations we wish to see safeguarded and assured, should be accorded the freest opportunity of autonomous development.

XI. Rumania, Serbia, and Montenegro should be evacuated; occupied territories restored; Serbia accorded free and secure access to the sea; and the relations of the several Balkan states to one another determined by friendly counsel along historically established lines of allegiance and nationality; and international guarantees of the political and economic independence and territorial integrity of the several Balkan states should be entered into.

XII. The Turkish portions of the present Ottoman Empire should be assured a secure sovereignty, but the other nationalities which are now under Turkish rule should be assured an undoubted security of life and an absolutely unmolested opportunity of autonomous development, and the Dardanelles should be permanently opened as a flee passage to the ships and commerce of all nations under international guarantees.

XIII. An independent Polish state should be erected which should include the territories inhabited by indisputably Polish populations, which should be assured a free and secure access to the sea, and whose political and economic independence and territorial integrity should be guaranteed by international covenant.

XIV. A general association of nations must be formed under specific covenants for the purpose of affording mutual guarantees of political independence and territorial integrity to great and small states alike.

In regard to these essential rectifications of wrong and assertions of right we feel ourselves to be intimate partners of all the governments and peoples associated together against the Imperialists. We cannot be separated in interest or divided in purpose. We stand together until the end.

For such arrangements and covenants we are willing to fight and to continue to fight until they are achieved; but only because we wish the fight to prevail and desire a just and stable peace such as can be secured only by removing the chief provocations to war, which this program does not remove. We have no jealousy of German greatness, and there is nothing in this program that impairs it. We grudge her no achievement or distinction of learning or of pacific enterprise such as have made her record very bright and very enviable. We do not wish to injure her or to block in any way her legitimate influ-ence or power. We do not wish to fight her either with arms or with hostile arrangements of trade if she is willing to associate herself with us and the other peace-loving nations of the world in covenants of justice and law and fair dealing. We wish her only to accept a place of equality among the peoples of the world,—the new world in which we now live,—instead of a place of mastery.

Neither do we presume to suggest to her any alteration or modification of her institutions. But it is necessary, we must frankly say, and necessary as a preliminary to any intelligent dealings with her on our part, that we should know whom her spokesmen speak for when they speak to us, whether for the Reichstag majority or for the military party and the men whose creed is imperial domination.

We have spoken now, surely, in terms too concrete to admit of any doubt or question. An evident principle runs through the whole program I have outlined. It is the principle of justice to all peoples and nationalities, and their right to live on equal terms of liberty and safety with one another, whether they be strong or weak. Unless this principle be made its foundation no part of the structure of international justice can stand. The people of the United States could act upon no other principle; and to the vindication of this principle they are ready to devote their lives, their honor, and everything that they possess. The moral climax of this the culminating and final war for human liberty has come, and they are ready to put their own strength; their own highest purpose, their own integrity and devotion to the test.

* * * * * *

1. *Examine the first five points and the next eight as two separate groups. What basic issues do the two groups address?*

2. *Compare the Fourteen Points with Wilson's war message (Document 22–3). What similarities in tone and substance do you find between these two statements?*

chapter 23

The Twenties, 1921–1929

23–1 Motion Picture Diaries

During the 1920s, the Hollywood-based movie industry became the most popular form of mass culture in America. A national audience in the tens of millions went to the movies regularly and followed the lives of the stars with an almost religious fervor. Young people in particular responded to the allure of motion pictures. The following excerpts from diaries kept by young moviegoers during the 1920s provide a look at how they felt about and responded to the new medium.

SOURCE: Herbert Blumer, *Movies and Conduct* (Macmillan, 1933), pp. 220–223, 232–247, 251–257.

STUDENTS' "MOTION PICTURE AUTOBIOGRAPHIES"

A GIRL OF 22, COLLEGE SENIOR, NATIVE WHITE PARENTS

I have tried to remember the first time that I went to a movie. It must have been when I was very young because I cannot recall the event. My real interest in motion pictures showed itself when I was in about fourth grade at grammar school. There was a theater on the route by which I went home from school and as the picture changed every other day I used to spend the majority of my time there. A gang of us little tots went regularly....

Goodness knows, you learn plenty about love from the movies. That's their long run; you learn more from actual experience, though! You do see how the gold-digger systematically gets the poor fish in tow. You see how the sleek-haired, long-earringed, languid-eyed siren lands the men. You meet the flapper, the good girl, 'n' all the feminine types and their little tricks of the trade. We pick up their snappy comebacks which are most handy when dispensing with an unwanted suitor, a too ardent one, too backward one, etc. And believe me, they observe and remember, too.

I can remember when we all nudged one another and giggled at the last close-up in a movie. I recall when during the same sort of close-up when the boy friend squeezes your arm and looks soulfully at you. Oh, it's lotsa fun! No, I never fell in love with my movie idol. When I don't know a person really, when I know I'll never have a chance with 'em, I don't bother pining away

over them and writing them idiotic letters as some girls I've known do. I have imagined playing with a movie hero many times though; that is while I'm watching the picture. I forget about it when I'm outside the theater. Buddy Rogers and Rudy Valentino have kissed me oodles of times, but they don't know it. God bless 'em!

Yes, love scenes have thrilled me and have made me more receptive to love. I was going with a fellow whom I liked as a playmate, so to speak; he was a little younger than me and he liked me a great deal. We went to the movie—Billie Dove in it. Oh, I can't recall the name but Antonio Moreno was the lead, and there were some lovely scenes which just got me all hot 'n' bothered. After the movie we went for a ride 'n' parked along the lake; it was a gorgeous night. Well, I just melted (as it were) in his arms, making him believe I loved him, which I didn't. I sort of came to, but I promised to go steady with him. I went with him 'til I couldn't bear the sight of him. Such trouble I had trying to get rid of him, and yet not hurt his feelings, as I had led him to believe I cared more than I did. I've wished many times that we'd never seen the movie. Another thing not exactly on the subject but important, I began smoking after watching Dolores Costello, I believe it was, smoke, which hasn't added any joy to my parents' lives.

COLLEGE GIRL, 18, NATIVE BORN OF WEALTHY SWEDISH PARENTS

Upon going to my first dance I asked the hairdresser to fix my hair like Greta Garbo's. Of course I did not tell the hairdresser that I was copying this intriguing and fascinating actress or she would think I had gone insane. I, the "nicest" girl, whom mothers to this day set as an example to their daughters and young sons. Oh, the unconscious cruelty of father when he forbade me pleasures other children had and have, and I partly made up this injustice to myself by seeing a picture once or twice a year and living them over and over again. I lived the life of the heroine and used my little sister for the rival or unpleasant character, very seldom the good character. The rival afforded me more opportunity to be dramatic. In speaking on graduation day I did my best to finish with the swaying-like curtsy which Pola Negri taught me from the stage.

Somehow or other Dolores Costello has not taught me mannerisms, but what beauty is. When I see her I cannot help but truly believe that there is a God, creator of the beautiful. She brings to me that deep feeling of beauty and all that goes with beauty—love, truth, sympathy, etc.

Only at one time did the movies decide my yielding to a temptation which my better self condemned. I regret it very much. I had been fond of a dark boy, somewhat like John Gilbert, who had proposed many times while I was a sophomore in high school. He seemed perfect to me at the time. His family are among the best known aristocrats and he was supposedly intelligent. How I dislike him for this lack of the "supposed intelligence." He did not realize what he was asking me to do but they are not all of that type. One evening after he had built more alluring castles than usual, I decided it would be romantic to run away with him. No longer would I be under my dear but misunderstanding father's strict rules.

At that time we lived some distance from here in an enormous home with a beautiful garden surrounding it. My "hero" was to wait near the thick bushes, and to help me to get out through the windows as soon as it was dark. I had scarcely flashed the light as the signal, when father came into my room. He had been told by the gardener or someone else that somebody was lurking among the trees. He came to warn me about closing my windows, and found me with my clothes packed. No one outside of father, the boy, and I will ever know this, but it hurt all of us.

Because my father had been very strict in his beliefs, regarding marriage, rights of women, and these beliefs gave me many chances to rebel unsuccessfully, I was in a mood to listen and see other beliefs. Sometimes before this again unsuccessful rebellion I had seen a runaway marriage which had impressed me tremendously— I did think that having a hero like this dark boy to protect me from father's anger and strictness would be heaven. Curiously enough I was more interested in the details of escaping—how the girl got her clothes down, how she got down, what he did to help her down—all these details I watched more carefully than the rest of the play in the runaway marriage....

A BOY OF 17, HIGH SCHOOL SENIOR, NATIVE BLACK PARENTS

The earliest movie stars that I can remember were Wm. S. Hart and Tom Mix who played entirely in Western stories. I liked to see them shoot the villain and save the girl and "live happily ever after." It caused me to shout as loudly, or louder, than the rest. Following them came Douglas Fairbanks, who seemed so carefree and light that he won nearly everyone with his personality. He would jump, use a lasso, thrust a sword, and fight in a way to satisfy any child's desire for action. Now I have no special star but I think Emil Jannings is a great actor because he seems to put his heart and soul into his work.

As a boy, I went with nearly every one to the theater; my mother, father, sister or brother, relatives, and friends. Usually I went in the afternoon or evening, anywhere from one to five times a week. Now I still go with my relatives occasionally but mostly with friends or alone.

I cannot recall anything that I have done that I had seen in the movies except try to make love. It happened that when I was small there were no boys in my neighborhood and I had to go several blocks before I could play with some my size or age. But there were a few girls in my neighborhood my size. Seeing Douglas Fairbanks woo his maiden I decided to try some of "Doug's stuff" on one of the girl friends. I know I was awkward and it proved more or less a flop.

Several times on seeing big, beautiful cars which looked to be bubbling over with power and speed, I dreamed of having a car more powerful and speedier than all the rest. I saw this car driven by myself up to the girl friend's door and taking her for a ride. (I was then eight years old and in my dreams I was no older.)

* * * * * *

1. *What aspect of movies makes the deepest impression on these young people? Which fantasies and emotions seem most touched?*

2. *What do the diaries suggest about how people used movies in relation to their family lives and friends?*

23–2 Herbert Hoover, American Individualism, 1922

Herbert Hoover's influence on American politics and society was perhaps second to none during the 1920s. He was widely admired for his administrative and humanitarian work during World War I. As Secretary of Commerce Hoover exerted enormous influence over the modernizing economy. His philosophy offered an appealing synthesis that celebrated both national progress and traditional individualism. Hoover's presidency failed to respond to the human tragedy of the Great Depression, but the ideas expressed in his 1922 book American Individualism *struck a chord with millions.*

SOURCE: From *American Individualism* by Herbert Hoover, Copyright © 1922 by Herbert Hoover Presidential Library Association, Inc. Reprinted by permission.

Five or six great social philosophies are at struggle in the world for ascendancy. There is the Individualism of America. There is the Individualism of the more democratic states of

Europe with its careful reservations of castes and classes. There are Communism, Socialism, Syndicalism, Capitalism, and finally there is Autocracy—whether by birth, by possessions, militarism, or divine right of kings. Even the Divine Right still lingers on although our lifetime has seen fully two-thirds of the earth's population, including Germany, Austria, Russia, and China, arrive at a state of angry disgust with this type of social motive power and throw it on the scrap heap.

All these thoughts are in ferment today in every country in the world. They fluctuate in ascendancy with times and places. They compromise with each other in daily reaction on governments and peoples. Some of these ideas are perhaps more adapted to one race than another. Some are false, some are true. What we are interested in is their challenge to the physical and spiritual forces of America.

The partisans of some of these other brands of social schemes challenge us to comparison; and some of their partisans even among our own people are increasing in their agitation that we adopt one or another or parts of their devices in place of our tried individualism. They insist that our social foundations are exhausted, that like feudalism and autocracy America's plan has served its purpose—that it must be abandoned.

There are those who have been left in sober doubt of our institutions or are confounded by bewildering catchwords of vivid phrases. For in this welter of discussions there is much attempt to glorify or defame social and economic forces with phrases. Nor indeed should we disregard the potency of some of these phrases in their stir to action.—"The dictatorship of the Proletariat," "Capitalistic nations," "Germany over all," and a score of others. We need only to review those that have jumped to horseback during the last ten years in order that we may be properly awed by the great social and political havoc that can be worked where the bestial instincts of hate, murder, and destruction are clothed by the demagogue in the fine terms of political idealism.

For myself, let me say at the very outset that my faith in the essential truth, strength, and vitality of the developing creed by which we have hitherto lived in this country of ours has been confirmed and deepened by the searching experiences of seven years of service in the backwash and misery of war. Seven years of contending with economic degeneration, with social disintegration, with incessant political dislocation, with all of its seething and ferment of individual and class conflict, could but impress me with the primary motivation of social forces, and the necessity for broader thought upon their great issues to humanity. And from it all I emerge an individualist—an unashamed individualist. But let me say also that I am an American individualist. For America has been steadily developing the ideals that constitute progressive individualism.

No doubt, individualism run riot, with no tempering principle, would provide a long category of inequalities, of tyrannies, dominations, and injustices. America, however, has tempered the whole conception of individualism by the injection of a definite principle, and from this principle it follows that attempts at domination, whether in government or in the processes of industry and commerce, are under an insistent curb. If we would have the values of individualism, their stimulation to initiative, to the development of hand and intellect, to the high development of thought and spirituality, they must be tempered with that firm and fixed ideal of American individualism—*an equality of opportunity*. If we would have these values we must soften its hardness and stimulate progress through that sense of service that lies in our people.

Therefore, it is not the individualism of other countries for which I would speak, but the individualism of America. Our individualism differs from all others because it embraces these great ideals: *that while we build our society upon the attainment of the individual, we shall safeguard to every individual an equality of opportunity to take that position in the community to which his intelligence, character, ability, and ambition entitle him; that we keep the social solution free from frozen strata of classes; that we shall stimulate effort of each individual to achievement; that through an enlarging sense of responsibility and understanding we shall assist him to this attainment; while he in turn must stand up to the emery wheel of competition.*

Individualism cannot be maintained as the foundation of a society if it looks to only legalistic justice based upon contracts, property, and political equality. Such legalistic safeguards are themselves not enough. In our individualism we have long since abandoned the laissez faire of the 18th Century—the notion that it is "every man for himself and the devil take the hindmost." We abandoned that when we adopted the ideal of equality of opportunity—the fair chance of Abraham Lincoln. We have confirmed its abandonment in terms of legislation, of social and economic justice,—in part because we have learned that it is the hindmost who throws the bricks at our social edifice, in part because we have learned that the foremost are not always the best nor the hindmost the worst—and in part because we have learned that social injustice is the destruction of justice itself. We have learned that the impulse to production can only be maintained at a high pitch if there is a fair division of the product. We have also learned that fair division can only be obtained by certain restrictions on the strong and the dominant....

The will-o'-the wisp of all breeds of socialism is that they contemplate a motivation of human animals by altruism alone. It necessitates a bureaucracy of the entire population, in which, having obliterated the economic stimulation of each member, the fine gradations of character and ability are to be arranged in relative authority by ballot of more likely by a Tammany Hall or a Bolshevist party, or some other form of tyranny. The proof of the futility of these ideas as a stimulation to the development and activity of the individual does not lie alone in the ghastly failure of Russia, but also lies in our own failure in attempts at nationalized industry.

Likewise the basic foundations of autocracy, whether it be class government or capitalism in the sense that a few men through unrestrained control of property determine the welfare of great numbers, is as far apart from the rightful expression of American individualism as the two poles. The will-o'-the-wisp of autocracy in any form is that it supposes that the good Lord endowed a special few with all the divine attributes. It contemplates one human animal dealing to the other human animals his just share of earth, of glory, and of immortality. The proof of the futility of these ideas in the development of the world does not lie alone in the grim failure of Germany, but it lies in the damage to our moral and social fabric from those who have sought economic domination in America, whether employer or employee.

We in America, have had too much experience of life to fool ourselves into pretending that all men are equal in ability, in character, in intelligence, in ambition. That was part of the claptrap of the French Revolution. We have grown to understand that all we can all hope to assure to the individual through government is liberty, justice, intellectual welfare, equality of opportunity, and stimulation to service.

It is in maintenance of a society fluid to these human qualities that our individualism departs from the individualism of Europe. There can be no rise for the individual through the frozen strata of classes, or of castes, and no stratification can take place in a mass livened by the free stir of its particles. This guarding of our individualism against stratification insists not only in preserving in the social solution an equal opportunity for the able and ambitious to rise from the bottom; it also insists that the sons of the successful shall not by any mere right of birth or favor continue to occupy their fathers' places of power against the rise of a new generation in process of coming up from the bottom. The pioneers of our American individualism had the good sense not to reward Washington and Jefferson and Hamilton with hereditary dukedoms and fixtures in landed estates, as Great Britain rewarded Marlborough and Nelson. Otherwise our American fields of opportunity would have been clogged with long generations inheriting their fathers' privileges without their fathers' capacity for service.

That high and increasing standards of living and comfort should be the first of considerations in public mind and in government needs no apology. We have long since realized that the basis of an advancing civilization must be a high and growing standard of living for all the people, not for a single class; that education, food, clothing, housing, and the spreading use of what we so often term non-essentials, are the real fertilizers of the soil from which spring the finer flowers of life. The economic development of the past fifty years has lifted the general standard of comfort far beyond the dreams of our forefathers. The only road to further advance in the standard of living is by greater invention, greater elimination of waste, greater production and better distribution of commodities and services, for by increasing their ratio to our numbers and dividing them justly we each will have more of them.

* * * * * *

1.   How does Hoover appeal to American history and the sense that the country is unique among nations?

2.   What part do economics and standards of living play in Hoover's argument?

23-3   *Bruce Barton, Jesus Christ as Businessman, 1925*

The popular culture of the 1920s celebrated the businessman and business values more intensively than did the popular culture of any previous era. This was no doubt linked to the political ascendancy of Republican conservatives such as Warren Harding, Calvin Coolidge, and Herbert Hoover. It also reflected the growth of the advertising and public relations industries, which identified the glories of consumer culture with American mass production and business know-how. The Man Nobody Knows, *a best seller written by advertising executive Bruce Barton, argued that Jesus Christ was the model for the modern businessman.*

SOURCE: Reprinted with the permission of Macmillan Publishing Company from *The Man Nobody Knows* by Bruce Barton. Copyright © 1925 by the Bobbs-Merrill Company, Inc., renewed 1952 by Brute Barton.

Chapter 6

HIS WAY IN OUR WORLD

When Jesus was twelve years old, his father and mother took him to the Feast at Jerusalem.

It was the big national vacation; even peasant families saved their pennies and looked forward to it through the year. Towns like Nazareth were emptied of their inhabitants except for the few old folks who were left behind to look after the very young ones. Crowds of cheerful pilgrims filled the highways, laughing their way across the hills and under the stars at night.

In such a mass of folk it was not surprising that a boy of twelve should be lost. When Mary and Joseph missed Him on the homeward trip, they took it calmly and began a search among the relatives.

The inquiry produced no result. Some remembered having seen Him in the Temple, but no one had seen Him since. Mary grew frightened; where could He be? Back there in the city alone? Wandering hungry and tired through the friendless streets? Carried away by other travelers into a distant country? She pictured a hundred calamities. Nervously she and Joseph hurried back over the hot roads, through the suburbs, up through the narrow city streets, up to the courts of the Temple itself.

And there He was.

Not lost; not a bit worried. Apparently unconscious that the feast was over, He sat in the midst of a group of old men, who were questioning Him and applauding the shrewd common sense of His replies.

Involuntarily His parents halted—they were simple folk, uneasy among strangers and disheveled by their haste. But after all they were His parents, and a very human feeling of irritation quickly overcame their diffidence. Mary stepped forward and grasped His arm.

"Son, why hast thou thus dealt with us?" she demanded. "Behold, thy father and I have sought thee sorrowing."

I wonder what answer she expected to receive. Did she ever know exactly what He was going to say: Did any one in Nazareth quite understand this keen eager lad who had such curious moments of abstraction and was forever breaking out with remarks that seemed so far beyond His years?

He spoke to her now with deference as always, but in words that did not dispel but rather added to her uncertainty.

"How is it that ye sought me?" He asked. "Wist ye not that I must be about my father's business?"...

What interests us most in this one recorded incident of His boyhood is the fact that for the first time He defined here and at this age the purpose of His career. He did not say, "Wist ye not that I must practise preaching?" or "Wist ye not that I must get ready to meet the arguments of men like these?" The language and intent were quite different. "Wist ye not that I must be about my father's *business?*" He said. He thought of his life as *business.* What did he mean by business? To what extent are the principles by which he conducted his business applicable to ours? And if he were among us again, in our highly competitive world, would his business philosophy work?

It was on the afternoon when James and John came to ask Him what promotion they might expect. They were two of the most energetic of the lot, called "Sons of Thunder," by the rest, being noisy and always in the midst of some sort of a storm. They had joined the ranks because they liked Him, but with no very definite idea of what it was all about. Now they wanted to know where the enterprise was heading and just what there would be in it for them.

"Master," they said, "we want to ask what plans you have in mind for us. You're going to need big men around you when you establish your kingdom; our ambition is to sit on either side of you, one on your right hand and the other on your left."

Can we really object to that attitude? Each of us has asked as hoped for advancement. If we want a better place, we usually ask for it.

Jesus answered with a sentence of great poetry. But wouldn't it have sounded absurd to the sons of thunder?

"Whosoever will be great among you, shall be your minister," He said, "and whosoever of you will be the chiefest, shall be servant of all."

Grand sounding, yes. But isn't it contradictory? Be a good servant and you will be great; be the best possible servant and you will occupy the highest possible place. A splendid speech—but utterly impractical; nothing to take seriously in a common-sense world. That is just what men thought for some hundreds of years; and then, quite suddenly, great enterprises... woke up to a great discovery. For several decades now that discovery proclaimed more and more widely as something distinctly modern....

The principle that he who serves best accomplishes most spreads to every area. I observe most closely what is closest to me, and I know that business and industry have learned that a real understanding of and regard for the individual and the social or business community, large or small, must be part of every aspect of work. The huge plants and financial strength of, say, an automobile manufacturer rest on the willingness and ability not only to provide for your safety, comfort and convenience but to feel—and convince you of it—a genuine concern for your pleasure in the product, your benefit from it.

Of course the manufacturer has a profit motive. But to say that as if it made the service a mere sales trick is to misread the record and miss the point entirely. Some self-interest (not selfishness) can be shown in almost any human enterprise, and it may well be a vital worthy part of most. The important fact is that we seem to be increasing our awareness that worthiness is related to any advancement or gain.

The evidence of this new attitude is overwhelming. Manufacturers of building equipment, of clothes, of food; presidents of railroads and steamship companies; the heads of banks and investment houses—all of them tell the same story. They call it the "spirit of modern business"; they sup-

pose, most of them, that it is something very new. Jesus preached it more than nineteen hundred years ago.

* * * * * *

1.   *What elements of modern advertising do you find in Barton's interpretation and style?*

2.   *Why do you think his book was such a big seller? Who do you think was the main audience for the book?*

23–4   *Eleanor Wembridge, Petting and Necking, 1925*

The so-called moral revolution fascinated social scientists and journalists in the 1920s. Sex was more openly and frankly discussed in the press and elsewhere, and there is evidence that unmarried couples engaged in more overtly sexual activities, although the extent of this activity is difficult to gauge. Certainly the influence of the works of Sigmund Freud and Havelock Ellis, who insisted that sexual drive was natural and the key to understanding human behavior, contributed to the new openness. In the following excerpt, journalist Eleanor Wembridge comments on the practices of "petting" and "necking" in a 1925 article.

SOURCE: Eleanor Wembridge, "Petting and Necking," *Survey*, July 1, 1925, pp. 393–395.

... [In 1924] I was at a student conference of young women comprised of about eight hundred college girls from the middle western states. The subject of petting was very much on their minds, both as to what attitude they should take toward it with the younger girls, (being upperclassmen themselves) and also how much renunciation of this pleasurable pastime is required of them. If I recall correctly, two entire mornings were devoted discussing the matter, two evenings, and another overflow meeting.

So far as I could judge from their discussion groups, the girls did not advise younger classmen not to pet—they merely advised them to be moderate about it, not lose their heads, not go too far—in fact the same line of conduct which is advised for moderate drinking. Learn temperance in doing, not abstinence.

Before the conference I made it my business to talk to as many college girls as possible. I consulted as many, both in groups and privately, as I had time for at the conference. And since it is all to be repeated in another state

this summer, I have been doing so, when opportunity offered, ever since. Just what does petting consist in? What ages take it most seriously? Is it a factor in every party? Do "nice" girls do it, as well as those who are not "nice"? Are they "stringing" their elders, by exaggerating the prevalence of petting, or is there more of it than they admit? These are samples of the questions I have asked, and have heard them ask each other in the discussions where I have listened in.

One fact is evident, that whether or not they pet, they hesitate to have someone believe that they do not. It is distinctly the *mores* of the time to be considered as ardently sought after, and as not too priggish to respond. As one girl said—"I don't particularly care to be kissed by some of the fellows I know, but I'd let them do it any time rather than think I wouldn't dare. As a matter of fact, there are lots of fellows I don't kiss. It's the very young kids that never miss a chance."

That petting should lead to actual illicit relations between the petters is not advised nor countenanced among the girls with whom I discussed it. They drew the line quite sharply. That it often did so lead, they admitted, they were not ready to allow that there were any more of such affairs than there had always been. School and college scandals, with their sudden departures and hasty marriages, have always existed to some extent, and they still do. But only accurate statistics, hard to arrive at, can prove either or not the sex carelessness of the present day extends to an increase of sex immorality, or whether since so many more people go to college there is an actual decrease in the amount of it, in proportion to the number of students. The girls seemed to feel that those who went too far were more fools than knaves, and that in most cases they married. They thought that hasty and secret marriages, of which most of them could report several, were foolish, but after all about as likely to turn out well as any others. Their attitude toward such contingencies was disapproval, but it was expressed with a slightly amused shrug, a shrug which one can imagine might have sat well on the shoulders of Voltaire. In fact the writer was torn, in her efforts to sum up their attitude, between classifying them as eighteenth century realists and as Greek nymphs existing before the dawn of history!

I sat with one pleasant college Amazon, a total stranger, beside a fountain in the park, while she asked if I saw any harm in her kissing a young man whom she liked, but whom she did not want to marry. "It's terribly exciting. We get such a thrill. I think it is natural to want nice men to kiss you, so why not do what is natural?" There was no embarrassment in her manner. Her eyes and her conscience were equally untroubled. I felt as if a girl from the Parthenon frieze had stepped down to ask if she might not sport in the glade with a handsome faun. Why not indeed? Only an equally direct forcing of twentieth century science on primitive simplicity could bring us even to the same level in our conversation, and at that, the stigma of impropriety seemed to fall on me, rather than on her. It was hard to tell whether her infantilism were real, or half-consciously assumed in order to have a child's license and excuse to do as she pleased. I am inclined to think that both with her and with many others, it is assumed. One girl said, "When

I have had a few nights without dates I nearly go crazy. I tell my mother she must expect me to go out on a fearful necking party." In different parts of the country, *petting* and *necking* have opposite meanings. One locality calls necking (I quote their definition) "petting only from the neck up." Petting involves anything else you please. Another section reverses the distinction, and the girl in question was from the latter area. In what manner she announces to her mother her plans to neck, and in what manner her mother accepts the announcement; I cannot be sure....

*   *   *   *   *   *

1.   *What is the author's attitude towards petting and necking? Is there evidence that her attitude is generational?*

2.   *What connections can you make between this document and the ones dealing with movies (23–1)?*

23–5   Paul Morand, Speakeasies in New York, 1929

The Eighteenth Amendment banned the manufacture and sale of alcoholic beverages, starting in 1920. But Prohibition proved difficult to enforce, especially in the nation's cities, and turned millions of citizens into routine lawbreakers. It also contributed to an enormous increase in organized crime, as the promise of staggering profits attracted many to the illicit liquor trade. Paul Morand was a French author and diplomat whose colorful account of New York depicted the more sensational sides of big-city life in the 1920s.

SOURCE: From *New York* by Paul Morand, translated by Hamish Miles. Copyright © 1930 by Flammarion. Reprinted by permission of Flammarion.

Open a book or newspaper of a few years ago and you will seek the term "speakeasy" in vain. It was born of Prohibition. The speakeasy (the name suggests a whispered password) is a clandestine refreshment-bar selling spirits or wine. They must be visited to understand present-day New York.... There are a few in the downtown streets, but they are mainly set up between Fortieth Street and Sixtieth Street; they are usually situated downstairs and are identifiable by the large number of empty cars standing at their doors. The door is closed, and is only opened after you have been scrutinized through a door-catch or a barred opening. At night an electric torch suddenly gleams through a pink

silk curtain. There is a truly New York atmosphere of humbug in the whole thing. The interior is that of a criminal house; shutters are closed in full daylight, and one is caught in the smell of a cremation furnace, for the ventilation is defective and grills are prepared under the mantel-piece of the fireplace. Italians with a too familiar manner, or plump, blue pseudo-bullfighters, carrying bunches of monastic keys, guide you through the deserted rooms of the abandoned house. Facetious inscriptions grimace from the walls. There are a few very flushed diners. At one table some habitués are asleep, their heads sunk on their arms; behind a screen somebody is trying to restore a young woman who has had an attack of hysteria....The food is almost always poor, the service deplorable; the staff regard you with the eyes of confederates and care not two pins about you. The Sauterne is a sort of glycerine; it has to go with a partridge brought from the refrigerator of a French vessel; the champagne would not be touched at a Vincennes wedding-party.

Yet the speakeasy pervades Manhattan with a fascinating atmosphere of mystery. If only one could drink water there! Some speakeasies are disguised behind florists' shops, or behind undertakers' coffins. I know one, right in Broadway, which is entered through an imitation telephone-box; it has excellent beer; appetizing sausages and Welsh rabbits are sizzling in chafing-dishes and are given to customers without extra charge; drunks are expelled through a side-door which seems to open out into the nether world, as in *Chicago Nights*. In the poorer quarters many former saloons for the ordinary people have secretly reopened. All these secret shrines are readily accessible, for there are, it is said, 20,000 speakeasies in New York, and it is unlikely that the police do not know them; I think myself that they are only forced to close down when they refuse to make themselves pleasant to persons in authority, or when they sell too much poison.…The speakeasy is very popular in all classes of society; women go there gladly, even a few young girls.…

An intelligent lady remarked to me once that Prohibition was very pleasant. "Before it," she said, "no decent woman could go into a bar, but now nobody is surprised at our being there."…

A town of contrasts, puritan and libertine; the two-sided picture of a well-policed America and a savage continent, of East and West; a few yards from the luxury of Fifth Avenue and one is in battered and dirty Eighth Avenue. New York is the symbol of America, and half of its population is foreign; it is a center of Anglo-Saxon culture, speaking Yiddish;…after making you rich in a week, it ruins you in one morning.…

New York's supreme beauty, its truly unique quality, is its violence. Violence gives it nobility, excuses it, makes its vulgarity forgettable. For New York is vulgar; it is stronger, richer, newer than anything you like, but it is common.…

People are always moving.… The only permanent addresses are those of banks. People change jobs as they change houses. The town is no less changing. One builds for thirty years; those buildings have no past and no future either. Some districts alter their appearance in one season.…

Night is abolished.…We have seen restaurants full at dawn—with people who will be at work four hours later. New York is a town that never halts, never slacks off. Subways and street-cars run up and down all night long, twenty-four hours a day.…

Everything goes fast.…

New York is a perpetual thunderstorm.

* * * * * *

1.   What distinctions does the author observe among speakeasies and the people who frequent them?

2.   How do you think accounts like Morand's made the city seem attractive and/or repellent to Americans outside New York?

3.   How has Prohibition changed the drinking habits of American men and women?

23–6   U.S. Congress, Debating Immigration Restriction, 1921

The movement to place legal limits on immigration to the United States succeeded with the enactment of the so-called "quota laws" of 1921 and 1924. The laws targeted mainly people from southern and eastern Europe, the main source of the immigration flow since 1890. Restrictionists found new support for their views in the conservative political climate following World War I. The following speeches made on the floor of the House of Representatives exemplify the attitudes and arguments of those favoring immigration restriction.

SOURCE: *Congressional Record,* April 20, 1921, p. 450; December 10, 1921, p. 177.

Mr. [Lucian Walton] PARISH [D.-Tex.]. We should stop immigration entirely until such a time as we can amend our immigration laws and so write them that hereafter no one shall be admitted except he be in full sympathy with our Constitution and laws, willing to declare himself obedient to our flag, and willing to release himself from any obligations he may owe to the flag of the country from which he came.

It is time that we act now, because within a few short years the damage will have been done. The endless tide of immigration will have filled our country with a foreign and unsympathetic element. Those who are out of sympathy with our Constitution and the spirit of our Government will be here in large numbers, and the true spirit of Americanism left us by our fathers will gradually become poisoned by this uncertain element.

The time once was when we welcomed to our shores the oppressed and downtrodden people from all the world, but they came to us because of oppression at home and with the sincere purpose of making true and loyal American citizens, and in truth and in fact they did adapt themselves to our ways of thinking and contributed in a substantial sense to the progress and development that our civilization has made. But that time has passed now; new and strange conditions have arisen in the countries over there; new and strange doctrines are being taught. The Governments of the Orient are being overturned and destroyed, and anarchy and bolshevism are threatening the very foundation of many of them, and no one can foretell what the future will bring to many of those countries of the Old World now struggling with these problems.

Our country is a self-sustaining country. It has taught the principles of real democracy to all the nations of the earth; its flag has been the synonym of progress, prosperity, and the preservation of the rights of the individual, and there can be nothing so dangerous as for us to allow the undesirable foreign element to poison our civilization and thereby threaten the safety of the institutions that our forefathers have established for us.

Now is the time to throw about this country the most stringent immigration laws and keep from our shores forever those who are not in sympathy with the American ideas. It is the time now for us to act and act quickly, because every month's delay increases the difficulty in which we find ourselves and renders the problems of government more difficult of solution. We must protect ourselves from the poisonous influences that are threatening the very foundation of the Governments of Europe; we must see to it that those who come here are loyal and true to our Nation and impress upon them that it means something to have the privileges of American citizenship. We must hold this country true to the American thought and the American ideals....

Mr. [James V.] McCLINTIC [D.-Okla.]. Some time ago it was my privilege to visit Ellis Island, not as a member of the committee but as a private citizen interested in obtaining information relative to the situation which exists at that place. I stood at the end of a hall with three physicians, and I saw them examine each immigrant as they came down the line, rolling back the upper eyelid in order to gain some information as to the individual's physical condition. I saw them place the chalk marks on their clothing which indicated that they were in a diseased condition, so that they could be separated when they reached the place where they were to undergo certain examinations. Afterwards I went to a large assembly hall where immigrants came before the examiners to take the literacy test, and the one fact that impressed me more than anything else was that practically every single immigrant examined that day had less than $50 to his credit....

Practically all of them were weak, small of stature, poorly clad, emaciated, and in a condition which showed that the environment surrounding them in their European homes were indeed very bad.

It is for this reason that I say the class of immigrants coming to the shores of the United States at this time are not the kind of people we want as citizens in this country. It is a well-known fact that the majority of immigrants coming to this country at the present time are going into the large industrial centers instead of the agricultural centers of the United States, and when it is taken into consideration that the large centers are already crowded to the extent that there is hardly sufficient living quarter to take care of the people it can be readily seen that this class of people, instead of becoming of service to the communities where they go, they will become charges to be taken care of by charitable institutions. The week I visited Ellis Island I was told that 25,000 immigrants had been unloaded at that port. From their personal appearance they seemed to be the offcasts of the countries from which they came....

* * * * * *

1.   *What kinds of arguments do the congressmen make regarding the political and intellectual capabilities of recent immigrants? About their physical qualities?*

2.   *How do that they claim new immigrants differ from those in earlier periods of American history?*

23–7   *Hiram Evans, The Klan's Fight for Americanism, 1926*

The revived Ku Klux Klan of the 1920s differed markedly from the Klan in the Reconstruction era. It was strongest in midwestern and western communities, including many small cities, and its main targets were Catholics and Jews rather than African Americans. The revived Klan combined hatred of "un-American" ideologies with the rituals and sociability of a fraternal order. It also achieved significant political power in hundreds of local communities and in the national Democratic Party. Hiram Evans, the Klan's Imperial Wizard, published this essay in 1926.

SOURCE: From "Klan's Fight for Americanism," by Hiram Evans. *NORTH AMERICAN REVIEW 123* (March–May 1926), 33–63. Reprinted by permission.

The real indictment against the Roman Church is that it is, fundamentally and irredeemably, in its leadership, in politics, in thought, and largely in membership, actually and actively alien, un-American and usually anti-American. The old stock Americans, with the exception of the few such of Catholic faith—who are in a class by themselves, standing tragically torn between their faith and their racial and national patriotism—see in the Roman Church today the chief leader of alienism, and the most dangerous alien power with a foothold inside our boundaries. It is this and nothing else that has revived hostility to Catholicism. By no stretch of the imagination can it fairly be called religious prejudice, though, now that the hostility has become active, it does derive some strength from the religious schism.

We Americans see many evidences of Catholic alienism. We believe that its official position and its dogma, its theocratic autocracy and its claim to full authority in temporal as well as spiritual matters, all make it impossible for it as a church, or for its members if they obey it, to coöperate in a free democracy in which Church and State have been separated. It is true that in this country the Roman Church speaks very softly on these points, so that many Catholics do not know them. It is also true that the Roman priests preach Americanism, subject to their own conception of Americanism, of course. But the Roman Church itself makes a point of the divine and unalterable character of its dogma, it has never seen fit to abandon officially any of these un-American attitudes, and it still teaches them in other countries. Until it does renounce them, we cannot believe anything except that they all remain in force, ready to be called into action whenever feasible, and temporarily hushed up only for expediency.

The hierarchical government of the Roman Church is equally at odds with Americanism. The Pope and the whole hierarchy have been for centuries almost wholly Italian. It is nonsense to suppose that a man, by entering a church, loses his race or national loyalties. The Roman Church today, therefore, is just what its name says— Roman; and it is impossible for its hierarchy or the policies they dictate to be in real sympathy with Americanism. Worse, the Italians have proven to be one of the least assimilable of people. The autocratic nature of the Catholic Church organization, and its suppression of free conscience or free decision, need not be discussed; they are unquestioned. Thus it is fundamental to the Roman Church to demand a supreme loyalty, overshadowing national or race loyalty, to a power that is inevitably alien, and which at the best must inevitably inculcate ideals un-American if not actively anti-American....

The facts are that almost everywhere, and especially in the great industrial centers where the Catholics are strongest, they vote almost as a unit, under control of leaders of their own faith, always in support of the interests of the Catholic Church and of Catholic candidates without regard to other interests, and always also in support of alienism whenever there is an issue raised. They vote, in short, not as American citizens, but as aliens and Catholics! They form the biggest, strongest, most cohesive of all the alien *blocs*. On many occasions they form alliances with other alien *blocs* against American interests, as with the Jews in New York today, and with others in the case of the recent opposition to immigrant restriction....

There are three of these great racial instincts, vital elements in both the historic and the present attempts to build an America which shall fulfill the aspirations and justify the heroism of the men who made the nation. These are the instincts of loyalty to the white race, to the traditions of America, and to the spirit of Protestantism, which has been an essential part of Americanism ever since the days of Roanoke and Plymouth Rock. They are condensed into the Klan slogan: "Native, white, Protestant supremacy."

First in the Klansman's mind is patriotism— America for Americans. He believes religiously that a betrayal of Americanism or the American race is treason to the most sacred of trusts, a trust from his fathers and a trust from God. He believes, too, that Americanism can only be achieved if the pioneer stock is kept pure....

Americanism, to the Klansman, is a thing of the spirit, a purpose and a point of view, that can only come through instinctive racial understanding. It has, to be sure, certain defined principles, but he does not believe that many aliens understand those principles, even when they use our words in talking about them. Democracy is one, fairdealing, impartial justice, equal opportunity, religious liberty, independence, self-reliance, courage, endurance, acceptance of individual responsibility as well as individual rewards for effort, willingness to sacrifice for the good of his family, his nation and his race before anything else but God, dependence on enlightened *conscience* for guidance, the right to unhampered development—these are fundamental. But within the bounds they fix there must be the utmost freedom, tolerance, liberalism. In short, the Klansman believes in the greatest possible diversity and individualism within the limits of the American spirit. But he believes also that few aliens can understand that spirit, that fewer try to, and that there must be resistance, intolerance even, toward anything that threatens it, or the fundamental national unity based upon it.

The second word in the Klansman's trilogy is "white." The white race must be supreme, not only in America but in the world. This is equally undebatable, except on the ground that the races might live together, each with full regard for the rights and interests of others, and that those rights and interests would never conflict. Such an idea, of course, is absurd; the colored races today, such as Japan, are clamoring not for equality but for their supremacy. The whole history of the world, on its broader lines, has been one of race conflicts, wars, subjugation or extinction. This is not pretty, and certainly disagrees with the maudlin theories of cosmopolitanism, but it is truth. The world has been so made that each race must fight for its life, must conquer, accept slavery or die. The Klansman believes that the whites will not become slaves, and he does not intend to die before his time.

Moreover, the future of progress and civilization depends on the continued supremacy of the white race. The forward movement of the world for centuries has come entirely from it. Other races each had its chance and either failed or stuck fast, while white civilization shows no sign of having reached its limit. Until the whites falter, or some colored civilization has a miracle of awakening, there is not a single colored stock that can claim even equality with the white; much less supremacy.

The third of the Klan principles is that Protestantism must be supreme; that Rome shall not rule America. The Klansman believes this is not merely because he is a Protestant, nor even because the Colonies that are now our nation were settled for the purpose of wresting America from the control of Rome and establishing a land of free conscience. He believes it also because Protestantism is an essential part of Americanism; without it America could never have been created and without it she cannot go forward. Roman rule would kill it.

* * * * * *

1.   *What is the basis for the Klan's anti-Catholic*

bias? Why do you think the Klan is so obsessed with "aliens"?

2.   *How does the Klan define "Americanism?" How does this definition reflect the social and cultural changes of the previous generation?*

23–8   Charles S. Johnson, The City Negro, 1925

By the 1920s the "great migration" of southern African Americans had created new and vital black communities in dozens of northern cities. African-American cultural influence flowered in music and literature; at the same time, the new urban environment brought changes to African American life. Charles S. Johnson, a leading African American social scientist and editor of his day, examined the significance of black urbanization in a 1925 essay that appeared in the famous anthology The New Negro.

SOURCE: Charles S. Johnson, "The New Frontage on American Life," in Alain Locke, ed., *The New Negro* (1925).

A new type of Negro is evolving—a city Negro. He is being evolved out of those strangely divergent elements of the general background. And this is a fact overlooked by those students of human behavior, who with such quick comprehension detect the influence of the city in the nervousness of the Jew, the growing nervous disorders of city dwellers in general to the tension of city life. In ten years, Negroes have been actually transplanted from one culture to another.

Where once there were personal and intimate relations, in which individuals were in contact at practically all points of their lives, there are now group relations in which the whole structure is broken up and reassorted, casting them in contact at only one or two points of their lives. The old controls are no longer expected to operate. Whether apparent or not, the newcomers are forced to reorganize their lives, to enter a new status and adjust to it that eager restlessness which prompted them to leave home....

If the Negroes in Harlem show at times less courtesy toward white visitors than is required by the canons of good taste, this is bad, but understandable. It was remarked shortly after the first migration that the newcomers on boarding street cars invariably strode to the front even if there were seats in the rear. This is, perhaps, a mild example of tendencies expressed more strikingly in other directions, for with but few exceptions they are forced to sit in the rear of street cars throughout the South.

The difference between the background of northern and southern Negroes is even wider than it seems. In the two there are utterly different packets of stored up memories marking out channels of conduct. The southern Negro directs his ambitions at those amenities of which the northern Negro boasts, and until the first wonderment and envy subside, ignores his reservations. This is the hectic period of transition, so noticeable after huge accessions—inevitably in the wake of the newcomers north, whether the numbers are large or small. There comes the testing of long cherished desires, the thirst for forbidden fruit—and disillusionment, partial or complete, almost as inevitably....

The violent sub-currents of recent years, which have shifted the economic base of Negro life—as indeed they have affected all other groups—have brought about a new orientation throughout, and have accentuated group attitudes among both black and white, sometimes favorably, sometimes unfavorably; here in a spurt of progress, there in a backwash of reaction.

Take the case of Negro business. It is only within recent years that a coldly practical eye has been turned to the capital created by that body of black workers; to the very obvious fact that a certain affluence breeds certain respect; that where the pressure is heaviest, and unjust restrictions imposed, there is a politely effective boycott possible in "racial solidarity" which diverts Negro capital from disinterested hands into the coffers of "race institutions." Instance the Negro insurance companies, of which there are now sixty-seven, with over $250,000,000 worth of insurance in force, flourishing out of the situation of special premium rates for Negroes instituted by some companies, and a policy of total exclusion practiced by others. No work for young Negro men and women in general business? Then they will establish their own businesses and borrow from the sentimental doctrine of "race pride" enough propulsion to compensate for the initial deficiencies of capital. But is this entirely representative of the new Negro thought? It is not. This increased activity is largely an opportunistic policy, with its firmest foothold in the South. Where it exists in the North it has been almost wholly transplanted by southern Negroes. The cities of the North where conditions tend most, in special instances to approach the restrictions of the South, become the most active business centers. The greater the isolation, the more pronounced and successful this intensive group commercialism.

Or, to take another angle of this picture: Mr. Marcus Garvey has been accused of inspiring and leading a movement for the "re-exaltation" of things black, for the exploitation of Negro resources for the profit of Negroes, and for the re-establishment of prestige to things Negro. As a fact, he has merely had the clairvoyance to place himself at the head of a docile sector of a whole population which, in different degrees, has been expressing an indefinable restlessness and broadening of spirit. The Garvey movement itself is an exaggeration of this current mood which attempts to reduce these vague longings to concrete symbols of faith. In this great sweep of the Negro population are comprehended the awkward gestures of the awakening black peasantry, the new desire of Negroes for an independent status, the revolt against a culture which has but partially (and again unevenly) digested the Negro masses—the black peasants least of all. It finds a middle ground in the feelings of kinship with all oppressed dark peoples, as articulated so forcefully by the Negro press, and takes, perhaps, its highest expression in the objectives of the Pan-African Congress.

New emotions accompany these new objectives. Where there is ferment and unrest, there is change. Old traditions are being shaken and rooted up by the percussion of new ideas. In this the year of our Lord, 1925, extending across the entire country are seventeen cities in violent agitation over Negro residence areas, and where once there was acquiescence, silent or ineffectually grumbly, there are now in evidence new convictions which more often prompt to resistance. It is this spirit, aided by increased living standards and refined tastes, that has resulted in actual housing clashes, the most notorious of which have been occurring in Detroit, Michigan, where, with a Negro population increase of more than 500 per cent in the past ten years, this new resistance has clashed with the spirit of the South, likewise drawn there by the same economic forces luring and pushing the Negroes. This same spirit was evidenced in the serious racial clashes which flared up in a dozen cities after the first huge migration of Negroes northward, and which took a sad toll in lives. Claude McKay, the young Negro poet, caught the mood of the new Negro in this, and molded it into fiery verse which Negro newspapers copied and recopied:

> If we must die, let it not be like hogs,
> Hunted and penned in an inglorious spot...

Nor does this embrace all of the ragged pattern: Silently and yet with such steady persistence that it has the aspect of an utterly distinct movement, the newer spirits are beginning to free themselves from the slough of that servile feeling (now happily classified by the psychologists as the "inferiority complex") inherited from slavery and passed along with virulence for over fifty years. The generation in whom lingered memories of the painful degradation of slavery could not be expected to cherish even those pearls of song and poetry born of suffering. They would be expected to do just as they did: rule out the Sorrow Songs as the product of ignorant slaves, taboo dialect as incorrect English, and the priceless folk lore as the uncultured expression of illiterates, an utterly conscious effort to forget the past, and take over, suddenly, the symbols of that culture which had so long ground their bodies and spirits in the dirt. The newer voices, at a more comfortable distance, are beginning to find a new beauty in these heritages, and new values in their own lives.

Less is heard of the two historic "schools of thought" clashing ceaselessly and loud over the question of industrial and higher education for the Negro. Both schools are, sensibly, now taken for granted as quite necessary. The new questions of the industrial schools are concerned with adjusting their curricula to the new fields of industry in which Negro workers will play an ever mounting role, and with expanding their academic and college courses; while the new question of the universities is that of meeting the demand for trained Negroes for business, the professions, and the arts. The level of education has been lifted through the work of both, and the new level, in itself, is taking care of the sentiment about the division.

Thus the new frontier of Negro life is flung out in a jagged, uneven but progressive pattern. For a group historically retarded and not readily assimilated, contact with its surrounding culture breeds quite uneven results. There is no fixed racial level of culture. The lines cut both vertically and horizontally. There are as great differences, with reference to culture, education, sophistication, among Negroes as between the races. (This overlapping is probably what the new psychologists have been trying to point out with their elaborately documented intelligence measurements.) And just as these currents move down and across and intersect, so may one find an utter maze of those rationalizations of attitudes of differently placed Negro groups toward life in general, and their status in particular. But a common purpose is integrating these energies born of new conflicts, and it is not at all improbable that the culture which has both nourished and abused these strivings will, in the end, be enriched by them.

* * * * * *

1.   According to Johnson, how have cities changed the lives and behavior of black migrants from the

South? How has the southern heritage made itself felt in the North?

2.   *What is the relationship between racial segregation and black economic activity?*

3.   *What changes does Johnson see in the level and meaning of "racial solidarity?"*

23–9   *Motion Picture Production Code, 1930*

Hollywood had long been subject to attacks from groups which believed that movies degraded morality. With the advent of sound in motion pictures in the late 1920s, pressure for stricter controls intensified. To stave off criticism and threats of legal censorship, Hollywood producers created an internal code that set the boundaries of movie content. Movie producers hoped that this self-censorship would placate the film industry's critics.

SOURCE: Motion Picture Producers and Distributors of America, "The Motion Picture Production Code of 1930," in Olga J. Martin, *Hollywood's Movie Commandments* (H. W. Wilson, 1937).

General Principles

I.   Theatrical motion pictures, that is, pictures intended for the theatre as distinct from pictures intended for churches, schools, lecture halls, educational movements, social reform movements, etc., are primarily to be regarded as *Entertainment.*

Mankind has always recognized the importance of entertainment and its value in rebuilding the bodies and souls of human beings.

But it has always recognized that entertainment can be of a character *harmful* to the human race, and, in consequence, has clearly distinguished between:

Entertainment which tends to improve the race, or, at least, to re-create and rebuild human beings exhausted with the realities of life; and
Entertainment which tends to degrade human beings, or to lower their standards of life and living.

Hence the moral importance of entertainment is something which has been universally recognized. It enters intimately into the lives of men and women and affects them closely; it occupies their minds and affections during leisure hours, and ultimately touches the whole of their lives. A man may be judged by his standard of entertainment as easily as by the standard of his work.

So correct entertainment raises the whole standard of a nation.
Wrong entertainment lowers the whole living condition and moral ideals of a race.
NOTE, for example, the healthy reactions to healthful moral sports like baseball, golf; the unhealthy reactions to sports like cockfighting, bullfighting, bear-baiting, etc. Note, too, the effect on a nation of gladiatorial combats, the obscene plays of Roman times, etc.

II.   Motion pictures are very important as *Art.*

Though a new art, possibly a combination art, it has the same object as the other arts, the presentation of human thoughts, emotions and experiences, in terms of an appeal to the soul thru the senses.

Here, as in entertainment:

Art enters intimately into the lives of human beings.

Art can be morally good, lifting men to higher levels.

This has been done thru good music, great painting, authentic fiction, poetry, drama.

Art can be morally evil in its effects. This is the case clearly enough with unclean art, indecent books, suggestive drama. The effect on the lives of men and women is obvious.

NOTE: It has often been argued that art in itself is unmoral, neither good nor bad. This is perhaps true of the *thing* which is music, painting, poetry, etc. But the thing is the *product* of some person's mind, and that mind was either good or bad morally when it produced the thing. And the thing has *its effect* upon those who come into contact with it. In both these ways, as a product and the cause of definite effects, it has a deep moral significance and an unmistakable moral quality.

HENCE: The motion pictures which are the most popular of modern arts for the masses, have their moral quality from the minds which produce them and from their effects on the moral lives and reactions of their audiences. This gives them a most important morality.

1)   They *reproduce* the morality of the men who use the pictures as a medium for the expression of their ideas and ideals.

2)   They *affect* the moral standards of those who thru the screen take in these ideas and ideals.

In the case of the motion pictures, this effect may be particularly emphasized because no art has so quick and so widespread an appeal to the masses. It has become in an incredibly short period, *the art of the multitudes.*

III.   The motion picture has special *Moral obligations:*

A)   Most arts appeal to the mature. This art appeals at once to every class—mature, immature, developed, undeveloped, law-abiding, criminal. Music has its grades for different classes; so has literature and drama. This art of the motion picture, combining as it does the two fundamental appeals of looking at a picture and listening to a story, at once reaches every class of society.

B)   Because of the mobility of a film and the case of picture distribution, and because of the possibility of duplicating positives in large quantities, this art *reaches places* unpenetrated by other forms of art.

C)   Because of these two facts, it is difficult to produce films intended for only *certain classes of people.* The exhibitor's theatres are for the masses, for the cultivated and the rude, mature and immature, self-restrained and inflammatory, young and old, law-respecting and criminal. Films, unlike books and music, can with difficulty be confined to certain selected groups.

D)   The latitude given to film material cannot, in consequence, be as wide as the latitude given to *book material.* In addition:

(a)   A book describes; a film vividly presents.

(b)   A book reaches the mind thru words merely; a film reaches the eyes and ears thru the reproduction of actual events.

(c)   The reaction of a reader to a book depends largely on the keenness of the reader; the reaction to a film depends on the vividness of presentation.

E)   This is also true when comparing the film with the newspapers. Newspapers present by description, films by actual presentation. Newspapers are after the fact and present things that have taken place; the film gives the events in the process of enactment and with apparent reality of life.

F)   Everything possible in a *play* is not possible in a film.

(a)   Because of the larger audience of the film, and its consequently mixed character. Psychologically, the larger the audience, the lower the moral mass resistance to suggestion.

(b)   Because thru light, enlargement of character presentation, scenic emphasis, etc., the screen story is brought closer to the audience than the play.

(c)   The enthusiasm for and interest in the film *actors and actresses,* developed beyond anything of the sort in history, makes the audience largely sympathetic toward the characters they portray and the stories in which they figure. Hence they are more ready to confuse the actor and character, and they are most receptive of the emotions and ideals portrayed and presented by their favorite stars.

G)   Small communities, remote from sophistication and from the hardening process which often takes place in the ethical and moral standards of larger cities, are easily and readily reached by any sort of film.

H)   The grandeur of mass meetings, large action, spectacular features, etc., affects and arouses more intensely the emotional side of the audience.

IN GENERAL: The mobility, popularity, accessibility, emotional appeal, vividness, straight-forward presentation of fact in the films makes for intimate contact on a larger audience and greater emotional appeal. Hence the larger moral responsibilities of the motion pictures.

SECOND SECTION

Working Principles

I.   No picture should lower the moral standards of those who see it. This is done:

(a)   When evil is made to appear *attractive,* and good is made to appear *unattractive.*

(b)   When the *sympathy* of the audience is thrown on the side of crime, wrong-doing, evil, sin. The same thing is true of a film that would throw sympathy against goodness, honor, innocence, purity, honesty.

NOTE: *Sympathy with a person who sins,* is not the same as sympathy with the sin or crime of which he is guilty. We may feel sorry for the plight of the murderer or even understand the circumstances which led him to his crime; we may not feel sympathy with the wrong which he has done.

The presentation of evil is often essential for art, or fiction, or drama. This in itself is not wrong, provided:

(a)   That evil is *not presented alluringly.* Even if later on the evil is condemned or punished, it must not be allowed to appear so attractive that the emotions are drawn to desire or approve so strongly that later they forget the condemnation and remember only the apparent joy of the sin.

(b)   That thruout the presentation, *evil and good are never confused* and that evil is always recognized clearly as evil.

(c)   That in the end the audience feels that *evil is wrong and good is right.*

II.   Law, natural or divine, must not be belittled, ridiculed, nor must a sentiment be created against it.

A)   The *presentation of crimes* against the law, human or divine, is often necessary for the carrying out of the plot. But the presentation must not throw sympathy with the criminal as against the law, nor with the crime as against those who punish it.

B)   The *courts* of the land should not be presented as *unjust.*

III.   As far as possible, life should not be misrepresented, at least not in such a way as to place in the mind of youth false values on life.

NOTE: This subject is touched just in passing. The attention of the producers is called, however, to the magnificent possibilities of the screen for character development, the building of right ideals, the inculcation in story-form of right principles. If motion pictures consistently held up high types of character, presented stories that would affect lives for the better, they could become the greatest natural force for the improvement of mankind.

* * * * * *

1.   *How does the Code attempt to universalize values? What does it define as the movies' moral responsibility?*

2.   *Compare the General Principleswith to the Working Principles. How do they differ, and how do they complement each other?*

chapter 24

The Great Depression and the New Deal, 1929–1939

24-1 Bob Stinson, Flint Sit-Down Strike, 1936

The successful Flint sit-down strike of 1936–37 was an historic breakthrough for the United Automobile Workers union. It gave a critical boost as well to the larger, nationwide drive to organize mass-production workers, a campaign led by John L. Lewis and the Committee for Industrial Organization (CIO). Bob Stinson was a UAW activist who began working at the Fisher Body plant in Flint in 1917. He recalled the momentous forty-four-day strike and its meaning for auto workers in an interview given in 1970.

SOURCE: From Hard Times: *An Oral History of the Great Depression* by Studs Terkel, Copyright © 1970 by Studs Terkel. Reprinted by permission of Pantheon Books, a Division of Random House, Inc.

THE FLINT SIT-DOWN happened Christmas Eve, 1936. I was in Detroit, playing Santa Claus to a couple of small nieces and nephews. When I came back, the second shift had pulled the plant. It took about five minutes to shut the line down. The foreman was pretty well astonished. (Laughs.)

The boys pulled the switches and asked all the women who was in Cut-and-Sew to go home. They informed the supervisors they could stay, if they stayed in their office. They told the plant police they could do their job as long as they didn't interfere with the workers.

We had guys patrol the plant, see that nobody got involved in anything they shouldn't. If anybody got careless with company property—such as sitting on an automobile cushion without putting burlap over it—he was talked to. You couldn't paint a sign on the wall or anything like that. You used bare springs for a bed. 'Cause if you slept on a finished cushion, it was no longer a new cushion.

Governor Murphy said he hoped to God he would never have to use National Guard against people. But if there was damage to property, he would do so. This was right down our alley, because we invited him to the plant and see how well we were taking care of the place.

They'd assign roles to you. When some of the guys

at headquarters wanted to tell some of the guys in the plant what was cookin', I carried the message. I was a scavenger, too.

The merchants cooperated. There'd be apples, bushels of potatoes, crates of oranges that was beginnin' to spoil. Some of our members were also little farmers, they come up with a couple of baskets of junk.

The soup kitchen was outside the plant. The women handled all the cooking, outside of one chef who came from New York. He had anywhere from ten to twenty women washing dishes and peeling potatoes in the strike kitchen. Mostly stews, pretty good meals. They were put in containers and hoisted up through the window. The boys in there had their own plates and cups and saucers.

Didn't the guys want a drink now and then...?

That was one of the hard ones. Even though you had strict discipline in there, anybody wanted to climb through the window, you couldn't stop him. He could leave any time he wanted. There was always some of the boys who would take a day off, go out and see how the old woman was doing. When they'd come back in, if somebody didn't search 'em, why, there'd be a pint.

The plant police would start bringin' in some women. That was damn quickly stopped.

We had 'em outnumbered. They may have been anti-union at the time, but it wasn't more than three or four years later before the plant guards' union was organized. I don't blame 'em. They were dependent on their supervisors for jobs just like we were.

Most of the men had their wives and friends come down, and they'd stand inside the window and they'd talk. Find out how the family was. If the union supplied them with enough coal....

We had a ladies' auxiliary. They'd visit the homes of the guys that was in the plant. They would find out if there was any shortage of coal or food. Then they'd maneuver around amongst themselves until they found some place to get a ton of coal. Some of them even put the arm on Consumer Power if there was a possibility of having her power shut off.

Any of the wives try to talk the guys into coming out?

Some of 'em would have foremen come to their homes: "Sorry, your husband was a very good operator. But if he don't get out of the plant and away from the union, he'll never again have a job at General Motors." If this woman was the least bit scared, she'd come down and cry on her husband's shoulder. He'd more than likely get a little disturbed, get a hold of his strike captain.... Maybe we'd send a couple of women out there. Sometimes you just had to let 'em go. Because if you kept them in there, they'd worry so damn much over it, that'd start ruinin' the morale of the rest of the guys.

Morale was very high at the time. It started out kinda ugly because the guys were afraid they put their foot in it and all they was gonna do is lose their jobs. But as time went on, they begin to realize they could win this darn thing, 'cause we had a lot of outside people comin' in showin' their sympathy.

Time after time, people would come driving by the plant slowly. They might pull up at the curb and roll down the window and say, "How you guys doin'?" Our guys would be lookin' out the windows, they'd be singin' songs and hollerin.' Just generally keeping themselves alive.

Sometimes a guy'd come up to you on the street and say, "How the guys doin'?" You say, "They're doin' all right." Then he'd give ya a song and dance: "I hear the boys at Chevrolet are gonna get run out tonight." I'd say, "Hogwash." He'd end with sayin': "Well, I wish you guys the best of luck because, God damn, when I worked there it was a mess." The guy'd turn around and walk away.

Nationally known people contributed to our strike fund. Mrs. Roosevelt for one. We even had a member of Parliament come from England and address us.

Lotta things worked for the union we hadn't even anticipated. Company tried to shut off the heat. It was a bluff. Nobody moved for half an hour, so they turned it back on again. They didn't want the pipes to get cold. (Laughs.) If the heat was allowed to drop, then the pipes will separate—they were all jointed together—and then you got a problem.

Some of the time you were scared, because there was all kinds of rumors going around. We had a sheriff—he came in one night at Fisher One and read the boys the riot act. He told 'em they had to leave. He stood there, looked at 'em a few minutes. A couple of guys began to curse 'im, and he turned around and left himself.

National Guard troops were there. Some from Pontiac, some from Detroit. I lived within a block where they camped. I would pass these young fellas every day. One boy, pretty young, he had a union button on. Was it his union button or was it his dad's? I walked up to him. "Your captain allow you to wear that button?" He says, "I don't know, but I'm gonna find out." (Laughs.) They were twenty-year olds. Well-behaved boys. No rough stuff, nothing untoward happened.

The men sat in there for forty-four days. Governor Murphy—I get emotional over him (laughs)—was trying to get both sides to meet on some common ground. I think he lost many a good night's sleep. We wouldn't use force. Mr. Knudsen was head of General Motors and, of course, there was John L. Lewis. They'd reach a temporary agreement and invariably the Flint Alliance or GM headquarters in Detroit would throw a monkey wrench in it. So every morning, Murphy got up with an unsolved problem.

John L. was as close to a Shakespearean actor as any I've ever listened to. He could get up there and damn all the adversaries—he had more command of language. He made a speech that if they shoot the boys out at the plant, they'd have to shoot him first.

There were a half a dozen false starts at settlement. Finally, we got the word: THE THING IS SETTLED. My God, you had to send about three people, one right after the other, down to some of those plants because the guys didn't believe it. Finally, when they did get it, they may marched out of the plants with the flag flyin' and all that stuff.

You'd see some guys comin' out of there with whiskers as long as Santa Claus. They made a rule they wasn't gonna shave until the strike was over. Oh, it was just like—you've gone through the Armistice delirium, haven't you? Everybody was runnin' around shaking everybody by the hand, sayin', "Jesus, you look strange, you got a beard on you now." (Laughs.) Women kissin' their husbands. There was a lotta drunks on the streets that night.

When Mr. Knudsen put his name to a piece of paper and says that General Motors recognizes the UAW-CIO—until that moment, we were non-people, we didn't even exist. (Laughs.) That was the big one. (His eyes are moist.)

* * * * * *

1. How were the sit-downers able to maintain unity and discipline? What obstacles did they face to keeping up morale?

2. What role did support groups outside the plant play in the sitdowner's success?

24–2   Meridel Le Sueur, Women on the Breadlines, 1932

Mass unemployment meant hunger and despair for millions of American families during the Great Depression. Long lines at free soup kitchens and employment bureaus were a common sight, especially in large cities. Like many writers of the era, Meridel Le Sueur felt compelled to report on the human misery brought on by the Depression. Le Sueur later joined the Communist Party and wrote journalism and fiction depicting the labor and political struggles of the day. Here she describes the despair she found among unemployed women in Minneapolis.

SOURCE: Meridel Le Sueur, "Women on the Breadlines," *New Masses* (1932).

I am sitting in the city free employment bureau. It's the woman's section. We have been sitting here now for four hours. We sit here every day, waiting for a job. There are no jobs. Most of us have had no breakfast. Some have had scant rations for over a year. Hunger makes a human being lapse into a state of lethargy, especially city hunger. Is there any place else in the world where a human being is supposed to go hungry amidst plenty without an outcry, without protest, where only the boldest steal or kill for bread, and the timid crawl the streets, hunger like the beak of a terrible bird at the vitals?

We sit looking at the floor. No one dares think of the coming winter. There are only a few more days of summer. Everyone is anxious to get work to lay up something for that long siege of bitter cold. But there is no work. Sitting in the room we all know it. That is why we don't talk much. We look at the floor dreading to see that knowledge in each other's eyes. There is a kind of humiliation in it. We look away from each other. We look at the floor. Its too terrible to see this animal terror in each other's eyes.

So we sit hour after hour, day after day, waiting for a job to come in. There are many women for a single job. A thin sharp woman sits inside the wire cage looking at the book. For four hours we have watched her looking at that book. She has a hard little eye. In the small bare room there are half a dozen women sitting on the benches waiting. Many come and go. Our faces are all familiar to each other, for we wait here everyday.

This is a domestic employment bureau. Most of the women who come here are middle aged, some have families, some raised their families and are now alone, some have men who are out of work. Hard times and the man leaves to hunt for work. He doesn't find it. He drifts on. The woman probably doesn't hear from him for a long time. She expects it. She isn't surprised. She struggles alone to feed the many mouths. Sometimes she gets help from the charities. If she's clever she can get herself a good living from the charities, if she's naturally a lick spittle, naturally a little docile and cunning. If she's proud then she starves silently, leaving her children to find work, coming home after a day's searching to wrestle with her house, her children.

Some such story is written on the faces of all these women. There are young girls too, fresh from the country. Some are made brazen too soon by the city. There is a great exodus of girls from the farms into the city now. Thousands of farms have been vacated completely in Minnesota. The girls are trying to get work. The prettier ones can get jobs in the stores when there are any, or waiting on tables but these jobs are only for the attractive and the adroit, the others, the real peasants have a more difficult time....

It's one of the great mysteries of the city where women go when they are out of work and hungry. There are not many women in the bread line. There are no flop houses for women as there are for men, where a bed can be had for a quarter or less. You don't see women lying on the floor at the mission in the free flops. They obviously don't sleep in the jungle or under newspapers in the park. There is no law I suppose against their being in these places but the fact is they rarely are.

Yet there must be as many women out of jobs in cities and suffering extreme poverty as there are men. What happens to them? Where do they go? Try to get into the Y.W. without any money or looking down at heel. Charities take care of very few and only those that are called "deserving." The lone girl is under suspicion by the virgin women who dispense charity.

I've lived in cities for many months broke, without help, too timid to get in bread lines. I've known many women to live like this until they simply faint on the street from privations, without saying a word to anyone. A woman will shut herself up in a room until it is taken away from her, and eat a cracker a day and be as quiet as a mouse so there are no social statistics concerning her.

I don't know why it is, but a woman will do this unless she has dependents, will go for weeks, verging on starvation, crawling in some hole, going through the streets ashamed, sitting in libraries, parks, going for days without speaking to a living soul like some exiled beast, keeping the runs mended in her stockings, shut up in terror in her own misery, until she becomes too super sensitive and timid to even ask for a job.

Bernice says even strange men she has met in the park have sometimes, that is in better days, given her a loan to pay her room rent. She has always paid them back.

In the afternoon the young girls, to forget the hunger and the deathly torture and fear of being jobless, try and pick up a man to take them to a ten cent show. They never go to more expensive ones, but they can always find a man willing to spend a dime to have the company of a girl for the afternoon.

Sometimes a girl facing the night without shelter will approach a man for lodging. A woman always asks a man for help. Rarely another woman. I have known girls to sleep in men's rooms for the night, on a pallet without molestation, and given breakfast in the morning.

Its no wonder these young girls refuse to marry, refuse to rear children. They are like certain savage tribes, who, when they have been conquered refuse to breed.

Not one of them but looks forward to starvation, for the coming winter. We are in a jungle and know it. We are beaten, entrapped. There is no way out. Even if there were a job, even if that thin acrid woman came and gave everyone in the room a job for a few days, a few hours, at thirty cents an hour, this would all be repeated tomorrow, the next day and the next.

Not one of these women but knows, that despite years of labour there is only starvation, humiliation in front of them....

So we sit in this room like cattle, waiting for a non-existent job, willing to work to the farthest atom of energy, unable to work, unable to get food and lodging, unable to bear children; here we must sit in this shame looking at the floor, worse than beasts at a slaughter.

It is appalling to think that these women sitting so listless in the room may work as hard as it is possible for a human being to work, may labour night and day, like Mrs. Gray wash street cars from midnight to dawn and offices in the early evening, scrubbing for fourteen and fifteen hours a day, sleeping only five hours or so, doing this their whole lives, and never earn one day of security, having always before them the pit of the future. The endless labour, the bending back, the water soaked hands, earning never more than a weeks wages, never having in their hands more life than that.

It's not the suffering, not birth, death, love that the young reject, but the suffering of endless labour without dream, eating the spare bread in bitterness, a slave without the security of a slave.

* * * * * *

1. *How does Le Sueur differentiate the plight of unemployed women from that of men?*

2. *What strategies for survival does she find among women?*

24–3   Franklin D. Roosevelt, First Inaugural Address, 1933

Franklin D. Roosevelt took office at the lowest point of the Great Depression. Over one-quarter of the work force was unemployed and the American economic system teetered on collapse. In his inaugural address, FDR conceived his primary task as restoring the confidence of a badly shaken nation. Roosevelt proved a very effective radio speaker, and this speech was the first of many in which he effectively exploited the new medium to reach Americans directly in their homes.

SOURCE: *Public Papers and Addresses of Franklin D. Roosevelt,* Vol. 2 (1933).

I am certain that my fellow Americans expect that on my induction into the Presidency I will address them with a candor and a decision which the present situation of our Nation impels. This is preeminently the time to speak the truth, the whole truth, frankly and boldly. Nor need we shrink from honestly facing conditions in our country today. This great Nation will endure as it has endured, will revive and will prosper. So, first of all, let me assert my firm belief that the only thing we have to fear is fear itself—nameless, unreasoning, unjustified terror which paralyzes needed efforts to convert retreat into advance. In every dark hour of our national life a leadership of frankness and vigor has met with that understanding and support of the people themselves which is essential to victory. I am convinced that you will again give the support to leadership in these critical days.

In such a spirit on my part and on yours we face our common difficulties. They concern, thank God, only material things. Values have shrunken to fantastic levels; taxes have risen; our ability to pay has fallen; government of all kinds is faced by serious curtailment of income; the means of exchange are frozen in the currents of trade; the withered leaves of industrial enterprise lie on every side; farmers find no markets for their produce; the savings of many years in thousands of families are gone.

More important, a host of unemployed citizens face the grim problem of existence, and an equally great number toil with little return. Only a foolish optimist can deny the dark realities of the moment.

Yet our distress comes from no failure of substance. We are stricken by no plague of locusts. Compared with the perils which our forefathers conquered because they believed and were not afraid, we have still much to be thankful for. Nature still offers her bounty and human efforts have multiplied it. Plenty is at our doorsteps, but a generous use of it languishes in the very sight of the supply. Primarily this is because the rulers of the exchange of mankind's goods have failed, through their own stubbornness and their own incompetence, have admitted their failure, and abdicated. Practices of the unscrupulous money changers stand indicted in the court of public opinion, rejected by the hearts and minds of men....

Happiness lies not in the mere possession of money; it lies in the joy of achievement, in the thrill of creative effort. The joy and moral stimulation of work no longer must be forgotten in the mad chase of evanescent profits. These dark days will be worth all they cost us if they teach us that our true destiny is not to be ministered unto but to minister to ourselves and to our fellow men....

Our greatest primary task is to put people to work. This is no unsolvable problem if we face it wisely and courageously. It can be accomplished in part by direct recruiting by the Government itself, treating the task as we would treat the emergency of a war, but at the same time, through this employment, accomplishing greatly needed projects to stimulate and reorganize the use of our natural resources.

Hand in hand with this we must frankly recognize the overbalance of population in our industrial centers and, by engaging on a national scale in a redistribution, endeavor to provide a better use of the land for those best fitted for the land. The task can be helped by definite efforts to raise the values of agricultural products and with this the power to purchase the output of our cities. It can be helped by preventing realistically the tragedy of the growing loss through foreclosure of our small homes and our farms. It can be helped by insistence that the Federal, State, and local governments act forthwith on the demand that their cost be drastically reduced. It can be helped by the unifying of relief activities which to-day are often scattered, uneconomical, and unequal. It can be helped by national planning for and supervision of all forms of transportation and of communications and other utilities which have a definitely public character. There are many ways in which it can be helped, but it can never be helped merely by talking about it. We must act and act quickly.

Finally, in our progress toward a resumption of work we require two safeguards against a return of the evils of the old order; there must be a strict supervision of all banking and credits and investments; there must be an end to speculation with other people's money, and there must be provision for an adequate but sound currency.

There are the lines of attack. I shall presently urge upon a new Congress in special session detailed measures for their fulfillment, and I shall seek the immediate assistance of the several States. Through this program of action we address ourselves to putting our own national house in order and making income balance outgo....

In the field of world policy I would dedicate this Nation to the policy of the good neighbor—the neighbor who resolutely respects himself and, because he does so, respects the rights of others—the neighbor who respects his obligations and respects the sanctity of his agreements in and with a world of neighbors.

If I read the temper of our people correctly, we now realize as we have never realized before our interdependence on each other; that we can not merely take but we must give as well; that if we are to go forward, we must move as a trained and loyal army willing to sacrifice for the good of a common discipline, because without such discipline no progress is made, no leadership becomes effective. We are, I know, ready and willing to submit our lives and property to such discipline, because it makes possible a leadership which aims at a larger good. This I propose to offer, pledging that the larger purposes will bind upon us all as a sacred obligation with a unity of duty hitherto evoked only in time of armed strife.

With this pledge taken, I assume unhesitatingly the leadership of this great army of our people dedicated to a disciplined attack upon our common problems.

Action in this image and to this end is feasible under the form of government which we have inherited from our ancestors. Our Constitution is so simple and practical that it is possible always to meet extraordinary needs by changes in emphasis and arrangement without loss of essential form. That is why our constitutional system has proved itself the most superbly enduring political mechanism the modern world has produced. It has met every stress of vast expansion of territory, of foreign wars, of bitter internal strife, of world relations.

It is to be hoped that the normal balance of executive and legislative authority may be wholly adequate to meet the unprecedented task before us. But it may be that an unprecedented demand and need for undelayed action may call for temporary departure from that normal balance of public procedure.

I am prepared under my constitutional duty to recommend the measures that a stricken nation in the midst of a stricken world may require. These measures, or such other measures as the Congress may build out of its experience and wisdom, I shall seek, within my constitutional authority, to bring to speedy adoption.

But in the event that the Congress shall fail to take one of these two courses, and in the event that the national emergency is still critical, I shall not evade the clear course of duty that will then confront me. I shall ask the Congress for the one remaining instrument to meet the crisis—broad Executive power to wage a war against the emergency, as great as the power that would be given to me if we were in fact invaded by a foreign foe.

* * * * * *

1.   What rhetorical strategies does Roosevelt use to

restore confidence? How does he define or explain the crisis facing America?

2.   *What appeals does he make to citizens?*

3.   *What specific measures does Roosevelt propose to deal with the crisis at hand?*

24–4   Huey Long,
Share Our Wealth, 1935

As governor of Louisiana, Huey Long won a fiercely loyal popular following by using state power to improve social services, build roads and schools, and reform tax codes. In 1932, Long moved to the U.S. Senate, where he at first supported Franklin D. Roosevelt. But the ambitious Long soon broke with the President and launched the national "Share Our Wealth" movement as an alternative to the New Deal. Before he was assassinated in 1935, Long loomed as a potential political rival to FDR.

SOURCE: Congressional Record, 73rd Congress, 2nd Sess. (1934).

Here is the whole sum and substance of the Share Our Wealth movement:

1.   Every family to be furnished by the government a homestead allowance, free of debt, of not less than one-third the average family wealth of the country, which means, at the lowest, that every family shall have the reasonable comforts of life up to a value of from $5,000 to $6,000: No person to have a fortune of more than 100 to 300 times the average family fortune, which means that the limit to fortune is between $1,500,000 and 5,000,000, with annual capital levy taxes imposed on all above 1,000,000.

2.   The yearly income of every family shall be not less than one-third of the average family income, which means that, according to the estimates of the statisticians of the U.S. Government and Wall Street, no family's annual income would be less than from $2,000 to $2,500: No yearly income shall be allowed to any person larger than from 100 to 300 times the size of the average family income, which means that no person would be allowed to earn in any year more than $600,000 to $1,800,000, all to be subject to present income tax laws.

3.   To limit or regulate the hours of work to such an extent as to prevent over-production; the most modern and efficient machinery would be encouraged so that as much would be produced as possible so as to satisfy all demands of the people, but also to allow the maximum time to the workers for recreation, convenience, education, and luxuries of life.

4.   An old age pension to the persons over 60.

5.   To balance agricultural production with what can be consumed according to the laws of God, which includes the preserving and storing of surplus commodities to be paid for and held by the Government for emergencies when such are needed. Please bear in mind, however, that when the people of America have had money to buy things they needed, we have never had a surplus of any commodity. This plan of God does not call for destroying any of the things raised to eat or wear, nor does it countenance whole destruction of hogs, cattle or milk.

6.   To pay the veterans of our wars what we owe them and to care for their disabled.

7.   Education and training for all children to be equal in opportunity in all schools, colleges, universities and other institutions for training in the professions and vocations of life; to be regulated on the capacity of children to learn, and not on the ability of parents to pay the costs. Training for life's work to be as much universal and thorough for all walks in life as has been the training in the arts of killing.

8.   The raising of revenues and taxes for the support of this program to come from the reduction of swollen fortunes from the top, as well as for the support of public works to give employment whenever there may be any slackening necessary in private enterprise.

* * * * * *

1.   What does Long's program promise the ordinary people of Depression-era America? How does he propose to implement it?

2.   Compare Long's program to that of the Populist Party of the 1890s (Document 20–4). What similarities and differences do you see between the two programs?

24–5   *National Labor Relations Act, 1935*

The National Labor Relations Act guaranteed the right of workers to collective bargaining. It established the National Labor Relations Board to oversee elections in which workers could choose whether they wanted union representation and, if so, which specific bargaining unit they preferred. The NLRB was also empowered to investigate and stop unfair labor practices by employers, employees, or unions. One of the most popular New Deal measures, the Act contributed substantially to the Democratic landslide of 1936 and to the successful organizing drives of the Committee for Industrial Organization (CIO).

SOURCE: U.S. Statutes at Large, Vol. XLIX.

FINDINGS AND POLICY

SECTION 1. The denial by employers of the right of employees to organize and the refusal by employers to accept the procedure of collective bargaining lead to strikes and other forms of industrial strife or unrest, which have the intent or the necessary effect of burdening or obstructing commerce by (a) impairing the efficiency, safety, or operation of the instrumentalities of commerce; (b) occurring in the current of commerce; (c) materially affecting, restraining, or controlling the flow of raw materials or manufactured or processed goods from or into the channels of commerce, or the prices of such materials or goods in commerce; or (d) using diminution of employment and wages in such volume as substantially to impair or disrupt the market for goods flowing from or into the channels of commerce.

The inequality of bargaining power between employees who do not possess full freedom of association or actual liberty of contract, and employers who are organized in the corporate or other forms of ownership association substantially burdens and affects the flow of commerce, and tends to aggravate recurrent business depressions, by depressing wage rates and the purchasing power of wage earners in industry and by preventing the stabilization of competitive wage rates and working conditions within and between industries.

Experience has proved that protection by law of the right of employees to organize and bargain collectively safeguards commerce from injury, impairment, or interruption, and promotes the flow of commerce by removing certain recognized sources of industrial strife and unrest, by encouraging practices fundamental to the friendly adjustment of industrial disputes arising out of differences as to wages, hours, or other working conditions, and by restoring equality of bargaining power between employers and employees.

It is hereby declared to be the policy of the United States to eliminate the causes of certain substantial obstructions to the free flow of commerce and to mitigate and eliminate these obstructions when they have occurred by encouraging the practice and procedure of collective bargaining and by protecting the exercise by workers of full freedom of association, self-organization, and designation of representatives of their own choosing, for the purpose of negotiating the terms and conditions of their employment or other mutual aid or protection....

NATIONAL LABOR RELATIONS BOARD

SEC. 3. (a) There is hereby created a board, to be known as the "National Labor Relations Board," which shall be composed of three members, who shall be appointed by the President, by and with the advice and consent of the Senate. One of the original members shall be appointed for a term of one year, one for a term of three years, and one for a term of five years, but their successors shall be appointed for terms of five years each, except that any individual chosen to fill a vacancy shall be appointed only for the unexpired term of the member whom he shall succeed. The President shall designate one member to serve as chairman of the Board. Any member of the Board may be removed by the President, upon notice and hearing, for neglect of duty or malfeasance in office, but for no other cause....

SEC. 4. (a) Each member of the Board shall receive a salary of $10,000 a year, shall be eligible for reappointment, and shall not engage in any other business, vocation, or employment...The Board may establish or utilize such regional, local, or other agencies, and utilize such voluntary and uncompensated services, as may from time to time be needed....

SEC. 6. (a) The Board shall have authority from time to time to make, amend, and rescind such rules and regulations as may be necessary to carry out the provisions of this Act. Such rules and regulations shall be effective upon publication in the manner which the Board shall prescribe.

RIGHTS OF EMPLOYEES

SEC. 7. Employees shall have the right of self-organization, to form, join, or assist labor organizations, to bargain collectively through representatives of their own choosing, and to engage in concerted activities, for the purpose of collective bargaining or other mutual aid or protection.

SEC. 8. It shall be an unfair labor practice for an employer—

(1) To interfere with, restrain, or coerce employees in the exercise of the rights guaranteed in section 7.

(2) To dominate or interfere with the formation or administration of any labor organization or contribute financial or other support to it: *Provided,* That subject to rules and regulations made and published by the Board pursuant to section 6 (a), an employer shall not be prohibited from permitting employees to confer with him during working hours without loss of time or pay.

(3) By discrimination in regard to hire or tenure of employment or any term or condition of employment to encourage or discourage membership in any labor organization: *Provided,* That nothing in this Act, or in the National Industrial Recovery Act (U.S. C., Supp. VII, title 15, secs. 701–712), as amended from time to time, or in any code or agreement approved or prescribed thereunder, or in any other statute of the United States, shall preclude an employer from making an agreement with a labor organization (not established, maintained, or assisted by any action defined in this Act as an unfair labor practice) to require as a condition of employment membership therein, if such labor organization is the representative of the employees as provided in section 9 (a), in the appropriate collective bargaining unit covered by such agreement when made.

(4) To discharge or otherwise discriminate against an employee because he has filed charges or given testimony under this Act.

(5) To refuse to bargain collectively with the representatives of his employees, subject to the provisions of Section 9 (a).

REPRESENTATIVES AND ELECTIONS

SEC. 9. (a) Representatives designated or elected for the purposes of collective bargaining by the majority of the employees in a unit appropriate for such purposes, shall be the exclusive representatives of all the employees in such unit for the purposes of collective bargaining in respect to rates of pay, wages, hours of employment, or other conditions of employment: *Provided,* That any individual employee or a group of employees shall have the right at any time to present grievances to their employer.

(b) The Board shall decide in each case whether, in order to insure to employees the full benefit of their right to self-organization and to collective bargaining, and otherwise to effectuate the policies of this Act, the unit appropriate for the purposes of collective bargaining shall be the employer unit, craft unit, plant unit, or subdivision thereof.

(c) Whenever a question affecting commerce arises concerning the representation of employees, the Board may investigate such controversy and certify to the parties, in writing, the name or names of the representatives that have been designated or selected. In any such investigation, the Board shall provide for an appropriate hearing upon due notice, either in conjunction with a proceeding under section 10 or otherwise, and may take a secret ballot of employees, or utilize any other suitable method to ascertain such representatives.

(d) Whenever an order of the Board made pursuant to section 10 (c) is based in whole or in part upon facts certified following an investigation pursuant to subsection (c) of this section, and there is a petition for the movement or review of such order, such certification and the record of such investigation shall be included in the transcript of the entire record required to be filed under subsections 10 (e) or 10 (f), and thereupon the decree of the court enforcing, modifying, or setting aside in whole or in part the order of the Board shall be made and entered upon the pleadings, testimony, and proceedings set forth in such transcript.

PREVENTION OF UNFAIR LABOR PRACTICES

SEC. 10. (a) The Board is empowered, as hereinafter provided, to prevent any person from engaging in any unfair labor practice (listed in section 8) affecting commerce. This power shall be exclusive, and shall not be affected by any other means of adjustment or prevention that has been or may be established by agreement, code, law, or otherwise.

(b) Whenever it is charged that any person has engaged in or is engaging in any such unfair labor practice, the Board, or any agent or agency designated by the Board for such purposes, shall have power to issue and cause to be served upon such person a complaint stating the charges in that respect, and containing a notice of hearing before the Board or a member thereof, or before a designated agent or agency, at a place therein fixed, not less than five days after the serving of said complaint.

Any such complaint may be amended by the member, agent, or agency conducting the hearing or the Board in its discretion at any time prior to the issuance of an order based thereon. The person so complained shall have the right to file an answer to the original amended complaint and to appear in person or otherwise and give testimony at the place and time fixed in the complaint. In the discretion of the member, agent or agency conducting the hearing of the Board, any other person may be allowed to intervene in the said proceeding and to present testimony. In any such proceeding the rules of evidence prevailing in courts of law or equity shall not be controlling.

(c) The testimony taken by such member, agent or agency or the Board shall be reduced to writing and filed with the Board. Thereafter, in its discretion, the Board upon notice may take further testimony or hear argument. If upon all the testimony taken the Board shall be of the opinion that any person named in the complaint has engaged in or is engaging in any such unfair labor practice, then the Board shall state its findings of fact and shall issue and cause to be served on such person an order requiring such person to cease and desist from such unfair labor practice, and to take such affirmative action, including reinstatement of employees with or without back pay, as will effectuate the policies of this Act. Such order may further require such person to make reports from time to time showing the extent to which it has complied with the order. If upon all the testimony taken the Board shall be of the opinion that no person named in the complaint has engaged in or is engaging in any such unfair labor practice, then the Board shall state its find-

ings of fact and shall issue an order dismissing the said complaint....

(e) The Board shall have power to petition any circuit court of appeals of the United States, or if all the circuit courts of appeals to which application may be made are in vacation, any district court of the United States, within any circuit or district, respectively, wherein the unfair labor practice in question occurred or wherein such person resides or transacts business, for the enforcement of such order and for appropriate temporary relief or restraining order, and shall certify and file in the court a transcript of the entire record in the proceeding, including the pleadings and testimony upon which such order was entered and the findings and order of the Board. Upon such filing, the court shall cause notice thereof to be served upon such person, and thereupon shall have jurisdiction of the proceeding and of the question determined therein, and shall have power to grant such temporary relief or restraining order as it deems just and proper, and to make and enter upon the pleadings, testimony, and proceedings set forth in such transcript a decree enforcing, modifying, and enforcing as so modified, or setting aside in whole or in part the order of the Board....

* * * * * *

1. *What arguments does the Act make in favor of collective bargaining? How does it define unfair labor practices?*

2. *What mechanisms does the Act include for enforcement?*

24–6   U.S. Senate, Investigation of Strikebreaking, 1939

Although the National Labor Relations Act guaranteed a legal right to collective bargaining, labor organizers still faced fierce, sometimes violent, opposition from employers opposed to unions. Between 1936 and 1939, the Civil Liberties Subcommittee of the Senate Committee on Education and Labor conducted a lengthy investigation of interference with attempts at union organizing. The following excerpt details the use of strikebreakers by employers during the labor wars of the 1930s.

SOURCE: U.S. Senate, Committee on Education and Labor, *Strikebreaking Services*, 76th Congress, 1st Sess., Report No. 6 (1939).

SECTION 1. THE BUSINESS OF FURNISHING STRIKE SERVICES

The committee makes the following findings concerning the commercial aspects of the business of furnishing strike services:

(a) Many detective agencies engage in the business of furnishing and supervising strikebreakers, strikeguards, and propagandists, missionaries or street operators. Most, if not all of the detective agencies engaged in the business of furnishing these three classes of strike employees, or any one of them, also offer the service of spying on the union affiliations and union activities of employees. The three functions of furnishing strike services, labor espionage, and industrial munitions are related in purpose, and are sometimes carried on by the same detective agency.

(b) Some employers' associations, committed to a policy of antiunionism, furnish strikeguards or strike-

breakers as a part of their services to assist employers to fight against the recognition of unions.

(c) A considerable body of men in our great industrial centers are available for, and seek employment in, strike situations. These are the men recruited by detective agencies or employers' associations to serve as strikebreakers, strikeguards, or missionaries. They go from strike to strike and some of them make this work their vocation. An underworld profession of strikebreaking exists.

(d) Detective agencies and employers' associations furnishing strike services recruit strikeguards and strikebreakers through strike lieutenants, leaders of the strikebreaking profession, who have a wide acquaintance among those available for strike work. If they can establish a clientele of employers, strike lieutenants sometimes set up in business for themselves.

(e) The profits made by detective agencies from strikebreaking are enormous, ranging from 25 to 100 percent.

(f) Such profits are increased by the prevailing attitude of antiunion employers toward strikebreaking services. In time of strike even large and carefully run corporations seem to experience a collapse of proper accounting procedure, and vast sums are turned over to the leaders of the strikebreaking class without question or investigation.

(g) Taking advantage of the opportunities offered by such financial laxity, and by the racketeering character of their vocation, professional strike followers cheat employers through padded pay rolls, deceit, and other forms of graft. It is such sums of money and such opportunities for fraud that constitute the lifeblood of the strikebreaking profession and maintain it in existence.

SECTION 2. THE PURPOSE OF COMMERCIALIZED STRIKE SERVICES

The committee finds that strike services are offered by detective agencies and employers' associations not so much for the purpose of assisting employers to protect property and maintain operations during strikes but rather for the purpose of destroying unions and the processes of collective bargaining. This conclusion does not question the right of the employers to engage watch-men to protect their premises, nor the right permanently to replace employees for good cause by other skilled and competent workmen. These acknowledged rights of the employer, however, cannot be invoked to justify employment of the strikebreakers, strikeguards, and missionaries furnished in the usual course of business by detective agencies, strikebreaking agencies, or employers' associations for the following reasons:

(a) The strikebreaker furnished as a part of strike service by the above-mentioned agencies, is, in most cases, not a qualified workman but an incompetent mercenary, posing as a workman for the purpose of breaking strikes. He usually receives compensation higher than that of the regular employees, and is discharged after the strike.

(b) The strikeguard furnished by the agencies mentioned above, is not a man trained and qualified for police and patrol duty. He is, for the most part, a specialized kind of ruffian, a "regular fink" well versed in violence, often dishonest, and sometimes a gangster.

(c) The propagandist, missionary, or street operator furnished by the organizations mentioned above, practices deception and deceit, and often performs in the role of agent provocateur or spy.

No employer who has accepted the principle of collective bargaining in good faith can consider using such persons against his employees. Not only do such persons tend to provoke violence and disorder, but their purpose is to discredit and destroy instruments of collective bargaining and make amicable settlement of disputes an impossibility. Through their acts of intimidation, coercion, and provocation such persons violate the rights of free speech and free assembly and the freedom of association of employees. Furthermore, during the period of this committee's investigation, the use of such strike services, and the business of purveying them, violated the policy of labor relations enunciated by the Congress.

SECTION 3. RELATIONS BETWEEN STRIKE SERVICES AND STRIKE VIOLENCE

The committee finds that commercialized strike services have constituted an important cause of violence occurring in strikes in which they have been used, for the following reasons:

(a) Commercialized strike services tend to produce violence and disorder. Such violence comes partly as a result of the natural hostility and resentment of workingmen against the use of industrial mercenaries, but is more directly attributable to the activities of professional strike followers and the employers who use them.

(b) In most cases professional strikebreakers or strikeguards have a pecuniary incentive to create and maintain a state of disorder and violence in the strike on which they serve. Detective agencies have been known to create or feign violence in order to extend and increase the services which they render.

(c) In some cases employers have directed detective agencies to perform acts of violence, or have instigated such acts, or have made their commission inevitable. This has been done either to discredit strikers because of such acts, to break their morale by the use of physical force, or to create a disorderly situation of such proportions that the armed intervention of the State will be required to suppress it.

(d) Professional strikeguards and strikebreakers are worse than useless in preventing or policing acts of lawlessness or violence by strikers. Instead of controlling or pacifying such situations, they embitter them and add further fuel to the flames....

* * * * * *

1.   *According to the report, how is strikebreaking organized as a commercial business? What people are employed in this line of work?*

2.   *What are the main techniques? What do these suggest about the motives and interests of employers who use them?*

24–7   *Republican Party Platform, 1936*

Not all Americans supported the New Deal. In fact, millions of Americans reviled Franklin D. Roosevelt and his policies. The Republican Party Platform of 1936 outlines conservative complaints against the New Deal. The campaign that year was filled with bitter, often personal, denunciations of Roosevelt. But the overwhelming Democratic landslide in both the presidential race and in the Congress amounted to a strong vote of confidence in the President's policies.

SOURCE: Proceedings, 21st Republican National Convention.

America is in peril. The welfare of American men and women and the future of our youth are at stake. We dedicate ourselves to the preservation of their political liberty, their individual opportunity and their character as free citizens, which today for the first time are threatened by Government itself.

For three long years the New Deal Administration has dishonored American traditions and flagrantly betrayed the pledges upon which the Democratic Party sought and received public support.

The powers of Congress have been usurped by the President.

The integrity and authority of the Supreme Court have been flouted.

The rights and liberties of American citizens have been violated.

Regulated monopoly has displaced free enterprise.

The New Deal Administration constantly seeks to usurp the rights reserved to the States and to the people.

It has insisted on the passage of laws contrary to the Constitution.

It has intimidated witnesses and interfered with the right of petition.

It has dishonored our country by repudiating its most sacred obligations.

It has been guilty of frightful waste and extravagance, using public funds for partisan political purposes.

It has promoted investigations to harass and intimidate American citizens, at the same time denying investigations into its own improper expenditures.

It has created a vast multitude of new offices, filled them with its favorites, set up a centralized bureaucracy, and sent out warms of inspectors to harass our people.

It had bred fear and hesitation in commerce and industry, thus discouraging new enterprises, preventing employment and prolonging the depression.

It secretly has made tariff agreements with our foreign competitors, flooding our markets with foreign commodities.

It has coerced and intimidated voters by withholding relief from those opposing its tyrannical policies.

It has destroyed the morale of many of our people and made them dependent upon Government.

Appeals to passion and class prejudice have replaced reason and tolerance.

To a free people these actions are insufferable. This campaign cannot be waged on the traditional differences between the Republican and Democratic parties. The responsibility of this election transcends all previous political divisions. We invite all Americans, irrespective of party, to join us in defense of American institutions.

CONSTITUTIONAL GOVERNMENT AND FREE ENTERPRISE

WE PLEDGE OURSELVES:

1.   To maintain the American system of constitutional and local self government, and to resist all attempts to impair the authority of the Supreme Court of the United States, the final protector of the rights of our citizens against the arbitrary encroachments of the legislative and executive branches of Government. There can be no individual liberty without an independent judiciary.

2. To preserve the American system of free enterprise, private competition, and equality of opportunity, and to seek its constant betterment in the interests of all.

REEMPLOYMENT

The only permanent solution of the unemployment problem is the absorption of the unemployed by industry and agriculture. To that end, we advocate:

Removal of restrictions on production.

Abandonment of all New Deal policies that raise production costs, increase the cost of living, and thereby restrict buying, reduce volume and prevent reemployment.

Encouragement instead of hindrance to legitimate business.

Withdrawal of Government from competition with private payrolls.

Elimination of unnecessary and hampering regulations.

Adoption of such policies as will furnish a chance for individual enterprise, industrial expansion, and the restoration of jobs.

RELIEF

The necessities of life must be provided for the needy, and hope must be restored pending recovery. The administration of relief is a major failure of the New Deal. It has been faithless to those who most deserve our sympathy. To end confusion, partisanship, waste and incompetence,

WE PLEDGE:

1. The return of responsibility for relief administration to non-political local agencies familiar with community problems.

2. Federal grants-in-aid to the States and Territories while the need exists, upon compliance with these conditions: (a) a fair proportion of the total relief burden to be provided from the revenues of States and local governments; (b) all engaged in relief administration to be selected on the basis of merit and fitness; (c) adequate provision to be made for the encouragement of those persons who are trying to become self-supporting.

3. Undertaking of Federal public works only on their merits and separate from the administration of relief.

4. A prompt determination of the facts concerning relief and unemployment.

Security

Real security will be possible only when our productive capacity is sufficient to furnish a decent standard of living for all American families and to provide a surplus for future needs and contingencies. For the attainment of that ultimate objective, we look to the energy, self-reliance and character of our people, and to our system of free enterprise.

Society has an obligation to promote the security of the people, by affording some measure of protection against involuntary unemployment and dependency in old age. The New Deal policies, while purporting to provide social security, have, in fact, endangered it.

We propose a system of old age security....

We propose to encourage adoption by the States and Territories of honest and practical measures for meeting the problems of unemployment insurance.

The unemployment insurance and old age annuity sections of the present Social Security Act are unworkable and deny benefits to about two-thirds of our adult population, including professional men and women and all those engaged in agriculture and domestic service, and the self employed, while imposing heavy tax burdens upon all. The so-called reserve fund estimated at forty-seven billion dollars for old age insurance is no reserve at all, because the fund will contain nothing but the Government's promise to pay, while the taxes collected in the guise of premiums will be wasted by the Government in reckless and extravagant political schemes.

LABOR

The welfare of labor rests upon increased production and the prevention of exploitation. We pledge ourselves to:

Protect the right of labor to organize and to bargain collectively through representatives of its own choosing without interference from any source.

Prevent governmental job holders from exercising autocratic powers over labor.

Support the adoption of State laws and interstate compacts to abolish sweatshops and child labor, and to protect women and children with respect to maximum hours, minimum wages and working conditions. We believe that this can be done within the Constitution as it now stands.

AGRICULTURE

The farm problem is an economic and social, not a partisan problem, and we propose to treat it accordingly....

Our paramount object is to protect and foster the family type of farm, traditional in American life, and to promote policies which will bring about an adjustment of agriculture to meet the needs of domestic and foreign markets. As an emergency measure, during the agricultural depression, Federal benefit payments or grants-in-aid when administered within the means of the Federal Government are consistent with a balanced budget.

WE PROPOSE:

1. To facilitate economical production and increased consumption on a basis of abundance instead of scarcity.

2. A national land-use program, including the acquisition of abandoned and non-productive farm lands by voluntary sale or lease, subject to approval of the legislative and executive branches of the States concerned, and the devotion of such land to appropriate public use, such as watershed protection and flood prevention, reforestation, recreation, and conservation of wild life.

3. That an agricultural policy be pursued for the protection and restoration of the land resources, designed to bring about such a balance between soil-building and soil-depleting crops as will permanently insure productivity, with reasonable benefits to cooperating farmers on family-type farms, but so regulated as to eliminate the New Deal's destructive policy towards the dairy and livestock industries.

4. To extend experimental aid to farmers developing new crops suited to our soil and climate....

REGULATION OF BUSINESS

We recognize the existence of a field within which governmental regulation is desirable and salutary. The authority to regulate should be vested in an independent tribunal acting under clear and specific laws establishing definite standards. Their determinations on law and facts should be subject to review by the Courts. We favor Federal regulation, within the Constitution, of the marketing of securities to protect investors. We favor also Federal regulation of the interstate activities of public utilities....

GOVERNMENT FINANCE

The New Deal Administration has been characterized by shameful waste and general financial irresponsibility. It has piled deficit upon deficit. It threatens national bankruptcy and the destruction through inflation of insurance policies and savings bank deposits.

WE PLEDGE OURSELVES TO:

Stop the folly of uncontrolled spending.

Balance the budget—not by increasing taxes but by cutting expenditures, drastically and immediately.

Revise the Federal tax system and coordinate it with State and local tax systems.

Use the taxing power for raising revenue and not for punitive or political purposes.

MONEY AND BANKING

We advocate a sound currency to be preserved at all hazards.

The first requisite to a sound and stable currency is a balanced budget.

We oppose further devaluation of the dollar.

We will restore to the Congress the authority lodged with it by the Constitution to coin money and regulate the value thereof by repealing all the laws delegating this authority to the Executive.

We will cooperate with other countries toward stabilization of currencies as soon as we can do so with due regard for our national interests and as soon as other nations have sufficient stability to justify such action.

CONCLUSION

We assume the obligations and duties imposed upon Government by modern conditions. We affirm our unalterable conviction that, in the future as in the past, the fate of the nation will depend, not so much on the wisdom and power of Government, as on the character and virtue, self-reliance, industry and thrift of the people and on their willingness to meet the responsibilities essential to the preservation of a free society.

Finally, as our party affirmed in its first Platform in 1856: "Believing that the spirit of our institutions as well as the Constitution of our country guarantees liberty of conscience and equality of rights among our citizens, we oppose all legislation tending to impair them," and "we invite the affiliation and cooperation of the men of all parties, however differing from us in other respects, in support of the principles herein declared."

The acceptance of the nomination tendered by this Convention carries with it, as a matter of private honor and public faith, an undertaking by each candidate to be true to the principles and program herein set forth.

* * * * * *

1. *What underlying philosophical differences with the New Deal are expressed here?*

2. *What specific alternatives do the Republicans offer? How do some of these suggest that they have reluctantly accepted some of the New Deal's approach?*

24–8   Carey McWilliams, Okies in California, 1939

The combination of the Dust Bowl and a depressed economy caused a mass migration of hundreds of thousands seeking a better life in California. Most came from the hard-hit rural regions of the Midwest and Southwest. Migrants usually endured poor living conditions in California and found few prospects for employment or land ownership. Journalist Carey McWilliams investigated migrant communities and gave the following testimony to a House committee looking into the problem.

SOURCE: Carey McWilliams, Testimony, U.S. Congress House Select Committee to Investigate the Interstate Migration of Destitute Citizens, *Hearings,* 76th Cong., 3rd Sess. (1941).

The most characteristic of all housing in California in which migrants reside at the moment is the shacktown or cheap subdivision. Most of these settlements have come into existence since 1933 and the pattern which obtains is somewhat similar throughout the State. Finding it impossible to rent housing in incorporated communities on their meager incomes, migrants have created a market for a very cheap type of subdivision of which the following may be taken as being representative:

In Monterey County, according to a report of Dr. D. M. Bissell, county health officer, under date of November 28, 1939, there are approximately three well-established migrant settlements. One of these, the development around the environs of Salinas, is perhaps the oldest migrant settlement of its type in California. In connection with this development I quote a paragraph of the report of Dr. Bissell:

"This area is composed of all manners and forms of housing without a public sewer system. Roughly, 10,000 persons are renting or have established homes there. A chief element in this area is that of refugees from the Dust Bowl who inhabit a part of Alisal called Little Oklahoma. Work in lettuce harvesting and packing and sugar beet processing have attracted these people who, seeking homes in Salinas without success because they aren't available, have resorted to makeshift adobes outside the city limits. Complicating the picture is the impermeable substrata which makes septic tanks with leaching fields impractical. Sewer wells have resulted

with the corresponding danger to adjacent water wells and to the water wells serving the Salinas public. Certain districts, for example, the Airport Tract and parts of Alisal, have grown into communities with quite satisfactory housing, but others as exemplified by the Graves district are characterized by shacks and lean-tos which are unfit for human habitation.".…

Typical of the shacktown problem are two such areas near the city limits of Sacramento, one on the east side of B Street, extending from Twelfth Street to the Sacramento city dump and incinerator; and the other so-called Hoovertown, adjacent to the Sacramento River and the city filtration plant. In these two areas there were on September 17, 1939, approximately 650 inhabitants living in structures that, with scarcely a single exception, were rated by the inspectors of this division as "unfit for human occupancy." The majority of the inhabitants were white Americans, with the exception of 50 or 60 Mexican families, a few single Mexican men, and a sprinkling of Negroes. For the most part they are seasonally employed in the canneries, the fruit ranches, and the hop fields of Sacramento County. Most of the occupants are at one time or another upon relief, and there are a large number of occupants in these shacktowns from the Dust Bowl area. Describing the housing, an inspector of this division reports:

"The dwellings are built of brush, rags, sacks, boxboard, odd bits of tin and galvanized iron, pieces of canvas and whatever other material was at hand at the time of construction."

Wood floors, where they exist, are placed directly upon the ground, which because of the location of the camps with respect to the Sacramento River, is damp most of the time. To quote again from the report:

"Entire families, men, women, and children, are crowded into hovels, cooking and eating in the same room. The majority of the shacks have no sinks or cesspools for the disposal of kitchen drainage, and this, together with garbage and other refuse, is thrown on the surface of the ground."

Because of the high-water table, cesspools, where they exist, do not function properly; there is a large overflow of drainage and sewage to the surface of the ground. Many filthy shack latrines are located within a few feet of living quarters. Rents for the houses in these shacktowns range from $3 to $20 a month. In one instance a landlord rents ground space for $1.50 to $5 a month, on which tenants are permitted to erect their own dugouts. The Hooverville section is composed primarily of tents and trailers, there being approximately 125 tent structures in this area on September 17, 1939. Both areas are located in unincorporated territory. They are not subject at the present time to any State or county building regulation. In Hooverville, at the date of the inspection, many families were found that did not have even a semblance of tents or shelters. They were cooking and sleeping on the ground in the open and one water tap at an adjoining industrial plant was found to be the source of the domestic water supply for the camp....

******

1.   *What were the difficulties faced by migrant communities in California?*

2.   *How does their situation seem worse than that of Depression victims in big cities?*

24–9   Hiram Sherman, *The Federal Theater Project, 1936*

The Works Progress Administration (WPA) established several federally funded arts programs designed to create employment for artists and support cultural activities around the nation. Among the most innovative of these was the Federal Theater Project, which encouraged artistic experimentation and building new audiences for theater. Hiram Sherman was a New York–based actor who performed in many Federal Theater productions.

SOURCE: From *Hard Times: An Oral History of the Great Depression* by Studs Terkel. Copyright © 1970 by Studs Terkel. Reprinted by permission of Pantheon Books, a Division of Random House, Inc.

In 1936, I joined the Federal Theater. I was assigned to Project 891. The directors and producers were Orson Welles and John Houseman. The theater we had taken over was the Maxine Elliott. A lot of theaters went dark during the Depression, and the theater owners were happy to lease them to the Government.

One of the marvelous things about the Federal Theater, it wasn't bound by commercial standards. It could take on poetic drama and do it. And experimental theater. The Living Newspaper made for terribly exciting productions. Yet it was theater by bureaucracy. Everything had to go to a higher authority. There were endless chits to be approved. There were comic and wasteful moments all over the country. But it was forward-thinking in so many ways. It anticipated some of today's problems. The Unit I was in was integrated. We did Marlowe's *Doctor Faustus*. Mephistopheles was played by a Negro, Jack Carter. Orson Welles played Faustus.

Our next production was *Cradle Will Rock*, words and music by Marc Blitzstein. And we rehearsed those eight hours a day. We worked every moment, and sometimes we worked overtime because we loved it.

Cradle Will Rock was for its day a revolutionary piece. It was an attack on big business and the corruption involved. It was done *à la* Brecht. We had it fully rehearsed.

On opening night, when the audience was assembling in the street, we found the doors of the Maxine Elliott closed. They wouldn't admit the audience because of an edict from Washington that this was revolutionary fare. And we would have no performance. Somebody had sent down the word.

Well, when you have an alert company, who are all keyed up at this moment, and a master of publicity such as Orson Welles, this is just grist for their mills. (Laughs.)

It's a nice evening in May—late May or April. Balmy evening. An audience not able to get into a theater, but not leaving because the directors of 891, Orson Welles and John Houseman, were haranguing them in the street: "Don't leave!" They expected to get a reversal of the edict. We're told not to make up. We're told not to go home. We don't know what's going to happen.

No reversal came from Washington. So Orson and John Houseman got their friends on the phone: What theater could we do this in? Somebody suggested the Jolson Theater. An announcement was made to all these people, without benefit of microphone: if you go to the Jolson Theater you will see the show. And we marched. Walking with our audience around into Broadway and then up Seventh Avenue to Fifty-ninth Street, we acquired an even larger audience.

Walking down the middle of the street?

Oh yes. Walking with no police permit. (Laughs.) Just overflowing the sidewalks. Obviously something was afoot. The Jolson Theater hadn't had a booking for months and was very dusty. But it was open.

Word came from Actors Equity that proper bonding arrangements had not been made. The actors would not be allowed to appear on the stage. Because now you're not under the aegis of the Federal Theater. You're under some obscure private management. You don't know what, because you haven't found out yet.

This didn't daunt us. We had a colloquy right in the alley. We decided, well, if we can't go on the stage, we could wheel out the piano and Marc Blitzstein could do what he had done in so many auditions: describe the setting and such, and we'll all sit in the audience. Equity didn't say we couldn't sit in the audience. When our cues come, we will rise and give them. So, that we did.

The theater filled. I don't know how the extra people, who didn't hold tickets for the opening, how they got in. I've often wondered. Did the box office open or did they just say: come in for the laughs? But it was packed with people. The stage was bare, the curtain was up, and suddenly missed all your fellow actors. You couldn't find them. We were in different parts of the house.

Eventually the house lights lowered a little. Marc Blitzstein came out and laid the setting and played a few bars and then said: "Enter the whore." I didn't know where Olive Stanton, who played the whore, was. Suddenly you could hear Olive's very clear high voice, from over left. A spotlight suddenly found her and she stood up. She was in the lower left-hand box. One by one, as we were called up, we joined in. We turned around if we were down front, and faced the audience. People were scattered all over. It was a most exciting evening. The audience reaction was tremendous.

One of those summers, '38, '39, I don't know which—Marc Blitzstein corraled most of us who'd been in the original company and asked us if we'd give up Sunday to go give a performance of *Cradle Will Rock* in Bethlehem, Pennsylvania. I thought this was marvelous. Because we're now going to take *Cradle Will Rock* to the workers, to the people for whom he wrote this piece. We were all corraled into a bus and off we went on a nice, hot summer's day. I thought, well, pretty soon the mills will close down and the steel workers will pour into this amusement park, as twilight comes, and they'll hear this marvelous saga. No one showed up.

A few men drifted in, and the first thing you find out is that many of them do not understand or speak English. And this was written in, supposedly, common American speech. Here we were preparing an opera for the proletariat, and the proletariat neither wants nor understands it. It's a rather shocking occurrence. But you don't give up.

You're in a hot, sort of open auditorium. And Will Geer, never to be discouraged, scrounging around for an audience. He found a picnic of church ladies over an adjoining hill. They were spreading out their picnic baskets and he asked: "Would you like to be entertained with an opera?" They allowed as how they would, and they packed their gingham table cloths, all the sandwiches and brought them over to this little amusement place. And sat down.

Marc Blitzstein came out and announced the name of this piece was *Cradle Will Rock,* the setting was Steeltown, U.S.A., and it begins on a street corner at night, and enter the whore. When he said those words, our audience got up and packed up their picnic baskets and left us. We never did do *Cradle Will Rock* in Bethlehem, Pennsylvania.

We were to report back to the Federal Theater, to Project 891. We had no assignment at the moment. But all of us in the stock company had to spend eight hours a day in the Maxine Elliott Theater. We could bring no food in the theater. We had a lunch hour. We could read, but we could not write. We couldn't deface anything, we couldn't rehearse. We sat. Forced sitting, with nothing to keep you interested, is one of the most grueling punishments I've ever been through. I've never been in jail as yet, I expect to. But prisoners are paid for work.

I don't know if I'm partisan to the underdog or whether I'm the underdog. My political convictions were my own. But this is not the case in life. You're stigmatized, anything you do. I was active in my union, I was playing benefits—there was Spanish relief, you know, the Spanish Civil War. My life was very full. I didn't sleep very much. I got excited about everything. They were tearing down the Sixth Avenue Elevated and selling the scrap iron to Japan. I was going to protest.... (Laughs.) There was a cause every second.

I was horrified one morning to find that a Congressman from Kansas had stated in the Congressional Record that I was one of the seven Communists that dominated the Council of the Actors Equity Association. I thought that was unusual. So I sent the Congressman a wire and I said: I read this news story, and if you'll repeat your accusations outside the halls of Congress, I would sue you for loss of employment. I never heard from him again.

******

1. *How did the Project allow artists to create productions that might have been impossible to produce in the commercial theater? How did these productions reflect the political issues of the day?*

2. *What do Sherman's frustrations with the Project suggest about the limits of federally funded arts programs?*

chapter 25

World War II, 1930s–1945

25–1   Bernice Brode, Tales of Los Alamos, 1943

Bernice Brode lived at Los Alamos for two years with her husband, an experimental physicist, and their two children. Like many Los Alamos wives, she also worked as a computer technician after receiving training there. She wrote this account some thirty-five years after the war ended.

SOURCE: Lawrence Badash et al., eds., *Reminiscences of Los Alamos, 1943–1945* (Boston: Reidel 1980), 138–146.

Los Alamos was a very unusual community. Beginning with its remote location high on the mesa, it was closed tight.... Only visitors or VIPs from high places in Washington, who were directly connected with the Manhattan Project, were allowed in. It was unusual because it was a young community, with an average age of around twenty-five years. There were practically no old people. Those of us in our early forties were the senior citizens. We had no invalids, no in-laws, no unemployed, no idle rich, no poor, and no jails....

The Army Engineers proceeded in the early spring of 1943 to erect barracks in the technical area. Barracks were built for the Army personnel and dormitories for the single civilians. We also had a trailer area for maintenance people at the edge of the mesa. The sanitary conditions were a disgrace and many of our socially minded ladies tried to get improvements, but in our last hectic days of '45, when the trailer area grew alarmingly, the authorities were too pressed to take any steps. Well, this then was the town where the first atomic bomb was made. Plain, utilitarian, and quite ugly, but surrounded by some of the most spectacular scenery in America. We could gaze beyond the town, fenced in by steel wire, and watch the seasons come and go. The aspens turning gold in the fall, the dark evergreens, blizzards piling up snow in winter, the pale green of spring buds, and the dry desert wind whistling through the pines in summer. It was surely a touch of genius to establish our strange town on the mesa top, although many sensible people have very sensibly said that Los Alamos was a city that never should have been.

The strangest feature of all to us was the security.

We were quite literally fenced in by a tall barbed wire barricade surrounding the entire site and patrolled along the outside by armed MPs. In our first weeks we heard shots but never knew why. Actually we felt cozy and safe, free from robbers and mountain bears. We never locked our doors. In our second year, extra MPs were sent to guard the homes of the Oppenheimers and Parsons, making round-the-clock patrols. No one, not even the families themselves could go in without a pass. If they had forgotten their pass, they had a hard time getting in. Some of the practical housewives cooked up a scheme to use these MPs as babysitters in the immediate neighborhood. What could be safer than a man with a gun guarding the precious small-fry? The children were sure to be impressed and behave accordingly. Martha Parsons never hired a babysitter as long as the MPs remained around her house, and Kitty Oppenheimer once got real service when the guard came to the front door of the house she was visiting to tell her that little Peter was crying. Soon after, the sergeant in charge put his foot down, no more babysitting for his crack MPs! a group that was specially picked for duty at the number-one government project. The patrol outside the fence soon ceased except for an occasional mounted patrol. There was little temptation to conquer the fence and no one tried, except dogs and children, to dig holes underneath it. Rather the fence became a symbol. We felt protected and very important, and tended to act accordingly, griping at everything, including our fenced-in condition. Although we could leave the mesa at will with a pass, we did have to keep within the boundaries roughly defined by Albuquerque, Cuba, Las Vegas and Lamy, all in New Mexico. We would go to Mesa Verde, Denver, Carlsbad Caverns or El Paso, with special permission. We could not talk to strangers or friends on trips and it was common knowledge that we were being watched by the Army G-2 and the FBI. In general, we were not allowed to send children to camp or away to school. If they were already in school they could not come up for vacations. Our driver's licenses had numbers instead of names and were not signed. All our occupations were listed 'Engineers' and our addresses as Post Office Box 1663, Santa Fe. With gas rationing in effect, most of the traffic between Lamy and Santa Fe and Taos was ours....

In the fall of 1943 the daily bulletin delivered by a soldier and thrust in the kitchen door suddenly announced that all mail, incoming and outgoing, would be censored. The announcement caused quite a stir and a number of questions about its fairness, necessity and legality. We were always accusing Army management of being dramatic about such things. As censorship began we had to apply for cards to send to relatives stating that mail was being opened for security purposes and asking that they destroy the cards and not mention the censorship ever. We sent our mail unsealed with the understanding that it would be read, sealed up and sent on. If something inside did not meet with the censor's approval, it would be returned to the writer with a slip indicating what rule had been broken. We each had a book of rules describing what not to say. We could not mention last names, give distances or places nearby, and the worst word, "physicist," was strictly forbidden. I might say we could write "theoretical" or "experimental," and the censors wouldn't know, but our friends would…. Since Los Alamos, or more strictly speaking, P.O. Box 1663, was the only place in the United States where mail was censored, envelopes with the censor's seal are now collector's items. I destroyed I don't know how many before we left for home, alas. We continued to live in a security-minded atmosphere for nearly three years. Actually, anyone who had wanted to could have given away secrets. But enough of us, while poking fun at the security regulations, took our trusted positions very seriously. Some of the neighborhood philosophers at Los Alamos foresaw implications in the secrecy formula. Hans Staub, who was a Swiss physicist, went around asking in emphatic tones of prophecy, "are these big tough MPs with their guns here to keep us in or to keep the rest of the world out? There is an important distinction here, and before I leave this place I would like to know the answer."

The U.S. Army Corps of Engineers Manhattan District ran the project in those early years. Most of us were civilians at Los Alamos. We found living in an Army post unique and I'm sure the Army regarded us, all of us, as equally strange. Ordinarily Army officers run any post to suit themselves, setting the standards and following strict protocol. At Los Alamos things did not work that way at all. Of all civilians, probably free-wheeling scientists with their tradition of non-conformity, are the least likely to measure up to proper military standards. Furthermore, there was a feeling that we were slumming it up there in our secluded mesa, far from city and university life and free from the need to keep up appearances. We truly believed in plain living and high thinking. To counteract the Army regime, the civilians had a town council, appointed at first and later elected as the town grew. The council was most unorthodox on an Army post but Oppenheimer believed that a civilian governing body, though lacking in real authority, would serve a useful purpose. And it did….

….The sign 'Oppenheimer' was placed over baby Tony's crib and people filed by in the corridor for days to view the boss's baby girl. General Groves complained about the rapid increase in the population which immediately increased the housing problem and eventually would increase the school troubles. Rumor had it that the General ordered the commanding officer to do something

about it. It is not clear what, if anything, was ever done. Our population was young and vigorous and the babies were free, so what could the General expect?…

The technical area, called T-area, Tech Area or just simply T, where the main work of the project was done, resembled a small factory—a two-storey clapboard building painted green, of course. The windows were large and pleasant, like those in our houses, although innocent of any washing since the original putty was smeared on. This one building designed as a laboratory only was built along the west road, but it soon grew in several directions and added wings whenever possible.

The physicists were divided, roughly speaking, into two varieties, the theoretical and the experimental. The distinction often made among themselves was that the former knew what was the matter with the doorbell while the latter also knew how to fix it. (Whether they did fix it is something else altogether.) Everyone wore casual clothes, jeans or old unpressed trousers, open shirts and no ties. I don't recall seeing a shined pair of shoes during working hours. They all seemed to be enjoying themselves as scientists always do when they ponder their problems together. No one has to drive them; they drive themselves when they have an intriguing problem. And so it was at Los Alamos. Even an outsider like myself, with no idea what the problem was, could feel the inner urge for scientific solution.

I suppose I heard a lot of talk which is even now stamped top secret, and I used to ask facetious questions when the talk seemed to get bigger than usual. I once asked Emilio Segrè what on earth we were hatching up there? To put me in my place he answered, "now, just you listen to me, what we do here, if we do it will make a revolution, like electricity did." I knew we were engaged in an important aspect of the war effort, but as to Emilio's revolution, I continued to discount it. But later I suppose he was proved right. Each night after everyone had gone home, the MPs came into the T area to check out security violations. If they found anything, they would simply write an appeal in the Bulletin next day, for more diligence. But once in a while they cracked down. One night, after midnight, Hans Bethe was selected as their victim. He had left something out of the safe, so two MPs came to his house, woke him up and insisted he return to T and put the stuff away, himself, to teach him a lesson. Everyone was more careful from then on….

* * * * * *

1.   *How did the constraints of military secrecy shape day-to-day life in the scientific community at Los Alamos? What effects did it have on families?*

2.   *What sorts of hierarchical distinctions emerged within the community?*

3.   *How did the Los Alamos residents respond to the pressure placed upon them, especially with regard to secrecy and their lack of knowledge about the larger project of building an atomic bomb?*

25–2   Franklin D. Roosevelt, The Four Freedoms, 1941

President Roosevelt used his State of the Union address in January 1941 to formulate an American response to the spreading world war. The sense of urgency had grown with the recent fall of France; only Great Britain continued to resist the Nazi onslaught. In this speech, Roosevelt in effect prepared the nation for at least a limited involvement in the war, and he defined the ideals for which he believed the nation was willing to fight.

SOURCE: Public Papers and Documents of Franklin D. Roosevelt, Vol. 9 (1941).

…I suppose that every realist knows that the democratic way of life is at this moment being directly assailed in every part of the world—assailed either by arms or by secret spreading of poisonous propaganda by those who seek to destroy unity and promote discord in nations that are still at peace….

Our national policy is this:

First, by an impressive expression of the public will and without regard to partisanship, we are committed to all-inclusive national defense.

Second, by an impressive expression of the public will and without regard to partisanship, we are committed to full support of all those resolute people everywhere who are resisting aggression and are thereby keeping war away from our hemisphere. By this support we express our determination that the democratic cause shall prevail, and we strengthen the defense and the security of our own nation.

Third, by an impressive expression of the public will and without regard to partisanship, we are committed to the proposition that principles of morality and considerations for our own security will never permit us to acquiesce in a peace dictated by aggressors and sponsored by appeasers. We know that enduring peace cannot be bought at the cost of other people's freedom….

Therefore, the immediate need is a swift and driving increase in our armament production….

Let us say to the democracies: "We Americans are vitally concerned in your defense of freedom. We are putting forth our energies, our resources and our organizing powers to give you the strength to regain and maintain a free world. We shall send you in ever-increasing numbers, ships, planes, tanks, guns. That is our purpose and our pledge."…

As men do not live by bread alone, they do not fight by armaments alone. Those who man our defenses and those behind them who build our defenses must have the stamina and the courage which come from an unshakable belief in the manner of life which they are defending. The mighty action that we are calling for cannot be based on a disregard of all the things worth fighting for.

The nation takes great satisfaction and much strength from the things which have been done to make its people conscious of their individual stake in the preservation of democratic life in America. Those things have toughened the fibre of our people, have renewed their faith and strengthened their devotion to the institutions we make ready to protect.

Certainly this is no time for any of us to stop thinking about the social and economic problems which are the root cause of the social revolution which is today a supreme factor in the world. For there is nothing mysterious about the foundations of a healthy and strong democracy.

The basic things expected by our people of their political and economic systems are simple. They are:

Equality of opportunity for youth and for others.
Jobs for those who can work.
Security for those who need it.
The ending of special privilege for the few.
The preservation of civil liberties for all.
The enjoyment of the fruits of scientific progress in a wider and constantly rising standard of living.

These are the simple, the basic things that must never be lost sight of in the turmoil and unbelievable complexity of our modern world. The inner and abiding strength of our economic and political systems is dependent upon the degree to which they fulfill these expectations….

In the future days which we seek to make secure, we look forward to a world founded upon four essential human freedoms.

The first is freedom of speech and expression—everywhere in the world.

The second is freedom of every person to worship God in his own way—everywhere in the world.

The third is freedom from want—which, translated into world terms, means economic understandings which will secure to every nation a healthy peacetime life for its inhabitants—everywhere in the world.

The fourth is freedom from fear, which, translated into world terms, means a world-wide reduction of armaments to such a point and in such a thorough manner that no nation will be in a position to commit an act of physical aggression against any neighbor—anywhere in the world.

That is no vision of a distant millennium. It is a definite basis for a kind of world attainable in our own time and generation. That kind of world is the very antithesis of the so-called "new order" of tyranny which the dictators seek to create with the crash of a bomb.

To that new order we oppose the greater conception—the moral order. A good society is able to face schemes of world domination and foreign revolutions alike without fear.

Since the beginning of our American history we have been engaged in change, in a perpetual, peaceful revolution, a revolution which goes on steadily, quietly, adjusting itself to changing conditions without the concentration camp or the quick-lime in the ditch. The world order which we seek is the co-operation of free countries, working together in a friendly, civilized society.

This nation has placed its destiny in the hands, heads and hearts of its millions of free men and women, and its faith in freedom under the guidance of God. Freedom means the supremacy of human rights everywhere. Our support goes to those who struggle to gain those rights and keep them. Our strength is in our unity of purpose.

To that high concept there can be no end save victory.

* * * * * *

1.   *How does Roosevelt propose to keep the nation out of the war? What warnings does he make to the American people?*

2.   *What are the "four freedoms"? How does FDR use them to connect foreign policy with his domestic programs?*

25–3   Burton K. Wheeler, Radio Address on Lend-Lease, 1941

In early 1941, President Roosevelt proposed that the United States become the "arsenal for Democracy" by offering material aid to Great Britain in its battle with Germany. That March, Congress approved the Lend-Lease Act, which allowed the President to transfer arms and other war materiel to any nation whose defense he thought vital to America's national defense. Isolationists, such as Democratic Senator Burton K. Wheeler of Montana, vehemently opposed Lend-Lease for pushing the nation a step closer toward war.

SOURCE: Congressional Record, 77th Congress, 1st Sess., Appendix, (194).

The lend-lease policy, translated into legislative form, stunned a Congress and a nation wholly sympathetic to the cause of Great Britain. The Kaiser's blank check to Austria-Hungary in the first World War was a piker compared to the Roosevelt blank check of World War II. It warranted my worst fears for the future of America, and it definitely stamps the President as war-minded.

The lend-lease-give program is the New Deal's triple A foreign policy; it will plow under every fourth American boy.

Never before have the American people been asked or compelled to give so bounteously and so completely of their tax dollars to any foreign nation. Never before has the Congress of the United States been asked by any President to violate international law. Never before has this Nation resorted to duplicity in the conduct of its foreign affairs. Never before has the United States given to one man the power to strip this Nation of its defenses. Never before has a Congress coldly and flatly been asked to abdicate.

If the American people want a dictatorship—if they want a totalitarian form of government and if they want war—this bill should be steam-rollered through Congress, as is the wont of President Roosevelt.

Approval of this legislation means war, open and complete warfare. I, therefore, ask the American people before they supinely accept it, Was the last World War worth while?

If it were, then we should lend and lease war materials. If it were, then we should lend and lease American boys. President Roosevelt has said we would be repaid by England. We will be. We will be repaid, just as England repaid her war debts of the first World War—repaid those dollars wrung from the sweat of labor and the toil of farmers with cries of "Uncle Shylock." Our boys will be returned—returned in caskets, maybe; returned with bodies maimed; returned with minds warped and twisted by sights of horrors and the scream and shriek of high-powered shells.

Considered on its merits and stripped of its emotional appeal to our sympathies, the lend-lease-give bill is both ruinous and ridiculous. Why should we Americans pay for war materials for Great Britain who still has $7,000,000,000 in credit or collateral in the United States? Thus far England has fully maintained rather than depleted her credits in the United States. The cost of the lend-lease-give program is high in terms of American tax dollars, but it is even higher in terms of our national defense. Now it gives to the President the unlimited power to completely strip our air forces of its every bomber, of its every fighting plane.

It gives to one man—responsible to no one—the power to denude our shores of every warship. It gives to one individual the dictatorial power to strip the American Army of our every tank, cannon, rifle, or antiaircraft gun. No one would deny that the lend-lease-give bill contains provisions that would enable one man to render the United States defenseless, but they will tell you, "The President would never do it." To this I say, "Why does he ask the power if he does not intend to use it?" Why not, I say, place some check on American donations to a foreign nation?

Is it possible that the farmers of America are willing to sell their birthright for a mess of pottage?

Is it possible that American labor is to be sold down the river in return for a place upon the Defense Commission, or because your labor leaders are entertained at pink teas?

Is it possible that the American people are so gullible that they will permit their representatives in Congress to sit supinely by while an American President demands totalitarian powers—in the name of saving democracy?

I say in the kind of language used by the President—shame on those who ask the powers—and shame on those who would grant them.

You people who oppose war and dictatorship, do not be dismayed because the war-mongers and interventionists control most of the avenues of propaganda, including the motion-picture industry.

Do not be dismayed because Mr. Willkie, of the Commonwealth & Southern, agrees with Mr. Roosevelt.

This merely puts all the economic and foreign "royalists" on the side of war.

Remember, the interventionists control the money bags, but you control the votes.

* * * * * *

1.   *What is Wheeler's constitutional argument against Lend-Lease?*

2.   *How does he use the American experience in World War I to make the isolationist case?*

25–4   *Ernie Pyle, The Toughest Beachhead in the World, 1944*

On June 6, 1944 an Allied task force launched the long awaited invasion of France, on the Normandy peninsula. General Dwight D. Eisenhower commanded the largest military operation in history, including nearly 3 million troops and 5,000 ships and landing craft. Of the 34,000 Americans who landed on Utah and Omaha Beaches the first morning, 7,300 were killed. War correspondent Ernie Pyle cabled this report of the fighting one day after the initial assault. Pyle himself was killed the next year in the Pacific.

SOURCE: "The Toughest Beachhead in the World" in *SCIENCE DIGEST*, Vol. 16, September 1994, pp. 13–14, as condensed from *BRAVE MEN* by Ernie Pyle, Copyright © 1943, 1944 by Scripps-Howard Newspaper Alliance. Copyright © 1971, 1972 by Henry Holt and Company, Inc. Reprinted by permission of Henry Holt and Company, Inc.

Now that it is over, it seems to me a pure miracle we ever took the beach at all. For some it was easy, but in this special sector where I now am, our troops faced such odds that our getting to shore would be like me whipping Joe Louis down to a pulp.

Ashore, facing us were more enemy troops than we had in our assault waves. The advantages were all theirs. The disadvantages all ours.

The Germans were dug into positions they had been working on for months. Still they weren't yet all complete. A 100-foot bluff a couple of hundred yards back from the beach had great concrete gun emplacements built right into the hilltops. They opened to the sides instead of the front, thus making it very hard for naval fire from the ships to reach them, and enabling the Germans to shoot parallel with the beach and cover every foot of it for miles with artillery fire.

Then they had hidden machine-gun nests on the forward slopes with cross-fire taking in every inch of beach. These nests are connected with the networks of trenches so that German gunners could move about without exposing themselves.

Throughout the length of the beach, running zig-zag a couple of hundred yards back from the shoreline, was an immense V-shaped ditch, 15 deep feet. Nothing could cross it, not even men on foot, until it had been partially filled.

And in other places at the far ends of the beach where the ground was flatter they had great concrete walls which had been blasted by naval gunfire or by hand-set explosives after we got ashore. Our only exits from the beach were several valleys, each about 100 yards wide.

The Germans made the most of these funnellike traps, literally sowing their bottom sides with buried mines. They contained, too, barbed-wire entanglements with mines attached, hidden ditches and machine guns firing from the slopes. That is what was on shore.

But our men had to go through a maze nearly as deadly before they even got ashore. The underwater obstacles were terrific. The Germans had whole fields of evil devices under the water to catch our boats.

The Germans had masses of those great six-pronged spiders made of railroad iron and standing shoulder high in places just beneath the surface of the water for our landing craft to run into. They also had huge logs, buried in the sand, pointing upward and outward, their tops just below the water. Attached to these logs were mines.

In addition to these obstacles, they had floating mines in the beach waters, land mines buried on the sand beach, and more mines in checkerboard rows in the tall grass beyond the sand. And the enemy had four men on shore for every three men we had approaching shore.

And yet we got on.

Now that the fighting has moved inland, human litter extends in a thin little line, just like a high water mark, for miles along the beach. This is the strewn personal gear, gear that will never be needed again, of those who fought and died to give us our entrance into Europe.

Here in a jumbled row for mile on mile are soldiers' packs. Here are socks and shoe polish, sewing kits, diaries, Bibles and hand grenades. Here are the latest letters from home, with the address on each one neatly razored out—one of the security precautions enforced before the boys embarked.

Here are toothbrushes and razors and snapshots of families back home staring up at you from the sand. Here are pocketbooks, metal mirrors, extra trousers, and bloody, abandoned shoes. Here are broken-handled shovels, and portable radios smashed almost beyond recognition, and mine detectors twisted and ruined.

Soldiers carry strange things ashore with them. In every invasion you'll find at least one soldier hitting the beach at H-Hour with a banjo slung over his shoulder. The most ironic piece of equipment marking our beach—this beach of first despair, then victory—is a tennis racket that some soldier had brought along.

Two of the most dominant items in the beach refuse are cigarettes and writing paper. Each soldier was issued a carton of cigarettes just before he started. Today these canons by the thousand, water-soaked and spilled out, mark the line of our first savage blow.

Writing paper and air-mail envelopes come second. The boys had intended to do a lot of writing in France. Letters that would have filled those blank, abandoned pages.

The strong, swirling tides of the Normandy coastline shift the contours of the sandy beach as they move in and out. They carry soldiers' bodies out to sea, and later they return them. They cover the bodies of heroes with sand, and then in their whims they uncover them.

As I plowed out over the wet sand of the beach on that first day ashore, I walked around what seemed to be a couple of pieces of driftwood sticking out of the sand.

They were a soldier's two feet. He was completely covered by the shifting sands except for his feet. The toes of his G.I. shoes pointed toward the land he had come so far to see, and which he saw so briefly.

* * * * * *

1.   *Ernie Pyle had a reputation for writing about the war from "the soldier's view." How does this dispatch reflect that?*

2.   *How and why does Pyle try to connect the battlefront with the home front?*

25–5   R. L. Duffus, A City That Forges Thunderbolts, 1943

American communities experienced unprecedented social dislocation during World War II. Everywhere, people were on the move: to training camps, to front lines overseas, to new jobs and homes. Industrial centers such as Detroit underwent especially rapid and intense changes in the service of war mobilization. The following account details what the war meant for the city's workers, businesses, neighborhoods, and cultural life. Just six months after this article appeared, Detroit suffered the worst race riot in its history up to that time.

SOURCE: From "A City That Forges Thunderbolts" by R. L. Duffus in *THE NEW YORK TIMES MAGAZINE*, January 10, 1943, Copyright © 1943 by the New York Times Company. Reprinted by permission.

…The visitor who has spent a week in the city's war plants, sweets and public places and who has talked to some of those who frequent them may still be puzzled. He is likely to see past, present and future in a jumble almost as chaotic as the sprawling pattern of the city itself, where towers testify to a peacetime grandeur, new factories to a present strength and determination, miles of jerry-built houses and thousands of families crowded into small rooms, shacks and trailer camps to an inability to solve a great problem over night, and acres of untenanted prairie to possibilities not yet realized.

Detroit, as they say, has changed over. The expression is not quite correct. Apart from what is going on in the plants there is still some surprise and confusion in the city itself, as people try to adjust themselves to a new congestion, new habits of working and living, and new problems of human relations.

There is no precedent for a thing quite like this happening to a city like Detroit. For that matter, there is no city like Detroit. There are no accustomed symptoms to look for. What one expected would happen has not happened. What one didn't expect has taken place.

The re-visiting traveler, descending from his train, doesn't get the full impact at once. The outward and visible downtown city hasn't altered much. Uniforms in the street crowds, American, Canadian, Australian, tell of the war, but so do they in every city nowadays. Motor cars, despite gas rationing, still move in comparatively greater numbers and with greater speed than they do in New York City. Neither the sternness of war nor the effervescence of a frantic prosperity is at first noticeable in Detroit.

These things are there, but you do have to look for them. You look for them in your hotel. You find that the bellboy who carries your bags is from Atlanta and has been on his job for two days. You know that within a month or so he will he in the Army or in a war factory. You find that the middle-aged woman who cleans your room would like to work in a factory, but has been told she can't because she has only her first citizenship papers. You learn that the room itself is under Army lease and that you can be turned out if the Army wishes to move in. The Army doesn't move in, but you feel precarious.

You hear that there are 20,000 newly arrived Federal employes in Detroit, and more on the way—representatives of a consumer who intends to receive just what he ordered. You become acquainted with a bartender, who tells you that munitions workers drink "shots and shells"—a double shot of rye whiskey and a shell of beer.

You hear all sorts of tall stories about "Hill Billies" (this term is said to include every one who has migrated into Detroit from south of the Michigan line, and hence might even, because of the way the line runs around Detroit, take in a few Canadians), who are not accustomed to wearing shoes, and whose wives buy them boxes of three-for-fifty cigars. Your taxi driver says he knows for a fact that one new arrival mailed a letter in a fire-alarm box before he had been in town half an hour.

You hear stories, but perhaps they tell more about the old settlers than about the new arrivals. You look for the reality. You don't find it at a theatre where a musical comedy is being shown. There are a few males in sweaters and with no ties in the orchestra, but half the seats are empty. You don't find much of it in saloons, expensive restaurants or the obvious night spots. You get a sense of it in a downtown drugstore, where you have to fight your way to get to the refreshment counter at midnight; in advertisements for help wanted; in department store crowds; in your inability to get a messenger to run an errand for you; in the recorded fact that is one Detroit toolmaker reached the dizzy height of $2.75 an hour for his straight time, time and a half for overtime and double for the seventh day, and didn't mind working long hours; in a 30 per cent increase in trucking accidents, ascribed to green drivers replacing experienced men who had gone into the factories; in sixty-nine trucks out of one firm's fleet of 450 tied up on a Saturday night, not by a strike, but by lack of drivers.

If you simmer down what you see and what you hear and believe you begin to understand what has happened to Detroit. The great war migration into the city is a fact. Within two years, by Census Bureau estimates, the metropolitan area of Detroit has added 336,000 people to its population, to make a total of more than 600,000 engaged there in the war industries.

This is something, but it isn't enough. Detroit not only has to deal with existing congestion. It has to decide how much more congestion it can stand without having people stepping on each other's toes all over the place. Some authorities say that 100,000 more workers will be needed from outside the area, in addition to at least 40,000 Detroit women who have said they would take war jobs. Others say that immigration into the area will have to be discouraged because there will not be enough beds for the newcomers to sleep in or enough street cars, buses and automobiles (or gas) to carry them to and from their work.

There is one other contradiction in the Detroit picture. The area has about 200,000 Negroes. Negro leaders say their labor has not been fully utilized, and that those employed are often working below the level of their skills. "Idle Negro workers here," said one reliable spokesman, "are baffled by talk of a manpower shortage." There are some signs that necessity will take care of this situation.

High wages are a statistical fact. A union contract signed last August with a typical war materials company lists more than 130 jobs, of which the highest pays $1.88 an hour for tool and die workers, the lowest 75 cents an a hour for some of the women. The unskilled worker under that contract gets 85 cents an hour.

Some shops run an average payroll of $80 to $90 a week. The average working week is close to fifty hours and would be higher if it were not pulled down by individual absenteeism, shortage of materials, changes in production plants, such as the current shift from tanks, guns and ammunition to planes and ships, and the unavoidable delays of the not quite complete changeover. It will surely run higher as the new production lines get rid of their "bugs." The average Detroit war worker now gets something like $50 in his weekly pay envelope, and when he works longer he will naturally get more.

This isn't hay. Neither is it fantastic wealth for those accustomed to the automobile industry. The fantastic element is introduced when this much money comes into the hands of rural newcomers who have been accustomed neither to much income nor to large cities. The veterans trot along about as they always did when times were good. They live, by and large, where they have always lived.

It is the late arrivals who change Detroit and are changed by it. Add to their numbers the regiments of newly employed women and of men drifting in from other occupations and you have something to think about. Inject into the situation the tension between white migrants from the South and the new and old Negro workers (there were about 25,000 in the automobile and allied industries at the peak of civilian production), and there is more to think about.

This tension is felt in the shops. When you visit the plants you usually see Negroes working by themselves, or engaged in pushing, hauling or lifting occupations which differentiate them from the whites. The Negro forms about 10 per cent of the population of Detroit. The problem isn't simple for him, nor for those who wish him well. It ties in with housing, because he has always been the worst housed in Detroit.

There are trailer camps—maybe miles of them altogether. They are pretty well organized. One such camp has a trailer with a front porch, very neat, permanent-looking and homelike. This camp also has an air-raid shelter. Across the road, a few hundred feet away, were houses which looked as though they had cost between $15,000 and $25,000. Outlying Detroit is pretty well scrambled—no doubt about it.

Rows and rows of little houses, mostly white-painted or unpainted wood, but sometimes faced with brick, bloom at intervals over the flatlands. Between the groups are occasional farmhouses and fields where corn grew last Summer.

You see signs urging you to buy a share in America at so much down and so much ever after. Some of these signs are new. The little houses don't cure the housing shortage. The plan to turn vacant stores into apartments holds out some promise. Another proposal is to make use of country clubs.

Linked to housing is transportation. Many a Detroit worker is accustomed to driving from ten to as much as twenty-five miles to work, alone or in company. The great parking lots around the larger plants are astounding, even with gas rationing in force. If the worker falls back on street car or bus lines he finds scant remedy. The city-owned Detroit street railways are carrying nearly a third more passengers than they did a year ago, which means that 200,000 new passengers are making round trips daily.

But even bad housing and congested public vehicles and all the other troubles that are intensified when a city has to take care of 15 per cent more people than it is equipped for are endurable when there is full employment, and a stir of something worth working for.

Detroit's working population tastes the joys of being very much wanted. The first effect of this state of affairs, especially on the new residents, was to cause a good deal of restless shopping around for the ideal job among all the jobs offered. The labor turnover in many instances has been remarkable. One Detroit manufacturing corporation hired 2,700 employes in a recent month. It lost 2,000 for various reasons, chief among them the lure of other jobs, although dislike of city life, dissatisfaction with working hours, and "vacations" also figured. A 10 per cent turnover monthly has been no rarity. It may be too early to determine how much the stabilization order of Manpower Director Paul V. McNutt will do to relieve this situation. Some action of the kind was undeniably needed.

The old hands don't shift. They know what seniority means in slack times, and they know what slack times have meant in the past and can mean in the future. But the drifters, the new hands, are not necessarily idlers. They have been shopping, as often as not, for more work and longer shifts—for more overtime.

The whistles blow, by day and by night, and the crowds come surging out. Some are dog-tired. You get that way in a long shift. They want food and sleep. If they seek amusement they are likely to turn to neighborhood movie houses, beer saloons, dance halls. The Southern whites have brought the square dances with them. Halls where these can be performed are crowded, with waiting lines stamping feet to the music within.

What does this army of workers think about? Is it aware of the great issue it is helping to determine? It probably does think about that issue, and it is probably as serious about it as the men who are doing the fighting. Soldiers think and talk about their personal affairs, their relatives, their girls, their food, and so do workers in munitions factories. They are embarrassed by heroic generalities. When they talk about the war they are likely to mention their own buddies who are in it. Or they scrawl something about Hitler and Tojo on a tank and let it go at that. Generally they appear to give more attention to the Japanese than to the Germans.

But they do want to get on with the job. They may stop working for a minute or two when visitors appear, especially if one of the visitors carries a camera and seems about to use it, but they want that overhead crane brought over, they want that forging—quick. They lean over precise machines, with something like affection in their eyes. And they complain of things which stop or interrupt the work—not of the work itself. There is no oratory in their natures. They do want to get the stuff out.

Against the night sky are the chimneys of great factories. Lights blaze. Machinery roars and thunders. A democracy at war has its troubles and its weaknesses. But the work gets done. It does get done. And this is Detroit at the beginning of 1943—a city amazed and often confused, but a miraculous city, a city forging thunderbolts.

* * * * * *

1.   *How do Detroit's citizens respond to overcrowding? To newfound prosperity?*

2.   *Who are the new people coming to Detroit? How well do they adjust to life there?*

3.   *What evidence does the author find of growing racial tensions in the city?*

25–6   *Virginia Snow Wilkinson, From Housewife to Shipfitter, 1943*

War brought extraordinary demands for labor in defense plants and other sectors of the economy as millions entered the armed forces. Women and African Americans, who had been largely excluded from high-wage and skilled factory work in the past, now found new opportunities to obtain quality jobs. The Office of War Information and the mass media now encouraged women to do their patriotic duty and work in defense plants. The following magazine piece describes one woman's experience with defense work.

...Over and over for months I had heard from the radio the call for women to enter war work. I had been delaying for one reason or another but I finally recognized these arguments in favor of my going to the shipyards: my children, now in their teens, were able to take some responsibility for our home; I wanted to help out the war effort more than I had been doing through a few voluntary services; and with living costs always going up and the children's education looming ahead, we could use the money. So I had taken the aptitude test at the U.S. Employment Office, had attended a defense class for shipfitters, and was now on my way to an actual job at Richmond.

...When I reached the shipyards...I was borne along by the crowd and permitted to enter through the guarded gate when I had shown my temporary pass. I stood in a long line to receive papers; I stood in another line to receive tool checks (for every tool borrowed, a chip from your stack). At last some sixty of us women were herded to a personnel building, where a young man addressed us on safety precautions, the woman counselor for the day shift advised us about our clothing, and then, after a tour of the yard, we were divided into the trades for which we had been employed. The names of the welders were called and responded to. An escort was assigned to take them to their locations. The burners were selected, the flangers, the chippers, the checkers. Only a sparse group remained to be grouped as shipfitters' helpers—six women besides myself, Negro and white. Again we started out en masse; this time to a little cottage which was labeled "Master Shipfitter." The man upon whom the cottage door opened was small and harassed. We were presented to him a little apologetically, I thought, by our guide.

"What have you got there?" the shipfitter asked.

"Just a few shipfitter helpers, Mr. Jepson."

"Oh, my God! Women shipfitters. Why do they treat me like this? Women shipfitters...."

...I was sent to work on a nearly completed hull in one of the concrete basins—a hull which had been constructed up to its weather deck. I found myself on the rusty black steel more amazed than ever before.

I was assigned to a leaderman working high on the side of the ship.

"You come along with me, duchess. I'll teach you how to make scuppers. Come on."

To "come on" meant to clamber over the side of the ship until I felt the scaffolding beneath me. The simplest way seemed to be to jump from the deck to the scaffold, for I was not going to be caught lagging behind the men here where I was the only woman on the side of the hull. Sometimes a worker would extend a hand of assistance. I refused to see it. I jumped from deck to scaffold, catching myself by a clutch at a handy pipe; I squeezed to the outer edge of the support to allow another worker to pass; I ran along the scaffold planks. All this in abysmal ignorance of where I was. It was hours later, I think, when my leaderman, standing beside me, tossed a little piece of wood or rag overboard and I heard no sound from it as it fell or lighted. I looked over and down, and down, and then crept by inches back to the security of the hull's side. No soft billowy water lay beneath us, but a great depth of brutal concrete.

"Do people often fall off the scaffold?" I asked, shaking.

"Not often," my leaderman assured me. "Only once."

I did not allow the firm surface of the hull to get out of my clasp for the remainder of the afternoon, not, that is, until later, when a piece of red-hot steel just skinned between me and the hull I was clinging to. It landed at my feet still glowing. I looked up at the men above me, who were preoccupied with the burning of a hole.

"Never mind, darling," the leaderman soothed. "I think they saw you."

But later I heard him berating these same burners. "You let a red-hot clip fall within an inch of her—what the hell you trying to do?"

The next day Mr. Jepson sent me out to an assembly way where I was entered upon the foreman's books as a shipfitter's helper. Here are made the double bottoms which hold water and oil for the ship's needs and for necessary ballast and, I suppose, give a second bottom when the first is missing. These units look much like the honeycomb of a wasp's nest—with the wasps still crawling about chipping, marking, and welding. They are built up off the ground about five feet on skids of heavy timber and iron....

I walked along the skids and bumped into a man in tan, apparently an engineer. We talked.

"Tell me," I asked, "Do you think I have misjudged my job? Do you think if I keep trying I can find something to do?"

"Let me tell you," he said. "I have degrees from four different universities. I helped build Singapore and Pearl Harbor. And *I* can't find a job for myself."

I took my problem to Mr. Jepson.

"Can't you find a job with something for me to do?" I asked him.

"You've got a job, haven't you?"

"You mean I've been employed. But I can't go on taking money for doing nothing. I've got to respect myself or leave."

"My God, all day long they come in here wanting me to find them a job with more to do. What do you think I am? I can't revolutionize the industry. What people don't understand is that this is shipfitting. You can't build ships the way you do other things." He spread out his arms. "There are times while the work is getting laid out when few people are needed but then, after it shapes up, everyone around, and more, can be thrown on it. There just has to be a period of lull. If this were a peacetime activity the boss would be around with more work than anyone could do, shouting, 'Get the hell on to the job.' But by God, woman, this is war. What can you expect?"

Later, my foreman, answering the same inquiry, said, "The management does employ more men and women than it can put to work at once but they are here on hand, taking on new experience, learning new terminology—port, starboard, bulkhead, and vertical keel. Some will drop out but eventually the others will be drawn in on the job. Some of those will be no good. The others will build ships. You've got to have a lot of people to draw from in order to get even some good workmen. They shake the basket after a while and the capable come to the top."

"And the women?" I asked.

"And the women too have got to be used. The men don't like the idea; they voted against it in their unions; but they'll get used to women in time and think nothing of it. They used to feel the same way about women in the plate shop, but it's full of women now—they run the show—and there's no real hostility there toward them any more. Women haven't been seen much on ships yet but they'll be seen as the war goes on."

I was glad he mentioned the war. I had been wondering whether it was because there were no radio news reports here that no one spoke of the war, that great events shaping outside were diminished and pushed back from the consciousness of men. Was it because there were no clocks—for never a one could you find in the yard—that there seemed to be so little realization of the time that was so late? It was hard indeed to remember the urgency of the voices on the air, my own struggle against a sense of guilt and conscience, and the compulsion that had finally brought me to this job I was not doing. Should I leave? I remembered my husband's and children's absurd pride in my being here and decided to give myself two months to find something real to do.

…It must have been a fortnight or so later that I was given my first real shipfitting job…I was taught to put chocks on the double bottom. Chocks act as supports when the unit is turned over and put into the waiting hull. For weeks the craftsmen of our skids had worked on a huge section of double bottom, labeled XAK, which was at last passed as finished. It was prepared by the riggers to be lifted by the cranes—and then the whistle blew and we all went home. In the morning we learned that while the cranes were lifting the sixty tons—on the graveyard shift, mind you—the great weight suddenly broke loose and dropped, breaking a crane, smashing the roadway and concrete walk, and quite ruining the unit itself.

If the work in the basin on Hull 6 was not to be held up we had to rush a new XAK to replace the other. All hands were thrown upon it—even my hands. I was told to locate the chocks on the blueprint, to measure for them, to find the chocks, to get a welder to put them on, and to check to see that they were square.…

A few mornings later, as soon as we stepped upon the skids, we perceived that something new was astir. The shipfitting women—there were three of us—were called together.

"We're going to give you your own unit to work on together," the leaderman said. "XAK is your baby now. Study your print, square your frame lines down the vertical keel, and get the crane to bring you your steel."

Alice, our naive nineteen-year-old, glowed. "Golly," she said. "Really?" The colored girl was more sophisticated but we were all pleased.

"Let's be so accurate and careful that they won't be able to find a thing wrong. Let's check and recheck everything.…"

"We'll work it out together. If one of us makes a mistake we'll tell her and correct it and no bad feelings…" "We'll all stand and fall together on it." That was the way we talked.

I never saw such a change in three workmen as in these three girls. We became integrated persons working together on a project which focused all our interests. I noticed how quickly we ran our own errands, how conscientious we were in checking, how we abhorred sloppy measurements. For once we had been given responsibility, for once we had been put on our own, for once we had enough to do.

"When we finish we'll hold open house and invite you in to tea," we told our leaderman.

Our enjoyment was such that we did not notice that something was amiss until late in the afternoon. Then we became gradually aware of the hostility of the men. Our woman burner reported that they were "seething with resentment" that women should be given a unit to construct. The women checkers said, "You should just hear what we hear outside our checking shed, my dears." This was the first time I had come up against the hostility of one sex toward another and I could not believe it. The men had always been so decent, so respectful, so kindly. But this was the first time that we had been seen in the light of competitors. We had been amusing little creatures only too happy to take what crumbs of jobs were dropped to us.

Our leaderman said, "I know, but pay no attention. They'll have to get used to women shipfitters. Half these men may be in the Army this January. They might as well accept the fact that women will have to take their places."

Our woman checker said, "In September I was one of the first women ever to be admitted out here in the yards. You could have cut the resentment with a knife and spread it thick. But it's gradually being worn away."

The next day, with no explanation, our XAK, "our baby," was taken from us and given to the men. We had to stand aside and see the men working on what we felt was our project. Cora, whose boy friend was one of the group, said the men were afraid the assemblies would become like the plate shop—overrun by women. She took herself over to the unit where her friend was working, to lean against the steel. Alice took out her lipstick: "Oh, what the heck do I care so long as I get my dollar five an hour. But it *was* fun."

I tried to reflect that there must be another side to this thing. Maybe the men who were heads of families, straining to take care of several dependents, and who had known the bitter struggle for a living—maybe these men resented the fact that any eighteen-year-old could come out without a day's training, without a grain of tool sense or mechanical sense, and draw the same pay as they and rise at the same rate—even these girls who would go at once into debt for fur coats and "perfectly adorable" evening gowns. The pay was too high for the beginner, I knew—for the boy who had quit high school as well as for the girl. The experienced workman might easily feel resentment. But this I knew too; that the responsibility placed upon these girls had made them almost in one day into serious workmen.…

I had promised myself two months in which to find myself here in the shipyards but my probation was not to last so long. It seemed that we, the women, were being assimilated gradually, if slowly. For a while we had floated on top, undissolved, but the broth was big enough with a little stirring and stewing to absorb us all—or almost all.

The great need was for experienced workmen, men or women; and time on the job, doing this and a little of that, adds up finally to experience. I was given more and more to do. (When I told my leader-man that I liked having more to do he answered, "Well, neither you nor I nor the shipyards are as new and green as we were; we're all getting under way.") Six weeks from the date of my arrival at the yard I was given a unit to handle by myself. I guess it was not so much but it was my own.

* * * * * *

1. *What are the most difficult obstacles facing Wilkinson on her new job? How does she deal with them?*

2. *How does her work as a shipfitter change Wilkinson?*

25–7 *Earl B. Dickerson, The Fair Employment Practices Committee, 1941–43*

Despite the high demand for wartime labor, African Americans continued to face discrimination in the defense industry. In 1941, several African-American leaders threatened to lead a march on Washington unless action was taken. In response, President Roosevelt issued Executive Order 8802, forbidding racial discrimination by defense contractors and creating a Fair Employment Practices Committee to investigate charges of racial bias. Earl B. Dickerson, an African-American lawyer from Chicago appointed by FDR to serve on the FEPC, recalled his experience.

SOURCE: From *The Good War: An Oral History of World War II* by Studs Terkel. Copyright © 1984 by Studs Terkel. Reprinted by permission of Pantheon Books, a Division of Random House, Inc.

Around 1940, '41, the war industries were set in motion: Lockheed, Boeing, all the rest. If this was a war to see that democracy prevails, preparations should involve all our people equally. Since blacks had been to a large extent excluded, A. Philip Randolph and Walter White planned a march on Washington. I knew both men intimately. To prevent this from happening, Mr. Roosevelt put forth Executive Order 8802. This set up the Fair Employment Practices Committee. I was one of the first named. Because I was the only lawyer in this group, I was always sent out in advance of any hearing. With some investigators, I prepared the cases for the committee when it met.

One of the first hearings was here in Chicago at City Hall. It was a wonderful three days, examining these people from industry. I remember some fellow from LaGrange. It was one of these General Motors subsidiaries. We had him on the stand: "How many Negroes do you employ?" He replied, "One."

I distinctly remember the hearings in Los Angeles. I had gone out a week before the hearings with a couple of investigators. Lockheed had employed some twenty thousand people in the war effort. No Negroes. Not until the morning of the hearings did they employ any. I asked the head of personnel, "Are you familiar with the contents of Executive Order 8802?" He said yes. I said, "Do you have any Negroes in your employ?" He said yes. "How many do you have?" He said nine. I said, "In what department?" He said, "In the custodial department." That meant they were sweeping floors. (Wryly) Well, that was a beginning.

Another company, there were no black bricklayers. The reason given: one or two couldn't work alongside whites. They'd have to get enough to work one side of the building. Since they couldn't find that many, they'd employ none.

I distinctly remember the hearings in Birmingham. One of my colleagues on the committee, a southern newspaper publisher, called me on the phone a few days before the scheduled hearings: "Earl, perhaps you shouldn't go down there. There have been all sorts of threats." I said, "I want you to read Executive Order 8802 again. It says, 'the jurisdiction of this committee shall be in all states and territories of the United States.'" I had it before me. "The question I ask you now is, 'Is Birmingham within the jurisdiction of the United States?'" He said yes. I said, "That being the case, I'll be there."

When I got off the plane at Birmingham to walk to the terminal, a man about six feet four, a tall Caucasian, came to me and said, "Are you Mr. Earl B. Dickerson?" I said yes. He said, "I'm the United States marshal in this district and I have been requested by the Justice Department to protect you during your trip here." In those days, blacks couldn't stay in hotels in Birmingham. So he would come and pick me up each of those three days. And in the federal court, where the hearings were held, he stood beside me the whole three days.

There was another black fellow on the committee. He was very black and I'm sort of brown. The newspapers came out and described us as the black and brown babies from Chicago. That was around 1942.

You must remember Roosevelt had to be pushed. I had no personal relationship with President Roosevelt until he issued Executive Order 8802. It was June 25, 1941.

We had hearings in Washington, D.C., from time to time. The streetcar system did not employ blacks as motormen or conductors. This was during the war, and every day there were ads in the papers advertising for people to apply for jobs as motormen and conductors. The civil rights people there told blacks to apply for these jobs. They had no luck. We set a date for the hearings on this. I was the acting chairman at the time and prepared the case. It was in all the newspapers.

Just the day before the hearing, I got a call from a fellow named Mcintyre. He was Roosevelt's secretary. He said, "We understand you are having hearings tomorrow. President Roosevelt has asked me to request that you postpone the hearings until some later date." I said that all the newspapers not only here but throughout the United States know about these hearings tomorrow. We have prepared the case, a noted lawyer from New York has come in, and it will be at Dumbarton Oaks. I said, "I can't go out to the public and postpone this case unless Mr. Roosevelt himself would tell me."

This was about one o'clock in the afternoon. He called me right back. "At two-thirty this afternoon, the President will meet with you in the White House." When I walked in the White House, Mrs. Mary McLeod Bethune was sitting just outside his office. She was the most influential black around, very close to Mrs. Roosevelt. I think Mrs. Roosevelt was one of the sparkplugs behind Executive Order 8802. After she hugged me, Mrs. Bethune said, "The President asked that I be in on this conversation."

Well, the President simply told me he wanted permission to defer the hearings. I said, "I'm just wondering why it is, Mr. President—" He said, "I want it delayed until I return." I said, "Very well, Mr. President." Of course, the next morning we read about Mr. Roosevelt having flown to Yalta to meet with Churchill and Stalin.

Soon after this, Attorney General Francis Biddle came up with a proposal to reorganize the commission. All the members were reappointed except me. It was one of my major disappointments in life. I knew it was because I had been so aggressive. I had been the leader of all the agitation that went on in the committee.

What did they give as the reason?

They didn't have to, did they? Oh, they had hearings, but not the kind of aggressive ones I'd been pushing. Nobody ever criticized me. I was in all the newspapers throughout the country.

Roosevelt wanted to go slow. I was taking 'em too fast. When you talk about him, he was not unlike any other Caucasian in that position. The blacks had never challenged authority like that before, except for individuals. Here was a collective attack on the practices of the American people.

Do you know that my work on that committee has affected my life? Years later, when Governor Kerner appointed me as one of the first members of the Illinois Fair Employment Practices Committee, I had to be confirmed by the state senate. This fellow Broyles was chairman of the Illinois Un-American Activities Committee. On the day of the hearings, on the wall of that room, they had my files posted. My membership in the Soviet-American Friendship Committee, my membership in the National Lawyers' Guild—and all my activities on the Fair Employment Practices Committee. The fifteen Republicans voted no, the thirteen Democrats voted yes. I was not confirmed.

It was in World War Two—because it was so clear, it was against Hitler—that the blacks began to measure the rights they had as against the rights that the whites were given. Now I tell you, this measuring will never end. Not until they have the rights the others have.

* * * * * *

1.   *What differences, if any, did Dickerson find between doing the Committee's work in northern and southern cities?*

2.   *What does his experience suggest about the FEPC's effectiveness? About Roosevelt's position on civil rights?*

25–8   *Barbara Wooddall and Charles Taylor, Letters to and from the Front, 1941–1944*

Barbara Wooddall and Charles Taylor, like many thousands of other couples, had to fit their romance, marriage, and family in between the demands of wartime. In August 1941, they met on a blind date while Charles was in basic training. A year later they married. For the next two years they moved from base to base, and in 1943 they had a baby girl, Sandra. In June 1944, Charles left for combat in Europe; he did not return until November 1945. Through it all they corresponded regularly, leaving a detailed account of how the war deeply shaped a generation's personal lives.

SOURCE: From *Miss You: The World War II Letters of Barbara Wooddall Taylor and Charles E. Taylor* by J. Linoff, D. Smith, B. Taylor, and C. Taylor. Copyright © 1990 by the University of Georgia Press, Letters of Barbara Wooddall Taylor and Charles E. Taylor. Copyright © by Taylor Thomas Lawson.

Fairburn, Georgia   December 11, 1941

Dearest Charlie,

....Well, what about this WAR business. Oh, Charlie, will you still get your Christmas leave? You must get it because I'm counting big on being with you again. I hope I feel just the way I did the first night I had a date with you, remember? We had such a good time and I've never been so knocked for a loop. I remember exactly what I thought about you and I wonder if I will think it again when you come. We must be sure and we will be sure....

A man here in the office just said that Italy had declared WAR on the USA. What's going to happen to us? There is no doubt in my mind as to whom shall win this WAR, but how long will it take us? It makes you feel like getting the best of everything before it's all gone. Now I know that isn't the right way to feel, is it Charlie????

Charlie, please don't threaten me. I just want to wait until I see you and I already know what I'll say and do. I can hardly wait.
Must close now,
Sincerely,   Barbara

Ft. Leonard Wood, Missouri   14 July 1942
Dear Mr. Wooddall:

Perhaps this letter from me will come as a surprise to you, but it seems to me that even in these extraordinary circumstances in which we find ourselves today, formalities should still be observed.

I realize that you are completely aware that Barbara and I have plans for marriage upon her arrival in St. Louis, but before we go any further in our plans, I would like to have your consent. I already have the consent of my family, they are very proud to add such a wonderful person as Barbara to their family.

Sir, I am sorry that we are in War, which does not afford Barbara and I time, under the circumstances, to have the luxury of a normal peace-time wedding. However, there could be nothing about a big formal wedding that could have any effect upon the life and beauty of Barbara's and my life as husband and wife....

Needless to say, I am looking forward to the day when I shall become a member of your happy family.

Respectfully yours,   Charles E. Taylor

Evansville, Indiana   August 16, 1942
My dearest sweetheart,

I am now in Evansville and it is 3:10 p.m. Guess you are well on your way to Ft. Leonard Wood and I would give all I have to be with you. Darling, how will I ever do without you—even for a day!...

I was so proud of you when the train started moving in St. Louis. There you were smiling at me and waving, and, darling, it just made me feel good to know that you were my husband and I was your wife. When I couldn't see you any longer, well, I cried *just a little bit* and the lady sitting with me started crying. Jimminy cricket! say I, everything happens to me! Soon I found out that she had been to see her husband at Jefferson Barracks for the weekend. There were two girls across the aisle from me whose husbands are at Jefferson Barracks and Ft. Leonard Wood....

I'm here with a girl from Kansas who is going to see her boy friend at Macon, Georgia. She's rather cute and I'm glad she's here. At least it's nice having someone to talk with.

You know, we have the most beautiful love in the whole wide world. These last two weeks mean a lot more to me than happiness at the moment—they mean that I have a husband who loves me just as much as I do him—they mean that I don't have to live from day-to-day any longer, but that *we* can live for the future when the WAR is over and we are together forevermore.

You certainly did more than your part to make our honeymoon a success and I love you for everything.
I love you,
Your loving wife,   Barbara
P.S. A conductor just called a St. Louis train and it took all the self-control and will-power I have not to jump up and run to train that would take me back to you.

Fairburn, Georgia   July 22, 1943
My dearest sweetheart,

Well, this time next month, you will be a "papa," we hope, eh? Won't that be simply grand! Honestly, I can't even imagine what it's going to be like to have a little ole baby, of our very own!...

Just Your Barbie

At Sea   21 June 1944
My Dearest Darling,

I haven't written you a letter for two days but it is the same for there is nothing much for me to writ except the same old things. I was just lying there on my bunk last night trying to visualize you and Sandra Lee [their daughter]. Gee, it would be a wonderful thing just to see you two. My Barbie, you are so brave and good and oh, so nice to have as a wife. Darling, you must send me some kodak pictures and also some pictures of everything. Gee, I'd give a lot to see you all….By the way, send my mail Air Mail or "V-Mail" so it will come in record time: Also check the addresses on your letters and see that you have the correct address on them….

You know me and my feelings, well, they are still with me and now instead of just feeling I am coming back, I know I will be back. I'll keep up the war front—you keep up the home front. o.k.?

Barbie, listen to the news as often as you can. See if you can sorta keep up with the people I have soldiered with or the people we know. Write things to me so I'll not be too dumb about the people I used to know.

Darling, you must love me now and forever for we really are matched for this life on earth. The longer I live the surer I become of it, don't you? We may have a lot of things to look forward to that we can't see so live on the theory of today and don't worry about tomorrow—let the engineers build your bridges as you need them. Just be happy and think about all the things you and I have and will have as the years go by….

Live on my love and my regard for your purity and be as good to Sandra Lee as possible. She is good enough to be spoiled so that you can. Give her a hug and kiss from me and save a million for yourself.

Lovingly forever,   Charlie

Fairburn, Georgia   May 23, 1945
My dearest sweetheart,

… I liked your letter very much. It was nice and long—just what I needed. Sure I want you to get out of the Army as soon as possible—and I don't think it's the wrong way to feel at all. You've done more than your share already—so it's time someone else stepped in your place—in my opinion.

I agree with you about the diaphragm—but, may I be so bold as to ask where you learned so much about the article! After all, Charlie. Anyway, it's a great idea—and although I do want *several* children—not just two, if you please—I would like to plan for the next ones. So, with a diaphragm it would be better, of course. Do you mean that you want me to get a diaphragm *now?* You once said to wait until you were sure of coming home—so let me know, I mean ans. this pronto! I do think they're well worth the money. No, I wouldn't feel funny getting pregnant on my second honeymoon—but, frankly, I'd rather not. Just re-read the above sentence "you were sure of coming home"—I don't mean it that way—for I'm sure you're coming home *someday*—I meant until you were really on the way home, see?

The only disadvantage of a diaphragm—if I am capable of explaining what I mean—anyhow, well, most sensible people (from what I hear) only have one sexual intercourse in one evening—but some others (me, for instance, when I really get excited—and I'm sure I will when I see you again—for it gives me goose-pimples to even think about your coming home!!). Anyway, as I started to say—well, in the case of more than one SI in an evening—it isn't satisfactory, on account of—well, guess you know what I mean. Therefore, *one* has to be good—therefore, you, my friend, will have to control your feelings, in order to make it good. See? So, it's all up to you, as usual….

Write as often as possible and remember I love you.
Always,   Your Barbie

France   9 August 1945
My Dearest Darling:

…What do you think of this new bomb? Wow, it is really a new and bad thing for the Jap[anese], isn't it? I do hope that it is kept in the right hands for even a little nation could surely harness the world with a destructive weapon as that. I feel sure that if it is as powerful as the papers state it is then the War with Japan will be short from here on. They will surely give up soon with a weapon like that against them—plus Russia declaring war on them, all within 48 hours. They will be extremely foolish if they don't give up, eh?…

Say, I'll just bet that you are getting to be a good cook. From the things you talk about you must have really learned a lot about the kitchen business, haven't you. And truly I do love vegetables alone, honest!
Lovingly,   Your Charlie

Fairburn, Georgia,   August 16, 1945
My dearest sweetheart,

THE WAR IS OVER—oh, Charlie baby, this is what we waited for so long. Even yet, I can't believe it. I'm so grateful to God. Let's be humble and live such a life that we can show Him how thankful we are. Mother and I were listening to the radio when the news first came on—and we were laughing and crying together. I kept saying, "I want to go to Paris"—meaning, I wanted to go on the air by radio—and sure enough—we did go to Paris—and I felt as if we were there together. I've been wondering if you did go into Paris.

We could hardly settle down to eat—and Mother wanted me to go to the Community Meeting at the church. So, I quickly took a bath and dressed, listening to the radio all the time....

Well, I sat in the choir at church and felt good all over singing "My country 'Tis of Thee" etc....

Everyone has a holiday today of course—so we're going swimming this afternoon. And, gasoline is NOT rationed—man, that's wonderful. Honestly, things are happening so fast, well, I just can't grasp it all.

Always,   Your Barbie

* * * * * *

1. *How do the letters of Barbara and Charles differ in tone and subject? What do they suggest about the different strains of wartime upon men and women?*

2. *How does the correspondence evolve over time?*

25-9   *Korematsu v. United States, 1944*

Shortly after Pearl Harbor, President Roosevelt bowed to pressure from military leaders and West Coast residents by authorizing the removal and internment of Japanese Americans as a national defense measure. The move was defended on the grounds that the Japanese were "an enemy race." About 100,000 Japanese Americans, including 70,000 native-born American citizens, were sent to "relocation centers" in the interior of the country. In this 1944 case brought by civil libertarians, the Supreme Court upheld the order, with Justice Murphy dissenting.

SOURCE: 323 U.S. 214 (1944).

JUSTICE BLACK DELIVERED THE OPINION OF THE COURT

It should be noted, to begin with, that all legal restrictions which curtail the civil rights of a single racial group are immediately suspect. That is not to say that all such restrictions are unconstitutional. It is to say that courts must subject them to the most rigid scrutiny. Pressing public necessity may sometimes justify the existence of such restrictions; racial antagonism never can....

Exclusion of those of Japanese origin was deemed necessary because of the presence of an unascertained number of disloyal members of the group, most of whom we have no doubt were loyal to this country. It was because we could not reject the finding of the military authorities that it was impossible to bring about an immediate segregation of the disloyal from the loyal that we sustained the validity of the curfew order as applying to the whole group. In the instant case, temporary exclusion of the entire group was rested by the military on the same ground. The judgment that exclusion of the whole group was for the same reason a military imperative answers the contention that the exclusion was in the nature of group punishment based on antagonism to those of Japanese origin. That there were members of the group who retained loyalties in Japan has been confirmed by investigations made subsequent to the exclusion. Approximately five thousand American citizens of Japanese ancestry refused to swear unqualified allegiance to the United States and to renounce allegiance to the Japanese Emperor, and several thousand evacuees requested repatriation to Japan.

We uphold the exclusion order as of the time it was made and when the petitioner violated it.... In doing so, we are not unmindful of the hardships imposed by it upon a large group of American citizens.... But hardships are part of war, and war is an aggregation of hardships. All citizens alike, both in and out of uniform, feel the impact of war in greater or lesser measure. Citizenship has its responsibilities as well as its privileges, and in time of war the burden is always heavier. Compulsory exclusion of large groups of citizens from their homes, except under circumstances of direct emergency and peril, is inconsistent with our basic governmental institutions. But when under conditions of modern warfare our shores are threatened by hostile forces, the power to protect must be commensurate with the threatened danger....

It is said that we are dealing here with the case of imprisonment of a citizen in a concentration camp solely because of his ancestry, without evidence or inquiry concerning his loyalty and good disposition towards the United States. Our task would be simple, our duty clear, were this a case involving the imprisonment of a loyal citizen in a concentration camp because of racial prejudice. Regardless of the true nature of the assembly and relocation centers—and we deem it unjustifiable to call them concentration camps with all the ugly connotations that term implies—we are dealing specifically with nothing but an exclusion order. To cast this case into outlines of racial prejudice, without reference to the real military dangers which were presented, merely confuses the issue. Korematsu was not excluded from the Military Area because of hostility to him or his race. He *was* excluded because we are at war with the Japanese Empire, because the properly constituted military authorities feared an invasion of our West Coast and felt constrained to take proper security measures, because they decided that the military urgency of the situation demanded that all citizens of Japanese ancestry be segregated from the West Coast temporarily, and finally, because Congress, reposing its confidence in this time of war in our military leaders—as inevitably it must—determined that they should have the power to do just this. There was evidence of disloyalty on the part of some, the military authorities considered that the need for action was great, and time was short. We cannot—by availing ourselves of the calm perspective of hindsight—now say that at that time these actions were unjustified.

JUSTICE MURPHY, DISSENTING

This exclusion of "all persons of Japanese ancestry, both alien and non-alien," from the Pacific Coast area on a plea of military necessity in the absence of martial law ought not to be approved. Such exclusion goes over "the very brink of constitutional power" and falls into the ugly abyss of racism.

In dealing with matters relating to the prosecution and progress of a war, we must accord great respect and consideration to the judgments of the military authorities who are on the scene and who have full knowledge of the military facts. The scope of their discretion must, as a matter of necessity and common sense, be wide. And their judgments ought not to be overruled lightly by those whose training and duties ill-equip them to deal intelligently with matters so vital to the physical security of the nation.

At the same time, however, it is essential that there be definite limits to military discretion, especially where martial law has not been declared. Individuals must not be left impoverished of their constitutional rights on a plea of military necessity that has neither substance nor support....

That this forced exclusion was the result in good measure of this erroneous assumption of racial guilt rather than bona fide military necessity is evidenced by the Commanding General's Final Report on the evacuation from the Pacific Coast area. In it he refers to all individuals of Japanese descent as "subversive," as belonging to "an enemy race" whose "racial strains are undiluted," and as constituting "over 112,000 potential enemies...at large today" along the Pacific Coast. In support of this blanket condemnation of all persons of Japanese descent, however, no reliable evidence is cited to show that such individuals were generally disloyal, or had generally so conducted themselves in this area as to constitute a special menace to defense installations or war industries, or had otherwise by their behavior furnished reasonable ground for their exclusion as a group.

Justification for the exclusion is sought, instead, mainly upon questionable racial and sociological grounds not ordinarily within the realm of expert military judgment, supplemented by certain semi-military conclusions drawn from an unwarranted use of circumstantial evidence....

No one denies, of course, that there were some disloyal persons of Japanese descent on the Pacific Coast who did all in their power to aid their ancestral land. Similar disloyal activities have been engaged in by many persons of German, Italian and even more pioneer stock in our country. But to infer that examples of individual disloyalty prove group disloyalty and justify discriminatory action against the entire group is to deny that under our system of law individual guilt is the sole basis for deprivation of rights.... To give constitutional sanction to that inference in this case, however well-intentioned may have been the military command on the Pacific Coast, is to adopt one of the cruelest of the rationales used by our enemies to destroy the dignity of the individual and to encourage and open the door to discriminatory actions against other minority groups in the passions of tomorrow....

I dissent, therefore, from this legalization of racism. Racial discrimination in any form and in any degree has no justifiable part whatever in our democratic way of life. It is unattractive in any setting but it is utterly revolting among a free people who have embraced the principles set forth in the Constitution of the United States. All residents of this nation are kin in some way by blood or culture to a foreign land. Yet they are primarily and necessarily a part of the new and distinct civilization of the United States. They must accordingly be treated at all times as the heirs of the American experiment and as entitled to all the rights and freedoms guaranteed by the Constitution.

* * * * * *

1. *How does the Court avoid the racial aspects of the case? How does it deal with the issue of the violation of citizenship rights?*

2. *How does Murphy invoke the racial issue in his dissent?*

chapter 26

The Cold War, 1945–1952

26–1 Clark Clifford, Memorandum to President Truman, 1946

White House Special Counsel Clark Clifford prepared this private memorandum for President Truman in 1946. Clifford was particularly influenced by George Kennan's diplomatic cables from Moscow, which emphasized the need for U.S. "containment" of Soviet aggression. The memo also reflects the view of the Secretaries of State, War, and Navy, as well as the Joint Chiefs of Staff. Clifford deftly summarized the "hard line" view toward the Soviet Union, then emerging as the consensus position among administration officials.

SOURCE: Clark Clifford to President Truman, September 24, 1946. Clark Clifford Papers, Harry S. Truman Library, in William Chafe and Harvard Sitkoff, eds., *A History of Our Time* (Oxford, 1991).

A direct threat to American security is implicit in Soviet foreign policy which is designed to prepare the Soviet Union for war with the leading capitalistic nations of the world. Soviet leaders recognize that the United States will be the Soviet Union's most powerful enemy if such a war as that predicted by Communist theory ever comes about and therefore the United States is the chief target of Soviet foreign and military policy....

The most obvious Soviet threat to American security is the growing ability of the USSR to wage an offensive war against the United States. This has not hitherto been possible, in the absence of Soviet long-range strategic air power and an almost total lack of sea power. Now, however, the USSR is rapidly developing elements of her military strength which she hitherto lacked and which will give the Soviet Union great offensive capabilities. Stalin has declared his intention of sparing no effort to build up the military strength of the Soviet Union. Development of atomic weapons, guided missiles, materials for biological warfare, a strategic air force, submarines of great cruising range, naval mines and mine craft, to name the most important, are extending the effective range of Soviet military power well into areas which the United States regards as vital to its security.... The primary objective of United States policy toward the Soviet Union is to convince Soviet leaders that it is in their interest to participate in a system of world cooperation, that there are no funda-

mental causes for war between our two nations, and that the security and prosperity of the Soviet Union, and that of the rest of the world as well, is being jeopardized by the aggressive militaristic imperialism such as that in which the Soviet Union is now engaged.

However, these same leaders with whom we hope to achieve an understanding on the principles of international peace appear to believe that a war with the United States and the other leading capitalistic nations is inevitable. They are increasing their military power and the sphere of Soviet influence in preparation for the "inevitable" conflict, and they are trying to weaken and subvert their potential opponents by every means at their disposal. So long as these men adhere to these beliefs, it is highly dangerous to conclude that hope of international peace lies only in "accord," "mutual understanding," or "solidarity" with the Soviet Union.

Adoption of such a policy would impel the United States to make sacrifices for the sake of Soviet-U.S. relations, which would only have the effect of raising Soviet hopes and increasing Soviet demands, and to ignore alternative lines of policy, which might be much more compatible with our own national and international interests.

The Soviet government will never be easy to "get along with." The American people must accustom themselves to this thought, not as a cause for despair, but as a fact to be faced objectively and courageously. If we find it impossible to enlist Soviet cooperation in the solution of world problems, we should be prepared to join with the British and other Western countries in an attempt to build up a world of our own which will pursue its own objectives and will recognize the Soviet orbit as a distinct entity with which conflict is not predestined but with which we cannot pursue common aims.

As long as the Soviet government maintains its present foreign policy, based upon the theory of an ultimate struggle between communism and capitalism, the United States must assume that the USSR might fight at any time for the two-fold purpose of expanding the territory under Communist control and weakening its potential capitalist opponents. The Soviet Union was able to flow into the political vacuum of the Balkans, Eastern Europe, the Near East, Manchuria and Korea because no other nation was both willing and able to prevent it. Soviet leaders were encouraged by easy success and they are now preparing to take over new areas in the same way. The Soviet Union, as Stalin euphemistically phrased it, is preparing "for any eventuality."

Unless the United States is willing to sacrifice its future security for the sake of "accord" with the USSR now, this government must, as a first step toward world stabilization, seek to prevent additional Soviet aggression.... This government should be prepared, while scrupulously avoiding any act which would be an excuse for the Soviets to begin a war, to resist vigorously and successfully any efforts of the USSR to expand into areas vital to American security.

The language of military power is the only language which disciples of power politics understand. The United States must use that language in order that Soviet leaders will realize that our government is determined to uphold the interests of its citizens and the rights of small nations. Compromise and concessions are considered, by the Soviets, to be evidences of weakness and they are encouraged by our "retreats" to make new and greater demands.

The main deterrent to Soviet attack on the United States, or to attack on areas of the world which are vital to our security, will be the military power of this country. It must be made apparent to the Soviet government that our strength will be sufficient to repel any attack and sufficient to defeat the USSR decisively if a war should start. The prospect of defeat is the only sure means of deterring the Soviet Union.

The Soviet Union's vulnerability is limited due to the vast area over which its key industries and natural resources are widely dispersed, but it is vulnerable to atomic weapons, biological warfare, and long-range power. Therefore, in order to maintain our strength at a level which will be effective in restraining the Soviet Union, the United States must be prepared to wage atomic and biological warfare. A highly mechanized army, which can be moved either by sea or by air, capable of seizing and holding strategic areas, must be supported by powerful naval and air forces. A war with the USSR would be "total" in a more horrible sense than any previous war and there must be constant research for both offensive and defensive weapons.

Whether it would actually be in this country's interest to employ atomic and biological weapons against the Soviet Union in the event of hostilities is a question which would require careful consideration in the light of the circumstances prevailing at the time. The decision would probably be influenced by a number of factors, such as the Soviet Union's capacity to employ similar weapons, which can not now be estimated. But the important point is that the United States must be prepared to wage atomic and biological warfare if necessary. The mere fact of preparedness may be the only powerful deterrent to Soviet aggressive action and in this sense the only sure guaranty of peace.

The United States, with a military potential composed primarily of [highly] effective technical weapons, should entertain no proposal for disarmament or limitation of armament as long as the possibility of Soviet aggression exists. Any discussion on the limitation of armaments should be pursued slowly and carefully with the knowledge constantly in mind that proposals on outlawing atomic warfare and long-range offensive weapons would greatly limit United States strength, while only moderately affecting the Soviet Union. The Soviet Union relies primarily on a large infantry and artillery force and the result of such arms limitation would be to deprive the United States of its most effective weapons without impairing the Soviet Union's ability to wage a quick war of aggression in Western Europe, the Middle East or the Far East....

In addition to maintaining our own strength, the United States should support and assist all democratic countries which are in any way menaced or endangered by the USSR. Providing military support in case of attack is a last resort; a more effective barrier to communism is strong economic support. Trade agreements, loans and technical missions strengthen our ties with friendly nations and are effective demonstrations that capitalism is at least the equal of communism. The United States can do much to ensure that economic opportunities, personal freedom and social equality are made possible in countries outside the Soviet sphere by generous financial assistance. Our policy on reparations should be directed toward strengthening the areas we are endeavoring to keep outside the Soviet sphere. Our efforts to break down trade barriers, open up rivers and international waterways, and bring about economic unification of countries, now divided by occupation armies, are also directed toward the re-establishment of vigorous and healthy non-Communist economies.

In conclusion, as long as the Soviet government adheres to its present policy, the United States should maintain military forces powerful enough to restrain the Soviet Union and to confine Soviet influence to its present area. All nations not now within the Soviet sphere should be given generous economic assistance and political support in their opposition to Soviet penetration. Economic aid may also be given to the Soviet government and private trade with the USSR permitted provided the results are beneficial to our interests....

Even though Soviet leaders profess to believe that the conflict between Capitalism and Communism is irreconcilable and must eventually be resolved by the triumph of the latter, it is our hope that they will change their minds and work out with us a fair and equitable settlement when they realize that we are too strong to be beaten and too determined to be frightened.

* * * * * *

1. How does Clifford define the essential threat of the U.S.S.R.? To what extent does he base his analysis on Soviet ideology, as compared to Soviet behavior?

2. What military measures does Clifford recommend to meet the threat? What economic policies does he suggest?

26–2   Henry Wallace, Letter to President Truman, 1946

Secretary of Commerce Henry Wallace found himself a lone voice of dissent within the Truman administration. An ardent New Dealer, Wallace had served as Secretary of Agriculture and Vice President under President Roosevelt. If he had not been removed from the Democratic ticket in 1944 to placate southern conservatives, Wallace rather than Truman would have succeeded FDR. Wallace was deeply disturbed by what he thought was a reversal of the wartime policy of cooperation with the U.S.S.R. He expressed his views privately here, but when he publicly broke with the president two months later, Truman fired him.

SOURCE: Henry Wallace to President Truman, July 23, 1946. Harry Truman Papers, Harry S. Truman Library, in William Chafe and Harvard Sitkoff, eds., *A History of Our Times* (Oxford, 1991).

I have been increasingly disturbed about the trend of international affairs since the end of the war, and I am even more troubled by the apparently growing feeling among the American people that another war is coming and the only way that we can head it off is to arm ourselves to the teeth. Yet all of past history indicates that an armaments race does not lead to peace but to war. The months just ahead may well be the crucial period which will decide whether the civilized world will go down in destruction after the five or ten years needed for several nations to arm themselves with atomic bombs. Therefore I want to give you my views on how the present trend toward conflict might be averted....

How do American actions since V-J Day appear to other nations? I mean by actions the concrete things like $13 billion for the War and Navy Departments, the Bikini tests of the atomic bomb and continued production of bombs, the plan to arm Latin America with our weapons, production of B-29s and planned production of B-36s, and the effort to secure air bases spread over half the globe from which the other half of the globe can be bombed. I cannot but feel that these actions must make it look to the rest of the world as if we were only paying lipservice to peace at the conference table.

These facts rather make it appear either (1) that we are preparing ourselves to win the war which we regard as inevitable or (2) that we are trying to build up a predominance of force to intimidate the rest of mankind. How would it look to us if Russia had the atomic bomb and we did not, if Russia had 10,000-mile bombers and air bases within a thousand miles of our coastlines, and we did not?

Some of the military men and self-styled "realists" are saying: "What's wrong with trying to build up a predominance of force? The only way to preserve peace is for this country to be so well armed that no one will dare attack us. We know that America will never start a war."

The flaw in this policy is simply that it will not work. In a world of atomic bombs and other revolutionary new weapons, such as radioactive poison gases and biological warfare, a peace maintained by a predominance of force is no longer possible.

Why is this so? The reasons are clear:

FIRST. Atomic warfare is cheap and easy compared with old-fashioned war. Within a very few years several countries can have atomic bombs and other atomic weapons. Compared with the cost of large armies and the manufacture of old-fashioned weapons, atomic bombs cost very little and require only a relatively small part of a nation's production plant and labor force.

SECOND. So far as winning a war is concerned, having more bombs—even many more bombs—than the other fellow is no longer a decisive advantage. If another nation had enough bombs to eliminate all of our principal cities and our heavy industry, it wouldn't help us very much if we had ten times as many bombs as we needed to do the same to them.

THIRD. And most important, the very fact that several nations have atomic bombs will inevitably result in neurotic, fear-ridden, itching-trigger psychology in all the peoples of the world, and because of our wealth and vulnerability we would be among the most seriously affected. Atomic war will not require vast and time-consuming preparations, the mobilization of large armies, the conversion of a large proportion of a country's industrial plants to the manufacture of weapons. In a world armed with atomic weapons, some incident will lead to the use of those weapons.

There is a school of military thinking which recognizes these facts, recognizes that when several nations have atomic bombs, a war which will destroy modern civilization will result and that no nation or combination of nations can win such a war. This school of thought therefore advocates a "preventive war," an attack on Russia *now* before Russia has atomic bombs.

This scheme is not only immoral, but stupid. If we should attempt to destroy all the principal Russian cities and her heavy industry, we might well succeed. But the immediate countermeasure which such an attack would call forth is the prompt occupation of all Continental Europe by the Red Army. Would we be prepared to destroy the cities of all Europe in trying to finish what we had started? This idea is so contrary to all the basic instincts and principles of the American people that any such action would be possible only under a dictatorship at home....

Our basic distrust of the Russians, which has been greatly intensified in recent months by the playing up of conflict in the press, stems from differences in political and economic organization. For the first time in our history defeatists among us have raised the fear of another system as a successful rival to democracy and free enterprise in other countries and perhaps even our own. I am convinced that we can meet that challenge as we have in the past by demonstrating that economic abundance can be achieved without sacrificing personal, political and religious liberties. We cannot meet it as Hitler tried to by an anti-Comintern alliance.

It is perhaps too easy to forget that despite the deep-seated differences in our cultures and intensive anti-Russian propaganda of some twenty-five years' standing, the American people reversed their attitudes during the crisis of war. Today, under the pressure of seemingly insoluble international problems and continuing deadlocks, the tide of American public opinion is again turning against Russia. In this reaction lies one of the dangers to which this letter is addressed.

I should list the factors which make for Russian distrust of the United States and of the Western world as follows. The first is Russian history, which we must take into account because it is the setting in which Russians see all actions and policies of the rest of the world. Russian history for over a thousand years has been a succession of attempts, often unsuccessful, to resist invasion and conquest—by the Mongols, the Turks, the Swedes, the Germans and the Poles. The scant thirty years of the existence of the Soviet Government has in Russian eyes been a continuation of their historical struggle for national existence. The first four years of the new regime, from 1917 through 1921, were spent in resisting attempts at destruction by the

Japanese, British and French, with some American assistance, and by the several White Russian armies encouraged and financed by the Western powers. Then, in 1941, the Soviet State was almost conquered by the Germans after a period during which the Western European powers had apparently acquiesced in the rearming of Germany in the belief that the Nazis would seek to expand eastward rather than westward. The Russians, therefore, obviously see themselves as fighting for their existence in a hostile world.

Second, it follows that to the Russians all of the defense and security measures of the Western powers seem to have an aggressive intent. Our actions to expand our military security system—such steps as extending the Monroe Doctrine to include the arming of the Western Hemisphere nations, our present monopoly of the atomic bomb, our interest in outlying bases and our general support of the British Empire—appear to them as going far beyond the requirements of defense. I think we might feel the same if the United States were the only capitalistic country in the world, and the principal socialistic countries were creating a level of armed strength far exceeding anything in their previous history. From the Russian point of view, also, the granting of a loan to Britain and the lack of tangible results on their request to borrow for rehabilitation purposes may be in regarded as another evidence of strengthening an anti-Soviet bloc.

Finally, our resistance to her attempts to obtain warm-water ports and her own security system in the form of "friendly" neighboring states seems, from the Russian point of view, to clinch the case. After twenty-five years of isolation and after having achieved the status of a major power, Russia believes that she is entitled to recognition of her new status. Our interest in establishing democracy in Eastern Europe, where democracy by and large has never existed, seems to her is an attempt to re-establish the encirclement of unfriendly neighbors which was created after the last war, and which might serve as a springboard of still another an effort to destroy her....

We should make an effort to counteract the irrational fear of Russia which is being systematically built up in the American people by certain individuals and publications. The slogan that communism and capitalism, regimentation and democracy, cannot continue to exist in the same world is, from a historical point of view, pure propaganda. Several religious doctrines, all claiming to be the only true gospel and salvation, have existed side by side with a reasonable degree of tolerance for centuries. This country was for the first half of its national life a democratic island in a world dominated in by absolutist governments.

We should not act as if we too felt that we were threatened in today's world. We are by far the most powerful nation in the world, the only Allied nation which came out of the war without devastation and much stronger than before the war. Any talk on our part about the need for strengthening our defenses further is bound to appear hypocritical to other nations....

The real test lies in the achievement of international unity. It will be fruitless to continue to seek solutions for the many specific problems that face us in the making of the peace and in the establishment of an enduring international order without first achieving an atmosphere of mutual trust and confidence. The task admittedly is not an easy one....

Fundamentally, this comes down to the point discussed earlier in this letter, that even our own security, in the sense that we have known it in the past, cannot be preserved by military means in a world armed with atomic weapons. The only type of security which can be maintained by our own military force is the type described by a military man before the Senate Atomic Energy Commission—a security against invasion after all our cities and perhaps 40 million of our city population have been destroyed by atomic weapons. That is the best that "security" on the basis of armaments has to offer us. It is not the kind of security that our people and the people of the other United Nations are striving for.

* * * * * *

1. *Why does Wallace believe that the current American military policy is flawed? What alternatives does he offer?*

2. *Compare Wallace's treatment of Soviet motives with Clifford's. How do the two men differ in their interpretation of Russian history and foreign policy?*

3. *What is Wallace's vision for international security?*

26–3   *The Truman Doctrine, 1947*

In March 1947 President Truman appealed to Congress for $400 million in foreign aid to the governments of Greece and Turkey, both of which were fighting to repress civil rebellions. Truman's speech marked a new course in American foreign policy by asserting a responsibility to stop the spread of communism anywhere in the world. Truman's vision divided the world neatly into two camps, and it assumed that all social revolution was being directed from Moscow. The Truman Doctrine placed Cold War principles at the very foundation of American foreign policy for decades to come.

SOURCE: *Congressional Record*, March 12, 1947.

The gravity of the situation which confronts the world today necessitates my appearance before a joint session of the Congress. The foreign policy and the national security of this country are involved.

One aspect of the present situation, which I wish to present to you at this time for your consideration and decision, concerns Greece and Turkey.

The United States has received from the Greek Government an urgent appeal for financial and economic assistance. Preliminary reports from the American Economic Mission now in Greece and reports from the American Ambassador in Greece corroborate the statement of the Greek Government that assistance is imperative if Greece is to survive as a free nation.

I do not believe that the American people and the Congress wish to turn a deaf ear to the appeal of the Greek Government.

The very existence of the Greek state is today threatened by the terrorist activities of several thousand armed men, led by Communists, who defy the Government's authority at a number of points, particularly along the northern boundaries. A commission appointed by the United Nations Security Council is at present investigating disturbed conditions in Northern Greece and alleged border violations along the frontiers between Greece on the one hand and Albania, Bulgaria and Yugoslavia on the other.

Meanwhile, the Greek Government is unable to cope with the situation. The Greek Army is small and poorly equipped. It needs supplies and equipment if it is to restore the authority to the Government throughout Greek territory.

Greece must have assistance if it is to become a self-supporting and self-respecting democracy. The United States must supply this assistance. We have already extended to Greece certain types of relief and economic aid but these are inadequate. There is no other country to which democratic Greece can turn. No other nation is willing and able to provide the necessary support for a democratic Greek Government.

The British Government, which has been helping Greece, can give no further financial or economic aid after March 31. Great Britain finds itself under the necessity of reducing or liquidating its commitments in several parts of the world, including Greece....

Greece's neighbor, Turkey, also deserves our attention. The future of Turkey as an independent and economically sound state is clearly no less important to the freedom-loving peoples of the world than the future of Greece. The circumstances in which Turkey finds itself today are considerably different from those of Greece. Turkey has been spared the disasters that have beset Greece. And during the war, the United States and Great Britain furnished Turkey with material aid. Nevertheless, Turkey now needs our support.

Since the war Turkey has sought additional financial assistance from Great Britain and the United States for the purpose of effecting the modernization necessary for the maintenance of its national integrity. That integrity is essential to the preservation of order in the Middle East.

The British Government has informed us that, owing to its own difficulties, it can no longer extend financial or economic aid to Turkey. As in the case of Greece, if Turkey is to have the assistance it needs, the United States must supply it. We are the only country able to provide that help....

To ensure the peaceful development of nations, free from coercion, the United States has taken a leading part in establishing the United Nations. The United Nations is designed to make possible lasting freedom and independence for all its members. We shall not realize our objectives, however, unless we are willing to help free peoples to maintain their free institutions and their national integrity against aggressive movements that seek to impose on them totalitarian regimes. This is no more than a frank recognition that totalitarian regimes imposed on free peoples, by direct or indirect aggression, undermine the foundations of international peace and hence the security of the United States.

The peoples of a number of countries of the world have recently had totalitarian regimes forced upon them against their will. The Government of the United States has made frequent protests against coercion and intimidation, in violation of the Yalta Agreement, in Poland, Rumania and Bulgaria. I must also state that in a number of other countries there have been similar developments.

At the present moment in world history nearly every nation must choose between alternative ways of life. The choice is too often not a free one.

One way of life is based upon the will of the majority, and is distinguished by free institutions, representative government, free elections, guarantees of individual liber-ty, freedom of speech and religion, and freedom from political oppression.

The second way of life is based upon the will of the minority forcibly imposed upon the majority. It relies upon terror and oppression, a controlled press and radio, fixed elections, and the suppression of personal freedoms.

I believe that it must be the policy of the United States to support free peoples who are resisting attempted subjugation by armed minorities or by outside pressures.

I believe that we must assist free peoples to work out their own destinies in their own way.

I believe that our help should be primarily through economic and financial aid which is essential to economic stability and orderly political processes.

The world is not static, and the status quo is not sacred. But we cannot allow changes in the status quo in violation of the charter of the United Nations by such methods as coercion, or by such subterfuges as political infiltration. In helping free and independent nations to maintain their freedom, the United States will be giving effect to the principles of the charter of the United Nations.

It is necessary only to glance at a map to realize that the survival and integrity of the Greek nation are of grave importance in a much wider situation. If Greece should fall under the control of an armed minority, the effect upon its neighbor, Turkey, would be immediate and serious. Confusion and disorder might well spread throughout the entire Middle East.

Moreover, the disappearance of Greece as an independent state would have a profound effect upon those countries in Europe whose peoples are struggling against great difficulties to maintain their freedoms and their independence while they repair the damages of war.

It would be an unspeakable tragedy if these countries, which have struggled so long against overwhelming odds, should lose that victory for which they sacrificed so much. Collapse of free institutions and loss of independence would be disastrous not only for them but for the world. Discouragement and possibly failure would quickly be the lot of neighboring peoples striving to maintain their freedom and independence.

Should we fail to aid Greece and Turkey in this fateful hour, the effect will be far reaching to the west as well as to the east. We must take immediate and resolute action.

I therefore ask the Congress to provide authority for assistance to Greece and Turkey in the amount of $400,000,000 for the period ending June 30, 1948.

In addition to funds, I ask the Congress to authorize the detail of American civilian and military personnel to Greece and Turkey, at the request of those countries, to assist in the tasks of reconstruction, and for the purpose of supervising the use of such financial and material assistance as may be furnished. I recommend that authority also be provided for the instruction and training of selected Greek and Turkish personnel.

Finally, I ask that the Congress provide authority which will permit the speediest and most effective use, in terms of needed commodities, supplies, and equipment, of such funds as may be authorized.

This is a serious course upon which we embark. I would not recommend it except that the alternative is much more serious.

The United States contributed $341,000,000,000 toward winning World War II. This is an investment in world freedom and world peace.

The assistance that I am recommending for Greece and Turkey amounts to little more than 1 tenth of 1 per cent of this investment. It is only common sense that we should safeguard this investment and make sure that it was not in vain.

The seeds of totalitarian regimes are nurtured by misery and want. They spread and grow in the evil soil of poverty and strife. They reach their full growth when the

hope of a people for a better life has died. We must keep that hope alive. The free peoples of the world look to us for support in maintaining their freedoms.

If we falter in our leadership, we may endanger the peace of the world—and we shall surely endanger the welfare of this nation.

Great responsibilities have been placed upon us by the swift movement of events. I am confident that the Congress will face these responsibilities squarely.

* * * * * *

1.   *How does the Doctrine define "national security"? Why does Truman believe the "national security" of the United States to be at stake here?*

2.   *What consequences does Truman foresee if the United States fails to aid Greece and Turkey?*

3.   *What does Truman define as the two "alternative ways of life" available to nations?*

26–4   *The Truman Loyalty Order, 1947*

Amid Republican charges that his Administration was "soft on communism," Truman formulated a domestic accompaniment to his anticommunist foreign policy. In 1947, he issued an executive order establishing a Loyalty Review Board for the federal civil service. The board was empowered to investigate and dismiss employees suspected of disloyalty. The Attorney General was directed to draw up a list of "subversive" organizations that would provide a basis for investigation. The Loyalty Order legitimized, and further stimulated, the frenzy of anticommunist activity in all phases of American life.

SOURCE: *The New York Times,* March 23, 1947.

Part I

INVESTIGATION OF APPLICANTS

1. There shall be a loyalty investigation of every person entering the civilian employment of any department or agency of the Executive Branch of the Federal Government.

   A.   Investigations of persons entering the competitive service shall be conducted by the Civil

Service Commission, except in such cases as are covered by a special agreement between the commission and any given department or agency.

   B.   Investigations of persons other than those entering the competitive service shall be conducted by the employing department or agency. Departments and agencies without investigative organizations shall utilize the investigative facilities of the Civil Service Commission.

2. The investigations of persons entering the employ of the Executive Branch may be conducted after any such person enters upon actual employment therein, but in any such case the appointment of such person shall be conditioned upon a favorable determination with respect to his loyalty....

3. An investigation shall be made of all applicants at all available pertinent sources of information and shall include reference to:

   A.   Federal Bureau of Investigation files.

   B.   Civil Service Commission files.

   C.   Military and Naval Intelligence files.

   D.   The files of any other appropriate government investigative or intelligence agency.

E.   House Committee on un-American Activities files.

F.   Local law-enforcement files at the place of residence and employment of the applicant, including municipal, county and state law-enforcement files.

G.   Schools and colleges attended by applicant.

H.   Former employers of applicant.

I.   References given by applicant.

J.   Any other appropriate source.

4. Whenever derogatory information with respect to loyalty of an applicant is revealed, a full field investigation shall be conducted. A full field investigation shall also be conducted of those applicants, or of applicants for particular positions, as may be designated by the head of the employing department or agency, such designations to be based on the determination by any such head of the best interests of national security.

Part II

INVESTIGATION OF EMPLOYEES

1. The head of each department and agency in the Executive Branch of the Government shall be personally responsible for an effective program to assure that disloyal civilian officers or employees are not retained in employment in his department or agency.

A.   He shall be responsible for prescribing and supervising the loyalty determination procedures of his department or agency, in accordance with the provisions of this order, which shall be considered as providing minimum requirements.

B.   The head of a department or agency which does not have an investigative organization shall utilize the investigative facilities of the Civil Service Commission.

2. The head of each department and agency shall appoint one or more loyalty boards, each composed of not less than three representatives of the department or agency concerned, for the purpose of hearing loyalty cases arising within such department or agency and making recommendations with respect to the removal of any officer or employee of such department or agency on grounds relating to loyalty, and he shall prescribe regulations for the conduct of the proceedings before such boards.

A.   An officer or employee who is charged with being disloyal shall have a right to an administrative hearing before a loyalty board in the employing department or agency. He may appear before such board personally, accompanied by counsel or representative of his own choosing, and present evidence on his own behalf, through witnesses or by affidavit.

B.   The officer or employee shall be served with a written notice of such hearing in sufficient time, and shall be informed therein of the nature of the charges against him in sufficient detail, so that he will be enabled to prepare his defense. The charges shall be stated as specifically and completely as, in the discretion of the employing department or agency, security considerations permit, and the officer or employee shall be informed in the notice (1) of his right to reply to such charges in writing within a specified reasonable period of time, (2) of his right to an administrative hearing on such charges before a loyalty board, and (3) of his right to appear before such board personally, to be accompanied by counsel or representative of his own choosing, and to present evidence on his behalf, through witness or by affidavit.

3. A recommendation of removal by a loyalty board shall be subject to appeal by the officer or employee affected, prior to his removal, to the head of the employing department or agency or to such person or persons as may be designated by such head, under such regulations as may be prescribed by him, and the decision of the department or agency concerned shall be subject to appeal to the Civil Service Commission's Loyalty Review Board, hereinafter provided for, for an advisory recommendation.

4. The rights of hearing, notice thereof, and appeal therefrom shall be accorded to every officer or employee prior to his removal on grounds of disloyalty, irrespective of tenure, or of manner, method, or nature of appointment, but the head of the employing department or agency may suspend any officer or employee at any time pending a determination with respect to loyalty.

5. The loyalty boards of the various departments and agencies shall furnish to the Loyalty Review Board, hereinafter provided for, such reports as may be requested concerning the operation of the loyalty program in any such department or agency.

Part III

RESPONSIBILITIES OF CIVIL SERVICE COMMISSION

1. There shall be established in the Civil Service Commission a Loyalty Review Board of not less than

three impartial persons, the members of which shall be officers or employees of the commission.

   A.   The board shall have authority to review cases involving persons recommended for dismissal on grounds relating to loyalty by the loyalty board of any department or agency and to make advisory recommendations thereon to the head of the employing department or agency. Such cases may be referred to the board either by the employment department or agency, or by the officer or employee concerned.

   B.   The board shall make rules and regulations, not inconsistent with the provisions of this order, deemed necessary to implement statutes and executive orders relating to employee loyalty.

   C.   The Loyalty Review Board shall also:
      1.   Advise all departments and agencies on all problems relating to employee loyalty.
      2.   Disseminate information pertinent to employee loyalty programs.
      3.   Coordinate the employee loyalty policy and procedures of the several departments and agencies.
      4.   Make reports and submit recommendations to the Civil Service Commission for transmission to the President from time to time as may be necessary to the maintenance of the employee loyalty program.

2. There shall also be established and maintained in the Civil Service Commission a central master index covering all persons on whom loyalty investigations have been made by any department or agency since Sept. 1, 1939. Such master index shall contain the name of each person investigated, adequate identifying information concerning each such person, and a reference to each department and agency which has conducted a loyalty investigation concerning the person involved....

   B.   The reports and other investigative material and information developed by the investigating department or agency shall be retained by such department or agency in each case...

3. The Loyalty Review Board shall currently be furnished by the Department of Justice the name of each foreign or domestic organization, association, movement, group or combination of persons which the Attorney General, after appropriate investigation and determination, designates as totalitarian, Fascist, Communist or subversive, or as having adopted a policy of advocating or approving the commission of acts of force or violence to deny others their rights under the Constitution of the United States, or as seeking to alter the form of government of the United States by unconstitutional means.

   A.   The Loyalty Review Board shall disseminate such information to all departments and agencies.

Part IV

SECURITY MEASURES IN INVESTIGATIONS

1. At the request of the head of any department or agency of the Executive Branch an investigative agency shall make available to such head, personally, all investigative material and information collected by the investigative agency concerning any employee or prospective employee of the requesting department or agency, or shall make such material and information available to any officer or officers designated by such head and approved by the investigative agency.

2. Notwithstanding the foregoing requirement, however, the investigative agency may refuse to disclose the names of confidential informants, provided it furnishes sufficient information about such informants on the basis of which the requesting department or agency can make an adequate evaluation of the information furnished by them, and provided it advises the requesting department or agency in writing that it is essential to the protection of the informants or to the investigation of other cases that the identity of the informants not be revealed. Investigative agencies shall not use this discretion to decline to reveal sources of information where such action is not essential.

3. Each department and agency of the Executive Branch should develop and maintain, for the collection and analysis of information relating to the loyalty of its employees and prospective employees, a staff specially trained in security techniques, and an effective security control system for protecting such information generally and for protecting confidential sources of such information particularly.

Part V

STANDARDS

1. The standard for the refusal of employment or the removal from employment in an executive department or agency on grounds relating to loyalty shall be that, on all the evidence, reasonable grounds exist for belief that the

person involved is disloyal to the Government of the United States.

2. Activities and associations of an applicant or employee which may be considered in connection with the determination of disloyalty may include one or more of the following:

A. Sabotage, espionage, or attempts or preparations therefor, knowingly associating with spies or saboteurs;

B. Treason or sedition or advocacy thereof;

C   Advocacy of revolution of force or violence to alter the constitutional form of Government of the United States.

D. Intentional, unauthorized disclosure to any person, under circumstances which may indicate disloyalty to the United States, of documents or information of a confidential or non-public character obtained by the person making the disclosure as a result of his employment by the Government of the United States;

E. Performing or attempting to perform his duties, or *otherwise acting, so as to serve the interests of*

another government in preference to the interests of the United States.

F. Membership in, affiliation with or *sympathetic association* with any foreign or *domestic* organization, association, movement, *group or combination* of persons, designated by the Attorney General as totalitarian, Fascist, Communist, or *subversive,* or as having adopted a policy of advocating or approving the commission of acts of force or violence to deny other persons their rights under the Constitution of the United States, or as seeking to alter the form of Government of the United States by unconstitutional means....

* * * * * *

1. *How does the order define disloyalty? How does the Loyalty Review Board obtain information about employee loyalty?*

2. *What provisions does the order make for legal appeal of its decisions?*

26–5   American Medical Association, Campaign against Compulsory Health Insurance, 1949

After his narrow reelection in 1948, President Truman made an effort to extend New Deal liberalism with his "Fair Deal" program. But 1930s-style liberalism was in retreat, weakened by a combination of a resurgent Republican Party, reactionary southern Democrats in Congress, and powerful interest-group lobbies. The politics of anticommunism provided a convenient cover for antiliberalism. When Truman introduced an ambitious plan for national health insurance, the American Medical Association denounced it as "socialized medicine" and launched a vigorous public relations campaign against it.

SOURCE: Clem Whitaker and Leone Baxter, National Education Campaign of the American Medical Association, February 21, 1949.

The general strategy, major issues and fundamental procedures of the campaign were fully outlined during the meeting of State Medical Society leaders with A.M.A. representatives and the campaign management in Chicago, February 12.

This skeletonized Plan of Campaign is simply a working blueprint, designed to define the separate responsibilities of the National, State and County organizations—and to outline the basic steps in getting the job in operation.

There is no need to review the general program, except to underline two major objectives:

First, this is *an affirmative campaign.* Defeating compulsory health insurance is the immediate job, but stopping the agitation for compulsory health insurance, by enrolling the people in sound voluntary health insurance systems, is our most important objective. That's the only way to resolve this problem.

Second, this must be *a broad, public campaign*—with leaders in every walk of life participating—not just a doctors' campaign. But the work of getting the people alerted and recruited for the battle, that's the responsibility of doctors and their lay representatives.

In setting up State and County campaigns, this basic precept of sound campaigning should be kept in mind:

A simple campaign program, vigorously and carefully carried out, is much more effective than an ambitious, complicated program, with some of the bases left uncovered.

Start with a program you know you can handle with the money and manpower available. Then amplify it later.

Tireless personal work and unbounded enthusiasm for your cause are the most important factors in successful campaigning.

THE NATIONAL CAMPAIGN STRUCTURE

The Coordinating Committee of the American Medical Association, headed by Dr. Elmer L. Henderson, Chairman of the Board of Trustees, is charged with over-all responsibility for the conduct of the campaign and is *the policy-making board of the campaign.*

The Campaign Directors are responsible to The Coordinating Committee.

The Coordinating Committee, in turn, is responsible to The House of Delegates.

THE JOB AT NATIONAL HEADQUARTERS

The job at National Campaign Headquarters, eliminating activities which cannot be covered in a thumb-nail sketch of operations, breaks down as follows:

1. Development and direction of *national planning and campaign strategy.*
2. Direction of *the National publicity campaign,* utilizing, largely, the existing, normal channels—the press associations, major newspapers, radio networks and television, the great national magazines, trade publications, newsletters, et cetera. *The first objective in this phase of the National campaign will be to get medicine off the defensive, and to conduct an affirmative program of education.* An intensive campaign *for* voluntary health insurance will be conducted concurrently with the drive *against* compulsory health insurance.
3. Direction of *the National-organization endorsement drive,* designed to mobilize hundreds of the great National organizations in support of medicine's cause. This is a vital step in broadening the campaign into a public crusade. The National Headquarters will need constant aid from the State Societies in carrying out this part of the program. (Kansas spearheaded the work which brought an endorsement from the American Farm Bureau Federation; California first initiated the drive which brought favorable action from the American Legion National Convention.)
4. National *coordination of the work in the 48 States,* the District of Columbia and the several Territories. There will be a constant flow of information between National and State headquarters, with reports of changing conditions and vital developments in the campaign. Programs and ideas which have worked successfully in some of the States will be made available, through a National exchange service, to the others.
5. *Production of all basic campaign literature and materials,* including posters, pamphlets, leaflets, reprints, form resolutions and form speeches, cartoons and mats, publicity which can be adapted for State use, lists of organizations, conventions, etc. This is one of the biggest and most urgent jobs in National Headquarters—and the materials will start to flow to the States just as fast as copy-writers, artists, engravers and printers can turn out finished products. As an indication of the tremendous production problems involved, in carrying our story direct to the American people, press runs of pamphlets and other materials are expected to total 100 million copies during the first twelve months of the campaign. About one-third of that stockpile of "ammunition" will be released directly through National facilities, with the remaining two-thirds destined for distribution through the States.
6. Organization and direction of *a National Speakers Bureau* to cover top-assignment speaking engagements. State Medical Societies are urgently requested to send in the names of dynamic speakers (either doctors or laymen) who are *qualified* and *willing* to take out-of-State assignments. Our immediate goal: *Two top men from each State!*
7. Direction of *a National Women's Campaign,* geared to bring the support of the major women's organizations, and to arouse women throughout the Nation to the threat of socialized medicine.
8. Active *cooperation with the pre-paid medical and hospital plans and the accident and health insurance companies in an all-out drive to provide the American people with voluntary health insurance coverage.* Special literature will be produced for use of the voluntary systems—and the A.M.A. campaign will be closely meshed with the promotional work of the Blue Shield, Blue Cross and private indemnity companies.

THE STATE MEDICAL SOCIETIES' JOB

One of the first jobs of every State Medical Society (where it hasn't already been done) will be to organize every County Society into a hard-driving campaign organization.

Due to varying local conditions, each State, of course, will work out its own campaign structure—and the relationship between the State and County Societies in the conduct of the campaign. Many of the States already have scheduled meetings of County representatives, patterned somewhat after the National meeting of State leaders in Chicago on February 12. In other States, battle orders are going out by letter, telegraph and telephone.

AUXILIARIES

Above all, don't overlook or discount the Auxiliaries in setting up your State-County campaign organization. The women may be one of the answers to your problem of literature distribution; they certainly should be of positive assistance in getting endorsements from women's clubs, in talking to club editors on the newspapers, in helping to build an effective Speakers' Bureau. A doctor's wife usually has more time than a busy doctor—and she has a personal stake in this campaign!

* * * * * *

1.   Why did the A.M.A. turn to a public relations firm for help? What does this suggest about the nature of postwar politics?

2.   What are the key elements in the campaign as outlined here? How does the A.M.A. hope to discredit national health care and improve its own image?

3.   What reasons would the A.M.A. have for opposing national health insurance?

26–6   Ronald Reagan and Albert Maltz, Testimony before HUAC, 1947

The House Un-American Activities Committee began to investigate charges of alleged communist influence in the movie industry in the fall of 1947. The hearings attracted an enormous amount of press attention due to the glamour associated with Hollywood celebrities. HUAC began with a group of so-called "friendly" witnesses who cooperated with the investigation for a variety of reasons, including a desire to settle old political scores. The Committee then moved to the "unfriendly" witnesses. These included some who were or had been members of the Communist Party, but all of whom rejected HUAC's intrusion into their political beliefs.

Ronald Reagan, a friendly witness, was president of the Screen Actors Guild. Albert Maltz, an unfriendly witness, was active in the Screen Writers Guild.

SOURCE: U.S. Congress, House, Committee on Un-American Activities. *Hearings* (1947).

Testimony of Ronald Reagan

Mr. Stripling: Are you the president of the guild at the present time?

Mr. Reagan: Yes, sir....

Mr. Stripling: Have you ever held any other position in the Screen Actors Guild?

Mr. Reagan: Yes, sir. Just prior to the war I was a member of the board of directors, and just after the war, prior to my being elected president, I was a member of the board of directors.

Mr. Stripling: As a member of the board of directors, as president of the Screen Actors Guild, and as an active member, have you at any time observed or noted within the organization a clique of either Communists or Fascists who were attempting to exert influence or pressure on the guild?

Mr. Reagan: Well, sir, my testimony must be very similar to that of Mr. [George] Murphy and Mr. [Robert] Montgomery. There has been a small group within the Screen Actors Guild which has consistently opposed the policy of the guild board and officers of the guild, as evidenced by the vote on various issues. That small clique referred to has been suspected of more or less following the tactics that we associated with the Communist Party

Mr. Stripling: Would you refer to them as a disruptive influence within the guild?

Mr. Reagan: I would say that at times they have attempted to be a disruptive influence.

Mr.Stripling: You have no knowledge yourself as to whether or not any of them are members of the Communist Party?

Mr. Reagan: No, sir, I have no investigative force, or anything, and I do not know.

Mr. Stripling: Has it ever been reported to you that certain members of the guild were Communists?

Mr. Reagan: Yes, sir, I have heard different discussions and some of them tagged as Communists.

Mr. Stripling: Would you say that this clique has attempted to dominate the guild?

Mr. Reagan: Well, sir, by attempting to put over their own particular views on various issues, I guess you would have to say that our side was attempting to dominate, too, because we were fighting just as hard to put over our views, and I think we were proven correct by the figures—Mr. Murphy gave the figures—and those figures were always approximately the same, an average of ninety percent or better of the Screen Actors Guild voted in favor of those matters now guild policy.

Mr. Stripling: Mr. Reagan, there has been testimony to the effect here that numerous Communist-front organizations have been set up in Hollywood. Have you ever been solicited to join any of those organizations or any organization which you considered to be a Communist-front organization?

Mr. Reagan: Well, sir, I have received literature from an organization called the Committee for a Far-Eastern Democratic Policy. I don't know whether it is Communist or not. I only know that I didn't like their views and as a result I didn't want to have anything to do with them....

Mr. Stripling: Mr. Reagan, what is your feeling about what steps should be taken to rid the motion-picture industry of any Communist influences?

Mr. Reagan: Well, sir, ninety-nine percent of us are pretty well aware of what is going on, and I think, within the bounds of our democratic rights and never once stepping over the rights given us by democracy, we have done a pretty good job in our business of keeping those people's activities curtailed. After all, we must recognize them at present as a political party. On that basis we have exposed their lies when we came across them, we have opposed their propaganda, and I can certainly testify that in the case of the Screen Actors Guild we have been eminently successful in preventing them from, with their usual tactics, trying to run

a majority of an organization with a well-organized minority. In opposing those people, the best thing to do is make democracy work. in the Screen Actors Guild we make it work by insuring everyone a vote and by keeping everyone informed. I believe that, as Thomas Jefferson put it, if all the American people know all of the facts they will never make a mistake. Whether the Party should be outlawed, that is a matter for the Government to decide. As a citizen, I would hesitate to see any political party outlawed on the basis of its political ideology. We have spent a hundred and seventy years in this country on the basis that democracy is strong enough to stand up and fight against the inroads of any ideology. However, if it is proven that an organization is an agent of a foreign power, or in any way not a legitimate political party—and I think the Government is capable of proving that— then that is another matter. I happen to be very proud of the industry in which I work; I happen to be very proud of the way in which we conducted the fight. I do not believe the Communists have ever at any time been able to use the motion-picture screen as a sounding board for their philosophy or ideology.

TESTIMONY OF ALBERT MALTZ

THE CHAIRMAN. Mr. Maltz, the committee is unanimous in permitting you to read the statement.

MR. MALTZ. Thank you.

I am an American and I believe there is no more proud word in the vocabulary of man. I am a novelist and screen writer and I have produced a certain body of work in the past 15 years. As with any other writer, what I have written has come from the total fabric of my life—my birth in this land, our schools and games, our atmosphere of freedom, our tradition of inquiry, criticism, discussion, tolerance. Whatever I am, America has made me. And I, in turn, possess no loyalty as great as the one I have to this land, to the economic and social welfare of its people, to the perpetuation and development of its democratic way of life.

Now at the age of 39, I am commanded to appear before the House Committee on Un-American Activities. For a full week this committee has encouraged an assortment of well-rehearsed witnesses to testify that I and others are subversive and un-American. It has refused us the opportunity that any pickpocket receives in a magistrate's court—the right to cross-examine these witnesses, to refute their testimony, to reveal their motives, their history, and who, exactly, they are. Furthermore it grants these witnesses congressional immunity so that we may not sue them for libel for their slanders.

I maintain that this is an evil and vicious procedure; that it is legally unjust and morally indecent—and that it places in danger every other American, since if the right of any one citizen can be invaded, then the constitutional guaranties of every other American have been subverted and no one is any longer protected from official tyranny.

What is it about me that this committee wishes to destroy? My writings? Very well, let us refer to them.

My novel, *The Cross and the Arrow,* was issued in a special edition of 140,000 copies by a wartime Government agency, the armed services edition, for American servicemen abroad.

My short stories have been reprinted in over 30 anthologies, by as many American publishers—all subversive, no doubt.

My film, *The Pride of the Marines,* was premiered in 28 cities at Guadal-canal Day banquets under the auspices of the United States Marine Corps.

Another film, *Destination Tokyo,* was premiered aboard a United States submarine and was adopted by the Navy as an official training film.

My short film, *The House I Live In,* was given a special award by the Academy of Motion Picture Arts and Sciences for its contribution to racial tolerance.

My short story, *The Happiest Man on Earth,* won the 1938 O. Henry Memorial Award for the best American short story.

This, then, is the body of work for which this committee urges I be blacklisted in the film industry—and tomorrow, if it has its way in the publishing and magazine fields also.

By cold censorship, if not legislation, I must not be allowed to write. Will this censorship stop with me? Or with the others now singled out for attack? If it requires acceptance of the ideas of this committee to remain immune from the brand of un-Americanism, then who is ultimately safe from this committee except members of the Ku Klux Klan?

Why else does this committee now seek to destroy me and others? Because of our ideas, unquestionably. In 1801, when he was President of the United States, Thomas Jefferson wrote:

Opinion, and the just maintenance of it, shall never be a crime in my view; nor bring injury to the individual.

But a few years ago, in the course of one of the hearings of this committee, Congressman J. Parnell

Thomas said, and I quote from the official transcript:

I just want to say this now, that it seems that the New Deal is working along hand in glove with the Communist Party. The New Deal is either for the Communist Party or it is playing into the hands of the Communist Party.

Very well, then, here is the other reason why I and others have been commanded to appear before this committee—our ideas. In common with many Americans, I supported the New Deal. In common with many Americans I supported, against Mr. Thomas and Mr. Rankin, the anti-lynching bill. I opposed them in my support of OPA controls and emergency veteran housing and a fair employment practices law. I signed petitions for these measures, joined organizations that advocated them, contributed money, sometimes spoke from public platforms, and I will continue to do so. I will take my philosophy from Thomas Payne, Thomas Jefferson, Abraham Lincoln, and I will not be dictated to or intimidated by men to whom the Ku Klux Klan, as a matter of committee record, is an acceptable American institution.

I state further that on many questions of public interest my opinions as a citizen have not always been in accord with the opinions of the majority. They are not now nor have my opinions ever been fixed and unchanging, nor are they now fixed and unchangeable; but, right or wrong, I claim and I insist upon my right to think freely and to speak freely; to join the Republican Party or the Communist Party, the Democratic or the Prohibition Party; to publish whatever I please; to fix my mind or change my mind, without dictation from anyone; to offer any criticism I think fitting of any public official or policy; to join whatever organizations I please, no matter what certain legislators may think of them. Above all, I challenge the right of this committee to inquire into my political or religious beliefs, in any manner or degree, and I assent that not the conduct of this committee but its very existence are a subversion of the Bill of Rights.

If I were a spokesman for General Franco, I would not be here today. I would rather be here. I would rather die than be a shabby American, groveling before men whose names are Thomas and Rankin, but who now carry out activities in America like those carried out in Germany by Goebbels and Himmler.

The American people are going to have to choose between the Bill of Rights and the Thomas committee. They cannot have both. One or the other must be abolished in the immediate future.

THE CHAIRMAN. Mr. Stripling (pounding gavel). Mr. Stripling.

MR. STRIPLING. Mr. Maltz, what is your occupation?

MR. MALTZ. I am a writer.

MR. STRIPLING. Are you employed in the motion-picture industry?

MR. MALTZ. I work in various fields of writing and I have sometimes accepted employment in the motion-picture industry.

MR. STRIPLING. Have you written the scripts for a number of pictures?

MR. MALTZ. It is a matter of public record that I have written scripts for certain motion pictures.

MR. STRIPLING. Are you a member of the Screen Writers Guild?

THE CHAIRMAN. Louder, Mr. Stripling.

MR. STRIPLING. Are you a member of the Screen Writers Guild?

MR. MALTZ. Next you are going to ask me what religious group I belong to.

THE CHAIRMAN. No, no; we are not.

MR. MALTZ. And any such question as that—

THE CHAIRMAN. I know.

MR. MALTZ. Is an obvious attempt to invade my rights under the Constitution.

MR. STRIPLING. Do you object to answering whether or not you are a member of the Screen Writers Guild?

MR. MALTZ. I have not objected to answering that question. On the contrary, I point out that next you are going to ask me whether or not I am a member of a certain religious group and suggest that I be blacklisted from an industry because I am a member of a group you don't like.

(The chairman pounds gavel.)

MR. STRIPLING. Mr. Maltz, do you decline to answer the question?

MR. MALTZ. I certainly do not decline to answer the question. I have answered the question.

MR. STRIPLING. I repeat, Are you a member of the Screen Writers Guild?

MR. MALTZ. And I repeat my answer, sir, that any such question is an obvious attempt to invade my list of organizations as an American citizen and I would be a shabby American if I didn't answer as I have.

MR. STRIPLING. Mr. Maltz, are you a member of the Communist Party?

MR. MALTZ. Next you are going to ask what my religious beliefs are.

MR. McDOWELL. That is not answering the question.

MR. MALTZ. And you are going to insist before various members of the industry that since you do not like my religious beliefs I should not work in such industry. Any such question is quite irrelevant.

MR. STRIPLING. I repeat the question. Are you now or have you ever been a member of the Communist Party?

MR. MALTZ. I have answered the question, Mr. Stripling. I am sorry. I want you to know—

MR. McDOWELL. I object to that statement.

THE CHAIRMAN. Excuse the witness. No more questions. Typical Communist line....

* * * * * *

1. *What influences does Reagan believe that communists have in the Screen Actors Guild and in motion picture content?*

2. *What reasons does Reagan give for cooperating with the HUAC?*

3. *How does Maltz justify his refusal to answer questions? What does he think are the motives behind the HUAC investigation?*

26–7 *Joseph McCarthy, Speech at Wheeling, West Virginia, 1950*

Anticommunism had already become the dominant political issue of the day when Senator Joseph McCarthy (Republican, Wisconsin) burst upon the national scene with this 1950 speech. McCarthy injected a new level of hysteria and intensity into the debate over the communist threat. He claimed the State Department, the Democratic Party, even the Army, were riddled with traitors. He used the press, a wide network of sympathetic government officials, and his power *as chair of a Senate subcommittee to mount a one-man crusade against the Communist menace. Before his censure by the Senate in 1954, McCarthy's attacks, smears, and bullying tactics made him the most influential and feared politician in America.*

SOURCE: *Congressional Record*, 81st Congress, 2nd Sess., 1954–57.

Five years after a world war has been won, men's hearts should anticipate a long peace, and men's minds should be free from the heavy weight that comes with war. But this is not such a period—for this is not a period of peace. This is a time of the "cold war." This is a time when all the world is split into two vast, increasingly hostile armed camps—a time of a great armaments race....

Today we are engaged in a final, all-out battle between communistic atheism and Christianity. The modern champions of communism have selected this as the time. And, ladies and gentlemen, the chips are down—they are truly down....

Six years ago, at the time of the first conference to map out the peace—Dumbarton Oaks—there was within the Soviet orbit 180,000,000 people. Lined up on the anti-totalitarian side there were in the world at that time roughly 1,625,000,000 people. Today, only 6 years later, there are 800,000,000 people under the absolute domination of Soviet Russia—an increase of over 400 percent. On our side, the figure has shrunk to around 500,000,000. In other words, in less than 6 years the odds have changed from 9 to 1 in our favor to 8 to 5 against us. This indicates the swiftness of the tempo of Communist victories and American defeats in the cold war. As one of our outstanding historical figures once said, "When a great democracy is destroyed, it will not be because of enemies from without, but rather because of enemies from within."...

The reason why we find ourselves in a position of impotency is not because our only powerful potential enemy has sent men to invade our shores, but rather because of the traitorous actions of those who have been treated so well by this Nation. It has not been the less fortunate or members of minority groups who have been selling this Nation out, but rather those who have had all the benefits that the wealthiest nation on earth has had to offer—the finest homes, the finest college education, and the finest jobs in Government we can give.

This is glaringly true in the State Department. There the bright young men who are born with silver spoons in their mouths are the ones who have been the worst.... In my opinion the State Department, which is one of the most important government departments, is thoroughly infested with Communists.

I have in my hand 57 cases of individuals who would appear to be either card carrying members or certainly loyal to the Communist Party, but who nevertheless are still helping to shape our foreign policy....

I know that you are saying to yourself, "Well, why doesn't the Congress do something about it?" Actually, ladies and gentlemen, one of the important reasons for the graft, the corruption, the dishonesty, the disloyalty, the treason in high Government positions—one of the most important reasons why this continues is a lack of moral uprising on the part of the 140,000,000 American people. In the light of history, however, this is not hard to explain.

It is the result of an emotional hang-over and a temporary moral lapse which follows every war. It is the apathy to evil which people who have been subjected to the tremendous evils of war feel. As the people of the world see mass murder, the destruction of defenseless and innocent people, and all of the crime and lack of morals which go with war, they become numb and apathetic. It has always been thus after war.

However, the morals of our people have not been destroyed. They still exist. This cloak of numbness and apathy has only needed a spark to rekindle them. Happily, this spark has finally been supplied.

As you know, very recently the Secretary of State proclaimed his loyalty to a man guilty of what has always been considered as the most abominable of all crimes—of being a traitor to the people who gave him a position of great trust. The Secretary of State in attempting to justify his continued devotion to the man who sold out the Christian world to the atheistic world, referred to Christ's Sermon on the Mount as a justification and reason therefore, and the reaction of the American people to this would have made the heart of Abraham Lincoln happy.

When this pompous diplomat in striped pants, with a phony British accent, proclaimed to the American people that Christ on the Mount endorsed communism, high treason, and betrayal of a sacred trust, the blasphemy was so great that it awakened the dormant indignation of the American people.

He has lighted the spark which is resulting in a moral uprising and will end only when the whole sorry mess of twisted, warped thinkers are swept from the national scene so that we may have a new birth of national honesty and decency in government.

* * * * * *

1.   Why do you think McCarthy's Wheeling speech gained so much attention? What political motives might he have had?

2.   How does McCarthy's anticommunism differ from that expressed by Clark Clifford and Harry Truman (Documents 26–1, 26–3)?

26–8   *The Advertising Council, The Miracle of America, 1948*

In the immediate postwar years, American business spent millions of dollars on public relations campaigns that touted the benefits of the free-enterprise system. Some trade groups, such as the Chamber of Commerce and the National Association of Manufacturers, mounted aggressive drives aimed at rolling back liberal programs associated with the New Deal. This pamphlet, issued by a trade association of ad agencies, mass media, and corporate advertisers, offered a typically upbeat, optimistic view of the American economy.

SOURCE: The Advertising Council, *The Miracle of America* (1948).

*It all started…*when Junior looked up from his homework:

"It says here America is great and powerful on account of the American economic system. What's our economic system, Dad?"

Dad put his paper down and appeared to be thinking hard.

"I'd like to know, too," Mother put in. "I think in these times *every* American ought to be informed about what makes up the American way of life."

"So do I," Sis added.

"Well, I could give you all sorts of answers," Dad said. "But maybe we ought to get the story straight from the one who knows it best."

"Who's that?" asked Junior.

"You'll recognize him all right," Dad said. "Let's go!"

So they did…

Junior gasped. "Gee whiz—I know *him!*"

"Uncle Sam," Dad began, "my boy here wants to know what makes America great. You know—our economic system and all that. Fact is, I guess we all do."…

"In the early days, men and animals did most of our work.

"We even used the wind to run our machines.

"Then we began to use water power to turn millstones and run looms. But in some places no water power was to be had.

"We needed something better. Our inventors and business men kept testing and trying. There would be big rewards in our free market for reliable power that could be used *anywhere.*

"At last we had it—thanks to an ingenious Scotsman—James Watt. He invented an engine driven by steam made from coal!

"Later still Americans developed engines run by gasoline and electricity.

"Now we're looking for ways to use atomic power.…

"Americans are known as inventive people. Why? Because we have had the incentive to profit by making improvements—and backing them with our savings.

"When our people realized that they were free to shape their own destinies, they began to devise machines which multiplied each man's work power.

"In 1799, Eli Whitney, inventor of the cotton gin that did 50 men's work, made history with an order for

muskets awarded by the U.S. Army. Instead of building each gun separately, he turned out standard parts which could be used interchangeably on *any* gun.

"Hearing of this, the clocksmith Eli Terry started to make clocks on the same principle. With all the laborious fitting eliminated, he found that he could sell clocks for $10 apiece instead of the regular $25. In three years he and his partner, Seth Thomas sold 5,000.

"Eli Terry saw that if he cut his costs by mass production, and distributed a bigger volume more widely, he would benefit more people and make more money. And it worked out exactly that way!

"Pins had long been made by hand, selling as high as 20 cents each. Then a Connecticut man perfected machines to make *two million pins a week!*

"Down through the years, Americans invented hundreds of thousands of work-saving machines.

"Of course, it takes money to make and install those new, labor-saving machines in factories—more money than any one man could afford. A machine for one worker often costs thousands of dollars. So the owner took in many *partners*—thrifty men and women who received *stock* in exchange for their money. All these *partners* joined to form a *company* which they owned together. In order to make a profit in competition with other companies, they had to turn out better and less expensive products.

"The same new freedoms that made Americans ingenious and inventive made us better and better workers—no matter what our jobs.

"The planners and managers of industry found new and improved ways of designing factories and work flow—so that goods were turned out more quickly and cheaply.

"They found new and better ways to get those goods from the factories to the stores and into the homes. Advertising and selling opened up bigger markets by telling the story to millions.

"And the individual worker became steadily more skillful at his job. He realized that the more he could produce during the hours he worked, the more he would increase his own value. When many workers did that, it added up to national prosperity!

"Labor unions and collective bargaining strengthened the worker's sense of security and improved working conditions. The result is that America gradually developed the greatest group of skilled workers and technicians the world has ever seen.…

"It is because we Americans *produce* so much better for every hour we work that we *earn* more and can *buy* more.…

"…and the end is not yet. We have learned that *in the long run*

"When output per hour goes up, prices drop, so more people can buy and all of us gain.

"But when output per hour goes down, prices rise, so fewer people can buy and all of us lose.

"Of course, there are unusual periods when these principles don't seem to work—times when business is far above or far below normal. But over the long pull you'll find that these rules of productivity *do* apply.

"On the average, productivity has increased in the United States almost one-fifth every 10 years since 1850. We topped this in the 20 years 1920–1940, and we can do it again!"

"Can we keep right on doing it?" Dad asked.

"We certainly can!" Uncle Sam replied. "If every-body who plays a part in making things will team up to do it, we can raise productivity so far and so fast that we can share the benefits and have real security for *all* our people."

* * * * * *

1. *How does the pamphlet explain the success and uniqueness of the American economic system?*

2. *How does the Advertising Council's piece connect American economic policy and practice with patriotism?*

3. *What problems, if any, does it acknowledge?*

26–9   NSC-68, 1950

The National Security Act of 1946 reorganized the nation's military structure by creating a cabinet-level Department of Defense to coordinate all branches of the armed forces. It also created the National Security Council to advise the President and, under it, the Central Intelligence Agency. In 1950, at the request of President Truman, the NSC undertook a sweeping review of the nation's military and strategic needs. NSC-68 remained secret until 1975, but its analysis and recommendation of massive military buildup made it one of the key policy documents of the postwar era.

SOURCE: Excerpts from "NSC-68: A Report to the National Security Council," April 14, 1950, from The Naval War College Review 27/6, May/June 1975, pp. 51–108. Reprinted by permission of the Naval War College Review.

Within the past thirty-five years the world has experienced two global wars of tremendous violence. It has witnessed two revolutions—the Russian and the Chinese—of extreme scope and intensity. It has also seen the collapse of five empires—the Ottoman, the Austro-Hungarian, German, Italian and Japanese—and the drastic decline of two major imperial systems, the British and the French. During the span of one generation, the international distribution of power has been fundamentally altered. For several centuries it had proved impossible for any one nation to gain such preponderant strength that a coalition of other nations could not in time face it with greater strength. The international scene was marked by recurring periods of violence and war, but a system of sovereign and independent states was maintained, over which no state was able to achieve hegemony.

Two complex sets of factors have now basically altered this historical distribution of power. First, the defeat of Germany and Japan and the decline of the British and French Empires have interacted with the development of the United States and the Soviet Union in such a way that power has increasingly gravitated to these two centers. Second, the Soviet Union, unlike previous aspirants to hegemony, is animated by a new fanatic faith, antithetical to our own, and seeks to impose its absolute authority over the rest of the world. Conflict has, therefore, become endemic and is waged, on the part of the Soviet Union, by violent or non-violent methods in accordance with the dictates of expediency. With the development of increasingly terrifying weapons of mass destruction, every individual faces the ever-present possibility of annihilation should the conflict enter the phase of total war.

On the one hand, the people of the world yearn for relief from the anxiety arising from the risk of atomic war. On the other hand, any substantial further extension of the area under the domination of the Kremlin would raise the possibility that no coalition adequate to confront the Kremlin with greater strength could be assembled. It is in this context that this Republic and its citizens in the ascendancy of their strength stand in their deepest peril.

The issues that face us are momentous, involving the fulfillment or destruction not only of this Republic but of civilization itself. They are issues which will not await our deliberations. With conscience and resolution this Government and the people it represents must now take new and fateful decisions....

Our overall policy at the present time may be described as one designed to foster a world environment in which the American system can survive and flourish. It therefore rejects the concept of isolation and affirms the necessity of our positive participation in the world community.

This broad intention embraces two subsidiary policies. One is a policy which we would probably pursue even if there were no Soviet threat. It is a policy of attempting to develop a healthy international community. The other is the policy of "containing" the Soviet system. These two policies are closely interrelated and interact on one another. Nevertheless, the distinction between them is basically valid and contributes to a clearer understanding of what we are trying to do.

The policy of striving to develop a healthy international community is the long-term constructive effort which we are engaged in. It was this policy which gave rise to our vigorous sponsorship of the United Nations. It is of course the principal reason for our long continuing endeavors to create and now develop the Inter-American system. It, as much as containment, underlay our efforts to rehabilitate Western Europe. Most of our international economic activities can likewise be explained in terms of this policy.

In a world of polarized power, the policies designed to develop a healthy international community are more than ever necessary to our own strength....

A comprehensive and decisive program to win the peace and frustrate the Kremlin design should be so designed that it can be sustained for as long as necessary to achieve our national objectives. It would probably involve:

1.   The development of an adequate political and economic framework for the achievement of our long-range objectives.

2.   A substantial increase in expenditures for military purposes adequate to meet the requirements for the tasks listed in Section D–1.

3.   A substantial increase in military assistance programs, designed to foster cooperative efforts, which will adequately and efficiently meet the requirements of our allies for the tasks referred to in Section D–1–*e.*

4.   Some increase in economic assistance programs and recognition of the need to continue these programs until their purposes have been accomplished.

5.   A concerted attack on the problem of the United States balance of payments, along the lines already approved by the President.

6.   Development of programs designed to build and maintain confidence among other peoples in our strength and resolution, and to wage overt psychological warfare calculated to encourage mass defections from Soviet allegiance and to frustrate the Kremlin design in other ways.

7.   Intensification of affirmative and timely measures and operations by covert means in the fields of economic warfare and political and psychological warfare with a view to fomenting and supporting unrest and revolt in selected strategic satellite countries.

8.   Development of internal security and civilian defense programs.

9.   Improvement and intensification of intelligence activities.

10. Reduction of Federal expenditures for purposes other than defense and foreign assistance, if necessary by the deferment of certain desirable programs.

11. Increased taxes....

CONCLUSIONS AND RECOMMENDATIONS

The foregoing analysis indicates that the probable fission bomb capability and possible thermonuclear bomb capability of the Soviet Union have greatly intensified the Soviet threat to the security of the United States. This threat is of the same character as that described in NSC 20/4 (approved by the President on November 24, 1948) but is more immediate than had previously been estimated. In particular, the United States now faces the contingency that within the next four or five years the Soviet Union will possess the military capability of delivering a surprise atomic attack of such weight that the United States must have substantially increased general air, ground, and sea strength, atomic capabilities, and air and civilian defenses to deter war and to provide reasonable assurance, in the event of war, that it could survive the initial blow and go on to the eventual attainment of its objectives. In turn, this contingency requires the intensification of our efforts in the fields of intelligence and research and development....

In the light of present and prospective Soviet atomic capabilities, the action which can be taken under present programs and plans, however, becomes dangerously inadequate, in both timing and scope, to accomplish the rapid progress toward the attainment of the United States political, economic, and military objectives which is now imperative.

A continuation of present trends would result in a serious decline in the strength of the free world relative to the Soviet Union and its satellites. This unfavorable trend arises from the inadequacy of current programs and plans rather than from any error in our objectives and aims. These trends lead in the direction of isolation, not by deliberate decision but by lack of the necessary basis for a vigorous initiative in the conflict with the Soviet Union.

Our position as the center of power in the free world places a heavy responsibility upon the United States for leadership. We must organize and enlist the energies and resources of the free world in a positive program for peace which will frustrate the Kremlin design for world domination by creating a situation in the free world to which the Kremlin will be compelled to adjust. Without such a cooperative effort, led by the United States, we will have to make gradual withdrawals under pressure until we discover one day that we have sacrificed positions of vital interest.

It is imperative that this trend be reversed by a much more rapid and concerted build-up of the actual strength of both the United States and the other nations of the free world. The analysis shows that this will be costly and will involve significant domestic financial and economic adjustments.

The execution of such a build-up, however, requires that the United States have an affirmative program beyond the solely defensive one of countering the threat posed by the Soviet Union. This program must light the path to peace and order among nations in a system based on freedom and justice, as contemplated in the in Charter of the United Nations. Further, it must envisage the political and economic measures with which and the military shield behind which the free world can work to frustrate the Kremlin design by the strategy of the cold war: for every consideration of devotion to our fundamental values and to our national security demands that we achieve our objectives by the strategy of the cold war, building up our military strength in order that it may not have to be used. The only sure victory lies in the frustration of the Kremlin design by the steady development of the moral and material strength of the free world and its projection into the Soviet world in such a way as to bring about an internal change in the Soviet system. Such a positive program— harmonious with our fundamental national purpose and our objectives—is necessary if we are to regain and retain the initiative and to win and hold the necessary popular support and cooperation in the United States and the rest of the free world.

This program should include a plan for negotiation with the Soviet Union, developed and agreed with our allies and which is consonant with our objectives. The United States and its allies, particularly the United Kingdom and France, should always be ready to negotiate with the Soviet Union on terms consistent with our objectives. The present world situation, however, is one which militates against successful negotiations with the Kremlin—for the terms of agreements on important pend-

ing issues would reflect present realities and would therefore be unacceptable, if not disastrous, to the United States and the rest of the free world. After a decision and a start on building up the strength of the free world has been made, it might then be desirable for the United States to take an initiative in seeking negotiations in the hope that it might facilitate the process of accommodation by the Kremlin to the new situation. Failing that, the unwillingness of the Kremlin to accept equitable terms or its bad faith in observing them would assist in consolidating popular opinion in the free world in support of the measures necessary to sustain the build-up.

In summary, we must, by means of a rapid and sustained build-up of the political, economic, and military strength of the free world, and by means of an affirmative program intended to wrest the initiative from the Soviet Union, confront it with convincing evidence of the determination and ability of the free world to frustrate the Kremlin design of a world dominated by its will. Such evidence is the only means short of war which eventually may force the Kremlin to abandon its present course of action and to negotiate acceptable agreements on issues of major importance.

The whole success of the proposed program hangs ultimately on recognition by this Government, the American people, and all free peoples, that the cold war is in fact a real war in which the survival of the free world is at stake. Essential prerequisites to success are consultations with Congressional leaders designed to make the program the object of non-partisan legislative support, and a presentation to the public of a full explanation of the facts and implications of the present international situation. The prosecution of the program will require of us all the ingenuity, sacrifice, and unity demanded by the vital importance of the issue and the tenacity to persevere until our national objectives have been attained.

* * * * * *

1.   *How does NSC–68 contrast the current global balance of power with earlier historical eras? How does its analysis of Soviet society and objectives compare with that of the Clifford memorandum (Document 26–1)?*

2.   *How does NSC–68 link military and economic policy? What specific strategies does it recommend for "frustration of the Kremlin design"?*

chapter 27

America at Midcentury, 1952–1963

27-1 The Teenage Consumer, 1959

One consequence of the postwar "baby boom" was the emergence of a growing "teen market." For the first time, businesses designed product lines and advertising appeals aimed specifically at teenagers with money to spend. The following report from Life Magazine *outlines how teenage buying power had become an integral part of the larger consumer culture of the postwar era.*

SOURCE: "A Young $10 Billion Power," in *Life Magazine,* August 31, 1959. Courtesy of Life Magazine, © Time Warner.

Life Magazine Identifies the New Teenage Market, 1959

To some people the vision of a leggy adolescent happily squealing over the latest fancy present from Daddy is just another example of the way teen-agers are spoiled to death these days. But to a growing number of businessmen the picture spells out the profitable fact that the American teen-agers have emerged as a big-time consumer in the U.S. economy. They are multiplying in numbers. They spend more and have more spent on them. And they have minds of their own about what they want.

The time is past when a boy's chief possession was his bike and a girl's party wardrobe consisted of a fancy dress worn with a string of dime-store pearls. What Depression-bred parents may still think of as luxuries are looked on as necessities by their offspring. Today teen-agers surround themselves with a fantastic array of garish and often expensive baubles and amusements. They own 10 million phonographs, over a million TV sets, 13 million cameras. Nobody knows how much parents spend on them for actual necessities nor to what extent teen-agers act as hidden persuaders on their parents' other buying habits. Counting only what is spent to satisfy their special teen-age demands, the youngsters and their parents will shell out about $10 billion this year, a billion more than the total sales of GM.

Until recently businessmen have largely ignored the teen-age market. But now they are spending millions on advertising and razzle-dazzle promotional stunts. Their efforts so far seem only to have scratched the surface of a rich lode. In 1970, when the teen-age population expands from its present 18 million to 28 million, the market may be worth $20 billion. If parents have any idea of organized revolt, it is already too late. Teenage spending is so important that such action would send quivers through the entire national economy....

At 17 Suzie Slattery of Van Nuys, Calif. fits any businessman's dream of the ideal teen-age consumer. The daughter of a reasonably well-to-do TV announcer, Suzie costs her parents close to $4,000 a year, far more than average for the country but not much more than many of the upper middle income families of her town. In an expanding economy more and more teen-agers will be moving up into Suzie's bracket or be influenced as consumers by her example.

Last year $1,500 was spent on Suzie's clothes and $550 for her entertainment. Her annual food bill comes to $900. She pays $4 every two weeks at the beauty parlor. She has her own telephone and even has her own soda fountain in the house. On summer vacation days she loves to wander with her mother through fashionable department stores, picking out frocks or furnishings for her room or silver and expensive crockery for the hope chest she has already started.

As a high school graduation present, Suzie was given a holiday cruise to Hawaii and is now in the midst of a new clothes-buying spree for college. Her parents' constant indulgence has not spoiled Suzie. She takes for granted all the luxuries that surround her because she has had them all her life. But she also has a good mind and some serious interests. A top student in her school, she is entering Occidental College this fall and will major in political science....

SOME FASCINATING FACTS ABOUT A BOOMING MARKET

FOOD: Teen-agers eat 20% more than adults. They down 3 1/2 billion quarts of milk every year, almost four times as much as is drunk by the infant population under 1. Teen-agers are a main prop of the ice cream industry, gobbling 145 million gallons a year.

BEAUTY CARE: Teen-agers spent $20 million on lipstick last year, $25 million on deodorants (a fifth of total sold), $9 million on home permanents. Male teenagers own 2 million electric razors.

ENTERTAINMENT: Teen-agers lay out more than $1.5 billion a year for entertainment. They spend about $75 million on single pop records. Although they create new musical idols, they are staunchly faithful to the old. Elvis Presley, still their favorite, has sold 25 million copies of single records in four years, an all-time high.

HOMEMAKERS: Major items like furniture and silver are moving into the teen-age market because of a growing number of teen-age marriages. One-third of all 18- and 19-year-old girls are already married. More than 600,000 teen-agers will be married this year. Teen-agers are now starting hope chests at 15.

CREDIT RISKS: Some 800,000 teen-agers work at full-time jobs and can buy major items on credit.

* * * * * *

1. *To what extent is the new youth market a product of money earned by teenagers, as opposed to money earned by their parents?*

2. *Many parents and social scientists of the day expressed anxiety over the emergence of a separate teenage culture. Did the business community express any similar fears?*

27–2   *Dwight D. Eisenhower, Farewell Address, 1961*

As Supreme Commander of Allied forces during World War II, Dwight D. Eisenhower had won wide admiration for forging an effective fighting force out of a huge agglomeration of disparate armies and military leaders. As president, Eisenhower's conservative managerial style emphasized national unity in the face of conflict. His conservatism also caused him to worry over the rapid growth of the arms race and the "military-industrial complex."

SOURCE: Papers of the Presidents: Dwight D. Eisenhower (1960–1961).

Three days from now, after half a century in the service of our country, I shall lay down the responsibilities of office as, in traditional and solemn ceremony, the authority of the Presidency is vested in my successor....

We now stand ten years past the midpoint of a century that has witnessed four major wars among great nations. Three of them involved our own country. Despite these holocausts America is today the strongest, the most influential and most productive nation in the world. Understandably proud of this pre-eminence we yet realize that America's leadership and prestige depend, not merely upon our unmatched material progress, riches and military strength, but on how we use our power in the interests of world peace and human betterment.

Throughout America's adventure in free government, our basic purposes have been to keep the peace; to foster progress in human achievement, and to enhance liberty, dignity and integrity among people and among nations. To strive for less would be unworthy of a free and religious people. Any failure traceable to arrogance, or our lack of comprehension or readiness to sacrifice would inflict upon us grievous hurt both at home and abroad.

Progress toward these noble goals is persistently threatened by the conflict now engulfing the world. It commands our whole attention, absorbs our very beings. We face a hostile ideology—global in scope, atheistic in character, ruthless in purpose, and insidious in method.

Unhappily the danger it poses promises to be of indefinite duration. To meet it successfully, there is called for, not so much the emotional and transitory sacrifices of crisis, but rather those which enable us to carry forward steadily, surely, and without complaint the burdens of a prolonged and complex struggle—with liberty the stake. Only thus shall we remain, despite every provocation, on our charted course toward permanent peace and human betterment....

A vital element in keeping the peace is our military establishment. Our arms must be mighty, ready for instant action, so that no potential aggressor may be tempted to risk his own destruction.

Our military organization today bears little relation to that known by any of my predecessors in peacetime, or indeed by the fighting men of World War II or Korea.

Until the latest of our world conflicts, the United States had no armaments industry. American makers of plowshares could, with time and as required, make swords as well. But now we can no longer risk emergency improvisation of national defense; we have been compelled to create a permanent armaments industry of vast proportions. Added to this, three and a half million men and women are directly engaged in the defense establishment. We annually spend on military security more than the net income of all United States corporations.

This conjunction of an immense military establishment and a large arms industry is new in the American experience. The total influence—economic, political, even spiritual—is felt in every city, every statehouse, every office of the federal government. We recognize the imperative need for this development. Yet we must not fail to comprehend its grave implications. Our toil, resources, and livelihood are all involved; so is the very structure of our society.

In the councils of government, we must guard against the acquisition of unwarranted influence, whether sought or unsought, by the military-industrial complex. The potential for the disastrous rise of misplaced power exists and will persist. We must never let the weight of this combination endanger our liberties or democratic processes. We should take nothing for granted. Only an alert and knowledgeable citizenry can compel the proper meshing of the huge industrial and military machinery of defense with our peaceful methods and goals, so that security and liberty may prosper together.

Akin to, and largely responsible for the sweeping changes in our industrial-military posture, has been the technological revolution during recent decades.

In this revolution, research has become central; it also becomes more formalized, complex, and costly. A steadily increasing share is conducted for, by, or at the direction of, the federal government....

The prospect of domination of the nation's scholars by federal employment, project allocations, and the power of money is ever present—and is gravely to be regarded.

Yet, in holding scientific research and discovery in respect, as we should, we must also be alert to the equal and opposite danger that public policy could itself become the captive of a scientific-technological elite.

It is the task of statesmanship to mold, to balance, and to integrate these and other forces, new and old, within the principles of our democratic system—ever aiming toward the supreme goals of our free society.

Another factor in maintaining balance involves the element of time. As we peer into society's future, we—you and I, and our government—must avoid the impulse to live only for today, plundering, for our own ease and convenience, the precious resources of tomorrow. We cannot mortgage the material assets of our grandchildren without risking the loss also of their political and spiritual heritage. We want democracy to survive for all generations to come, not to become the insolvent phantom of tomorrow.

Down the long lane of the history yet to be written America knows that this world of ours, ever growing smaller, must avoid becoming a community of dreadful fear and hate, and be, instead, a proud confederation of mutual trust and respect.

Such a confederation must be one of equals. The weakest must come to the conference table with the same confidence as do we, protected as we are by our moral, economic, and military strength. That table, though scarred by many past frustrations, cannot be abandoned for the certain agony of the battlefield.

Disarmament, with mutual honor and confidence, is a continuing imperative. Together we must learn how to compose differences, not with arms, but with intellect and decent purpose. Because this need is so sharp and apparent I confess that I lay down my official responsibilities in this field with a definite sense of disappointment. As one who has witnessed the horror and the lingering sadness of war—as one who knows that another war could utterly destroy this civilization which has been so slowly and painfully built over thousands of years—I wish I could say tonight that a lasting peace is in sight.

Happily, I can say that war has been avoided. Steady progress toward our ultimate goal has been made. But, so much remains to be done. As a private citizen, I shall never cease to do what little I can to help the world advance along that road....

* * * * * *

1. *Dwight D. Eisenhower had been a military man all his life. Why did he choose to focus on the dangers of military buildup in his farewell to the American people?*

2. *What specific threats does Eisenhower see posed to the nation's domestic life by "an immense military establishment"? To its foreign policy?*

27–3 *John F. Kennedy Inaugural Address, 1961*

John F. Kennedy won the presidency by a tiny margin in 1960. He had promised "to get the country moving again" during his campaign, telling the nation that "We stand on the edge of a New Frontier." He cultivated an image of youthful vitality, designed to distinguish him from the Eisenhower–Nixon administration. His inaugural address, written by aide Theodore C. Sorensen, captured the themes and goals of his campaign and presidency.

SOURCE: Public Papers of the Presidents: John F. Kennedy (1961).

We observe today not a victory of party but a celebration of freedom—symbolizing an end as well as a beginning—signifying renewal as well as change. For I have sworn before you and Almighty God the same solemn oath our forebears prescribed nearly a century and three-quarters ago.

The world is very different now. For man holds in his mortal hands the power to abolish all forms of human poverty and all forms of human life. And yet the same revolutionary beliefs for which our forebears fought are still at issue around the globe—the belief that the rights of man come not from the generosity of the state but from the hand of God.

We dare not forget today that we are the heirs of that first revolution. Let the word go forth from this time and place, to friend and foe alike, that the torch has been passed to a new generation of Americans—born in this century, tempered by war, disciplined by a hard and bitter peace, proud of our ancient heritage—and unwilling to witness or permit the slow undoing of those human rights to which this nation has always been committed, and to which we are committed today at home and around the world.

Let every nation know, whether it wishes us well or ill, that we shall pay any price, bear any burden, meet any hardship, support any friend, oppose any foe to assure the survival and the success of liberty.

This much we pledge—and more.

To those old allies whose cultural and spiritual origins we share, we pledge the loyalty of faithful friends. United, there is little we cannot do in a host of cooperative ventures. Divided, there is little we can do—for we dare not meet a powerful challenge at odds and split asunder.

To those new states whom we welcome to the ranks of the free, we pledge our word that one form of colonial control shall not have passed away merely to be replaced by a far more iron tyranny. We shall not always expect to find them supporting our view. But we shall always hope to find them strongly supporting their own freedom—and to remember that, in the past, those who foolishly sought power by riding the back of the tiger ended up inside.

To those people in the huts and villages of half the globe struggling to break the bonds of mass misery, we pledge our best efforts to help them help themselves, for whatever period is required—not because the Communists may be doing it, not because we seek their votes, but because it is right. If a free society cannot help the many who are poor, it cannot save the few who are rich.

To our sister republics south of the border, we offer a special pledge—to convert our good words into good deeds—in a new alliance for progress—to assist free men and free governments in casting off the chains of poverty. But this peaceful revolution of hope cannot become the prey of hostile powers. Let all our neighbors know that we shall join with them to oppose aggression or subversion anywhere in the Americas. And let every other power know that this hemisphere intends to remain the master of its own house.

To that world assembly of sovereign states, the United Nations, our last best hope in an age where the instruments of war have far outpaced the instruments of peace, we renew our pledge of support—to prevent it from becoming merely a forum for invective—to strengthen its shield of the new and the weak—and to enlarge the area in which its writ may run.

Finally, to those nations who would make themselves our adversary, we offer not a pledge but a request: that both sides begin anew the quest for peace, before the dark powers of destruction unleashed by science engulf all humanity in planned or accidental self-destruction.

We dare not tempt them with weakness. For only when our arms are sufficient beyond doubt can we be certain beyond doubt that they will never be employed.

But neither can two great and powerful groups of nations take comfort from our present course—both sides overburdened by the cost of modern weapons, both rightly alarmed by the steady spread of the deadly atom, yet both racing to alter that uncertain balance of terror that stays the hand of mankind's final war.

So let us begin anew—remembering on both sides that civility is not a sign of weakness, and sincerity is always subject to proof. Let us never negotiate out of fear. But let us never fear to negotiate.

Let both sides explore what problems unite us instead of belaboring those problems which divide us.

Let both sides, for the first time, formulate serious and precise proposals for the inspection and control of arms—and bring the absolute power to destroy other nations under the absolute control of all nations.

Let both sides seek to invoke the wonders of science instead of its terrors. Together let us explore the stars, conquer the deserts, eradicate disease, tap the ocean depths, and encourage the arts and commerce.

Let both sides unite to heed in all corners of the earth the command of Isaiah—to "undo the heavy burdens...[and] let the oppressed go free."

And if a beachhead of co-operation may push back the jungle of suspicion, let both sides join in creating a new endeavor, not a new balance of power, but a new world of law, where the strong are just and the weak secure and the peace preserved.

All this will not be finished in the first one hundred days. Nor will it be finished in the first one thousand days, nor in the life of this administration, nor even perhaps in our lifetime on this planet. But let us begin.

In your hands, my fellow citizens, more than mine, will rest the final success or failure of our course. Since this country was founded, each generation of Americans has been summoned to give testimony to its national loyalty. The graves of young Americans who answered the call to service surround the globe.

Now the trumpet summons us again—not as a call to bear arms, though arms we need,—not as a call to battle, though embattled we are—but a call to bear the burden of a long twilight struggle, year in and year out, "rejoicing in hope, patient in tribulation"—a struggle against the common enemies of man: tyranny, poverty, disease, and war itself.

Can we forge against these enemies a grand and global alliance, North and South, East and West, that can assure a more fruitful life for all mankind? Will you join in that historic effort?

In the long history of the world, only a few generations have been granted the role of defending freedom in its hour of maximum danger. I do not shrink from this .responsibility—I welcome it. I do not believe that any of us would exchange places with any other people or any other generation. The energy, the faith, the devotion which we bring to this endeavor will light our country and all who serve it—and the glow from that fire can truly light the world.

And so, my fellow Americans: ask not what your country can do for you—ask what you can do for your country.

My fellow citizens of the world: ask not what America will do for you, but what together we can do for the freedom of man.

Finally, whether you are citizens of America or citizens of the world, ask of us here the same high standards of strength and sacrifice which we ask of you. With a good conscience our only sure reward, with history the final judge of our deeds, let us go forth to lead the land we love, asking His blessing and His help, but knowing that here on earth God's work must truly be our own.

* * * * * *

1. *How does Kennedy's address reflect the rhetoric and imagery of the Cold War?*

2. *What weight does Kennedy give to domestic issues, as compared with foreign relations? How would you interpret the balance between these two?*

3. *Compare Kennedy's speech with Eisenhower's farewell in terms of both style and substance.*

27–4   Newton Minow, Address to the National Association of Broadcasters, 1961

Established in 1934 to regulate the nation's public airwaves, the Federal Communications Commission made little effort to interfere with the program policies of commercial broadcasters. President Kennedy appointed Newton Minow Chairman of the FCC in 1961. In his first major policy statement, Minow shook up the broadcasting industry by candidly criticizing what he saw on television. His remarks set off a national debate over the quality and growing influence of television in American life.

SOURCE: Newton Minow, Address to the National Association of Broadcasters, 1961.

…Your industry possesses the most powerful voice in America. It has an inescapable duty to make that voice ring with intelligence and with leadership. In a few years this exciting industry has grown from a novelty to an instrument of overwhelming impact on the American people. It should be making ready for the kind of leadership that newspapers and magazines assumed years ago, to make our people aware of their world.

Ours has been called the jet age, the atomic age, the space age. It is also, I submit, the television age. And just as history will decide whether the leaders of today's world employed the atom to destroy the world or rebuild it for mankind's benefit, so will history decide whether today's broadcasters employed their powerful voice to enrich the people or debase them….

Like everybody, I wear more than one hat. I am the chairman of the FCC. I am also a television viewer and the husband and father of other television viewers. I have seen a great many television programs that seemed to me eminently worthwhile, and I am not talking about the much-bemoaned good old days of "Playhouse 90" and "Studio One."

I am talking about this past season. Some were wonderfully entertaining, such as "The Fabulous Fifties," the "Fred Astaire Show" and the "Bing Crosby Special"; some were dramatic and moving, such as Conrad's "Victory" and "Twilight Zone"; some were marvelously informative, such as "The Nation's Future," "CBS Reports," and "The Valiant Years." I could list many more—programs that I am sure everyone here felt enriched his own life and that of his family. When television is good, nothing—not the theater, not the magazines or newspapers—nothing is better.

But when television is bad, nothing is worse. I invite you to sit down in front of your television set when your station goes on the air and stay there without a book, magazine, newspaper, profit-and-loss sheet, or rating book to distract you—and keep your eyes glued to that set until the station signs off. I can assure you that you will observe a vast wasteland.

You will see a procession of game shows, violence, audience participation shows, formula comedies about totally unbelievable families, blood and thunder, mayhem, violence, sadism, murder, Western badmen, Western good men, private eyes, gangsters, more violence and cartoons. And, endlessly, commercials—many screaming, cajoling, and offending. And, most of all, boredom. True, you will see a few things you will enjoy. But they will be very, very few. And if you think I exaggerate, try it.

Is there one person in this room who claims that broadcasting can't do better?...

Why is so much of television so bad? I have heard many answers: demands of your advertisers; competition for ever higher ratings; the need always to attract a mass audience; the high cost of television programs; the insatiable appetite for programming material—these are some of them. Unquestionably these are tough problems not susceptible to easy answers.

But I am not convinced that you have tried hard enough to solve them. I do not accept the idea that the present overall programming is aimed accurately at the public taste. The ratings tell us only that some people have their television sets turned on, and, of that number, so many are tuned to one channel and so many to another. They don't tell us what the public might watch if they were offered half a dozen additional choices. A rating, at best, is an indication of how many people saw what you gave them. Unfortunately it does not reveal the depth of the penetration or the intensity of reaction, and it never reveals what the acceptance would have been if what you gave them had been better—if all the forces of art and creativity and daring and imagination had been unleashed. I believe in the people's good sense and good taste, and I am not convinced that the people's taste is as low as some of you assume....

Certainly I hope you will agree that ratings should have little influence where children are concerned. The best estimates indicate that during the hours of 5 to 6 P.M., 60 percent of your audience is composed of children under twelve. And most young children today, believe it or not, spend as much time watching television as they do in the schoolroom. I repeat—let that sink in—most young children today spend as much time watching television as they do in the schoolroom. It used to be said that there were three great influences on a child: home, school, and church. Today there is a fourth great influence, and you ladies and gentlemen control it.

If parents, teachers, and ministers conducted their responsibilities by following the ratings, children would have a steady diet of ice cream, school holidays, and no Sunday school. What about your responsibilities? Is there no room on television to teach, to inform, to uplift, to stretch, to enlarge the capacities of our children? Is there no room for programs deepening their understanding of children in other lands? Is there no room for a children's news show explaining something about the world to them at their level of understanding? Is there no room for reading the great literature of the past, teaching them the great traditions of freedom? There are some fine children's shows, but they are drowned out in the massive doses of cartoons, violence, and more violence. Must these be your trademarks? Search your consciences and see if you cannot offer more to your young beneficiaries whose future you guide so many hours each and every day.

What about adult programming and ratings? You know, newspaper publishers take popularity ratings too. The answers are pretty clear; it is almost always the comics, followed by the advice-to-the-lovelorn columns. But, ladies and gentlemen, the news is still on the front page of all newspapers, the editorials are not replaced by more comics, the newspapers have not become one long collection of advice to the lovelorn. Yet newspapers do not need a license from the government to be in business—they do not use public property. But in television— where your responsibilities as public trustees are so plain—the moment that the ratings indicate that Westerns are popular, there are new imitations of Westerns on the air faster than the old coaxial cable could take us from Hollywood to New York....

Let me make clear that what I am talking about is balance. I believe that the public interest is made up of many interests. There are many people in this great country, and you must serve all of us. You will get no argument from me if you say that, given a choice between a Western and a symphony, more people will watch the Western. I like Westerns and private eyes too—but a steady diet for the whole country is obviously not in the public interest. We all know that people would more often prefer to be entertained than stimulated or informed. But your obligations are not satisfied if you look only to popularity as a test of what to broadcast. You are not only in show business; you are free to communicate ideas as well as relaxation. You must provide a wider range of choices, more diversity, more alternatives. It is not enough to cater to the nation's whims— you must also serve the nation's needs....

Let me address myself now to my role, not as a viewer but as chairman of the FCC.... I want to make clear some of the fundamental principles which guide me.

First, the people own the air. They own it as much in prime evening time as they do at 6 o'clock Sunday morning. For every hour that the people give you, you owe them something. I intend to see that your debt is paid with service.

Second, I think it would he foolish and wasteful for us to continue any worn-out wrangle over the problems of payola, rigged quiz shows, and other mistakes of the past....

Third, I believe in the free enterprise system. I want to see broadcasting improved and I want you to do the job....

Fourth, I will do all I can to help educational television. There are still not enough educational stations, and major centers of the country still lack usable educational channels....

Fifth, I am unalterably opposed to governmental censorship. There will be no suppression of programming which does not meet with bureaucratic tastes. Censorship strikes at the taproot of our free society.

Sixth, I did not come to Washington to idly observe the squandering of the public's airwaves. The squandering of our airwaves is no less important than the lavish waste of any precious natural resource....

What you gentlemen broadcast through the people's air affects the people's taste, their knowledge, their opinions, their understanding of themselves and of their world. And their future. The power of instantaneous sight and sound is without precedent in mankind's history. This is an awesome power. It has limitless capabilities for good—and

for evil. And it carries with it awesome responsibilities—responsibilities which you and I cannot escape....

* * * * * *

1. How does Minow appeal to and define the "public interest"? What specific steps does he suggest for making the broadcasting industry more responsive to it?

2. Compare Minow's description of television fare with what you are familiar with today. Does television still merit his description as "a vast wasteland"?

27–5 John K. Galbraith, The Affluent Society, 1958

Harvard economist John K. Galbraith worked for the Office of Price Administration during World War II. His influential book The Affluent Society *surveyed the American economy in the postwar years. His title became a widely used shorthand description for postwar America, but Galbraith was in fact deeply troubled by the persistence of poverty and inequality. As an economic adviser to President Kennedy, Galbraith unsuccessfully pushed for greater federal spending on social services and job training programs.*

SOURCE: *The Affluent Society,* 4/e by John Kenneth Galbraith, Copyright © 1958, 1969, 1976, 1984 by John Kenneth Galbraith, Reprinted by permission of the Houghton Mifflin Co. All rights reserved.

The final problem of the productive society is what it produces. This manifests itself in an implacable tendency to provide an opulent supply of some things and a niggardly yield of others. This disparity carries to the point where it is a cause of social discomfort and social unhealth. The line which divides our area of wealth from our area of poverty is roughly that which divides privately produced and marketed goods and services from publicly rendered services. Our wealth in the first is not only in startling contrast with the meagerness of the latter, but our wealth in privately produced goods is, to a marked degree, the cause of crisis in the supply of public services. For we have failed to see the importance, indeed the urgent need, of maintaining a balance between the two.

This disparity between our flow of private and public goods and services is no matter of subjective judgment. On the contrary, it is the source of the most extensive comment which only stops short of the direct contrast being made here. In the years following World War II, the papers of any major city—those of New York were

an excellent example—told daily of the shortages and shortcomings in the elementary municipal and metropolitan services. The schools were old and overcrowded. The police force was under strength and underpaid. The parks and playgrounds were insufficient. Streets and empty lots were filthy, and the sanitation staff was underequipped and in need of men. Access to the city by those who work there was uncertain and painful and becoming more so. Internal transportation was overcrowded, unhealthful, and dirty. So was the air. Parking on the streets had to be prohibited, and there was no space elsewhere. These deficiencies were not in new and novel services but in old and established ones. Cities have long swept their streets, helped their people move around, educated them, kept order, and provided horse rails for vehicles which sought to pause. That their residents should have a nontoxic supply of air suggests no revolutionary dalliance with socialism.

The discussion of this public poverty competed, on the whole successfully, with the stories of ever-increasing opulence in privately produced goods. The Gross National Product was rising. So were retail sales. So was personal income. Labor productivity had also advanced. The automobiles that could not be parked were being produced at an expanded rate. The children, though without schools, subjected in the playgrounds to the affectionate interest of adults with odd tastes, and disposed to increasingly imaginative forms of delinquency, were admirably equipped with television sets. We had difficulty finding storage space for the great surpluses of food despite a national disposition to obesity. Food was grown and packaged under private auspices. The care and refreshment of the mind, in contrast with the stomach, was principally in the public domain. Our colleges and universities were severely overcrowded and underprovided, and the same was true of the mental hospitals.

The contrast was and remains evident not alone to those who read. The family which takes its mauve and cerise, air-conditioned, power-steered, and power-braked automobile out for a tour passes through cities that are badly paved, made hideous by litter, blighted buildings, billboards, and posts for wires that should long since have been put underground. They pass on into a countryside that has been rendered largely invisible by commercial art. (The goods which the latter advertise have an absolute priority in our value system. Such aesthetic considerations as a view of the countryside accordingly come second. On such matters we are consistent.) They picnic on exquisitely packaged food from a portable icebox by a polluted stream and go on to spend the night at a park which is a menace to public health and morals. Just before dozing off on an air mattress, beneath a nylon tent, amid the stench of decaying refuse, they may reflect vaguely on the curious unevenness of their blessings. Is this, indeed, the American genius?...

A feature of the years immediately following World War II was a remarkable attack on the notion of expanding and improving public services. During the depression years such services had been elaborated and improved partly in order to fill some small part of the vacuum left by the shrinkage of private production. During the war years the role of government was vastly expanded. After that came the reaction. Much of it, unquestionably, was motivated by a desire to rehabilitate the prestige of private production and therewith of producers. No doubt some who joined the attack hoped, at least tacitly, that it might be possible to sidestep the truce on taxation vis-à-vis equality by having less taxation of all kinds. For a time the notion that our public services had somehow become inflated and excessive was all but axiomatic. Even liberal politicians did not seriously protest. They found it necessary to aver that they were in favor of public economy too.

In this discussion a certain mystique was attributed to the satisfaction of privately supplied wants. A community decision to have a new school means that the individual surrenders the necessary amount, willy-nilly, in his taxes. But if he is left with that income, he is a free man. He can decide between a better car or a television set. This was advanced with some solemnity as an argument for the TV set. The difficulty is that this argument leaves the community with no way of preferring the school. All private wants, where the individual can choose, are inherently superior to all desires which must be paid for by taxation and with an inevitable component of compulsion....

Urgent warnings were issued of the unfavorable effects of taxation on investment—"I don't know of a surer way of killing off the incentive to invest than by imposing taxes which are regarded by people as punitive." This was at a time when the inflationary effect of a very high level of investment was causing concern. The same individuals who were warning about the inimical effects of taxes were strongly advocating a monetary policy designed to reduce investment. However, an understanding of our economic discourse requires an appreciation of one of its basic rules: men of high position are allowed, by a special act of grace, to accommodate their reasoning to the answer they need. Logic is only required in those of lesser rank.

Finally it was argued, with no little vigor, that expanding government posed a grave threat to individual liberties. "Where distinction and rank is achieved almost exclusively by becoming a civil servant of the state...it is too much to expect that many will long prefer freedom to security."

With time this attack on public services has somewhat subsided. The disorder associated with social imbalance has become visible even if the need for balance between private and public services is still imperfectly appreciated.

Freedom also seemed to be surviving. Perhaps it was realized that all organized activity requires concessions by the individual to the group. This is true of the policeman who joins the police force, the teacher who gets a job at the high school, and the executive who makes his way up the hierarchy of Du Pont. If there are differences between public and private organization, they are of kind rather than of degree. As this is written the pendulum has in fact swung back. Our liberties are now menaced by the conformity exacted by the large corporation and its impulse to create, for its own purposes, the organization man. This danger we may also survive.

Nonetheless, the postwar onslaught on the public services left a lasting imprint. To suggest that we canvass our public wants to see where happiness can be improved by more and better services has a sharply radical tone. Even public services to avoid disorder must be defended. By contrast the man who devises a nostrum for a nonexistent need and then successfully promotes both remains one of nature's noblemen.

* * * * * *

1. *How does Galbraith distinguish between private- and public-sector spending?*

2. *How does he explain the decline in public-service spending?*

27–6 Rachel Carson, Silent Spring, 1962

Rachel Carson was a marine biologist and writer who worked for many years with the U.S. Bureau of Fisheries. She combined the imagination of a creative writer with the scientific passion for fact, and her 1951 book The Sea Around Us *became a worldwide best-seller. More than any other individual, she alerted the world to the dangers of man-made pollution upon the natural environment. Her widely influential* Silent Spring *warned of the problems posed by the widespread use of chemical pesticides and helped to launch the modern environmental movement.*

The history of life on earth has been a history of interaction between living things and their surroundings. To a large extent, the physical form and the habits of the earth's vegetation and its animal life have been molded by the environment. Considering the whole span of earthly time, the opposite effect, in which life actually modifies its surroundings, has been relatively slight. Only within the moment of time represented by the present century has one species—man—acquired significant power to alter the nature of his world.

During the past quarter century this power has not only increased to one of disturbing magnitude but it has changed in character. The most alarming of all man's assaults upon the environment is the contamination of air, earth, rivers, and sea with dangerous and even lethal materials. This pollution is for the most part irrecoverable; the chain of evil it initiates not only in the world that must support life but in living tissues is for the most part irreversible. In this now universal contamination of the environment, chemicals are the sinister and little-recognized partners of radiation in changing the very nature of the world—the very nature of its life. Strontium 90, released through nuclear explosions into the air, comes to the earth in rain or drifts down as fallout, lodges in soil, enters into the grass or corn or wheat grown there, and in time takes up its abode in the bones of a human being, there to remain until his death. Similarly, chemicals sprayed on croplands or forests or gardens lie long in the soil, entering into living organisms, passing from one to another in a chain of poisoning and death. Or they pass mysteriously by underground streams until they emerge and, through the alchemy of air and sunlight, combine into new forms that kill vegetation, sicken cattle, and

work unknown harm on those who drink from once pure wells. As Albert Schweitzer has said, "Man can hardly even recognize the devils of his own creation."

It took hundreds of millions of years to produce the life that now inhabits the earth—eons of time in which that developing and evolving and diversifying life reached a state of adjustment and balance with its surroundings. The environment, rigorously shaping and directing the life it supported, contained elements that were hostile as well as supporting. Certain rocks gave out dangerous radiation; even within the light of the sun, from which all life draws its energy, there were short-wave radiations with power to injure. Given time—time not in years but in millennia—life adjusts, and a balance has been reached. For time is the essential ingredient; but in the modern world there is no time.

The rapidity of change and the speed with which new situations are created follow the impetuous and heedless pace of man rather than the deliberate pace of nature. Radiation is no longer merely the background radiation of rocks, the bombardment of cosmic rays, the ultraviolet of the sun that have existed before there was any life on earth; radiation is now the unnatural creation of man's tampering with the atom. The chemicals to which life is asked to make its adjustment are no longer merely the calcium and silica and copper and all the rest of the minerals washed out of the rocks and carried in rivers to the sea; they are the synthetic creations of man's inventive mind, brewed in his laboratories, and having no counterparts in nature.

To adjust to these chemicals would require time on the scale that is nature's; it would require not merely the years of a man's life but the life of generations. And even this, were it by some miracle possible, would be futile, for the new chemicals come from our laboratories in an endless stream; almost five hundred annually find their way into actual use in the United States alone. The figure is staggering and its implications are not easily grasped—500 new chemicals to which the bodies of men and animals are required somehow to adapt each year, chemicals totally outside the limits of biologic experience.

Among them are many that are used in man's war against nature. Since the mid-1940s over 200 basic chemicals have been created for use in killing insects, weeds, rodents, and other organisms described in the modern vernacular as "pests"; and they are sold under several thousand different brand names.

These sprays, dusts, and aerosols are now applied almost universally to farms, gardens, forests, and homes—nonselective chemicals that have the power to kill every insect, the "good" and the "bad," to still the song of birds and the leaping of fish in the streams, to coat the leaves with a deadly film, and to linger on in the soil—all this though the intended target may be only a few weeds or insects. Can anyone believe it is possible to lay down such a barrage of poisons on the surface of the earth without making it unfit for all life? They should not be called "insecticides," but "biocides."

The whole process of spraying seems caught up in an endless spiral. Since DDT was released for civilian use, a process of escalation has been going on in which ever more toxic materials must be found. This has happened because insects, in a triumphant vindication of Darwin's principle of the survival of the fittest, have evolved super races immune to the particular insecticide used, hence a deadlier one has always to be developed— and then a deadlier one than that....

The "control of nature" is a phrase conceived in arrogance, born of the Neanderthal age of biology and philosophy, when it was supposed that nature exists for the convenience of man. The concepts and practices of applied entomology for the most part date from that Stone Age of science. It is our alarming misfortune that so primitive a science has armed itself with the most modern and terrible weapons, and that in turning them against the insects it has also turned them against the earth.

* * * * * *

1.   *Why does Carson maintain a "global" perspective on the issue of pollution?*

2.   *Why and how does she focus her critique on the most recent human abuses of the natural environment?*

27-7   *Jack Kerouac, On the Road, 1957*

The most influential and prodigious of the "Beat generation" writers, Jack Kerouac documented the lives of young people who had turned their backs on what they saw as the stifling conformity and materialism of postwar America. Although he had written it years earlier, Kerouac could not get On the Road *published until 1957. His difficulties with publishers, along with the vitriolic critical attacks on his work, helped drive Kerouac to alcoholism and death at age 47.*

SOURCE: Jack Kerouac, "On the Road" (1957), pp. 104–107, 110–112.

The parties were enormous; there were at least a hundred people at a basement apartment in the West Nineties. People overflowed into the cellar compartments near the furnace. Something was going on in every corner, on every bed and couch—not an orgy but just a New Year's party with frantic screaming and wild radio music. There was even a Chinese girl. Dean ran like Groucho Marx from group to group, digging everybody. Periodically we rushed out to the car to pick up more people. Damion came. Damion is the hero of my New York gang, as Dean is the chief hero of the Western. They immediately took a dislike to each other. Damion's girl suddenly socked Damion on the jaw with a roundhouse right. He stood reeling. She carried him home. Some of our mad newspaper friends came in from the office with bottles. There was a tremendous and wonderful snowstorm going on outside. Ed Dunkel met Lucille's sister and disappeared with her; I forgot to say that Ed Dunkel is a very smooth man with the women. He's six foot four, mild, affable, agreeable, bland, and delightful. He helps women on with their coats. That's the way to do things. At five o'clock in the morning we were all rushing through the backyard of a tenement and climbing in through a window of an apartment where a huge party was going on. At dawn we were back at Tom Saybrook's. People were drawing pictures and drinking stale beer. I slept on a couch with a girl called Mona in my arms. Great groups filed in from the old Columbia Campus bar. Everything in life, all the faces of life, were piling into the same dank room. At Ian MacArthur's the party went on. Ian MacArthur is a wonderful sweet fellow who wears glasses and peers out of them with delight. He began to learn "Yes!" to everything, just like Dean at this time, and hasn't stopped since. To the wild sounds of Dexter Gordon and Wardell Gray blowing "The Hunt," Dean and I played catch with Marylou over the couch; she was no small doll either. Dean went around with no undershirt, just his pants, barefoot, till it was time to hit the car and fetch more people. Everything happened. We found the wild, ecstatic Rollo Greb and spent a night at his house on Long Island. Rollo lives in a nice house with his aunt; when she dies the house is all his. Meanwhile she refuses to comply with any of his wishes and hates his friends. He brought this ragged gang of Dean, Marylou, Ed, and me, and began a roaring party. The woman prowled upstairs; she threatened to call the police. "Oh, shut up, you old bag!" yelled Greb. I wondered how he could live with her like this. He had more books than I've ever seen in all my life—two libraries, two rooms loaded from floor to ceiling around all four walls, and such books as the Apocryphal Something-or-Other in ten volumes. He played Verdi operas and pantomimed them in his pajamas with a great rip down the back. He didn't give a damn about anything. He is a great scholar who goes reeling down the New York waterfront with original seventeenth-century musical manuscripts under his arm, shouting. He crawls like a big spider through the streets. His excitement blew out of his eyes in stabs of fiendish light. He rolled his neck in spastic ecstasy. He lisped, he writhed, he flopped, he moaned, he howled, he fell back in despair. He could hardly get a word out, he was so excited with life. Dean stood before him with head bowed, repeating over and over again, "Yes...Yes...Yes." He took me into a corner. "That Rollo Greb is the greatest, most wonderful of all. That's what I was trying to tell you—that's what I want to be. I want to be like him. He's never hung-up, he goes every direction, he lets it all out, he knows times, he has nothing to do but rock back and forth. Man, he's the end! You see, if you go like him all the time you'll finally get it."

"Get what?"

"IT! IT! I'll tell you—now no time, we have no time now." Dean rushed back to watch Rollo Greb some more.

George Shearing, the great jazz pianist, Dean said, was exactly like Rollo Greb. Dean and I went to see Shearing at Birdland in the midst of the long, mad weekend. The place was deserted, we were the first customers, ten o'clock. Shearing came out, blind, led by the hand to his keyboard. He was a distinguished-looking Englishman with a stiff white collar, slightly beefy, blond, with a delicate English-summer's-night air about him that came out in the first rippling sweet number he played as the bass-player leaned to him reverently and thrummed the beat. The drummer, Denzil Best, sat motionless except for his wrists snapping the brushes. And Shearing began to rock; a smile broke over his ecstatic face; he began to rock in the piano seat, back and forth, slowly at first, then the beat went up, and he began rocking fast, his left foot jumped up with every beat, his neck began to rock crookedly, he brought his face down to the keys, he pushed his hair back, his combed hair dissolved, he began to sweat. The music picked up. The bass-player hunched over and socked it in, faster and faster, it seemed faster and faster, that's all. Shearing began to play his chords; they rolled out of the piano in great rich showers, you'd think the man wouldn't have time to line them up. They rolled and rolled like the sea. Folks yelled for him to "Go!" Dean was sweating; the sweat poured down his collar. "There he is! That's him! Old God! Old God Shearing! Yes! Yes! Yes!" And Shearing was conscious of the madman behind him, he could hear every one of Dean's gasps and imprecations, he could sense it though he couldn't see. "That's right!" Dean said. "Yes!" Shearing smiled; he rocked. Shearing rose from the piano, dripping with sweat; these were his great 1949 days before he became cool and commercial. When he was gone Dean pointed to the empty piano seat. "God's empty chair," he said. On the piano a horn sat; its golden shadow made a strange reflection along the desert caravan painted on the wall behind the drums. God was gone; it was the silence of his departure. It was a rainy night. It was the myth of the rainy night. Dean was popeyed with awe. This madness would lead nowhere. I didn't know what was happening to me, and I suddenly realized it was only the tea that we were smoking; Dean had bought some in New York. It made me think that everything was about to arrive—the moment when you know all and everything is decided forever.

It was drizzling and mysterious at the beginning of our journey. I could see that it was all going to be one big saga of the mist. "Whooee!" yelled Dean. "Here we go!" And he hunched over the wheel and gunned her; he was back in his element, everybody could see that. We were all delighted, we all realized we were leaving confusion and nonsense behind and performing our one and noble function of the time, *move*. And we moved! We flashed past the mysterious white signs in the night somewhere in New Jersey that say *SOUTH* (with an arrow) and *WEST* (with an arrow) and took the south one. New Orleans! It burned in our brains. From the dirty snows of "frosty fagtown New York," as Dean called it, all the way to the greeneries and river smells of old New Orleans at the washed-out bottom of America; then west. Ed was in the back seat; Marylou and Dean and I sat in front and had the warmest talk about the goodness and joy of life. Dean suddenly became tender. "Now dammit, look here, all of you, we all must admit that everything is fine and there's no need in the world to worry, and in fact we should realize what it would mean to us to *UNDERSTAND* that we're not *REALLY* worried about *ANYTHING*. Am I right?" We all agreed. "Here we go, we're all together.... What did we do in New York? Let's forgive." We all had our spats back there. "That's behind us, merely by miles and inclinations. Now we're heading down to New Orleans to dig Old Bull Lee and ain't that going to be kicks and listen will you to this old tenorman blow his top"—he shot up the radio volume till the car shuddered—"and listen to him tell the story and put down true relaxation and knowledge."

We all jumped to the music and agreed. The purity of the road. The white line in the middle of the highway unrolled and hugged our left front tire as if glued to our groove. Dean hunched his muscular neck, T-shirted in the winter night, and blasted the car along. He insisted I drive through Baltimore for traffic practice; that was all right, except he and Marylou insisted on steering while they kissed and fooled around. It was crazy; the radio was on full blast. Dean beat drums on the dashboard till a great sag developed in it; I did too. The poor Hudson—the slow boat to China—was receiving her beating.

"Oh man, what kicks!" yelled Dean. "Now Marylou, listen really, honey, you know that I'm hotrock capable of everything at the same time and I have unlimited energy—now in San Francisco we must go on living together. I know just the place for you—at the end of it the regular chain-gang run—I'll be home just a cut-hair less than every two days and for twelve hours at a stretch, and *man,* you know what we can do in twelve hours, darling. Meanwhile I'll go right on living at Camille's like nothin', see, she won't know. We can work it, we've done it before." It was all right with Marylou, she was really out for Camille's scalp. The understanding had been that Marylou would switch to me in Frisco, but I now began to see they were going to stick and I was going to be left alone on my butt at the other end of the continent. But why think about that when all the golden land's ahead of you and all kinds of

unforeseen events wait lurking to surprise you and make you glad you're alive to see?

* * * * * *

1. *What attraction do you think the character of Dean Moriarty held for readers?*

2. *Why do you think so many critics reviled the novel? In what ways does Kerouac reject the dominant values of 1950s America?*

3. *The Beat writers strongly identified with the art and lives of jazz musicians. How is this reflected in the excerpt?*

27–8   Betty Friedan, The Problem That Has No Name, 1963

A 1942 graduate of Smith College, Betty Friedan raised three children and worked as a freelance magazine writer after World War II. In 1957, she sent questionnaires to members of her Smith class, asking them to describe their lives since graduation. She combined their answers with more research and published The Feminine Mystique *in 1963. The book's pathbreaking analysis of the unhappiness felt by many suburban middle-class housewives helped spark the modern feminist movement. In 1966 Friedan helped found the National Organization for Women.*

SOURCE: From *The Feminine Mystique* by Betty Friedan. Copyright © 1963, 1973, 1974, 1983 by Betty Friedan. Reprinted by permission of W.W. Norton & Company, Inc.

The suburban housewife—she was the dream image of the young American women and the envy, it was said, of women all over the world. The American housewife—freed by science and labor-saving appliances from the drudgery, the dangers of childbirth and the illnesses of her grandmother. She was healthy, beautiful, educated, concerned only about her husband, her children, her home. She had found true feminine fulfillment. As a housewife and mother, she was respected as a full and equal partner to man in his world. She was free to choose automobiles, clothes, appliances, supermarkets; she had everything that women ever dreamed of.

In the fifteen years after World War II, this mystique of feminine fulfillment became the cherished and self-perpetuating core of contemporary American culture. Millions of women lived their lives in the image of those

pretty pictures of the American suburban housewife, kissing their husbands goodbye in front of the picture window, depositing their station-wagonsful of children at school, and smiling as they ran the new electric waxer over the spotless kitchen floor. They baked their own bread, sewed their own and their children's clothes, kept their new washing machines and dryers running all day. They changed the sheets on the beds twice a week instead of once, took the rug-hooking class in adult education, and pitied their poor frustrated mothers, who had dreamed of having a career. Their only dream was to be perfect wives and mothers; their highest ambition to have five children and a beautiful house, their only fight to get and keep their husbands. They had no thought for the unfeminine problems of the world outside the home; they wanted the men to make the major decisions. They gloried in their role as women, and wrote proudly on the census blank: "Occupation: housewife."

For over fifteen years, the words written for women, and the words women used when they talked to each other, while their husbands sat on the other side of the room and talked shop or politics or septic tanks, were about problems with their children, or how to keep their husbands happy, or improve their children's school, or cook chicken or make slipcovers. Nobody argued whether women were inferior or superior to men; they were simply different. Words like "emancipation" and "career" sounded strange and embarrassing; no one had used them for years. When a French-woman named Simone de Beauvoir wrote a book called *The Second Sex,* an American critic commented that she obviously "didn't know what life was all about," and besides, she was talking about French women. The "woman problem" in America no longer existed.

If a woman had a problem in the 1950s and 1960s, she knew that something must be wrong with her marriage, or with herself. Other women were satisfied with their lives, she thought. What kind of a woman was she if she did not feel this mysterious fulfillment waxing the kitchen floor? She was so ashamed to admit her dissatisfaction that she never knew how many other women shared it. If she tried to tell her husband, he didn't understand what she was talking about. She did not really understand it herself. For over fifteen years women in America found it harder to talk about this problem than about sex. Even the psychoanalysts had no name for it. When a woman went to a psychiatrist for help, as many women did, she would say, "I'm so ashamed," or "I must be hopelessly neurotic." "I don't know what's wrong with women today," a suburban psychiatrist said uneasily. "I only know something is wrong because most of my patients happen to be women. And their problem isn't sexual." Most women with this problem did not go to see a psychoanalyst, however. "There's nothing wrong really," they kept telling themselves. "There isn't any problem."

But on an April morning in 1959, I heard a mother of four, having coffee with four other mothers in a suburban development fifteen miles from New York, say in a tone of quiet desperation, "the problem." And the others knew, without words, that she was not talking about a problem with her husband, or her children, or her home. Suddenly they realized they all shared the same problem, the problem that has no name. They began, hesitantly, to talk about it. Later, after they had picked up their children at nursery school and taken them home to nap, two of the women cried, in sheer relief, just to know they were not alone.

Gradually I came to realize that the problem that has no name was shared by countless women in America. As a magazine writer I often interviewed women about problems with their children, or their marriages, or their houses, or their communities. But after a while I began to recognize the telltale signs of this other problem. I saw the same signs in suburban ranch houses and split-levels on Long Island and in New Jersey and Westchester County; in colonial houses in a small Massachusetts town; on patios in Memphis; in suburban and city apartments; in living rooms in the Midwest. Sometimes I sensed the problem, not as a reporter, but as a suburban housewife, for during this time I was also bringing up my own three children in Rockland County, New York. I heard echoes of the problem in college dormitories and semiprivate maternity wards, at PTA meetings and luncheons of the League of Women Voters, at suburban cocktail parties, in station wagons waiting for trains, and in snatches of conversation overheard at Schrafft's. The groping words I heard from other women, on quiet afternoons when children were at school or on quiet evenings when husbands worked late, I think I understood first as a woman long before I understood their larger social and psychological implications....

If I am right, the problem that has no name stirring in the minds of so many American women today is not a matter of loss of femininity or too much education, or the demands of domesticity. It is far more important than anyone recognizes. It is the key to these other new and old problems which have been torturing women and their husbands and children, and puzzling their doctors and educators for years. It may well be the key to our future as a nation and a culture. We can no longer ignore that voice within women that says: "I want something more than my husband and my children and my home."

* * * * * *

1. *What does Friedan mean by "the mystique of feminine fulfillment"?*

2. *How do men contribute to the "feminine mystique" and the "problem that has no name"?*

3. *Why does Friedan think it so important to "name" the problem?*

27–9 Jerry Lee Lewis and Sam Phillips Discuss "Great Balls of Fire," 1957

Jerry Lee Lewis was one of the most dynamic pioneers of early rock 'n' roll. His first record, the 1957 "rockabilly" tune "Whole Lotta' Shakin'," was a huge hit for Sam Phillips's Sun Records in Memphis. When Phillips presented Lewis with a follow-up song, "Great Balls of Fire," the young singer balked at recording it. The following is a transcription of their argument in the Sun

studio. Phillips prevailed, and "Great Balls of Fire" became another big hit for Lewis.

SOURCE: Greil Marcus, *Mystery Train* (1975), pp. 265–267.

Jerry Lee Lewis and Sam Phillips, 1957

JERRY LEE LEWIS: H—E—L—L!

SAM PHILLIPS: I don't believe it.

JLL: Great Godamighty, great balls of fire!

SP: I don't believe it.

JLL: It says, WAKE MAN! To the Joy of God! Only! But when it comes to *worldly music* [Jerry Lee is already high on a pulpit]—that's rock 'n'roll....

JLL: —or anything like that, you have done brought your-self into the world, and you're in the world, and you hadn't come on out of the world, *and you're still a sinner.*

You're a sinner—and when you be saved—*and borned again*—and be made *as a little child—and walk before God—*

And be holy—

And brother, I mean that you got to be so pure! No sin shall enter there: *No Sin!*

For it says, *No Sin.* It don't say just a little bit, it says, NO SIN SHALL ENTER THERE—broth-er, not one little bit! You've got to walk and *talk* with God to go to Heaven. You've got to be *so* good....

SP: Alright. Now look, Jerry. Religious conviction—doesn't mean anything—resembling extremism. [Phillips suddenly picks up speed.] *Do you mean to tell me* that you're gonna take the Bible, you're gonna take God's word, and you gonna *revolutionize the whole universe?* Now listen! Jesus Christ was sent here by God Almighty. Did he convince, did he *save,* all the people in the world?

JLL: Naw, but he tried to!

SP: *He sure did.* NOW WAIT JUST A MINUTE. Jesus Christ—came into this world. He *tolerated* man. He didn't preach from one pulpit. He went around, and he *did good.*

JLL: That's right! He preached *everywhere!*

SP: Everywhere!

JLL: He preached on land!

SP: Everywhere! That's right! That's right!

JLL: He preached on the water!

SP: That's right, that's exactly right! Now—

JLL: And then he done everything! He *healed!*

SP: Now, now,—here' s, *here's the difference—*

JLL: [Speaking as if horns have sprouted on Phillip's head]: *Are you followin' Those That Heal?* Like Jesus Christ?

SP: [Confused]: Whata you mean, I, I, what—

JLL: [Triumphant]: Well, it's happening everyday! *The blind* had eyes opened. *The lame* were made to walk.

SP: *Jerry—*

JLL: *The crippled* were made to walk.

SP: Alright now. Jesus Christ, in my opinion, is just as *real today,* as He was when He came into this world.

JLL: Right, right, you're so right you don't know what you're sayin'.

SP: [Back on the offensive]: Now, then! I will say, *more so—*

SP: Wait, wait, wait just a minute, we can't, we got to—Now, look. Now, listen. I'm tellin' you outa

my heart. I have studied the Bible, a little bit—

JLL: Well, I have too.

SP: I've studied it through and through and through and through and Jerry, Jerry—If you think, that you can't, can't do good, if you're a rock 'n' roll exponent—

JLL: *You can do good,* Mr. Phillips, don't get me wrong—

SP: Now, wait, wait listen, when I say *do good—*

JLL: YOU CAN HAVE A KIND HEART!

SP: [Suddenly angry]: I don't *mean,* I don't *mean* just—

JLL: You can help people!

SP: *You can save souls!*

JLL: [Appalled]: No. NO! No, no!

SP: Yes!

JLL: How can the DEVIL save souls? *What are you talkin' about?*

SP: Lissen, Lissen…

JLL: I have the Devil in me! If I didn't I'd be a Christian!

SP: Well, you may *have* him—

JLL: [Fighting for his life]: JESUS! Heal this man! He cast the Devil out, the Devil says, Where can I go? He says, Can I go into this *swine?* He says, Yeah, go into him. Didn't he go into him?

SP: Jerry. The point I'm tryin' to make is—if you believe in what you're singin'—you got no alter-native whatsoever—out of—LISTEN!—out of—

JLL: Mr. Phillips! I don't care, it ain't what you believe, it's [as if explaining to a child], *it's what's written in the Bible!*

SP: Well, wait a minute.

JLL: It's what is *there,* Mr. Phillips.

SP: No, no.

JLL: It's just what's there.

SP: No, by gosh, if it's not what you believe [and Phillips hits the clincher] *then how do you inter-pret the Bible!…*

SP: Huh! How do you interpret the Bible if it's not what you believe!

JLL: [Confused]: Well, it's just *not* what you believe, you just *can't….*

* * * * * *

1.   *Jerry Lee Lewis had spent some time at the Southwest Bible School before becoming a professional musician. Why does he object to recording the song?*

2.   *What does this exchange suggest about the relationship between early rock 'n' roll and religion?*

27–10 John F. Kennedy, Speech at American University, 1963

The Cuban missile crisis of 1962 had brought the world perilously close to nuclear disaster. In its aftermath, leaders of both the United States and the Soviet Union looked for ways to reduce diplomatic tensions and initiate discussions about disarmament. President Kennedy's commencement address at American University in June 1963 suggested that he had begun to rethink some of the basic issues defining Soviet–American relations and the Cold War.

SOURCE: Public papers of the Presidents: John F. Kennedy (1965).

Some say that it is useless to speak of world peace or world law or world disarmament—and that it will be useless until the leaders of the Soviet Union adopt a more enlightened attitude. I hope they do. I believe we can help them do it. But I also believe that we must reexamine our own attitude—as individuals and as a Nation—for our attitude is as essential as theirs. And every graduate of this school, every thoughtful citizen who despairs of war and wishes to bring peace, should begin by looking inward—by examining his own attitude toward the possibilities of peace, toward the Soviet Union, toward the course of the cold war and toward freedom and peace here at home.

First: Let us examine our attitude toward peace itself. Too many of us think it is impossible. Too many think it unreal. But that is a dangerous, defeatist belief. It leads to the conclusion that war is inevitable—that mankind is doomed—that we are gripped by forces we cannot control....

Second: Let us reexamine our attitude toward the Soviet Union....

No government or social system is so evil that its people must be considered as lacking in virtue. As Americans, we find communism profoundly repugnant, as a negation of personal freedom and dignity. But we can still hail the Russian people for their many achievements—in science and space, in economic and industrial growth, in culture and in acts of courage.

Among the many traits the peoples of our two countries have in common, none is stronger than our mutual abhorrence of war. Almost unique, among the major world powers, we have never been at war with each other. And no nation in the history of battle ever suffered more than the Soviet Union suffered in the course of the Second World War. At least 20 million lost their lives. Countless millions of homes and farms were burned or sacked. A third of the nation's territory, including nearly two thirds of its industrial base, was turned into a wasteland—a loss equivalent to the devastation of this country east of Chicago.

Today, should total war ever break out again—no matter how—our two countries would become the primary targets. It is an ironic but accurate fact that the two strongest powers are the two in the most danger of devastation. All we have built, all we have worked for, would be destroyed in the first 24 hours. And even in the cold war, which brings burdens and dangers to so many countries, including this Nation's closest allies—our two countries bear the heaviest burdens. For we are both devoting massive sums of money to weapons that could be better devoted to combating ignorance, poverty, and disease. We are both caught up in a vicious and dangerous cycle in which suspicion on one side breeds suspicion on the other, and new weapons beget counter weapons.

In short, both the United States and its allies, and the Soviet Union and its allies, have a mutually deep interest in a just and genuine peace and in halting the arms race. Agreements to this end are in the interests of the Soviet Union as well as ours—and even the most hostile nations can be relied upon to accept and keep those treaty obligations, and only those treaty obligations, which are in their own interest.

So, let us not be blind to our differences—but let us also direct attention to our common interests and to the means by which those differences can be resolved. And if we cannot end now our differences, at least we can help make the world safe for diversity. For, in the final analysis, our most basic common link is that we all inhabit this small planet. We all breathe the same air. We all cherish our children's future. And we are all mortal.

Third: Let us reexamine our attitude toward the cold war, remembering that we are not engaged in debate, seeking to pile up debating points. We are not here distributing blame or pointing the finger of judgment. We must deal with the world as it is, and not as it might have been had the history of the last 18 years been different....

...The United States will make no deal with the Soviet Union at the expense of other nations and other peoples, not merely because they are our partners, but also because their interests and ours converge.

Our interests converge, however, not only in defending the frontiers of freedom, but in pursuing the paths of peace. It is our hope—and the purpose of allied policies—to convince the Soviet Union that she, too should let each nation choose its own future, so long as that choice does not interfere with the choices of others. The Communist drive to impose their political and economic system on others is the primary cause of world tension today. For there can be no doubt that, if all nations could refrain from interfering in the self-determination of others, the peace would be much more assured.

This will require a new effort to achieve world law—a new context for world discussions. It will require increased understanding between the Soviets and ourselves. And increased understanding will require increased contact and communication. One step in this direction is the proposed arrangement for a direct line between Moscow and Washington, to avoid on each side the dangerous delays, misunderstandings, and misreadings of the other's actions which might occur at a time of crisis.

We have also been talking in Geneva about other first-step measures of arms control, designed to limit the intensity of the arms race and to reduce the risks of accidental war. Our primary long-range interest in Geneva, however, is general and complete disarmament—designed to take place by stages, permitting parallel political developments to build the new institutions of peace which would take the place of arms. The pursuit of disarmament has been an effort of this Government since the 1920s. It has been urgently sought by the past three administrations. And however dim the prospects may be today, we intend to continue this effort—to continue it in order that all countries, including our own, can better grasp what the problems and possibilities of disarmament are.

The one major area of these negotiations where the end is in sight, yet where a fresh start is badly needed, is in a treaty to outlaw nuclear tests. The conclusion of such a treaty, so near and yet so far, would check the spiraling arms race in one of its most dangerous areas. It would place the nuclear powers in a position to deal more effectively with one of the greatest hazards which man faces in 1963, the further spread of nuclear arms. It would increase our security—it would decrease the prospects of war. Surely this goal is sufficiently important to require our steady pursuit, yielding neither to the temptation to give up the whole effort nor the temptation to give up our insistence on vital and responsible safeguards.

I am taking this opportunity, therefore, to announce two important decisions in this regard.

First: Chairman Khrushchev, Prime Minister Macmillan, and I have agreed that high-level discussions will shortly begin in Moscow looking toward early agreement on a comprehensive test ban treaty. Our hopes must be tempered with the caution of history—but with our hopes go the hopes of all mankind.

Second: To make clear our good faith and solemn convictions on the matter, I now declare that the United States does not propose to conduct nuclear tests in the atmosphere so long as other states do not do so. We will not be the first to resume. Such a declaration is no substitute for a formal binding treaty, but I hope it will help us achieve one. Nor would such a treaty be a substitute for disarmament, but I hope it will help us achieve it....

...The United States, as the world knows, will never start a war. We do not want a war. We do not now expect a war. This generation of Americans has already had enough—more than enough—of war and hate and oppression. We shall be prepared if others wish it. We shall be alert to try to stop it. But we shall also do our part to build a world of peace where the weak are safe and the strong are just. We are not helpless before that task or hopeless of its success. Confident and unafraid, we labor on—not toward a strategy of annihilation but toward a strategy of peace.

* * * * * *

1.   *Compare the tone and substance of this address with those of Kennedy's inaugural two-and-a-half years earlier.*

2.   *Why and how does Kennedy emphasize the mutual interests and commonalities between the United States and the Soviet Union? How does he suggest using these similarities to achieve a "thaw" in the Cold War?*

3.   *Kennedy's speech focuses on improving U.S.–U.S.S.R. relations. Yet at the same time his administration began the buildup of American military forces in southeast Asia. How would you explain this seeming contradiction?*

chapter 28

The Civil Rights Movement, 1945–1966

28–1   Jo Ann Gibson Robinson, The Montgomery Bus Boycott, 1955

The successful year-long boycott waged against segregated bus lines launched the non-violent, mass-protest phase of the civil rights movement. Rosa Parks's arrest for refusing to give up her seat to a white man provided the spark. The boycott catapulted the Rev. Martin Luther King, Jr., the minister at Dexter Avenue Baptist Church, into a national leadership role among civil rights activists. After Mrs. Parks's arrest, Jo Ann Gibson Robinson, an English teacher at Alabama State College and a member of the black Women's Political Council, made the first crucial organizing effort within Montgomery's African-American community.

SOURCE: From *The Montgomery Bus Boycott and the Women Who Started It: The Memoir of Jo Ann Gibson Robinson,* edited with a Foreword by David J. Garrow, Copyright © 1987 University of Tennessee Press. Used with permission.

It was the first time the soft-spoken, middle-aged woman had been arrested. She maintained decorum and poise, and the word of her arrest spread. Mr. E. D. Nixon, a longtime stalwart of our NAACP branch, along with liberal white attorney Clifford Durr and his wife Virginia, went to the jail and obtained Mrs. Parks's release on bond. Her trial was scheduled for Monday, December 5, 1955.

The news traveled like wildfire into every black home. Telephones jangled; people congregated on street corners and in homes and talked. But nothing was done. A numbing helplessness seemed to paralyze everyone. Very few stayed off the buses the rest of that day or the next. There was fear, discontent, and uncertainty. Everyone seemed to wait for someone to *do* something, but nobody made a move. For that day and a half black Americans rode the buses as before, as if nothing had happened. They were sullen and uncommunicative, but they rode the buses. There was a silent, tension-filled waiting. For blacks were not talking loudly in public places—they were quiet, sullen, waiting. Just waiting!

Thursday evening came and went. Thursday night was far spent, when, at about 11:30 P.M., I sat alone in my peaceful single-family dwelling on a quiet street. I was thinking about the situation. Lost in thought, I was startled by the telephone's ring. Black attorney Fred Gray, who had been out of town all day, had just gotten back and was returning the phone message I had left for him about Mrs. Parks's arrest. Attorney Gray, though a very young man, had been one of my most active colleagues in our previous meetings with bus company officials and Commissioner Birmingham. A Montgomery native who had attended Alabama State and been one of my students, Fred Gray had gone on to law school in Ohio before returning to his home town to open a practice with the only other black lawyer in Montgomery, Charles Langford.

Fred Gray and his wife Bernice were good friends of mine, and we talked often. In addition to being a lawyer, Gray was a trained, ordained minister of the gospel, actively serving as assistant pastor of Holt Street Church of Christ.

Tonight his voice on the phone was very short and to the point. Fred was shocked by the news of Mrs. Parks's arrest. I informed him that I already was thinking that the WPC should distribute thousands of notices calling for all bus riders to stay off the buses on Monday, the day of Mrs. Parks's trial. "Are you ready?" he asked. Without hesitation, I assured him that we were. With that he hung up, and I went to work.

I made some notes on the back of an envelope: "The Women's Political Council will not wait for Mrs. Parks's consent to call for a boycott of city buses. On Friday, December 2, 1955, the women of Montgomery will call for a boycott to take place on Monday, December 5."

Some of the WPC officers previously had discussed plans for distributing thousands of notices announcing a bus boycott. Now the time had come for me to write just such a notice. I sat down and quickly drafted a message and then called a good friend and colleague, John Cannon, chairman of the business department at the college, who had access to the college's mimeograph equipment. When I told him that the WPC was staging a boycott and needed to run off the notices, he told me that he too had suffered embarrassment on the city buses. Like myself, he had been hurt and angry. He said that he would happily assist me. Along with two of my most trusted senior students, we quickly agreed to meet almost immediately, in the middle of the night, at the college's duplicating room. We were able to get three messages to a page, greatly reducing the number of pages that had to be mimeographed in order to produce the tens of thousands of leaflets we knew would be needed. By 4 A.M. Friday, the sheets had been duplicated, cut in thirds, and bundled. Each leaflet read:

Another Negro woman has been arrested and thrown in jail because she refused to get up out of her seat on the bus for a white person to sit down. It is the second time since the Claudette Colvin came that a Negro woman has been arrested for the same thing. This has to be stopped. Negroes have rights, too, for if Negroes did not ride the buses, they could not operate. Three-fourths of the riders are Negroes, yet we are arrested, or have to stand over empty seats. If we do not do something to stop these arrests, they will continue. The next time it may be you, or your daughter, or mother. This woman's case will come up on Monday. We are, therefore, asking every Negro to stay off the buses Monday in protest of the arrest and trial. Don't ride the buses to work, to town, to school, or anywhere on Monday. You can afford to stay out of school for one day if you have no other way to go except by bus. You can also afford to stay out of town for one day. If you work, take a cab, or walk. But please, children and grown-ups, don't ride the bus at all on Monday. Please stay off of all buses Monday.

Between 4 and 7 A.M., the two students and I mapped out distribution routes for the notices. Some of the WPC officers previously had discussed how and where to deliver thousands of leaflets announcing a boycott, and those plans now stood me in good stead. We outlined our routes, arranged the bundles in sequences, stacked them in our cars, and arrived at my 8 A.M. class, in which both young men were enrolled, with several minutes to spare. We weren't even tired or hungry. Just like me, the two students felt a tremendous sense of satisfaction at being able to contribute to the cause of justice.

After class my two students and I quickly finalized our plans for distributing the thousands of leaflets so that one would reach every black home in Montgomery. I took out the WPC membership roster and called the former president, Dr. Mary Fair Burks, then the Pierces, the Glasses, Mrs. Mary Cross, Mrs. Elizabeth Arrington, Mrs. Josie Lawrence, Mrs. Geraldine Nesbitt, Mrs. H. Councill Trenholm, Mrs. Catherine N. Johnson, and a dozen or more others. I alerted all of them to the forthcoming distribution of the leaflets, and enlisted their aid in speeding and organizing the distribution network. Each would have one person waiting at a certain place to take a package of notices as soon as my car stopped and the young men could hand them a bundle of leaflets.

Then I and my two student helpers set out. Throughout the late morning and early afternoon hours we dropped off tens of thousands of leaflets. Some of our bundles were dropped off at schools, where both students and staff members helped distribute them further and spread the word for people to read the notices and then pass them on to neighbors. Leaflets were also dropped off

at business places, storefronts, beauty parlors, beer halls, factories, barber shops, and every other available place. Workers would pass along notices both to other employees as well as to customers.

During those hours of crucial work, nothing went wrong. Suspicion was never raised. The action of all involved was so casual, so unconcerned, so nonchalant, that suspicion was never raised, and neither the city nor its people ever suspected a thing! We never missed a spot. And no one missed a class, a job, or a normal routine. Everything was done by the plan, with perfect timing. By 2 o'clock, thousands of the mimeographed handbills had changed hands many times. Practically every black man, woman, and child in Montgomery knew the plan and was passing the word along. No one knew where the notices had come from or who had arranged for their circulation, and no one cared. Those who passed them on did so efficiently, quietly, and without comment. But deep within the heart of every black person was a joy he or she dared not reveal....

On Friday morning, December 2, 1955, a goodly number of Montgomery's black clergymen happened to be meeting at the Hilliard Chapel A.M.E. Zion Church on Highland Avenue. When the Women's Political Council officers learned that the ministers were assembled in that meeting, we felt that God was on our side. It was easy for my two students and me to leave a handful of our circulars at the church, and those disciples of God could not truthfully have told where the notices came from if their very lives had depended on it. Many of the ministers received their notices of the boycott at the same time, in the same place. They all felt equal, included, appreciated, needed. It seemed predestined that this should be so.

One minister read the circular, inquired about the announcements, and found that all the city's black congregations were quite intelligent on the matter and were planning to support the one-day boycott with or without their ministers' leadership. It was then that the ministers decided that it was time for them, the leaders, to catch up with the masses. If the people were really determined to stage this one-day protest, then they would need moral support and Christian leadership. The churches could serve as channels of communication, as well as altars where people could come for prayer and spiritual guidance. Since the ministers were servants of the people and of God, and believed in the gospel of social justice, and since the churches were institutions supported by the people, the clerics could serve as channels through which all the necessary benefits could flow. Thus, for the first time in the history of Montgomery, black ministers united to lead action for civic improvement. There was no thought of denomination. Baptists, Presbyterians, Episcopalians, Lutherans, Congregationalists, and others joined together and became one band of ministerial brothers, offering their leadership to the masses. Had they not done so, they might have alienated themselves from their congregations and indeed lost members, for the masses were ready, and they were united!

The black ministers and their churches made the Montgomery Bus Boycott of 1955–1956 the success that it was. Had it not been for the ministers and the support they received from their wonderful congregations, the outcome of the boycott might have been different. The ministers gave themselves, their time, their contributions, their minds, their prayers, and their leadership, all of which set examples for the laymen to follow. They gave us confidence, faith in ourselves, faith in them and their leadership, that helped the congregations to support the movement every foot of the way.

Under the aegis of the Interdenominational Ministerial Alliance a meeting was called for that Friday evening at the Dexter Avenue Baptist Church, of which the Reverend Dr. Martin Luther King, Jr., was pastor. To this meeting were invited all the ministers, all club presidents and officers, all church organization heads, and any interested persons.

In the meantime, domestic workers who worked late into the day toyed with the slips of paper carrying the important information of the protest. Most of them destroyed the evidence, buried the information in their memories, and went merrily on their way to work. However, one lone black woman, a domestic loyal to her "white lady," in spite of her concern over the plight of her black peers and without any sense of obligation to her people, carried the handbill to her job and did not stop until the precious paper was safe in her "white lady's" hands. It was only a matter of minutes before the bus company, the City Commission, the chief of police, and the press knew its contents. The *Alabama Journal,* Montgomery's afternoon newspaper, ran a story on Saturday. Another article appeared in the *Montgomery Advertiser* on Sunday. The two local television stations and the four radio stations completed the coverage. The secret was out.

In recalling this particular incident later, the leaders of the boycott wondered if that woman's action had been providential, part of a divine plan to make the boycott succeed. If this was the case, she was not disloyal to her people, but rather was following the dictates of a higher authority!

The original intention had been that the whole affair would come as a complete surprise to whites. Then if all the darker set did not cooperate, no one would be the wiser. But now the news was out, and some misgivings and fear among blacks followed. Southern blacks, who had never been known to stick together as a group, to follow leadership, or to keep their mouths shut from exposing secrets, were on the spot!

One good thing, however, came from the revelation: the few black citizens in remote corners of the city who might not have gotten the news of the boycott, knew it now. The news that circulated through the newspapers, radio, television, and other channels of communication covered every possible isolated place not reached by the leaflets.

Publicity given the Monday boycott probably accounted, too, for the very large attendance which turned out for the Friday night meeting at Dexter Avenue Baptist Church. More than one hundred leaders were present.

There the organization of the boycott began. Special committees were set up. The main one focused on transportation. To help the walking public, volunteer cars had to be pooled, taxis had to be contacted, and donations had to be determined through cooperative means. Routes had to be mapped out to get workers to all parts of the city. Regular bus routes had to be followed so that workers who "walked along" the streets could be picked up. This committee, headed by Alfonso Campbell and staffed by volunteer workers, worked all night Friday to complete this phase of the program. The pickup system was so effectively planned that many writers described it as comparable in precision to a military operation.

What the ministers failed to do at that meeting was to select one person who would head the boycott. Those present discussed it, pointing out the leadership preparation of various individuals, but no definite decision was made. That had to wait until Monday afternoon, when the ministers realized that the one-day boycott was going to be successful. Then they met again, and Dr. Martin Luther King, Jr., agreed to accept the leadership post.

* * * * * *

1. *What does Robinson's narrative suggest about the sources and history of civil rights consciousness within the city's African-American community?*

2. *What were the differences between the boycott's organizers and participants and those who became its leaders? How did the ministers alter the original plans?*

28–2   *Brown v. Board of Education, 1954*

Throughout the 1940s and early 1950s, the NAACP mounted a series of court challenges to the "separate but equal" ruling that had protected legal segregation since the 1896 Plessy v. Ferguson *decision. It had won some limited victories, but it had not yet persuaded the Court to rule on the basic issue of whether segregated facilities were inherently unequal.* Brown *combined five different cases challenging segregated school systems. New Chief Justice Earl Warren gave the decision greater weight by achieving a unanimous verdict. He did so by omitting any language that would seem "forcing" to school districts.*

SOURCE: 347 U.S 483 (1954).

Chief Justice Warren Delivered the Opinion of the Court

These cases come to us from the States of Kansas, South Carolina, Virginia, and Delaware. In each of the cases, minors of the Negro race seek the aid of the courts in obtaining admission to the public schools of community on a nonsegregated basis. In each instance, they had been denied admission to schools by white children under laws requiring or permitting segregation according to race. This segregation was alleged to deprive the plaintiffs of the equal protection of the laws under the 14th Amendment.... The plaintiffs contend that segregated public schools are not "equal" and cannot be made "equal," and that hence they are deprived of the equal protection of the laws. Argument was heard in the 1952 Term, and reargument heard this Term on certain questions propounded by the Court.

Reargument was largely devoted to the circumstances surrounding the adoption of the 14th Amendment in 1868. It covered exhaustively consideration of the Amendment in Congress, ratification by the states, then existing practices in racial segregation, and the views of proponents and opponents of the Amendment. This discussion and our own investigation convince us although these sources cast some light, it is not enough to resolve the problem with which we are faced. At best, they are inconclusive. The most avid proponents of the post-War Amendments undoubtedly intended them to remove all legal distinctions among "all persons born or naturalized in the United States." Their opponents, just as certainly, were antagonistic to both the letter and the spirit of the Amendments and wished them to have the most limited effect. What others in Congress and the state legislatures had in mind cannot be determined with any degree of certainty.

An additional reason for the inconclusive nature of the Amendment's history, with respect to segregated schools, is the status of public education at that time. In the South, the movement toward free common schools supported by general taxation, had not yet taken hold. Education of white children was largely in the hands of private groups. Education of Negroes was almost nonexistent, and practically all of the race were illiterate. In fact, any education of Negroes was forbidden by law in some states. Today, in contrast, many Negroes have achieved outstanding success in the arts and sciences as well as in the business and professional world. It is true that public school education had advanced further in the North, but the effect of the Amendment on Northern States was generally ignored in the congressional debates. Even in the North, the conditions of public education did not approximate those existing today. The curriculum was usually rudimentary; ungraded schools were common in rural areas; the school term was but three months a year in many states; and compulsory attendance was virtually unknown. As a consequence, it is not surprising that there should be so little in the history of the 14th Amendment relating to its intended effect on public education.

In the first cases in this Court construing the 14th Amendment, decided shortly after its adoption, the Court interpreted it as proscribing all state-imposed discriminations against the Negro race. The doctrine of but "separate but equal" did not make its appearance in this Court until 1896....involving not education but transportation. In this Court, there have been six cases involving the "separate but equal" doctrine in the field of public education. In *Cumming v. County Board of Education...*and *Gong Lum v. Rice...*the validity of the doctrine itself was not challenged. In more recent cases, all on the graduate school level, inequality was found in that specific benefits enjoyed by white students were denied to Negro students of the same educational qualifications....In none of these cases was it necessary to reexamine the doctrine to grant relief to the Negro plaintiff. And in *Sweatt v. Painter,* the Court expressly reserved decision on the question whether *Plessy v. Ferguson* should be held inapplicable to public education. In the instant cases, that question is directly presented. Here, unlike *Sweatt v. Painter,* there are findings below that the Negro and white schools involved have been equalized or are being equalized, with respect to buildings, curricula, qualifications and salaries of teachers, and other "tangible" factors. Our decision, therefore, cannot turn on merely a comparison of these tangible factors in the Negro and white schools involved in each of the cases. We must look instead to the effect of segregation itself on public education.

In approaching this problem, we cannot turn the clock back to 1868 when the Amendment was adopted, or even to 1896 when *Plessy* was written. We must consider public education in the light of its full development and its present place in American life throughout the Nation. Only in this way can it be determined if segregation in public schools deprives these plaintiffs of the equal protection of the laws. Today, education is perhaps the most important function of state and local governments. Compulsory school attendance laws and the great expenditures for education both demonstrate our recognition of the importance of education to our democratic society. It is required in the performance of our most basic public responsibilities, even service in the armed forces. It is the very foundation of good citizenship. Today it is a principal instrument in awakening the child to cultural values, in preparing him for later professional training, and in helping him to adjust normally to his environment. In these days, it is doubtful that any child may reasonably be expected to succeed in life if he is denied the opportunity of an education. Such an opportunity, where the state has undertaken to provide it, is a right which must be made available to all on equal terms.

We come then to the question presented: Does segregation of children in public schools solely on the basis of race, even though the physical facilities and other "tangible" factors may be equal, deprive the children of the minority group of equal educational opportunities? We believe that it does. In *Sweatt* in finding that a segregated law school for Negroes could not provide them equal educational opportunities, this Court relied in large part on "those qualities which are incapable of objective measurement but which make for greatness in a law school." In *McLaurin*, the Court, in requiting that a Negro admitted to a white graduate school be treated like all other students, again resorted to intangible considerations: "[his] ability to study, to engage in discussions and exchange views with other students, and, in general, to learn his profession." Such considerations apply with added force to children in grade and high schools. To separate them from others of similar age and qualifications solely because of their race generates a feeling of inferiority as to their status in the community that may affect their hearts and minds in a way unlikely ever to be undone. The effect of this separation on their educational opportunities was well stated by a finding in the Kansas case by a court which nevertheless felt compelled to rule against the Negro plaintiffs: "Segregation of white and colored children in public schools has a detrimental effect upon the colored children. The impact is greater when it has the sanction of the law; for the policy of separating the races is usually interpreted as denoting the inferiority of the negro group. A sense of inferiority affects the motivation of a child to learn. Segregation with the sanction of law, therefore, has a tendency to retard the educational and mental development of Negro children and to deprive them of some of the benefits they would receive in a [racially] integrated school system." Whatever may have been the extent of psychological knowledge at the time of *Plessy v. Ferguson,* this finding is amply supported by modern authority. Any language in *Plessy v. Ferguson* contrary to this finding is rejected.

We conclude that in the field of public education the doctrine of "separate but equal" has no place. Separate educational facilities are inherently unequal. Therefore, we hold that the plaintiffs and others similarly situated for whom the actions have been brought are, by reason of the segregation complained of, deprived of the equal protection of the laws guaranteed by the 14th Amendment. This disposition makes unnecessary any discussion whether such segregation also violates the Due Process Clause of the 14th Amendment. Because these are class actions, because of the wide applicability of this decision, and because of the great variety of local conditions, the formulation of decrees in these cases presents problems of considerable complexity. On reargument, the consideration of appropriate relief was necessarily subordinated to the primary question—the constitutionality of segregation in public education. We have now announced that such segregation is a denial of the equal protection of the laws. In order that we may have the full assistance of the parties in formulating decrees, the cases will be restored to the docket, and the parties are requested to present further argument....

It is so ordered.

* * * * * *

1. *How does the Court's decision reflect a consideration of nonlegal factors, such as culture and social psychology?*

2. *Contrast the arguments delivered here with those in Plessy v. Ferguson.*

3. *The Court makes no provision for enforcing its order. Why, then, were civil rights groups so encouraged by the decision?*

28–3   Southern Manifesto on Integration, 1956

The Court issued a follow-up to the Brown *decision in 1955, addressing the issue of implementation. It ruled that desegregation must proceed "with all deliberate speed," beginning with states submitting timetables and oversight left to federal district courts. Meanwhile, political and legal resistance to desegregation gained strength throughout the white South. The militant White Citizens Councils quickly claimed a half-million members in eleven states. In 1956, 101 southern members of the Senate and House signed the following manifesto opposing the* Brown *decision and the reasoning behind it.*

SOURCE: *New York Times,* March 12, 1956.

We regard the decision of the Supreme Court in the school cases as clear abuse of judicial power. It climaxes a trend in the Federal judiciary undertaking to legislate, in derogation of the authority of Congress, and to encroach upon the reserved rights of the states and the people.

The original Constitution does not mention education. Neither does the Fourteenth Amendment nor any other amendment. The debates preceding the submission of the Fourteenth Amendment clearly show that there was no intent that it should affect the systems of education maintained by the states.

The very Congress which proposed the amendment subsequently provided for segregated schools in the District of Columbia.

When the amendment was adopted in 1868, there were thirty-seven states of the Union. Every one of the twenty-six states that had any substantial racial differences among its people either approved the operation of segregated schools already in existence or subsequently established such schools by action of the same law-making body which considered the Fourteenth Amendment.

As admitted by the Supreme Court in the public school case (*Brown v. Board of Education*), the doctrine of separate but equal schools "apparently originated in *Roberts v. City of Boston* (1849), upholding school segregation against attack as being violative of a state constitutional guarantee of equality." This constitutional doctrine began in the North—not in the South—and it was followed not only in Massachusetts but in Connecticut, New York, Illinois, Indiana, Michigan, Minnesota, New Jersey, Ohio, Pennsylvania and other northern states until they, exercising their rights as states through the constitutional processes of local self-government, changed their school systems.

In the case of *Plessy v. Ferguson* in 1896 the Supreme Court expressly declared that under the Fourteenth Amendment no person was denied any of his rights if the states provided separate but equal public facilities. This decision has been followed in many other cases. It is notable that the Supreme Court, speaking through Chief Justice Taft, a former President of the United States, unanimously declared in 1927 in *Lum v. Rice* that the "separate but equal" principle is "…within the discretion of the state in regulating its public schools and does not conflict with the Fourteenth Amendment." This interpretation, restated time and again, became a part of the life of the people of many of the states and confirmed their habits, customs, traditions and way of life. It is founded on elemental humanity and common sense, for parents should not be deprived by Government of the right to direct the lives and education of their own children. Though there has been no constitutional amendment or act of Congress changing this established legal principle almost a century old, the Supreme Court of the to United States, with no legal basis for such action, undertook to exercise their naked judicial power and substituted their personal political and social ideas for the established law of the land.

This unwarranted exercise of power by the court, contrary to the Constitution, is creating chaos and confusion in the states principally affected. It is destroying the amicable relations between the white and Negro races that have been created through ninety years of patient effort by the good people of both races. It has planted hatred and suspicion where there has been heretofore friendship and understanding. Without regard to the consent of the governed, outside agitators are threatening immediate and revolutionary changes in our public school systems. If done, this is certain to destroy the system of public education in some of the states. With the gravest concern for the explosive and dangerous condition created by this decision and inflamed by outside meddlers:

We reaffirm our reliance on the Constitution as the fundamental law of the land. We decry the Supreme Court's encroachments on rights reserved to the states and to the people, contrary to established law and to the Constitution.

We commend the motives of those states which it have declared the intention to resist forced integration by any lawful means.

We appeal to the states and people who are not directly affected by these decisions to consider the constitutional principles involved against the time when they too, on issues vital to them, may be the victims of judicial encroachment.

Even though we constitute a minority in the present Congress, we have full faith that a majority of the American people believe in the dual system of government which has enabled us to achieve our greatness and will in time demand that the reserved rights of the states and of the people be made secure against judicial usurpation.

We pledge ourselves to use all lawful means to bring about a reversal of this decision which is contrary to the Constitution and to prevent the use of force in its implementation.

In this trying period, as we all seek to right this wrong, we appeal to our people not to be provoked by the agitators and troublemakers invading our states and to scrupulously refrain from disorder and lawless acts.

* * * * * *

1. *How does the Manifesto's legal interpretation of the Fourteenth Amendment differ from the Court's? To what extent does it invoke nonlegal factors?*

2. *What are the Manifesto's assumptions about race relations in the South since the Civil War? How does it define states' rights?*

28–4 *Julian Bond, Sit-Ins and the Origins of SNCC, 1960*

The sit-in movement began in Greensboro, North Carolina, in early 1960 and quickly spread to cities across the South. it attracted thousands of young people, mostly African-American students, eager to challenge segregation in new ways. Julian Bond came from an educated, middle-class black family in Georgia. He attended Morehouse College, one of six historically black institutions that composed the Atlanta University Center. Bond emerged as a leader of the sit-in movement in Atlanta and the Student Non-Violent Coordinating Committee (SNCC), founded in the spring of 1960.

SOURCE: Reprinted by permission of The Putnam Publishing Group from *My Soul is Rested* by Howell Raines. Copyright © 1977 by Howell Raines.

JULIAN BOND: On about the third day of February, 1960, I was sitting in what was then Yates and Milton's Drugstore at the corner of Fair and Chestnut streets which was sort of a student hangout and served the function of a coffeehouse for Atlanta University Center students.* Sitting in the back there, just doing nothing, I guess, by myself. A fellow came over whom I knew to be Lonnie King. I knew him because he was a football player and had just run a touchdown against someone, a spectacular touchdown. Morehouse didn't have a good team. And he came up to me and he showed me a copy of the Atlanta *Daily World* which at that time was a daily paper. I know it was the third or fourth of February because the headline said. "Greensboro Student Sit-In, Third Day."
He said, "Have you seen that?" And I was sort of irritated and I said, "Yeah, you know, I read the papers." And he said, "What do you think about it?" And I said, "Well, it's

---

* The Atlanta University Center comprises Morehouse and five other black institutions. The AU schools, as they are called, occupy adjoining campuses near downtown Atlanta.

all right, pretty good stuff." And he said, "Don't you think it ought to happen here?" And I said, "It probably will." And he said, "Let's make it happen." And I should have said, "What do you mean, *let's?*" [Laughs] But I didn't. You know, Lonnie's a very persuasive guy, and I didn't know him at all except by reputation as an athlete. And he said. "You take this side of the drugstore and I'll take the other and we'll call a meeting for Sale Hall Annex [a building on the campus] for noon today to talk about it." So I took half the drugstore, and he took half, and we had a meeting of a small group of people, about twenty people. And the next day enlarged it to more and more, and that began the student movement....

Our original plan was to hit all of the five-and-dimes, Woolworth's and W.T. Grant's and Kresge's and all those places, and we went to the Atlanta University Center presidents...and they suggested—Dr. Clement, rather, suggested—what I see in retrospect was a delaying move. He suggested that if we demonstrated nobody would know why we were demonstrating, which, of course, was foolish. Of course, they would know why. The lunch counters were segregated and we wanted them integrated.

But he said, "Atlanta students are always different; we have to do it better than anyone else." So he suggested that we publish in the paper, in the two daily papers and the *World,* a statement of grievances about what we thought was wrong and how it could be set right....

It was called "An Appeal for Human Rights" and Dr. Clement somehow got the money for that to be published as a full page ad in the *Journal* and *Constitution* and the *World.* Now I say all this to say that what Dr. Clement really wanted to do was just have us put off the initial demonstration, believing that if we ever did begin we couldn't be stopped, and he did succeed in having us delay it until the fifteenth of March. We were ready in the middle of February to do something. He, through this delaying tactic, put us off until the middle of March.

See, the sit-ins had been going on all over the country at the time and most of them were at private places like Woolworth's, and there was some legal question as to what your rights were when you went into a place that was private property. The businessman's position was that he had a right to run it the way he wanted to. There was no federal anti-discrimination law, and so some lawyers and the presidents suggested that if we wanted to go to some place where we would be on firm footing, to go to cafeterias in public buildings…the City Hall cafeteria, the state cafeteria, the bus station cafeterias, because they are involved in interstate commerce….

We didn't go to any private places that first day, and I was chosen to lead the group at City Hall. They had a big sign out in the front at the time which said "Cafeteria, Public Is Welcome." So we went in, very neat, neckties, and all the girls looking as sharp as they could, and I was so goddamn nervous I didn't know what to do. I had told all these kids, I had about twelve people with me, that we'd be in jail fifteen minutes at the most. There was a heavyset woman that I guess was the manager, and she said, "What do you want?" And we said, "We want to eat." And she said, "Well, we can't serve you here." And I said, "Well, the sign outside says the public is welcome." She said, "This is just for City Hall employees." We said, "That's not true, you've got a sign outside saying the public is welcome and we're the public and we want to eat." She said, "I'm going to call the police." She did, and a paddy wagon backed up to that door as you face the City Hall on the right side there, and we all got in, scared. They took us down to the old big jail, the one that's been torn down, the one they used to call Big Rock….

And a little later they…took us to a hearing before some judge. I don't remember who it was, but the two lawyers who defended me were Hollowell and A.T. Walden,* and Walden was in his dotage and literally fell asleep on his feet….I'm looking at Walden, and I said, "This guy's my lawyer and he's asleep." [Incredulous] And the judge said, "Well, how do you plead?" And I looked at Hollowell and I said, "How do I plead?" [Laughs] And Hollowell said, "Innocent, you fool." So I said, "Innocent, Your Honor."

And they bound me over to the grand jury and later I was indicted on nine counts—violation of the anti-trespass law; violation of the anti-mask law, which is an anti-Ku Klux Klan statute; conspiracy in restraint of trade; this enormous collection of charges. I just got them to dead docket it two years ago….I was indicted on enough charges to put me away for ninety-nine years, and you think I wasn't scared?…

Then they took us from the courtroom back across to the old jail and time kept passing and these guys kept

saying, "Bond, we've been here about six hours. You said we were getting out in about an hour." I said, "Don't worry about it, fellas, we'll be out in a minute." One or two people began to get nervous. None of us had ever been in jail before. Eventually we were bonded out, later that night, and went over to Paschal's, where Mr. Paschal graciously had a beautiful chicken dinner for us, a free meal. Then we went over to Spelman** where we could be heroes, you know, among the women, and that was it. That was my first and last time in jail.

He recalls the spirit of the times, the happiest of his life.

At one time we had almost fifteen hundred people on a picket line downtown, encircling all of downtown Atlanta. And we had two-way radios. We ran from a little church back over here, Providence Baptist Church, I think it was, a regular shuttle system, cars taking people down and taking them back. We had people coming to spend an hour on their breaks, to spend an hour picketing. [There were] special football coats for the girls, with big hoods, because there were a lot of thugs downtown throwing spitballs and stuff at them. We had special laminated signs that wouldn't wash off in the rain. We were hell. [Laughs]

I'll tell you something else that happened. The Student Nonviolent Coordinating Committee (SNCC) was formed Easter weekend of 1960, and it originally was to be exactly what its name said, a coordinating committee….

The Easter meeting of young sit-in veterans was at Shaw University in Raleigh, North Carolina.

Well, there were about three hundred people there from all over the South, as well as, I guess, about another hundred white students—white and black, but predominately white students from Northern schools—who were in support groups. And there were organizational representatives—the meeting was called by SCLC. Ella Baker was the executive director then. She was just being replaced by Wyatt Tee Walker. She was on the way out, and he was on the way in.

But she was very concerned about two things. One, she thought that SCLC *hadn't* been involved in the sit-in movement as much as it should have been, and by that I think she meant Dr. King. And secondly, she felt that the student movement was really directionless, that it had narrow vision and thought the whole world was nothing but lunch counters. And so she called this meeting together, I don't think with any idea that an organization would come out of it, or that may have been her plan. But there were people there from SCLC, the NAACP, and CORE, and each of them wanted us, the students, to

---

* Donald Hollowell, a well-known civil rights lawyer, was the younger partner of A.T. Walden, the pioneering black attorney consulted by Rev. Martin Luther King, Sr.

** The women's college of the AU complex.

become a part of them. The NAACP wanted us to be NAACP youth chapters, CORE wanted us to become CORE chapters, SCLC wanted us to become the youth wing of SCLC. We finally decided we'd be our own thing and set up what was then called the Temporary Student Nonviolent Coordinating Committee and elected Marion Barry the chairman.

There was a dynamite, a militant speech given by James Lawson, who was then at Vanderbilt and had been arrested in church while he was preaching one Sunday morning by the Nashville police for conspiracy or something. But there was the feeling among many of us that James Lawson was challenging King for leadership of this group of young people, that he was younger than King, that he was still a student himself at the Vanderbilt Divinity School, that he was in his definition of nonviolence more militant than King. He believed in radical nonviolence, chaining yourself to airplanes and that kind of stuff. Lunch counters were okay, but he was for bigger things. So he made a very aggressive speech, really stirred people up.

Miss Baker made a very thoughtful speech, the theme of which was "more than a hamburger," that we ought to be interested in more than integrating lunch counters, that there was a whole social structure to be changed here. And then King made a speech. Whatever it was, it left no real impression, except that this was Martin Luther King. We used to joke about King. He was a hometown boy…so it was hard for us to look at him as *Martin Luther King, Jr.* We used to joke and call him The Lord. But it was hard for us to revere him, I think, the way other people did. You know, no man is a prophet in his own hometown. But there was a lot of pressure for us to join these other groups, and we resisted and set up our own little group.

* * * * * *

1.   *How did the sit-ins differ from the Montgomery bus boycott in tactics and makeup of the protesters?*

2.   *What does Bond's account suggest about the impact of young people on the movement? What role did generational tensions play within the movement at this point?*

28–5   *Martin Luther King Jr., Letter from a Birmingham Jail, 1963*

In 1963, Martin Luther King Jr. and the Southern Christian Leadership Conference brought a campaign of nonviolent civil disobedience to Birmingham, Alabama. The city had long been a bastion of segregation and racial discrimination. King and his advisers were confident that they could provoke local authorities and bring the glare of national publicity to their cause. King was one of hundreds of people arrested, and while in jail he composed this letter to eight local clergymen who had publicly criticized his tactics.

You deplore the demonstrations that are presently taking place in Birmingham. But I am sorry that your statement did not express a similar concern for the conditions that brought the demonstrations into being. I am sure that each of you would want to go beyond the superficial social analyst who looks merely at effects, and does not grapple with underlying causes. I would not hesitate to say that it is unfortunate that so-called demonstrations are taking place in Birmingham at this time, but I would say in more emphatic terms that it is even more unfortunate that the white power structure of this city left the Negro community with no other alternative.

In any nonviolent campaign there are four basic steps: 1) collection of the facts to determine whether injustices are alive; 2) negotiation; 3) self-purification; and 4) direct action. We have gone through all of these steps in Birmingham. There can be no gainsaying of the fact that racial injustice engulfs this community. Birmingham is probably the most thoroughly segregated city in the United States. Its ugly record of police brutality is known in every section of this country. Its unjust treatment of Negroes in the courts is a notorious reality. There have been more unsolved bombings of Negro homes and churches in Birmingham than any city in this nation. These are the hard, brutal, and unbelievable facts….

We know through painful experience that freedom is never voluntarily given by the oppressor; it must be demanded by the oppressed. Frankly I have never yet engaged in a direct action movement that was "well timed," according to the timetable of those who have not suffered unduly from the disease of segregation. For years now I have heard the word "Wait!" It rings in the ear of every Negro with a piercing familiarity. This "wait" has almost always meant "never." It has been a tranquilizing Thalidomide, relieving the emotional stress for a moment, only to give birth to an ill-formed infant of frustration. We must come to see with the distinguished jurist of yesterday that "justice too long delayed is justice denied." We have waited for more than 340 years for our constitutional and God-given rights. The nations of Asia and Africa are moving with jet-like speed toward the goal of political independence, and we still creep at horse and buggy pace toward the gaining of a cup of coffee at a lunch counter....

You express a great deal of anxiety over our willingness to break laws. This is certainly a legitimate concern. Since we so diligently urge people to obey the Supreme Court's decision of 1954 outlawing segregation in the public schools, it is rather strange and paradoxical to find us consciously breaking laws. One may well ask, "How can you advocate breaking some laws and obeying others?" The answer is found in the fact that there are two types of laws: There are *just* laws and there are *unjust* laws. I would be the first to advocate obeying just laws. One has not only a legal but a moral responsibility to obey just laws. Conversely, one has a moral responsibility to disobey unjust laws. I would agree with Saint Augustine that "An unjust law is no law at all."

Now what is the difference between the two? How does one determine when a law is just or unjust? A just law is a man-made code that squares with the moral law or the law of God. An unjust law is a mode that is out of harmony with the moral law. To put it in the terms of Saint Thomas Aquinas, an unjust law is a human law that is not rooted in eternal and natural law. Any law that uplifts human personality is just. Any law that degrades human personality is unjust.

All segregation statutes are unjust because segregation distorts the soul and damages the personality. It gives the segregator a false sense of superiority and the segregated a false sense of inferiority. To use the words of Martin Buber, the great Jewish philosopher, segregation substitutes an "I-it" relationship for the "I-thou" relationship, and ends up relegating persons to the status of things. So segregation is not only politically, economically, and sociologically unsound, but it is morally wrong and sinful. Paul Tillich has said that sin is separation. Isn't segregation an existential expression of man's tragic separation, an expression of his awful estrangement, his terrible sinfulness? So I can urge men to obey the 1954 decision of the Supreme Court because it is morally right, and I can urge them to disobey segregation ordinances because they are morally wrong....

Let me give another explanation. An unjust law is a code inflicted upon a minority which that minority had no part in enacting or creating because it did not have the unhampered right to vote. Who can say the Legislature of Alabama which set up the segregation laws was democratically elected? Throughout the state of Alabama all types of conniving methods are used to prevent Negroes from becoming registered voters and there are some counties

without a single Negro registered to vote despite the fact that the Negro constitutes a majority of the population. Can any law set up in such a state be considered democratically structured?...

We can never forget that everything Hitler did in Germany was "legal" and everything the Hungarian freedom fighters did in Hungary was "illegal." It was "illegal" to aid and comfort a Jew in Hitler's Germany. But I am sure that, if I had lived in Germany during that time, I would have aided and comforted my Jewish brothers even though it was illegal. If I lived in a Communist country today where certain principles dear to the Christian faith are suppressed, I believe I would openly advocate disobeying these anti-religious laws....

We will have to repent in this generation not as merely for the vitriolic words and actions of the bad people, but for the appalling silence of good people. We must come to see that human progress never rolls in on wheels of inevitability. It comes through the tireless efforts and persistent work of men willing to be co-workers with God, and without this hard work time itself becomes an ally of the forces of social stagnation....

You spoke of our activity in Birmingham as extreme. At first I was rather disappointed that fellow clergymen would see my nonviolent efforts as those of the extremist. I started thinking about the fact that I stand in the middle of two opposing forces in the Negro community. One is a force of complacency made up of Negroes who, as a result of long years of oppression, have been so completely drained of self-respect and a sense of "somebodiness" that they have adjusted to segregation, and of a few Negroes in the middle class who, because of a degree of academic and economic security, and because at points they profit by segregation, have unconsciously become insensitive to the problems of the masses. The other force is one of bitterness and hatred and comes perilously close to advocating violence. It is expressed in the various black nationalist groups that are springing up over the nation, the largest and best known being Elijah Muhammad's Muslim movement. This movement is nourished by the contemporary frustration over the continued existence of racial discrimination. It is made up of people who have lost faith in America, who have absolutely repudiated Christianity, and who have concluded that the white man is an incurable "devil."

I have tried to stand between these two forces saying that we need not follow the "donothingism" of the complacent or the hatred and despair of the black nationalist. There is the more excellent way of love and nonviolent protest. I'm grateful to God that, through the Negro church, the dimension of nonviolence entered our struggle. If this philosophy had not emerged I am convinced that by now many streets of the South would be flowing with floods of blood. And I am further convinced that if our white brothers dismiss us as "rabble rousers" and "outside agitators"—those of us who are working through the channels of nonviolent direct action—and refuse to support our nonviolent efforts, millions of Negroes, out of frustration and despair, will seek solace and security in black nationalist ideologies, a development that will lead inevitably to a frightening racial nightmare.

Oppressed people cannot remain oppressed forever. The urge for freedom will eventually come. This is what has happened to the American Negro. Something within has reminded him of his birthright of freedom; something without has reminded that he can gain it....

But as I continued to think about the matter I gradually gained a bit of satisfaction from being considered an extremist. Was not Jesus an extremist in love? "Love your enemies, bless them that curse you, pray for them that despitefully use you." Was not Amos an extremist for justice—"Let justice roll down like waters and righteousness like a mighty stream." Was not Paul an extremist for the gospel of Jesus Christ—"I bear in my body the marks of the Lord Jesus." Was not Martin Luther an extremist— "Here I stand; I can do none other so help me God." Was not John Bunyan an extremist—"I will stay in jail to the end of my days before I make a butchery of my conscience." Was not Abraham Lincoln an extremist—"This nation cannot survive half slave and half free." Was not Thomas Jefferson an extremist—"We hold these truths to be self evident that all men are created equal."

So the question is not whether we will be extremist but what kind of extremist will we be. Will we be extremists for hate or will we be extremists for love? Will we be extremists for the preservation of injustice—or will we be extremists for the cause of justice?...

I have traveled the length and breadth of Alabama, Mississippi, and all the other Southern states. On sweltering summer days and crisp autumn mornings I have looked at her beautiful churches with their spires pointing heavenward. I have beheld the impressive outlay of her massive religious education buildings. Over and over again I have found myself asking: "Who worships here? Who is their God? Where were their voices when the lips of Governor Barnett dripped with words of interposition and nullification? Where were they when Governor Wallace gave the clarion call for defiance and hatred?"...The contemporary Church is so often a weak, ineffectual voice with an uncertain sound. It is so often the arch-supporter of the *status quo*. Far from being disturbed by the presence of the Church, the power structure of the average community is consoled by the Church's silent and often vocal sanction of things as they are.

But the judgment of God is upon the Church as never before. If the Church of today does not recapture the sacrificial spirit of the early Church, it will lose its authentic ring, forfeit the loyalty of millions and be dis-

missed as an irrelevant social club with no meaning for the 20th century.... I am thankful to God that some noble souls from the ranks of organized religion have broken loose from the paralyzing chains of conformity and joined us as active partners in the struggle for freedom...they have gone with the faith that right defeated is stronger than evil triumphant. These men have been the leaven in the lump of the race. Their witness has been the spiritual salt that has preserved the true meaning of the Gospel in these troubled times. They have carved a tunnel of hope through the dark mountain of disappointment.... But even if the Church does not come to the aid of justice, I have no despair about the future. I have no fear about the outcome of our struggle in Birmingham, even if our motives are presently misunderstood. We will reach the goal of freedom in Birmingham and all over the nation, because the goal of America is freedom. Abused and scorned though we may be, our destiny is tied up with the destiny of America.... One day the South will recognize its real heroes. They will be the James Merediths, courageously and with a majestic sense of purpose, facing jeering and hostile mobs and the agonizing loneliness that characterizes the life of the pioneer. They will be old, oppressed, battered Negro women, symbolized in a 72-year-old woman of Montgomery, Alabama, who rose up with a sense of dignity and with her people decided not to ride the segregated buses, and responded to one who inquired about her tiredness with ungrammatical profundity: "My feets is tired, but my soul is rested." They will be young high school and college students, young ministers of the Gospel and a host of the elders, courageously and nonviolently sitting in at lunch counters and willingly going to jail for conscience's sake. One day the South will know that when these disinherited children of God sat down at lunch counters they were in reality standing up for the best in the American dream and the most sacred values in our Judeo-Christian heritage, and thus carrying our whole nation back to great wells of democracy which were dug deep by the founding fathers in the formulation of the Constitution and the Declaration of Independence....

* * * * * *

1. How does King use theological and ethical arguments, familiar to his critics, to defend his actions? What specific elements of Judeo-Christian tradition does he invoke?

2. What political and legal points does he combine with these?

3. How does King answer the charges of extremism?

28-6 Fannie Lou Hamer, Voting Rights in Mississippi, 1962–1964

Fannie Lou Hamer grew up in Sunflower County, Mississippi, where she sharecropped cotton with her husband. In 1962, she responded to the efforts of SNCC workers who were attempting to encourage voter registration among the black population. At the time, Mississippi had the lowest percentage of black voters in the South. Hamer became a local leader of the civil rights movement, and she endured frightful beatings for her activism. She went on to help found the Mississippi Freedom Democratic Party. At the 1964 Democratic National Convention, she riveted delegates and a national television audience with her story.

SOURCE: Reprinted by permission of The Putnam Publishing Group from *My Soul is Rested* by Howell Raines. Copyright © 1977 by Howell Raines.

Fannie Lou Hamer

Well, we were living on a plantation about four and a half miles east of here.... Pap had been out there thirty years, and I had been out there eighteen years, 'cause we had been married at that time eighteen years. And you know, things were just rough.... I don't think that I ever remember working for as much as four dollars a day. Yes, one year I remember working for four dollars a day, and I was gettin' as much as the men, 'cause I kept up with the time....But anyway, I just knowed things wasn't right.

So then that was in 1962 when the civil rights workers came into this county. Now, I didn't know anything about voter registration or nothin' like that, 'cause people had never been told that they could register to vote. And livin' out in the country, if you had a little radio, by the time you got in at night, you'd be too tired to listen at what was goin' on.... So they had a rally. I had gone to church that Sunday, and the minister announced that they were gon' have a mass meeting that Monday night. Well, I didn't know what a mass meeting was, and I was just curious to go to a mass meeting. So I did...and they was talkin' about how blacks had a right to register and how they had a right to *vote*....Just listenin' at 'em, I could just see myself votin' people outa office that I know was wrong and didn't do nothin' to help the poor. I said, you know, that's sumpin' I really wanna be involved in, and finally at the end of that rally, I had made up my mind that I was gonna come out there when they said you could go down that Friday to try to register.

She remembers the date precisely: August 31, 1962. She and seventeen others climbed aboard an old bus owned by a black man from neighboring Bolivar County. SNCC had chartered it for the thirty-mile ride to the county, seat in Indianola. Once there, she was the first into the registrar's office.

...He brought a big old book out there, and he gave me the sixteenth section of the Constitution of Mississippi, and that was dealing with de facto laws, and I didn't know nothin' about no de facto laws, didn't know nothin' about any of 'em. I could copy it like it was in the book...but after I got through copying it, he told me to give a reasonable interpretation and tell the meaning of that section that I had copied. Well, I flunked out....

So then we started back to Ruleville and on our way back to Ruleville, this same highway patrolman that I had seen steady cruisin' around this bus stopped us. We had crossed that bridge, coming over from Indianola. They got out the cars, flagged the bus down. When they flagged the bus down, they told all of us to get off of the bus. So at this time, we just started singing "Have a Little Talk with Jesus," and we got off the bus, and all they wanted then was for us to get back on the bus. They arrested Bob[*] and told the bus driver he was under arrest. So we went back then to Indianola. The bus driver was fined one hundred dollars for driving a bus with too much yellow in it. Now ain't that ridiculous?

For what?

Too much yellow. Said the bus looked too much like a school bus. That's funny, but it's the truth. But you see, it was to frighten us to death. This same bus had been used year after year hauling cotton choppers and cotton pickers to Florida to try to make a livin' that winter, and he had never been arrested before. But the day he tried...to carry us to Indianola, they fined him a hundred dollars, and I guess it was so ridiculous that they finally cut the fine down to thirty dollars, and all of us *together*—not one, but all us together—had enough to pay the fine. So we paid the fine, and then we got back on the bus and come on to Ruleville.

So Rev. Jeff Summers, who live on Charles Street, just the next street over, he carried me out there on the Marlowe Plantation where I had worked for eighteen years. And when I got out there, my little girl—she's dead now, Dorothy—she met me and one of Pap's cousins, and said that man [who owned the plantation] had been raising a lot of Cain ever since we left, that he had been in the

---

[*] Bob Moses, who had come back to Ruleville to accompany the group to the courthouse.

field more times than he usually come a day, because I had gone to the courthouse. See, the people at the courthouse would call and tell it. So they was kinda scared, and quite natural I began to feel nervous, but I knowed I hadn't done nothin' wrong. So after my little girl told me, wasn't too long 'fore Pap got off, and he was tellin' me the same thing that the other kids had told me.

I went on in the house, and I sat down on a little old bed that belonged to the little girl, and when I sat down on the bed, this man [who owned the plantation] he come up and he asked Pap, "Did you tell Fannie Lou what I said?" And Pap said, "Yessir, I sho' did." And I got up and walked to the door, and then he asked me, "Did Pap tell you what I said?" I said, "He told me." And he said, "I mean that. You'll have to go back to Indianola and withdraw, or you have to leave this place." So I said, "Mr. Dee, I didn't go down there to register for you. I went down there to register for myself." And that made him madder, you know.

So he told me, "I want your answer now, yea or nay." And he said, "They gon'"—now, I don't know who the *they* were, whether it was the white Citizens Council or the Ku Klux Klan, 'cause I don't think one is no worse than the other—"they gon' worry me tonight. They gon' worry the hell outa me, and I'm gon' worry hell outa you. You got 'til in the mornin' to tell me. But if you don't go back there and withdraw, you got to leave the plantation."

So I knowed I wasn't goin' back to withdraw, so wasn't nothin' for me to do but leave the plantation. So Pap brought me out that same night and I come to Mrs. Tucker's, a lady live over on Byron Street. I went to her house, and I stayed, and Pap began to feel nervous when he went to the shop* and saw some buckshot shells. And they don't have buckshot shells to *play* with in August and September, because you ain't huntin' or nothin' like that.

> *On September tenth—again she recalls the date precisely—came the nightrider attack. The riders shot into the McDonald home, where the SNCC workers were staying, and into the Tucker home, where Mrs. Hamer had been given shelter. "They shot in that house sixteen times, tryin' to kill me," she remembers. She fled to the home of a niece in Tallahatchie County when the night-time terrorism continued on into the fall.*

I stayed away, 'cause things then—you could see 'em at night. They would have fires in the middle of the road.... You wouldn't see no Klan signs, but just make a fire in the middle of the road. And it was *so dangerous,* I stayed in Tallahatchie County all of September and then October, and then November I come back to Ruleville. I was comin', I didn't know why I was comin', but I was just sick of runnin' and hadn't done nothin'.... I started tryin' to find a place to stay, 'cause we didn't have nothin'.

> *The woman who had been her sixth-grade school teacher put her in touch with a black woman who had a three-room house for rent "for eighteen dollars a month and that was a lotta money." She and her family moved in on December 3.*

That was on a Sunday, and that Monday, the fourth of December, I went back to Indianola to the circuit clerk's office and I told him who I was and I was there to take that literacy test again.

I said, "Now, you cain't have me fired 'cause I'm already fired, and I won't have to move now, because I'm not livin' in no white man's house." I said, "I'll be here every thirty days until I become a registered voter." 'Cause that's what you would have to do: go every thirty days and see had you passed the literacy test....I went back then the tenth of January in 1963, and I had become registered....I passed the second one, because at the second time I went back, I had been studying sections of the Mississippi Constitution, so I would know if I got one that was simple enough that I might could pass it.

I passed that second test, but it made us become like criminals. We would have to have our lights out before dark. It was cars passing that house all times of the night, driving real slow with guns, and pickups with white mens in it, and they'd pass that house just as slow as they could pass it...three guns lined up in the back. All of that. This was the kind of stuff. Pap couldn't get nothin' to do....

So I started teachin' citizenship class, and I became the supervisor of the citizenship class in this county. So I moved around the county to do citizenship education, and later on I become a field secretary for SNCC—I guess being about one of the oldest people at that time that was a field secretary, 'cause they was real young.

> *Once more the classic Southern story was repeated. White oppression created a Movement heroine. She became a leader in the Mississippi Freedom Democratic Party and, at the 1964 Democratic Convention, a national celebrity with her televised testimony before the Credentials Committee about that "woesome time for us when we was arrested in Winona." That time came in the summer of 1963. She was with a group returning from a voter-registration workshop in South Carolina. Their bus stopped in Winona, a central Mississippi town which had not bowed to the ICC's bus-depot ruling. "Some of the folks got off to go in to get food, and some of 'em got off to go in the washroom. Well, they went in what at that time was called the white side, and you just didn't go in the white side of a restaurant." She was one of seven arrested.*

They carried us on to the county jail. It wasn't the city jail. The county jail, so we could be far enough out, they didn't care how loud we hollered, wasn't nobody

---

* The maintenance shop on the plantation.

gon' hear us….I was put in the cell with…I cain't think of this child's name…Evester Simpson. She's Mrs. Morris now. But anyway, I was in the cell with her, and they left Miss Ponder[*] and somebody else out, and I started hearing screaming like I had never heard. And I could hear the sounds of the licks, but I couldn't see nobody. And I hear somebody when they say, "Cain't you say yessir, nigger? Cain't you say yessir, bitch?"

And I could understand Miss Ponder's voice. She said, "Yes, I can say yessir." He said, "Well, say it." She said, "I don't know you well enough." She never would say yessir, and I could hear when she would hit the flo', and then I could hear them licks just soundin'. [Softly] That was somethin'. That's a experience—that's a experience that I wouldn't want to go through again. But anyway, she kept screamin', and they kept beatin' on her, and finally she started prayin' for 'em, and she asked God to have mercy on 'em, because they didn't know what they was doin'.

And after then…I heard some real *keen* screams, and that's when they passed my cell with a girl, she was fifteen years old, Miss Johnson. June Johnson. They passed my cell, and the blood was runnin' down in her face, and they put her in another cell.

And then finally they come to my room, and one of them men told me, "Get up from there, fatso," and he carried me outa that cell. They first asked me, when at they first come to the cell, they asked me where I was from, and I told 'em. And they said, "We gon' check that out," and I reckon they was callin' the white folks here. Well, the white folks here knowed I had tried to register, so they was gon' give me as much trouble as possible, 'cause when they come back, the man say, "You from Ruleville, all right." Said, "You, bitch, you, we gon' make you wish you was dead." And let me tell you, before they stopped beatin' me, I wish they would me have hit me one lick that could have ended the misery me that they had me in. They had me to lay down on this bunk bed with my face down, and they had two black prisoners. You know, a lot of folks would say, "Well, I woulda died before I'd done that." But nobody know the condition that those prisoners was in, before they were s'posed to beat me. And I heard that highway patrolman tell that black man, said, "If you don't beat her, you *know* what we'll do to you." And he didn't have no other choice.

So they had me lay down on my face, and they bea with a thick leather thing that was wide. And it had sumpin' in it *heavy*. I don't know what that was, rocks or lead. But everytime they hit me, I got just as hard, and I put my hands behind my back, and they beat me in my hands 'til my hands…my hands was as navy blue as anything you ever seen…that blood, I guess, and then beatin' it 'til it just turned black.

And then after the first one beat, they ordered the second one to beat me, and when the second one started beatin', it was just—it was just too much. I started wigglin'…you know, kickin' my feet back there. The highway patrolman walked over there and had that first one had beat, told him to sit on my feet…while the second one beat But anyway, they finally told me to get up, and I just couldn't hardly get up, and they kept on tellin' me to get up. I finally could get up, but when I got back to my cell bed, I couldn't set down. I would *scream*. It hurted me to set down.

After I got beat, I didn't hardly see my family in 'bout a month, 'cause I went on to Atlanta, from Atlanta to Washington, and from Washington to New York, because they didn't want my family to see me in the shape I was in. I had been beat 'til I was real hard, just hard like a piece of wood or somethin'. A person don't know what can happen to they body if they beat with something like I was beat with.

Less than four years after she failed that first literacy test at the Sunflower County Courthouse, less than three years after that devastating beating in Winona, Mississippi *magazine named her as one of six "Women of Influence" in the state. The magazine carried her picture next to that of another woman of influence—an aristocratic Delta matron who wrote a newspaper column entitled "Dis an' Dat." Within ten years Ruleville had held Fannie Lou Hamer Day. The white mayor who had once clapped her husband in jail for an overdue water bill said she would go down in history as a champion of her people.*

* * * * * *

1. What does Hamer's account reveal about the connection between economics and politics in Mississippi?

2. What does her story suggest about the political evolution of grassroots leaders in the movement? What impact did her activism have on family life?

---

[*] Annelle Ponder, one of two SCLC voter-education teachers permanently stationed in Mississippi.

28–7   *Letters from Mississippi Freedom Summer, 1964*

Over one thousand young volunteers, most of them northern white college students, took part in the Mississippi Freedom Summer Project. Sponsored by SNCC and the Congress of Racial Equality (CORE), the Project's goals included voter registration, the establishment of "Freedom Schools," and bringing the glare of national publicity to racial oppression in the state. The disappearance and brutal murder of three project volunteers, James Chaney, a local African American, and Michael Schwerner and Andrew Goodman, two northern whites, brought enormous attention to the project. It also stirred resentment among young African-American activists who bitterly noted that if the murdered volunteers had all been black, there would have been far less national concern.

Mileston, August 18

Dear folks,

One can't move onto a plantation cold; or canvas a plantation in the same manner as the Negro ghetto in town. It's far too dangerous. Many plantations—homes included—are posted, meaning that no trespassing is permitted, and the owner feels that he has the prerogative to shoot us on sight when we are in the house of one of *his* Negroes.

Before we canvas a plantation, our preparation includes finding out whether the houses are posted, driving through or around the plantation without stopping, meanwhile making a detailed map of the plantation. We're especially concerned with the number of roads in and out of the plantation. For instance, some houses could be too dangerous to canvas because of their location near the boss man's house and on a dead end road. In addition to mapping, we attempt to talk to some of the tenants when they are off the plantation, and ask them about conditions. The kids often have contacts, and can get on the plantation unnoticed by the boss man, with the pretense of just visiting friends. Our canvassing includes not only voter registration, but also extensive reports on conditions—wages, treatment by the boss man, condition of the houses, number of acres of cotton, etc. Much more such work needs to be done. The plantation

system is crucial in Delta politics and economics, and the plantation system must be brought to an end if democracy is to be brought to the Delta....

Love,
Joel

July 18

...Four of us went to distribute flyers announcing the meeting. I talked to a woman who had been down to register a week before. She was afraid. Her husband had lost his job. Even before we got there a couple of her sons had been man-handled by the police. She was now full of wild rumors about shootings and beatings, etc. I checked out two of them later. They were groundless. This sort of rumorspreading is quite prevalent when people get really scared....

At 6 P.M. we returned to Drew for the meeting, to be held in front of a church (they wouldn't let us meet inside, but hadn't told us not to meet outside). A number of kids collected and stood around in a circle with about 15 of us to sing freedom songs. Across the street perhaps 100 adults stood watching. Since this was the first meeting in town, we passed out mimeoed song sheets. Fred Miller, Negro from Mobile, stepped out to the edge of the street to give somebody a sheet. The cops nabbed him. I was about to follow suit so he wouldn't he alone, but Mac's policy [Charles McLaurin, SNCC—a civil rights group— project director] was to ignore the arrest. We sang on mightily "Ain't going to let no jailing turn me around." A group of girls was sort of leaning against the cars on the periphery of the meeting. Mac went over to encourage them to join us. I gave a couple of song sheets to the girls. A cop rushed across the street and told me to come along. I guess I was sort of aware that my actions would get me arrested, but felt that we had to show these girls that we were not afraid. I was also concerned with what might happen to Fred if he was the only one.

...The cop at the station was quite scrupulous about letting me make a phone call. I was then driven to a little concrete structure which looked like a power house. I could hear Fred's courageous, off-key rendition of a freedom song from inside and joined him as we approached. He was very happy to see me. Not long thereafter, four more of our group were driven up to make their calls...

The Drew jail consists of three small cells off a wide hall. It was filthy, hot and stuffy. A cop came back to give us some toilet paper. We sang songs for a while, and yelled greetings to Negroes who drove by curiously. One of the staff workers had been in jail 106 times. I asked the cop if he could open another cell as there were not enough beds accessible to us. He mumbled something about how that would be impossible and left. They hadn't confiscated anything and one of the guys had a battered copy of *The Other America,* so we divided up the chapters. I got the dismal one on the problems of the aged.... To be old and forgotten is certainly a worse sentence than mine (I wouldn't recommend that book for those planning to do time)...

Well, the night was spent swatting mosquitoes. An old Negro couple walked by in front of the jail and asked how we were doing. They said they supported us and the old lady said, "God bless you all." This, in the context of a tense town with a pretty constant stream of whites in cars driving by....

Holly Spring

Dear Mom and Dad:

The atmosphere in class is unbelievable. It is what every teacher dreams about—real, honest enthusiasm and desire to learn anything and everything. The girls come to class of their own free will. They respond to everything that is said. They are excited about learning. They drain me of everything that I have to offer so that I go home at night completely exhausted but very happy....

I start out at 10:30 teaching what we call the Core Curriculum, which is Negro History and the History and Philosophy of the Movement, to about fifteen girls ranging from 15 to 25 years of age. I have one girl who is married with four children, another who is 23 and a graduate from a white college in Tennessee, also very poorly educated. The majority go to a Roman Catholic High School in Holly Springs and have therefore received a fairly decent education by Mississippi standards. They can, for the most part, express themselves on paper but their skills in no way compare to juniors and seniors in northern suburban schools.

In one of my first classes, I gave a talk on Haiti and the slave revolt which took place at the end of the eighteenth century. I told them how the French government (during the French Revolution) abolished slavery all over the French Empire. And then I told them that the English decided to invade the island and take it over for a colony of their own. I watched faces fall all around me. They knew that a small island, run by former slaves, could not defeat England. And then I told them that the people of Haiti succeeded in keeping the English out. I watched a smile spread slowly over a girl's face. And I felt the girls sit up and look at me intently. Then I told them that Napoleon came to power, reinstated slavery, and sent an expedition to reconquer Haiti. Their faces began to fall again. They waited for me to tell them that France defeated the former slaves, hoping against hope I that I would say that they didn't. But when I told them that the French generals tricked the Haitian leader Toussaint to come aboard their ship, captured him and sent him back to France to die, they knew that there was no hope. They

waited for me to spell out the defeat. And when I told them that Haiti did succeed in keeping out the European powers and was recognized finally as an independent republic, they just looked at me and smiled. The room stirred with a gladness and a pride that this could have happened. And I felt so happy and so humble that I could have told them this little story and it could have meant so much.

We have also talked about what it means to be a Southern white who wants to stand up but who is alone, rejected by other whites and not fully accepted by the Negroes. We have talked about their feelings about Southern whites. One day three little white girls came to our school and I asked them to understand how the three girls felt by remembering how it feels when they are around a lot of whites. We agreed that we would not stare at the girls but try to make them feel as normal as possible.

Along with my Core class I teach a religion class at one every afternoon and a class on non-violence at four-fifteen. All my classes are approximately an hour. Both these classes are made up of four to six girls from my morning class and about four boys of the same age group. In religion they are being confronted for the first time with people whom they respect who do not believe in God and with people who believe in God but do not take the Bible literally. It's a challenging class because I have no desire to destroy their belief, whether Roman Catholic or Baptist, but I want them to learn to look at all things critically and to learn to separate fact from interpretation and myth in all areas, not just religion.

Every class is beautiful. The girls respond, respond, respond. And they disagree among themselves. I have no doubt that soon they will be disagreeing with me. At least this is one thing that I am working towards. They are a sharp group. But they are under-educated and starved for knowledge. They know that they have been cheated and they want anything and everything that we can give them.

I have a great deal of faith in these students. They are very mature and very concerned about other people. I really think that they will be able to carry on without us. At least this is my dream...

Love,
Pam

Biloxi, Aug. 16

In the Freedom School one day during poetry writing, a 12-year-old girl handed in this poem to her teacher:

What Is Wrong?
What is wrong with me everywhere I go
  No one seems to look at me.
Sometimes I cry.
I walk through woods and sit on a stone.
  I look at the stars and I sometimes wish.

Probably if my wish ever comes true,
  Everyone will look at me.

Then she broke down crying in her sister's arms. The Freedom School here had given this girl the opportunity of meeting someone she felt she could express her problems to...

                                                    Ruleville

To my brother,

    Last night, I was a long time before sleeping, although I was extremely tired. Every shadow, every noise—the bark of a dog, the sound of a car—in my fear and exhaustion was turned into a terrorist's approach. And I believed that I heard the back door open and a Klansman walk in, until he was close by the bed. Almost paralyzed by the fear, silent, I finally shone my flashlight on the spot where I thought he was standing...I tried consciously to overcome this fear. To relax, I began to breathe deep, think the words of a song, pull the sheet up close to my neck...still the tension. Then I rethought why I was here, rethought what could be gained in view of what could be lost. All this was in rather personal terms, and then in larger scope of the whole Project. I remembered Bob Moses saying he had felt justified in asking hundreds of students to go to Mississippi because he was not asking anyone to do something that he would not do...I became aware of the uselessness of fear that immobilizes an individual. Then I began to relax.

    "We are not afraid. Oh Lord, deep in my heart, I do believe. We Shall Overcome Someday" and then I think I began to truly understand what the words meant. Anyone who comes down here and is not afraid I think must be crazy as well as dangerous to this project where security is quite important. But the type of fear that they mean when they, when we, sing "we are not afraid" is the type that immobilizes....The songs help to dissipate the fear. Some of the words in the songs do not hold real meaning on their own, others become rather monotonous—but when they are sung in unison, or sung silently by oneself they take on new meaning beyond words or rhythm...There is almost a religious quality about some of these songs, having little to do with the usual concept of a god. It has to do with the miracle that youth has organized to fight hatred and ignorance. It has to do with the holiness of the dignity of man. The god that makes such miracles is the god I do believe in when we sing "God is on our side." I know I am on that god's side. And I do hope he is on ours.

    Jon, please be considerate to Mom and Dad. The fear I just expressed, I am sure they feel much more intensely without the relief of being here to know exactly how things are. Please don't go defending me or attacking them if they are critical of the Project....

    They said over the phone "Did you know how much

it takes to make a child?" and I thought of how much it took to make a Herbert Lee (or many others whose names I do not know)...I thought of how much it took to be a Negro in Mississippi twelve months a year for a lifetime. How can such a thing as a life be weighed?...

                                        With constant love,
                                                    Heather

                                        Greenwood, June 29
    We have heard rumors twice to the effect that the three men were found weighted down in that river. Both stories, though the same, were later completely dropped in an hour or so. How do you like that guy Gov. Johnson saying that they might be hiding in the North or maybe in Cuba for all he knew....

                                            Tchula, July 16
    Yesterday while the Mississippi River was being dragged looking for the three missing civil rights workers, two bodies of Negroes were found—one cut in half and one without a head. Mississippi is the only state where you can drag a river any time and find bodies you were not expecting. Things are really much better for rabbits—there's a closed season on rabbits.

                                            Como, August 3
    About three weeks ago there was a flying rumor that they had been found in a rural jail. Tonight it was said that three graves had been found near Philadelphia. How the ghosts of those three shadow all our work! "Did you know them?" I am constantly asked. Did I need to?

                                        Meridian, August 4
    Last night Pete Seeger was giving a concert in Meridian. We sang a lot of freedom songs, and every time a verse like 'No more lynchings' was sung, or 'before I'd be a slave I'd be buried in my grave,' I had the flash of understanding that sometimes comes when you suddenly think about the meaning of a familiar song....I wanted to stand up and shout to them, "Think about what you are singing—people really have died to keep us all from being slaves." Most of the people there still did not know that the bodies had been found. Finally just before the singing of "We Shall Overcome," Pete Seeger made the announcement. "We must sing 'We Shall Overcome' now," said Seeger. "The three boys would not have wanted us to weep now, but to sing and understand this song." That seems to me the best way to explain the greatness of this project—that death can have this meaning. Dying is not an everpresent possibility in Meridian, the way some reports may suggest. Nor do any of us want to die. Yet in a moment like last night, we can feel that anyone who did die for the Project would wish to be remembered not by tributes or grief but by understanding and continuation of what he was doing....

As we left the church, we heard on the radio the end of President Johnson's speech announcing the air attacks on Vietnam....I could only think "This must not be the beginning of a war. There is still a freedom fight, and we are winning. We must have time to live and help Mississippi to be alive." Half an hour before, I had understood death in a new way. Now I realized that Mississippi, in spite of itself, has given real meaning to life. In Mississippi you never ask, "What is the meaning of life?" or "Is there any point to it all?" but only that we may have enough life to do all that there is to be done....

Meridian, August 5

At the Freedom school and at the community center, many of the kids had known Mickey and almost all knew Jimmy Chaney. Today we asked the kids to describe Mickey and Jimmy because we had never known them.

"Mickey was a big guy. He wore blue jeans all the time"...I asked the kids, "What did his eyes look like?" and they told me they were "friendly eyes nice eyes" ("nice" is a lovely word in a Mississippi accent). "Mickey was a man who was at home everywhere and with anybody," said the 17-year-old girl I stay with. The littlest kids, the 6, 7, 8 years olds, tell about how he played "Frankenstein" with them or took them for drives or talked with them about Freedom. Many of the teenage boys were delinquents until Mickey went down to the bars and jails and showed them that one person at least would respect them if they began to fight for something important....And the grownups too, trusted him. The lady I stay with tells with pride of how Mickey and Rita came to supper at their house, and police cars circled around the house all during the meal. But Mickey could make them feel glad to take the risk.

People talk less about James Chaney here, but feel more. The kids describe a boy who played with them—whom everyone respected but who never had to join in is fights to maintain this respect—a quiet boy but very sharp and very understanding when he did speak. Mostly we know James through his sisters and especially his 12-year-old brother, Ben. Today Ben was in the Freedom School. At lunchtime the kids have a jazz band (piano, washtub bass, cardboard boxes and bongos as drums) and tiny Ben was there leading all even with his broken arm, with so much energy and rhythm that even Senator Eastland would have had to stop and listen if he'd been walking by....

Laurel, August 11

Dear Folks,

...The memorial service began around 7:30 with over 120 people filling the small, wooden-pew lined church. David Dennis of CORE [a civil rights group], the Assistant Director for the Mississippi Summer Project, spoke for COFO [an amalgam of civil rights organizations]. He talked to the Negro people of Meridian—it was a speech to move people, to end the lethargy, to make people stand up. It went something like this:

"I am not here to memorialize James Chaney, I am not here to pay tribute—I am too sick and tired. Do YOU hear me, I am S-I-C-K and T-I-R-E-D. I have attended too many memorials, too many funerals. This has got to stop. Mack Parker, Medgar Evers, Herbert Lee, Lewis Allen, Emmett Till, four little girls in Birmingham, a 13-year-old boy in Birmingham, and the list goes on and on. I have attended these funerals and 5 memorials and I am SICK and TIRED. But the trouble is that YOU are NOT sick and tired and for that reason YOU, yes YOU, are to blame. Everyone of your damn souls. And if you are going to let this continue now then you are to blame, yes YOU. Just as much as the monsters of hate who pulled the trigger or brought down the club; just as much to blame as the sheriff and the chief of police, as the governor in Jackson who said that he 'did not have time' for Mrs. Schwerner when she went to see him, and just as much to blame as the President and Attorney General in Washington who wouldn't provide protection for Chaney, Goodman and Schwerner when we told them that protection was necessary in Neshoba County....Yes, I am angry, I AM. And it's high time that you got angry too, angry enough to go up to the courthouse Monday and register—everyone of you. Angry enough to take five and then other people with you. Then and only then can these brutal killings be stopped. Remember it is your sons and your daughters who have been killed all these years and you have done nothing about it, and if you don't do nothing NOW baby, I say God Damn Your Souls...."

Mileston, August 9

Dear Blake,

...Dave finally broke down and couldn't finish and the Chaney family was moaning and much of the audience and I were also crying. It's such an impossible thing to describe but suddenly again, as I'd first realized when I heard the three men were missing when we were still training up at Oxford [Ohio], I felt the sacrifice the Negroes have been making for so long. How the Negro people are able to accept all the abuses of the whites—all the insults and injustices which make me ashamed to be white—and then turn around and say they want to love us, is beyond me. There are Negros who want to kill whites and many Negros have much bitterness but still the majority seem to have the quality of being able to look for a future in which whites will love the Negroes. Our kids talk very critically of all the whites around here and still they have a dream of freedom in which both races understand and accept each other. There is such an overpowering task ahead of these kids that sometimes I can't do anything but cry for them. I hope they are up to the task, I'm not sure I would be if I were a

Mississippi Negro. As a white northerner I can get involved whenever I feel like it and run home whenever I get bored or frustrated or scared. I hate the attitude and position of the Northern whites and despise myself when I think that way. Lately I've been feeling homesick and longing for pleasant old Westport and sailing and swimming and my friends. I don't quite know what to do because I can't ignore my desire to go home and yet I feel I am a much weaker person than I like to think I am because I do have these emotions. I've always tried to avoid situations which aren't so nice, like arguments and dirty houses and now maybe Mississippi. I asked my father if I could stay down here for a whole year and I was almost glad when he said "no" that we couldn't afford it because it would mean supporting me this year in addition to three more years of college. I have a desire to go home and to read a lot and go to Quaker meetings and be by myself so I can think about all this rather than being in the middle of it all the time. But I know if my emotions run like they have in the past, that I can only take that pacific sort of life for a little while and then I get the desire to be active again and get involved with knowing other people. I guess this all sounds crazy and I seem to always think out my problems as I write to you. I am angry because I have a choice as to whether or not to work in the Movement and I am playing upon that choice and leaving here. I wish I could talk with you 'cause I'd like to know if you ever felt this way about anything. I mean have you ever despised yourself for your weak conviction or something. And what is making it worse is that all those damn northerners are thinking of me as a brave hero....

Martha

* * * * * *

1. *What do the volunteers think they are accomplishing, aside from promoting voting rights and holding classes? What are they learning about themselves, as well as the people of Mississippi?*

2. *How do the reactions to the murder of Chaney, Schwerner, and Goodman differ between white and black volunteers?*

28–8   *The Civil Rights Act, 1964*

The growing strength of the Civil Rights Movement provided the political pressure to pass the Civil Rights Act of 1964. After John F. Kennedy's assassination, Lyndon B. Johnson guided the legislation through a thicket of congressional opposition, including a three-month filibuster. It was by far the strongest civil rights measure since Reconstruction. But even so, it lacked real teeth for the enforcement of voting rights; those would come the following year in the Voting Rights Act.

SOURCE: *78 U.S. Statutes at Large* ff. Public Law 88–352.

Title I
Voting Rights

SEC. 101 (2). No person acting under color of law shall—

(A) in determining whether any individual is qualified under State law or laws to vote in any Federal election, apply any standard, practice, or procedure different from the standards, practices, or procedures applied under such law or laws to other individuals within the same county, parish, or similar political subdivision who have been found by State officials to be qualified to vote;...

(C) employ any literacy test as a qualification for voting in any Federal election unless (i) such test is administered to each individual wholly in writing; and (ii) a certified copy of the test and of the answers given by the individual is furnished to him within twenty-five days of the submission of his request made within the period of time during which records and papers are required to be retained and preserved pursuant to title III of the Civil Rights Act of 1960....

Title II
Injunctive Relief Against Discrimination in Places of Public Accommodation

SEC. 201. (a) All persons shall be entitled to the full and equal enjoyment of the goods, services, facilities, privileges, advantages, and accommodations of any place of public accommodation, as defined in this section, without discrimination or segregation on the ground of race, color, religion, or national origin.

(b) Each of the following establishments which serves the public is a place of public accommodation within the meaning of this title if its operations affect commerce, or if discrimination or segregation by it is supported by State action:

(1) any inn, motel, or other establishment which provides lodging to transient guests, other than an establishment located within a building which contains not more than five rooms for rent or hire and which is actually occupied by the proprietor of such establishment as his residence;

(2) any restaurant, cafeteria, lunch room, lunch counter, soda fountain, or other facility principally

engaged in selling food for consumption on the premises....

(3) any motion picture house, theater, concert hall, sports arena, stadium or other place of exhibition or entertainment....

(d) Discrimination or segregation by an establishment is supported by State action within the meaning of this title if such discrimination or segregation (1) is carried on under color of any law, statute, ordinance, or regulation; or (2) is carried on under color of any custom or usage required or enforced by officials of the State or political subdivision thereof....

SEC. 202. All persons shall be entitled to be free, at any establishment or place, from discrimination or segregation of any kind on the ground of race, color, religion, or national origin, if such discrimination or segregation is or purports to be required by any law, statute, ordinance, regulation, rule, or order of a State or any agency or political subdivision thereof....

SEC. 206. (a) Whenever the Attorney General has reasonable cause to believe that any person or group of persons is engaged in a pattern or practice of resistance as to the full enjoyment of any of the rights secured by this title, the Attorney General may bring a civil action in the appropriate district court of the United States by filing with it a complaint...requesting such preventive relief, including an application for a permanent or temporary injunction, restraining order or other order against the person or persons responsible for such pattern or practice, as he deems necessary to insure the full enjoyment of the rights herein described.

Title VI
Nondiscrimination in Federally Assisted Programs

SEC. 601. No person in the United States shall, on the ground of race, color, or national origin, be excluded from participation in, be denied the benefits of, or be subjected to discrimination under any program or activity receiving Federal financial assistance.

******

1. *What specific forms of discrimination does the Act outlaw? In which realms?*

2. *What kinds of discrimination does the Act ignore?*

28–9 Michael Harrington, The Other America, 1962

Michael Harrington was a journalist who had been active in socialist and Catholic reform groups. His 1962 book offered a startling exposé of poverty in the midst of plenty. Writing with passion and precision, he showed how millions of poor people were consigned to invisibility by a culture and political system too intent on celebrating "the affluent society." Harrington's book helped bring the issue of poverty and economic inequality to the national consciousness, and it provided some of the intellectual ammunition for the War on Poverty.

SOURCE: Reprinted with the permission of Macmillan Publishing Company from *THE OTHER AMERICA* by Michael Harrington. Copyright © 1962 by Michael Harrington.

The Invisible Land

THERE IS a familiar America. It is celebrated in speeches and advertised on television and in the magazines. It has the highest mass standard of living the world has ever known.

In the 1950s this America worried about itself, yet even its anxieties were products of abundance. The title of a brilliant book was widely misinterpreted, and the familiar America began to call itself "the affluent society." There was introspection about Madison Avenue and tail fins; there was discussion of the emotional suffering taking place in the suburbs. In all this, there was an implicit assumption that the basic grinding economic problems had been solved in the United States. In this theory the nation's problems were no longer a matter of basic human needs, of food, shelter, and clothing. Now they were seen as qualitative, a question of learning to live decently amid luxury.

While this discussion was carried on, there existed another America. In it dwelt somewhere between 40,000,000 and 50,000,000 citizens of this land. They were poor. They still are.

To be sure, the other America is not impoverished in the same sense as those poor nations where millions cling to hunger as a defense against starvation. This country has escaped such extremes. That does not change the fact that tens of millions of Americans are, at is this very moment, maimed in body and spirit, existing at levels beneath those necessary for human decency. If these people are not starving, they are hungry, and sometimes fat with hunger, for that is what cheap foods do. They are without adequate housing and education and medical care.

The Government has documented what this means to the bodies of the poor, and the figures will be cited throughout this book. But even more basic, this poverty twists and deforms the spirit. The American poor are pessimistic and defeated, and they are victimized by mental suffering to a degree unknown in Suburbia.

This book is a description of the world in which these people live; it is about the other America. Here are the unskilled workers, the migrant farm workers, the aged, the minorities, and all the others who live in the economic underworld of American life. In all this, there will be statistics, and that offers the opportunity for disagreement among honest and sincere men. I would ask the reader to respond critically to every assertion, but not to allow statistical quibbling to obscure the huge, enormous, and intolerable fact of poverty in America. For, when all is said and done, that fact is unmistakable, whatever its exact dimensions, and the truly human reaction can only be outrage. As W. H. Auden wrote:

Hunger allows no choice
To the citizen or the police;
We must love one another or die.

I

The millions who are poor in the United States tend to become increasingly invisible. Here is a great mass of people, yet it takes an effort of the intellect and will even to see them.

I discovered this personally in a curious way. After I wrote my first article on poverty in America, I had all the statistics down on paper. I had proved to my satisfaction that there were around 50,000,000 poor in this country. Yet, I realized I did not believe my own figures. The poor existed in the Government reports; they were percentages and numbers in long, close columns, but they were not part of my experience. I could prove that the other America existed, but I had never been there.

My response was not accidental. It was typical of what is happening to an entire society, and it reflects profound social changes in this nation. The other America, the America of poverty, is hidden today in a way that it never was before. Its millions are socially invisible to the rest of us. No wonder that so many misinterpreted Galbraith's title and assumed that "the affluent society" meant that everyone had a decent standard of living....

Then, many of the poor are the wrong age to be seen. A good number of them (over 8,000,000) are sixty-five years of age or better; an even larger number are under eighteen. The aged members of the other America are often sick, and they cannot move. Another group of them live out their lives in loneliness and frustration: they sit in rented rooms, or else they stay close to a house in a neighborhood that has completely changed from the old days. Indeed, one of the worst aspects of poverty among the aged is that these people are out of sight and out of mind, and alone.

The young are somewhat more visible, yet they too stay close to their neighborhoods. Sometimes they advertise their poverty through a lurid tabloid story about a gang killing. But generally they do not disturb the quiet streets of the middle class.

And finally, the poor are politically invisible. It is one of the cruelest ironies of social life in advanced countries that the dispossessed at the bottom of society are unable to speak for themselves. The people of the other America do not, by far and large, belong to unions, to fraternal organizations, or to political parties. They are without lobbies of their own; they put forward no legislative program. As a group, they are atomized. They have no face; they have no voice.

Thus, there is not even a cynical political motive for caring about the poor, as in the old days. Because the slums are no longer centers of powerful political organizations, the politicians need not really care about their inhabitants. The slums are no longer visible to the middle class, so much of the idealistic urge to fight for those who need help is gone. Only the social agencies have a really direct involvement with the other America, and they are without any great political power....

II

...Poverty in America forms a culture, a way of life and feeling. It is crucial to generalize this idea, for it profoundly affects how one moves to destroy poverty.

The most obvious aspect of this interrelatedness is in the way in which the various subcultures of the other America feed into one another. This is clearest with the aged. There the poverty of the declining years is, for some millions of human beings, a function of the poverty of the earlier years. If there were adequate medical care for everyone in the United States, there would be less misery for old people. It is as simple as that. Or there is the relation between the poor farmers and the unskilled workers. When a man is driven off the land because of the impoverishment worked by technological progress, he leaves one part of the culture of poverty and joins another. If something were done about the low income farmer, that would immediately tell in the statistics of urban unemployment and the economic underworld. The same is true of the rest of the society. The second nation in our midst, the other America, must be brought into the Union.

In order to do this, there is a need for planning. It is literally incredible that this nation knows so much about poverty, that it has made so many inventories of misery, and that it has done so little. The material for a comprehensive program is already available. It exists in congressional reports and the statistics of Government agencies. What is needed is that the society make use of its knowledge in a rational and systematic way. As this book is being written, there are proposals for a Department of Urban Affairs in the Cabinet (and it will probably be a reality by the time these words are published). Such an agency could be the coordinating center for a crusade against the other America. In any case, if there is not planning, any attempt to deal with the problem of poverty will fail, at least in part.

Then there are some relatively simple things that could be done, involving the expansion of existing institutions and programs. Every American should be brought under the coverage of social security, and the payments should be enough to support a dignified old age. The principle already exists. Now it must be extended to those who need help the most. The same is true with minimum wage. The spectacle of excluding the most desperate from coverage must come to an end. If it did, there would be a giant step toward the elimination of poverty itself.

In every subculture of the other America, sickness and disease are the most important agencies of continuing misery. *The New York Times* publishes a list of the "neediest cases" each Christmas. In 1960 the descriptions of personal tragedy that ran along with this appeal involved in the majority of cases the want of those who had been struck down by illness. If there were adequate medical care, this charity would be unnecessary.

Today the debate on medical care centers on the aged. And indeed, these are the people who are in the most desperate straits. Yet it would be an error of the first magnitude to think that society's responsibility begins with those sixty-five years of age. As has been pointed out several times, the ills of the elderly are often the inheritance of the earlier years. A comprehensive medical program, guaranteeing decent care to every American, would actually reduce the cost of caring for the aged. That, of course, is only the hardheaded argument for such an approach. More importantly, such a program would make possible a human kind of existence for everyone in the society.

And finally, it must be remembered that none of these objectives can be accomplished if racial prejudice is to continue in the United States. Negroes and other minorities constitute only 25 per cent of the poor, yet their degradation is an important element in maintaining the entire culture of poverty. As long as there is a reservoir of cheap Negro labor, there is a means of keeping the poor whites down. In this sense, civil-rights legislation is an absolutely essential component in any campaign to end poverty in the United States. In short, the welfare provisions of American society that now help the upper two-thirds must be extended to the poor. This can be done if

the other Americans are motivated to take advantage of the opportunities before them, if they are invited into the society. It can be done if there is a comprehensive program that attacks the culture of poverty at every one of its strong points.

But who will carry out this campaign?…There is no place to look except toward the Federal Government. And indeed, even if there were alternate choices, Washington would have to play an important role, if only because of the need for a comprehensive program and for national planning. But in any case there is no argument, for there is only one realistic possibility: only the Federal Government has the power to abolish poverty.

In saying this, it is not necessary to advocate complete central control of such a campaign. Far from it. Washington is essential in a double sense: as a source of the considerable funds needed to mount a campaign against the other America, and as a place for coordination, for planning, and the establishment of national standards. The actual implementation of a program to abolish poverty can be carried out through myriad institutions, and the closer they are to the specific local area, the better the results. There are, as has been pointed out already, housing administrators, welfare workers, and city planners with dedication and vision. They are working on the local level, and their main frustration is the lack of funds. They could be trusted actually to carry through on a national program. What they lack now is money and the support of the American people.

There is no point in attempting to blueprint or detail the mechanisms and institutions of a war on poverty in the United States. There is information enough for action. All that is lacking is political will.

Thus the difficult, hardheaded question about poverty that one must answer is this: Where is the political will coming from? The other America is systematically underrepresented in the Government of the United States. It cannot really speak for itself. The poor, even in politics, must always be the object of charity (with the major exception of the Negroes, who, in recent times, have made tremendous strides forward in organization).

Indeed, part of the invisibility of poverty in American life is a result of party structure. Since each major party contained differences within itself greater than the differences between it and the other party, politics in the fifties and early sixties tended to have an issueless character. And where issues were not discussed, the poor did not have a chance. They could benefit only if elections were designed to bring new information to the people, to wake up the nation, to challenge, and to call to action.

In all probability there will not be a real attack on the culture of poverty so long as this situation persists. For the other America cannot be abolished through concessions and compromises that are almost inevitably made at the expense of the poor. The spirit, the vision that are required if the nation is to penetrate the wall of pessimism and despair that surrounds the impoverished millions cannot be produced under such circumstances.

What is needed if poverty is to be abolished is a return of political debate, a restructuring of the party system so that there can be clear choices, a new mood of social idealism.

* * * * * *

1.   *How does Harrington explain the "invisibility" of so many millions of people?*

2.   *What does he mean by the claim that poverty "forms a culture, a way of life and feeling"?*

3.   *Does Harrington believe that poverty can be eliminated? What strategies does he offer for attacking the problem?*

28-10   Stokely Carmichael, Black Power, 1966

By 1966, a new consciousness had emerged among young African Americans active in the civil rights struggle. The cry of "Black Power" had replaced "We Shall Overcome" within the more militant sectors of the movement. Stokely Carmichael, a veteran of the Freedom Rides and voting rights campaigns in the Deep South, first articulated the philosophy behind Black Power when he became chairman of SNCC in 1966. His essay lays out the origin and meaning of the term that began winning support from young black activists and making white liberals increasingly uneasy.

SOURCE: From "What We Want," by Stokely Carmichael, as appeared in *New York Review of Books,* September 22, 1966. Reprinted by permission of Kwanie Ture, formerly Stokely Carmichael.

One of the tragedies of the struggle against racism is that up to now there has been no national organization which could speak to the growing militancy of young black people in the urban ghetto. There has been only a civil rights movement, whose tone of voice was adapted to an audience of liberal whites. It served as a sort of buffer zone between them and angry young blacks. None of its so-called leaders could go into a rioting community and be listened to. In a sense, I blame ourselves—together with the mass media—for what has happened in Watts, Harlem, Chicago, Cleveland, Omaha. Each time the people in those cities saw Martin Luther King get slapped, they became angry; when they saw four little black girls bombed to death, they were angrier; and when nothing happened, they were steaming. We had nothing to offer that they could see, except to go out and be beaten again. We helped to build their frustration.

For too many years, black Americans marched and had their heads broken and got shot. They were saying to

the country, "Look, you guys are supposed to be nice guys and we are only going to do what we are supposed to do—why do you beat us up, why don't you give us what we ask, why don't you straighten yourselves out?" After years of this, we are at almost the same point because we demonstrated from a position of weakness. We cannot be expected any longer to march and have our heads broken in order to say to whites: come on, you're nice guys. For you are not nice guys. We have found you out.

An organization which claims to speak for the needs of a community—as does the Student Nonviolent Coordinating Committee—must speak in the tone of that community, not as somebody else's buffer zone. This is the significance of black power as a slogan. For once, black people are going to use the words they want to use—not just the words whites want to hear. And they will do this no matter how often the press tries to stop the use of the slogan by equating it with racism or separatism.

An organization which claims to be working for the needs of a community—as SNCC does—must work to provide that community with a position of strength from which to make its voice heard. This is the significance of black power beyond the slogan.

Black power can be clearly defined for those who do not attach the fears of white America to their questions about it. We should begin with the basic fact that black Americans have two problems: they are poor and they are black. All other problems arise from this two-sided reality: lack of education, the so-called apathy of black men. Any program to end racism must address itself to that double reality.

Almost from its beginning, SNCC sought to address itself to both conditions with a program aimed at winning political power for impoverished Southern blacks. We had to begin with politics because black Americans are a propertyless people in a country where property is valued above all. We had to work for power, because this country does not function by morality, love, and nonviolence, but by power. Thus we determined to win political power, with the idea of moving on from there into activity that would have economic effects. With power, the masses could *make or participate in making* the decisions which govern their destinies, and thus create basic change in their day-to-day lives.

But if political power seemed to be the key to self-determination, it was also obvious that the key had been thrown down a deep well many years earlier. Disenfranchisement, maintained by racist terror, made it impossible to talk about organizing for political power in 1960. The right to vote had to be won, and SNCC workers devoted their energies to this from 1961 to 1965. They set up voter registration drives in the Deep South. They created pressure for the vote by holding mock elections in Mississippi in 1963 and by helping to establish the Mississippi Freedom Democratic Party (MFDP) in 1964. That struggle was eased, though not won, with the passage of the 1965 Voting Rights Act. SNCC workers could then address themselves to the question: "Who can we vote for, to have our needs met—how do we make our vote meaningful?"

SNCC had already gone to Atlantic City for recognition of the Mississippi Freedom Democratic Party by the Democratic convention and been rejected; it had gone with the MFDP to Washington for recognition by Congress and been rejected. In Arkansas, SNCC helped thirty Negroes to run for School Board elections; all but one were defeated, and there was evidence of fraud and intimidation sufficient to cause their defeat. In Atlanta, Julian Bond ran for the state legislature and was elected—twice—and unseated—twice. In several states, black farmers ran in elections for agricultural committees which make crucial decisions concerning land use, loans, etc. Although they won places on a number of committees, they never gained the majorities needed to them....

This is the specific historical experience from which SNCC's call for "black power" emerged on the Mississippi march last July. But the concept of "black power" is not a recent or isolated phenomenon: It has out grown of the ferment of agitation and activity by different people and organizations in many black communities over the years. Our last year of work in Alabama added a new concrete possibility. In Lowndes county, for example, black power will mean that if a Negro is elected sheriff, he can end police brutality. If a black man is elected tax assessor, he can collect and channel funds for the building of better roads and schools serving black people—thus advancing the move from political power into the economic arena. In such areas as where black men have a majority, they will attempt to use it to exercise control. This is what they seek: control. Where Negroes lack a majority, black power means proper representation and sharing of control. It means the creation of power bases

from which black people can work to change statewide or nationwide patterns of oppression through pressure from strength—instead of weakness. Politically, black power means what it has always meant to SNCC: the coming-together of black people to elect representatives and *to force those representatives to speak to their needs.* It does not mean merely putting black faces into office. A man or woman who is black and from the slums cannot be automatically expected to speak to the needs of black people. Most of the black politicians we see around the country today are not what SNCC means by black power. The power must be that of a community, and emanate from there....

Ultimately, the economic foundations of this country must be shaken if black people are to control their lives. The colonies of the United States—and this includes the black ghettoes within its borders, north and south—must be liberated. For a century, this nation has been like an octopus of exploitation, its tentacles stretching from Mississippi and Harlem to South America, the Middle East, southern Africa, and Vietnam; the form of exploitation varies from area to area but the essential result has been the same—a powerful few have been maintained and enriched at the expense of the poor and voiceless colored masses. This pattern must be broken. As its grip loosens here and there around the world, the hopes of black Americans become more realistic. For racism to die, a totally different America must be born.

This is what the white society does not wish to face; this is why that society prefers to talk about integration. But integration speaks not at all to the problem of poverty, only to the problem of blackness. Integration today means the man who "makes it," leaving his black brothers behind in the ghetto as fast as his new sports car will take him. It has no relevance to the Harlem wino or to the cottonpicker making three dollars a day. As a lady I know in Alabama once said, "the food that Ralph Bunche eats doesn't fill my stomach."

Integration, moreover, speaks to the problem of blackness in a despicable way. As a goal, it has been based on complete acceptance of the fact that *in order to have* a decent house or education, blacks must move into a white neighborhood or send their children to a white school. This reinforces, among both black and white, the idea that "white" is automatically better and "black" is by definition inferior. This is why integration is a subterfuge for the maintenance of white supremacy. It allows the nation to focus on a handful of Southern children who get into white schools, at great price, and to the 94 percent who are left behind in unimproved all-black schools. Such situations will not change until black people have power—to control their own school boards, in this case. Then Negroes become equal in a way that means something, and integration ceases to be a one-way street. Then integration doesn't mean draining skills and energies from the ghetto into white neighborhoods; then it can mean white people moving from Beverly Hills into Watts, white people joining the Lowdnes County Freedom Organization. Then integration becomes relevant....

White America will not face the problem of color, the reality of it. The well-intended say: "We're all human, everybody is really decent, we must forget color." But color cannot be "forgotten" until its weight is recognized and dealt with. White America will not acknowledge that the ways in which this country sees itself are contradicted by being black—and always have been. Whereas most of the people who settled this country came here for freedom or for economic opportunity, blacks were brought here to be slaves. When the Lowndes County Freedom Organization chose the black panther as its symbol, it was christened by the press "the Black Panther Party"—but the Alabama Democratic Party, whose symbol is a rooster, has never been called the White Cock Party. No one ever talked about "white power" because power in this country *is* white. All this adds up to more than merely identifying a group phenomenon by some catchy name or adjective. The furor over that black panther reveals the problems that white America has with color and sex; the furor over "black power" reveals how deep racism runs and the great fear which is attached to it.

Whites will not see that I, for example, as a person oppressed because of my blackness, have common cause with other blacks who are oppressed because of blackness. This is not to say that there are no white people who see things as I do, but that it is black people I must speak to first. It must be the oppressed to whom SNCC addresses itself primarily, not to friends from the oppressing group.

From birth, black people are told a set of lies about themselves. We are told that we are lazy—yet I drive through the Delta area of Mississippi and watch black people picking cotton in the hot sun for fourteen hours. We are told, "If you work hard, you'll succeed"—but if that were true, black people would own this country. We are oppressed because we are black—not because we are ignorant, not because we are lazy, not because we're stupid (and got good rhythm), but because we're black.

I remember that when I was a boy, I used to go to see Tarzan movies on Saturday. White Tarzan used to beat up the black natives. I would sit there yelling, "Kill the beasts, kill the savages, kill 'em!" I was saying: Kill *me.* It was as if a Jewish boy watched Nazis taking Jews off to concentration camps and cheered them on. Today, I want the chief to beat hell out of Tarzan and send him back to Europe. But it takes time to become free of the lies and their shaming effect on black minds. It takes time to reject

the most important lie; that black people inherently can't do the same things white people can do, unless white people help them.

The need for psychological equality is the reason why SNCC today believes that blacks must organize in the black community. Only black people can convey the revolutionary idea that black people are able to do things themselves. Only they can help create in the community an aroused and continuing black consciousness that will provide the basis for political strength. In the past, white allies have furthered white supremacy without the whites involved realizing it—or wanting it, I think. Black people must do thing themselves; they must get poverty money they will control and spend themselves, they must conduct tutorial programs themselves so that black children can identify with black people. This is one reason Africa has such importance. The reality of black men ruling their own nations gives blacks elsewhere a sense of possibility, of power, which they do not now have.

This does not mean we don't welcome help, or friends. But we wanted the right to decide whether anyone is, in fact, our friend. In the past, black Americans have been almost the only people whom everybody and his momma could jump up and call their friends. We have been tokens, symbols, objects—as I was in high school to many young whites, who liked having "a Negro friend." We want to decide who is our friend, and we will not accept someone who comes to us and says: "If you do X, Y, and Z, then I'll help you." We will not be told whom we should choose as allies. We will not be isolated from any group or nation except by our own choice. We cannot have any oppressors telling the oppressed how to rid themselves of the oppressor.

I have said that most liberal whites react to "black power" with the question, What about me?, rather than saying: Tell me what you want me to do and I'll see if I can do it. There are answers to the right question. One of the most disturbing things about almost all white supporters of the movement has been that they are afraid to go into their own communities—which is where the racism exists—and work to get rid of it. They want to run from Berkeley to tell us what to do in Mississippi; let them look instead at Berkeley. They admonish blacks to be nonviolent; let them preach nonviolence in the white community. They come to teach me Negro history, let them go to the suburbs and open up freedom schools for whites. Let them work to stop America's racist foreign policy; let them press this government to cease supporting the economy of South Africa.

There is a vital job to be done among poor whites. We hope to see, eventually, a coalition between poor blacks and poor whites. That is the only coalition which seems acceptable to us, and we see such a coalition as major internal instrument of change in American society. SNCC has tried several times to organize poor whites; we are trying again now, with an initial training program in Tennessee. It is purely academic today to talk about bringing poor blacks and whites together, but the job of creating a poor white power bloc must be attempted. The main responsibility for it falls upon whites. Black and white can work together in the white community where possible, it is not possible, however, to go into a poor Southern town and talk about integration. Poor whites everywhere are becoming more hostile—not less—partly because they see the nation's attention focused on black poverty and nobody coming to them. Too many young middle-class Americans, like some sort of Pepsi generation, have wanted to come alive....

But our vision is not merely of a society in which all black men have enough to buy the good things of life. When we urge that black money go into black pockets, we mean the communal pocket. We want to see money go back into the community and used to benefit it. We want to see the cooperative concept applied in business and banking. We want to see black ghetto residents demand that an exploiting landlord or storekeeper sell them, at minimal cost, a building or a shop that they will own and improve cooperatively; they can back their demand with a rent strike, or a boycott, and a community so unified behind them that no one else will move into the building or buy at the store. The society we seek to build among black people, then, is not a capitalist one. It is a society in which the spirit of community and humanistic love prevail. The word love is suspect; black expectations of what it might produce have been betrayed too often. But those were expectations of a response from the white community, which failed us. The love we seek to encourage is within the black community, the only American community where men call each other "brother" when they meet. We can build a community of love only where we have the ability and power to do so: among blacks.

As for white America, perhaps it can stop crying out against "black supremacy," "black nationalism," "racism in reverse," and begin facing reality. The reality is that this nation, from top to bottom, is racist; that racism is not primarily a problem of "human relations" but of an exploitation maintained—either actively or through silence—by the society as a whole. Camus and Sartre have asked, can a man condemn himself? Can whites, particularly liberal whites, condemn themselves? Can they stop blaming us, and blame their own system? Are they capable of the shame which might become a revolutionary emotion?

We have found that they usually cannot condemn themselves, and so we have done it. But the rebuilding of this society, if at all possible, is basically the responsibility of whites—not blacks. We won't fight to save the present society, in Vietnam or anywhere else. We are just going to work, in the way we see fit, and on goals we define, not for civil rights but for all our human rights.

* * * * * *

1.   How does Carmichael see Black Power as growing directly out of the civil rights struggles of the early 60s? What future does he see, if any, for integration and black–white political alliances?

2.   How does Black Power express both political and economic goals? To what extent does it offer a fundamental critique of American society?

3.   What similarities and differences do you see between Carmichael's rhetoric and that of Julian Bond? (Document 28–4).

chapter 29

War Abroad, War at Home, 1965–1974

29–1 Students for a Democratic Society, The Port Huron Statement, 1962

In 1962, a group of student activists with experience in the civil rights and peace movements founded the Students for a Democratic Society (SDS). Their manifesto gave voice to the growing alienation of college students and envisioned a new kind of politics based on "participatory democracy." Although decentralized and informal, SDS became the leading intellectual and political force within the New Left. Its members played key roles in civil rights work, the anti-war and anti-draft campaigns, student protest, and the early women's liberation movement. SDS dissolved amidst bitter factional disputes in 1969.

SOURCE: "The Port Huron Statement" by Tom Hayden, et al. Copyright © 1962 by Tom Hayden. Reprinted by permission of Tom Hayden.

We are people of this generation, bred in at least modest comfort, housed now in universities, looking uncomfortably to the world we inherit.

When we were kids the United States was the wealthiest and strongest country in the world: the only one with the atom bomb, the least scarred by modern war, an initiator of the United Nations that we thought would distribute Western influence throughout the world. Freedom and equality for each individual, government of, by, and for the people—these American values we found good principles by which we could live as men. Many of us began maturing in complacency.

As we grew, however, our comfort was penetrated by events too troubling to dismiss. First, the permeating and victimizing fact of human degradation, symbolized by the Southern struggle against racial bigotry, compelled most of us from silence to activism. Second, the enclosing fact of the Cold War, symbolized by the presence of the Bomb, brought awareness that we ourselves, and our friends, and millions of abstract "others" we knew more directly because of our common peril, might die at any time. We might deliberately ignore, or avoid, or fail to feel all other human problems, but not these two, for these were too immediate and crushing in their impact, too

challenging in the demand that we as individuals take the responsibility for encounter and resolution.

While these and other problems either directly oppressed us or rankled our consciences and became our own subjective concerns, we began to see complicated and disturbing paradoxes in our surrounding America. The declaration "all men are created equal…" rang hollow before the facts of Negro life in the South and the big cities of the North. The proclaimed peaceful intentions of the United States contradicted its economic and military investments in the Cold War status quo.

We witnessed, and continue to witness, other paradoxes. With nuclear energy whole cities can easily be powered, yet the dominant nation-states seem more likely to unleash destruction greater than that incurred in all wars of human history. Although our own technology is destroying old and creating new forms of social organization, men still tolerate meaningless work and idleness. While two-thirds of mankind suffers under-nourishment, our own upper classes revel amidst superfluous abundance. Although world population is expected to double in forty years, the nations still tolerate anarchy as a major principle of international conduct and uncontrolled exploitation governs the sapping of the earth's physical resources. Although mankind desperately needs revolutionary leadership, America rests in national stalemate, its goals ambiguous and tradition-bound instead of informed and clear, its democratic system apathetic and manipulated rather than "of, by, and for the people."

Not only did tarnish appear on our image of American virtue, not only did disillusion occur when the hypocrisy of American ideals was discovered, but we began to sense that what we had originally seen as the American Golden Age was actually the decline of an era. The worldwide outbreak of revolution against colonialism and imperialism, the entrenchment of totalitarian states, the menace of war, overpopulation, international disorder, supertechnology—these trends were testing the tenacity of our own commitment to democracy and freedom and our abilities to visualize their application to a world in upheaval.

Our work is guided by the sense that we may be the last generation in the experiment with living. But we are a minority—the vast majority of our people regard the temporary equilibriums of our society and world as eternally-functional parts. In this is perhaps the outstanding paradox: we ourselves are imbued with urgency, yet the message of our society is that there is no viable alternative to the present. Beneath the reassuring tones of the politicians, beneath the common opinion that America will "muddle through," beneath the stagnation of those who have closed their minds to the future, is the pervading feeling that there simply are no alternatives, that our times have witnessed the exhaustion not only of Utopias, but of any new departures as well. Feeling the press of complexity upon the emptiness of life, people are fearful of the thought that at any moment things might thrust out of control. They fear change itself, since change might smash whatever invisible framework seems to hold back chaos for them now. For most Americans, all crusades are suspect, threatening. The fact that each individual sees apathy in his fellows perpetuates the common reluctance to organize for change. The dominant institutions are complex enough to blunt the minds of their potential critics, and entrenched enough to swiftly dissipate or entirely repel the energies of protest and reform, thus limiting human expectancies. Then, too, we are a materially improved society, and by our own improvements we seem to have weakened the case for further change.

Some would have us believe that Americans feel contentment amidst prosperity—but might it not better be called a glaze above deeply-felt anxieties about their role in the new world? And if these anxieties produce a developed indifference to human affairs, do they not as well produce a yearning to believe there *is* an alternative to the present, that something *can* be done to change circumstances in the school, the workplaces, the bureaucracies, the government? It is to this latter yearning, at once the spark and engine of change, that we direct our present appeal. The search for truly democratic alternatives to the present, and a commitment to social experimentation with them, is a worthy and fulfilling human enterprise, one which moves us and, we hope, others today. On such a basis do we offer this document of our convictions and analysis: as an effort in understanding and changing the conditions of humanity in the late twentieth century, an effort rooted in the ancient, still unfulfilled conception of man attaining determining influence over his circumstances of life....

Making values explicit—an initial task in establishing alternatives—is an activity that has been devalued and corrupted. The conventional moral terms of the age, the politician moralities—"free world," "people's democracies"—reflect realities poorly, if at all, and seem to function more as ruling myths than as descriptive principles. But neither has our experience in the universities brought us moral enlightenment. Our professors and administrators sacrifice controversy to public relations; their curriculums change more slowly than the living events of the world; their skills and silence are purchased by investors in the arms race; passion is called unscholastic. The questions we might want raised—what is really important? can we live in a different and better way? if we wanted to change society, how would we do it?—are not thought to be questions of a "fruitful, empirical nature," and thus are brushed aside.

In suggesting social goals and values, therefore, we are aware of entering a sphere of some disrepute. Perhaps matured by the past, we have no sure formulas, no closed theories—but that does not mean values are beyond discussion and tentative determination. A first task of any social movement is to convince people that the search for orienting theories and the creation of human values is complex but worthwhile. We are aware that to avoid platitudes we must analyze the concrete conditions of social order. But to direct such an analysis we must use the guideposts of basic principles. Our own social values involve conceptions of human beings, human relationships, and social systems.

We regard *men* as infinitely precious and possessed of unfulfilled capacities for reason, freedom, and love. In affirming these principles we are aware of countering perhaps the dominant conceptions of man in the twentieth century: that he is a thing to be manipulated, and that he is inherently incapable of directing his own affairs. We oppose the depersonalization that reduces human beings to the status of things—if anything, the brutalities of the twentieth century teach that means and ends are intimately related, that vague appeals to "posterity" cannot justify the mutilations of the present. We oppose, too, the doctrine of human incompetence because it rests essentially on the modern fact that men have been "competently" manipulated into incompetence—we see little reason why men cannot meet with increasing skill the complexities and responsibilities of their situation, if society is organized not for minority, but for majority, participation in decision-making.

Men have unrealized potential for self-cultivation, self-direction, self-understanding, and creativity. It is this potential that we regard as crucial and to which we appeal, not to the human potentiality for violence, unreason, and submission to authority. The goal of man and society should be human independence: a concern not with image of popularity but with finding a meaning in life that is personally authentic; a quality of mind not compulsively driven by a sense of powerlessness, nor one which unthinkingly adopts status values, nor one which represses all threats to its habits, but one which has full, spontaneous access to present and past experiences, one which easily unites the fragmented parts of personal history, one which openly faces problems which are troubling and unresolved; one with an intuitive awareness of possibilities, an active sense of curiosity, an ability and willingness to learn.

This kind of independence does not mean egoistic individualism—the object is not to have one's way so much as it is to have a way that is one's own. Nor do we deify man—we merely have faith in his potential.

Human relationships should involve fraternity and honesty. Human interdependence is contemporary fact;

human brotherhood must be willed however, as a condition of future survival and as the most appropriate form of social relations. Personal links between man and man are needed, especially to go beyond the partial and fragmentary bonds of function that bind men only as worker to worker, employer to employee, teacher to student, American to Russian.

Loneliness, estrangement, isolation describe the vast distance between man and man today. These dominant tendencies cannot be overcome by better personnel management, nor by improved gadgets, but only when a love of man overcomes the idolotrous worship of things by man.

As the individualism we affirm is not egoism, the selflessness we affirm is not self-elimination. On the contrary, we believe in generosity of a kind that imprints one's unique individual qualities in the relation to other men, and to all human activity. Further, to dislike isolation is not to favor the abolition of privacy; the latter differs from isolation in that it occurs or is abolished according to individual will. Finally, we would replace power and personal uniqueness rooted in possession, privilege, or circumstance by power and uniqueness rooted in love, effectiveness, reason, and creativity.

As a *social system* we seek the establishment of a democracy of individual participation, governed by two central aims: that the individual share in those social decisions determining the quality and direction of his life; that society be organized to encourage independence in men and provide the media for their common participation.

In a participatory democracy, the political life would be based in several root principles:

- that decision-making of basic social consequence be carried on by public groupings;
- that politics be seen positively, as the art of collectively creating an acceptable pattern of social relations;
- that politics has the function of bringing people out of isolation and into community, thus being a necessary, though not sufficient, means of finding meaning in personal life;
- that the political order should serve to clarify problems in a way instrumental to their solution; it should provide outlets for the expression of personal grievance and aspiration; opposing views should be organized so as to illuminate choices and facilitate the attainment of goals; channels should be commonly available to relate men to knowledge and to power so that private problems—from bad recreation facilities to personal alienation—are formulated as general issues.

The economic sphere would have as its basis the principles:

- that work should involve incentives worthier than money or survival. It should be educative, not stultifying; creative, not mechanical; self-direct, not manipulated, encouraging independence, a respect for others, a sense of dignity and a willingness to accept social responsibility, since it is this experience that has crucial influence on habits, perceptions and individual ethics;
- that the economic experience is so personally decisive that the individual must share in its full determination;
- that the economy itself is of such social importance that its major resources and means of production should be open to democratic participation and subject to democratic social regulation.

Like the political and economic ones, major social institutions—cultural, education, rehabilitative, and others—should be generally organized with the well-being and dignity of man as the essential measure of success.

In social change or interchange, we find violence to be abhorrent because it requires generally the transformation of the target, be it a human being or a community of people, into a depersonalized object of hate. It is imperative that the means of violence be abolished and the institutions—local, national, international—that encourage nonviolence as a condition of conflict be developed.

These are our central values, in skeletal form. It remains vital to understand their denial or attainment in the context of the modern world.

* * * * * *

1. *How does the statement define the deep alienation that exists within the unprecedented prosperity of American society? What are its sources?*

2. *What new kind of community does the statement envision? How is that vision connected to a new kind of political activism?*

3. *In what ways is the Port Huron Statement a "radical" document? In what ways is it moderate?*

29–2   *Casey Hayden and Mary King Respond to Sexism in the Movement, 1965*

Casey Hayden and Mary King were civil rights activists who participated in SNCC and later became involved with in SDS. (Hayden was at one time married to SDS co-founder Tom Hayden.) In 1965, in response to the treatment of women within the Civil Rights and emerging New Left movements, Hayden and King co-authored "A Kind of Memo."

SOURCE: Sara Evans, *Personal Politics* (Knopf, 1979).

We've talked a lot, to each other and to some of you, about our own and other women's problems in trying to live in our personal lives and in our work as independent and creative people. In these conversations we've found what seem to be recurrent ideas or themes. Maybe we can look at these things many of us perceive, often as a result of insights learned from the movement:

Sex and caste: There seem to be many parallels that can be drawn between treatment of Negroes and treatment of women in our society as a whole. But in particular, women we've talked to who work in the movement seem to be caught up in a common-law caste system that operates, sometimes subtly, forcing them to work around or outside hierarchical structures of power which may exclude them. Women seem to be placed in the same position of assumed subordination in personal situations too. It is a caste system which, at its worst, uses and exploits women.

This is complicated by several facts, among them: 1) The caste system is not institutionalized by law (women have the right to vote, to sue for divorce, etc.); 2) Women can't withdraw from the situation (a la nationalism) or overthrow it; 3) There are biological differences (even though those biological differences are usually discussed or accepted without taking present and future technology into account so we probably can't be sure what these differences mean). Many people who are very hip to the implications of the racial caste system, even people in the movement, don't seem to be able to see the sexual caste system and if the question is raised they respond with: "That's the way it's supposed to be. There are biological differences." Or with other statements which recall a white segregationist confronted with integration.

Women and problems of work: The caste system perspective dictates the roles assigned to women in the movement, and certainly even more to women outside the movement. Within the movement, questions arise in situations ranging from relationships of women organizers to men in the community, to who cleans the freedom house, to who holds leadership positions, to who does secretarial work, and who acts as spokesman for groups. Other problems arise between women with varying degrees of awareness of themselves as being as capable as men but held back from full participation, or between women who see themselves as needing more control of their work than other women demand. And there are problems with relationships between white women and black women.

Women and personal relations with men: Having learned from the movement to think radically about the personal worth and abilities of people whose role in society had gone unchallenged before, a lot of women in the movement have begun trying to apply those lessons to their own relations with men. Each of us probably has her own story of the various results, and of the internal struggle occasioned by trying to break out of very deeply learned fears, needs, and self-perceptions, and of what happens when we try to replace them with concepts of people and freedom learned from the movement and organizing.

Institutions: Nearly everyone has real questions about those institutions which shape perspectives on men and women: marriage, child rearing patterns, women's (and men's) magazines, etc. People are beginning to think about and even to experiment with new forms in these areas.

Men's reactions to the questions raised here: A very few men seem to feel, when they hear conversations involving these problems, that they have a right to be present and participate in them, since they are so deeply involved. At the same time, very few men can respond non-defensively, since the whole idea is either beyond their comprehension or threatens and exposes them. The usual response is laughter. That inability to see the whole issue as serious, as the strait-jacketing of both sexes, and as societally determined often shapes our own response so that we learn to think in their terms about ourselves and to feel silly rather than trust our inner feelings. The problems we're listing here, and what others have said about them, are therefore largely drawn from conversations among women only—and that difficulty in establishing dialogue with men is a recurring theme among people we've talked to.

Lack of community for discussion: Nobody is writing, or organizing or talking publicly about women, in any way that reflects the problems that various women in the movement come across and which we've tried to touch above. Consider this quote from an article in the centennial issue of *The Nation:*

> However equally we consider men and women, the work plans for husbands and wives cannot be given equal weight. A woman should not aim for "a second-level career" because she is a *woman;* from girlhood on she should recognize that, if she is also going to be a wife and mother, she will not be able to give as much to her work as she would if single. That is, she should not feel that she cannot aspire to directing the laboratory simply because she is a woman, but rather because she is also a wife and mother, as such, her work as a lab technician (or the equivalent in another field) should bring both satisfaction and the knowledge that, through it, she is fulfilling an additional role, making an additional contribution.

And that's about as deep as the analysis goes publicly, which is not nearly so deep as we've heard many of you go in chance conversations.

The reason we want to try to open up dialogue is mostly subjective. Working in the movement often intensifies personal problems, especially if we start trying to apply things we're learning there to our personal lives. Perhaps we can start to talk with each other more openly than in the past and create a community of support for each other so we can deal with ourselves and others with integrity and can therefore keep working.

Objectively, the chances seem nil that we could start a movement based on anything as distant to general American thought as a sex-caste system. Therefore, most of us will probably want to work full time on problems such as war, poverty, race. The very fact that the country

can't face, much less deal with, the questions we're raising means that the movement is one place to look for some relief. Real efforts at dialogue within the movement and with whatever liberal groups, community women, or students might listen are justified. That is, all the problems between men and women and all the problems of women functioning in society as equal human beings are among the most basic that people face. We've talked in the movement about trying to build a society which would see basic human problems (which are now seen as private troubles), as public problems and would try to shape institutions to meet human needs rather than shaping people to meet the needs of those with power. To raise questions like those above illustrates very directly that society hasn't dealt with some of its deepest problems and opens discussion of why that is so. (In one sense, it is a radicalizing question that can take people beyond legalistic solutions into areas of personal and institutional change.) The second objective reason we'd like to see discussion begin is that we've learned a great deal in the movement and perhaps this is one area where a determined attempt to apply ideas we've learned there can produce some new alternatives.

* * * * * *

1. *What specific parallels does the memo make between the situation of African Americans in society and women in SNCC? How are the racial and sex caste systems different?*

2. *How does the memo attempt to redefine politics to include issues of interpersonal relations?*

3. *Why has discussion of these issues proven so difficult within SNCC?*

29–3   Lyndon B. Johnson, The Great Society, 1964

SOURCE: Lyndon B. Johnson, Address at Ann Arbor, Michigan, May 22, 1964, in *Public Papers of the Presidents of the United States, Lyndon B. Johnson, 1964* (Washington, D.C.: United States Printing Office), pp. 704–707.

When Lyndon B. Johnson became president after the assassination of John F. Kennedy in November 1963, Kennedy's advisers were already at work on an anti-poverty program, inspired, in part, by Michael Harrington's The Other America *(see Document 28-9, previous chapter). Two years after the Port Huron statement, Johnson spoke in Ann Arbor at the University of Michigan. In making an explicit generational appeal, Johnson sought to tap into the youthful idealism of his audience and the New Left in general. In this speech, he outlined an ambitious program of domestic programs that he called "The Great Society."*

I have come today from the turmoil of your Capital to the tranquillity of your campus to speak about the future of your country.

The purpose of protecting the life of our Nation and preserving the liberty of our citizens is to pursue the happiness of our people. Our success in that pursuit is the test of our success as a Nation.

For a century we labored to settle and to subdue a continent. For half a century we called upon unbounded invention and untiring industry to create an order of plenty for all of our people.

The challenge of the next half century is whether we have the wisdom to use that wealth to enrich and elevate our national life, and to advance the quality of our American civilization.

Your imagination, your initiative, and your indignation will determine whether we build a society where progress is the servant of our needs, or a society where old values and new visions are buried under unbridled growth. For in your time we have the opportunity to move not only toward the rich society and the powerful society, but upward to the Great Society.

The Great Society rests on abundance and liberty for all. It demands an end to poverty and racial injustice, to which we are totally committed in our time. But that is just the beginning.

The Great Society is a place where every child can find knowledge to enrich his mind and to enlarge his talents. It is a place where leisure is a welcome chance to build and reflect, not a feared cause of boredom and restlessness. It is a place where the city of man serves not only the needs of the body and the demands of commerce but the desire for beauty and the hunger for community.

It is a place where man can renew contact with nature. It is a place which honors creation for its own sake and for what it adds to the understanding of the race. It is a place where men are more concerned with the quality of their goals than the quantity of their goods.

But most of all, the Great Society is not a safe harbor, a resting place, a final objective, a finished work. It is a challenge constantly renewed, beckoning us toward a destiny where the meaning of our lives matches the marvelous products of our labor.

So I want to talk to you today about three places where we begin to build the Great Society—in our cities, in our countryside, and in our classrooms.

Many of you will live to see the day, perhaps 50 years from now, when there will be 400 million Americans—four-fifths of them in urban areas. In the remainder of this century urban population will double, city land will double, and we will have to build homes, highways, and facilities equal to all those built since this country was first settled. So in the next 40 years we must rebuild the entire urban United States.

Aristotle said: "Men come together in cities in order to live, but they remain together in order to live the good life." It is harder and harder to live the good life in American cities today.

The catalog of ills is long: there is the decay of the centers and the despoiling of the suburbs. There is not enough housing for our people or transportation for our traffic. Open land is vanishing and old landmarks are violated.

Worst of all expansion is eroding the precious and time honored values of community with neighbors and communion with nature. The loss of these values breeds loneliness and boredom and indifference.

Our society will never be great until our cities are great. Today the frontier of imagination and innovation is inside those cities and not beyond their borders.

New experiments are already going on. It will be the task of your generation to make the American city a place where future generations will come not only to live but to live the good life.

I understand that if I stayed here tonight I would see that Michigan students are really doing their best to live the good life.

This is the place where the Peace Corps was started. It is inspiring to see how all of you, while you are in this country, are trying so hard to live at the level of the people.

A second place where we begin to build the Great Society is in our countryside. We have always prided ourselves on being not only America the strong and America the free, but America the beautiful. Today that beauty is in danger. The water we drink, the food we eat, the very air that we breathe are threatened with pollution. Our parks are overcrowded, our seashores overburdened. Green fields and dense forests are disappearing.

A few years ago we were greatly concerned about the "Ugly American." Today we must act to prevent an ugly America.

For once the battle is lost, once our natural splendor is destroyed, it can never be recaptured. And once man can no longer walk with beauty or wonder at nature his spirit will wither and his sustenance be wasted.

A third place to build the Great Society is in the classrooms of America. There your children's lives will be shaped. Our society will not be great until every young mind is set free to scan the farthest reaches of thought and imagination. We are still far from that goal.

Today, 8 million adult Americans, more than the entire population of Michigan, have not finished 5 years of school. Nearly 20 million have not finished 8 years of school. Nearly 54 million—more than one-quarter of all America—have not even finished high school.

Each year more than 100,000 high school graduates, with proved ability do not enter college because they cannot afford it. And if we cannot educate today's youth, what will we do in 1970 when elementary school enrollment will be 5 million greater than 1960? And high school enrollment will rise by 5 million. College enrollment will increase by more than 3 million.

In many places, classrooms are overcrowded and curricula are outdated. Most of our qualified teachers are underpaid, and many of our paid teachers are unqualified. So we must give every child a place to sit and a teacher to learn from. Poverty must not be a bar to learning, and learning must offer an escape from poverty.

But more classrooms and more teachers are not enough. We must seek an educational system which grows in excellence as it grows in size. This means better training for our teachers. It means preparing youth to enjoy their hours of leisure as well as their hours of labor. It means exploring new techniques of teaching, to find new ways to stimulate the love of learning and the capacity for creation.

These are three of the central issues of the Great Society. While our Government has many programs directed at those issues, I do not pretend that we have the full answer to those problems.

But I do promise this: We are going to assemble the best thought and the broadest knowledge from all over the world to find those answers for America. I intend to establish working groups to prepare a series of White House conferences and meetings—on the cities, on natural beauty, on the quality of education, and on other emerging challenges. And from these meetings and from this inspiration and from these studies we will begin to set our course toward the Great Society.

The solution to these problems does not rest on a massive program in Washington, nor can it rely solely on the strained resources of local authority. They require us to create new concepts of cooperation, a creative federalism, between the National Capital and the leaders of local communities. Woodrow Wilson once wrote: "Every man sent out from his university should be a man of his Nation as well as a man of his time."

Within your lifetime powerful forces, already loosed, will take us toward a way of life beyond the realm of our experience, almost beyond the bounds of our imagination.

For better or for worse, your generation has been appointed by history to deal with those problems and to lead America toward a new age. You have the chance never before afforded to any people in any age. You can help build a society where the demands of morality, and the needs of the spirit, can be realized in the life of the Nation.

So, will you join in the battle to give every citizen the full equality which God enjoins and the law requires, whatever his belief, or race, or the color of his skin?

Will you join in the battle to give every citizen an escape from the crushing weight of poverty?

Will you join in the battle to make it possible for all nations to live in enduring peace—as neighbors and not as mortal enemies?

Will you join in the battle to build the Great Society, to prove that our material progress is only the foundation on which we will build a richer life of mind and spirit?

There are those timid souls who say this battle cannot be won; that we are condemned to a soulless wealth. I do not agree. We have the power to shape the civilization that we want. But we need your will, your labor, your hearts, if we are to build that kind of society.

Those who came to this land sought to build more than just a new country. They sought a new world. So I have come here today to your campus to say that you can make their vision our reality. So let us from this moment begin our work so that in the future men will look back and say: It was then, after a long and weary way, that man turned the exploits of his genius to the full enrichment of his life.

* * * * * *

1. How does Johnson's "Great Society" compare with the utopian views expressed in the Port Huron Statement? How does he propose to achieve it?

2. How does he try to make his vision especially relevant to young people?

29–4   *Lyndon B. Johnson, Why We Are in Vietnam, 1965*

By the summer of 1964, the Johnson Administration had already made secret plans to escalate the American military presence in Vietnam. But during the 1964 election campaign, LBJ stressed his differences with the hawkish views of Republican candidate Barry Goldwater. The President publicly rejected the idea of getting "tied down in a land war in Asia." But in the spring of 1965, Johnson ordered the first massive bombings of North Vietnam and began the buildup of American troop levels, soon to reach over 500,000. Speaking at Johns Hopkins University, Johnson tried to justify his policy.

SOURCE: Lyndon B. Johnson, "Peace Without Conquest." Address at Johns Hopkins University, April 6, 1905. Department of State Bulletin, April 26, 1965.

Tonight Americans and Asians are dying for a world where each people may choose its own path to change.

This is the principle for which our ancestors fought in the valleys of Pennsylvania. It is the principle for which our sons fight tonight in the jungles of Vietnam.

Vietnam is far away from this quiet campus. We have no territory there, nor do we seek any. The war is dirty and brutal and difficult. And some 400 young men, born into an America that is bursting with opportunity and promise, have ended their lives on Vietnam's steaming soil.

Why must we take this painful road?

Why must this Nation hazard its ease, and its interest, and its power for the sake of a people so far away?

We fight because we must fight if we are to live in a world where every country can shape its own destiny. And only in such a world will our own freedom be finally secure.

This kind of world will never be built by bombs or bullets. Yet the infirmities of man are such that force must often precede reason, and the waste of war, the works of peace.

We wish that this were not so. But we must deal with the world as it is, if it is ever to be as we wish.

The world as it is in Asia is not a serene or peaceful place.

The first reality is that North Vietnam has attacked the independent nation of South Vietnam. Its object is total conquest.

Of course, some of the people of South Vietnam are participating in an attack on their own government. But trained men and supplies, orders and arms, flow in a constant stream from north to south.

This support is the heartbeat of the war.

And it is a war of unparalleled brutality. Simple farmers are the targets of assassination and kidnapping. Women and children are strangled in the night because their men are loyal to their government. And helpless villages are ravaged by sneak attacks. Large-scale raids are conducted on towns, and terror strikes in the heart of cities.

The confused nature of this conflict cannot mask the fact that it is the new face of an old enemy.

Over this war—and all Asia—is another reality: the deepening shadow of Communist China. The rulers in Hanoi are urged on by Peking. This is a regime which has destroyed freedom in Tibet, which has attacked India, and has been condemned by the United Nations for aggression in Korea. It is a nation which is helping the forces of violence in almost every continent. The contest in Vietnam is part of a wider pattern of aggressive purposes.

Why are these realities our concern? Why are we in South Vietnam?

We are there because we have a promise to keep. Since 1954 every American President has offered support to the people of South Vietnam. We have helped to build, and we have helped to defend. Thus, over many years, we have made a national pledge to help South Vietnam defend its independence.

And I intend to keep that promise.

To dishonor that pledge, to abandon this small and brave nation to its enemies, and to the terror that must follow, would be an unforgivable wrong.

We are also there to strengthen world order. Around the globe, from Berlin to Thailand, are people whose well-being rests, in part, on the belief that they can count on us if they are attacked. To leave Vietnam to its fate would shake the confidence of all these people in the value of an American commitment and in the value of America's word. The result would be increased unrest and instability, and even wider war.

We are also there because there are great stakes in the balance. Let no one think for a moment that retreat from Vietnam would bring an end to conflict. The battle would be renewed in one country and then another. The central lesson of our time is that the appetite of aggression is never satisfied. To withdraw from one battlefield means only to prepare for the next. We must say in southeast Asia—as we did in Europe—in the words of the Bible: "Hitherto shalt thou come, but no further."

There are those who say that all our effort there will be futile—that China's power is such that it is bound to dominate all southeast Asia. But there is no end to that argument until all of the nations of Asia are swallowed up.

There are those who wonder why we have a responsibility there. Well, we have it there for the same reason that we have a responsibility for the defense of Europe. World War II was fought in both Europe and Asia, and when it ended we found ourselves with continued responsibility for the defense of freedom.

Our objective is the independence of South Vietnam, and its freedom from attack. We want nothing for ourselves—only that the people of South Vietnam be allowed to guide their own country in their own way.

We will do everything necessary to reach that objective. And we will do only what is absolutely necessary.

In recent months attacks on South Vietnam were stepped up. Thus, it became necessary for us to increase our response and to make attacks by air. This is not a change of purpose. It is a change in what we believe that purpose requires.

We do this in order to slow down aggression.

We do this to increase the confidence of the brave people of South Vietnam who have bravely borne this brutal battle for so many years with so many casualties.

And we do this to convince the leaders of North Vietnam—and all who seek to share their conquest—of a very simple fact:

We will not be defeated.

We will not grow tired.

We will not withdraw, either openly or under the cloak of a meaningless agreement.

We know that air attacks alone will not accomplish all of these purposes. But it is our best and prayerful judgment that they are a necessary part of the surest road to peace.

We hope that peace will come swiftly. But that is in the hands of others besides ourselves. And we must be prepared for a long continued conflict. It will require patience as well as bravery, the will to endure as well as the will to resist.

I wish it were possible to convince others with words of what we now find it necessary to say with guns and planes: Armed hostility is futile. Our resources are equal to any challenge. Because we fight for values and we fight for principles, rather than territory or colonies, our patience and our determination are unending.

Once this is clear, then it should also be clear that the only path for reasonable men is the path of peaceful settlement.

Such peace demands an independent South Vietnam—securely guaranteed and able to shape its own relationships to all others—free from outside interference—tied to no alliance—a military base for no other country.

These are the essentials of any final settlement....

This war, like most wars, is filled with terrible irony. For what do the people of North Vietnam want? They want what their neighbors also desire: food for their hunger; health for their bodies; a chance to learn; progress for their country; and an end to the bondage of material misery. And they would find all these things far more readily in peaceful association with others than in the endless course of battle....

We often say how impressive power is. But I do not find it impressive at all. The guns and the bombs, the rockets and the warships, are all symbols of human failure. They are necessary symbols. They protect what we cherish. But they are witness to human folly.

A dam built across a great river is impressive.

In the countryside where I was born, and where I live, I have seen the night illuminated, and the kitchens warmed, and the homes heated, where once the cheerless night and the ceaseless cold held sway. And all this happened because electricity came to our area along the humming wires of the REA [Rural Electrification Administrative]. Electrification of the countryside—yes, that, too, is impressive.

A rich harvest in a hungry land is impressive.

The sight of healthy children in a classroom is impressive.

These—not mighty arms—are the achievements which the American Nation believes to be impressive.

And, if we are steadfast, the time may come when all other nations will also find it so.

Every night before I turn out the lights to sleep I ask myself this question: Have I done everything that I can do to unite this country? Have I done everything I can to help unite the world, to try to bring peace and hope to all the peoples of the world? Have I done enough?

Ask yourselves that question in your homes—and in this hall tonight. Have we, each of us, all done all we could? Have we done enough?

We may well be living in the time foretold many years ago when it was said: "I call heaven and earth to record this day against you, that I have set before you life and death, blessing and cursing: therefore choose life, that both thou and thy seed may live."

This generation of the world must choose: destroy or build, kill or aid, hate or understand.

We can do all these things on a scale never dreamed of before.

Well, we will choose life. In so doing we will prevail over the enemies within man, and over the natural enemies of all mankind....

* * * * * *

1.   *How does Johnson put his policy in global perspective?*

2.   *Who is the enemy in Vietnam? What are the American objectives in fighting there?*

3.   *What connections do you see between this speech and the idea of "The Great Society" (Document 29–3)?*

29–5 *Martin Luther King, Jr., Conscience and the Vietnam War, 1967*

As American military involvement in Vietnam deepened, so, too, did opposition to the war. By 1967, hundreds of thousands of Americans had engaged in mass protest demonstrations on campuses and in cities around the nation. That year, Martin Luther King, Jr., addressed an antiwar rally of more than 125,000 gathered at the United Nations Plaza in New York City. King's outspoken antiwar views drew a storm of criticism from many civil rights leaders, white politicians, and others who thought he had no business meddling in foreign-policy issues. But for King, separating the war from the issues of racism and poverty had become impossible.

It is many months now since I found myself obliged by conscience to end my silence and to take a public stand against my country's war in Vietnam. The considerations which led me to that painful decision have not disappeared; indeed, they have been magnified by the course of events since then. The war itself is intensified, the impact on my country is even more destructive.

I cannot speak about the great themes of violence and nonviolence, of social change and of hope for the future without reflecting on the tremendous violence on Vietnam.

Since the spring of 1967, when I first made public my opposition to my government's policy, many persons have questioned me about the wisdom of my decision. "Why *you*" they have said. "Peace and civil rights don't mix. Aren't you hurting the cause of your people?" And when I hear such questions, I have been greatly saddened, for they mean that the inquirers have never really known me, my commitment, or my calling. Indeed, that question suggests that they do not know the world in which they live.

In explaining my position, I have tried to make it clear that I remain perplexed—as I think everyone must be perplexed—by the complexities and ambiguities of Vietnam. I would not wish to underrate the need for a collective solution to this tragic war. I would wish neither to present North Vietnam or the National Liberation Front as paragons of virtue, nor to overlook the role they can play in the successful resolution of the problem. While they both may have justifiable reason to be suspicious of the good faith of the United States, life and history give eloquent testimony to the fact that conflicts are never resolved without trustful give-and-take on both sides.

Since I am a preacher by calling, I suppose it is not surprising that I had several reasons for bringing Vietnam into the field of my moral vision. There is at the outset a very obvious and almost facile connection between the war in Vietnam and the struggle I and others have been waging in America. A few years ago there was a shining moment in that struggle. It seemed as if there was a real promise of hope for the poor, both black and white, through the poverty program. There were experiments, hopes, new beginnings. Then came the build-up in Vietnam, and I watched the program broken and eviscerated as if it were some idle political plaything of a society

gone mad on war, and I knew that America would never invest the necessary funds or energies in rehabilitation of its poor so long as adventures like Vietnam continued to draw men and skills and money like some demonical destructive suction tube. And so I was increasingly compelled to see the war not only as a moral outrage but also as an enemy of the poor, and to attack it as such.

Perhaps a more tragic recognition of reality took place when it became clear to me that the war was doing far more than devastating the hopes of the poor at home. It was sending their sons and their brothers and their husbands to fight and to die and in extraordinarily higher proportions relative to the rest of the population. We were taking the black young men who had been crippled by our society and sending them eight thousand miles away to guarantee liberties in Southeast Asia which they had not found in southwest Georgia and East Harlem. And so we have been repeatedly faced with the cruel irony of watching Negro and white boys on TV screens as they kill and die together for a nation that has been unable to seat them together in the same schools. We watch them in brutal solidarity burning the huts of a poor village, but we realize that they would never live on the same block in Detroit. I could not be silent in the face of such cruel manipulation of the poor.

My third reason moves to an even deeper level of awareness, but it grows out of my experience in the ghettos of the North over the last three years—especially the last three summers. As I have walked among the desperate, rejected, angry young men, I have told them that Molotov cocktails and rifles would not solve their problems. I have tried to offer them my deepest compassion, while maintaining my conviction that social change comes most meaningfully through nonviolent action. But, they asked, and rightly so, what about Vietnam? They asked if our own nation wasn't using massive doses of violence to solve its problems, to bring about the changes it wanted. Their questions hit home, and I knew that I could never again raise my voice against the violence of the oppressed in the ghettos without having first spoken clearly to the greatest purveyor of violence in the world today: my own government. For the sake of those boys, for the sake of this government, for the sake of the hundreds of thousands trembling under our violence, I cannot be silent.

For those who ask the question "Aren't you a civil rights leader?"—and thereby mean to exclude me from the movement for peace—I answer by saying that I have worked too long and hard now against segregated public accommodations to end up segregating my moral concern. Justice is indivisible. It must also be said that it would be rather absurd to work passionately and unrelentingly for integrated schools and not be concerned about the survival of a world in which to be integrated. I must say further that something in the very nature of our organizational structure in the Southern Christian Leadership Conference led me to this decision. In 1957, when a group of us formed that organization, we chose as our motto: "To save the soul of America." Now it should be incandescently clear that no one who has any concern for the integrity and life of America today can ignore the present war.

As if the weight of such a commitment were not enough, another burden of responsibility was placed upon me in 1964: I cannot forget that the Nobel Prize for Peace was also a commission—a commission to work harder than I had ever worked before for "the brotherhood of man." This is a calling which takes me beyond international allegiances, but even if it were not present, I would yet have to live with meaning of my commitment to the ministry of Jesus Christ. To me the relation of this ministry to the making of peace is so obvious that I sometimes marvel at those who ask me why I am speaking against the war. We are called to speak for the weak, for the voiceless, for the victims of our nation, and for those it calls enemy, for no document from human hands can make these humans any less our brothers.

And as I ponder the madness of Vietnam and search within myself for ways to understand and respond in compassion, my mind goes constantly to the people of that peninsula. I speak now not of the soldiers of each side, not of the junta in Saigon, but simply of the people who have been living under the curse of war for almost three continuous decades now. I think of them, too, because it is clear to me that there will be no meaningful solution until some attempt is made to know them and to hear their broken cries.

Somehow this madness must cease. We must stop now. I speak as a child of God and brother to the suffering poor of Vietnam. I speak for those whose land is being laid waste, whose homes are being destroyed, whose culture is being subverted. I speak for the poor of America who are paying the double price of smashed hopes at home and death and corruption in Vietnam. I speak as a citizen of the world, for the world as it stands aghast at the path we have taken. I speak as an American to the leaders of my own nation. The great initiative in this war is ours. The initiative to stop it must be ours.

In the spring of 1967, I made public the steps I consider necessary for this to happen. I should add now only that while many Americans have supported the proposals, the government has so far not recognized one of them. These are the times for real choices and not false ones. We are at the moment when our lives must be placed on the line if our nation is to survive its own folly. Every man of humane convictions must decide on the protest that best suits his convictions, but we must all protest.

There is something seductively tempting about stopping there and going off on what in some circles has become a popular crusade against the war in Vietnam. I say we must enter that struggle, but I wish to go on now to say something even more disturbing. The war in Vietnam is but a symptom of a far deeper malady within the American spirit.

In 1957 a sensitive American official overseas said that it seemed to him that our nation was on the wrong side of a world revolution. I am convinced that if we are to get on the right side of the world revolution we as a nation must undergo a radical revolution of values. A true revolution of values will soon cause us to question the fairness and justice of many of our past and present policies. A true revolution of values will soon look uneasily on the glaring contrast between poverty and wealth. With righteous indignation, it will look across the seas and see individual capitalists of the West investing huge sums of money in Asia, Africa, and South America only to take the profits out with no concern for the social betterment of the countries, and say: "This is not just." It will look at our alliance with the landed gentry of Latin America and say: "This is not just." The Western arrogance of feeling that it has everything to teach others and nothing to learn from them is not just. A true revolution of values will lay hands on the world order and say of war: "This way of settling differences is not just." This business of burning human beings with napalm, of filling our nation's homes with orphans and widows, of injecting poisonous drugs of hate into the veins of peoples normally humane, of sending men home from dark and bloody battlefields physically handicapped and psychologically deranged, cannot be reconciled with wisdom, justice, and love. A nation that continues year after year to spend more money on military defense than on programs of social uplift is approaching spiritual doom.

This kind of positive revolution of values is our best defense against Communism. War is not the answer. Communism will never be defeated by the use of atomic bombs or nuclear weapons.

These are revolutionary times; all over the globe men are revolting against old systems of exploitation and oppression. The shirtless and barefoot people of the land are rising up as never before. "The people that walked in darkness have seen a great light." We in the West must support these revolutions. It is a sad fact that because of comfort, complacency, a morbid fear of Communism, and our proneness to adjust to injustice, the Western nations that initiated so much of the revolutionary spirit of the modern world have now become the arch-antirevolutionaries. This has driven many to feel that only Marxism has the revolutionary spirit. Therefore, Communism is a judgment against our failure to make democracy real and follow through on the revolutions that we initiated. We must move past indecision to action. We must find new ways to speak for peace in Vietnam and for justice throughout the developing world, a world that borders on our doors. If we do not act, we shall surely be dragged down the long, dark, and shameful corridors of time reserved for those who possess power without compassion, might without morality, and strength without sight.

* * * * * *

1. *How does King connect the violence in Vietnam with the violence on the streets of American cities? with the plight of poor people?*

2. *How does he invoke the values of the civil rights movement to address the crisis in American foreign policy?*

29–6 Report of the National Advisory Committee on Civil Disorders, 1968

During the "long hot summer" of 1967, black ghetto rebellions exploded in Detroit and Newark, and scores of other cities experienced smaller riots. The magnitude of violence, death, and destruction was unprecedented, as was the level of response from federal and local authorities. President Johnson appointed a National Advisory Committee on Civil Disorders, chaired by Illinois Governor Otto Kerner, to investigate the causes of the rioting. The committee's final report painted a grim picture of the social and economic conditions in the nation's inner cities.

SOURCE: Wicker, Tom. Report of the National Advisory Committee on Civil Disorders (New York: Bantam Books, 1968), pp. 203–206.

We have seen what happened. Why did it happen?

In addressing this question we shift our focus from the local to the national scene, from the particular events of the summer of 1967 to the factors within the society at large which have brought about the sudden violent mood of so many urban Negroes.

The record before this Commission reveals that the causes of recent racial disorders are imbedded in a massive tangle of issues and circumstances—social, economic, political, and psychological—which arise out of the historical pattern of Negro-white relations in America.

These factors are both complex and interacting; they vary significantly in their effect from city to city and from year to year; and the consequences of one disorder, generating new grievances and new demands, become the causes of the next. It is this which creates the "thicket of tension, conflicting evidence and extreme opinions" cited by the President.

Despite these complexities, certain fundamental matters are clear. Of these, the most fundamental is the racial attitude and behavior of white Americans toward black Americans. Race prejudice has shaped our history decisively in the past; it now threatens to do so again. White racism is essentially responsible for the explosive mixture which has been accumulating in our cities since the end of World War II. At the base of this mixture are three of the most bitter fruits of white racial attitudes:

Pervasive discrimination and segregation. The first is surely the continuing exclusion of great numbers of Negroes from the benefits of economic progress through discrimination in employment and education, and their enforced confinement in segregated housing and schools. The corrosive and degrading effects of this condition and the attitudes that underlie it are the source of the deepest bitterness and at the center of the problem of racial disorder.

Black migration and white exodus. The second is the massive and growing concentration of impoverished Negroes in our major cities resulting from Negro migration from the rural South, rapid population growth and the continuing movement of the white middle-class to the suburbs. The consequence is a greatly increased burden on the already depleted resources of cities, creating a growing crisis of deteriorating facilities and services and unmet human needs.

Black ghettos. Third, in the teeming racial ghettos, segregation and poverty have intersected to destroy opportunity and hope and to enforce failure. The ghettos too often mean men and women without jobs, families without men, and schools where children are processed instead of educated, until they return to the street—to crime, to narcotics, to dependency on welfare, and to bitterness and resentment against society in general and white society in particular.

These three forces have converged on the inner city in recent years and on the people who inhabit it. At the same time, most whites and many Negroes outside the ghetto have prospered to a degree unparalleled in the history of civilization. Through television—the universal appliance in the ghetto—and the other media of mass communications, this affluence has been endlessly flaunted before the eyes of the Negro poor and the jobless ghetto youth.

As Americans, most Negro citizens carry within themselves two basic aspirations of our society. They seek to share in both the material resource of our system and its intangible benefits—dignity, respect and acceptance. Outside the ghetto many have succeeded in achieving a decent standard of life, and in developing the inner resources which give life meaning and dedication. Within the ghetto, however, it is rare that either aspiration is achieved.

Yet these facts alone—fundamental as they are—cannot be said to have caused the disorders. Other and more immediate factors help explain why these events happened now.

Recently, three powerful ingredients have begun to catalyze the mixture.

Frustrated hopes. The expectations aroused by the great judicial and legislative victories of the civil rights movement have led to frustration, hostility and cynicism in the face of the persistent gap between promise and fulfillment. The dramatic struggle for equal rights in the South has sensitized Northern Negroes to the economic inequalities reflected in the deprivation of ghetto life.

Legitimization of violence. A climate that tends toward the approval and encouragement of violence as a form of protest has been created by white terrorism directed against nonviolent protest, including instances of abuse and even murder of some civil rights workers in the South; by the open defiance of law and federal authority by state and local officials resisting desegregation; and by some protest groups engaging in civil disobedience who turn their backs on nonviolence, go beyond the Constitutionally protected rights of petition and free assembly, and resort to violence to attempt to compel alteration of laws and policies with which they disagree. This condition has been reinforced by a general erosion of respect for authority in American society and reduced effectiveness of social standards and community restraints on violence and crime. This in turn has largely resulted from rapid urbanization and the dramatic reduction in the average age of the total population.

Powerlessness. Finally, many Negroes have come to believe that they are being exploited politically and economically by the white "power structure." Negroes, like people in poverty everywhere, in fact lack the channels of communication, influence and appeal that traditionally have been available to ethnic minorities within the city and which enabled them—unburdened by color—to scale the walls of the white ghettos in an earlier era. The frustrations of powerlessness have led some to the conviction that there is no effective alternative to violence as a means of expression and redress, as a way of "mov-

ing the system." More generally, the result is alienation and hostility toward the institutions of law and government and the white society which controls them. This is reflected in the reach toward racial consciousness and solidarity reflected in the slogan "Black Power."

These facts have combined to inspire a new mood among Negroes, particularly among the young. Self-esteem and enhanced racial pride are replacing apathy and submission to "the system." Moreover, Negro youth, who make up over half of the ghetto population, share the growing sense of alienation felt by many white youth in our country. Thus, their role in recent civil disorders reflects not only a shared sense of deprivation and victimization by white society but also the rising incidence of disruptive conduct by a segment of American youth throughout the society.

INCITEMENT AND ENCOURAGEMENT OF VIOLENCE

These conditions have created a volatile mixture of attitudes and beliefs which needs only a spark to ignite mass violence. Strident appeals to violence, first heard from white racists, were echoed and reinforced last summer in the inflammatory rhetoric of black racists and militants. Throughout the year, extremists criss-crossed the country preaching a doctrine of black power and violence. Their rhetoric was widely reported in the mass media; it was echoed by local "militants" and organizations; it became the ugly background noise of the violent summer.

We cannot measure with any precision the influence of these organizations and individuals in the ghetto, but we think it clear that the intolerable and unconscionable encouragement of violence heightened tensions, created a mood of acceptance and an expectation of violence, and thus contributed to the eruption of the disorders last summer.

THE POLICE

It is the convergence of all these factors that makes the role of the police so difficult and so significant. Almost invariably the incident that ignites disorder arises from police action. Harlem, Watts, Newark and Detroit—all the major outbursts of recent years—were precipitated by routine arrests of Negroes for minor offenses by white police.

But the police are not merely the spark. In discharge of their obligation to maintain order and insure public safety in the disruptive conditions of ghetto life, they are inevitably involved in sharper and more frequent conflicts with ghetto residents than with the residents of other areas. Thus, to many Negroes police have come to symbolize white power, white racism and white repression. And the fact is that many police do reflect and express these white attitudes. The atmosphere of hostility and cynicism is reinforced by a widespread perception among Negroes of the existence of police brutality and corruption, and of a "double standard" of justice and protection—one for Negroes and one for whites.

* * * * * *

1. *What did the committee find as the fundamental cause of racial disorders in the cities? How did it explain the intensity of violence?*

2. *How would you compare the committee's analysis of the state of urban black America with the ideas expressed by Stokely Carmichael two years earlier (Document 28–10)?*

29–7   Robin Morgan, Radical Feminism, 1975

The feminist movement of the late 1960s and early 1970s began as a critique by radical women of the male chauvinism they experienced within the New Left and counterculture. From there, feminism expanded outward to transform the lives of millions of women, as well as nearly every aspect of American life. Through its insistence on exposing and fighting sexual inequality, feminist thinking and action reshaped intellectual life, politics, the professions, and popular culture. Robin Morgan was a leading radical feminist, as well as a poet., mother, and director of the New York Women's Law Center. She wrote this essay as a "personal retrospective" on the women's movement.

SOURCE: From *Rights of Passage*, by Robin Morgan. Copyright © 1975 by Robin Morgan. Used by permission of Edite Kroll Literary Agency.

I call myself a radical feminist, and that means specific things to me. The etymology of the word "radical" refers to "one who goes to the root." I believe that sexism is the root oppression, the one which, until and unless we *uproot* it, will continue to put forth the branches of racism, war, class hatred, ageism, competition, ecological disaster, and economic exploitation. This means, to me, that all the so-called revolutions to date have been *coups d'état* between men, in a halfhearted attempt to prune the branches but leave the root embedded—for the sake of preserving their own male privileges. Yet this also means that I'm not out for us as women to settle for a "piece of the pie," equality in an unjust society, or for mere "top-down" change which can be corrupted into leaving the basic system unaltered. I think our feminist revolution gains momentum from a "ripple effect"—from each individual woman gaining self-respect and yes, power, over her own body and soul first, then within her family, on her block, in her town, state, and so on out from the center, overlapping with similar changes other women are expe-

riencing, the circles rippling more widely and inclusively as they go. This is a revolution in consciousness, rising expectations, and the actions which reflect that organic process.

In the past decade I have seen just such methods give birth to hundreds of alternate feminist institutions, created and sustained by women's energy—all concrete moves toward self-determination and power....

Whenever I hear certain men sonorously announce that the Women's Movement is dead (a prediction they have been promoting hopefully since 1968), I am moved to an awkwardly unmilitant hilarity. I know, of course, that they mean we seem less sensational: "Where are all those bra-burnings?" (none of which ever took place anyway, to my knowledge). Such death-knell articulations are not only (deliberately?) unaware of multiform alternate institutions that are mushrooming, but unconscious of the more profound and threatening-to-the-status-quo political *attitudes* which underlie that surface. It is, for example, a grave error to see feminists as "retrenching" when the reality is that we have been maturing beyond those aforementioned "ejaculatory tactics" into a long-term, committed attitude toward *winning*. We are digging in, since we know that patriarchy won't be unbuilt in a day; and the revolution we are making is one on *every* front: economic, social, political, cultural, personal, public, sexual, biological, and yes, even metaphysical.

The early ultra-egalitarianism and guilt-ridden "downward mobility" motifs of certain radical feminist groups, for instance, have modulated into a realization that women deserve to have credit for what we accomplish, whether that be the author's name signed to her article (after centuries of being "Anonymous"), or the right to be paid a living wage for her work at a feminist business (instead of falling prey to a new volunteerism—this one "for the revolution's sake"). The early antipathy toward any and all structure has given way to a recognition that we must evolve totally new ways of organizing ourselves, something else than chaotic spontaneity or masculinist hierarchy. The early excesses of collective tyranny have shifted into an understanding that there is a difference between individualism and individuality—and that the latter is precious and to be cherished. The emphases on women's studies reflect the welcome end of anti-intellectual trends (again picked up from male movements—a "line" created by privileged men who already had their college educations along with their charisma points in SDS or the counter-culture). We are daring to demand and explore the delights of hard intellectual work, both as personal challenge and as shared necessity. All the jargon exhorting us to "seize power" won't help if we "seize" the labs, for instance, and stand ignorantly gaping at the test tubes. We are daring to research our own cleverly buried herstorical past, even to develop new radical teaching methods as joint odysseys between teachers and students, without deification—or degradation—of either….

And where, my dear reader may well ask, does this Pollyanna writer see the dangers, the failures, the losses? Or is she so blind, the woman in the mirror, that she thinks we've really come a long way, baby? Hardly.

These arms have held the vomitous shudderings of a sister-prostitute undergoing forced jail-withdrawal from her heroin addiction. These eyes have wept over the suicide of a sister-poet. These shoulders have tightened at the vilifications of men—on the street, in the media, on the lecture platform. These fists have clenched at the reality of backlash against us: the well-financed "friends of the fetus" mobilizing again to retake what small ground we have gained in the area of abortion; the rise in rape statistics (not only because more women are daring to *report* rapes, but also because more rapes are *occurring*); the ghastly mutilation-murders of women rumored to be witches (in the Catskill and Appalachian regions during the past two years) as an ominous message to all women who challenge patriarchal definitions. This stomach has knotted at the anonymous phone calls, the unsigned death threats, the real bombs planted in real auditoriums before a poetry reading or speech, the real bullet fired from a real pistol at the real podium behind which I was standing. (Those who have real power over our lives recognize the threat we pose—even when we ourselves do not.)

And yes, these fingers have knotted *their* versions of "correct lines"—strangling my own neck and the necks of other sisters.

I have watched some of the best minds of *my feminist* generation go mad with impatience and despair. So many other "oldie" radical feminists lost, having themselves lost the vision in all its intricacy, having let themselves be driven into irrelevance: the analytical pioneer whose "premature" brilliance isolated her into solipsism and finally self-signed-in commitment for "mental treatment"; the theorist whose nihilistic fear of "womanly" emotion led her into an obfuscated style and a "negative charisma"— an obsessive "I accuse" acridity corrosive to herself and other women; the fine minds lost to alcohol, or to "per-

sonal solutions," or to inertia, or to the comforting central-committeeist neat blueprint of outmoded politics, or to the equally reassuring glaze of "humanism," a word often misused as a bludgeon to convince women that we must put our suffering back at the bottom of the priority list. Some of these women never actually worked on a tangible feminist project—store-front legal counseling or a nursery or a self-help clinic—or if they did so at one time they have long ago stopped, lost touch with women outside their own "feminist café society" circles. Such alienation from the world of women's genuine daily needs seems to have provoked in some of my sister "oldies" a bizarre new definition of "radical feminist"; that is, one who relentlessly assails any political effectiveness on the part of other feminists, while frequently choosing to do so in terms of personalities and with slashing cruelty. After so many centuries of spending all our compassion on men, could we not spare a little for each other?

I've watched the bloody internecine warfare between groups, between individuals. All that fantastic energy going to fight each other instead of our oppression! (It is, after all, safer to attack "just women.") So much false excitement, self-righteousness and judgmental posturing! Gossip, accusations, counter-accusations, smears—all leapt to, spread, and sometimes believed without the impediments of such things as facts. I've come to think that we need a feminist code of ethics, that we need to create a new *women's* morality, an antidote of honor against this contagion by male supremacist values….

I would say to those few dear "oldies" who are burned out or embittered: you have forgotten that women are not fools, not sheep. We know about the dangers of commercialism and tokenism from the male right, and the dangers of manipulation and cooptation from the male left (the boys' establishment and the boys' movement). We are, frankly, bored by correct lines and vanguards and failurism and particularly by that chronic disease—guilt. Those of us who choose to struggle with men we love, well, we demand respect and support for that, and an end to psychological torture. Those of us who choose to relate solely to other women demand respect and support for *that,* and an end to the legal persecution and attitudinal bigotry that condemns freedom of sexual choice. Those of us who choose to have or choose *not* to have children demand support and respect for *that.* We know that the emerging women's art and women's spirituality are lifeblood for our survival—resilient cultures have kept oppressed groups alive even when economic analyses and revolutionary strategy have fizzled.

We know that serious, lasting change does not come about overnight, or simply, or without enormous pain and diligent examination and tireless, undramatic, everyday-a-bit-more-one-step-at-a-time work. We know that such change seems to move in cycles (thesis, antithesis, and synthesis—which itself in turn becomes a new thesis…), and we also know that those cycles are not merely going around in circles. They are, rather, an *upward spiral,* so that each time we reevaluate a position or place we've been before we do so from a new perspective. We are *in process,* continually evolving, and we will no longer be made to feel inferior or ineffectual for knowing and being what we are at any given moment.

Housewives across the nation stage the largest consumer boycott ever known (the meat boycott) and while it may not seem, superficially, a feminist action, *women* are doing this, women who ten years ago before this feminist movement, might have regarded such an action as unthinkable. The campaign for passage of the Equal Rights Amendment continues to gain supporters (like that fine closet feminist Betty Ford) despite all the combined right *and* left pieces of reaction against it. Consciousness-raising proliferates, in groups in individuals, in new forms and with new structures. The lines of communication begin to center around content instead of geography, and to stretch from coast to coast, so that women in an anti-rape project, for example, may be more in touch with other anti-rape groups nationally than with every latest development in the Women's Movement in their own backyards. I think this is to the good, it's a widening of vision, an exercising of muscle. It's Thinking Big….

This process has changed my life. Today, my sexuality unfolds in even more complex, beautiful, and self-satisfying layers. Today, I can affirm my mother and identify with her beyond all my intricate ambivalence. I can confront ersatz "sexual liberation" and its pornographic manifestos for what they are—degrading sexist propaganda. And I can confess my pride at an ongoing committed relationship with the husband I love and have always loved and whose transformation by feminism I have watched over and struggled with and marveled at. This process has given me the tools, as well, to affirm the woman I love, to help raise the child I love in new and freer ways. I have now curled round another spiral, and can admit that I *like* good food and enjoy cooking it (when that's not assumed to be my reason for existing). I have found my own appearance at last. No more "uniforms," but clothes that are comfortable, simple, pleasant, and *me;* hair that I cut or let grow as I choose, unconforming to fashion as dictated by *Vogue* or its inverse image, *Rolling Stone.* And this process, most of all, has given me the tools of self-respect as a woman artist, so that I am reclaiming my own shameless singing poet's voice beyond the untenable choices of "ivory tower, uninvolved" fake art or that grim "socialist-realist" polemical pseudo-art.

This ecstatic reclamation of my own and (and my brazen affirmation, indeed of *all art*) is inseparable from what I have lovingly named "metaphysical feminism"— the refusal to simplify or polarize the insatiable demand for a passionate, intelligent, complex, visionary, and *continuing* process which dares to include in its patterns everything from the scientific transformation which stars express as they nova, to the metaphorical use of that expression in a poem; a process which dares to celebrate contradiction and diversity, dares to see each field-daisy as miraculous, each pebble as profound, each sentient being as holy.

And also, more humbly, this process, this Women's Movement, has given me the chance to travel through it, to witness the splendor of women's faces all over America blossoming with hope, to hear women's voices rising in an at-first fragile, then stronger chorus of anger and determination. Pocatello, Idaho, and Escanaba, Michigan, and Lawrence, Kansas, and Sarasota, Florida, and Sacramento, California, and Portales, New Mexico, and Northampton, Massachusetts—and how many others? It has exhausted me, this Women's Movement, and sometimes made me cranky and guilty and gossipy and manipulative and self-pitying and self-righteous and sour. It has exasperated me, frustrated me, and driven me gloriously crazy.

But it is in my blood, and I love it, do you hear? I know in my bones that women's consciousness and our desire for freedom and the power to forge a humane world society will survive even the mistakes the Women's Movement makes—as if feminism were a card-carrying nitsy little sect and not what it *is,* a profoundly radical and perpetually enlarging vision of what can save this planet.…There are millions of us now, and the vision is expanding its process to include us all.

I trust that process with my life. I have learned to love that Women's Movement, that face in the mirror, it wearing its new, wry, patient smile; those eyes that have rained grief but can still see clearly; that body with its unashamed sags and stretch marks; that mind, with all its failings and its cowardices and its courage and its inexhaustible will to try again.

I want to say to that woman: we've only just of begun, and there's no stopping us. I want to tell her that she is maturing and stretching and daring and yes, succeeding, in ways undreamt until now. She will survive the naysayers, male *and* female, and she will coalesce in all her wondrously various forms and diverse lifestyles, ages, races, classes, and internationalities into one harmonious blessing on this agonized world. She is so very beautiful, and I love her. The face in the mirror is myself. And the face in the mirror is you.

Hayden and Mary King (Document 29-2)?

* * * * * *

1.   *How does Morgan define radical feminism, and how does she think it has changed society?*

2.   *What similarities and differences do you see between Morgan's ideas and those of Casey*

3.   *What evidence does Morgan offer for the social impact of the feminist idea that "the personal is political"?*

29–8   Spiro Agnew, The Dangers of Constant Carnival, 1969

The radical movements of the 1960s also were the catalyst for powerful conservative backlash. Political figures such as Richard Nixon and George Wallace were able to capitalize on youth revolt, ghetto riots, and the challenge to authority with thinly veiled appeals to racial fears and the desire for "law and order." Spiro Agnew, elected vice-president in 1968, emerged as an effective "hatchet man" for President Nixon, winning a broad following with his attacks upon the New Left and the allegedly liberal-dominated mass media. Agnew was forced to resign as vice-president in 1973 when he pleaded no contest to charges that he accepted bribes while in office.

SOURCE: Spiro Agnew, Address at Pennsylvania Republican Dinner, Harrisburg, October 30, 1969.

A little over a week ago, I took a rather unusual step for a Vice President. I said something. Particularly, I said something that was predictably unpopular with the people who would like to run the country without the inconvenience of seeking public office. I said I did not like some of the things I saw happening in this country. I criticized those who encouraged government by street carnival and suggested it was time to stop the carousel.

It appears that by slaughtering a sacred cow I triggered a holy war. I have no regrets. I do not intend to repudiate my beliefs, recant my words, or run and hide.

What I said before, I will say again. It is time for the preponderant majority, the responsible citizens of this country, to assert *their* rights. It is time to stop dignifying the immature actions of arrogant, reckless, inexperienced elements within our society. The reason is compelling. It is simply that their tantrums are insidiously destroying the fabric of American democracy.

By accepting unbridled protest as a way of life, we have tacitly suggested that the great issues of our times are best decided by posturing and shouting matches in the streets. America today is drifting toward Plato's classic definition of a degenerating democracy—a democracy that permits the voice of the mob to dominate the affairs of government.

Last week I was lambasted for my lack of "mental and moral sensitivity." I say that any leader who does not perceive where persistent street struggles are going to lead this nation lacks mental acuity. And any leader who does not caution this nation on the danger of this direction lacks moral strength.

I believe in Constitutional dissent. I believe in the people registering their views with their elected representatives, and I commend those people who care enough about their country to involve themselves in its great issues. I believe in legal protest within the Constitutional limits of free speech, including peaceful assembly and the right of petition. But I do not believe that demonstrations, lawful or unlawful, merit my approval or even my silence where the purpose is fundamentally unsound. In the case of the Vietnam Moratorium, the objective announced by the leaders—immediate unilateral withdrawal of all our forces from Vietnam—was not only unsound but idiotic. The tragedy was that thousands who participated wanted only to show a fervent desire for peace, but were used by the political hustlers who ran the event.

It is worth remembering that our country's founding fathers wisely shaped a Constitutional republic, not a pure democracy. The representative government they contemplated and skillfully constructed never intended that elected officials should decide crucial questions by counting the number of bodies cavorting in the streets. They recognized that freedom cannot endure dependent upon referendum every time part of the electorate desires it.

So great is the latitude of our liberty that only a subtle line divides use from abuse. I am convinced that our preoccupation with emotional demonstration, frequently crossing the line to civil disruption and even violence could inexorably lead us across that line forever.

Ironically, it is neither the greedy nor the malicious but the self-righteous who are guilty of history's worst atrocities. Society understands greed and malice and erects barriers of law to defend itself from these vices.

But evil cloaked in emotional causes is well disguised and often undiscovered until it is too late.

We have just such a group of self-proclaimed saviors of the American soul at work today. Relentless in their criticism of intolerance in America, they themselves are intolerant of those who differ with their views. In the name of academic freedom, they destroy academic freedom. Denouncing violence, they seize and vandalize buildings of great universities. Fiercely expressing their respect for truth, they disavow the logic and discipline necessary to pursue truth.

They would have us believe that they alone know what is good for America—what is true and right and beautiful. They would have us believe that their reflexive action is superior to our reflective action; that their revealed righteousness is more effective than our reason and experience.

Think about it. Small bands of students are allowed to shut down great universities. Small groups of dissidents are allowed to shout down political candidates. Small cadres of professional protesters are allowed to jeopardize the peace efforts of the President of the United States.

It is time to question the credentials of their leaders. And, if in questioning we disturb a few people, I say it is time for them to be disturbed. If, in challenging, we polarize the American people, I say it is time for a positive polarization.

It is time for a healthy in-depth examination of policies and a constructive realignment in this country. It is time to rip away the rhetoric and to divide on authentic lines. It is time to discard the fiction that in a country of 200 million people, everyone is qualified to quarterback the government.

For too long we have accepted superficial categorization—young versus old, white versus black, rich versus poor. Now it is time for an alignment based on principles and values shared by all citizens regardless of age, race, creed, or income. This, after all, is what America is all about.

America's pluralistic society was forged on the premise that what unites us in ideals is greater than what divides us as individuals. Our political and economic institutions were developed to enable men and ideas to compete in the marketplace on the assumption that the best would prevail. Everybody was deemed equal and by the rules of the game they could become superior. The rules were clear and fair: in politics, win an election; in economics, build a better mousetrap. And as time progressed, we added more referees to assure equal opportunities and provided special advantages for those whom we felt had entered life's arena at a disadvantage.

The majority of Americans respect these rules—*and with good reason.* Historically, they have served as a bulwark to prevent totalitarianism, tyranny, and privilege—the old world spectres which drove generations of immigrants to American sanctuary. Pragmatically, the rules of America work. This nation and its citizens—collectively and individually—have made more social, political, and economic progress than any civilization in world history.

The principles of the American system did not spring up overnight. They represent centuries of bitter struggle. Our laws and institutions are not even purely American—only our federal system bears our unique imprimatur.

We owe our values to the Judeo-Christian ethic which stresses individualism, human dignity, and a higher purpose than hedonism. We owe our laws to the political evolution of government by consent of the governed. Our nation's philosophical heritage is as diverse as its cultural background. We are a melting pot nation that has for over two centuries distilled something new and, I believe, sacred.

Now, we have among us a glib, activist element who would tell us our values are lies, and I call them impudent. Because anyone, who impugns a legacy of liberty and dignity that reaches back to Moses, is impudent.

I call them snobs for most of them disdain to mingle with the masses who work for a living. They mock the common man's pride in his work, his family, and his country. It has also been said that I called them intellectuals. I did not. I said that they characterized themselves as intellectuals. No true intellectual, no truly knowledgeable person, would so despise democratic institutions.

America cannot afford to write off a whole generation for the decadent thinking of a few. America cannot afford to divide over their demagoguery, to be deceived by their duplicity, or to let their license destroy liberty. We can, however, afford to separate them from our society—with no more regret than we should feel over discarding rotten apples from a barrel.

The leaders of this country have a moral as well as a political obligation to point out the dangers of unquestioned allegiance to any cause. We must be better than a charlatan leader of the French Revolution, remembered only for his words: "There go the people; I am their leader; I must follow them."

And the American people have an obligation, too—an obligation to exercise their citizenship with a precision that precludes excesses.

I recognize that many of the people who participated in the past Moratorium Day were unaware that its sponsors sought immediate unilateral withdrawal. Perhaps many more had not considered the terrible consequences of immediate unilateral withdrawal.

I hope that all citizens who really want peace will take the time to read and reflect on the problem. I hope that they will take into consideration the impact of abrupt termination; that they will remember the more than 3,000 innocent men, women, and children slaughtered after the Viet Cong captured Hue last year and the more than 15,000 doctors, nurses, teachers, and village leaders murdered by the Viet Cong during the war's early years. The only sin of these people was their desire to build their budding nation of South Vietnam.

Chanting "Peace Now" is no solution, if "Peace Now" is to permit a wholesale bloodbath. And saying that the President should understand the people's view is no solution. It is time for the people to understand the views of the President they elected to lead them.

First, foreign policy cannot be made in the streets.

Second, turning out a good crowd is not synonymous with turning out a good foreign policy.

Third, the test of a President cannot be reduced to a question of public relations. As the eighteenth-century jurist Edmund Burke wrote: "Your representative owes you not his industry only but his judgment; and he betrays instead of serving you, if he sacrifices it to your opinion."

Fourth, the impatience—the understandable frustration over this war—should be focused on the government that is stalling peace while continuing to threaten and invade South Vietnam—and that government's capital is not in Washington. It is in Hanoi.

This was not Richard Nixon's war, but it will be Richard Nixon's peace if we only let him make it.

Finally—and most important—regardless of the issue, it is time to stop demonstrating in the streets and start doing something constructive about our institutions. America must recognize the dangers of constant carnival. Americans must reckon with irresponsible leadership and reckless words. The mature and sensitive people of this country must realize that their freedom of protest is being exploited by avowed anarchists and communists who detest everything about this country and want to destroy it.

This is a fact. These are the few; these are not necessarily leaders. But they prey upon the good intentions of gullible men everywhere. They pervert honest concern to something sick and rancid. They are vultures who sit in trees and watch lions battle, knowing that win, lose, or draw, they will be fed.

Abetting the merchants of hate are the Parasites of passion. These are the men who value a cause purely for its political mileage. These are the politicians who temporize with the truth by playing both sides to their own advantage. They ooze sympathy for "the cause" but balance each sentence with equally reasoned reservations. Their interest is personal, not moral. They are ideological eunuchs whose most comfortable position is straddling the philosophical fence, soliciting votes from both sides.

Will Congress settle down to the issues of the nation and reform the institutions of America as our President asks? Can the press ignore the pipers who lead the parades? Will the heads of great universities protect the rights of all their students? Will parents have the courage to say no to their children? Will people have the intelligence to boycott pornography and violence? Will citizens refuse to be led by a series of Judas goats down tortuous paths of delusion and self-destruction?

Will we defend fifty centuries of accumulated wisdom? For that is our heritage. Will we make the effort to preserve America's bold, successful experiment in truly representative government? Or do we care so little that we will cast it all aside?

Because on the eve of our nation's 200th birthday, we have reached the crossroads. Because at this moment totalitarianism's threat does not necessarily have a foreign accent. Because we have a home-grown menace, made and manufactured in the U.S.A. Because if we are lazy or foolish, this nation could forfeit its integrity, never to be free again.

I do not want this to happen to America. And I do not think that you do either. We have something magnificent here, something worth fighting for, and now is the time for all good men to fight for the soul of their country. Let us stop apologizing for our past. Let us conserve and create for the future.

* * * * * *

1.   *How does Agnew seek to discredit the antiwar movement? How does he defend the Nixon administration's Vietnam policy?*

2.   *What political and rhetorical appeals does Agnew make to what Nixon called "the Silent Majority"? Whom does he blame for what he calls "the dangers of constant carnival"?*

29–9 John Kerry, Vietnam Veterans Against the War, 1971

President Richard Nixon ended the draft and began removing American ground troops from Vietnam. But he also increased the level of death and destruction through an escalated use of American air power, and he expanded the fighting to include Cambodia and Laos. As the war dragged on, the peace movement continued its struggle to end it. By 1970, the antiwar forces had attracted new elements, including significant numbers of Vietnam veterans. John Kerry, a Marine captain who helped found the Vietnam Veterans Against the War, received wide television coverage with the following testimony given to the Senate Foreign Relations Committee in 1971. Kerry won election to the U.S. Senate from Massachusetts in 1984.

SOURCE: Statement by John Kerry, Senate Committee of Foreign Relations, April 23, 1971.

I would like to talk on behalf of all those veterans and say that several months ago in Detroit we had an investigation at which over 150 honorably discharged, and many very highly decorated, veterans testified to war crimes committed in Southeast Asia. These were not isolated incidents but crimes committed on a day-to-day basis with the full awareness of officers at all levels of command.

It is impossible to describe to you exactly what did happen in Detroit—the emotions in the room and the feelings of the men who were reliving their experiences in Vietnam. They relived the absolute horror of what this country, in a sense, made them do.

They told stories that at times they had personally raped, cut off ears, cut off heads, taped wires from portable telephones to human genitals and turned up the power, cut off limbs, blown up bodies, randomly shot at civilians, razed villages in fashion reminiscent of Genghis Khan, shot cattle and dogs for fun, poisoned food stocks, and generally ravaged the countryside of South Vietnam in addition to the normal ravage of war and the normal and very particular ravaging which is done by the applied bombing power of this country.

We call this investigation the Winter Soldier Investigation. The term Winter Soldier is a play on words of Thomas Paine's in 1776 when he spoke of the Sunshine Patriots and summer time soldiers who deserted at Valley Forge because the going was rough.

We who have come here to Washington have come here because we feel we have to be winter soldiers now. We could come back to this country, we could be quiet, we could hold our silence, we could not tell what went on in Vietnam, but we feel because of what threatens this country, not the reds, but the crimes which we are committing that threaten it, that we have to speak out....

In our opinion and from our experience, there is nothing in South Vietnam which could happen that realistically threatens the United States of America. And to attempt to justify the loss of one American life in Vietnam, Cambodia or Laos by linking such loss to the preservation of freedom, which those misfits supposedly abuse, is to us the height of criminal hypocrisy, and it is that kind of hypocrisy which we feel has torn this country apart.

We found that not only was it a civil war, an effort by a people who had for years been seeking their libera-tion from any colonial influence whatsoever, but also we found that the Vietnamese whom we had enthusiastically molded after our own image were hard put to take up the fight against the threat we were supposedly saving them from.

We found most people didn't even know the difference between communism and democracy. They only wanted to work in rice paddies without helicopters strafing them and bombs with napalm burning their villages and tearing their country apart. They wanted everything to do with the war, particularly with this foreign presence of the United States of America, to leave them alone in peace, and they practiced the art of survival by siding with whichever military force was present at a particular time, be it Viet Cong. North Vietnamese or American.

We found also that all too often American men were dying in those rice paddies for want of support from their allies. We saw first hand how monies from American taxes were used for a corrupt dictatorial regime. We saw that many people in this country had a one-sided idea of who was kept free by our flag, and blacks provided the highest percentage of casualties. We saw Vietnam ravaged equally by American bombs and search and destroy missions, as well as by Viet Cong terrorism and yet we listened while this country tried to blame all of the havoc on the Viet Cong.

We rationalized destroying villages in order to save them. We saw America lose her sense of morality as she accepted very coolly at My Lai and refused to give up the image of American soldiers who hand out chocolate bars and chewing gum.

We learned the meaning of free fire zones, shooting anything that moves, and we watched while America placed a cheapness on the lives of Orientals.

We watched the United States falsification of body counts, in fact the glorification of body counts. We listened while month after month we were told the back of the enemy was about to break. We fought using weapons against "oriental human beings." We fought using weapons against those people which I do not believe this country would dream of using were we fighting in the European theater. We watched while men charged up hills because a general said that hill has to be taken, and after losing one platoon or two platoons they marched away to leave the hill for reoccupation by the North Vietnamese. We watched pride allow the most unimportant battles to be blown into extravaganzas, because we couldn't lose, and we couldn't retreat, and it because it didn't matter how many American bodies were lost to prove that point, and so there were Hamburger Hills and Khe Sanhs and Hill 81s and Fire Base 6s, and so many others.

Now we are told that the men who fought there must watch quietly while American lives are lost so that we can exercise the incredible arrogance of Vietnamizing the Vietnamese.

Each day to facilitate the process by which the United States washes her hands of Vietnam someone has to give up his life so that the United States doesn't have to admit something that the entire world already knows, so that we can't say that we have made a mistake. Someone has to die so that President Nixon won't be, and these are his words, "the first President to lose a war."

We are asking Americans to think about that because how do you ask a man to be the last man to die in Vietnam? How do you ask a man to be the last man to a die for a mistake?…We are here in Washington also to say that the problem of this war is not just a question of war and diplomacy. It is part and parcel of everything that we are trying as human beings to communicate to people in this country—the question of racism which is rampant in the military, and so many other questions such as the use of weapons; the hypocrisy in our taking umbrage at the Geneva Conventions and using that as justification for a continuation of this war when we are more guilty than any other body of violations of those Geneva Conventions: in the use of free fire zones, harassment interdiction fire, search and destroy missions, the bombings, the torture of prisoners, the killing of prisoners, all accepted policy by many units in South Vietnam. That is what we are trying to say. It is part and parcel of everything.

An American Indian friend of mine who lives in the Indian Nation of Alcatraz put it to me very succinctly. He told me how as a boy on an Indian reservation he had watched television and he used to cheer the cowboys when they came in and shot the Indians, and then suddenly one day he stopped in Vietnam and he said "my God, I am doing to these people the very same thing that was done to my people," and he stopped. And that is what we are trying to say, that we think this thing has to end.

We are here to ask, and we are here to ask vehemently, where are the leaders of our country? Where is the leadership? We're here to ask where are McNamara, Rostow, Bundy, Gilpatrick, and so many others? Where are they now that we, the men they sent off to war, have returned. These are commanders who have deserted their troops. And there is no more serious crime in the laws of war. The Army says they never leave their wounded. The marines say they never leave even their dead. These men have left all the casualties and retreated behind a pious shield of public rectitude. They've left the real stuff of their reputations bleaching behind them in the sun in this country….

We wish that a merciful God could wipe away our own memories of that service as easily as this administration has wiped away their memories of us. But all that they have done and all that they can do by this denial is to make more clear than ever our own determination to undertake one last mission—to search out and destroy the last vestige of this barbaric war, to pacify our own hearts, to conquer the hate and the fear that have driven this country these last ten years and more. And more. And so when thirty years from now our brothers go down the street without a leg, without an arm, or a face, and small boys ask why, we will be able to say "Vietnam" and not mean a desert, not a filthy obscene memory, but mean instead the place where America finally turned and where soldiers like us helped it in the turning.

* * * * * *

1.   Why does Kerry now oppose the American presence in Vietnam? How does he use the personal experiences of veterans to make his case?

2.   How does he hold the U.S. government accountable?

29–10   *Roe v. Wade (1973)*

No Supreme Court decision of this century, with the exception of Brown v. Board of Education, *has stirred as much controversy as* Roe v. Wade. *The case involved the challenge of a pregnant woman ("Jane Roe") and a doctor against a Texas law prohibiting abortion except by "medical advice for the purpose of saving the life of the mother." In a 6–3 vote, the Court struck down the Texas law and ruled that a woman's right to privacy included the*

right to have an abortion. Twenty years after Roe v. Wade, *abortion remains one of the most hotly contested social issues in American politics.*

SOURCE: 410 U.S. 113 (1973).

JUSTICE BLACKMUN DELIVERED THE OPINION OF THE COURT

We forthwith acknowledge our awareness of the sensitive and emotional nature of the abortion controversy, of the vigorous opposing views, even among physicians, and of the deep and seemingly absolute convictions that the subject inspires. One's philosophy, one's experience, one's exposure to the raw edges of human existence, one's religious training, one's attitudes toward life and family and their values, and the moral standards one establishes and seeks to observe, are all likely to influence and to color one's thinking and conclusions about abortion. In addition, population growth, pollution, poverty, and racial overtones tend to complicate and not to simplify the problem. Our task, of course, is to resolve the issue by constitutional measurement, free of emotion and of predilection. We seek earnestly to do this, and, because we do, we have inquired into, and in this opinion place some emphasis upon, medical and medical-legal history and what that history reveals about man's attitudes toward the abortion procedure over the centuries....

The principal thrust of appellant's attack on the Texas statutes is that they improperly invade a right, said to be possessed by the pregnant woman, to choose to terminate her pregnancy....

The Constitution does not explicitly mention any right of privacy. However, the Court has recognized that a right of personal privacy, or a guarantee of certain areas or zones of privacy, does exist under the Constitution. In varying contexts, the Court or individual Justices have, indeed, found at least the roots of that right in the First Amendment, in the Fourth and Fifth Amendments; in the penumbras of the Bill of Rights; in the Ninth Amendment; or in the concept of liberty guaranteed by the first section of the 14th Amendment. These decisions make it clear that only personal rights that can be deemed "fundamental" or "implicit in the concept of ordered liberty" are included in this guarantee of personal privacy. They also make it clear that the right has some extension to activities relating to marriage, procreation, contraception, family relationships, and child rearing and education.

This right of privacy, whether it be founded in the 14th Amendment's concept of personal liberty and restrictions upon state action, as we feel it is, or, as the District Court determined, in the Ninth Amendment's reservation of rights to the people, is broad enough to encompass a woman's decision whether or not to terminate her pregnancy. The detriment that the State would impose upon the pregnant woman by denying this choice altogether is apparent. Specific and direct harm medically diagnosable even in early pregnancy may be involved. Maternity, or additional offspring, may force upon the woman a distressful life and future. Psychological harm may be imminent. Mental and physical health may be taxed by child care. There is also the distress, for all concerned, associated with the unwanted child, and there is a problem of bringing a child into a family already unable, psychologically and otherwise, to care for it. In other cases, as in this one, the additional difficulties and continuing stigma of unwed motherhood may be involved. All these are factors the woman and her responsible physician necessarily will consider in consultation.

On the basis of elements such as these, appellants and some *amici* argue that the woman's right is absolute and that she is entitled to terminate her pregnancy at whatever time, in whatever way, and for whatever reason she alone chooses. With this we do not agree. The Court's decision recognizing a right of privacy also acknowledges that some state regulation in areas protected by that right is appropriate. A state may properly assert important interests in safeguarding health, in maintaining medical standards, and in protecting potential life. At some point in pregnancy, these respective interests become sufficiently compelling to sustain regulation of the factors that govern the abortion decision. The privacy right involved, therefore, cannot be said to be absolute. In fact, it is not clear to us that the claim asserted by some *amici* that one has an unlimited right to do with one's body as one pleases bears a close relationship to the right of privacy previously articulated in the Court's decisions. The Court has refused to recognize an unlimited right of this kind in the past. We, therefore, conclude that the right of personal privacy includes the abortion decision, but that this right is not unqualified and must be considered against important state interests in regulation.

A. The appellee and certain *amici* argue that the fetus is a "person" within the language and meaning of the 14th Amendment. In support of this, they outline at length and in detail the well-known facts of fetal development. If this suggestion of personhood is established, the appellant's case, of course, collapses, for the fetus' right to life is then guaranteed specifically by the Amendment. On the other hand, the appellee conceded that no case could be cited that holds that a fetus is a person within the meaning of the 14th Amendment....

B. The pregnant woman cannot be isolated in her privacy. She carries an embryo and, later, a fetus, if one accepts the medical definitions of the developing young in the human uterus. The situation therefore is inherently different from marital intimacy, or bedroom possession of obscene material, or marriage, or procreation, or education, with which these other cases were concerned. It is reasonable and appropriate for a State to decide that at some point in time another interest, that of health of the mother or that of potential human life, becomes significantly involved. The woman's privacy is no longer sole and any right of privacy she possesses must be measured accordingly.

Texas argues that, apart from the 14th Amendment, life begins at conception and is present throughout pregnancy, and that, therefore, the State has a compelling interest in protecting that life from and after conception. We need not resolve the difficult question of when life begins. When those trained in the respective disciplines of medicine, philosophy, and theology are unable to arrive at any consensus, the judiciary, at this point in the development of man's knowledge, is not in a position to speculate as to the answer. It should be sufficient to note briefly the wide divergence of thinking on this most sensitive and difficult question. There has always been strong support for the view that life does not begin until live birth. This was the belief of the Stoics. It appears to be the predominant, though not the unanimous, attitude of the Jewish faith. It may be taken to represent also the position of a large segment of the Protestant community. The common law found greater significance in quickening. Physicians and their scientific colleagues have regarded that event with less interest and have tended to focus either upon conception, upon live birth, or upon the interim point at which the fetus becomes "viable," that is, potentially able to live outside the mother's womb, albeit with artificial aid. Viability is usually placed at about seven months (28 weeks) but may occur earlier, even at 24 weeks. The Aristotelian theory of "mediate animation," that held sway throughout the Middle Ages and the Renaissance in Europe, continued to be official Roman Catholic dogma until the 19th century, despite opposition to this "ensoulment" theory from those in the church who would recognize the existence of life from the moment of conception. The latter is now, of course, the official belief of the Catholic Church. This is a view strongly held by many non-Catholics as well, and by many physicians. Substantial problems for precise definition of this view are posed, however, by new embryological data that purport to indicate that conception is a "process" over time, rather than an event, and by new medical techniques such as menstrual extraction, the "morning-after" pill, implantation of embryos, artificial insemination, and even artificial wombs. In areas other than criminal abortion, the law has been reluctant to endorse any theory that life, as we recognize it, begins before live birth or to accord legal rights to the unborn except in narrowly defined situations and except when the rights are contingent upon live birth.... In short, the unborn have never been recognized in the law as persons in the whole sense.

In view of all this, we do not agree that, by adopting one theory of life, Texas may override the rights of the pregnant woman that are at stake. We repeat, however, that the State does have an important and legitimate interest in preserving and protecting the health of the pregnant woman, whether she be a resident of the State or a nonresident who seeks medical consultation and treatment there, and that it has still *another* important and legitimate interest in protecting the potentiality of human life. These interests are separate and distinct. Each grows in substantiality as the woman approaches term and, at a point during pregnancy, each becomes "compelling."

With respect to the State's important and legitimate interest in the health of the mother, the "compelling" point, in the light of present medical knowledge, is at approximately the end of the first trimester. This is so because of the now established medical fact that until the end of the first trimester mortality in abortion is less than mortality in normal childbirth. It follows that, from and after this point, a State may regulate the abortion procedure to the extent that the regulation reasonably relates to the preservation and protection of maternal health. Examples of permissible state regulation in this area are requirements as to the qualifications of the person who is to perform the abortion; as to the licensure of that person; as to the facility in which the procedure is to be performed, that is, whether it must be a hospital or may be a clinic or some other place of less-than-hospital status; as to the licensing of the facility; and the like. This means, on the other hand, that for the period of pregnancy prior to this "compelling" point, the attending physician, in consultation with his patient, is free to determine, without regulation by the State, that, in his medical judgment, the patient's pregnancy should be terminated. If that decision is reached, the judgment may be effectuated by an abortion free of interference by the State.

This holding, we feel, is consistent with the relative weights of the respective interests involved, with the lessons and examples of medical and legal history, with the lenity of the common law, and with the demands of the profound problems of the present day. The decision leaves the State free to place increasing restrictions on abortion as the period of pregnancy lengthens, so long as those restrictions are tailored to the recognized state interests. The decision vindicates the right of the physician to administer medical treatment according to his professional judgment up to the points where important state interests provide compelling justifications for intervention. Up to those points, the abortion decision in all its aspects is inherently, and primarily, a medical decision, and basic responsibility for it must rest with the physician. If an individual practitioner abuses the privilege of exercising proper medical judgment, the usual remedies, judicial and intraprofessional, are available....

It is so ordered.

* * * * * *

1.   How does the Court argue for a "right to privacy," even though such a right is not mentioned in the Constitution?

2.   Does this ruling leave open the possibility of state regulation of abortion?

3.   How does the Court handle the issues of who defines when life begins?

29–11 Articles of Impeachment against Richard M. Nixon, 1974

Richard Nixon won an overwhelming reelection victory against Democrat George McGovern in 1972. But his presidency soon began unraveling as the full dimensions of the Watergate scandal began to emerge. A congressional investigation and a special prosecutor revealed Nixon's complicity in covering up the illegal attempt to bug Democratic Party headquarters. The contents of White House tapes also indicated that the President had misused the Internal Revenue Service, the FBI, and other federal agencies in a vendetta aimed at his political enemies. In the first such action since 1868, the House Judiciary Committee voted three articles of impeachment. Nixon resigned in August, 1974 rather than face certain impeachment by the House and conviction in the Senate.

SOURCE: House Judiciary Committee, *Report on the Impeachment of Richard M. Nixon*, House Report No. 1035, 93rd Cong., 2d Sess. (1974).

Impeaching Richard M. Nixon, President of the United States, of high crimes and misdemeanors.

Resolved. That Richard M. Nixon, President of the United States, is impeached for high crimes and misdemeanors, and that the following articles of impeachment be exhibited to the Senate:

Articles of impeachment exhibited by the House of Representatives of the United States of America in the name of itself and of all of the people of the United States of America, against Richard M. Nixon, President of the United States of America, in maintenance and support of its impeachment against him for high crimes and misdemeanors.

ARTICLE I

In his conduct of the office of President of the United States, Richard M. Nixon, in violation of his constitutional oath faithfully to execute the office of President of the United States and, to the best of his ability, preserve, protect, and defend the Constitution of the United States, and in violation of his constitutional duty to take care that the laws be faithfully executed, has prevented, obstructed, and impeded the administration of justice, in that:

On June 17, 1972, and prior thereto, agents of the Committee for the Re-election of the President committed unlawful entry of the headquarters of the Democratic National Committee in Washington, District of Columbia, for the purpose of securing political intelligence.

Subsequent thereto, Richard M. Nixon, using the powers of his high office, engaged personally and through his subordinates and agents, in a course of conduct or plan designed to delay, impede, and obstruct the investigation of such unlawful entry; to cover up, conceal, and protect those responsible; and to conceal the existence and scope of other unlawful covert activities.

The means used to implement this course of conduct or plan included one or more of the following:

(1) making or causing to be made false or misleading statements to lawfully authorized investigative officers and employees of the United States;

(2) withholding relevant and material evidence or information from lawfully authorized investigative officers and employees of the United States;

(3) approving, condoning, acquiescing in, and counseling witnesses with respect to the giving of false or misleading statements...;

(4) interfering or endeavoring to interfere with the conduct of investigations by the Department of Justice of the United States, the Federal Bureau of Investigation, the Office of Watergate Special Prosecution Force, and Congressional Committees;

(5) approving, condoning, and acquiescing in, the surreptitious payment of substantial sums of money for the purpose of obtaining the silence or influencing the testimony of witnesses, potential witnesses or individuals who participated in such unlawful entry and other illegal activities;

(6) endeavoring to misuse the Central Intelligence Agency, an agency of the United States;

(7) disseminating information received from officers [of] the Department of Justice of the United States to subjects of investigations [for] the purpose of aiding and assisting such subjects in their attempts to avoid criminal liability;

(8) making false or misleading public statements for the purpose of deceiving the people of the United States into believing that a thorough and complete investigation had been conducted with respect to allegations of misconduct on the part of personnel of the executive branch of the United States and personnel of the Committee for the Re-election of the President, and that there was no involvement of such personnel in such misconduct; or

(9) endeavoring to cause prospective defendants, and individuals duly tried and convicted, to expect favored treatment and consideration in return for their silence or false testimony, or rewarding individuals for their silence or false testimony.

In all of this, Richard M. Nixon has acted in a manner contrary to his trust as President and subversive of constitutional government, to the great prejudice of the cause of law and justice and to the manifest injury of the people of the United States.

Wherefore Richard M. Nixon, by such conduct, warrants impeachment and trial, and removal from office.

ARTICLE II

Using the powers of the office of President of the United States, Richard M. Nixon, in violation of his constitutional oath faithfully to execute the office of President of the United States and, to the best of his ability, preserve, protect, and defend the Constitution of the United States, and in disregard of his constitutional duty to take care that the laws be faithfully executed, has repeatedly engaged in conduct violating the constitutional rights of citizens, impairing the due and proper administration of justice and the conduct of lawful inquiries, or contravening the laws governing agencies of the executive branch and the purposes of these agencies.

This conduct has included one or more of the following:

(1) He has, acting personally and through his subordinates and agents, endeavored to obtain from the Internal Revenue Service, in violation of the constitutional rights of citizens, confidential information contained in income tax returns for purposes not authorized by law, and to cause, in violation of the constitutional rights of citizens, income tax audits or other income tax investigations to be initiated or conducted in a discriminatory manner.

(2) He misused the Federal Bureau of Investigation, the Secret Service, and other executive personnel, in violation or disregard of the constitutional rights of citizens, by directing or authorizing such agencies or personnel to conduct or continue electronic surveillance or other investigations for purposes unrelated to national security, the enforcement of laws, or any other lawful function of his office; he did direct, authorize, or permit the use of information obtained thereby for purposes unrelated to national security, the enforcement of laws, or any other lawful function of his office; and he did direct the concealment of certain records made by the Federal Bureau of Investigation of electronic surveillance.

(3) He has, acting personally and through his subordinates and agents, in violation or disregard of the constitutional rights of citizens, authorized and permitted to be maintained a secret investigative unit within the office of the President, financed in part with money derived from campaign contributions, which unlawfully utilized the resources of the Central Intelligence Agency, engaged in covert and unlawful activities, and attempted to prejudice the constitutional right of an accused to a fair trial.

(4) He has failed to take care that the laws were faithfully executed by failing to act when he knew or had reason to know that his close subordinates endeavored to impede and frustrate lawful inquiries by duly constituted executive,. judicial, and legislative entities concerning the unlawful entry into the headquarters of the Democratic National Committee, and the cover-up thereof, and concerning other unlawful activities, including those relating to the confirmation of Richard Kleindienst as Attorney General of the United States, the electronic surveillance of private citizens, the break-in into the offices of Dr. Lewis Fielding, and the campaign financing practices of the Committee to Re-elect the President.

(5) In disregard of the rule of law, he knowingly misused the executive power by interfering with agencies of the executive branch, including the Federal Bureau of Investigation, the Criminal Division, and the Office of Watergate Special Prosecution Force, of the Department of Justice, and the Central Intelligence Agency, in violation of his duty to take care that the laws he faithfully executed.

In all of this, Richard M. Nixon has acted in a manner contrary to his trust as President and subversive of constitutional government, to the great prejudice of the cause of law and justice and to the manifest injury of the people of the United States.

Wherefore Richard M. Nixon, by such conduct, warrants impeachment and trial, and removal from office.

ARTICLE III

In his conduct of the office of President of the United States, Richard M. Nixon, contrary to his oath faithfully to execute the office of President of the United States and, to the best of his ability, preserve, protect, and defend the Constitution of the United States, and in violation of his constitutional duty to take care that the laws be faithfully executed, has failed without lawful cause or excuse to produce papers and things as directed by duly authorized subpoenas issued by the Committee on the Judiciary of the House of Representatives on April 11, 1974, May 15, 1974, May 30, 1974, and June 24, 1974, and willfully disobeyed such subpoenas. The subpoenaed papers and things were deemed necessary by the Committee in order to resolve by direct evidence fundamental, factual questions relating to Presidential direction, knowledge, or approval of actions demonstrated by other evidence to be substantial grounds for impeachment of the President. In refusing to produce these papers and things, Richard M. Nixon, substituting his judgment as to what materials were necessary for the inquiry, interposed the powers of the Presidency against the lawful subpoenas of the House of Representatives, thereby assuming to himself functions and judgments necessary to the exercise of the sole power of impeachment vested by the Constitution in the House of Representatives.

In all of this, Richard M. Nixon has acted in a manner contrary to his trust as President and subversive of constitutional government, to the great prejudice of the cause of law and justice, and to the manifest injury of the people of the United States.

Wherefore Richard M. Nixon, by such conduct, warrants impeachment and trial, and removal from office.

* * * * * *

1. *What are the specific charges against Richard Nixon in the Articles of Impeachment? Are they serious enough to warrant impeachment? Why or why not?*

2. *To what extent do the articles reflect a constitutional struggle for power between the executive and legislative branches?*

chapter 30

The Conservative Ascendancy, 1974–1987

30–1 Town Meeting, Middletown, Pennsylvania, 1979

The nuclear accident at Three Mile Island brought home the risks of nuclear power to surrounding Pennsylvania communities. The near disaster left people suspicious of Metropolitan Edison, owners of the plant, as well as of state and scientific authorities. Local physicians and farmers testified to the harmful effects they believed released radiation had upon people and livestock. In communities that had long accepted nuclear power as a given, Three Mile Island created an enormous sense of unease, and it inspired a new generation of antinuclear skeptics and activists. These three citizens were among those who spoke at a town meeting held in Middletown three months after the TMI accident.

SOURCE: From *The People of Three Mile Island* by Robert del Tredici. Copyright ©1980 by Robert del Tredici. Reprinted by permission.

Richard Swartz

Ladies and gentlemen of Middletown, members of the Borough Council:

We didn't come here tonight to ask for better plans for evacuation, or seek the assurances from Metropolitan Edison or from our state government or our national government. Right here is why we came.

[A man in the audience holds up a child.]

How many watts is that kid worth? How many jobs is that kid worth? We're here because we feel endangered, and the next generation, and the next century, and their children. That's why we're here. Ladies and gentlemen, as long as there's faulty equipment operating in a nuclear power plant, as long as we have management and utility companies who care more for money than people, as long as there is the possibility of human error in the operation of nuclear power plants, considering Metropolitan Edison's past record and the fact that no one can any longer trust the people who control the nuclear situation in crisis events and in the day-to-day operation of these plants, I petition you tonight to not only slow down the reopening of Metropolitan Edison's Three Mile Island plant, but to close it down permanently.

A long time ago, some idiot had the idea of putting x-ray machines in shoe stores. They were dangerous. No

one knew it at the time, or those who knew weren't doing anything about it. The people of Pennsylvania were the first to outlaw those things. They took a stand. They fought the battle. Tonight I ask the people of Middletown to begin that battle and once again have Pennsylvanians in the forefront of the war against nuclear insecurity in our own neighborhood. You know Ralph Nader, a great American, said that nuclear power plants are technology's Viet Nam. We have it right here, baby. It's not 25,000 miles away. It's 2 1/2 miles away. Someone's going to die. Eventually there's going to be a disaster. You know it, if you don't shut them down. I don't want it to happen here. I can't look at these little kids sitting around here, the little one the man held up. Look at him. Do you want it to happen to him? It can't. That's why we're here. You know it's time that we all prepare to take this battle door to door, to the newspapers, the government, and to the gates of the Metropolitan Edison Three Mile Island plant if necessary.

[Applause]

Ladies and gentlemen, tonight I ask you to be patriots. For once, don't let them dictate to you. Don't listen to the big corporations. Don't listen to the big national government that can't, that doesn't touch you anymore. Ladies and gentlemen, be Americans. This is our town. This is our land. And these are our kids. Don't let them down.

Steven Reed

I heard one member of the council say that if he can receive assurances from the officials of Met Ed and the NRC, he would consider the opening of at least Unit One and maybe Unit Two. I must warn you all, citizens and collected officials alike, not to fall prey to that type of folly. To believe once again people who have systematically misled us, misrepresented their position, misstated and distorted and warped the facts and withheld the facts—something they are doing up to and including this date—I cannot believe that we could even give thought to placing credibility in their continued assurances for public safety after an accident happened that was not supposed to happen in the first place, according to them.

A combination of human error, lack of training, basic design flaws, failure of safety systems, failure of proper notification, failure to provide information with regard to public health and safety, failure to notify your mayor and others about what was going on, each of those factors alone should prove that they are not worthy of the trust and confidence the NRC has placed in them. Yet it appears, I'm sorry to say, ladies and gentlemen, it appears tonight that there has already been a decision made somewhere along the line at both the state and federal levels, that Unit One in fact is going to reopen. Therefore, the decision of Unit One is just as important because it includes Unit Two, whether it says so or not in your resolution. What you do sets a precedent throughout this nation maybe even throughout this globe. It cannot be overdramatized—and I will conclude on this—that the issue is more than just whether or not Met Ed is going to be held accountable. The issue goes a little bit further into whether or not there shall be a penalty for those who placed into jeopardy our lives and our children's future health. I don't like the way they ran it before and you can bet, if you didn't like it before, you're not going to like it any better in the future. Business as usual in Three Mile Island. The real issue is, and I can't emphasize it enough, is whether or not the people with the vested powers and financial interest in this country and in this area, sitting on this island, are in fact the ones who run the government or whether government is capable and willing to have the guts to represent public interest against special interests.

Kari Light

I live at 24 Ann Street in the first ward and I have my Ph.D. I don't have anything brilliant; I don't have anything documented, or anything political that I would like to share with you. But I would like you to know some of what this has meant to me personally and my relationship with this particular town. I have lived here literally since before I was born. My mother was pregnant here. And this has always been a safe, secure place for me. Like a lot of other people, when I was young and silly, I left town and I was away for a while; but I came back because this is where I felt I belonged, where I felt safe, and where I felt secure. That is gone. That is important to me. That was a major loss. I work away from here, I work on the West Shore, and I used to feel really good

when I'd be driving home. I'd be taking the Highspire Turnpike, and I'd be feeling good. Now I find any excuse I can not to come straight home. I no longer feel good getting back; I feel worse. That's important to me. Another very important thing to me is children. I work with children. Part of what I do is play therapy with children. And I love them. I enjoy them. There's hardly a child living that I can't feel joyful with, or at least that I couldn't feel joyful with. That also is gone. I can't look at children, play with children, enjoy children the way I could two or three months ago. I look at them and wonder what's going to happen to them. I wonder which ones of them are going to be able to produce children and which ones are not. I wonder which ones of them are going to have leukemia when they are older; I look at them and I grieve for them. They're not my children. I don't have children. And I'm grieving for your children, and you should be doing something about it.

I will never feel safe being pregnant in Middletown now. I can remember a time when women could be pregnant and feel good about it. I don't know a lot of women right now who are pregnant who are really comfortable. And I wouldn't want to have to go through that myself. That's another thing that I felt. Feelings about my own self and my own bearing and raising children here in Middletown. That's important to me.

* * * * * *

1. *How has the TMI accident changed the feelings these citizens have about their community?*

2. *What civic and political action do they advocate?*

30–2 *William Julius Wilson, The Urban Underclass, 1980*

Economic and social conditions among the nation's inner- city poor deteriorated during the 1970s. Some social scientists and government officials began referring to the growth of a new, permanent "under-class," made up of people who seemed locked into poverty across generations. The underclass debate focused on cause, with commentators giving different weight to factors such as racial discrimination, gender bias, cultural values, personal morality, and structural changes in the economy. Sociologist William Julius Wilson offered one of the more

sophisticated attempts to understand the phenomenon and debunk the more simplistic explanations.

SOURCE: William Julius Wilson. "The Underclass in Advanced Industrial Society," in Paul Peterson, ed., *The New Urban Reality*, 1985. Reprinted by permission of the Brookings Institution.

The increase in the number of female-headed families in the United States was dramatic during the 1970s. Whereas the total number of families grew by 12 percent from 1970 to 1979, the number of female-headed families increased by 51 percent. Moreover, the number of families headed by women with one or more of their children present in the home increased by 81 percent. If the change in family structure was notable for all families in the 1970s, it was close to phenomenal for blacks and Hispanics. Families headed by white women increased by 42 percent; families headed by black and Hispanic women grew by 73 and 77 percent, respectively.

In 1965 Moynihan expressed great concern that 25 percent of all black families were headed by women. That figure rose to 28 percent in 1969, 37 percent in 1976, and a startling 42 percent in 1980. By contrast, only 12 percent of white families and 22 percent of Hispanic families were headed by women in 1980, even though each group recorded a significant increase in female-headed families during the 1970s....

Even if a female householder is employed full time, her earnings are usually substantially less than that of a male worker and are not likely to be supplemented with income from a second full-time employed member of the household. For women who head families and are not employed (including those who have never been employed, have dropped out of the labor force to become full-time mothers, or are employed only part-time), the economic situation is often desperate. In 1980 the median income of female-headed families ($10,408) was only 45 percent of the median income of husband-wife families ($23,141); and the median income of families headed by black women ($7,425) was only 40 percent of the median income of husband-wife black families ($18,592). In 1978, of the roughly 3.2 million families who recorded incomes of less than $4,000, more than half were headed by women....

Economic hardship has become almost synonymous with black female-headed families: only 30 percent of all poor black families were headed by women in 1959, but by 1978 the proportion reached 74 percent (though it dipped to 70 percent in 1981). By contrast, 38 percent of all poor white families were headed by women in 1978. Reflecting the growth of black female-headed families, the proportion of black children in married-couple families dropped significantly, from 64 percent in 1970 to 56 percent in 1974 and 49 percent in 1978. Moreover, 41 percent of black children under 18 years of age resided in families whose incomes were below the poverty level in 1978, and three-fourths of those were in families headed by females.

The rise of female-headed families among blacks corresponds closely with the increase in the ratio of out-of-wedlock births. Only 15 percent of all black births in 1959 were out of wedlock. This figure jumped roughly 24 percent in 1965 and 53 percent in 1978, six times greater than the white ratio. Indeed, despite the far greater white population, the number of black babies born out of wedlock actually exceeded the number of illegitimate white babies in 1978. Although the proportion of black births that are outside of marriage is, in part, a function of the general decline in fertility among married blacks (a point dis-

cussed below), it is also a reflection of the growing prevalence of out-of-wedlock births among black teenagers. In 1978, 83 percent of the births to black teenagers (and 29 percent of the births to white teenagers) were outside of marriage.

These developments have significant implications for the problems of welfare dependency. In 1977 the proportion of black families receiving AFDC slightly exceeded the proportion of white females, despite the great difference in total population. It is estimated that about 60 percent of the children who are born out of wedlock and are alive and not adopted receive welfare. A study by the Urban Institute pointed out that "more than half of all AFDC assistance in 1975 was paid to women who were or had been teenager mothers."

I focus on female-headed families, out-of-wedlock births, and teenage pregnancy because they have become inextricably connected with poverty and dependency. The sharp increase in these and other forms of social dislocations in the inner city (including joblessness and violent crime) offers a difficult challenge to policy-makers. Because there has been so little recent systematic research on these problems and a paucity of thoughtful explanations for them, racial stereotypes of life and behavior in the urban ghetto have not been adequately challenged. The physical and social isolation of residents in the urban ghetto is thereby reinforced. The fundamental question is: why have the social conditions of the urban underclass deteriorated so rapidly since the mid-1960s?

To hold, as I do, that changes in economic and social situations will lead to changes in behavior patterns and norms, raises the issue of what public policy can deal effectively with the social dislocations that have plagued the urban underclass for the past several years. Any significant reduction of joblessness and related problems of crime, out-of-wedlock births, teenage pregnancies, single-parent homes, and welfare dependency requires a far more comprehensive program of economic and social reform than Americans have generally deemed appropriate or desirable. In short, it would require a radicalism that neither the Democratic nor the Republican party has been bold enough to propose.

A shift away from the convenient focus on "racism" would probably result in a greater understanding and appreciation of the complex factors associated with the recent increases in the rates of social dislocation among the urban underclass. Although present-day discrimination undoubtedly has contributed to their economic and social woes in the last twenty years, I have argued that these problems have been due far more to shifts in the American economy from manufacturing to service industries, which have produced extraordinary rates of joblessness in the inner city and exacerbated conditions generated by the historic flow of migrants, and to changes in the urban minority age structure and consequent population changes in the central city.

For all these reasons, the urban underclass has not benefited significantly from "race-specific" antidiscrimination policy programs, such as affirmative action, which have helped so many trained and educated blacks. If inner-city blacks are to be helped, they will be aided not by policies addressed primarily to poor minorities, but by policies designed to benefit all of the nation's poor. These will need to address the broader problems of generating full employment, developing sustained and balanced urban economic growth, and achieving effective welfare reform. Unless such problems are seriously faced, there is little hope for the effectiveness of other policies, including race-specific ones, in significantly reducing social dislocations among the urban underclass.

I am reminded in this connection of Bayard Rustin's plea during the early 1960s that blacks ought to recognize the importance of *fundamental* economic reform (including a system of national economic planning along with new education, manpower, and public works programs to help reach full employment) and the need for a broad-based coalition to achieve it. And since an effective political coalition will in part depend upon how the issues are defined, it is essential that the political message underline the need for economic and social reform that benefits all groups in the United States, not just poor minorities. Politicians and civil rights organizations, as two important examples, ought to shift or expand their definition of America's racial problems and broaden the scope of suggested policy programs to address them. They should, of course, continue to fight for an end to racial discrimination. But they must also recognize that poor minorities are profoundly affected by problems in America that go beyond racial considerations. The dislocations that follow these problems have made the underclass a reality of urban life, and if left alone they will continue to do so.

* * * * * *

1. *What connections does Wilson make between the growth of the underclass and the so-called "feminization of poverty"?*

2. *How have changes in the national and urban economy contributed to the underclass phenomenon? What policy recommendations does Wilson make for attacking the problem?*

30–3 *Affirmative Action in Atlanta, 1974*

The Civil Rights Movement and the Voting Rights Act of 1965 led to a sharp increase in the number of African Americans elected to office during the 1970s. In 1974, Atlanta, with a 50-percent black population, elected Maynard Jackson as its first African-American mayor. The Jackson administration made affirmative-action hiring of minority employees and businesses one of its top priorities. Here, Jackson and several of his aides recall their efforts to create a fairer, more racially inclusive climate through affirmative action in Atlanta.

SOURCE: From *Voices of Freedom* by Henry Hampton and Steve Fayer. Copyright © 1990 by Blackside, Inc. Used by permission of Bantam Books, a Division of Bantam Doubleday Dell Publishing Group, Inc.

MAYNARD JACKSON

When I became mayor, zero-point-five percent of all the contracts of the city of Atlanta went to Afro-Americans, in a city which at that time was fifty-fifty. There were no women department heads. This was not only a question of race; it was a question also of sexual discrimination and, you know, all the typical "isms." If there's one, normally there's a whole bunch of them, and they were all there. We had to change dramatically how the appointments to jobs went, normal hiring practices in city government went, the contracting process—not to reduce the quality, by the way, ever. We never ever, ever set up a lower standard. And those who say, "Well, affirmative action means you've got to lower the standard"—that's a real insult, in my opinion, to African-Americans and other minority Americans. We never did it, didn't have to do it.

EMMA DARNELL

The affirmative action program for the city of Atlanta, which we developed under the direction of Mayor Jackson in 1974, actually started with that first conference that I held with the mayor on the day that I was appointed. He said only one thing to me that day with respect to what he wanted done. He said words to this effect: "Emma, I want black people brought into this government. I want black people to have an opportunity to participate in not only the personnel operation with jobs, but in the purchasing and procurement operation." And, of course, this was new.

WALTER HUNTLEY

The construction of a new airport for the city of Atlanta was one of the major projects, if not the major project, in the

Jackson administration. There were a number of big construction projects between 1976 and 1979 or '80. But this was the crown jewel. And the reason was because the airport plays such a major role in Atlanta's overall economy. We have one of the busiest airports in the world, and we did at that time. And this was going to be the largest public construction project that had ever been undertaken by the city.

The magnitude of it was such that it was just very difficult to comprehend. It was about a seven-hundred-fifty-million-dollar project. And the anxiety, the anticipation, was high. There were the airlines, the elected officials, the private sector. The federal government was involved, and it was something that everyone knew that we had to do, and there was a lot riding on it. It had to be done right. And when Maynard indicated that he was going to make sure that blacks participate in every element of the process from the standpoint of construction, architectural services, legal services, the whole gamut, that's when basically, I guess you would say, the whole issue came under tremendous scrutiny.

MAYNARD JACKSON

The reaction was immediate. It was not all white. It was black and white. The surprise for me was the number of black friends, well-meaning, who were frightened by the aggressiveness of this program. And who cautioned me to slow down. They were concerned there might be a reaction against the black community. Well, our studies indicated to us that for the majority of black people, things could not get any worse.

I want to emphasize that as we moved toward affirmative action, we always saw that as an issue that had to be managed. And I think this is the key point. Affirmative action is not something that just happens when you sing songs and all of a sudden it jumps off the wall. That's not it. It has to be managed, and those in charge must produce. They must have goals to meet, and they must be judged as managers by their productivity, their success. So we had to build an airport, we had to do it well. We had to do it within budget. We had to do it within the time allocation, and simultaneously, it had to be done fairly. Black people, other minorities, and women had to have an equal—not superior—but an equal opportunity to participate in the bidding, the contracting, the conception, top to bottom, of this airport. And we did.

The result was that, when we announced how we were going to approach this, from a contract compliance point of view—contract compliance meaning, oh, five, six, seven, eight different items, including but not limited to affirmative action—I would have thought the heavens were falling down. We were threatened with litigation six,

seven times a day. A lot of litigation occurred. I was told that I was retarding the progress of Atlanta. Now, I'm the mayor who found an airport project that was eleven years old that nobody could do. They'd given up on it. They told me I couldn't do it. These are the longtime bureaucrats of the city, dedicated, Atlanta-loving people, but they had never sold encyclopedias, as I had, and had never trained people how to sell, and had never trained themselves in the positive attitude that is part of my life. I am a trained positive thinker. They told me, "You can't build this in that spot." I said "Why not?" They said, "Because Interstate 85 runs right through where you would have a terminal." I said, "Fine. We'll move the interstate." And they laughed at me.

EMMA DARNELL

More than two years before the airport expansion occurred, Maynard Jackson made it very clear publicly and privately, to representatives of the airlines, to representatives of the architect and engineer, to the general public, that the expansion of Hartsfield International Airport would involve significant minority participation. He also stated—and this became a rather controversial point—that with respect to the status of existing contracts at the airport, there were no existing contracts. And that all contracts for the expansion of the airport would be bidded. This, of course, created a great deal of controversy with respect to the architect and the engineer, because we had done business with one architect and one engineer at Atlanta airport for more than sixteen years.

GEORGE BERRY

I was one of those responsible for steering the course, and we simply took as a given that Mayor Jackson's position had to be met. That there was no alternative. That the alternative was that the project would not be done. And so we brought the architects, the engineers, the contractors in and told them that. We said, "Do you wish to do the job under these conditions? Or there will be no job at all."

There were several hundred men involved in the construction work, and as a result of our basic position, we were able to convince the architects, engineers, and contractors to modify their position and seek out minority joint-venture partners, to seek out qualified minority-owned contracting firms, and to reach his goal of twenty percent minority and another five percent small businesses. So small and minority groups together made up twenty-five percent of all construction work, which in the end, since the total construction amounted to five hundred million dollars, meant that roughly a hundred and twenty-five million dollars was done by minorities. In those days, that amount of money was historic!

Many of the critics were, in fact, correct that there were not that many experienced minority businesses and subcontractors in the Georgia area able to take on a hundred and twenty-five million dollars' worth of work in the normal and established way. So what happened was we encouraged majority-owned contractor firms to seek out smaller firms and give them more work than really those smaller firms had ever done before. And to take some risks. Many of them work beautifully. And many contractors today owe their start to this program. AMC Mechanical is one of them that comes to mind. It's owned by a man named Tom Cordy. He is now a major mechanical contractor here in Atlanta. He has done many airport projects across the country, specializing in fueling systems, airport fueling systems. Up until that time, AMC was a very small company, but because of the experience he got under this program, he is now a major company.

EMMA DARNELL

During this period, I learned, and all of us in power learned, that being black and being in power alone is nothing about the color. It's nothing about the genetics. It's nothing about the hair or the turban or the beads or the rhetoric. What it's about is what's on the inside. You know. Have you really been deeply and permanently affected by the blood that has been shed in order for you to sit behind the desk? Do you see Martin Luther King's grave as more than a white sepulchre with a quotation on it? Do you actually feel any sensitivity and responsibility to all of those folk out there in those churches and those programs who stand up and give you big applause, believing that you stayed on the case, or are you really in there trying to hold your ground, to get your house, get your car, get your BMW, get invited to the right receptions and be considered a leader?

I spoke at thirty-two churches a year. I spoke at twenty high schools a year. I spoke to Morehouse. I spoke to white and black business and nonbusiness segments of the community, because we were, for all practical purposes, engaged in a revolution. We knew that's what it was. It was still the civil rights revolution. Those persons during the sixties laid down their lives and died to put us into these positions of power. We did not consider these positions of power to be ends in and of themselves. We were to continue the revolution until we had accomplished the goal. So the steps that we took were, many of them, sound management tasks that are taken in order to accomplish a task. But there were political tasks that had to be done. People have to know what you're doing and how you're doing it. And that consumed a large amount of my own personal time.

When you begin to move in public policy areas that involve race, you can expect a great deal of emotion. And some of the emotion is fear. We underestimated, I might add, how controversial these practices [would be]. We were extremely naive. One of the things that made this whole program so controversial was that issues involving race in the South, and indeed throughout the nation, in 1974 still created very, very strong feelings. Another reason that I think that I became very controversial is because of my own style. Number one, I was black. Number two, female. Well, both: I was black and female. And also my style is not exactly one of a shrinking violet. I'm what some people call assertive. I have very strong convictions and I express them in a very strong way. In fact, my conduct and my style was very different from what people really expected from women in a leadership position.

White businessmen reacted to me and to the program which became identified with me with a great deal of fear and alarm. First of all, because they operate in an environment that is controlled by men. Okay? So they had a lot of problems with dealing with a woman as an equal.

* * * * * *

1.   *Why did the Jackson administration feel the strong need for an affirmative action program? In what areas did it pursue the program?*

2.   *What obstacles did the program face in Atlanta, and what did it achieve? What did Jackson's initiatives owe to the civil rights movement of the previous decade?*

30–4 Lois Gibbs, Love Canal, 1978

In the 1970s, the grim reality of nuclear and toxic wastes began hitting scores of American communities. One of the worst and most widely publicized stories involved the Love Canal in Niagara Falls, New York, where the Hooker Chemical Corporation had dumped chemical waste from 1920 to 1953. Houses and a school were built over the site in the 1950s. Residents complained about unusual odors, sludge, and sickness, but it was not until the late 1970s that New York State began investigating the situation and relocating families. Lois Gibbs was an activist who helped educate the community about the problem.

SOURCE: Lois Gibbs, *Love Canal: My Story* (State University of New York Press, 1982).

My Son Attending That School

Love Canal actually began for me in June 1978 with Mike Brown's articles in the Niagara Falls *Gazette*. At first, I didn't realize where the canal was. Niagara Falls has two sets of streets numbered the same. Brown's articles said Love Canal was between 99th and 97th streets, but I didn't think he meant the place where my children went to school or where I took them to play on the jungle gyms and swings. Although I read the articles, I didn't pay much attention to them. One article did stand out, though. In it, Mike Brown wrote about monkeys subjected to PCBs having miscarriages and deformed offspring.

One of his later articles pointed out that the school had been built over the canal. Still, I paid little attention. It didn't affect me, Lois Gibbs. I thought it was terrible; but I lived on the other side of Pine Avenue. Those poor people over there on the other side were the ones who had to worry; the problem didn't affect me, so I wasn't going to bother doing anything about it, and I certainly wasn't going to speak out about it. Then when I found out the 99th Street School was indeed on top of it, I was alarmed. My son attended that school. He was in kindergarten that year. I decided I needed to do some investigating.

I went to my brother-in-law, Wayne Hadley, a biologist and, at the time, a professor at the State University of New York at Buffalo. He had worked on environmental problems and knew a lot about chemicals. I asked him to translate some of that jibber-jabber in the articles into English. I showed Wayne Mike Brown's articles listing the chemicals in the canal and asked what they were. I was really alarmed by his answer. Some of the chemicals, he said, can affect the nervous system. Just a little

bit, even the amount that's in paint or gasoline, can kill brain cells. I still couldn't believe it; but if it *were* true, I wanted to get Michael out of that 99th Street School.

I went down to the offices of the *Gazette* and was surprised to learn how many articles there were on Love Canal. It not only surprised me, it panicked me! The articles listed the chemicals and described some reactions to them. One is damage to the central nervous system. (Michael had begun having seizures after he started school.) Another is leukemia and other blood diseases. (Michael's white blood cell count had gone down.) The doctor said that might have been caused by the medication he took for his epilepsy, but now I wasn't so sure. Michael had started school in September and had developed epilepsy in December; in February his white blood count dropped.

All of a sudden, everything seemed to fall into place. There's no history of epilepsy in either my family or my husband's. So why should Michael develop it? He had always been sensitive to medication. I could never give him an aspirin like a normal baby because he would get sick to his stomach or break out in a rash. I couldn't give him *anything* because of that sensitivity. If it were true that Michael was more sensitive than most other children, then whatever chemicals were buried under the school would affect him more than they did other children in the school, or even more than my daughter Missy, who has always been a strong, lively child. The chemicals probably would not affect Missy, at least not right away. I wasn't thinking then about long-term effects. (A year and a half later, Missy was hospitalized for a blood-platelet disorder, but later she was fine.)

I went over all the articles with Wayne, and decided Michael definitely should not attend that school—nor, for that matter, should any child. They shouldn't even play on that playground. Wayne was worried about his son Eric. He and my sister Kathy used to leave Eric for me to baby-sit while they were at work.

I was stunned that the school board had allowed a school to be built on such a location. Even today, it doesn't seem possible that, knowing there were dangerous chemicals buried there, someone could put up a *school* on the site. The 99th Street School had over 400 children that year, one of its lowest annual enrollments....

I was furious. [Her son could not be transferred to another school.] I wasn't going to send my child to a place that was poisoned. The thoughts that can go through a person's head. I thought that I, as a person, had rights, that I ought to have a choice, and that one of those choices was not to send my child to school in a contaminated place. Like many people, I can be stubborn whenI get angry. I decided to go door-to-door and see if the other parents in the neighborhood felt the same way. That way, maybe something could be done. At the time, though, I didn't really think of it as "organizing."

It wasn't just the phone call with the superintendent that convinced me I had to do something. I called the president of the 99th Street School PTA and asked her if she could help me, or if she could at least tell me whom to go to or what to do. She said she was about to go on vacation. I got the feeling she wasn't interested. She seemed to be pushing me away, as if she didn't want to have anything to do with me.

I was disappointed and angry. School would open again in two months, and I wasn't going to let my child go back to that school. I didn't care what I had to do to prevent it. I wasn't going to send him to a private school, either. First of all, we couldn't afford it; and second, I thought parents had the right to send their children to schools that were safe.

KNOCKING ON DOORS

As I said, I decided to go door-to-door with a petition. It seemed like a good idea to start near the school, to talk to the mothers nearest it. I had already heard that a lot of the residents near the school had been upset about the chemicals for the past couple of years. I thought they might help me. I had never done anything like this, however, and I was frightened. I was afraid a lot of doors would be slammed in my face, that people would think I was some crazy fanatic. But I decided to do it anyway. I went to 99th and Wheatfield and knocked on my first door. There was no answer. I just stood there, not knowing what to do. It was an unusually warm June day and I was perspiring. I thought: *What am I doing here? I must be crazy. People are going to think I am. Go home, you fool!* And that's just what I did.

It was one of those times when I had to sit down and face myself. I was afraid of making a fool of myself, I had scared myself, and I had gone home. When I got there, I sat at the kitchen table with my petition in my hand, thinking. *Wait. What if people do slam doors in your face? People may think you're crazy. But what's more important—what people think or your child's health? Either you're going to do something or you're going to have to admit you're a coward and not do it.* I decided to wait until the next day—partly to figure out exactly how I was going to do this but more, I think, to build my self-confidence.

A SICK COMMUNITY

As I proceeded down 99th Street, I developed a set speech. I would tell people what I wanted. But the speech

wasn't all that necessary. It seemed as though every home on 99th Street had someone with an illness. One family had a young daughter with arthritis. They couldn't understand why she had it at her age. Another daughter had had a miscarriage. The father, still a fairly young man, had had a heart attack. I went to the next house, and there, people would tell me *their* troubles. People were reaching out; they were telling me their troubles in hopes I would do something. But I didn't know anything to do. I was also confused. I just wanted to stop children from going to that school. Now look at all those other health problems! Maybe they were related to the canal. But even if they were, what could I do?

As I continued going door-to-door, I heard more. The more I heard, the more frightened I became. This problem involved much more than the 99th Street School. The entire community seemed to be sick! Then I remembered my own neighbors. One who lived on the left of my husband and me was suffering from severe migraines and had been hospitalized three or four times that year. Her daughter had kidney problems and bleeding. A woman on the other side of us had gastrointestinal problems. A man in the next house down was dying of lung cancer and he didn't even work in industry. The man across the street had just had lung surgery. I though about Michael; maybe there *was* more to it than just the school. I didn't understand how chemicals could get all the way over to 101st Street from 99th; but the more I thought about it, the more frightened I became—for my family and for the whole neighborhood.

Everything was unbelievable. I worried that I was exaggerating, or that people were exaggerating their complaints. I talked it over with Wayne. Luckily, he knew someone who might be able to help us—a Dr. Beverly Paigen, who is a biologist, geneticist, and cancer research scientist at the Roswell Park Memorial Institute, a world-famous research hospital in Buffalo. We went to see Dr. Paigen. She is a wonderful, brave person who, like Wayne, had been involved in environmental-pollution fights. She asked us to bring some soil samples so she could do an Ames test. The Ames test is a quick way of determining potentially dangerous effects of chemicals. When bacteria are exposed to mutagenic chemicals, Dr. Paigen told us, they reproduce abnormally.

I continued to go door-to-door. I was becoming more worried because of the many families with children who had birth defects. Then I learned something even more frightening: there had been five crib deaths within a few short blocks....

A REAL PROBLEM?

The New York State Health Department held a public meeting in June 1978. It was the first one I attended.

Dr. Nicholas Vianna and some of his staff explained that they were going to do environmental and health studies. They wanted to take samples—of blood, air, and soil, as well as from sump pumps. They wanted to find out if there really was a problem. They would study only the first ring of houses, though, the ones with backyards abutting Love Canal. Bob Matthews, Niagara Falls city engineer, was there to explain the city's plan for remedial construction. They all sat in front of a big, green chalkboard on the stage in the auditorium of the 99th Street School.

I didn't understand everything that was said, especially about determining whether there was a problem. A pretty young woman carefully dressed, with a lovely scarf, spoke articulately. Her dog's nose had been burned when it sniffed the ground in her yard. She kept asking Dr. Vianna: "What does this mean? How did he burn his nose?" She said the dog was suffering, that her children loved the dog and loved playing with him; but she was willing to have the dog put away if Dr. Vianna would first test the dog.

That was a new reaction to me, one I hadn't come across in my canvassing. How *did* the dog burn his nose? Did that mean chemicals were on the surface? I knew there were health problems, and I felt the school should be closed: but I hadn't actually *seen* any chemicals. I felt a chill. This was a new danger, and a more ominous one. A man got up and said he couldn't put his daughter out in his own backyard because if he did, the soles of her feet would burn. The man thought chemicals were causing it. His daughter was with him. She was a cute little thing, only eighteen months old, with curly dark hair. Imagine he couldn't let her play in his own backyard, and he didn't know why!

I asked Dr. Vianna if the 99th Street School was safe. He answered that the air readings on the school had come back clean. But there we were sitting in the school auditorium, smelling chemicals! I said: "You are telling me there are chemicals there....But you also tell us we can't eat the vegetables. How can these kids be safe walking on the playground? How can it be safe?" "Have the children walk on the sidewalk," Dr. Vianna said. "Make sure they don't cut across the canal or walk on the canal itself." I couldn't believe what I was hearing. I asked again: "How can you say all that when the playground is on the canal?" He didn't have an answer. He just said: "You are their mother. You can limit the time they play is on the canal." I wondered if he had any children. By now the audience was really frustrated, and so was I. People began walking out, muttering, furious. There were no answers. They didn't understand, and they were becoming frightened.

RAPIDLY LOSING MY FAITH

Every time I went to another house, I learned something new. In one home, I met a graying heavyset man with a pitted face. He couldn't walk very well. He had worked for Hooker at one time, and now he had chloracne, a condition that results from exposure to certain chemicals. I didn't know it then but chloracne is also a symptom of dioxin poisoning. Dioxin is toxic in parts per trillion. Later we learned that it was in Love Canal. The man was as nice and pleasant as he could be, but his face looked awful. It was all I could do to look at him. He wanted to go ahead with a class-action suit; but he was afraid to jeopardize his pension from Hooker.

I thought to myself: *How could you be so concerned about your pension? The law will protect you. Who cares about Hooker? Look what they've done to you in the plant, let alone what they've done to your family living here on one of their dump sites.* It was hard to understand why people were so afraid of Hooker, of what the company might do to them. Why weren't they angrier?

There were so many unbelievable things about the situation. In one house, a divorced woman with four children showed me a letter from the New York State Health Department. It was a thank-you letter, and a check was enclosed. I asked the woman what the check is was for. She said the health department had contacted her and asked if her son would go onto Love Canal proper, find two "hot" rocks, and put them in the jars they sent her. She had been instructed to give the rocks to Dr. Vianna or to someone at the 99th Street School headquarters of the health department. The so-called hot rocks were phosphorus rocks that the children would pick up and throw against cement, and, in the process, burn themselves. The rocks would pop like firecrackers. It amused the kids: but some had been burned on the eyes and skin. I just couldn't understand how a supposedly responsible agency would send an eleven-year-old child into a potentially dangerous area such as Love Canal and ask him to pick up something there that could harm him. To get the rocks, he had to climb a snow fence put there to keep children out. It amazed me that the health department would do such a thing. They are supposed to protect people's health, and here they were jeopardizing an innocent child. I used to have a lot of faith in officials, especially doctors and experts. Now I was losing that faith—fast!

I wanted Harry [my husband] to be tested also. I was worried that we were being affected even over there on 101st Street. Some of my neighbors thought it was silly to think we could be affected that far from the canal; but it was only a block and a half farther away. Most people on 101st said they wouldn't take the blood test. If I wanted to shut down the school, fine; but let's not carry it too far. "There's no problem over here," some said. "You have no business going over there. You're not a resident of 97th or 99th. Why don't you stay home and behave yourself!" Some of the women in the neighborhood would get together at a neighbor's house and gossip. "She's just doing it for publicity." But the gossip didn't bother me much. I was developing a pretty thick skin.

After weeks of carrying the petition door-to-door one door *was* slammed in my face. It wasn't as bad as I had feared, though. The woman who answered my knock recognized me immediately. She really laid it on. "What are you out here for? Why are you doing this? Look what you're doing to property values. When did you put your house up for sale?" She was a bitter woman, but her attack wasn't on me personally. She was just letting me know how she felt. She wouldn't sign my petition. That was the worst encounter I had with a neighbor. By then, such a rebuff made almost no difference. I was disappointed that she wouldn't sign, but I didn't lose any sleep over it.

The meeting had one good effect: it brought people together. People who had been feuding because little Johnny hit little Billy were now talking to each other. They had air readings in common or a dead plant or a dead tree. They compared readings, saying, "Hey, this is what I've got. What have you got?" The word spread fast and the community became close-knit. Everywhere you looked, there were people in little groups talking and wondering and worrying.

* * * * * *

1. *What range of reactions did Gibbs get from her neighbors? Why didn't more people support her efforts?*

2. *What kinds of indifference did she face from authority figures?*

30-5   *Jimmy Carter, The Crisis of Confidence, 1979*

Jimmy Carter's problems as president began almost as soon as he arrived in Washington. Elected as a self-defined "outsider," Carter had difficulty working with Congressional leaders and others in the Washington establishment. The growing energy crisis and the decline of American industrial competitiveness kept the economy sluggish. In July 1979, frustrated by his inability to get Congress to support his energy program, Carter appealed directly to the American people over television. The speech succeeded in identifying real feelings among the electorate, but it failed to produce any policy changes.

SOURCE: *New York Times*, July 16, 1979.

This is a special night for me. Exactly three years ago on July 15, 1976, I accepted the nomination of my party to run for President of the United States. I promised to you a President who is not isolated from the people, who feels your pain and shares your dreams and who draws his strength and his wisdom from you.

During the past three years, I've spoken to you on many occasions about national concerns: the energy crisis, reorganizing the Government, our nation's economy and issues of war, and especially peace. But over those years the subjects of the speeches, the talks and the press conferences have become increasingly narrow, focused more and more on what the isolated world of Washington thinks is important.

Ten days ago I had plans to speak to you again about a very important subject—energy. For the fifth time I would have described the urgency of the problem and laid out a series of legislative recommendations to the Congress, but as I was preparing to speak I began to ask myself the same question that I now know has been troubling many of you: Why have we not been able to get together as a nation to resolve our serious energy problem?

It's clear that the true problems of our nation are much deeper—deeper than gasoline lines or energy shortages. Deeper, even, than inflation or recession. And I realize more than ever that as President I need your help, so I decided to reach out and to listen to the voices of America. I invited to Camp David people from almost every segment of our society: business and labor; teachers and preachers; governors, mayors and private citizens.

And then I left Camp David to listen to other Americans. Men and women like you. It has been an extraordinary 10 days and I want to share with you what I heard.

First of all, I got a lot of personal advice. Let me quote a few of the typical comments that I wrote down.

This from a Southern Governor: "Mr. President, you're not leading this nation, you're just managing the Government."

"You don't see the people enough anymore."

"Some of your Cabinet members don't seem loyal. There's not enough discipline among your disciples."

Many people talked about themselves and about the condition of our nation. This from a young woman in Pennsylvania. "I feel so far from government. I feel like ordinary people are excluded from political power." And this from a young Chicano: "Some of us have suffered from recession all our lives. Some people have wasted energy but others haven't had anything to waste." And this from a religious leader: "No material shortage can touch the important things like God's love for us or our love for one another."

Several of our discussions were on energy, and I have a notebook full of comments and advice. I'll read just a few.

"We can't go on consuming 40 percent more energy than we produce. When we import oil, we are also importing inflation plus unemployment. We've got to use what we have. The Middle East has only 5 percent of the world's energy, but the United States has 24 percent."

And this is one of the most vivid statements: "Our neck is stretched over the fence and OPEC has the knife."

These 10 days confirmed my belief in the decency and the strength and the wisdom of the American people, but it also bore out some of my long-standing concerns about our nation's underlying problems. I know, of course, being President, that Government actions and legislation can be very important.

That's why I've worked hard to put my campaign promises into law, and I have to admit with just mixed success. But after listening to the American people I have been reminded again that all the legislatures in the world can't fix what's wrong with America.

So I want to speak to you tonight about a subject even more serious than energy or inflation. I want to talk to you right now about a fundamental threat to American democracy.

I do not mean our political and civil liberties. They will endure. And I do not refer to the outward strength of America—the nation that is at peace tonight everywhere in the world with unmatched economic power and military might. The threat is nearly invisible in ordinary ways. It is a crisis of confidence. It is a crisis that strikes at the very heart and soul and spirit of our national will.

We can see this crisis in the growing doubt about the meaning of our own lives and in the loss of a unity of purpose for our nation.

The erosion of our confidence in the future is threatening to destroy the social and the political fabric of America. The confidence that we have always had as a people is not simply some romantic dream or a proverb in a dusty book that we read just on the Fourth of July. It is the idea which founded our nation and which has guided our development as a people. Confidence in the future has supported everything else—public institutions and private enterprise, our own families and the very Constitution of the United States. Confidence has defined our course and has served as a link between generations.

We've always believed in something called progress. We've always had a faith that the days of our children would be better than our own.

Our people are losing that faith. Not only in Government itself, but in their ability as citizens to serve as the ultimate rulers and shapers of our democracy. As a people, we know our past and we are proud of it. Our progress has been part of the living history of America, even the world. We always believed that we were part of a great movement of humanity itself called democracy, involved in the search for freedom. And that belief has always strengthened us in our purpose. But just as we are losing our confidence in the future, we are also beginning to close the door on our past.

In a nation that was proud of hard work, strong families, close-knit communities and our faith in God, too many of us now tend to worship self-indulgence and consumption. Human identity is no longer defined by what one does but by what one owns.

But we've discovered that owning things and consuming things does not satisfy our longing for meaning.

We have learned that piling up material goods cannot fill the emptiness of lives which have no confidence or purpose. The symptoms of this crisis of the American spirit are all around us. For the first time in the history of our country a majority of our people believe that the next five years will be worse than the past five years. Two-thirds of our people do not even vote. The productivity of American workers is actually dropping and the willingness of Americans to save for the future has fallen below that of all other people in the Western world.

As you know there is a growing disrespect for Government and for churches and for schools, the news media and other institutions. This is not a message of happiness or reassurance but it is the truth. And it is a warning. These changes did not happen overnight. They've come upon us gradually over the last generation. Years that were filled with shocks and tragedy.

We were sure that ours was a nation of the ballot, not of the bullet, until the murders of John Kennedy and Robert Kennedy and Martin Luther King, Jr. We were taught that our armies were always invincible and our causes were always just only to suffer the agony of Vietnam. We respected the Presidency as a place of honor until the shock of Watergate. We remember when the phrase "sound as a dollar" was an expression of absolute dependability until 10 years of inflation began to shrink our dollar and our savings. We believed that our nation's resources were limitless until 1973, when we had to face a growing dependence on foreign oil.

These wounds are still very deep. They have never been healed.

Looking for a way out of this crisis, our people have turned to the Federal Government and found it isolated from the mainstream of our nation's life. Washington, D.C., has become an island. The gap between our citizens and our Government has never been so wide. The people are looking for honest answers, not easy answers, clear leadership, not false claims and evasiveness and politics as usual. What you see too often in Washington and elsewhere around the country is a system of government that seems incapable of action.

You see a Congress twisted and pulled in every direction by hundreds of well-financed and powerful special interests. You see every extreme position defended to the last vote, almost to the last breath, by one unyielding group or another.

Often you see paralysis and stagnation and drift. You don't like it.

And neither do I.

What can we do? First of all, we must face the truth and then we can change our course. We simply must have faith in each other. Faith in our ability to govern ourselves and faith in the future of this nation.

Restoring that faith and that confidence to America is a now the most important task we face.

Our fathers and mothers were strong men and women who shaped the new society during the Great Depression, who fought world wars and who carved out a new charter of peace for the world. We ourselves are the same Americans who just 10 years ago put a man on the moon. We are the generation that dedicated our society to the pursuit of human rights and equality.

And we are the generation that will win the war on the energy problem, and in that process rebuild the unity and confidence of America. We are at a turning point in our history. There are two paths to choose. One is the path I've warned about tonight—the path that leads to fragmentation and self-interest. Down that road lies a mistaken idea of freedom.

All the traditions of our past, all the lessons of our heritage, all the promises of our future point to another path: the path of common purpose and the restoration of American values. That path leads to true freedom for our nation and ourselves. We can take the first steps down that path as we begin to solve our energy problem. Energy will be the immediate test of our ability to unite this nation.

You know we can do it. We have the natural resources. We have more oil in our shale alone than several Saudi Arabias. We have more coal than any nation on earth. We have the world's highest level of technology. We have the most skilled work force, with innovative genius.

And I firmly believe we have the national will to win this war.

* * * * * *

1. *What is the crisis of spirit that Carter detects among Americans? What are its sources?*

2. *How does Carter's speech go against the grain of post–World War II political thought? What is he saying that most Americans do not care to hear?*

30–6 *Presidential Press Conference, 1979*

In early 1979 Islamic fundamentalists led by the Ayatollah Khomeini overthrew the Shah of Iran, a longtime U.S. ally and client. In November 1979, after the exiled Shah announced plans to seek medical treatment in the United States, Iranians students seized the U.S. Embassy in Teheran and took 54 Americans hostage. The hostage crisis proved a political disaster for Carter. It dragged on for 444 days, ending only when Ronald Reagan succeeded Jimmy Carter as president. These excerpts from a November 28 Carter press conference reflect some of the political gloom cast by the crisis and the mounting frustration over America's inability to control world events.

SOURCE: *President Carter, 1979* (Congressional Quarterly, 1980).

November 28, 1979

THE PRESIDENT: For the last 24 days our nation's concern has been focused on our fellow Americans being held hostage in Iran. We have welcomed some of them home to their families and their friends. But we will not rest nor deviate from our efforts until all have been freed from their imprisonment and their abuse.

We hold the Government of Iran fully responsible for the well-being and the safe return of every single person.

I want the American people to understand the situation as much as possible but there may be some questions tonight which I cannot answer fully because of my concern for the well-being of the hostages.

First of all I would like to say that I am proud of this great nation and I want to thank all Americans for their prayers, their courage, their persistence, their strong support and patience.

During these past days our national will, our courage and our maturity have all been severely tested. And history will show that the people of the United States have met every test.

In the days to come our determination may be even more sorely tried but we will continue to defend the security, the honor and the freedom of Americans everywhere.

This nation will never yield to blackmail. For all Americans our constant concern is the well-being and the safety of our fellow citizens who are being held illegally and irresponsibly hostage in Iran.

The actions of Iran have shocked the civilized world. For a government to applaud mob violence and terrorism, for a government actually to support and in effect participate in the taking and the holding of hostages is unprecedented in human history.

This violates not only the most fundamental precepts of international law but the common ethical and religious heritage of humanity.

There is no recognized religious faith on earth which condones kidnapping. There is no recognized religious faith on earth which condones blackmail. There is certainly no religious faith on earth which condones the sustained abuse of innocent people.

We are deeply concerned about the inhuman and degrading conditions imposed on the hostages. From every corner of the world, nations and people have voiced their strong revulsion and condemnation of Iran and have joined us in calling for the release of the hostages.

Last night, a statement of support was released and was issued by the president of the United Nations General Assembly, the Security Council, on behalf of all its members. We expect a further Security Council meeting on Saturday night at which more firm and official action may be taken to help in obtaining the release of the American hostages.

Any claims raised by government officials of Iran will ring hollow while they keep innocent people bound and abused and threatened.

We hope that this exercise of diplomacy and international law will bring a peaceful solution, because a peaceful solution is preferable to the other remedies available to the United States.

At the same time we pursue such a solution with grim determination, the Government of Iran must recognize the gravity of the situation which it has, itself, created. And the grave consequences which will result if harm comes to any of the hostages.

I want the American people to know—and I want the world to know—that we will persist in our efforts, through every means available, until every single American has been freed.

We must also recognize now as we never have before that it is our entire nation which is vulnerable because of our overwhelming and excessive dependence on oil from foreign countries. We have got to accept the fact that this dependence is a direct physical threat to our national security. And we must join together to fight for our nation's energy freedom.

We know the ways to win this war; more American energy and the more efficient use of what we have. The United States Congress is now struggling with this extremely important decision.

The way to victory is long and difficult. But we have the will and we have the human and the natural resources of our great nation.

However hard it might be to see into the future, one thing tonight is clear: We stand together. We stand as a nation unified; a people determined to protect the life and the honor of every American. And we are determined to make America an energy-secure nation once again.

It is unthinkable that we will allow ourselves to be dominated by any form of overdependence at home or any brand of terrorism abroad. We are determined that the freest nation on Earth shall protect and enhance its freedom.

I'll be glad to answer questions.

U.S. CREDIBILITY

Q: Mr. President, the Ayatollah Khomeini said the other day—and I'm using his words—that he doesn't believe you have the guts to use military force. He puts no credibility in our military deterrence. I'm wondering: How do we get out of this mess in Iran and still retain credibility with our allies and with our adversaries overseas?

P: We have the full support of our allies. And in this particular instance we have no adversaries overseas. There is no civilized country on earth which has not condemned the seizure and holding of the hostages by Iran.

It would not be advisable for me to explore publicly all the options open to our country. As I said earlier, I'm determined to do the best I can through diplomatic means and through peaceful means to ensure the safety of our hostages and their release. Other actions which I might decide to take would come in the future after those peaceful means have been exhausted. But I believe that the growing condemnation of the world community on Iran will have a beneficial effect.

FUTURE INCIDENTS

Q: What can the United States do now to prevent future incidents of the nature of Iran? How can you satisfy the public demand to end such embarrassments?

P: Well, this is an unprecedented and unique occurrence. Down through history we have had times when some of our people were captured by terrorists or who were abused, and there have obviously been instances of international kidnapping which occurred for the discomfiture of a people or a Government. So far as I know, this is the first time that such an activity has been encouraged by, and supported by, the Government itself. And I don't anticipate this kind of thing recurring.

We have taken steps already in view of the disturbances in the Middle East and the Persian Gulf region to guard our people more closely, to provide them with a higher degree of security and to make arrangements with the host governments to provide assistance if it's needed in the fastest possible way.

Many other nations have reduced severely the number of persons overseas. I think one of the points that should be made is that a year ago we had 70,000 Americans in Iran; 70,000! There were literally thousands of people who were killed in the Iranian revolution from all nations. We were able to extract Americans from Iran safely. It was a superb demonstration of cooperation and good conduct on the part of the State Department and other American officials.

So there will be disturbances in the future. But I think we are well protected as we possibly can be without withdrawing into a shell from protecting American interests in nations overseas. My own experience so far has been that the leaders of nations have recommitted themselves to provide security for embassies of all countries. I think we've learned a lesson from this instance. But because it is so unique in the high degree of irresponsibility of the Iranian Government leaders, I don't believe that we'll see another recurrence of it any time soon.

MOSLEM RELATIONS

Q: I would like to follow up Mr. Schorr's question. The consequences of the crisis in Iran is drifting the United States into almost a cold war with the Islamic countries. Watching TV news for 25 days Americans soon will believe the whole Moslem world is hating them. Moreover, they are not told that the Shiites are a very minor minority among the population of the Islamic world because the majority is Sunni. Don't you think you get any help from any Islamic country? And what will your policy be towards the Islamic countries under the circumstances?

P: Well the premise of your question is completely wrong. We're not approaching any sort of cold war with the Islamic countries. So far as I know every Islamic country has condemned Iran for its capture of our hostages and has been very supportive. This includes Moslem nations which in the past have not been close friends of ours—Iraq, Libya and others.

So I don't see this as a confrontation at all between our nation and the Islamic world. It's certainly not part of the Islamic faith to condone, as I said earlier, blackmail, or the persecution or harm of innocent people, or kidnapping, or terrorism.

So I think that we have a very good relationship with the people and the governments of the Islamic world and I don't think it's deteriorated in this instance. In some ways we've been drawn closer to these people because they see what has occurred in Iran as something of a disgrace for their own religious faith and they don't see this as typical of what Moslems believe.

I might add also that this is not typical of the Shiite faith, either. It's the misguided actions of a few people in Iran who are burning with hatred and a desire for revenge completely contrary to the teachings of the Moslem faith.

WAR POSSIBLE?

Q: Mr. President, there is a feeling of hostility throughout the country towards Iran because of hostages. Senator Long said the taking of our embassy in Iran, in his words, is an act of war. There are rumors—since denied—that our Navy has been called up for service. I ask you as our Commander in Chief, is war possible, is war thinkable?

P: It would be a mistake for the people of our country to have aroused within them hatred—toward anyone. Not against the people of Iran, and certainly not against Iranians who may be in our country as our guests.

We certainly do not want to be guilty of the same violation of human decency and basic human principles that have proven so embarrassing to many of the Iranian citizens themselves.

We obviously prefer to see our hostages protected and released completely through peaceful means. And that's my deepest commitment. And that will be my goal.

The United States has other options available to it which will be considered depending upon the circumstances, but I think it would not be well advised for me to speak of those specifically tonight.

U.S. POWER

Q: Mr. President, many Americans view the Iranian situation as one in a succession of events that proves that this country's power is declining. How can you assure Americans tonight that our power is not declining abroad and how are you reassessing priorities for the eighties in foreign policy?

P: The United States has neither the ability nor the will to dominate the world, to interfere in the internal affairs of other nations, to impose our will on other people whom we desire to be free to make their own decisions.

This is not part of the commitment of the United States.

Our country is the strongest on earth. We're the strongest militarily, politically, economically, and I think we're the strongest morally and ethically.

Our country has made great strides even since I've been in office.

I've tried to correct some of the defects that did exist. We have strengthened the military alliances of our country, for instance.

NATO now has a new spirit, a new confidence, a new cohesion, improving its military capabilities, much more able to withstand any threat from the East from the Soviet Union or the Warsaw Pact than it was before.

We've espoused again the principles that unite Americans and make us admired throughout the world, raising the banner of human rights. We're going to keep it high.

We have opened up avenues of communication, understanding, trade, with people that formerly were our enemies or excluded us—several countries in Africa, the vast people and the vast country of the People's Republic of China.

In doing so we have not alienated any of our previous friends. I think our country is strong within itself. There is not an embarrassment now about our Government, which did exist in a few instances in years gone by.

So I don't see at all that our country has become weak. We are strong and we are getting stronger, not weaker.

But if anybody thinks that we can dominate other people with our strength, military or political strength or economic strength, they're wrong. That's not the purpose of our country.

Our inner strength, our confidence in ourselves, I think is completely adequate and I believe the unity that the American people have shown in this instance, their patience, is not at all a sign of weakness. It is a sign of sure strength.

* * * * * *

1. *How is the hostage situation different from previous foreign-policy crises? Why is American military power not effective in this instance?*

2. *What does the crisis suggest about foreign policy problems that are not defined by Cold War categories?*

3. *How does the president respond to the claim that the hostage crisis reflects a decline in American power?*

30–7 Richard Viguerie, Why the New Right Is Winning, 1981

Ronald Reagan's presidential victory in 1980 owed a great deal to the perceived failures of the Carter Administration in both domestic and foreign policy. Reagan also benefited from the growing financial, intellectual, and political strength in the 1970s of the New Right. The New Right united fundamentalist religious organizations, conservative analysts and fund-raisers, single issue groups, and traditional conservatives in effectively exploiting voter anger and unease with the enormous social and cultural changes of the previous two decades. Richard Viguerie, who pioneered the techniques of computerized direct mail used by many New Right groups, offered the following analysis of their success.

SOURCE: Richard Viguerie, *The New Right: We're Ready to Lead* (Viguerie Company, 1981), pp. 1–7.

The election of 1980 came as a great shock to Americans who depended on the establishment media for their forecasts.

Not only did Ronald Reagan win the Presidency in an electoral landslide of historic proportions, for the first time in nearly a generation, Republicans took over the Senate.

Nationally known liberal Democrats—George McGovern, Frank Church, John Culver, Warren Magnuson, Gaylord Nelson, Birch Bayh—went down to defeat. The nation's leading liberal Republican senator (one of the few remaining after the 1978 elections) went down too: Jacob Javits lost to Alfonse D'Amato.

Americans learned early on the evening of November 4 that the election the media had called a "cliffhanger" was going to be, instead, a rout.

It was not until the next morning, when they woke to find the Senate in Republican hands, that they began to sense the full dimensions of the conservative revolution.

Suddenly it was the most cautious forecasters who looked most foolish. It was the people who had played it "safe" who had proved wildly wrong.

A few of us were not surprised. We in the New Right had been working for this moment for many years. We saw that our labors were bearing fruit, and we said so.

In the first edition of this book, written in the summer of 1980 and published six weeks *before* the election, I wrote:

"I firmly believe that we are on the brink of capturing one of those Houses, the U.S. Senate, perhaps this year and almost surely by 1982."

At the same time it must have sounded as if I hadn't been reading the papers!

On the night of November 4, history walked in on the liberals uninvited.

• Ronald Reagan, the country's foremost conservative politician since 1966, won the Presidency of the United States.

- His popular vote total topped that of the incumbent President, the highly-publicized third-party candidate John Anderson, and all the splinter-party standard-bearers combined.
- His electoral college margin—489 to 49—was among the greatest in history. And among challengers facing incumbents, only Franklin Roosevelt in 1932—with a three-year Depression on his side—did better.

Meanwhile, in the Senate races, the results were just as astonishing.

Backed by the support and organization of the New Right, conservatives like Steve Symms of Idaho, Don Nickles of Oklahoma, Bob Kasten of Wisconsin, Jeremiah Denton of Alabama, John East of North Carolina, Charles Grassley of Iowa, James Abdnor of South Dakota, Dan Quayle of Indiana, and the only woman to win, Paula Hawkins of Florida, stepped forth to offer the nation a new generation of conservative congressional leadership.

It has been obvious for a long time that conservatism is rising and liberalism is declining. Despite all the talk in the media about "trends," "cliffhangers," and "last-minute shifts," the plain truth is that more and more Americans are sick of liberalism—and aren't of afraid to say so.

The election of 1980 was the first modern conservative landslide. But it wasn't the first anti-liberal landslide.

In 1968 two anti-liberal candidates, Richard Nixon and George Wallace, won a combined 57 percent of the popular vote against the well-liked—but liberal—incumbent Vice President, Hubert Humphrey.

In 1972 Nixon, never very popular, won more than 60% of the total vote against the flamingly liberal George McGovern, who carried only one state (not even his home state of South Dakota).

Jimmy Carter didn't win election as a liberal. In the 1976 primaries he presented himself as the most conservative candidate in the field, and it was not until after he was safely in office that it became clear he intended to be a liberal President.

Even in 1980, when Democrats were sick of Carter, he won primaries—when his opponent was the even further left Edward Kennedy. Meanwhile, Ronald Reagan piled up victories against conservative, moderate and liberal candidates in his own party. After the televised debate a week before the election, an ABC phone-in poll gave Reagan a 2 to 1 edge over Carter. Many others in media denounced the poll as "unscientific."

Maybe it was. But the election on November 4 wasn't conducted in a laboratory either. The ABC poll was just one more sign of the times—for anyone who was interested.

All the signs pointed one way. They've been pointing that way for years, and years, and years. They still do.

America is basically a conservative country. The potential for conservative revolt has always been there, under the most favorable conditions. But those conditions have to be made.

That's where the New Right comes in.

For many years, conservatives were frustrated. We had no way to translate our vision into reality.

Most importantly, we lacked a vehicle to carry our message to the voters without going through the filter of the liberal-leaning news media.

During the 1950s, 1960s, and most of the 1970s liberal politicians were able to make speeches that sounded as if they were written by Barry Goldwater. The liberals could come home on weekends and make speeches calling for a strong America, attacking waste in Washington, and complaining about big government. Then, on Monday, they could go back to Washington and vote to block new weapons systems, to give away the Panama Canal, to increase taxes, to create new government agencies, and to weaken the CIA and FBI.

Occasionally, liberal politicians would visit Communist leaders like Fidel Castro and return to the U.S. with wonderful words of praise for the Cuban dictator, praise that most voters in South Dakota or Idaho never heard.

Why did the voters in South Dakota, Idaho, Iowa, Indiana, and Wisconsin not know about their congressmen's and senators' double lives—conservative-sounding at home, actively liberal in Washington or abroad?

Because most of the national (and some of the local) media didn't report the double life the politicians were leading.

Thanks to the New Right, the "people's right to know"—which the establishment media pay loud lip-service to, when it serves their own purposes—finally became a reality.

"You can't turn back the clock."

How often we hear this line from liberals. What they really mean is that we shouldn't try to correct their mistakes.

Well, the New Right has news for them. We aren't in the business of turning back clocks.

It's the Left that has tried to stop the clock and even bring back evils civilization has left behind.

- It's the Left that has re-introduced guild privileges based on compulsory unionism, government-imposed racial and sexual discrimination and oppressive taxes.
- It's the Left that favors a society based on state regulation, supervision, and coercion.
- It's the Left that has defended and even promoted pornography and abortion. (The clock has

stopped forever for eight million unborn American children.)

- It's the Left that focuses its compassion on the criminal rather than his victims.
- It's the Left that attacks our allies rather than our enemies.
- It's the Left that favors the non-producers over the people who work.
- It's the Left that encourages American women to feel that they are failures if they want to be wives and mothers.
- It's the Left that tears apart families and neighbors by the forced busing of children.
- It's the Left that has failed to protest Communist slavery and religious persecution—evils afflicting 1.8 *billion* human beings.
- It's the Left that's fought to keep prayer out of the schools.
- It's the Left that allowed ruthless Communist takeovers in Vietnam, Laos, Cambodia and Afghanistan.
- It's the Left that allowed the takeover of Iran, one of America's strongest allies, by a group of terrorists and extremists.
- It's the Left who crippled the CIA and FBI.
- It's the Left who sold the Russians computers and other sophisticated equipment used to oppress their people.

Liberalism has pitted itself against the best instincts of the American people. Journalist Tom Bethell says the abortion issue alone has destroyed the liberals' "moral monopoly."

Put simply, most Americans no longer look up to liberals. They look down on them.

Liberals have long sensed this. They have tried to make their mistakes irreversible and election-proof. As far as possible, they have sought to turn the powers of government over to the courts and administrative agencies—that is, to unelected and unaccountable public officials.

They have found other ways to impose their will. One of the most sophisticated has been deficit spending—producing an inflation that reduces blue-collar workers' real pay by pushing them into what used to be executive tax brackets. By such means liberals have increased government's grip on our wealth without openly raising tax rates.

Somebody had to call a halt to this devious elitism. What used to be liberalism has turned into socialism on the installment plan.

With the New Right, America has found a new voice. In 1980, that voice rang out—loud and clear.

The voters of Idaho and South Dakota finally got to know the *real* Frank Church and the *real* George McGovern—the ones Fidel Castro knows.

Because conservatives have mastered the new technology, we've been able to bypass the Left's near-monopoly of the national news media.

The New Right has also had its own ready-made network: the thousands of conservative Christian ministers whose daily broadcasts on local and national radio and TV reach an audience of 27 million. Every week, approximately 20 million people view just three such ministers—Jerry Falwell, Pat Robertson, and James Robison.

Until now this whole culture has been a dark continent to the Northeast, coastal-based national media. But these ministers are attacking issues the national media hardly mention: issues like worldwide Communist aggression, school prayer, sex on TV, the failures of the public schools. The conservative ministers are in touch with the people, and now they are in touch with each other.

The conservatism was always there. It took the New Right to give it leadership, organization, and direction.

The key word is *leadership.* Conservatives have had no lack of brilliant thinkers, brilliant writers, brilliant debaters, brilliant spokesmen. But none of these is the same thing as a leader.

George Gallup has found that 49% of registered voters in the U.S. now place themselves "right of center"—as against only 29% who say they are "left of center" and only 10% who call themselves "middle of the road."

And yet, with this tremendous potential support, the Republican Party has proved itself incapable of even mounting a consistent and effective opposition, much less rallying that 49% behind an agenda of its own. If it can't find its base with both hands, how is it going to lead the whole nation?

The New Right has proved it can lead. We're doing it. Leadership doesn't just show up on the first Tuesday in November. It has to be out there ahead of time—organizing, mailing, phoning, advertising, informing, getting names on the ballot.

The simple truth is that there is a new majority in America—and it's being led by the New Right.

* * * * * *

1. *Why does Viguerie believe that Reagan's election marks a historic turning point?*

2. *Why has liberalism declined, according to Viguerie? What does he mean by "the Left"?*

3. *How has the New Right created a new kind of effective conservative politics?*

chapter 31

Toward a Transitional America, since 1988

31-1 Jesse Jackson, Common Ground, 1988

Jesse Jackson began his political career in the civil rights movement, as an aide to the Rev. Martin Luther King, Jr., and the SCLC. After King's death Jackson used his base in Chicago to found Operation PUSH (People United to Save Humanity), a group focusing on economic empowerment for African Americans. In 1984 Jackson became the first African American to mount a serious campaign for president, attracting three million votes in Democratic primaries. In 1988, he won nearly seven million votes. His following included millions of non-black liberals and radicals attracted by his idealism and powerful oratory. He delivered this speech at the 1988 Democratic National Convention.

SOURCE: Vital Speeches Of the Day, Vol. 54 (1987–88).

When I look out at this convention, I see the face of America, red, yellow, brown, black and white, we're all precious in God's sight—the real rainbow coalition....

Dr. Martin Luther King Jr. lies only a few miles from us tonight.

Tonight he must feel good as he looks down upon us. We sit here together, a rainbow, a coalition—the sons and daughters of slave masters and the sons and daughters of slaves sitting together around a common table, to decide the direction of our party and our country. His heart would be full tonight....

Tonight there is a sense of celebration because we are moved, fundamentally moved, from racial battlegrounds by law, to economic common ground, tomorrow we will challenge to move to higher ground.

Common ground!

Think of Jerusalem—the intersection where many trails met. A small village that became the birthplace for three great religions—Judaism, Christianity and Islam.

Why was this village so blessed? Because it provided a crossroads where different people met, different cultures, and different civilizations could meet and find common ground.

When people come together, flowers always flourish and the air is rich with the aroma of a new spring.

Take New York, the dynamic metropolis. What makes New York so special?

It is the invitation of the Statue of Liberty—give me your tired, your poor, your huddled masses who yearn to breathe free.

Not restricted to English only.

Many people, many cultures, many languages—with one thing in common, the yearn[ing] to breathe free.

Common ground!....

We find common ground at the plant gate that closes on workers without notice. We find common ground at the farm auction where a good farmer loses his or her land to bad loans or diminishing markets. Common ground at the schoolyard where teachers cannot get adequate pay, and students cannot get a scholarship and can't make a loan. Common ground, at the hospital admitting room where somebody tonight is dying because they cannot afford to go upstairs to a bed that's empty, waiting for someone with insurance to get sick. We are a better nation than that. We must do better.

Common ground. What is leadership if not present help in a time of crisis? And so I met you at the point of challenge in Jay, Maine, where paper workers were striking for fair wages; in Greenfield, Iowa, where family farmers struggle for a fair price; in Cleveland, Ohio, where working women seek comparable worth; in McFarland, Calif., where the children of Hispanic farm workers may be dying from poison land, dying in clusters with Cancer; in the AIDS hospice in Houston, Texas, where the sick support one another, 12 are rejected by their own parents and friends.

Common ground.

America's not a blanket woven from one thread, one color, one cloth. When I was a child growing up in Greenville, S.C., and grandmother could not afford a blanket, she didn't complain and we did not freeze. Instead, she took pieces of old cloth—patches, wool, silk, gabardine, crockersack on the patches—barely good enough to wipe off your shoes with.

But they didn't stay that way very long. With sturdy hands and a strong cord, she sewed them together into a quilt, a thing of beauty and power and culture.

Now, Democrats, we must build such a quilt. Farmers, you seek fair prices and you are right, but you cannot stand alone. Your patch is not big enough. Workers, you fight for fair wages. You are right. But your patch labor is not big enough. Women, you seek comparable worth and pay equity. You are right. But your patch is not big enough. Women, mothers, who seek Head Start and day care and pre-natal care on the front side of life, rather than jail care and welfare on the back side of life, you're right, but your patch is not big enough.

Students, you seek scholarships. You are right. But your patch is not big enough. Blacks and Hispanics, when we fight for civil rights, we are right, but our patch is not big enough. Gays and lesbians, when you fight against discrimination and a cure for AIDS, you are right, but your patch is not big enough. Conservatives and progressives, when you fight for what you believe, right-wing, left-wing, hawk, dove—you are right, from your point of view, but your point of view is not enough.

But don't despair. Be as wise as my grandmama. Pool the patches and the pieces together, bound by a common thread. When we form a great quilt of unity and common ground we'll have the power to bring about health care and housing and jobs and education and hope to our nation.

I have a story. I wasn't always on television. Writers were not always outside my door. When I was born late one afternoon, October 8th, in Greenville, S.C., no writers asked my mother her name. Nobody chose to write down our address. My mama was not supposed to make it. And I was not supposed to make it. You see, I was born to a teen-age mother who was born to a teenage mother.

I understand. I know abandonment and people being mean to you, and saying you're nothing and nobody, and can never be anything. I understand. Jesse Jackson is my third name. I'm adopted. When I had no name, my grandmother gave me her name. My name was Jesse Burns until I was 12. So I wouldn't have a blank space, she gave me a name to hold me over. I understand when nobody knows your name. I understand when you have no name. I understand.

I wasn't born in the hospital. Mama didn't have insurance. I was born in the bed at home. I really do understand. Born in a three-room house, bathroom in the backyard, slop jar by the bed, no hot and cold running water. I understand. Wallpaper used for decoration? No. For a windbreaker. I understand. I'm a working person's person, that's why I understand you whether you're black or white. I understand work. I was not born with a silver spoon in my mouth. I had a shovel programmed for my hand. My mother, a working woman. So many days she went to work early with runs in her stockings. She knew better, but she wore runs in her stockings so that my brother and I could have matching socks and not be laughed at at school.

I understand. At 3 o'clock on Thanksgiving Day we couldn't eat turkey because mama was preparing someone else's turkey at 3 o'clock. We had to play football to entertain ourselves and then around 6 o'clock she would get off the Alta Vista bus; then we would bring up the leftovers and eat our turkey—leftovers, the carcass, the cranberries around 8 o'clock at night. I really do understand.

Every one of these funny labels they put on you, those of you who are watching this broadcast tonight in the projects, on the corners, I understand. Call you outcast, low down, you can't make it, you're nothing, you're from nobody, subclass, underclass—when you see Jesse Jackson, when my name goes in nomination, your name goes in nomination.

I was born in the slum, but the slum was not born in me. And it wasn't born in you, and you can make it. Wherever you are tonight you can make it. Hold your head high, stick your chest out. You can make it. It gets dark sometimes, but the morning comes. Don't you surrender. Suffering breeds character. Character breeds faith. In the end faith will not disappoint.

You must not surrender. You may or may not get there, but just know that you're qualified and you hold on and hold out. We must never surrender. America will get better and better. Keep hope alive. Keep hope alive. Keep hope alive.

* * * * * *

1.   *What does Jackson mean by "common ground"? How does he use that phrase to urge a more inclusive American political community?*

2.   *How does Jackson invoke his own childhood to make his political case?*

31–2 Cecelia Rosa Avila, Third-Generation Mexican American, 1988

Immigration from abroad increased enormously during the 1980s, especially from Asia, Latin America, and Central America. Newcomers fleeing extreme poverty and political instability tended to settle within already established immigrant communities. In California, Mexican Americans had long been an important political and cultural presence. Yet the ambiguities of identity remained. Cecelia Rosa Avila, seventeen-year-old daughter of a prominent Mexican American civil rights activist, expressed the sense of multiple identity common within immigrant communities of the 1980s.

SOURCE: From *Latinos* by Earl Shorris. Copyright ©1992 by Earl Shorris. Reprinted by permission of W. W. Norton & Company, Inc.

It's sad. It's scary. I get scared when I go outside to get the mail. I used to go outside and everything, but it just got too crazy, too many gangs, too many innocent people getting killed. Even if you just like wore a tie or sunglasses, you could get killed for that. Wrong color. Some people say they got killed for just wearing the wrong color sunglasses. It's just terrible. It's not getting any better. I mean, if President Reagan can't do anything, what makes you think Bush is going to do something? This world is terrible.

When I was little there wasn't as much violence. I could go out and play and not worry about nobody bothering me, no kidnappings or anything. I was with people I trusted. I would go over so-and-so's house and nothing would happen, but now things are so crazy, you know sometimes people walk down the street and they never come back. I knew of a girl, she went down to her neighbor's house, she never came back. She ended up dead the next day.

The Crips are blue and the Bloods are red. It used to be they just fought with fists, but now they fight with machine guns. And it's not like one on one, it's like ten on one, ten on ten. It's like group on group. They fight to kill. They don't fight to hurt, they fight to kill. They don't care. It's like they kill somebody tomorrow, they don't care. It's like they're used to it, so they just kill again.

Girls get involved in gangs very much, but I wouldn't. It's too crazy. And sometimes if somebody's going to jump you, they just like leave you there, they don't even jump in and help you, and they're supposed to be like your friends, backing you up in the gang, but they'll just like leave you.

I'm seventeen. I'll be eighteen in April [1989]. I used to know a lot of people and a lot of things, two years ago. Sometimes I hear things now. I know different things. I don't worry about it. I don't put myself in a position where I'll get hurt. I just go about my business. I don't do things in Compton. I go to my cousin's house or something. I don't do nothing in Compton.

I've been to Norwalk once. That's farther from here. It was pretty nice and pretty quiet. I would like to move; Compton is just too crazy. We'll probably move when I get married. We're…they're going to move to Idaho. That's what they want to do. My dad wants to go really bad, but he's going to wait 'til like later.

I would like to live somewhere far from here, but not out of the state, not in the country. I don't like the country, it's too quiet. It's different. You have to work really hard out there. Say you're a farmer, you have your crops and all that; you have to feed all your animals. You have to drink goat's milk and that's gross. It's too quiet. You have to walk like twenty miles to get to the nearest gas station or something. But in the city, everybody's like

for theirself. There's so much hate and so much rush—rushing here, rushing there—so much hate, but the country goes really slow. I would like to live in the city, but between, like in a rural/urban in-between, not too country, not too city, but just right, not too packed, but not too far away from each other.

When I was in junior high all my friends were black, and I always felt they were superior and this and that, so I started hanging around with them. I dressed like one. I wasn't proud to be a Mexican, you know, like, *I'm a Mexican, oh no!* I used to think Mexicans weren't nothing, I used to thought blacks were superior, you know. I guess because they walked around in big groups and all this and that, you know. I was in Ralph Bunche Junior High. It was mostly black, 70 percent black. The other kids were Mexican and maybe two or three Samoans. I had some friends who were Mexican, but I didn't hang around with them, because I didn't think they were anything. I didn't think they were important. I thought they were nerds or ugh! Mexican. I was telling myself, "I want to be black. I want to be black." So I used to hang around with black people when I thought I was black and all this.

I did little ridiculous things. I totally talked, you know, like slang, everything. I used to have a attitude. I used to like put my hair up high, like make it straight. You know, curl it. I used to buy all this like activator. I used to buy clothes for it and everything. I used to dress like it and everything. I wore like cords, tee shirts. Back then Pumas were in style, then Fila, then Booties and white socks and that. I'd you know chew my gum and like that and try and pop it all the time. The blacks acted like what I did was normal. They accepted me as being me.

Then I started getting older and my mind was maturing and all that and I said, "Why am I trying to be something I'm not. I should just be myself." Then by the tenth grade I started to realize different things. I should just be myself, Mexican.

Mexicans speak a different language, first of all, some do; second of all, different home styles, the way they're brought up, the way they cook—different cultures, two totally different cultures. The way they keep up their house, Mexicans have like a bunch of flowers or something in their front yard, sometimes they have dirt floors, like in Mexico. They have a lot of little kids. Black has kids, but not as much as Mexicans. Black, they have different ways, like in Africa they live like in huts or something. The food is different. We eat beans and rice and all that. That's not their everyday dish; they cook something else.

We all talk different. The blacks have like, "Child" and we have like *"O, mihija"* and *"hola"* and all this, you know. It's just different.

I wouldn't say Mexicans are more superior than the blacks. To me everybody's equal. Just because you're

Mexican doesn't mean you have to get all into it, like being from a gang just to prove you're proud of your race. You can be proud of your race just to be proud. It feels good to know you're from somewhere.

I'm Mexican American. I'm Mexican, but I wasn't born in Mexico. I'm not Caucasian. All my relatives are Mexican, plus I have a Mexican last name and everything, so I'm Mexican American. Caucasian people are not from Mexico just like African people aren't from Mexico. It's just a difference, a whole difference.

I was bilingual when I was little. I used to speak Spanish and English, but unfortunately, it wasn't kept up. I could speak Spanish a little bit: *No se creas,* that means "I don't believe it." *Yo tengo una lápiz.*

I've never been to Mexico. I would like to go really soon. All my relatives are there. I haven't seen nobody. I hardly know nobody. They live in Chihuahua, Mexico City, Guadalajara. Tijuana—I've been there. Tijuana was sad. I mean you think you don't have the richest house and you want more, but you should see what the people have. Sometimes they're like really poor. They sleep in boxes. Actually, it's really sad to see people living like that, but then there's a nice part. What really got me was the sad part, little kids coming up to cars begging for stuff and then they're selling little things they made. It's just really sad.

I go out with Mexicans. I used to like blacks. It doesn't matter to me, because I'm not prejudiced at all. I don't think anybody should be, because God created us all to be equal. But if a black comes up, that's fine with me as long as he treats me right and everything's right.

I don't try to be no cholo or anything because I don't have no feathers or big loops. Like Mexican girls wear really big loops so that they're chola, like in the girl gang, the Mexican gang. If I dressed that way, I would be rebelling. That's not the right way you're supposed to go. When you get into a gang, you're just asking for trouble. My hair's just me. I'm myself. My clothes I don't imitate nobody else; I'm myself.

I am sincere. I don't try to rule over people. I don't try to put people down. I care about people and what people think about me.

I work in a store in the Lakewood Mall. It's called Silverman's. I sell men's clothing, from leather to Cataricci pants, Carnegie sweaters, like really expensive stuff, really nice stuff. I like working, even though it is hard, but I enjoy it. I need to be responsible sometime, because I can't always be saying, "Daddy, I want this; Daddy, I want that." I gotta go out there and do for myself.

* * * * * *

1.   How does Avila deal with the gang warfare around her? How does she negotiate the complex issue of racial identity in Los Angeles?

2.   What does it mean for Avila to be a Mexican-American? In what sense is she simply an American?

31–3   *Howard Rheingold, Homesteading on the Electronic Frontier, 1993*

Howard Rheingold has written extensively on the philosophical and political implications of cyberspace, virtual reality, and the entire array of computer-mediated communications, known as CMC. He was an early and active member of the Whole Earth 'Lectronic Link (WELL), a virtual community in the San Francisco Bay area.

SOURCE: Howard Rheingold, *The Virtual Community* (Boston: Addison-Wesley, 1993), 4–8.

The technology that makes virtual communities possible has the potential to bring enormous leverage to ordinary citizens at relatively little cost—intellectual leverage, social leverage, commercial leverage, and most important, political leverage. But the technology will not in itself fulfill that potential; this latent technical power must be used intelligently and deliberately by an informed population. More people must learn about that leverage and learn to use it, while we still have the freedom to do so, if it is to live up to its potential. The odds are always good that big power and big money will find a way to control access to virtual communities; big power and big money always found ways to control new communications media when they emerged in the past. The Net is still out of control in fundamental ways, but it might not stay that way for long....

The potential social leverage comes from the power that ordinary citizens gain when they know how to connect two previously independent, mature, highly decentralized technologies: It took billions of dollars and decades to develop cheap personal computers. It took billions of dollars and more than a century to wire up the worldwide telecommunication network.... The important thing to keep in mind is that the worldwide, interconnected telecommunication network that we use to make telephone calls in Manhattan and Madagascar can also be used to connect computers together at a distance, and you don't have to be an engineer to do it.

The Net is an informal term for the loosely inter-connected computer networks that use CMC [computer-mediated communications] technology to link people around the world into public discussions.

Virtual communities are social aggregations that emerge from the Net when enough people carry on those public discussions long enough, with sufficient human feeling, to form webs of personal relationships in cyberspace.

Cyberspace, originally a term from William Gibson's science-fiction novel *Neuromancer,* is the name some people use for the conceptual space where words, human relationships, data, wealth, and power are manifested by people using CMC technology....

My direct observations on online behavior around the world over the past ten years have led me to conclude that whenever CMC technology becomes available to people anywhere, they inevitably build virtual communities with it, just as microorganisms inevitably create colonies.

I suspect that one of the explanations for this phenomenon is the hunger for community that grows in the breasts of people around the world as more and more informal public spaces disappear from our real lives. I also suspect that these new media attract colonies of enthusiasts because CMC enables people to do things with each other in new ways, and to do new kinds of things—just as telegraphs, telephones, and televisions did....

We need a clear citizens' vision of the way the Net ought to grow, a firm idea of the kind of media environment we would like to see in the future. If we do not develop such a vision for ourselves, the future will be shaped for us by large commercial and political powerholders.

The Net is so widespread and anarchic today because of the way its main sources converged in the 1980s, after years of independent, apparently unrelated development, using different technologies and involving different populations of participants. The technical and social convergences were fated, but not widely foreseen, by the late 1970s.

The wide-area CMC networks that span continents and join together thousands of smaller networks are a spinoff of American military research. The first computer network, ARPANET, was created in the 1970s so that Department of Defense-sponsored researchers could operate different computers at a distance; computer data, not person-to-person messages, were the intended content of the network, which handily happened to serve just as easily as a conduit for words. The fundamental technical idea on which ARPANET was based came from RAND, the think tank in Santa Monica that did a lot of work with top-secret thermonuclear war scenarios; ARPANET grew out of an older RAND scheme for a communication, com-mand, and control network that could survive nuclear attack by having no central control.

Computer conferencing emerged, also somewhat unexpectedly, as a tool for using the communication capacities of the networks to build social relationships across barriers of space and time. A continuing theme throughout the history of CMC is the way people adapt technologies designed for one purpose to suit their own very different, communication needs.... The programmers who created the first computer network installed electronic mail features; electronic mail wasn't the reason ARPANET was designed, but it was an easy thing to include once ARPANET existed. Then, in similar, ad hoc, do-it-yourself manner, computer conferencing grew out of the needs of U.S. policymakers to develop a communications medium for dispersed decision making....

The hobbyists who interconnect personal computers via telephone lines to make computer bulletin-board systems...have home-grown their part of the Net, a true grassroots use of technology. Hundreds of thousands of people around the world piggyback legally on the telecom network via personal computers and ordinary telephone lines. [This] is an extremely hard network to kill—just as the RAND planners had hoped. Information can take so many alternative routes when one of the nodes of the network is removed that the Net is almost immortally flexible. It is this flexibility that CMC telecom pioneer John Gilmore referred to when he said, "The Net interprets censorship as damage and routes around it.... "

The big hardwired networks spend a lot more money to create high-speed information conduits between high-capacity computing nodes. Internet, today's U.S. government-sponsored successor to ARPANET, is growing in every dimension at an astonishing pace....

ARPANET started around twenty years ago with roughly one thousand users, and now Internet is approaching ten million users.

* * * * * *

1.   What connections does Rheingold see between the rapid growth of CMC technologies and a hunger for community in modern America?

2.   How did Rheingold's involvement with WELL intersect with (and affect) his personal and family life?

3.   What disturbing dangers—and utopian possibilities—does he highlight? How are both of these embedded in the history of CMC technologies?

31–4 America Enters a New Century with Terror, 2001

The destruction of New York City's World Trade Center Towers on September 11, 2001, shocked the nation and the world. That day, two hijacked airplanes purposely slammed into the two towers, a third plane struck the Pentagon, and a fourth crashed into the Pennsylvania countryside. Within hours, all commercial aviation had ground to a halt. The devastation in New York City is detailed by New York Times *reporter N. R. Kleinfield in a September 12 article.*

SOURCE: *The New York Times*, September 12, 2001.

U.S. ATTACKED; HIJACKED JETS DESTROY TWIN TOWERS AND HIT PENTAGON IN DAY OF TERROR
By N. R. KLEINFIELD

It kept getting worse.

The horror arrived in episodic bursts of chilling disbelief, signified first by trembling floors, sharp eruptions, cracked windows. There was the actual unfathomable realization of a gaping, flaming hole in first one of the tall towers, and then the same thing all over again in its twin. There was the merciless sight of bodies helplessly tumbling out, some of them in flames.

Finally, the mighty towers themselves were reduced to nothing. Dense plumes of smoke raced through the downtown avenues, coursing between the buildings, shaped like tornadoes on their sides.

Every sound was cause for alarm. A plane appeared overhead. Was another one coming? No, it was a fighter jet. But was it friend or enemy? People scrambled for their lives, but they didn't know where to go. Should they go north, south, east, west? Stay outside, go indoors? People hid beneath cars and each other. Some contemplated jumping into the river.

For those trying to flee the very epicenter of the collapsing World Trade Center towers, the most horrid thought of all finally dawned on them: nowhere was safe.

For several panic-stricken hours yesterday morning, people in Lower Manhattan witnessed the inexpressible, the incomprehensible, the unthinkable. "I don't know what the gates of hell look like, but it's got to be like this," said John Maloney, a security director for an Internet firm in the trade center. "I'm a combat veteran, Vietnam, and I never saw anything like this."

The first warnings were small ones. Blocks away, Jim Farmer, a film composer, was having breakfast at a small restaurant on West Broadway. He heard the sound of a jet. An odd sound—too loud, it seemed, to be normal. Then he noticed: "All the pigeons in the street flew up.'"

It was the people outside, on the sidewalk, who saw the beginning. At 8:45, David Blackford was walking toward work in a downtown building. He heard a jet engine and glanced up. "I saw this plane screaming overhead," he said. "I thought it was too low. I thought it wasn't going to clear the tower.'"

Within moments, his fears were confirmed. The plane slammed into the north face of 1 World Trade Center. As he watched, he said, "You could see the concussion move up the building."

"It was a large plane flying low," said Robert Pachino, another witness. "There was no engine trouble. He didn't try to maneuver. This plane was on a mission."

Dark spots fell from the sides of the buildings, and at first it wasn't clear what they were. Sarah Sampino, who worked across the street, noticed black smoke outside and went to the window. "We saw bodies flying out of the windows," she said. "It was the 85th floor. I used to work on that floor."

James Wang, 21, a photography student snapping pictures of people doing tai chi at a nearby park, looked up and saw people high in the north tower. They seemed like tiny figurines, and he didn't know if they were awaiting rescue or merely looking out. "They were standing up there," he said. "And they jumped. One woman, her dress was billowing out."

Inside the towers, people felt it without knowing what it was. At about 15 minutes to 9, Anne Prosser, 29, rode the elevator to the 90th floor of Tower 1, where her global banking office was. As the doors opened, she heard what seemed like an explosion. She didn't know it, but the first plane had just hit several floors above her.

"I got thrown to the ground before I got to our suite," she said. "I crawled inside. Not everybody was at work." She said she tried to leave but there was so much debris in the air she couldn't breathe. Port Authority rescuers finally steered her to a stairway.

Tim Lingenfelder, 36, an office manager at a small investment banking firm, was sitting before his computer terminal on the 52nd floor of Tower 1. He had just sent an e-mail to his sister in Minnesota. Nothing special—just how was she and what he had had for breakfast.

The windows rattled. He heard a loud noise. The entire building shook. He looked up. Outside the windows, he noticed rubble falling, and he thought, "That can't be from here."

Only two others were at work, a father and son who were both bond traders. They said they had better get out. They hurried to the stairs and, along with flocks of others, began their descent.

"When I got to the 18th floor, my cell phone rang," Mr. Lingenfelder said. "It was my sister. She said a plane had hit and to get out now."

On the 32nd floor, the entourage was stuck for about 20 minutes because of smoke. Everyone ducked into offices on the floor to catch their breath. Mr. Lingenfelder peered out the window and saw a body lying on the roof of the hotel.

They returned to the stairs and made it out onto the plaza. Rubble and debris was all around. On the street there was endless paper and unmatched shoes.

John Cerqueira, 22, and Mike Ben Fanter, 36, were working on the 81st floor of 1 World Trade Center when they felt the collision. "People were freaking out," said Mr. Fanter, a sales manager. "I tried to get them in the center of the office. About 40 people. I led them to the hall down the steps."

He continued: "We stopped on the 68th floor. I could hear people screaming. There was a woman in a wheelchair. John and I carried her down from the 68th floor to the 5th floor, where we got out. We started to see people jumping from the top of the World Trade Center."

Teresa Foxx, 37, works at an investment banking firm a block from the World Trade Center, and she had dropped off her 15-month-old daughter, Trinity, at the Discovery Learning Center on the plaza level of 5 World Trade Center, the building adjacent to the two towers. While she was in her office, Ms. Foxx heard the blast and immediately knew it was a bomb. "Ever since I enrolled her in the World Trade Center, I keep thinking about the bombing that they had there," she said.

She grabbed her purse and went outside and began running toward the daycare center. Other people were speeding toward her, crying and screaming. She was crying herself. She had to get her daughter.

By the time she got to the center, the children had been evacuated several blocks away. She hurried over there and found her daughter. "I just grabbed her and held her," she said. "I was still crying, the other parents were still crying, but we all got our children."

When she got home, Ms. Foxx told her husband, "Now I understand why people run into burning buildings."

Within about 15 minutes of the first crash, the second plane struck the neighboring tower.

People in the street panicked and ran. Some tripped, fell, got knocked down, were pulled up. People lost their keys, their phones, their handbags, their shoes.

Brianne Woods, a student at Pace University, was walking to class, and as she passed a Burger King not a hundred feet from the trade center she heard a blast and felt the ground shake. She ran to a bank, where people were banging on the glass, breaking it, trying to get inside. "I saw a guy bleeding from the head right by the bank," she said. "People were getting stomped on under the crowd. I saw a

lady with no shoes, her feet were bleeding. I was probably in there for about 10 minutes, and I was hysterical."

Her brother worked in the World Trade Center and she didn't know if he was in there. She learned later that he had not gone to work.

She happened to have her cat, Oliver, with her, and she began wandering around, clutching her cat carrier, dazed. "I saw two people jump out," she said. "It was horrible. I felt I was in a bad nightmare."

Then a calm set in again. For blocks around, all the way up to 14th Street, the sidewalks were a mass of people, eerily quiet, for the incomprehension had struck them mute. As emergency vehicles, sirens blaring, sped downtown, people stood and gaped at the towers with holes in them. Many people were steadily inching downtown, not imagining anything worse was to come.

Marilyn Mulcahy, 31, had a business appointment at 9 at an office on Broadway a few blocks from the World Trade Center. She got off the subway at Chambers and Church Streets. She saw what she believed were pieces of a plane engine on the sidewalk, police officers running tape around it. She saw the holes in the towers and was dumbstruck.

Reason dictated caution, to get out of the area, but she was overcome with shock. Almost unknowingly, she walked to the office where her appointment was. Everyone had left. Even so, she took the time to scribble a note that she had been there and would call later.

Back on the street, fear caught up with her. She changed out of her heels into flat shoes she had in her bag and ran uptown.

On the corner of Vesey and Church Streets, across from the Borders Books and Music store in the corner of the trade center, a small-boned woman, her hair caked with blood, was sitting on the curb, shaking uncontrollably. One eye was clouded over. A man in a business suit was lying on a stretcher, being loaded into an ambulance. Emergency workers came to comfort the woman. Five feet away, another rescue worker crouched down next to a heavyset woman who was breathing through an inhaler and hugged her.

Some Trade Center workers blessed their luck at being late for work. Kathleen Dendy, 50, had gotten her hair cut and so never got to her office at her usual 8:30. She worked on the 99th floor. Rajesh Trivedi, 40, a computer programmer, normally reported at 7, but he had to drop his son off at school and so didn't get in. He worked on the 80th floor.

A plane was heard overhead and people looked up. Another one, they thought. "No, it's a fighter," someone said. "Ours."

"Are you sure?" a woman asked.

Many people were busy on cell phones, trying to reach friends and relatives they knew in the buildings or to alert their own loved ones that they were all right. But the circuits overloaded. Fear mounted.

And then it got even worse.

Police officers warned people in the vicinity to move north, that the buildings could fall, but most people found that unthinkable. They stayed put or gravitated closer.

Abruptly, there was an ear-splitting noise. The south tower shook, seemed to list in one direction and them began to come down, imploding upon itself.

"It looked like a demolition," said Andy Pollock.

"It started exploding," said Ross Milanytch, 57, who works at nearby Chase Manhattan Bank. "It was about the 70th floor. And each second another floor exploded out for about eight floors, before the cloud obscured it all."

Seth Bower was on Broadway when the force of the collapse knocked him over onto other people. Bodies fell on top of him—not all of them, he thought, alive.

A plume of smoke reminiscent of an atomic bomb rose upward and then descended to street level and sped uptown. People began running, chased by the smoke. The air rained white ash and plaster dust, coating people until they looked ghostlike.

Some people were screaming, and many were in shock. "Don't breathe the air," people shouted. "It could be toxic." People held their breath or covered their faces as best they could with cloths or their shirts.

Lisle Taylor, 26, a recruiter with Goldman, Sachs, had just gotten out of a nearby subway stop and saw hundreds of pieces of paper in the air. She thought it was a marketing campaign. Then she looked up and saw the tower collapsing. "A woman grabbed my hand," she said. "She was saying the Lord's Prayer."

For several blocks, everything was black. People found their eyes burned. Many wondered if they were seeing the very face of death.

Michael Clinch, a security officer for an Internet company, left his office soon after the first plane struck and was standing on Broadway talking to a police officer when the first tower fell. He saw a woman running, grabbed her and pulled her under a sport utility vehicle with him. "We got under the truck and waited until it got light again," he said. "There were cars just blowing up. They were trying to get equipment off this emergency truck and get it into a building and all these cars just blew up. One would blow up and set off the next one. It got so bad we just couldn't do anything any more and we had to get out of there."

Ten or so blocks north of the towers, the smoke had been outrun and it began to dissipate into the air. People stopped, turned and looked downtown. As the air cleared, an unthinkable site presented itself: empty space where a 110-story tower had been.

People gasped. They trembled. They sobbed.

"It can't be," an elderly woman said. "It just can't be. Where did it go? Oh, lord, where did it go?"

Many of the onlookers stayed put, frozen in horror. Slowly, the next thought crept into their consciousness: The other tower would come down too.

Several people voiced the thought: "Get out of here, the other tower's going to fall."

People started walking briskly north until the premonition became real—another horrifying eruption, as one floor after another seemed to detonate. Another giant cloud, soot, smoke streaming through the avenues. Again, people ran.

Many of them stopped at Canal Street and watched the smoke dissolve. People cried at what they saw: a crystalline sky with nothing in it.

"Oh my God," Tim Lingenfelder said, "there's nothing there."

That was when he lost it and began to cry.

People stood, numb, transfixed by what had to be a mirage. "All that were left of the buildings that you could see were the steel girders in like a triangular sail shape," said Ross Milanytch. "The dust was about an inch and a half thick on the ground."

Onlookers gathered in clumps and tried to understand. People with cars opened the doors and turned on the radios, and knots of people leaned close to hear what was happening. The news came across of of the plane at the Pentagon, the plane in Pittsburgh.

"It's like Pearl Harbor," said a middle-aged man at a small parking lot on Canal Street. "It's Pearl Harbor. It's war."

"It's sickos," someone else said. "Sickos."

"This is America," a man said. "How can it happen in America? How?"

A young man came around imploring people to report to St. Vincent's Manhattan Hospital to donate blood.

Lines five, eight deep developed at pay phones, but many of the phones didn't work. Most of the downtown businesses were closed. People borrowed cell phones, but the heavy phone traffic made communicating hard if not impossible. Countless people spent hours not knowing where a wife, a husband or a child was.

For hours, people lingered, uncertain where to go or what to do in a no longer plausible world. Some felt compelled to leave Manhattan, taking ferries to New Jersey. A man holding his weeping wife headed toward the Manhattan bridge, telling her, "Let's walk over the bridge to Brooklyn. They can't hurt us in Brooklyn."

Late in the afternoon, hundreds of rescue workers remained outside where the trade towers once loomed, watching the stubs of the buildings continue to burn into infinity. Several stories still stood, but it was hard to judge how many. Above the second story was nothing but an intense orange glow.

"It's eerie," said Monet Harris, 22, a transit worker. "You always look for those two buildings. You always know where you are when you see those two buildings. And now they're gone."

* * * * * *

1. *What events do the witnesses of the World Trade Center catastrophe remember most vividly?*

2. *What do most survivors' actions tell about the way people react in such a crisis?*